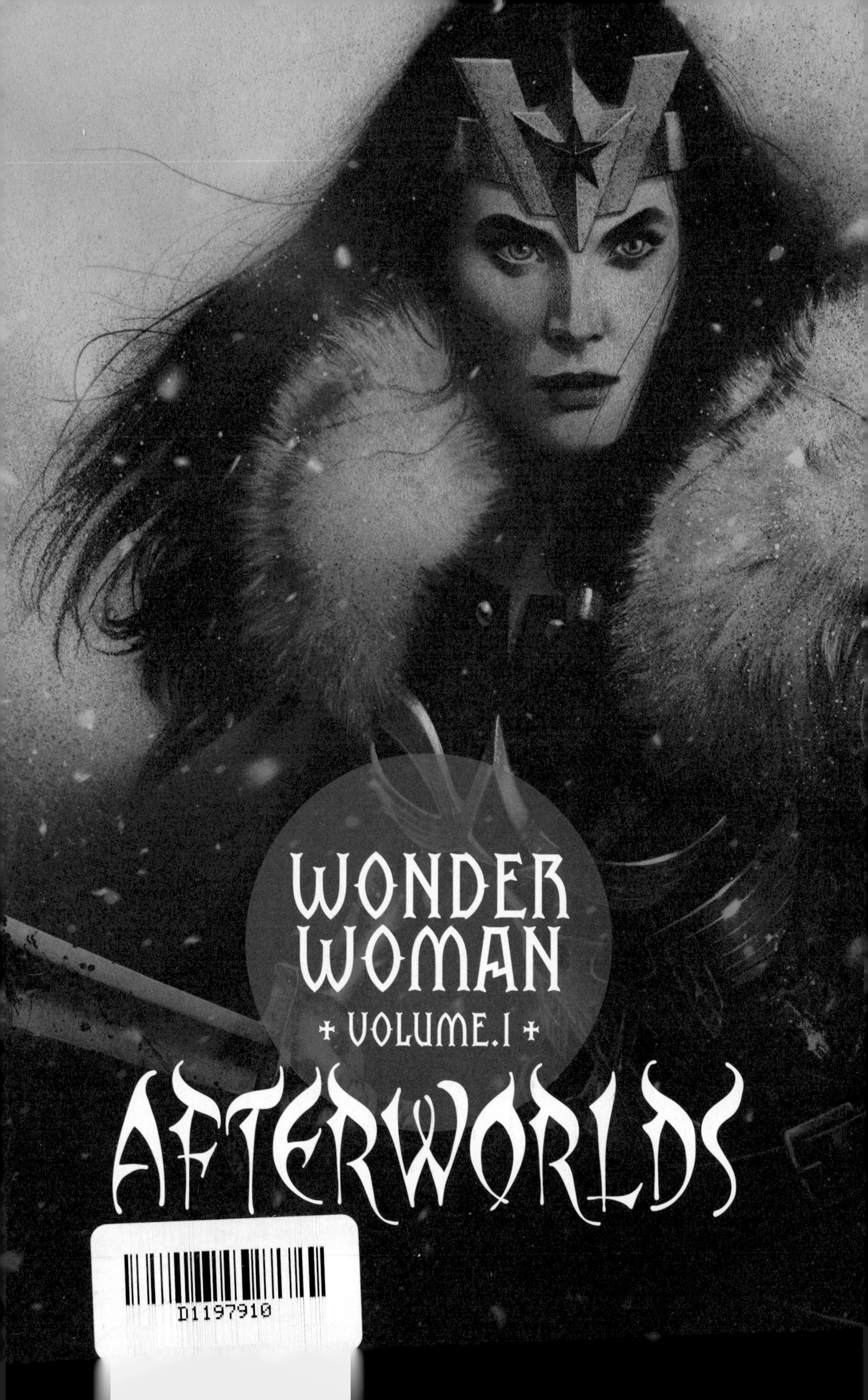
WONDER
WOMAN
+ VOLUME.1 +
AFTERWORLDS

MICHAEL W. CONRAD
WRITERS

TRAVIS MOORE
ANDY MacDONALD
EMANUELA LUPACCHINO
JILL THOMPSON
BECKY CLOONAN
PENCILLERS

TRAVIS MOORE
ANDY MacDONALD
WADE VON GRAWBADGER
JILL THOMPSON
BECKY CLOONAN
INKERS

TAMRA BONVILLAIN
NICK FILARDI
JORDIE BELLAIRE
JILL THOMPSON
COLORISTS

PAT BROSSEAU
LETTERER

TRAVIS MOORE AND
TAMRA BONVILLAIN
**COLLECTION
COVER ARTISTS**

WONDER WOMAN
CREATED BY
WILLIAM MOULTON MARSTON

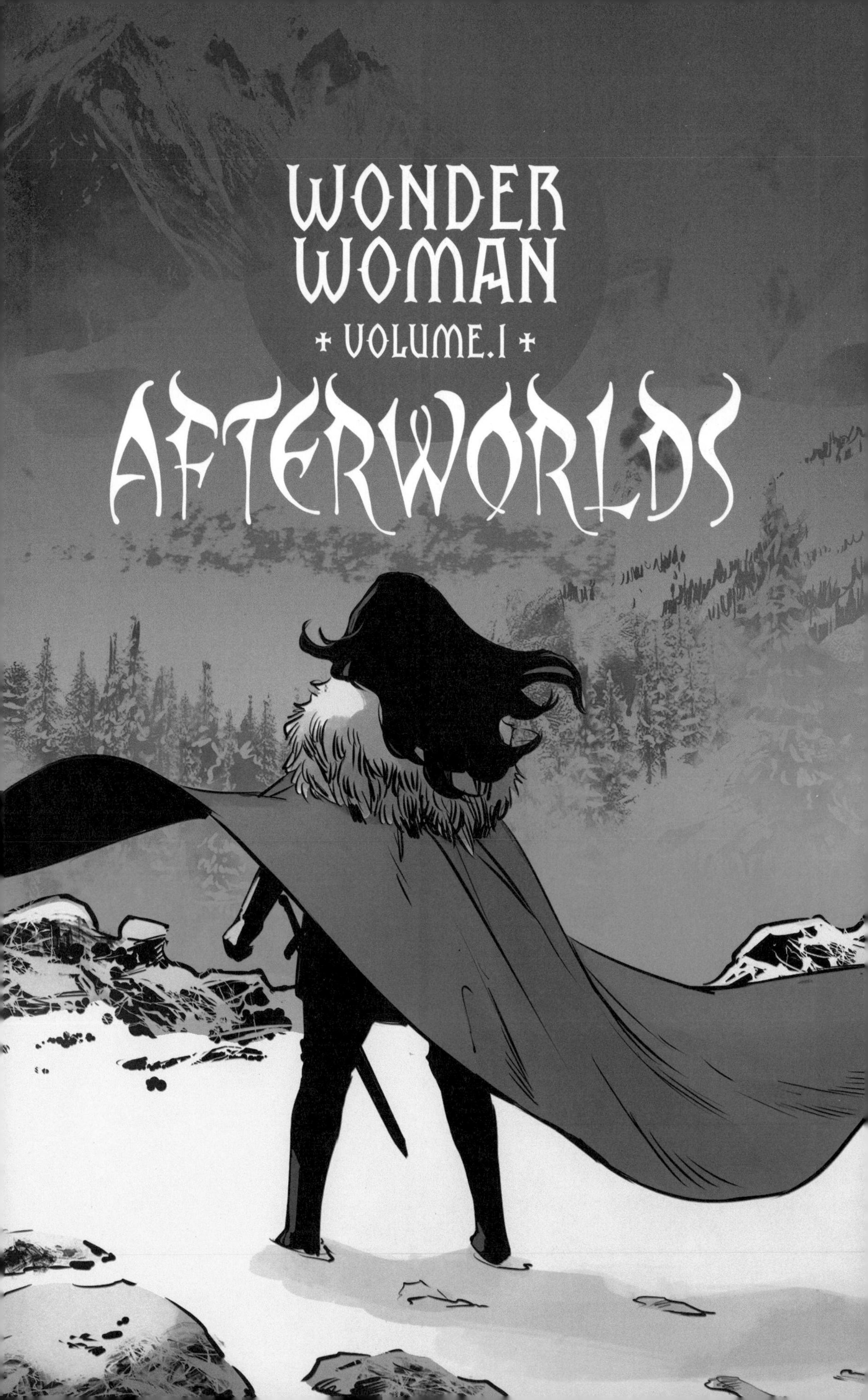
WONDER
WOMAN
VOLUME.1
AFTERWORLDS

Brittany Holzherr Editor – Original Series & Collected Edition
Bixie Mathieu Assistant Editor – Original Series
Steve Cook Design Director – Books & Publication Design
Suzannah Rowntree Publication Production

Marie Javins Editor-in-Chief, DC Comics

Daniel Cherry III Senior VP – General Manager
Jim Lee Publisher & Chief Creative Officer
Joen Choe VP – Global Brand & Creative Services
Don Falletti VP – Manufacturing Operations & Workflow Management
Lawrence Ganem VP – Talent Services
Alison Gill Senior VP – Manufacturing & Operations
Nick J. Napolitano VP – Manufacturing Administration & Design
Nancy Spears VP – Revenue

WONDER WOMAN VOL. 1: AFTERWORLDS

DC Comics, 2900 West Alameda Ave., Burbank, CA 91505
Printed by LSC Communications, Owensville, MO, USA. 11/5/21. First Printing.
ISBN: 978-1-77951-279-6

Library of Congress Cataloging-in-Publication Data is available.

PEFC Certified
This product is from sustainably managed forests and controlled sources
PEFC
PEFC/29-31-337
www.pefc.org

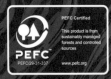

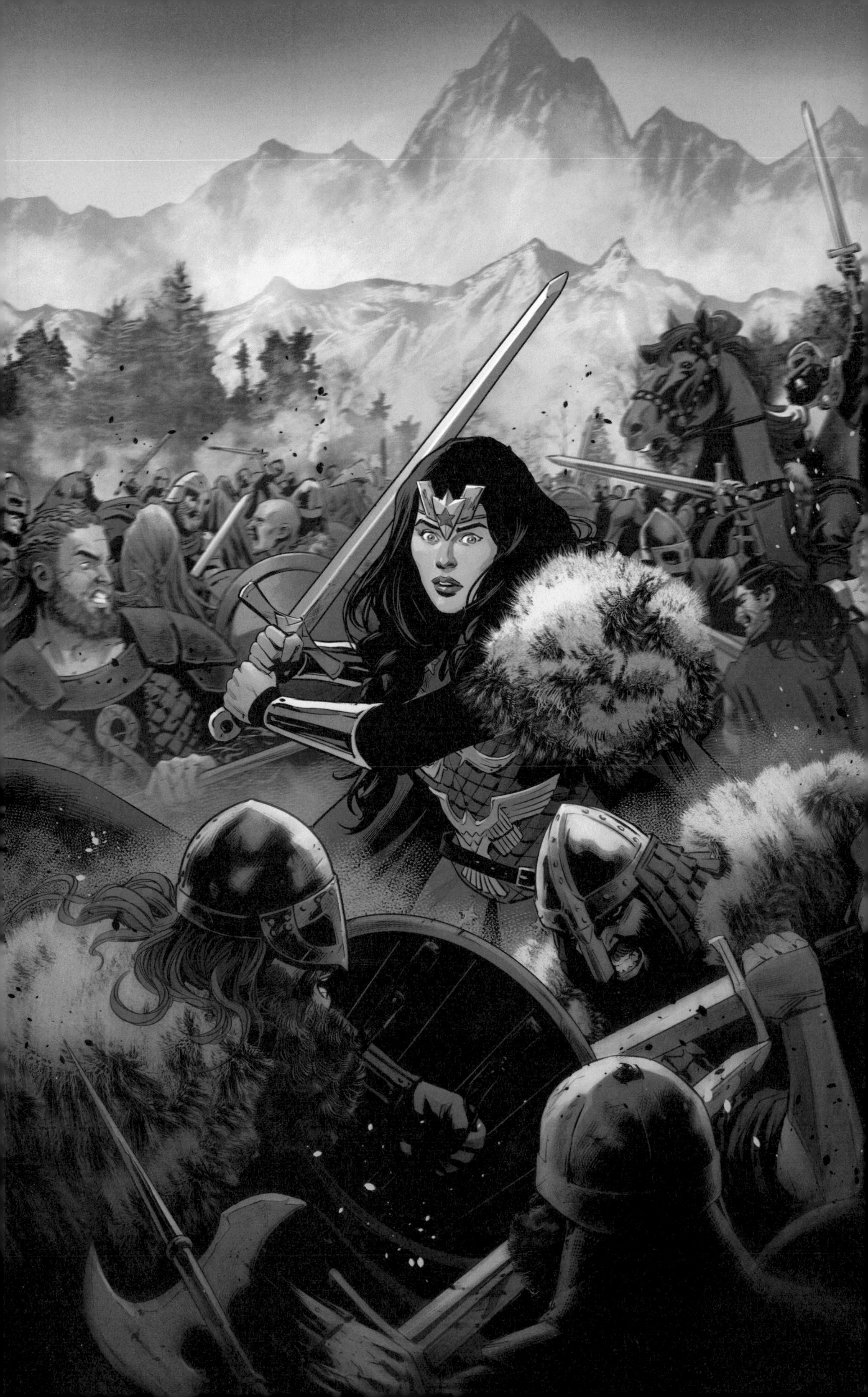

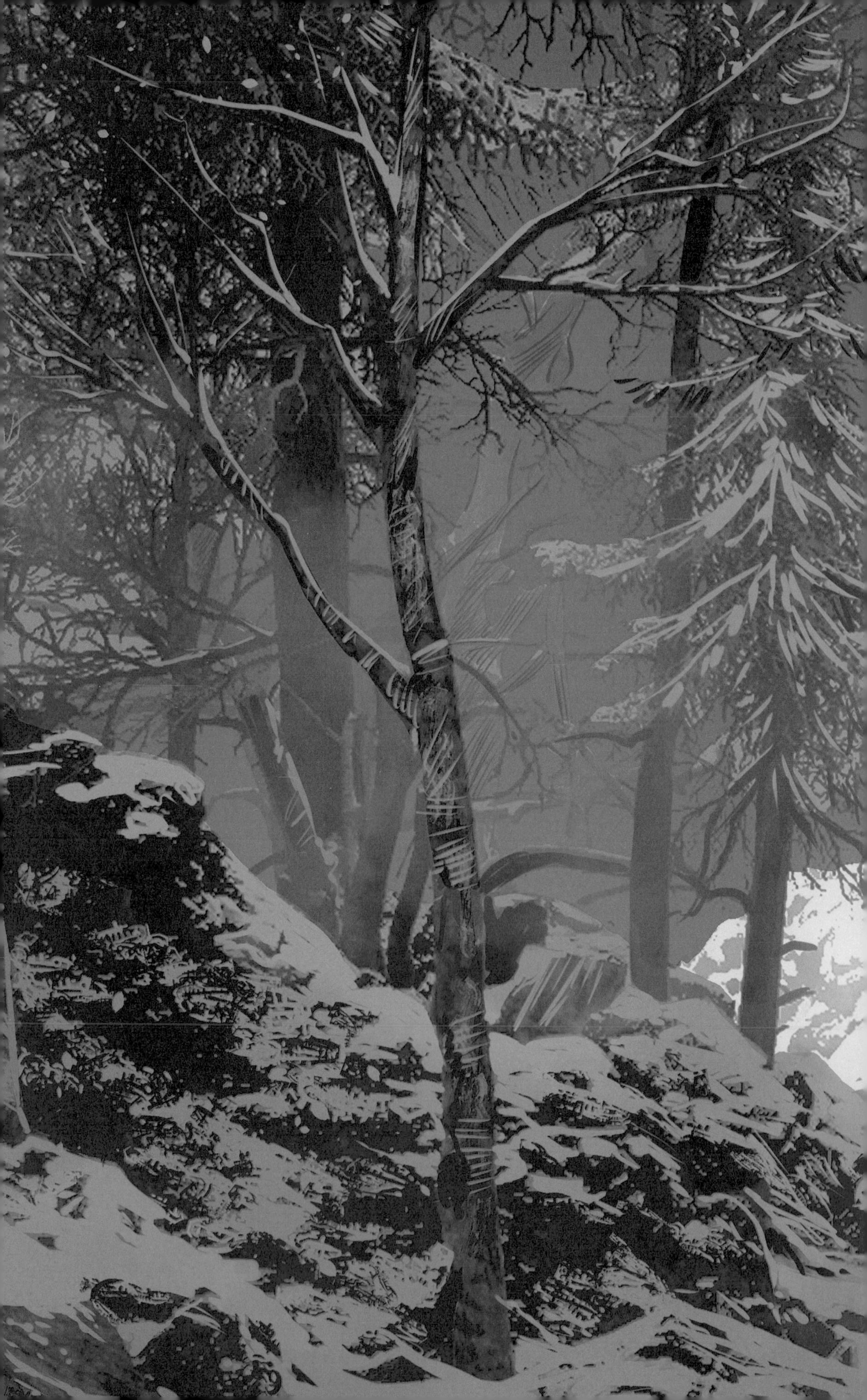

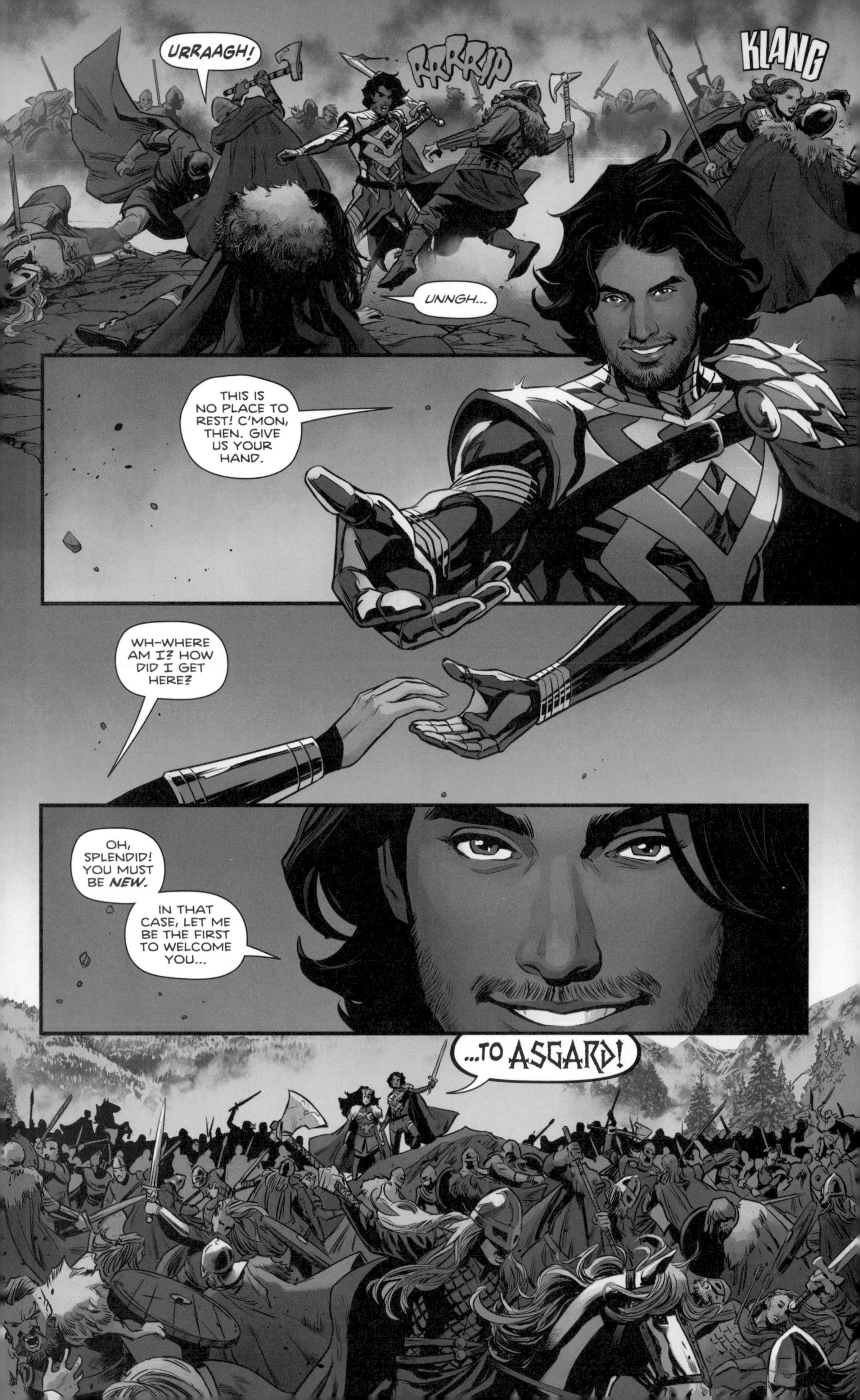
URRAAGH!
RRRRIP
KLANG
UNNGH...
THIS IS NO PLACE TO REST! C'MON, THEN. GIVE US YOUR HAND.
WH-WHERE AM I? HOW DID I GET HERE?
OH, SPLENDID! YOU MUST BE *NEW.*
IN THAT CASE, LET ME BE THE FIRST TO WELCOME YOU...
...TO ASGARD!

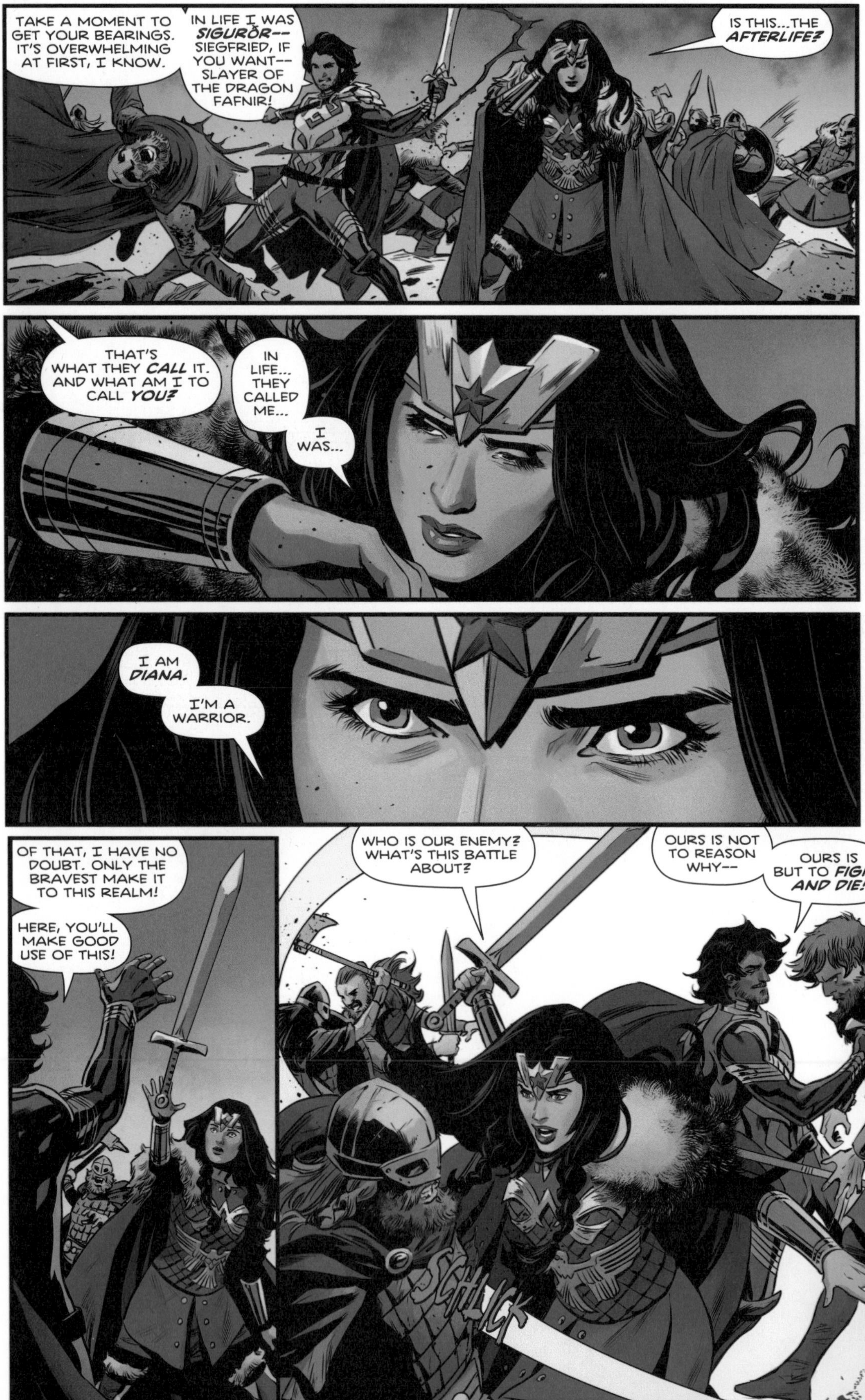

TAKE A MOMENT TO GET YOUR BEARINGS. IT'S OVERWHELMING AT FIRST, I KNOW.
IN LIFE I WAS SIGURÖR--SIEGFRIED, IF YOU WANT--SLAYER OF THE DRAGON FAFNIR!
IS THIS...THE AFTERLIFE?
THAT'S WHAT THEY CALL IT. AND WHAT AM I TO CALL YOU?
IN LIFE... THEY CALLED ME...
I WAS...
I AM DIANA.
I'M A WARRIOR.
OF THAT, I HAVE NO DOUBT. ONLY THE BRAVEST MAKE IT TO THIS REALM!
HERE, YOU'LL MAKE GOOD USE OF THIS!
WHO IS OUR ENEMY? WHAT'S THIS BATTLE ABOUT?
OURS IS NOT TO REASON WHY--
OURS IS BUT TO FIGHT AND DIE!
SCHLICK

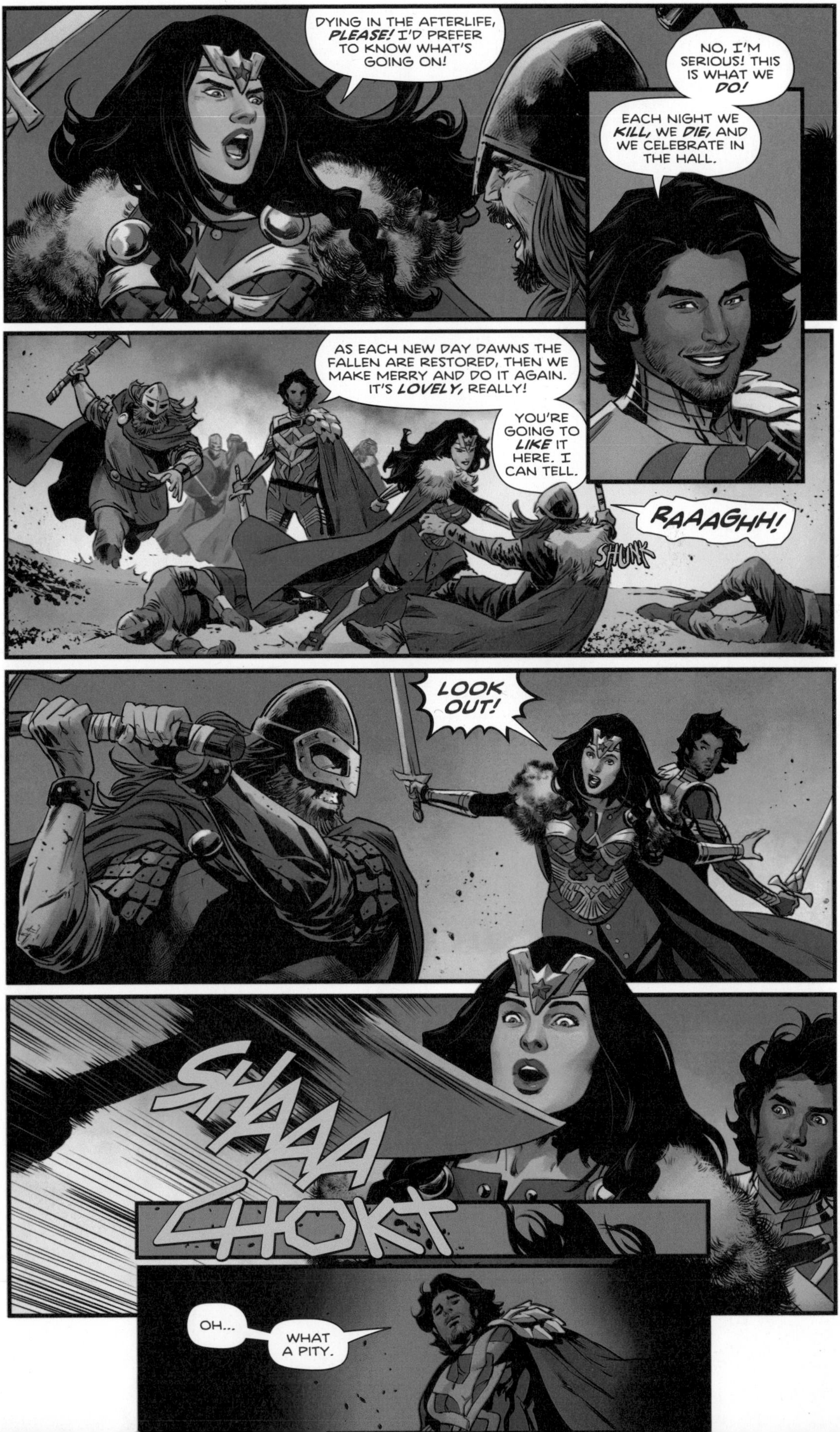
DYING IN THE AFTERLIFE, PLEASE! I'D PREFER TO KNOW WHAT'S GOING ON!
NO, I'M SERIOUS! THIS IS WHAT WE DO!
EACH NIGHT WE KILL, WE DIE, AND WE CELEBRATE IN THE HALL.
AS EACH NEW DAY DAWNS THE FALLEN ARE RESTORED, THEN WE MAKE MERRY AND DO IT AGAIN. IT'S LOVELY, REALLY!
YOU'RE GOING TO LIKE IT HERE. I CAN TELL.
RAAAGHH!
SHUNK
LOOK OUT!
SHAAA
CHOKT
OH...
WHAT A PITY.

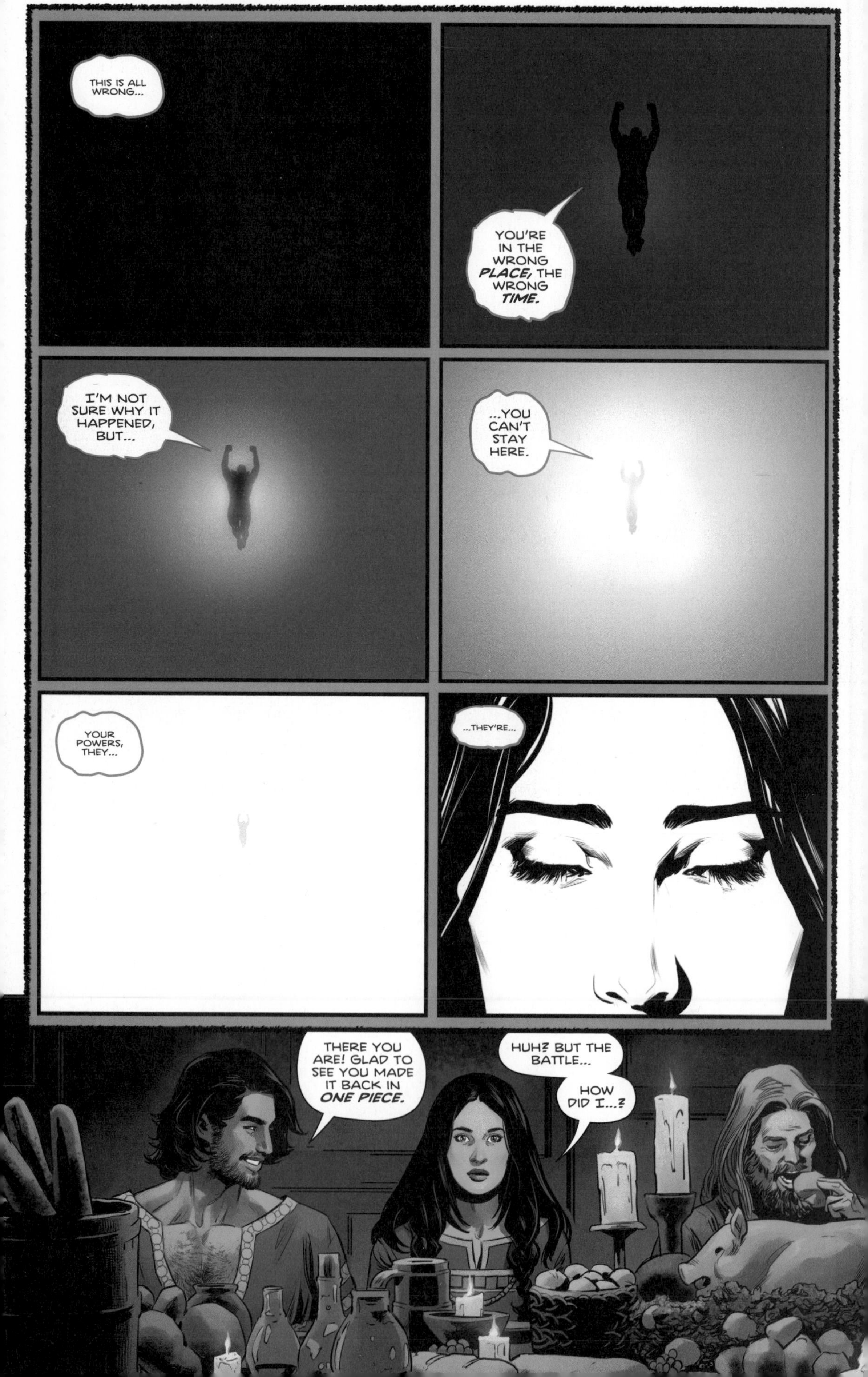
THIS IS ALL WRONG...
YOU'RE IN THE WRONG PLACE, THE WRONG TIME.
I'M NOT SURE WHY IT HAPPENED, BUT...
...YOU CAN'T STAY HERE.
YOUR POWERS, THEY...
...THEY'RE...
THERE YOU ARE! GLAD TO SEE YOU MADE IT BACK IN ONE PIECE.
HUH? BUT THE BATTLE...
HOW DID I...?

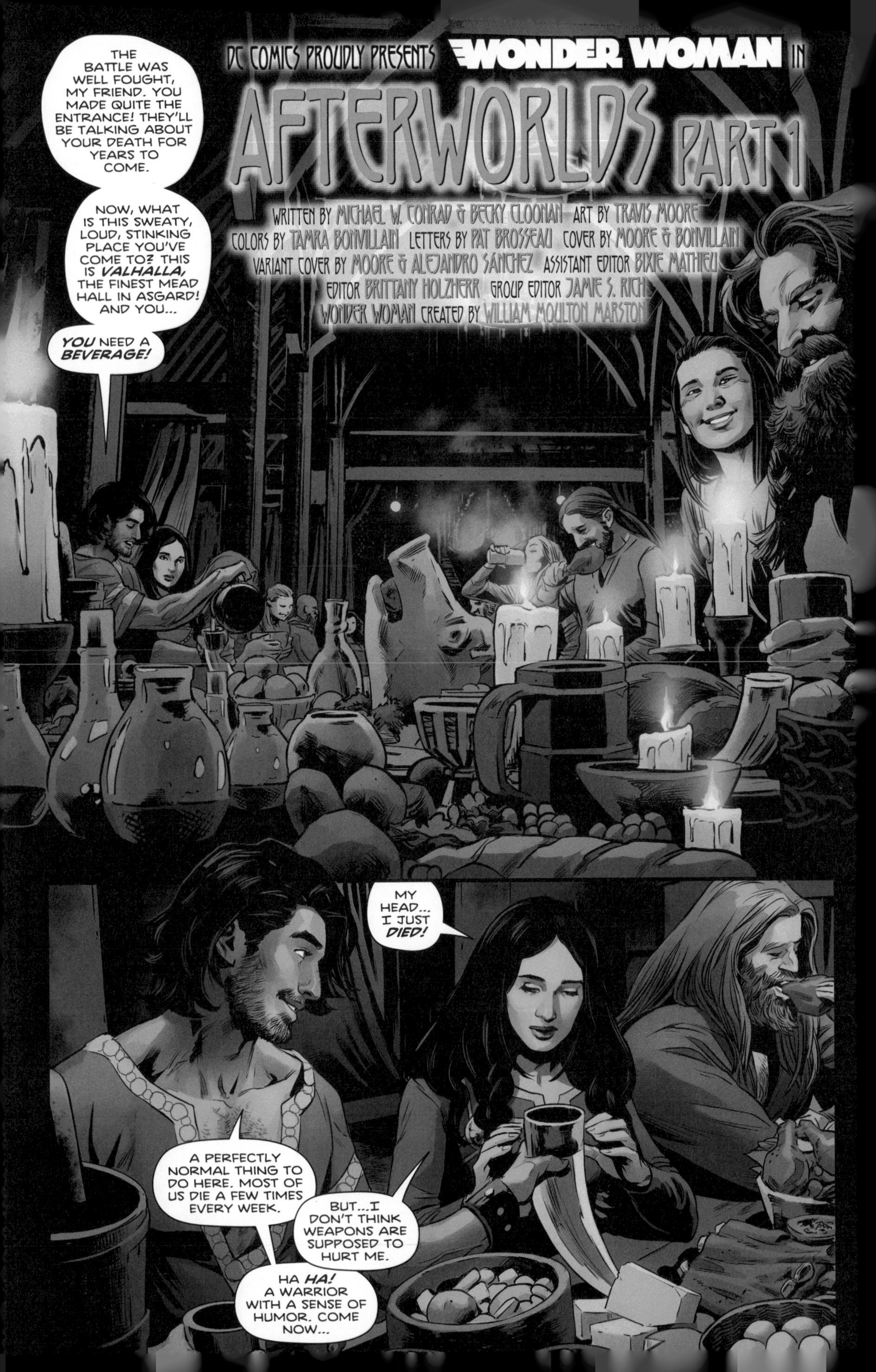
DC COMICS PROUDLY PRESENTS WONDER WOMAN IN
AFTERWORLDS PART 1
WRITTEN BY MICHAEL W. CONRAD & BECKY CLOONAN ART BY TRAVIS MOORE
COLORS BY TAMRA BONVILLAIN LETTERS BY PAT BROSSEAU COVER BY MOORE & BONVILLAIN
VARIANT COVER BY MOORE & ALEJANDRO SÁNCHEZ ASSISTANT EDITOR BIXIE MATHIEU
EDITOR BRITTANY HOLZHERR GROUP EDITOR JAMIE S. RICH
WONDER WOMAN CREATED BY WILLIAM MOULTON MARSTON
THE BATTLE WAS WELL FOUGHT, MY FRIEND. YOU MADE QUITE THE ENTRANCE! THEY'LL BE TALKING ABOUT YOUR DEATH FOR YEARS TO COME.
NOW, WHAT IS THIS SWEATY, LOUD, STINKING PLACE YOU'VE COME TO? THIS IS VALHALLA, THE FINEST MEAD HALL IN ASGARD! AND YOU...
YOU NEED A BEVERAGE!
MY HEAD... I JUST DIED!
A PERFECTLY NORMAL THING TO DO HERE. MOST OF US DIE A FEW TIMES EVERY WEEK.
BUT...I DON'T THINK WEAPONS ARE SUPPOSED TO HURT ME.
HA HA! A WARRIOR WITH A SENSE OF HUMOR. COME NOW...

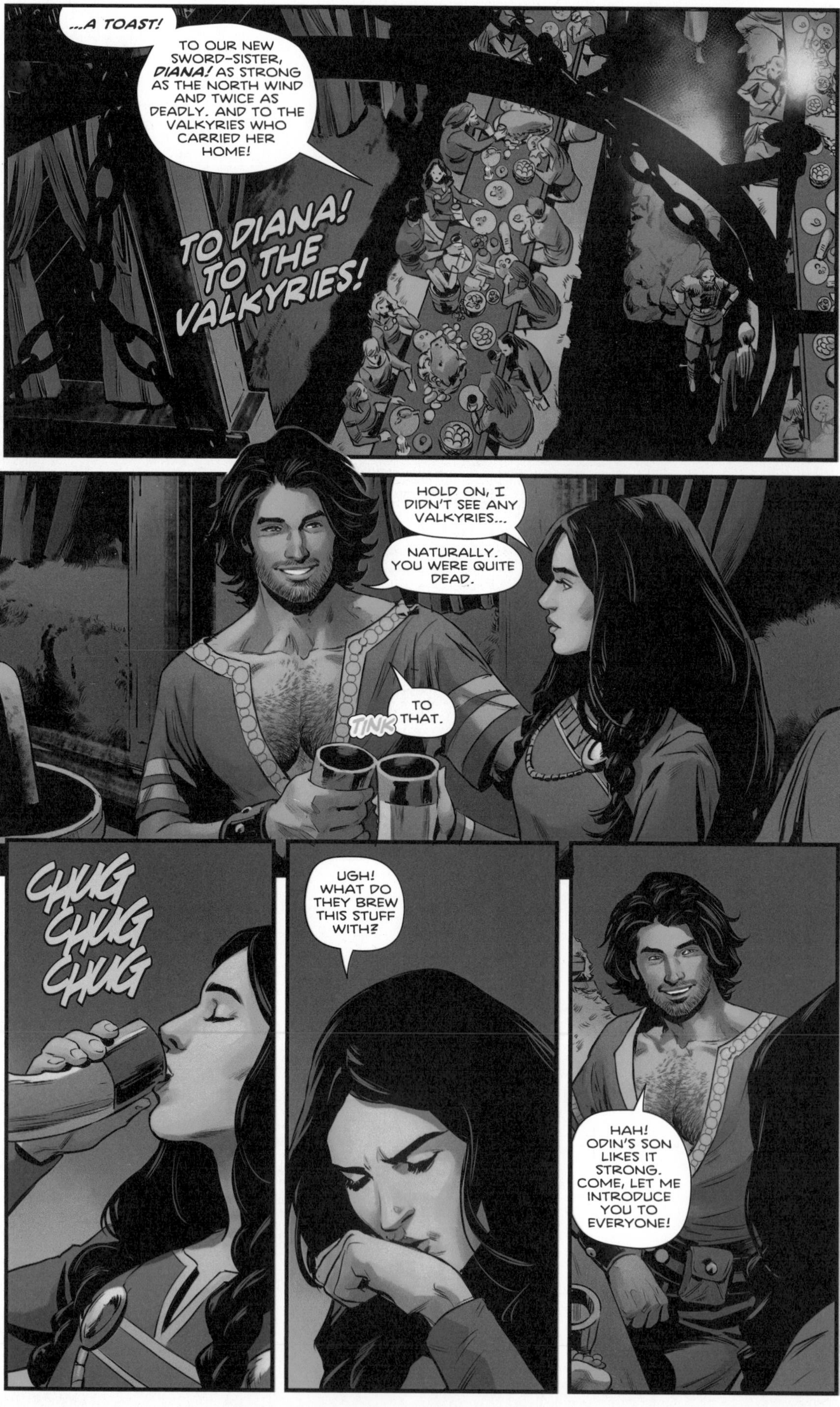
...A TOAST!
TO OUR NEW SWORD-SISTER, DIANA! AS STRONG AS THE NORTH WIND AND TWICE AS DEADLY. AND TO THE VALKYRIES WHO CARRIED HER HOME!
TO DIANA! TO THE VALKYRIES!
HOLD ON, I DIDN'T SEE ANY VALKYRIES...
NATURALLY. YOU WERE QUITE DEAD.
TO THAT.
TINK
CHUG CHUG CHUG
UGH! WHAT DO THEY BREW THIS STUFF WITH?
HAH! ODIN'S SON LIKES IT STRONG. COME, LET ME INTRODUCE YOU TO EVERYONE!

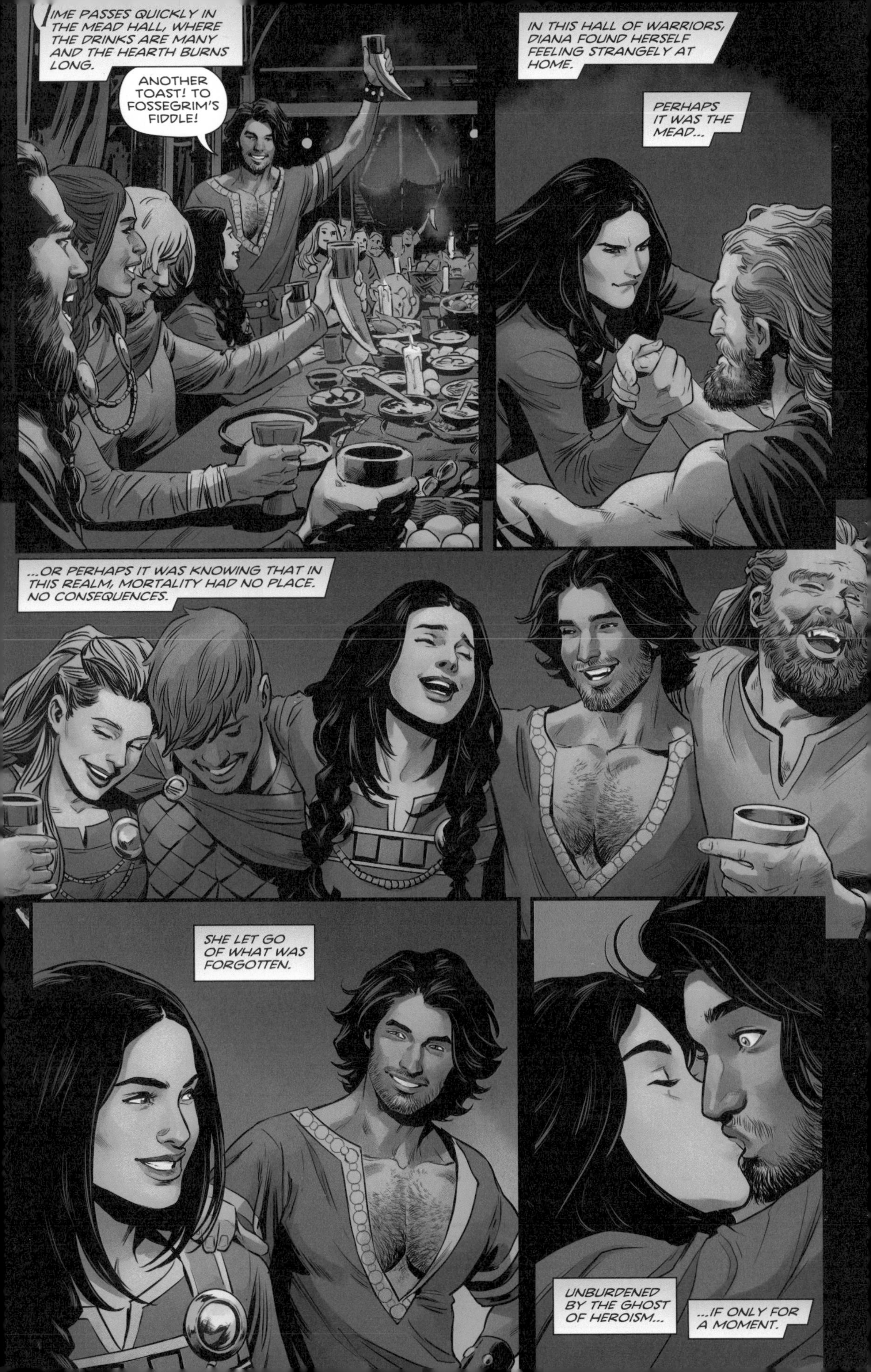
TIME PASSES QUICKLY IN THE MEAD HALL, WHERE THE DRINKS ARE MANY AND THE HEARTH BURNS LONG.
ANOTHER TOAST! TO FOSSEGRIM'S FIDDLE!
IN THIS HALL OF WARRIORS, DIANA FOUND HERSELF FEELING STRANGELY AT HOME.
PERHAPS IT WAS THE MEAD...
...OR PERHAPS IT WAS KNOWING THAT IN THIS REALM, MORTALITY HAD NO PLACE. NO CONSEQUENCES.
SHE LET GO OF WHAT WAS FORGOTTEN.
UNBURDENED BY THE GHOST OF HEROISM...
...IF ONLY FOR A MOMENT.

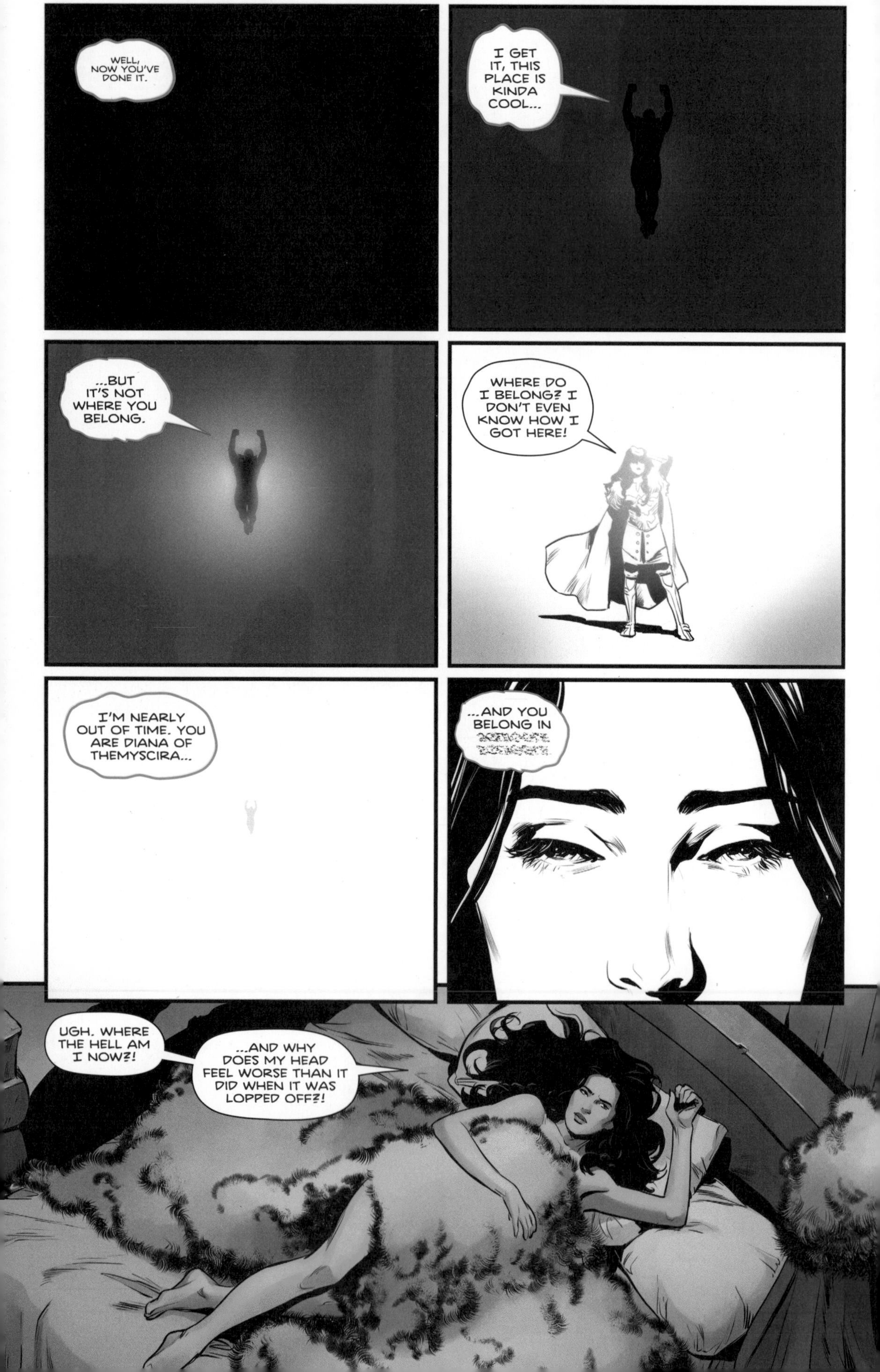
WELL, NOW YOU'VE DONE IT.
I GET IT, THIS PLACE IS KINDA COOL...
...BUT IT'S NOT WHERE YOU BELONG.
WHERE DO I BELONG? I DON'T EVEN KNOW HOW I GOT HERE!
I'M NEARLY OUT OF TIME. YOU ARE DIANA OF THEMYSCIRA...
...AND YOU BELONG IN
UGH. WHERE THE HELL AM I NOW?!
...AND WHY DOES MY HEAD FEEL WORSE THAN IT DID WHEN IT WAS LOPPED OFF?!

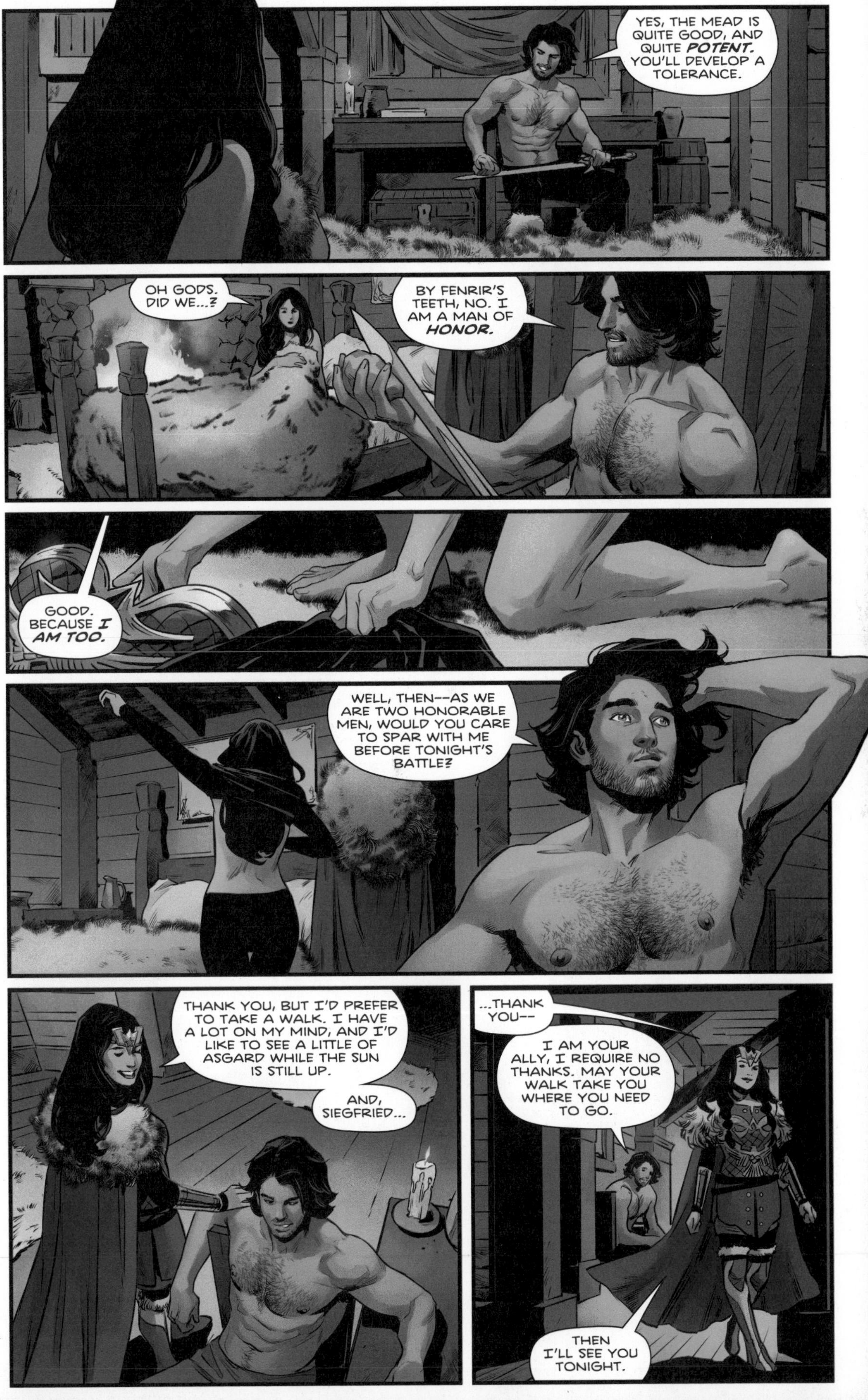
YES, THE MEAD IS QUITE GOOD, AND QUITE **POTENT.** YOU'LL DEVELOP A TOLERANCE.
OH GODS. DID WE...?
BY FENRIR'S TEETH, NO. I AM A MAN OF **HONOR.**
GOOD. BECAUSE ***I AM TOO.***
WELL, THEN--AS WE ARE TWO HONORABLE MEN, WOULD YOU CARE TO SPAR WITH ME BEFORE TONIGHT'S BATTLE?
THANK YOU, BUT I'D PREFER TO TAKE A WALK. I HAVE A LOT ON MY MIND, AND I'D LIKE TO SEE A LITTLE OF ASGARD WHILE THE SUN IS STILL UP.
AND, SIEGFRIED...
...THANK YOU--
I AM YOUR ALLY, I REQUIRE NO THANKS. MAY YOUR WALK TAKE YOU WHERE YOU NEED TO GO.
THEN I'LL SEE YOU TONIGHT.

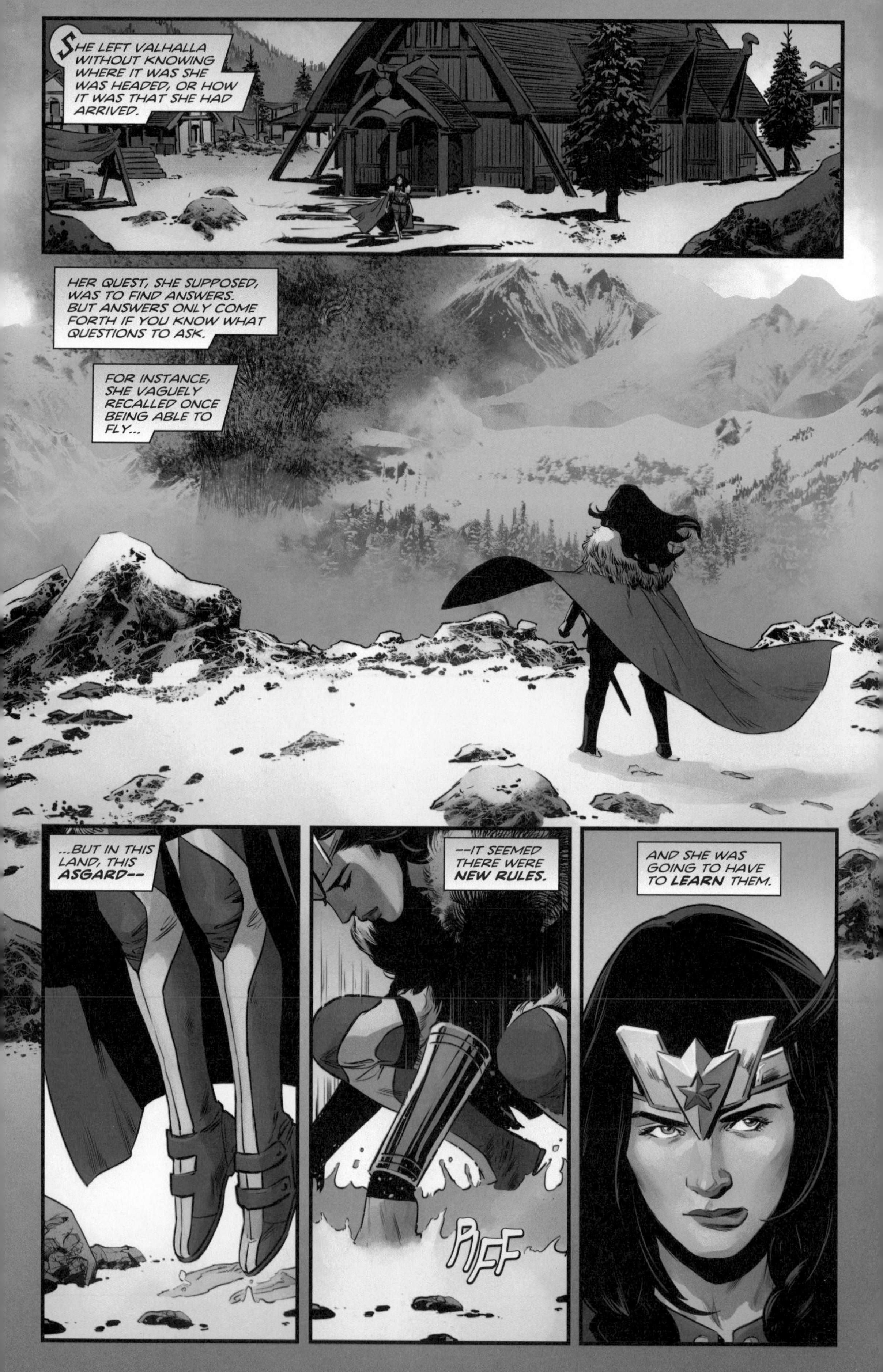
SHE LEFT VALHALLA WITHOUT KNOWING WHERE IT WAS SHE WAS HEADED, OR HOW IT WAS THAT SHE HAD ARRIVED.
HER QUEST, SHE SUPPOSED, WAS TO FIND ANSWERS. BUT ANSWERS ONLY COME FORTH IF YOU KNOW WHAT QUESTIONS TO ASK.
FOR INSTANCE, SHE VAGUELY RECALLED ONCE BEING ABLE TO FLY...
...BUT IN THIS LAND, THIS ASGARD--
--IT SEEMED THERE WERE NEW RULES.
PIFF
AND SHE WAS GOING TO HAVE TO LEARN THEM.

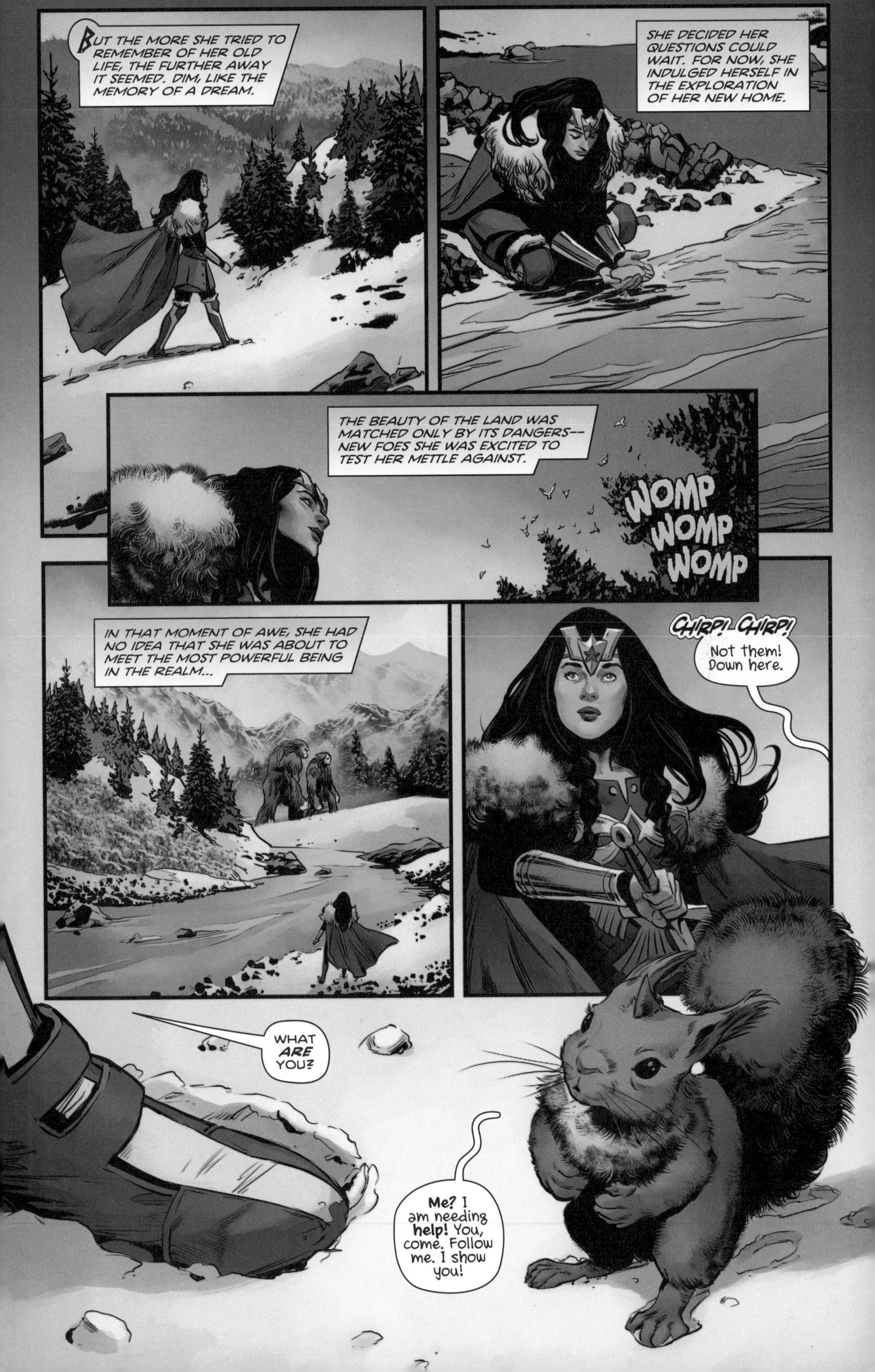

BUT THE MORE SHE TRIED TO REMEMBER OF HER OLD LIFE, THE FURTHER AWAY IT SEEMED. DIM, LIKE THE MEMORY OF A DREAM.
SHE DECIDED HER QUESTIONS COULD WAIT. FOR NOW, SHE INDULGED HERSELF IN THE EXPLORATION OF HER NEW HOME.
THE BEAUTY OF THE LAND WAS MATCHED ONLY BY ITS DANGERS-- NEW FOES SHE WAS EXCITED TO TEST HER METTLE AGAINST.
WOMP WOMP WOMP
IN THAT MOMENT OF AWE, SHE HAD NO IDEA THAT SHE WAS ABOUT TO MEET THE MOST POWERFUL BEING IN THE REALM...
CHIRP! CHIRP!
Not them! Down here.
WHAT ARE YOU?
Me? I am needing help! You, come. Follow me. I show you!

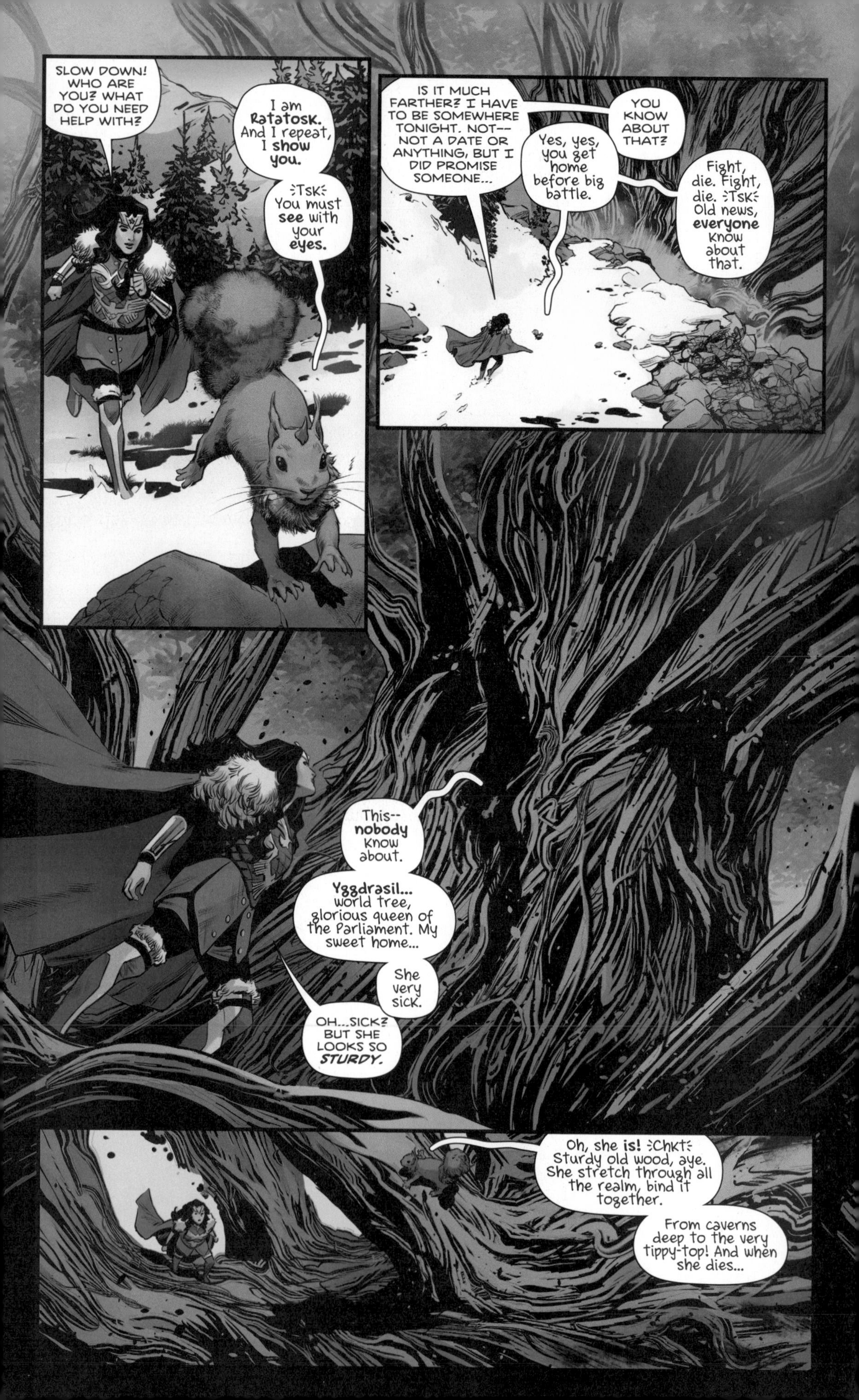
SLOW DOWN! WHO ARE YOU? WHAT DO YOU NEED HELP WITH?
I am **Ratatosk.** And I repeat, I **show you.**
⁝TSK⁝ You must **see** with your **eyes.**
IS IT MUCH FARTHER? I HAVE TO BE SOMEWHERE TONIGHT. NOT-- NOT A DATE OR ANYTHING, BUT I DID PROMISE SOMEONE...
Yes, yes, you get home before big battle.
YOU KNOW ABOUT THAT?
Fight, die. Fight, die. ⁝TSK⁝ Old news, **everyone** know about that.
This-- **nobody** know about.
Yggdrasil... world tree, glorious queen of the Parliament. My sweet home...
She very sick.
OH...SICK? BUT SHE LOOKS SO ***STURDY.***
Oh, she **is!** ⁝ChKt⁝ Sturdy old wood, aye. She stretch through all the realm, bind it together.
From caverns deep to the very tippy-top! And when she dies...

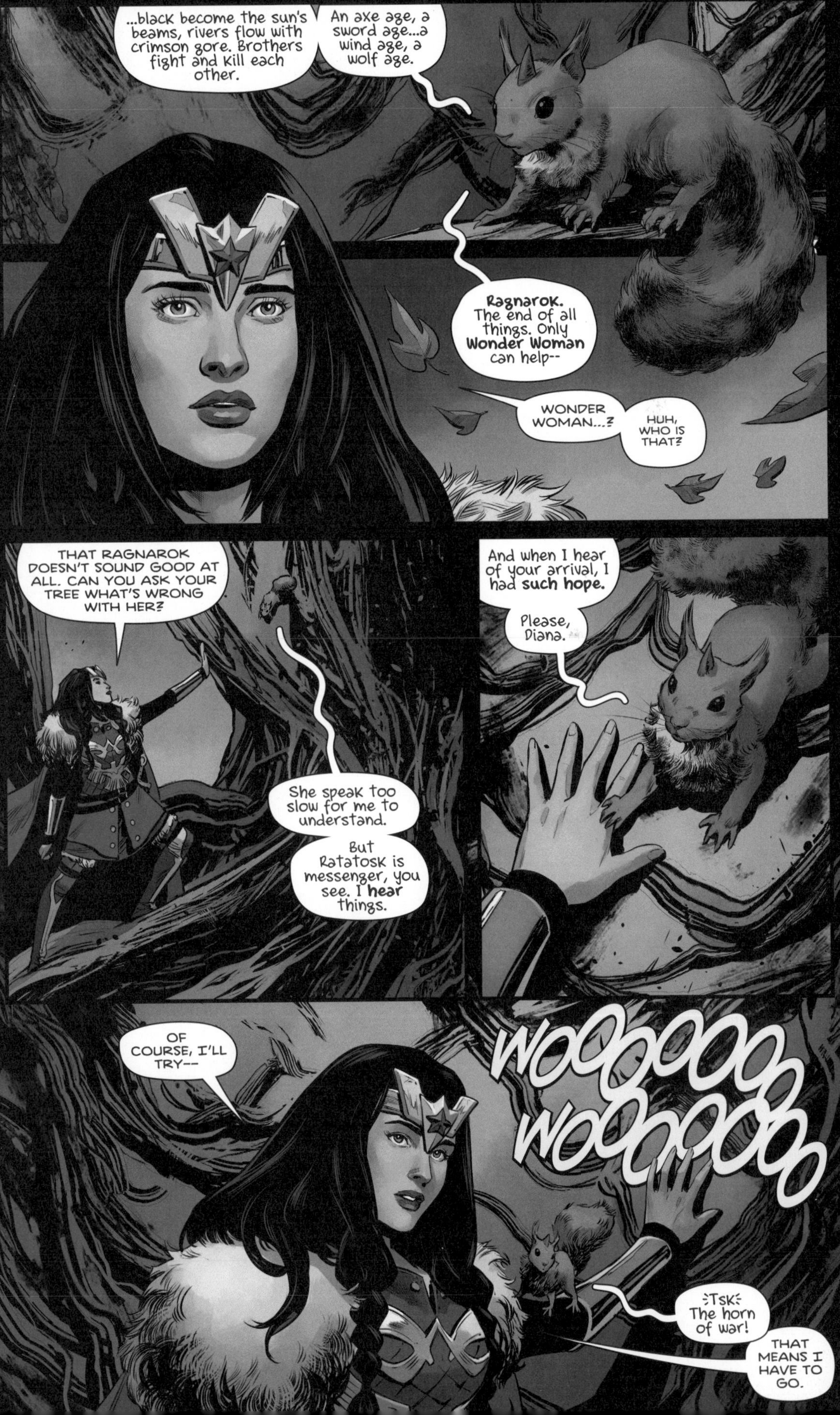
...black become the sun's beams, rivers flow with crimson gore. Brothers fight and kill each other.
An axe age, a sword age...a wind age, a wolf age.
Ragnarok. The end of all things. Only **Wonder Woman** can help--
WONDER WOMAN...?
HUH, WHO IS THAT?
THAT RAGNAROK DOESN'T SOUND GOOD AT ALL. CAN YOU ASK YOUR TREE WHAT'S WRONG WITH HER?
She speak too slow for me to understand.
But Ratatosk is messenger, you see. I **hear** things.
And when I hear of your arrival, I had **such hope.**
Please, Diana.
OF COURSE, I'LL TRY--
WOOOOOO WOOOOOOO
TSK The horn of war!
THAT MEANS I HAVE TO GO.

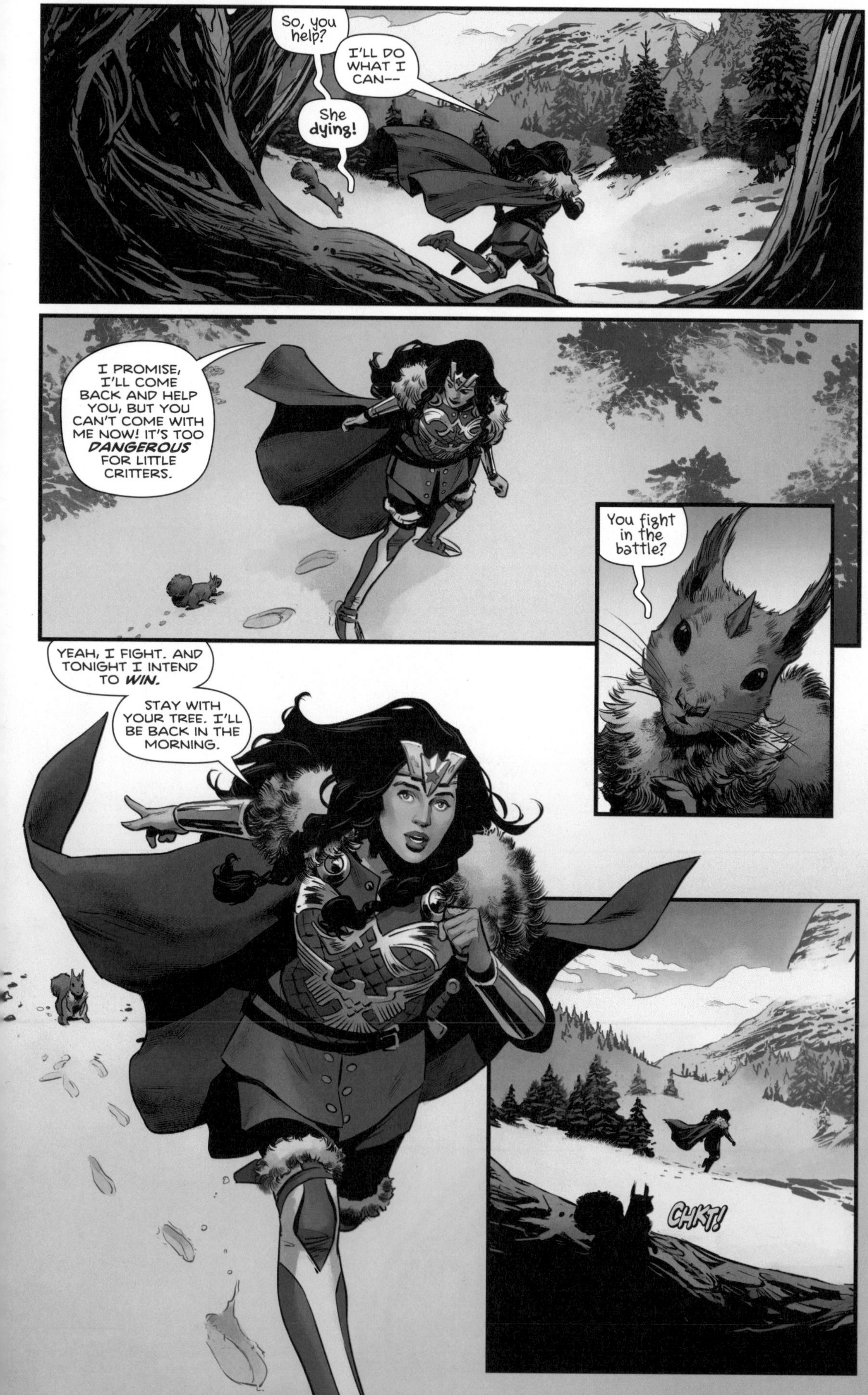
So, you help?
I'LL DO WHAT I CAN--
She dying!
I PROMISE, I'LL COME BACK AND HELP YOU, BUT YOU CAN'T COME WITH ME NOW! IT'S TOO DANGEROUS FOR LITTLE CRITTERS.
You fight in the battle?
YEAH, I FIGHT. AND TONIGHT I INTEND TO WIN.
STAY WITH YOUR TREE. I'LL BE BACK IN THE MORNING.
CHKT!

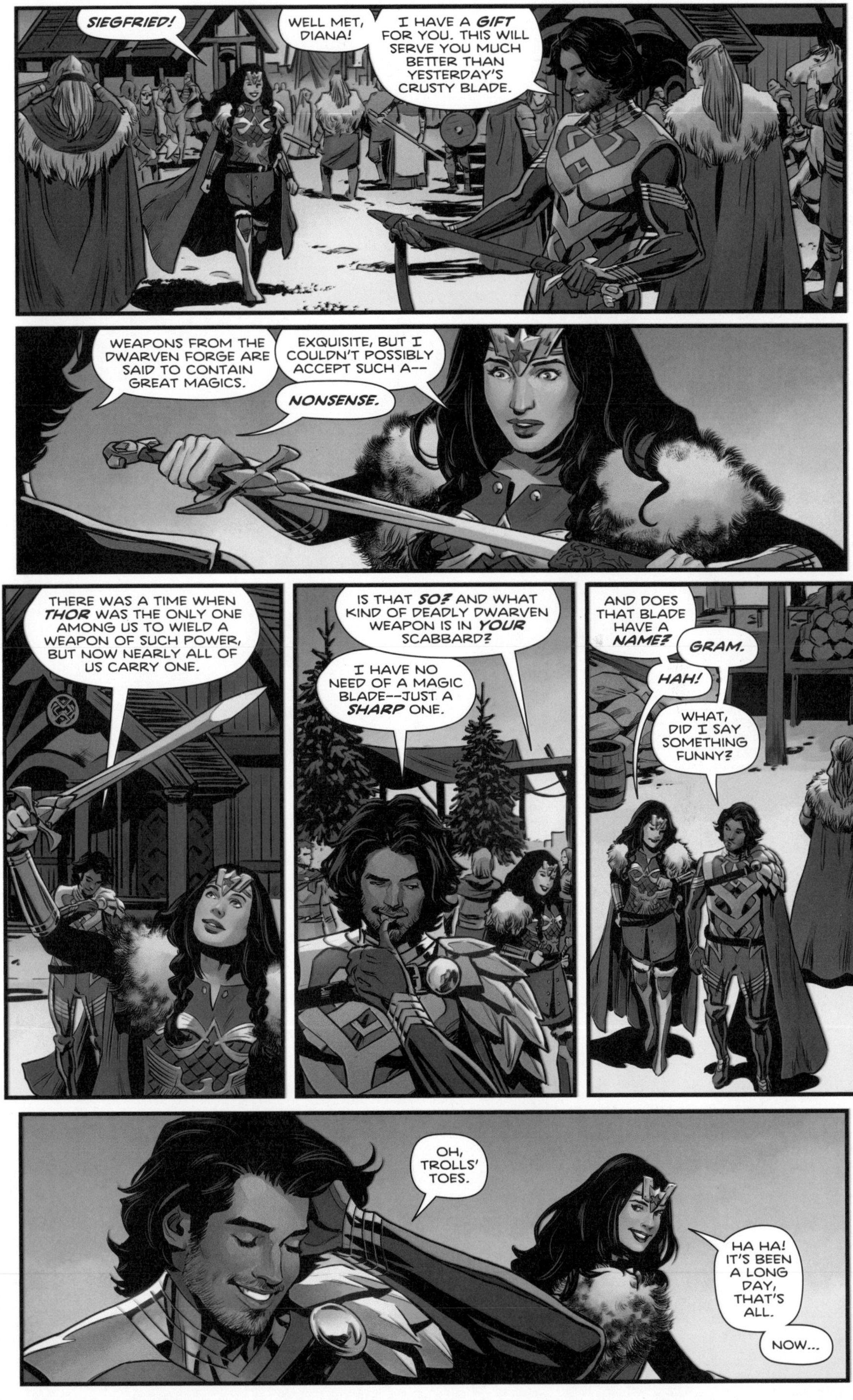
SIEGFRIED!
WELL MET, DIANA!
I HAVE A GIFT FOR YOU. THIS WILL SERVE YOU MUCH BETTER THAN YESTERDAY'S CRUSTY BLADE.
WEAPONS FROM THE DWARVEN FORGE ARE SAID TO CONTAIN GREAT MAGICS.
EXQUISITE, BUT I COULDN'T POSSIBLY ACCEPT SUCH A--
NONSENSE.
THERE WAS A TIME WHEN THOR WAS THE ONLY ONE AMONG US TO WIELD A WEAPON OF SUCH POWER, BUT NOW NEARLY ALL OF US CARRY ONE.
IS THAT SO? AND WHAT KIND OF DEADLY DWARVEN WEAPON IS IN YOUR SCABBARD?
I HAVE NO NEED OF A MAGIC BLADE--JUST A SHARP ONE.
AND DOES THAT BLADE HAVE A NAME?
GRAM.
HAH!
WHAT, DID I SAY SOMETHING FUNNY?
OH, TROLLS' TOES.
HA HA! IT'S BEEN A LONG DAY, THAT'S ALL.
NOW...

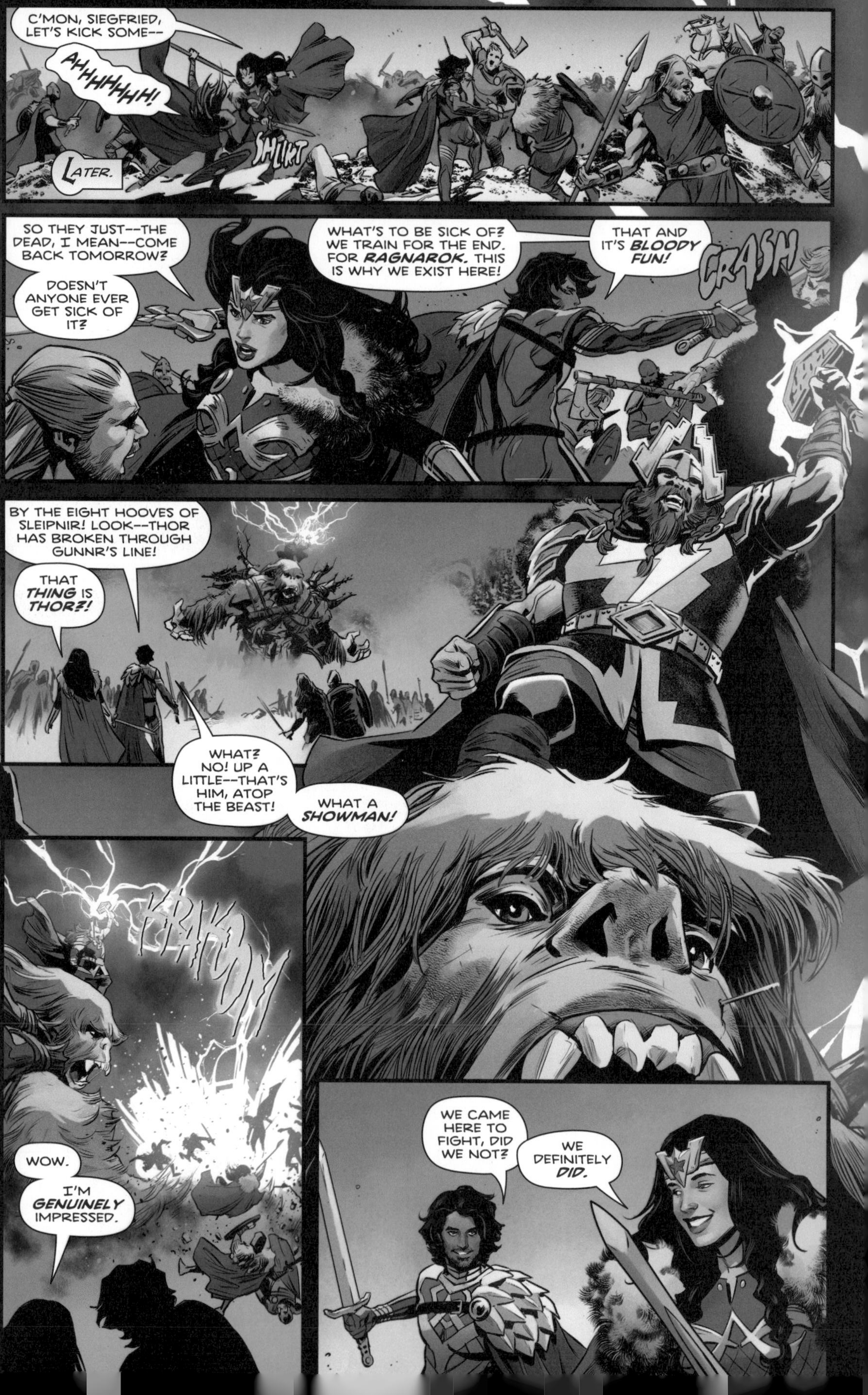
C'MON, SIEGFRIED, LET'S KICK SOME--
AHHHHHH!
SHLIRT
LATER.
SO THEY JUST--THE DEAD, I MEAN--COME BACK TOMORROW?
DOESN'T ANYONE EVER GET SICK OF IT?
WHAT'S TO BE SICK OF? WE TRAIN FOR THE END. FOR RAGNAROK. THIS IS WHY WE EXIST HERE!
THAT AND IT'S BLOODY FUN!
CRASH
BY THE EIGHT HOOVES OF SLEIPNIR! LOOK--THOR HAS BROKEN THROUGH GUNNR'S LINE!
THAT THING IS THOR?!
WHAT? NO! UP A LITTLE--THAT'S HIM, ATOP THE BEAST!
WHAT A SHOWMAN!
KRAKOOM
WOW.
I'M GENUINELY IMPRESSED.
WE CAME HERE TO FIGHT, DID WE NOT?
WE DEFINITELY DID.

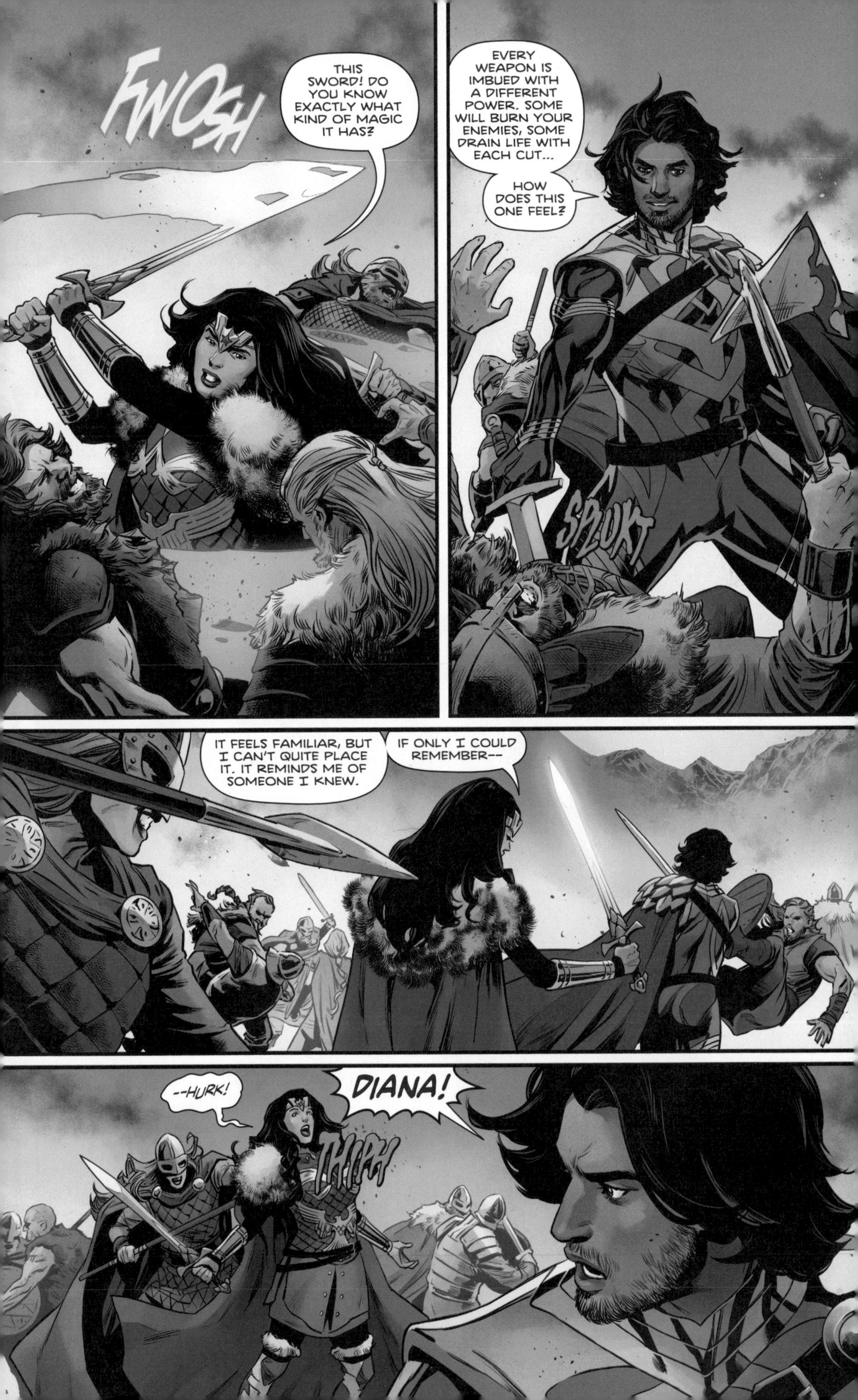
FWOSH
THIS SWORD! DO YOU KNOW EXACTLY WHAT KIND OF MAGIC IT HAS?
EVERY WEAPON IS IMBUED WITH A DIFFERENT POWER. SOME WILL BURN YOUR ENEMIES, SOME DRAIN LIFE WITH EACH CUT...
HOW DOES THIS ONE FEEL?
SPLUKT
IT FEELS FAMILIAR, BUT I CAN'T QUITE PLACE IT. IT REMINDS ME OF SOMEONE I KNEW.
IF ONLY I COULD REMEMBER--
--HURK!
DIANA!
THIPH

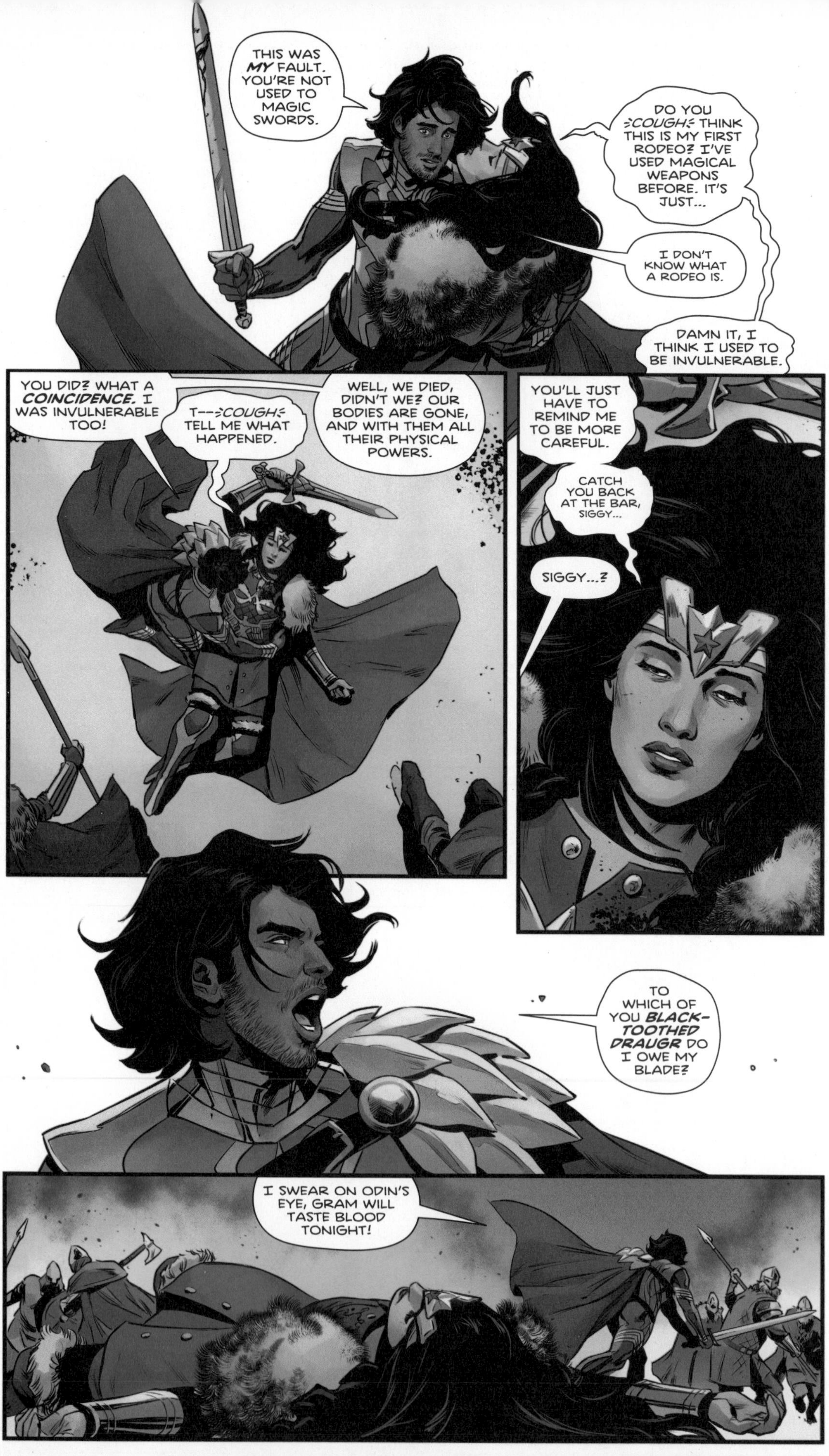
THIS WAS MY FAULT. YOU'RE NOT USED TO MAGIC SWORDS.
DO YOU -COUGH- THINK THIS IS MY FIRST RODEO? I'VE USED MAGICAL WEAPONS BEFORE. IT'S JUST...
I DON'T KNOW WHAT A RODEO IS.
DAMN IT, I THINK I USED TO BE INVULNERABLE.
YOU DID? WHAT A COINCIDENCE. I WAS INVULNERABLE TOO!
WELL, WE DIED, DIDN'T WE? OUR BODIES ARE GONE, AND WITH THEM ALL THEIR PHYSICAL POWERS.
T-- -COUGH- TELL ME WHAT HAPPENED.
YOU'LL JUST HAVE TO REMIND ME TO BE MORE CAREFUL.
CATCH YOU BACK AT THE BAR, SIGGY...
SIGGY...?
TO WHICH OF YOU BLACK-TOOTHED DRAUGR DO I OWE MY BLADE?
I SWEAR ON ODIN'S EYE, GRAM WILL TASTE BLOOD TONIGHT!

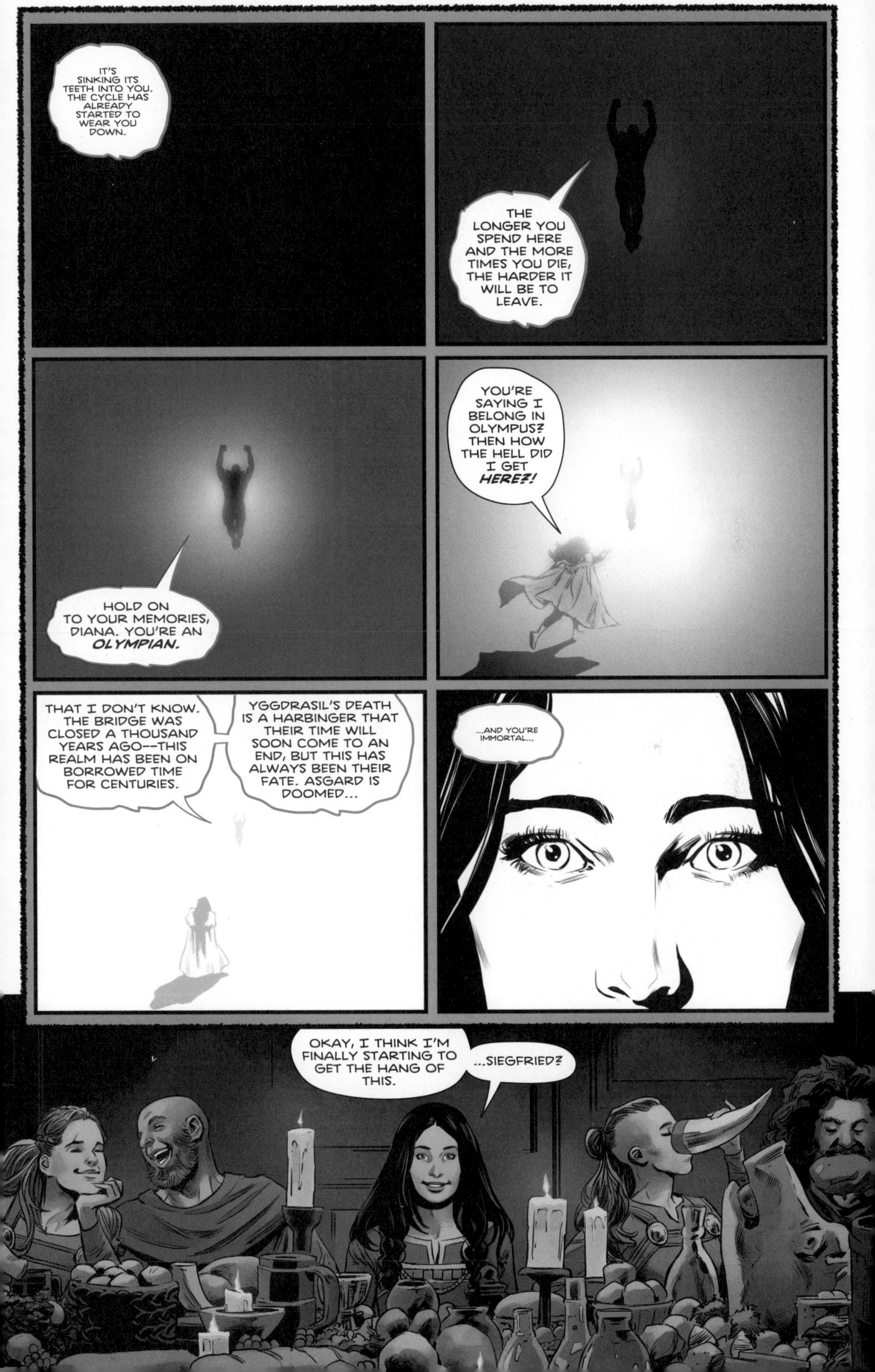
IT'S SINKING ITS TEETH INTO YOU. THE CYCLE HAS ALREADY STARTED TO WEAR YOU DOWN.
THE LONGER YOU SPEND HERE AND THE MORE TIMES YOU DIE, THE HARDER IT WILL BE TO LEAVE.
HOLD ON TO YOUR MEMORIES, DIANA. YOU'RE AN *OLYMPIAN.*
YOU'RE SAYING I BELONG IN OLYMPUS? THEN HOW THE HELL DID I GET *HERE?!*
THAT I DON'T KNOW. THE BRIDGE WAS CLOSED A THOUSAND YEARS AGO--THIS REALM HAS BEEN ON BORROWED TIME FOR CENTURIES.
YGGDRASIL'S DEATH IS A HARBINGER THAT THEIR TIME WILL SOON COME TO AN END, BUT THIS HAS ALWAYS BEEN THEIR FATE. ASGARD IS DOOMED...
...AND YOU'RE IMMORTAL...
OKAY, I THINK I'M FINALLY STARTING TO GET THE HANG OF THIS.
...SIEGFRIED?

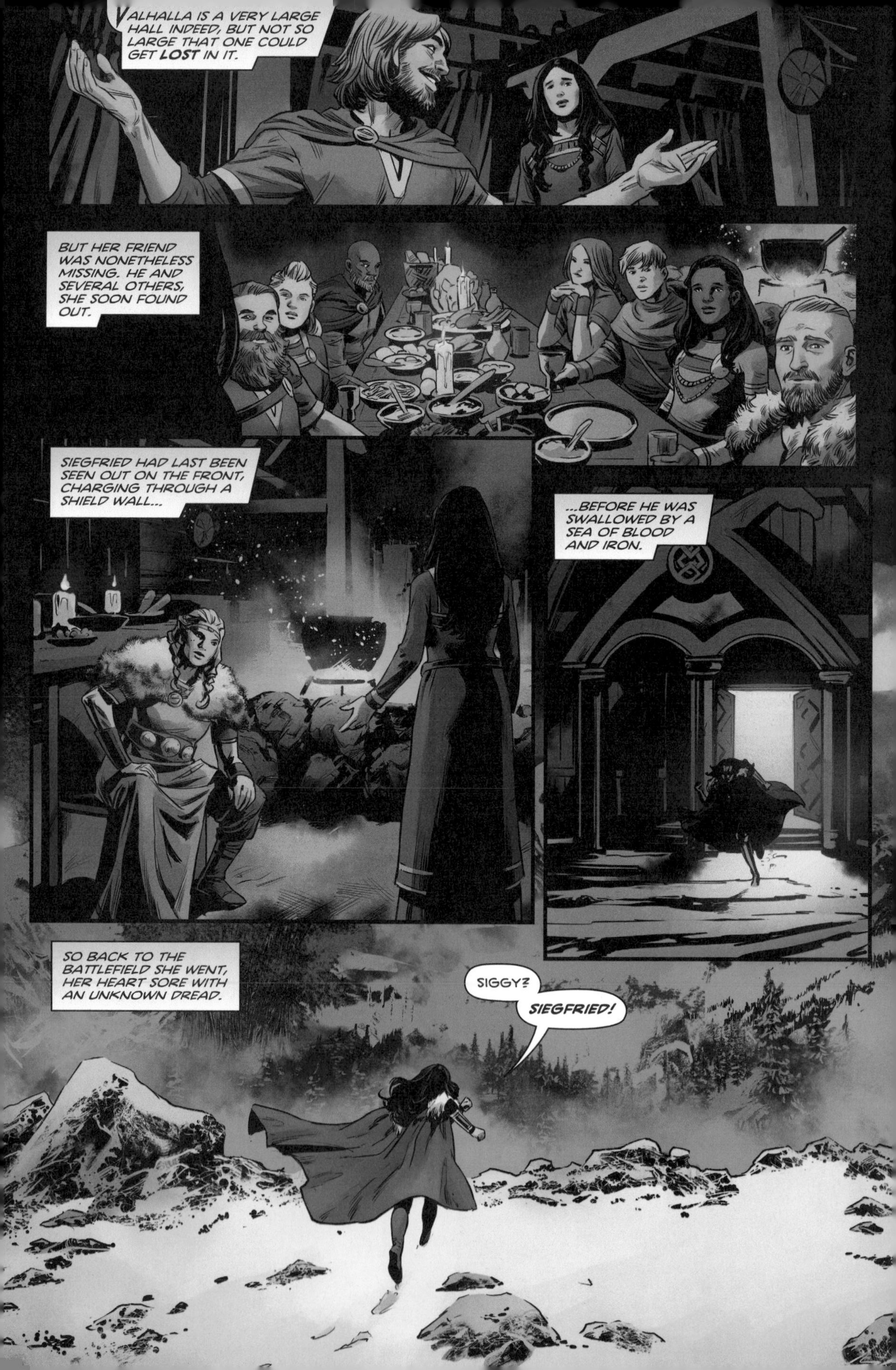
VALHALLA IS A VERY LARGE HALL INDEED, BUT NOT SO LARGE THAT ONE COULD GET LOST IN IT.
BUT HER FRIEND WAS NONETHELESS MISSING. HE AND SEVERAL OTHERS, SHE SOON FOUND OUT.
SIEGFRIED HAD LAST BEEN SEEN OUT ON THE FRONT, CHARGING THROUGH A SHIELD WALL...
...BEFORE HE WAS SWALLOWED BY A SEA OF BLOOD AND IRON.
SO BACK TO THE BATTLEFIELD SHE WENT, HER HEART SORE WITH AN UNKNOWN DREAD.
SIGGY?
SIEGFRIED!

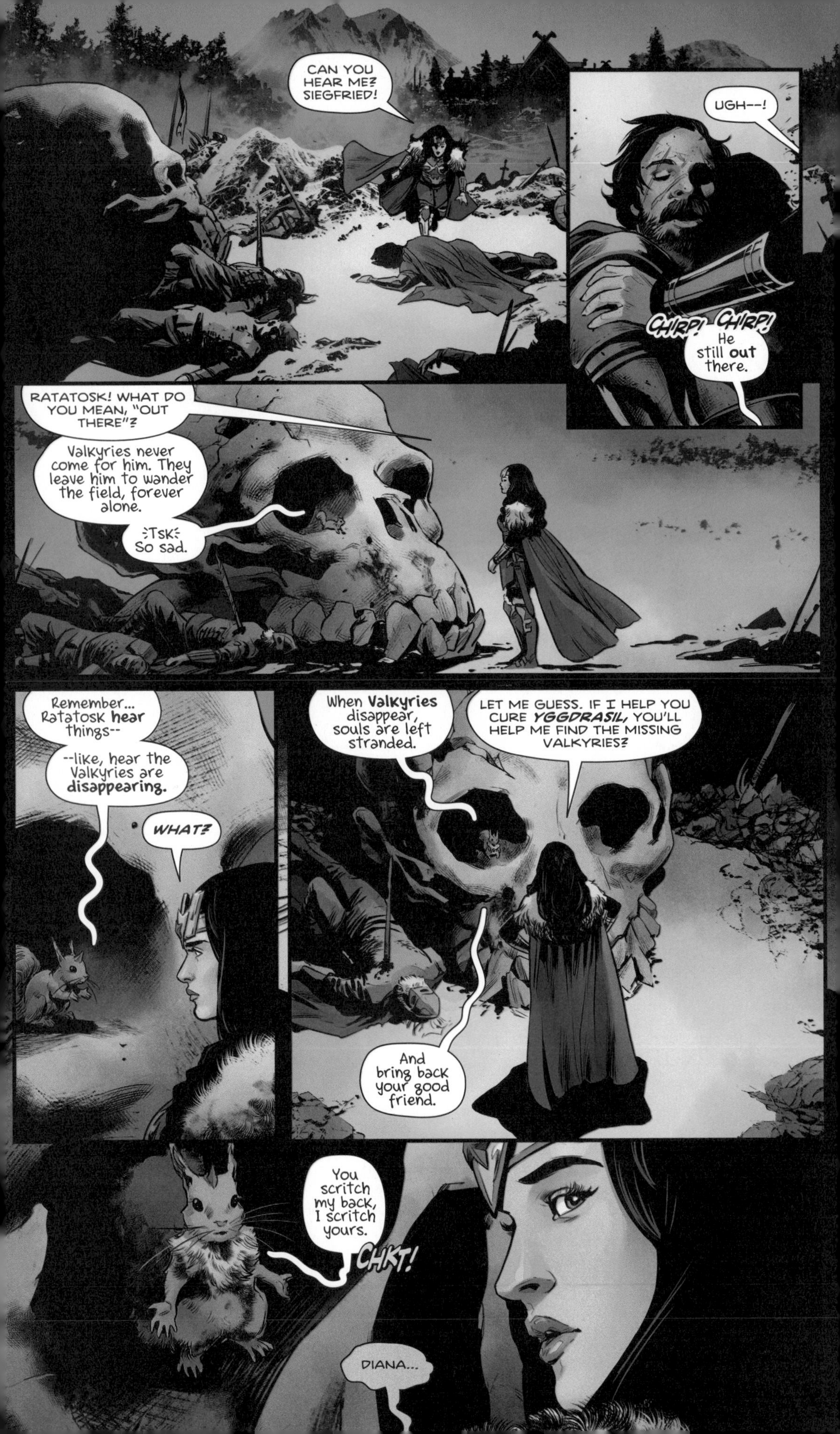
CAN YOU HEAR ME? SIEGFRIED!
UGH--!
CHIRP! CHIRP!
He still out there.
RATATOSK! WHAT DO YOU MEAN, "OUT THERE"?
Valkyries never come for him. They leave him to wander the field, forever alone.
Tsk So sad.
Remember... Ratatosk hear things--
--like, hear the Valkyries are disappearing.
WHAT?
When Valkyries disappear, souls are left stranded.
LET ME GUESS. IF I HELP YOU CURE YGGDRASIL, YOU'LL HELP ME FIND THE MISSING VALKYRIES?
And bring back your good friend.
You scritch my back, I scritch yours.
CHKT!
DIANA...

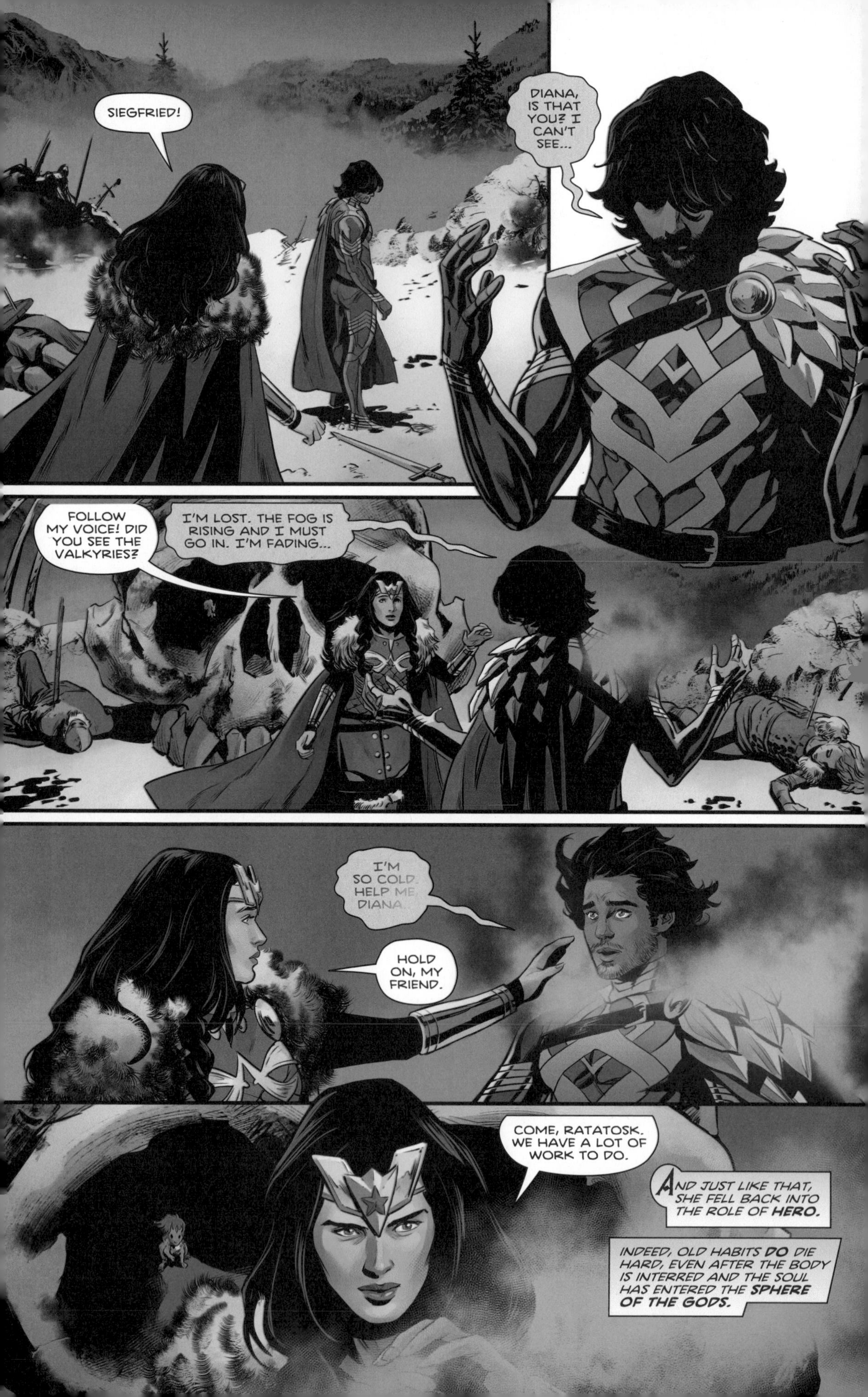
SIEGFRIED!
DIANA, IS THAT YOU? I CAN'T SEE...
FOLLOW MY VOICE! DID YOU SEE THE VALKYRIES?
I'M LOST. THE FOG IS RISING AND I MUST GO IN. I'M FADING...
I'M SO COLD. HELP ME, DIANA...
HOLD ON, MY FRIEND.
COME, RATATOSK. WE HAVE A LOT OF WORK TO DO.
AND JUST LIKE THAT, SHE FELL BACK INTO THE ROLE OF HERO.
INDEED, OLD HABITS DO DIE HARD, EVEN AFTER THE BODY IS INTERRED AND THE SOUL HAS ENTERED THE SPHERE OF THE GODS.

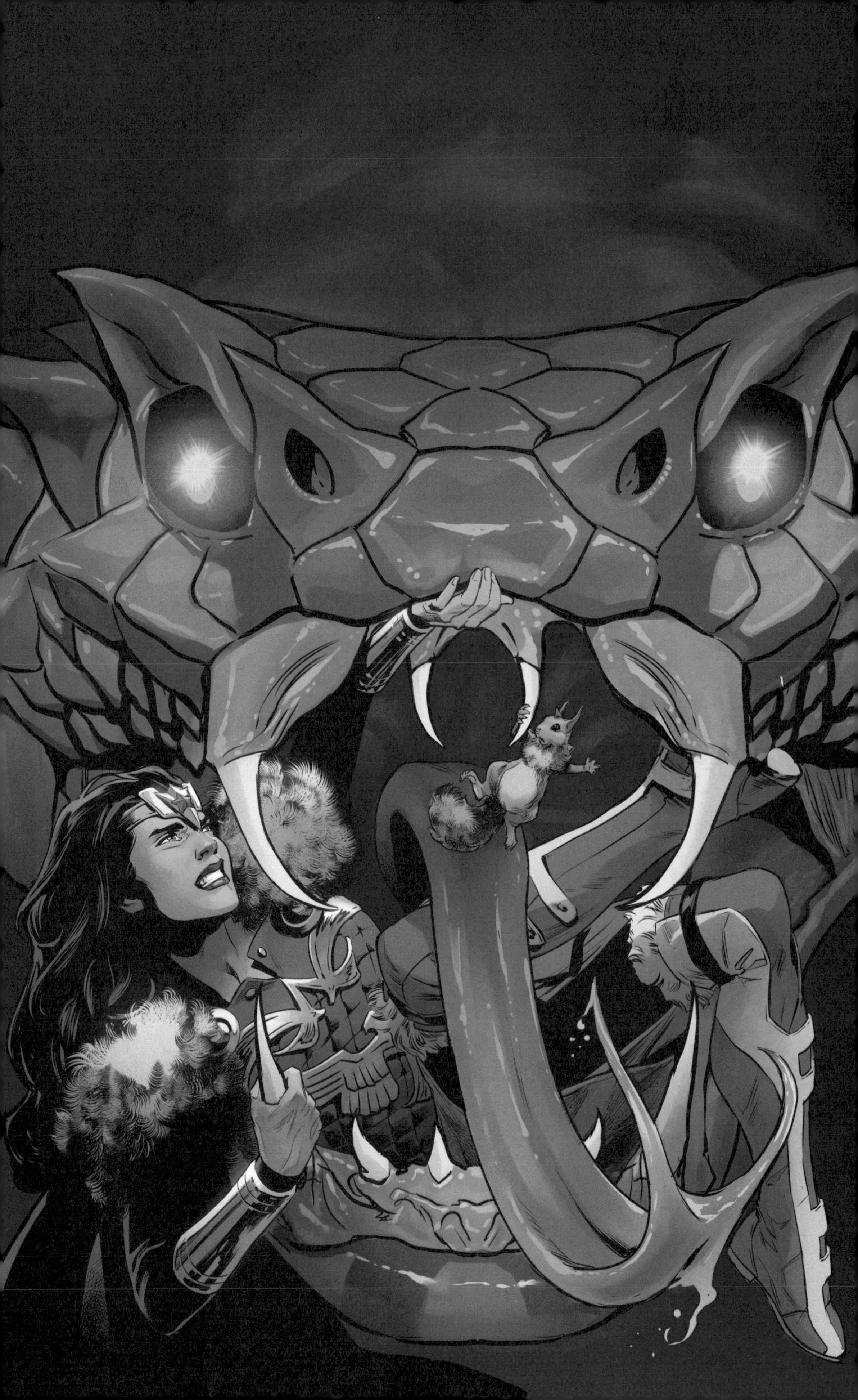

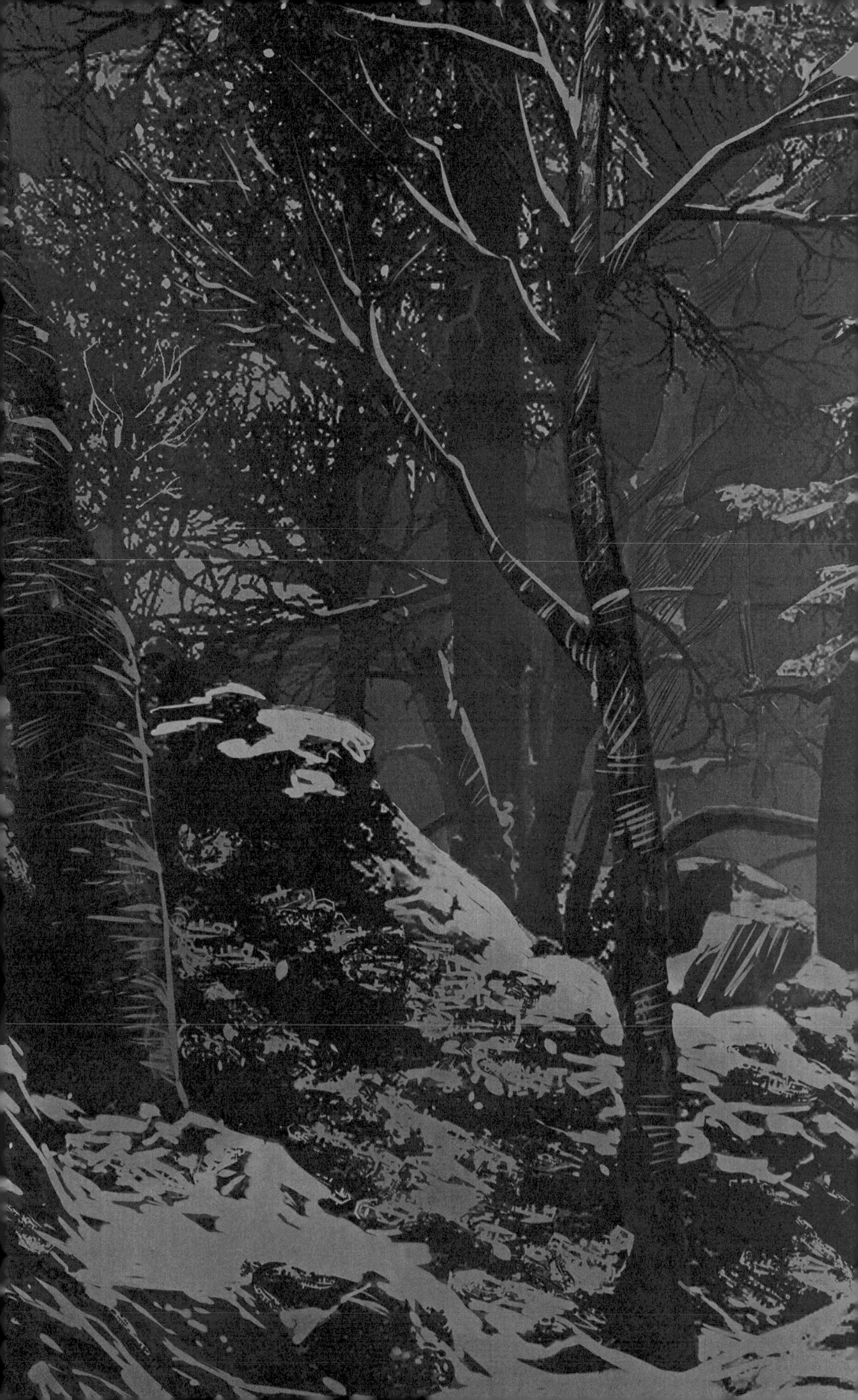

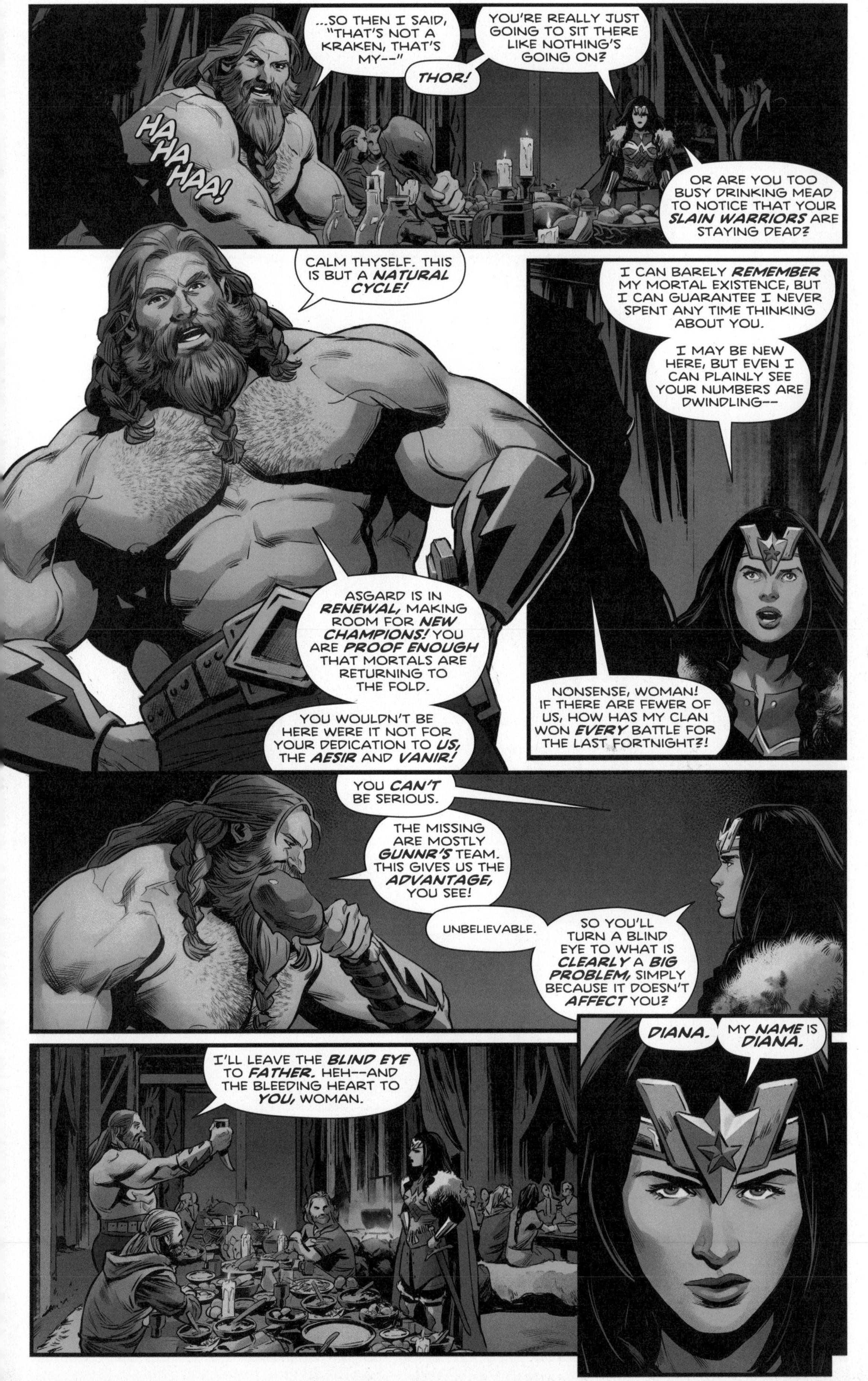
...SO THEN I SAID, "THAT'S NOT A KRAKEN, THAT'S MY--"
HAHAHAHAA!
THOR!
YOU'RE REALLY JUST GOING TO SIT THERE LIKE NOTHING'S GOING ON?
OR ARE YOU TOO BUSY DRINKING MEAD TO NOTICE THAT YOUR SLAIN WARRIORS ARE STAYING DEAD?
CALM THYSELF. THIS IS BUT A NATURAL CYCLE!
I CAN BARELY REMEMBER MY MORTAL EXISTENCE, BUT I CAN GUARANTEE I NEVER SPENT ANY TIME THINKING ABOUT YOU.
I MAY BE NEW HERE, BUT EVEN I CAN PLAINLY SEE YOUR NUMBERS ARE DWINDLING--
ASGARD IS IN RENEWAL, MAKING ROOM FOR NEW CHAMPIONS! YOU ARE PROOF ENOUGH THAT MORTALS ARE RETURNING TO THE FOLD.
YOU WOULDN'T BE HERE WERE IT NOT FOR YOUR DEDICATION TO US, THE AESIR AND VANIR!
NONSENSE, WOMAN! IF THERE ARE FEWER OF US, HOW HAS MY CLAN WON EVERY BATTLE FOR THE LAST FORTNIGHT?!
YOU CAN'T BE SERIOUS.
THE MISSING ARE MOSTLY GUNNR'S TEAM. THIS GIVES US THE ADVANTAGE, YOU SEE!
UNBELIEVABLE.
SO YOU'LL TURN A BLIND EYE TO WHAT IS CLEARLY A BIG PROBLEM, SIMPLY BECAUSE IT DOESN'T AFFECT YOU?
I'LL LEAVE THE BLIND EYE TO FATHER. HEH--AND THE BLEEDING HEART TO YOU, WOMAN.
DIANA.
MY NAME IS DIANA.

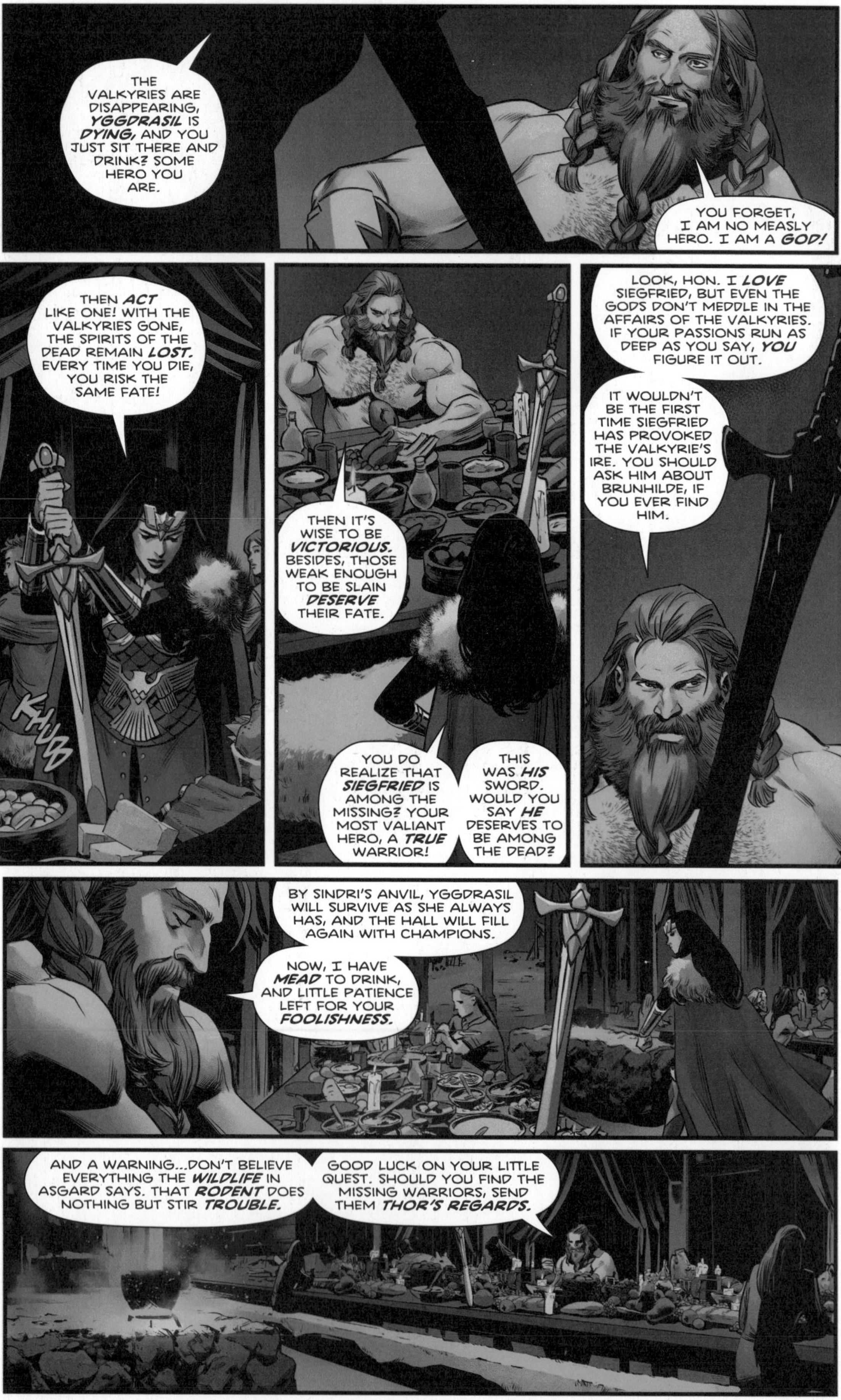
THE VALKYRIES ARE DISAPPEARING, YGGDRASIL IS DYING, AND YOU JUST SIT THERE AND DRINK? SOME HERO YOU ARE.
YOU FORGET, I AM NO MEASLY HERO. I AM A GOD!
THEN ACT LIKE ONE! WITH THE VALKYRIES GONE, THE SPIRITS OF THE DEAD REMAIN LOST. EVERY TIME YOU DIE, YOU RISK THE SAME FATE!
KHUD
THEN IT'S WISE TO BE VICTORIOUS. BESIDES, THOSE WEAK ENOUGH TO BE SLAIN DESERVE THEIR FATE.
YOU DO REALIZE THAT SIEGFRIED IS AMONG THE MISSING? YOUR MOST VALIANT HERO, A TRUE WARRIOR!
THIS WAS HIS SWORD. WOULD YOU SAY HE DESERVES TO BE AMONG THE DEAD?
LOOK, HON. I LOVE SIEGFRIED, BUT EVEN THE GODS DON'T MEDDLE IN THE AFFAIRS OF THE VALKYRIES. IF YOUR PASSIONS RUN AS DEEP AS YOU SAY, YOU FIGURE IT OUT.
IT WOULDN'T BE THE FIRST TIME SIEGFRIED HAS PROVOKED THE VALKYRIE'S IRE. YOU SHOULD ASK HIM ABOUT BRUNHILDE, IF YOU EVER FIND HIM.
BY SINDRI'S ANVIL, YGGDRASIL WILL SURVIVE AS SHE ALWAYS HAS, AND THE HALL WILL FILL AGAIN WITH CHAMPIONS.
NOW, I HAVE MEAD TO DRINK, AND LITTLE PATIENCE LEFT FOR YOUR FOOLISHNESS.
AND A WARNING...DON'T BELIEVE EVERYTHING THE WILDLIFE IN ASGARD SAYS. THAT RODENT DOES NOTHING BUT STIR TROUBLE.
GOOD LUCK ON YOUR LITTLE QUEST. SHOULD YOU FIND THE MISSING WARRIORS, SEND THEM THOR'S REGARDS.

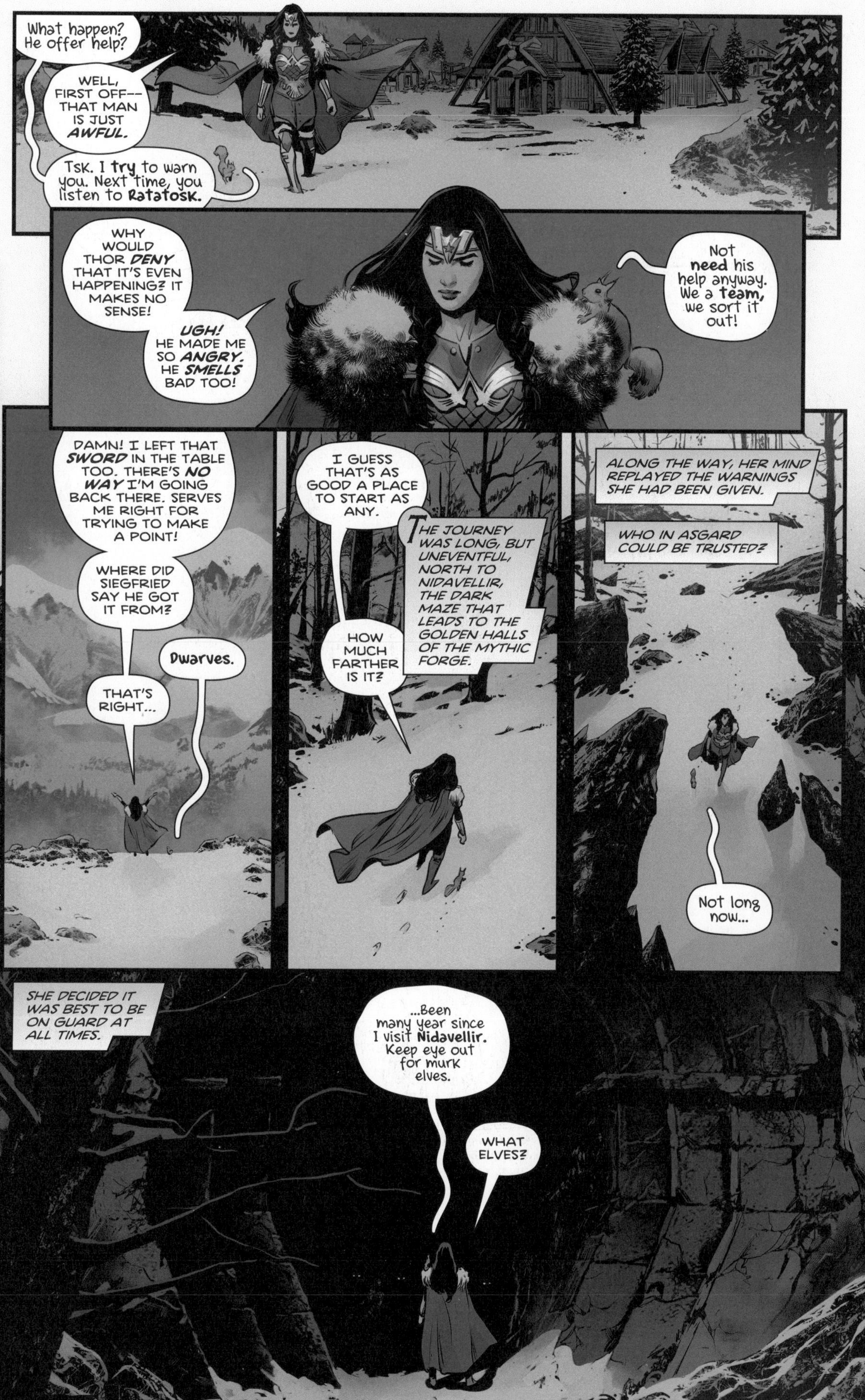

What happen? He offer help?
WELL, FIRST OFF-- THAT MAN IS JUST AWFUL.
Tsk. I try to warn you. Next time, you listen to Ratatosk.
WHY WOULD THOR DENY THAT IT'S EVEN HAPPENING? IT MAKES NO SENSE!
UGH! HE MADE ME SO ANGRY. HE SMELLS BAD TOO!
Not need his help anyway. We a team, we sort it out!
DAMN! I LEFT THAT SWORD IN THE TABLE TOO. THERE'S NO WAY I'M GOING BACK THERE. SERVES ME RIGHT FOR TRYING TO MAKE A POINT!
WHERE DID SIEGFRIED SAY HE GOT IT FROM?
Dwarves.
THAT'S RIGHT...
I GUESS THAT'S AS GOOD A PLACE TO START AS ANY.
THE JOURNEY WAS LONG, BUT UNEVENTFUL, NORTH TO NIDAVELLIR, THE DARK MAZE THAT LEADS TO THE GOLDEN HALLS OF THE MYTHIC FORGE.
HOW MUCH FARTHER IS IT?
ALONG THE WAY, HER MIND REPLAYED THE WARNINGS SHE HAD BEEN GIVEN.
WHO IN ASGARD COULD BE TRUSTED?
Not long now...
SHE DECIDED IT WAS BEST TO BE ON GUARD AT ALL TIMES.
...Been many year since I visit Nidavellir. Keep eye out for murk elves.
WHAT ELVES?

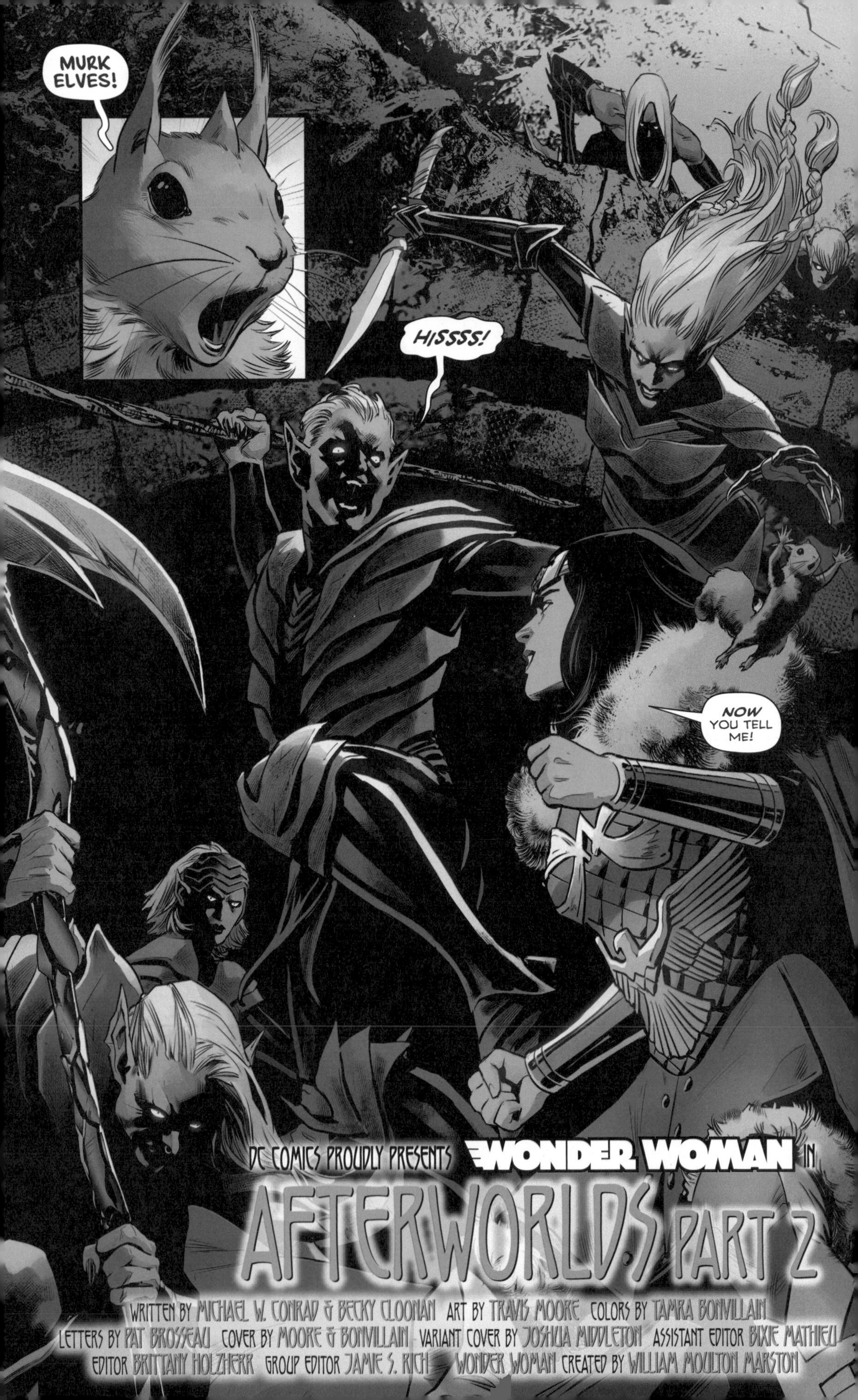
MURK ELVES!
HISSSS!
NOW YOU TELL ME!
DC COMICS PROUDLY PRESENTS WONDER WOMAN IN
AFTERWORLDS PART 2
WRITTEN BY MICHAEL W. CONRAD & BECKY CLOONAN ART BY TRAVIS MOORE COLORS BY TAMRA BONVILLAIN
LETTERS BY PAT BROSSEAU COVER BY MOORE & BONVILLAIN VARIANT COVER BY JOSHUA MIDDLETON ASSISTANT EDITOR BIXIE MATHIEU
EDITOR BRITTANY HOLZHERR GROUP EDITOR JAMIE S. RICH WONDER WOMAN CREATED BY WILLIAM MOULTON MARSTON

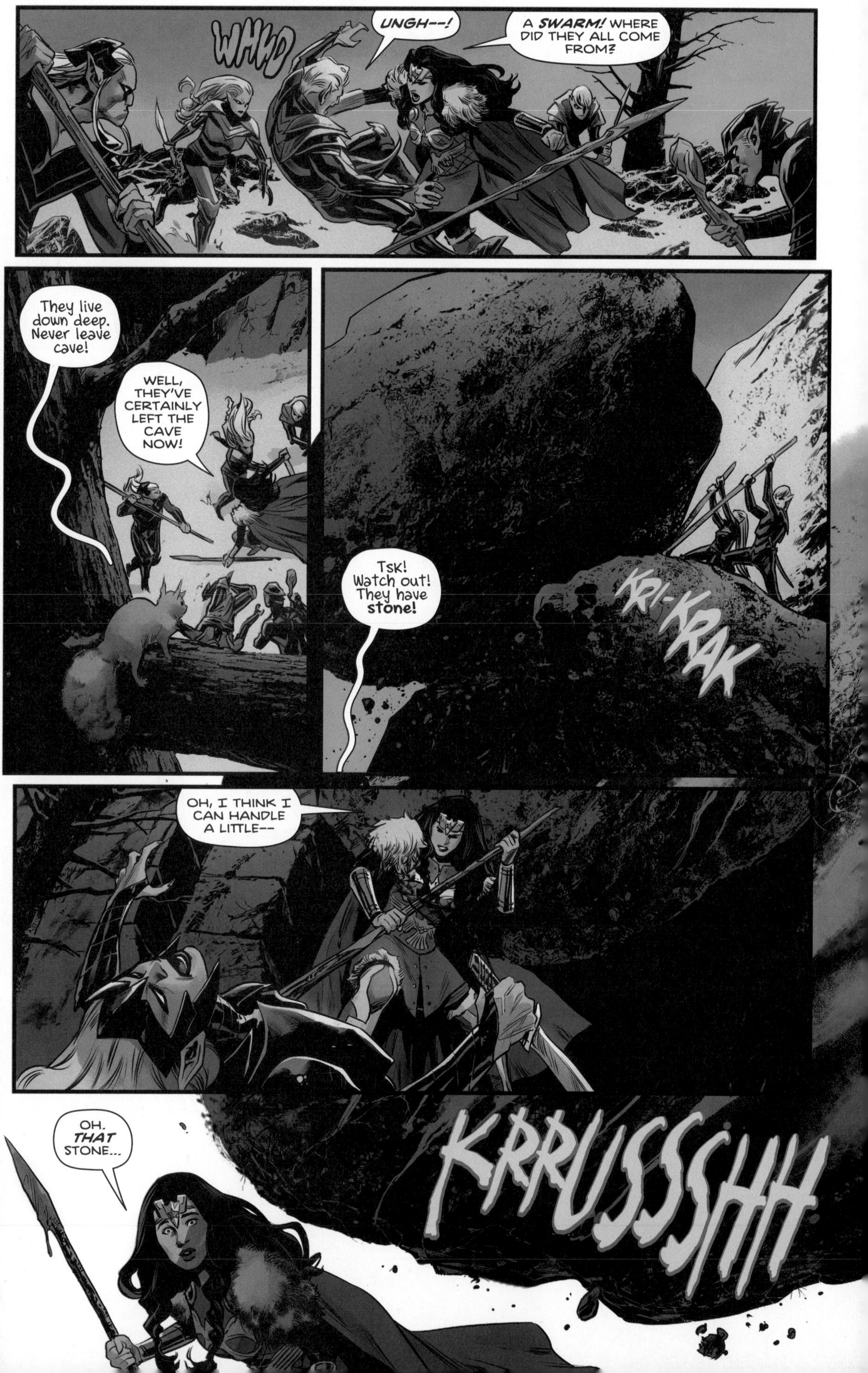
WHUD
UNGH--!
A SWARM! WHERE DID THEY ALL COME FROM?
They live down deep. Never leave cave!
WELL, THEY'VE CERTAINLY LEFT THE CAVE NOW!
Tsk! Watch out! They have stone!
KRI-KRAK
OH, I THINK I CAN HANDLE A LITTLE--
OH. THAT STONE...
KRRUSSSHH

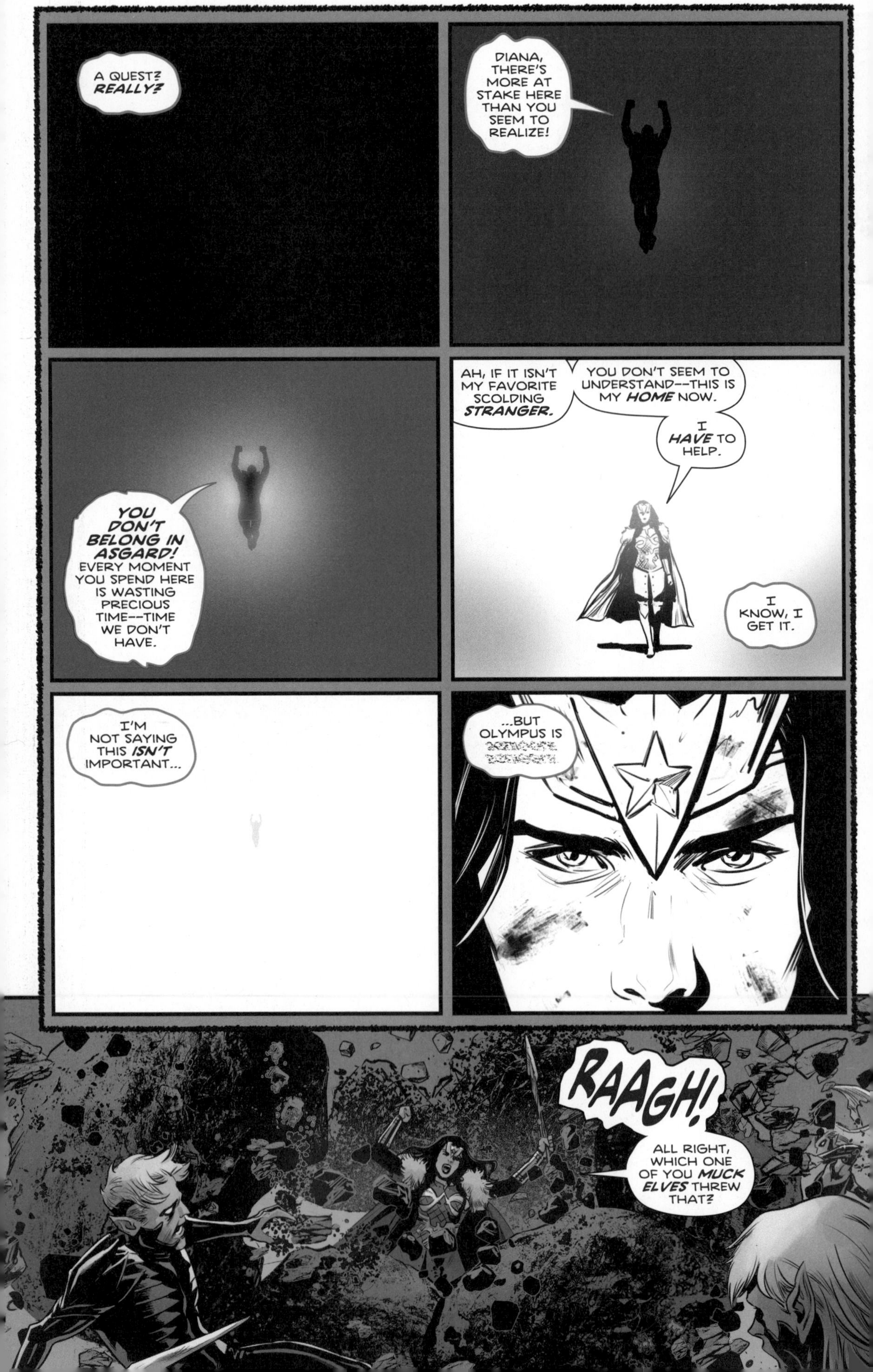
A QUEST? REALLY?
DIANA, THERE'S MORE AT STAKE HERE THAN YOU SEEM TO REALIZE!
YOU DON'T BELONG IN ASGARD! EVERY MOMENT YOU SPEND HERE IS WASTING PRECIOUS TIME--TIME WE DON'T HAVE.
AH, IF IT ISN'T MY FAVORITE SCOLDING STRANGER.
YOU DON'T SEEM TO UNDERSTAND--THIS IS MY HOME NOW.
I HAVE TO HELP.
I KNOW, I GET IT.
I'M NOT SAYING THIS ISN'T IMPORTANT...
...BUT OLYMPUS IS
RAAGH!
ALL RIGHT, WHICH ONE OF YOU MUCK ELVES THREW THAT?

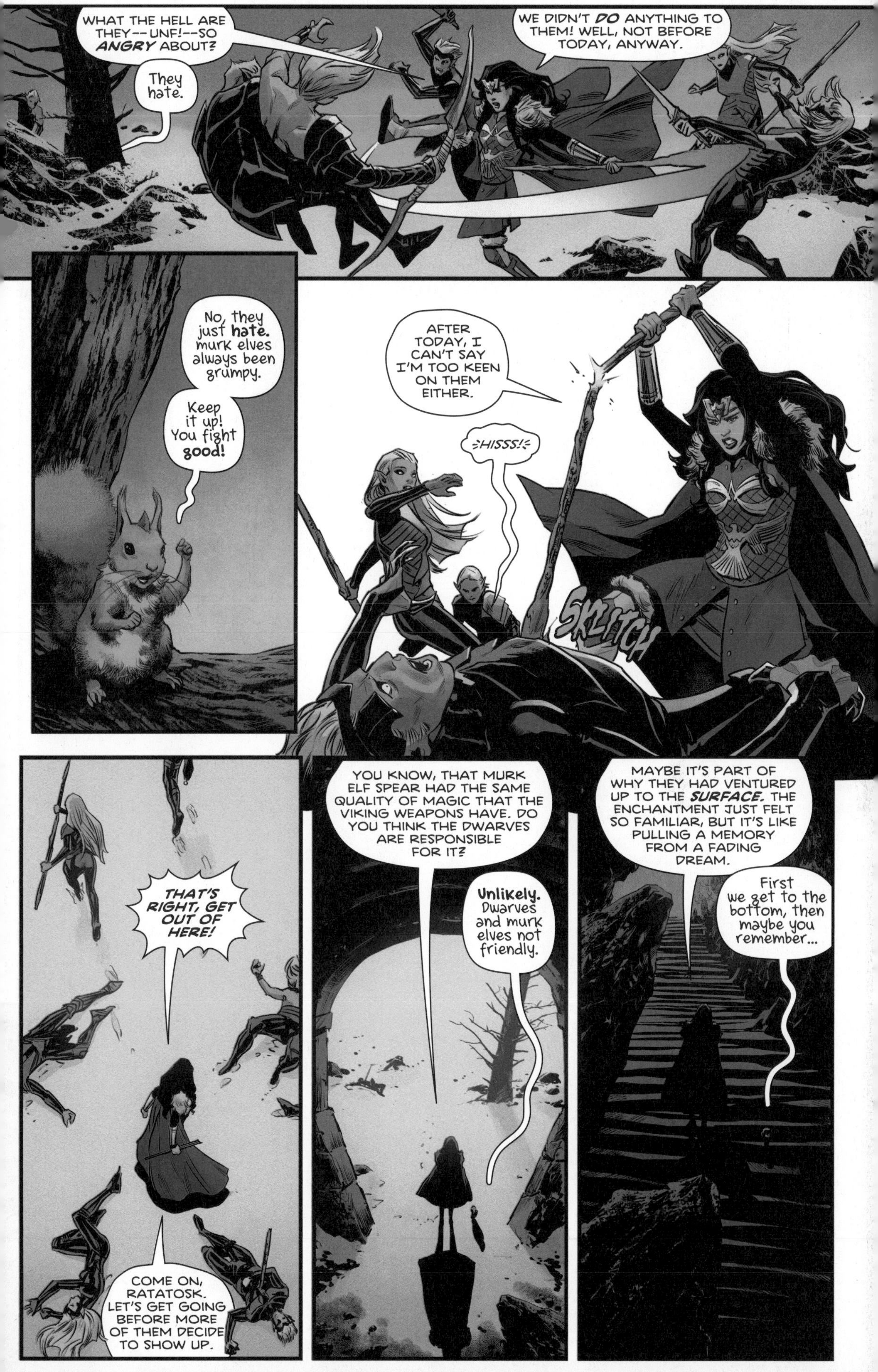

WHAT THE HELL ARE THEY--UNF!--SO ***ANGRY*** ABOUT?
They hate.
WE DIDN'T ***DO*** ANYTHING TO THEM! WELL, NOT BEFORE TODAY, ANYWAY.
No, they just **hate.** murk elves always been grumpy.
Keep it up! You fight **good!**
AFTER TODAY, I CAN'T SAY I'M TOO KEEN ON THEM EITHER.
HISSS!
SKLTCH
THAT'S RIGHT, GET OUT OF HERE!
COME ON, RATATOSK. LET'S GET GOING BEFORE MORE OF THEM DECIDE TO SHOW UP.
YOU KNOW, THAT MURK ELF SPEAR HAD THE SAME QUALITY OF MAGIC THAT THE VIKING WEAPONS HAVE. DO YOU THINK THE DWARVES ARE RESPONSIBLE FOR IT?
Unlikely. Dwarves and murk elves not friendly.
MAYBE IT'S PART OF WHY THEY HAD VENTURED UP TO THE ***SURFACE.*** THE ENCHANTMENT JUST FELT SO FAMILIAR, BUT IT'S LIKE PULLING A MEMORY FROM A FADING DREAM.
First we get to the bottom, then maybe you remember...

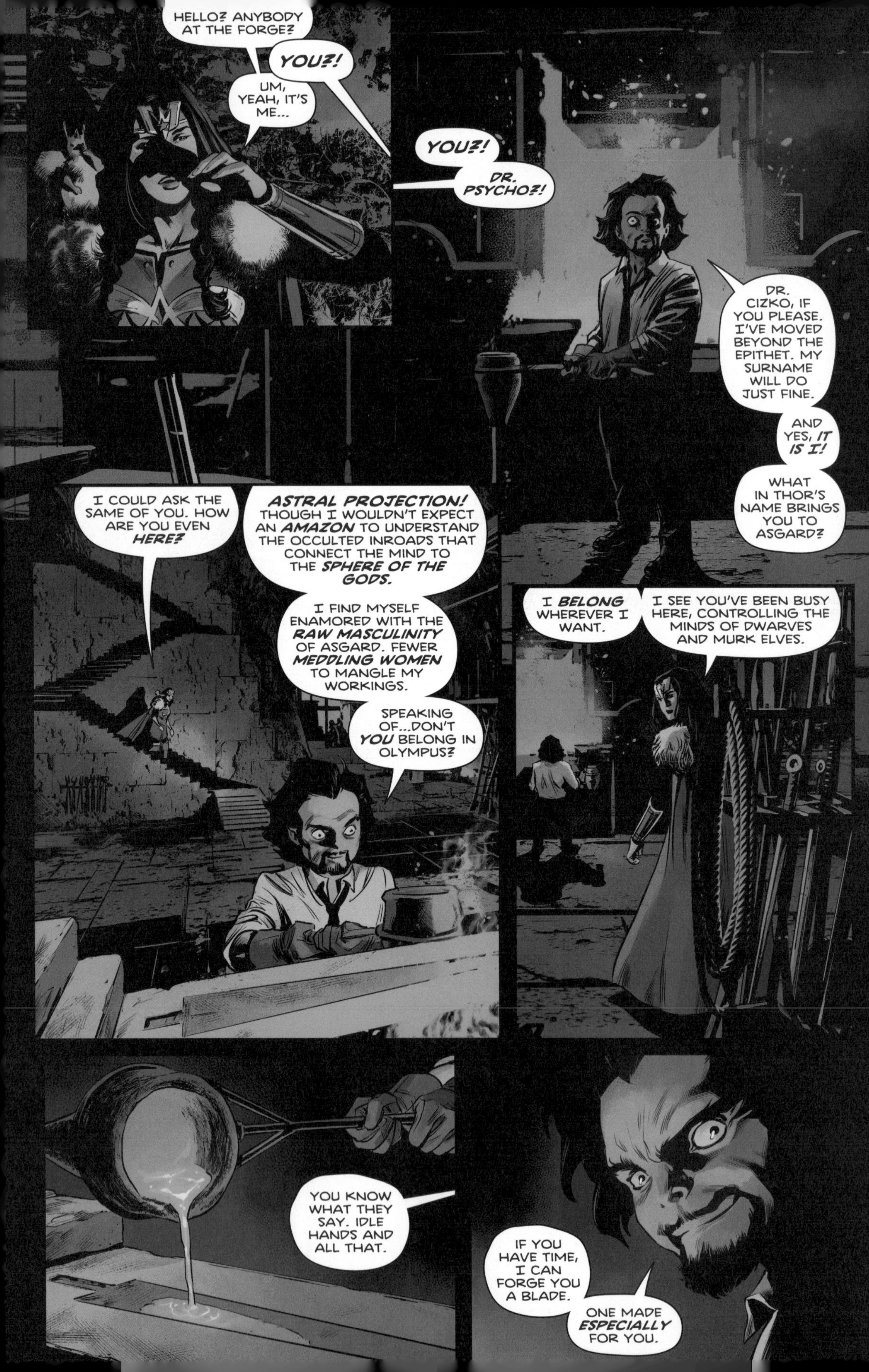
HELLO? ANYBODY AT THE FORGE?
YOU?!
UM, YEAH, IT'S ME...
YOU?!
DR. PSYCHO?!
DR. CIZKO, IF YOU PLEASE. I'VE MOVED BEYOND THE EPITHET. MY SURNAME WILL DO JUST FINE.
AND YES, IT IS I!
WHAT IN THOR'S NAME BRINGS YOU TO ASGARD?
I COULD ASK THE SAME OF YOU. HOW ARE YOU EVEN HERE?
ASTRAL PROJECTION! THOUGH I WOULDN'T EXPECT AN AMAZON TO UNDERSTAND THE OCCULTED INROADS THAT CONNECT THE MIND TO THE SPHERE OF THE GODS.
I FIND MYSELF ENAMORED WITH THE RAW MASCULINITY OF ASGARD. FEWER MEDDLING WOMEN TO MANGLE MY WORKINGS.
SPEAKING OF...DON'T YOU BELONG IN OLYMPUS?
I BELONG WHEREVER I WANT.
I SEE YOU'VE BEEN BUSY HERE, CONTROLLING THE MINDS OF DWARVES AND MURK ELVES.
YOU KNOW WHAT THEY SAY. IDLE HANDS AND ALL THAT.
IF YOU HAVE TIME, I CAN FORGE YOU A BLADE.
ONE MADE ESPECIALLY FOR YOU.

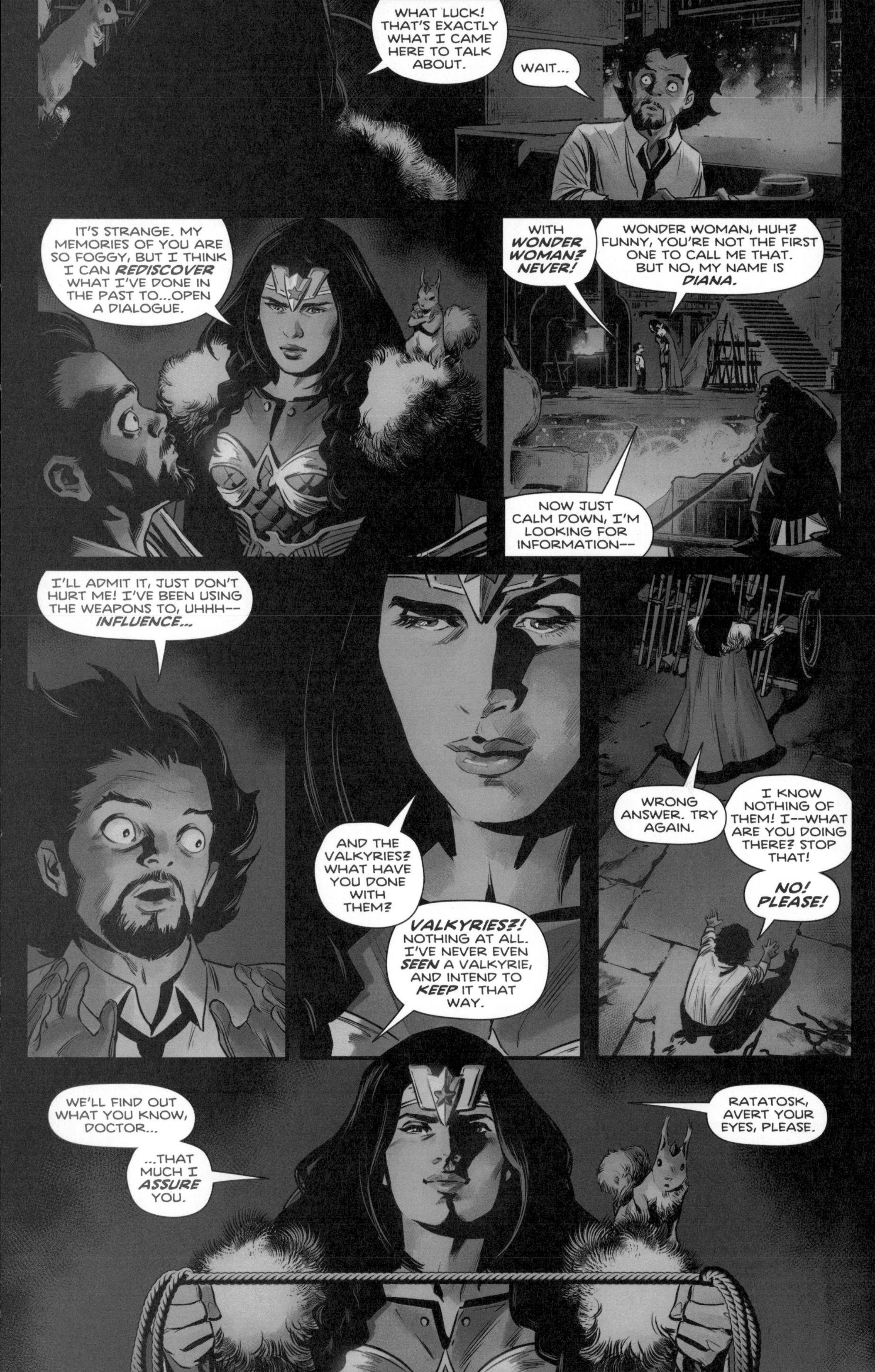
WHAT LUCK! THAT'S EXACTLY WHAT I CAME HERE TO TALK ABOUT.
WAIT...
IT'S STRANGE. MY MEMORIES OF YOU ARE SO FOGGY, BUT I THINK I CAN REDISCOVER WHAT I'VE DONE IN THE PAST TO...OPEN A DIALOGUE.
WITH WONDER WOMAN? NEVER!
WONDER WOMAN, HUH? FUNNY, YOU'RE NOT THE FIRST ONE TO CALL ME THAT. BUT NO, MY NAME IS DIANA.
NOW JUST CALM DOWN, I'M LOOKING FOR INFORMATION--
I'LL ADMIT IT, JUST DON'T HURT ME! I'VE BEEN USING THE WEAPONS TO, UHHH-- INFLUENCE...
AND THE VALKYRIES? WHAT HAVE YOU DONE WITH THEM?
VALKYRIES?! NOTHING AT ALL. I'VE NEVER EVEN SEEN A VALKYRIE, AND INTEND TO KEEP IT THAT WAY.
WRONG ANSWER. TRY AGAIN.
I KNOW NOTHING OF THEM! I--WHAT ARE YOU DOING THERE? STOP THAT!
NO! PLEASE!
WE'LL FIND OUT WHAT YOU KNOW, DOCTOR...
...THAT MUCH I ASSURE YOU.
RATATOSK, AVERT YOUR EYES, PLEASE.

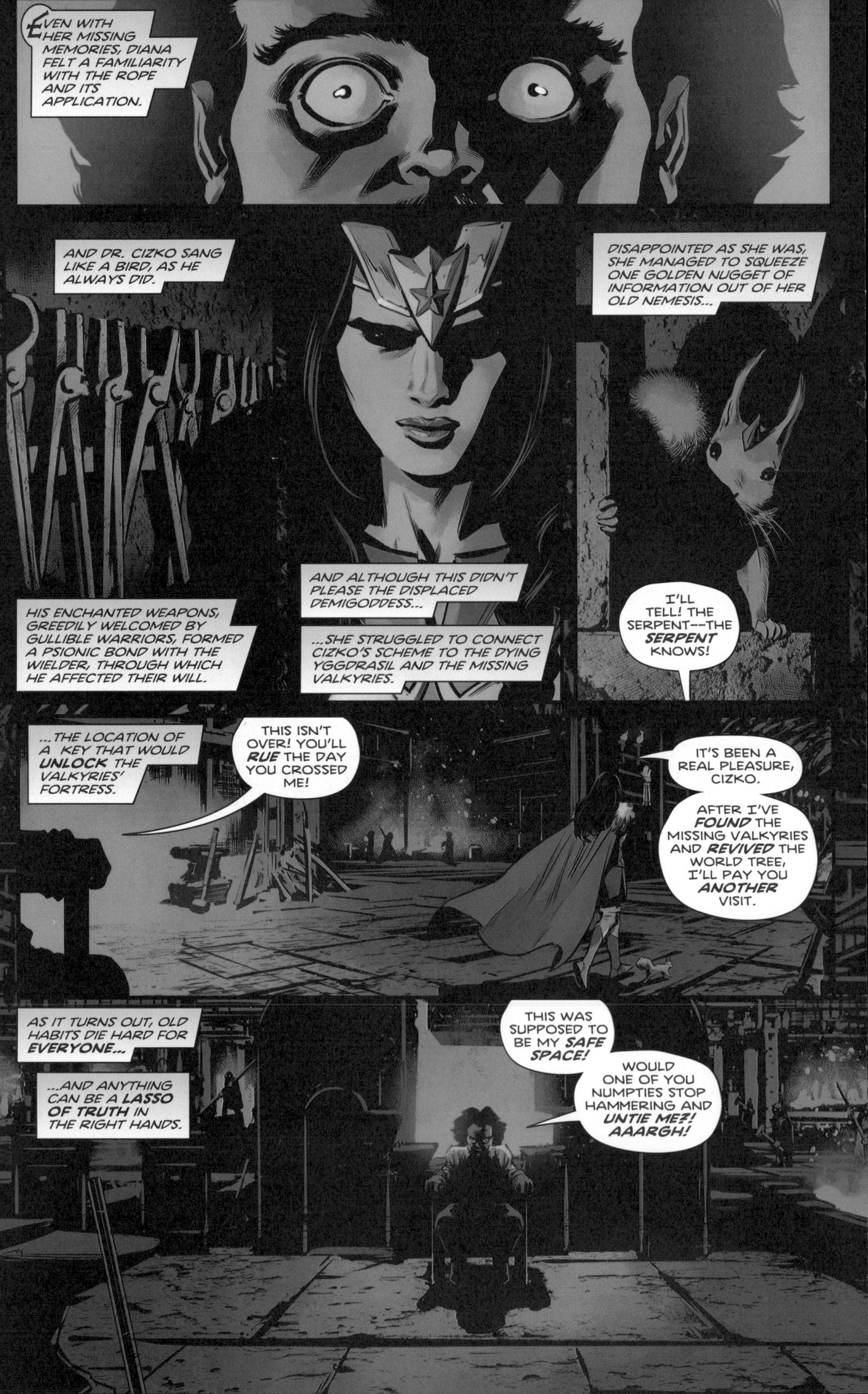
EVEN WITH HER MISSING MEMORIES, DIANA FELT A FAMILIARITY WITH THE ROPE AND ITS APPLICATION.
AND DR. CIZKO SANG LIKE A BIRD, AS HE ALWAYS DID.
HIS ENCHANTED WEAPONS, GREEDILY WELCOMED BY GULLIBLE WARRIORS, FORMED A PSIONIC BOND WITH THE WIELDER, THROUGH WHICH HE AFFECTED THEIR WILL.
AND ALTHOUGH THIS DIDN'T PLEASE THE DISPLACED DEMIGODDESS...
...SHE STRUGGLED TO CONNECT CIZKO'S SCHEME TO THE DYING YGGDRASIL AND THE MISSING VALKYRIES.
DISAPPOINTED AS SHE WAS, SHE MANAGED TO SQUEEZE ONE GOLDEN NUGGET OF INFORMATION OUT OF HER OLD NEMESIS...
I'LL TELL! THE SERPENT--THE SERPENT KNOWS!
...THE LOCATION OF A KEY THAT WOULD UNLOCK THE VALKYRIES' FORTRESS.
THIS ISN'T OVER! YOU'LL RUE THE DAY YOU CROSSED ME!
IT'S BEEN A REAL PLEASURE, CIZKO.
AFTER I'VE FOUND THE MISSING VALKYRIES AND REVIVED THE WORLD TREE, I'LL PAY YOU ANOTHER VISIT.
AS IT TURNS OUT, OLD HABITS DIE HARD FOR EVERYONE...
...AND ANYTHING CAN BE A LASSO OF TRUTH IN THE RIGHT HANDS.
THIS WAS SUPPOSED TO BE MY SAFE SPACE!
WOULD ONE OF YOU NUMPTIES STOP HAMMERING AND UNTIE ME?! AAARGH!

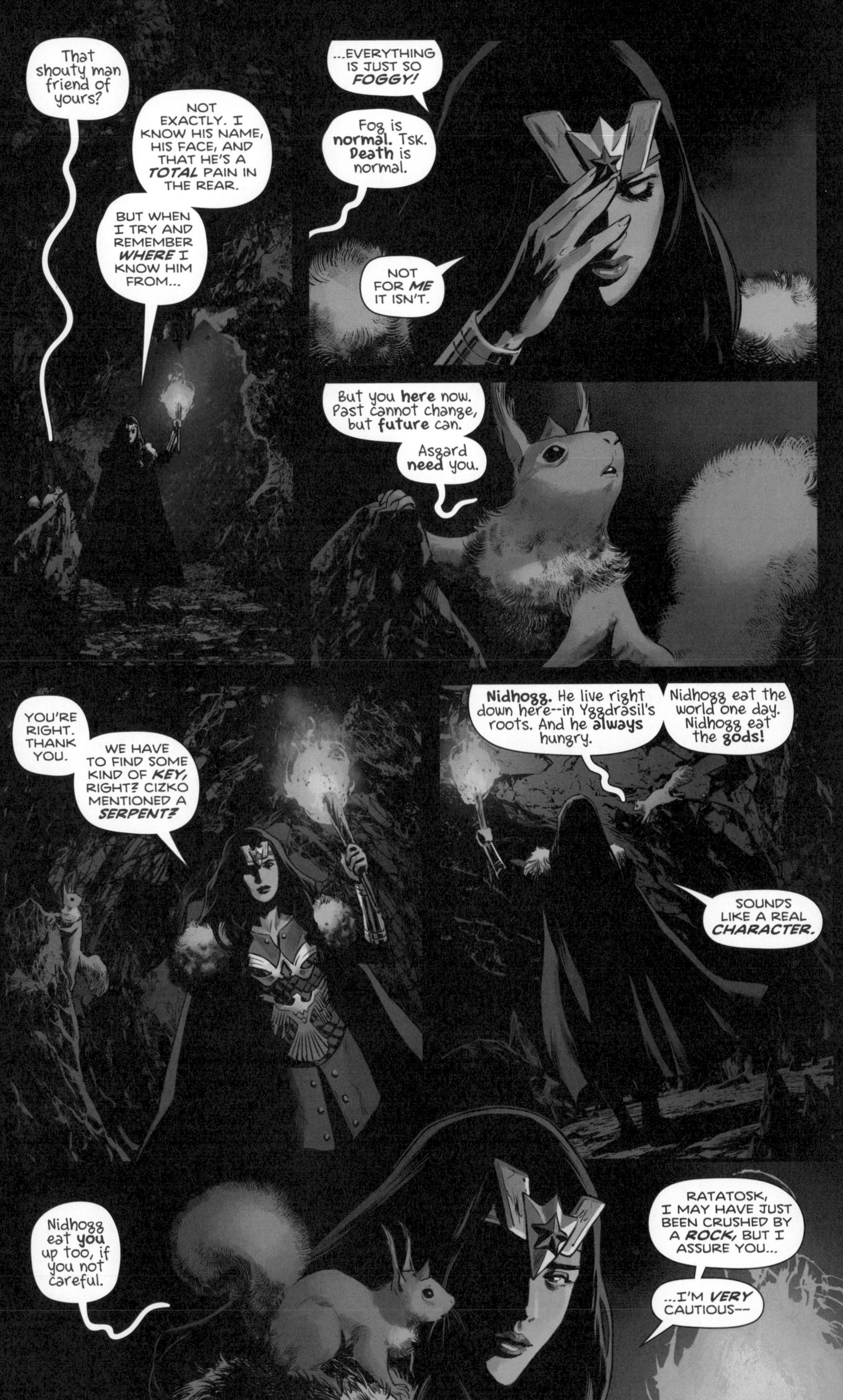

That shouty man friend of yours?
NOT EXACTLY. I KNOW HIS NAME, HIS FACE, AND THAT HE'S A TOTAL PAIN IN THE REAR.
BUT WHEN I TRY AND REMEMBER WHERE I KNOW HIM FROM...
...EVERYTHING IS JUST SO FOGGY!
Fog is normal. Tsk. Death is normal.
NOT FOR ME IT ISN'T.
But you here now. Past cannot change, but future can.
Asgard need you.
YOU'RE RIGHT. THANK YOU.
WE HAVE TO FIND SOME KIND OF KEY, RIGHT? CIZKO MENTIONED A SERPENT?
Nidhogg. He live right down here--in Yggdrasil's roots. And he always hungry.
Nidhogg eat the world one day. Nidhogg eat the gods!
SOUNDS LIKE A REAL CHARACTER.
Nidhogg eat you up too, if you not careful.
RATATOSK, I MAY HAVE JUST BEEN CRUSHED BY A ROCK, BUT I ASSURE YOU...
...I'M VERY CAUTIOUS--

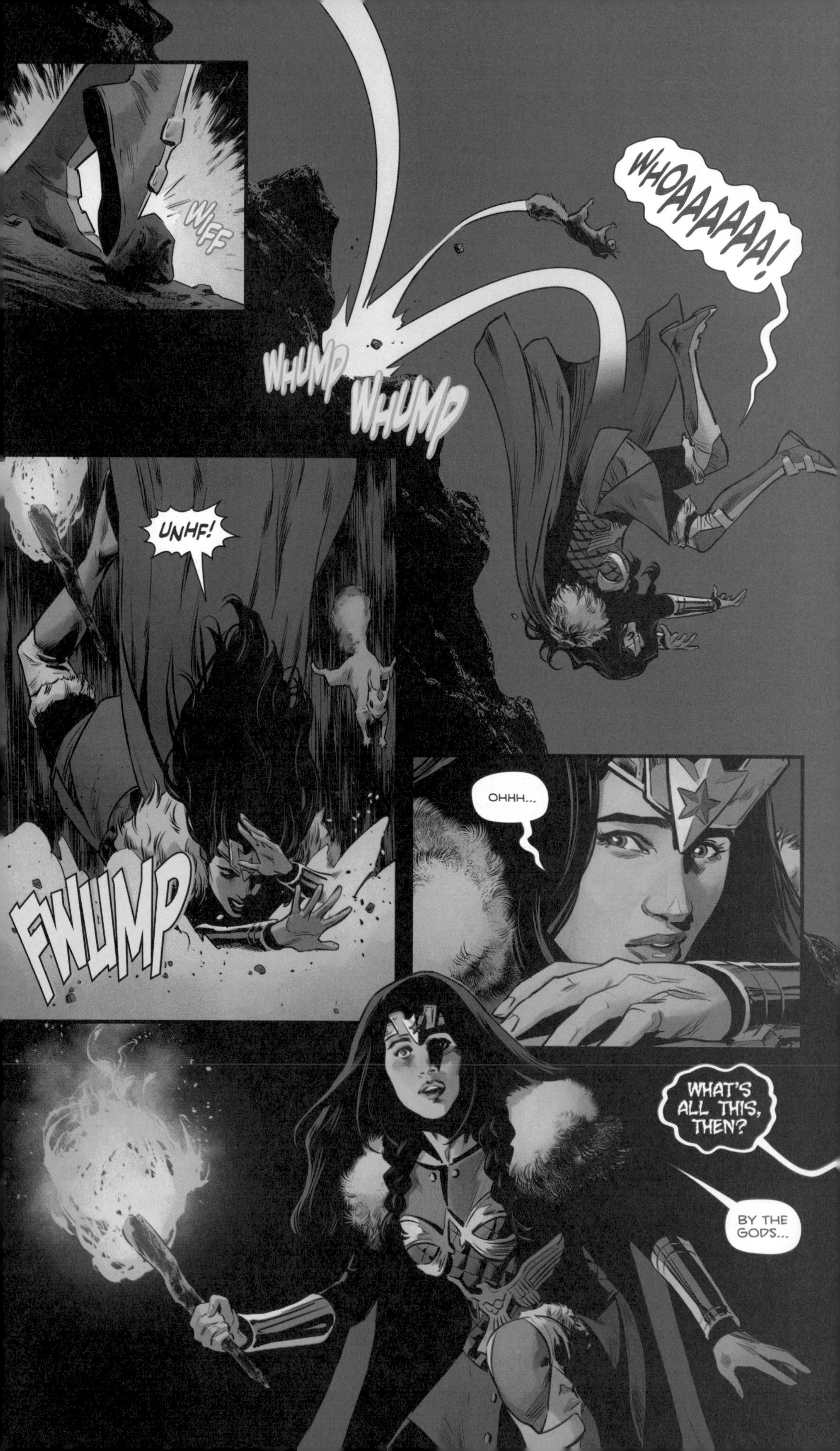
WIFF
WHUMP
WHUMP
WHOAAAAAA!
UNHF!
FWUMP
OHHH...
WHAT'S ALL THIS, THEN?
BY THE GODS...

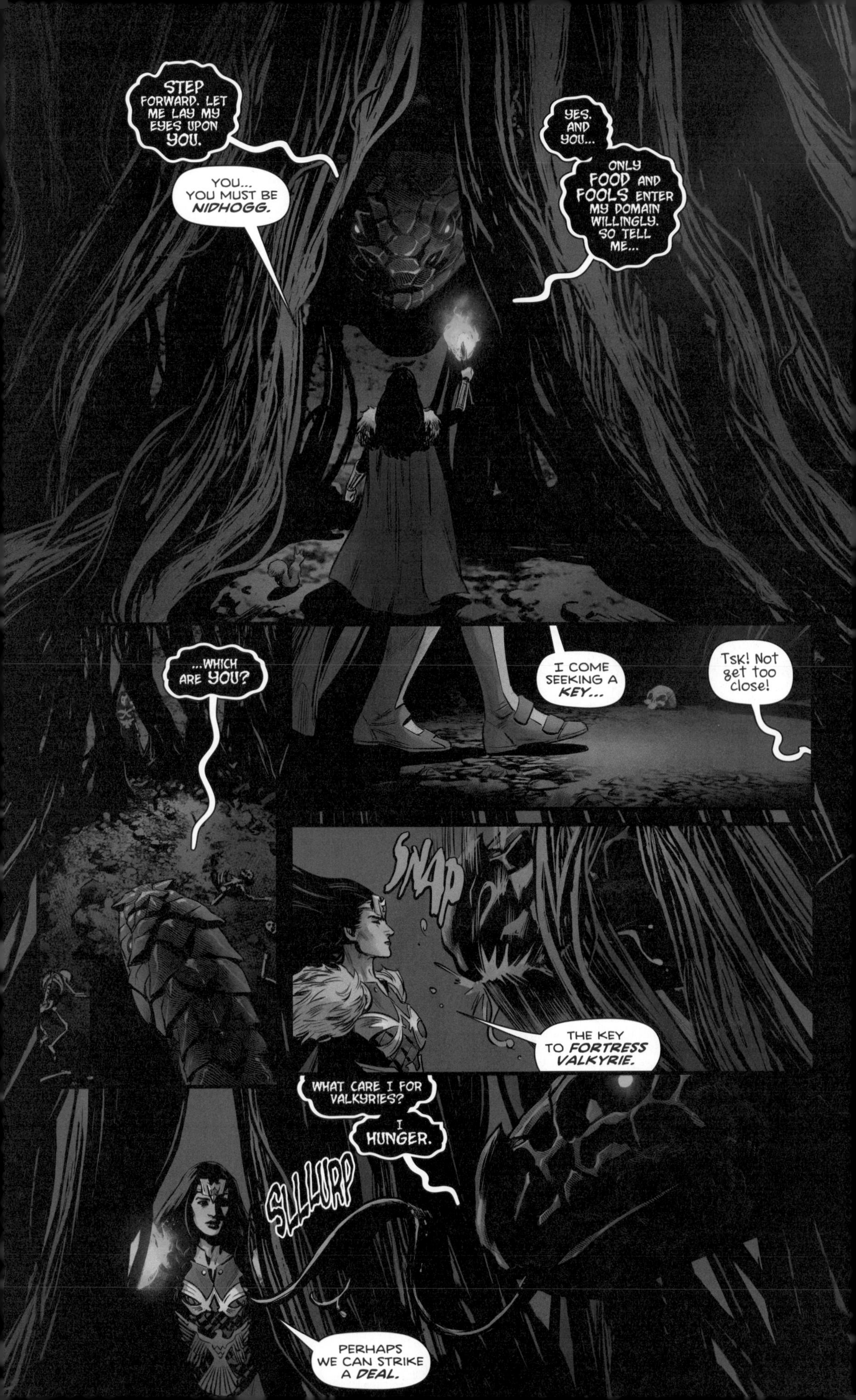

STEP FORWARD. LET ME LAY MY EYES UPON YOU.
YOU... YOU MUST BE NIDHOGG.
YES. AND YOU...
ONLY FOOD AND FOOLS ENTER MY DOMAIN WILLINGLY. SO TELL ME...
...WHICH ARE YOU?
I COME SEEKING A KEY...
Tsk! Not get too close!
SNAP
THE KEY TO FORTRESS VALKYRIE.
WHAT CARE I FOR VALKYRIES?
I HUNGER.
SLLLURP
PERHAPS WE CAN STRIKE A DEAL.

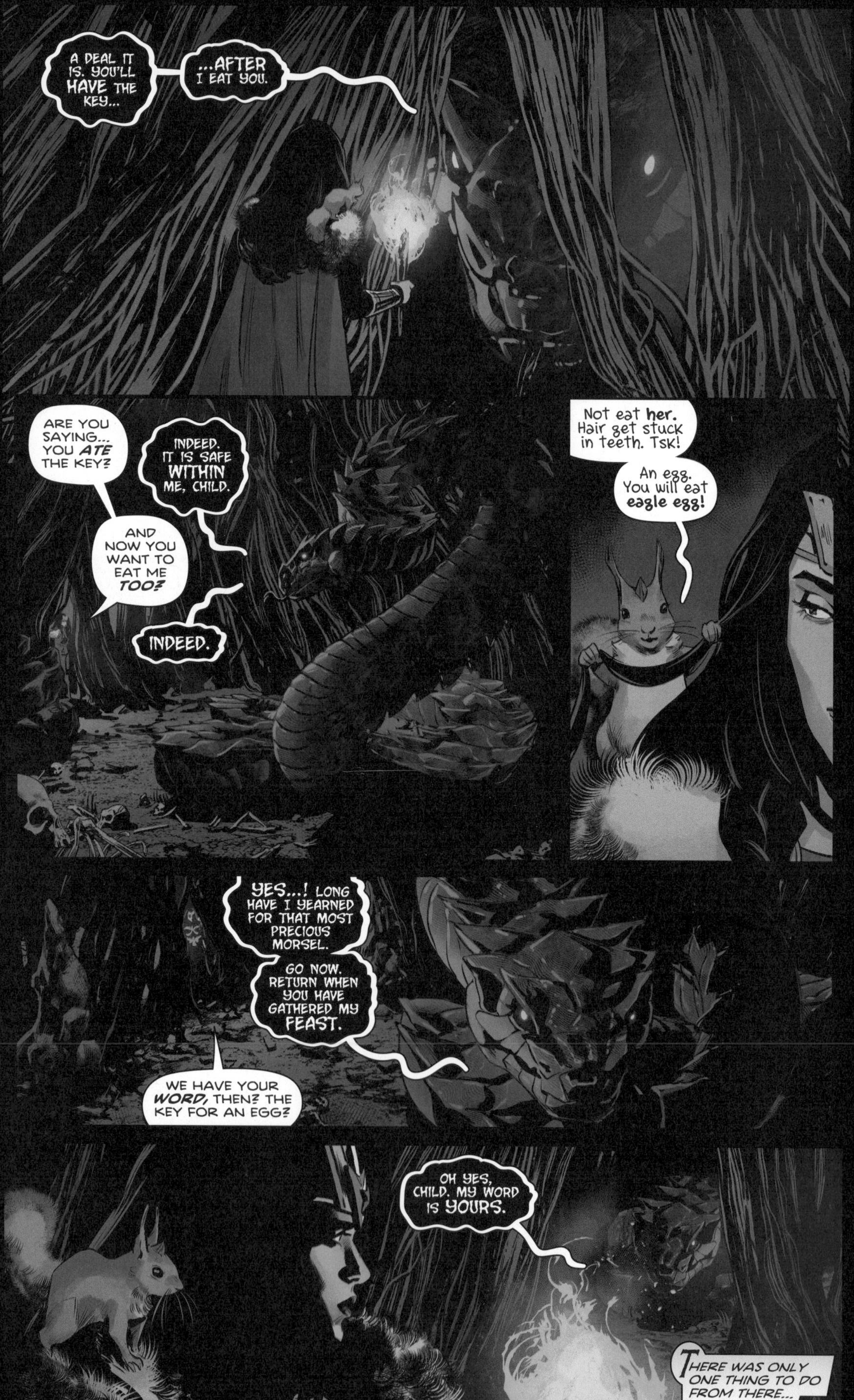

A DEAL IT IS. YOU'LL HAVE THE KEY...
...AFTER I EAT YOU.
ARE YOU SAYING... YOU ATE THE KEY?
INDEED. IT IS SAFE WITHIN ME, CHILD.
AND NOW YOU WANT TO EAT ME TOO?
INDEED.
Not eat her. Hair get stuck in teeth. Tsk!
An egg. You will eat eagle egg!
YES...! LONG HAVE I YEARNED FOR THAT MOST PRECIOUS MORSEL.
GO NOW. RETURN WHEN YOU HAVE GATHERED MY FEAST.
WE HAVE YOUR WORD, THEN? THE KEY FOR AN EGG?
OH YES, CHILD. MY WORD IS YOURS.
THERE WAS ONLY ONE THING TO DO FROM THERE...

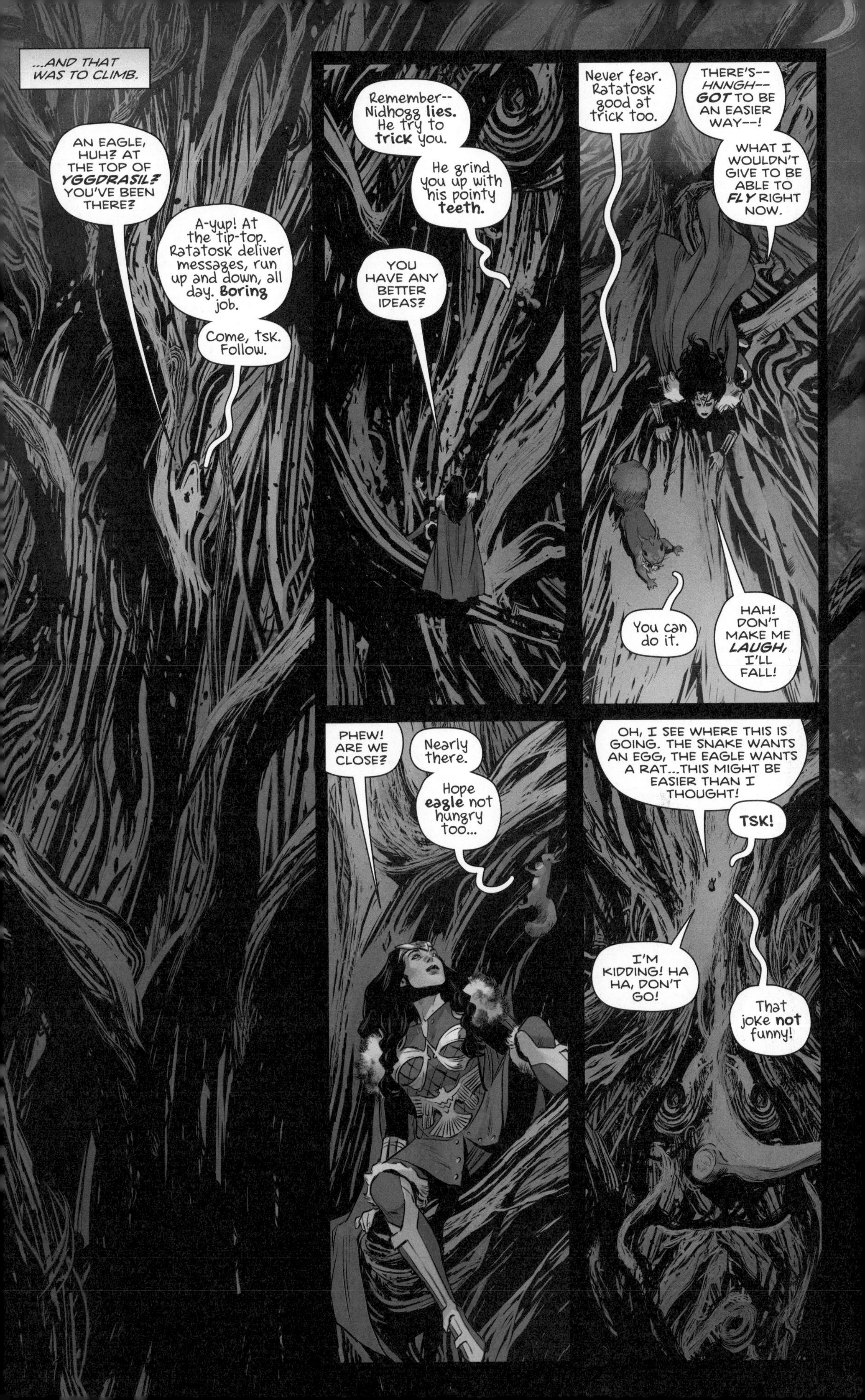
...AND THAT WAS TO CLIMB.
AN EAGLE, HUH? AT THE TOP OF YGGDRASIL? YOU'VE BEEN THERE?
A-yup! At the tip-top. Ratatosk deliver messages, run up and down, all day. Boring job.
Come, tsk. Follow.
Remember-- Nidhogg lies. He try to trick you.
He grind you up with his pointy teeth.
YOU HAVE ANY BETTER IDEAS?
Never fear. Ratatosk good at trick too.
THERE'S-- HNNGH-- GOT TO BE AN EASIER WAY--!
WHAT I WOULDN'T GIVE TO BE ABLE TO FLY RIGHT NOW.
You can do it.
HAH! DON'T MAKE ME LAUGH, I'LL FALL!
PHEW! ARE WE CLOSE?
Nearly there.
Hope eagle not hungry too...
OH, I SEE WHERE THIS IS GOING. THE SNAKE WANTS AN EGG, THE EAGLE WANTS A RAT...THIS MIGHT BE EASIER THAN I THOUGHT!
TSK!
I'M KIDDING! HA HA, DON'T GO!
That joke not funny!

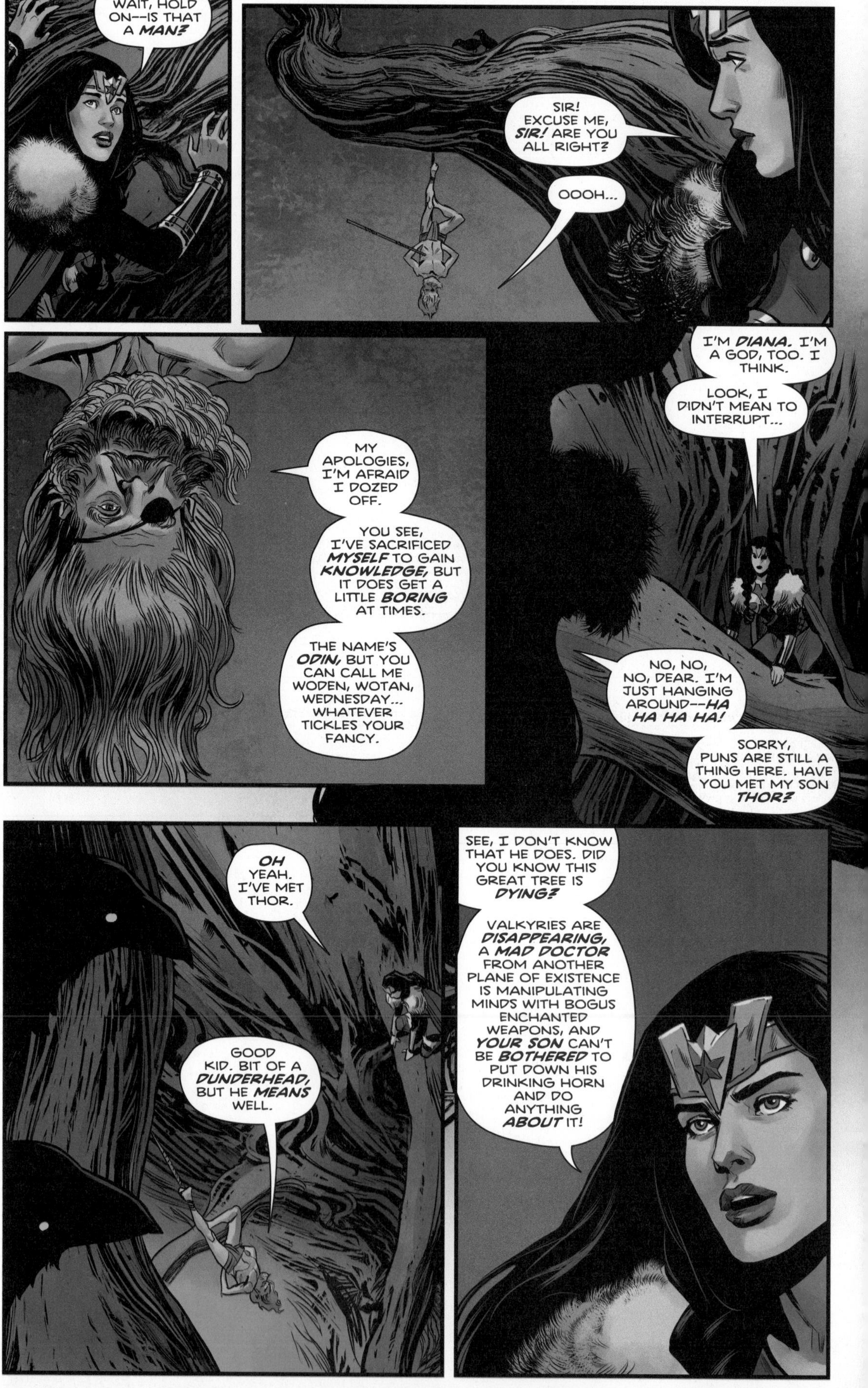
WAIT, HOLD ON--IS THAT A MAN?
SIR! EXCUSE ME, SIR! ARE YOU ALL RIGHT?
OOOH...
MY APOLOGIES, I'M AFRAID I DOZED OFF.
YOU SEE, I'VE SACRIFICED MYSELF TO GAIN KNOWLEDGE, BUT IT DOES GET A LITTLE BORING AT TIMES.
THE NAME'S ODIN, BUT YOU CAN CALL ME WODEN, WOTAN, WEDNESDAY... WHATEVER TICKLES YOUR FANCY.
I'M DIANA. I'M A GOD, TOO. I THINK.
LOOK, I DIDN'T MEAN TO INTERRUPT...
NO, NO, NO, DEAR. I'M JUST HANGING AROUND--HA HA HA HA!
SORRY, PUNS ARE STILL A THING HERE. HAVE YOU MET MY SON THOR?
OH YEAH. I'VE MET THOR.
GOOD KID. BIT OF A DUNDERHEAD, BUT HE MEANS WELL.
SEE, I DON'T KNOW THAT HE DOES. DID YOU KNOW THIS GREAT TREE IS DYING?
VALKYRIES ARE DISAPPEARING, A MAD DOCTOR FROM ANOTHER PLANE OF EXISTENCE IS MANIPULATING MINDS WITH BOGUS ENCHANTED WEAPONS, AND YOUR SON CAN'T BE BOTHERED TO PUT DOWN HIS DRINKING HORN AND DO ANYTHING ABOUT IT!

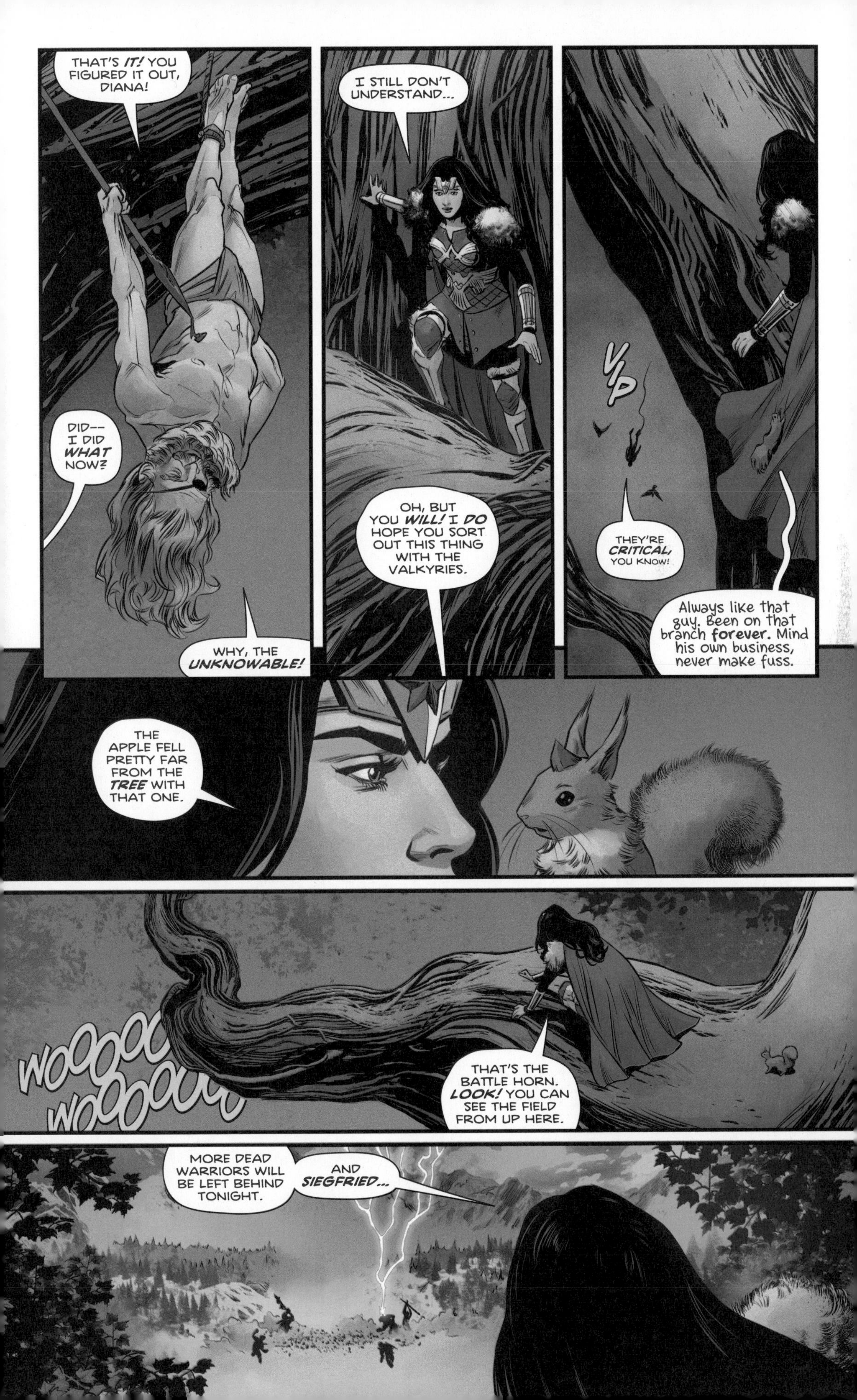

THAT'S IT! YOU FIGURED IT OUT, DIANA!
DID-- I DID WHAT NOW?
WHY, THE UNKNOWABLE!
I STILL DON'T UNDERSTAND...
OH, BUT YOU WILL! I DO HOPE YOU SORT OUT THIS THING WITH THE VALKYRIES.
VIP
THEY'RE CRITICAL, YOU KNOW!
Always like that guy. Been on that branch forever. Mind his own business, never make fuss.
THE APPLE FELL PRETTY FAR FROM THE TREE WITH THAT ONE.
WOOOOO
WOOOOOO
THAT'S THE BATTLE HORN. LOOK! YOU CAN SEE THE FIELD FROM UP HERE.
MORE DEAD WARRIORS WILL BE LEFT BEHIND TONIGHT.
AND SIEGFRIED...

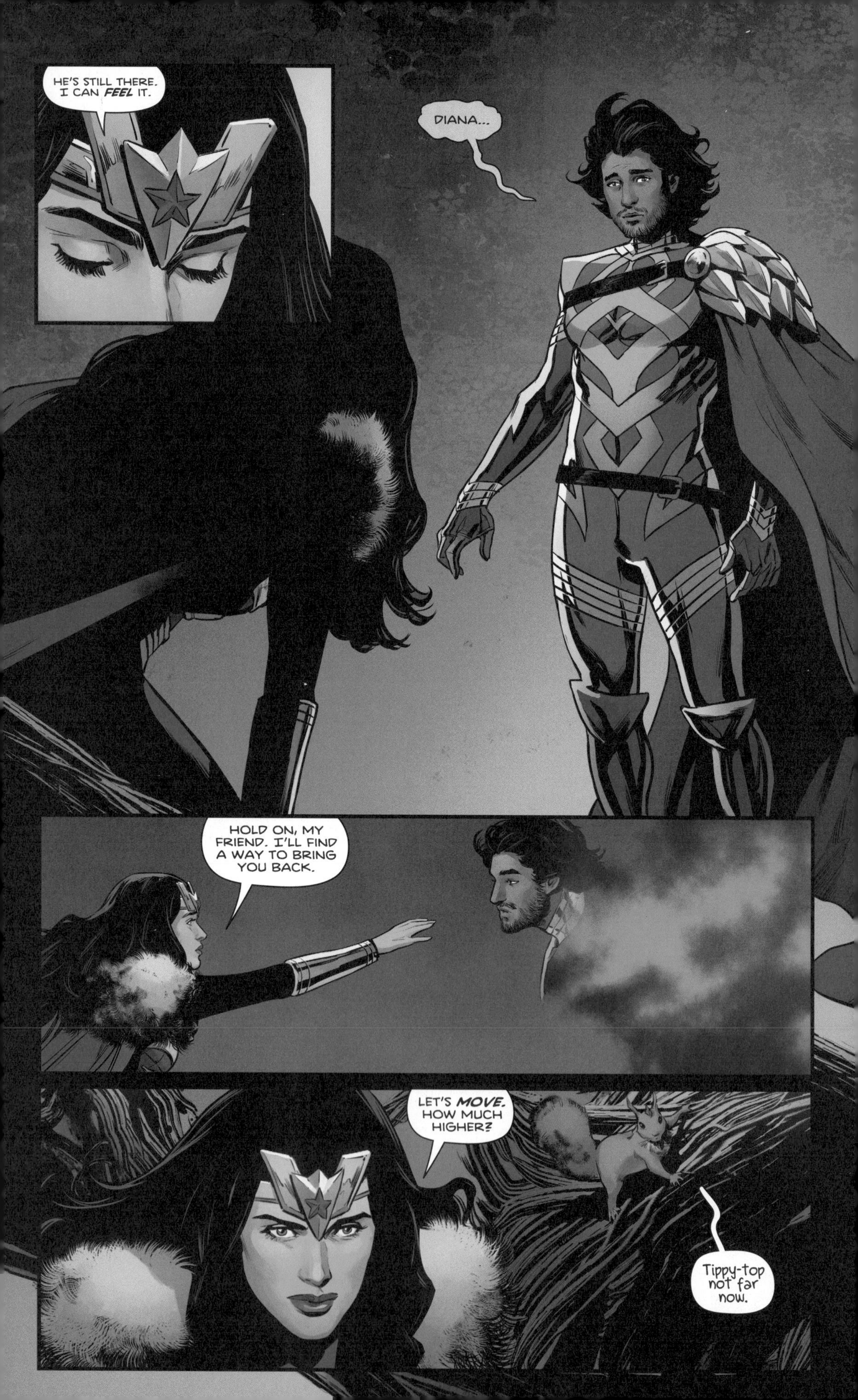
HE'S STILL THERE. I CAN FEEL IT.
DIANA...
HOLD ON, MY FRIEND. I'LL FIND A WAY TO BRING YOU BACK.
LET'S MOVE. HOW MUCH HIGHER?
Tippy-top not far now.

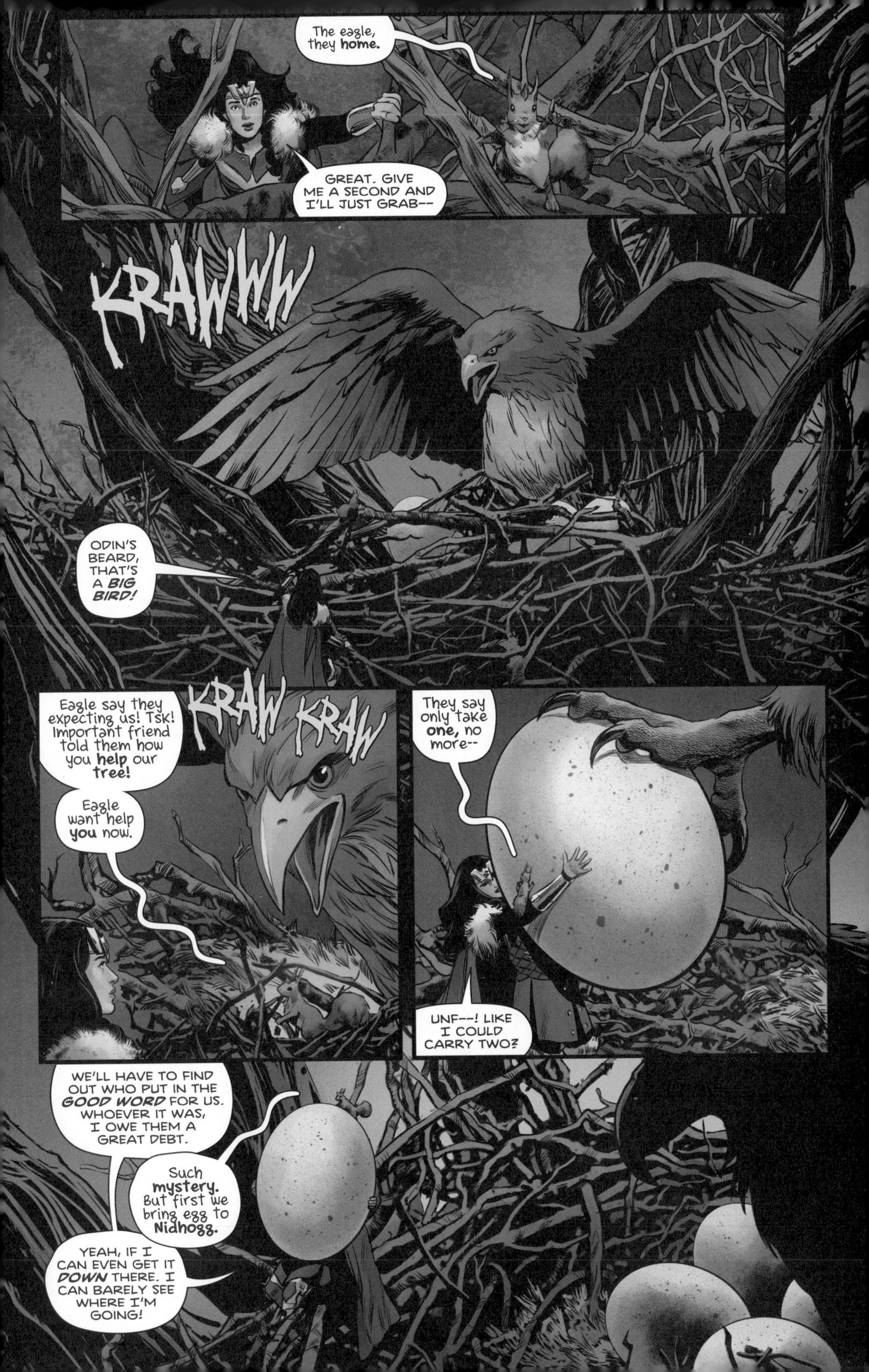

The eagle, they **home.**
GREAT. GIVE ME A SECOND AND I'LL JUST GRAB--
KRAWWW
ODIN'S BEARD, THAT'S A ***BIG BIRD!***
KRAW KRAW
Eagle say they expecting us! Tsk! Important friend told them how you **help** our **tree!**
Eagle want help **you** now.
They say only take **one,** no more--
UNF--! LIKE I COULD CARRY TWO?
WE'LL HAVE TO FIND OUT WHO PUT IN THE ***GOOD WORD*** FOR US. WHOEVER IT WAS, I OWE THEM A GREAT DEBT.
Such **mystery.** But first we bring egg to **Nidhogg.**
YEAH, IF I CAN EVEN GET IT ***DOWN*** THERE. I CAN BARELY SEE WHERE I'M GOING!

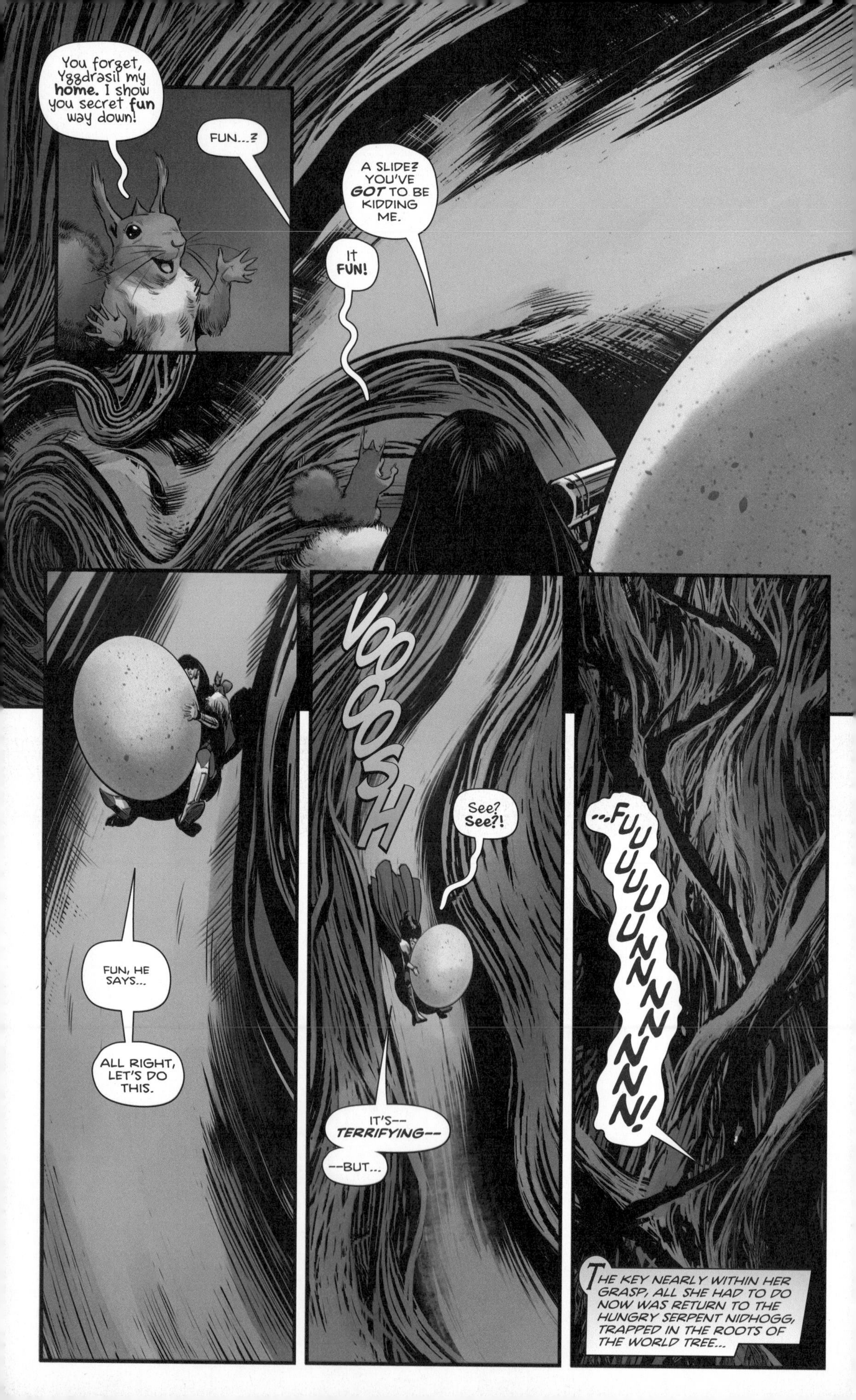

You forget, Yggdrasil my **home.** I show you secret **fun** way down!
FUN...?
A SLIDE? YOU'VE *GOT* TO BE KIDDING ME.
It **FUN!**
FUN, HE SAYS...
ALL RIGHT, LET'S DO THIS.
VOOOOOSH
See? **See?!**
IT'S-- *TERRIFYING--*
--BUT...
...FUUUUUNNNNNNN!
THE KEY NEARLY WITHIN HER GRASP, ALL SHE HAD TO DO NOW WAS RETURN TO THE HUNGRY SERPENT NIDHOGG, TRAPPED IN THE ROOTS OF THE WORLD TREE...

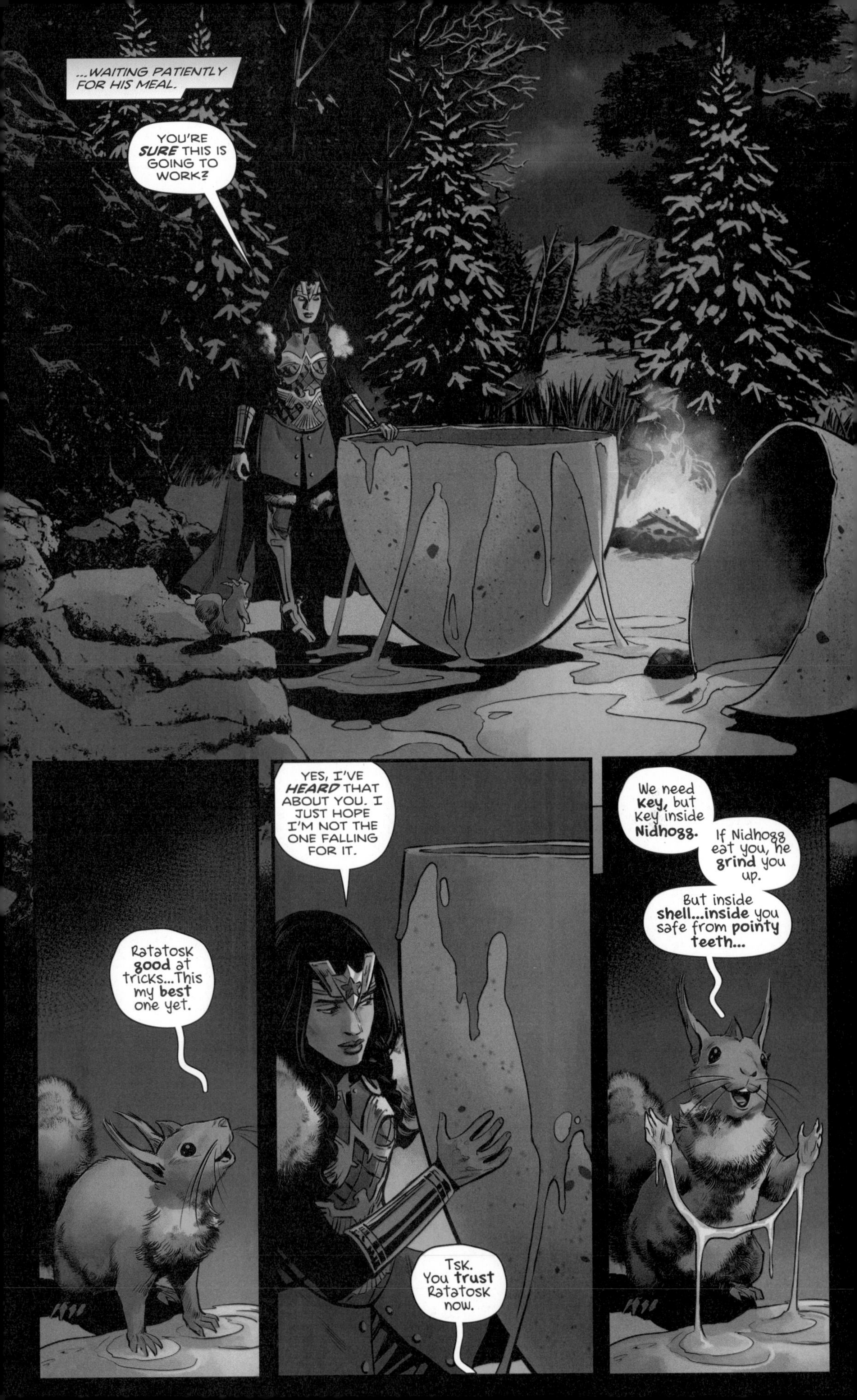
...WAITING PATIENTLY FOR HIS MEAL.
YOU'RE SURE THIS IS GOING TO WORK?
Ratatosk good at tricks...This my best one yet.
YES, I'VE HEARD THAT ABOUT YOU. I JUST HOPE I'M NOT THE ONE FALLING FOR IT.
Tsk. You trust Ratatosk now.
We need key, but key inside Nidhogg.
If Nidhogg eat you, he grind you up.
But inside shell...inside you safe from pointy teeth...

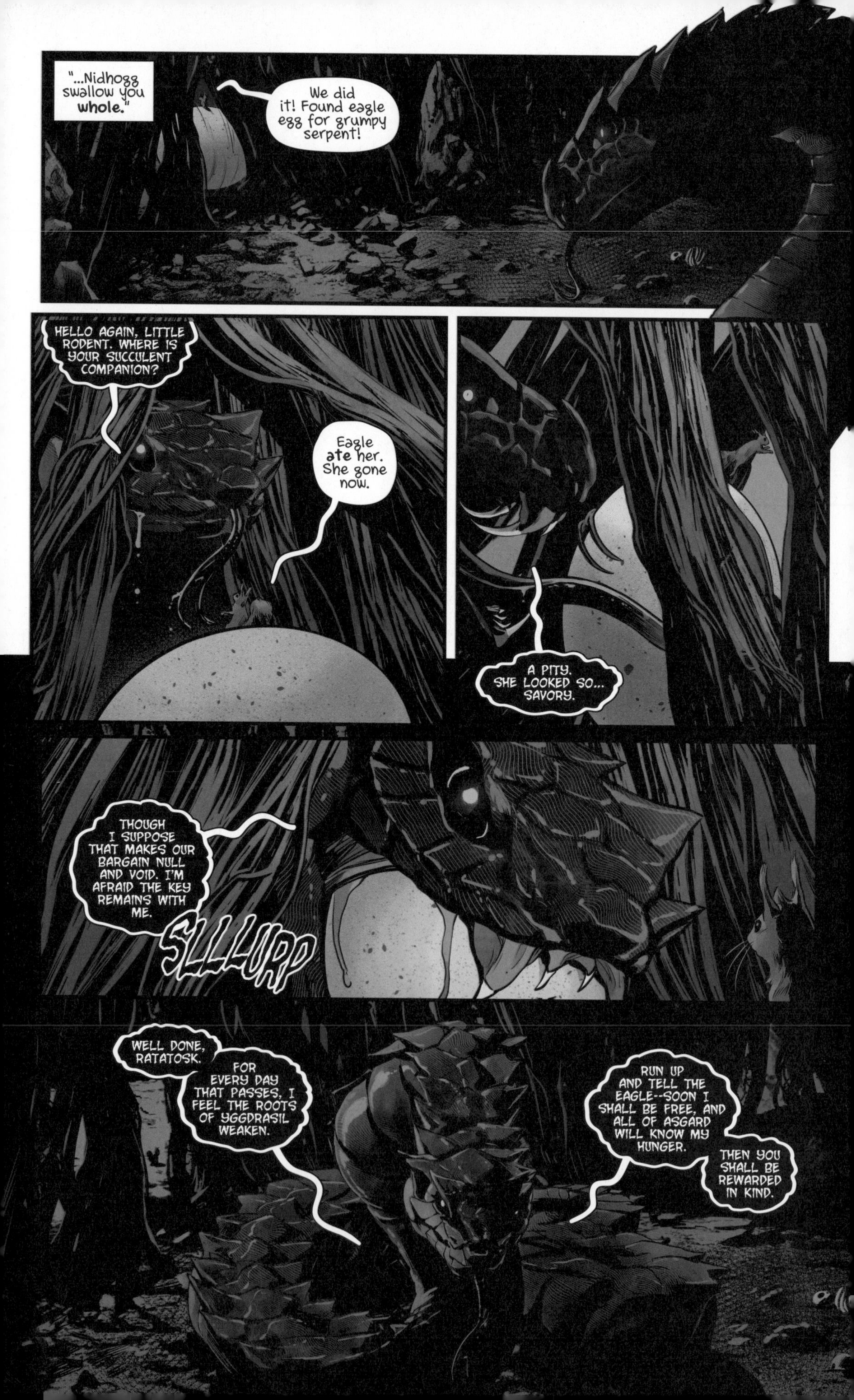
"...Nidhogg swallow you whole."
We did it! Found eagle egg for grumpy serpent!
HELLO AGAIN, LITTLE RODENT. WHERE IS YOUR SUCCULENT COMPANION?
Eagle ate her. She gone now.
A PITY. SHE LOOKED SO... SAVORY.
THOUGH I SUPPOSE THAT MAKES OUR BARGAIN NULL AND VOID. I'M AFRAID THE KEY REMAINS WITH ME.
SLLLURP
WELL DONE, RATATOSK.
FOR EVERY DAY THAT PASSES, I FEEL THE ROOTS OF YGGDRASIL WEAKEN.
RUN UP AND TELL THE EAGLE--SOON I SHALL BE FREE, AND ALL OF ASGARD WILL KNOW MY HUNGER.
THEN YOU SHALL BE REWARDED IN KIND.

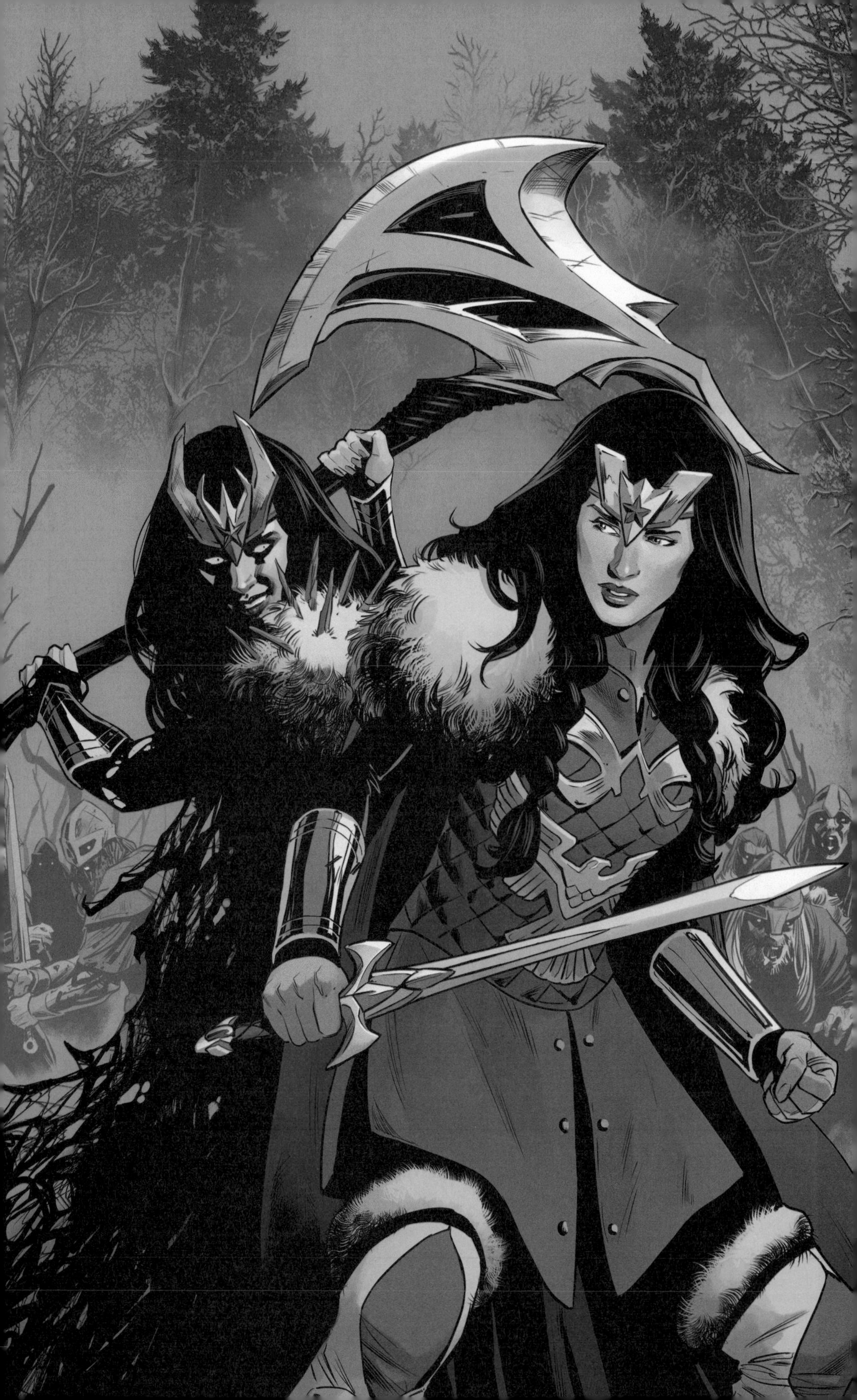

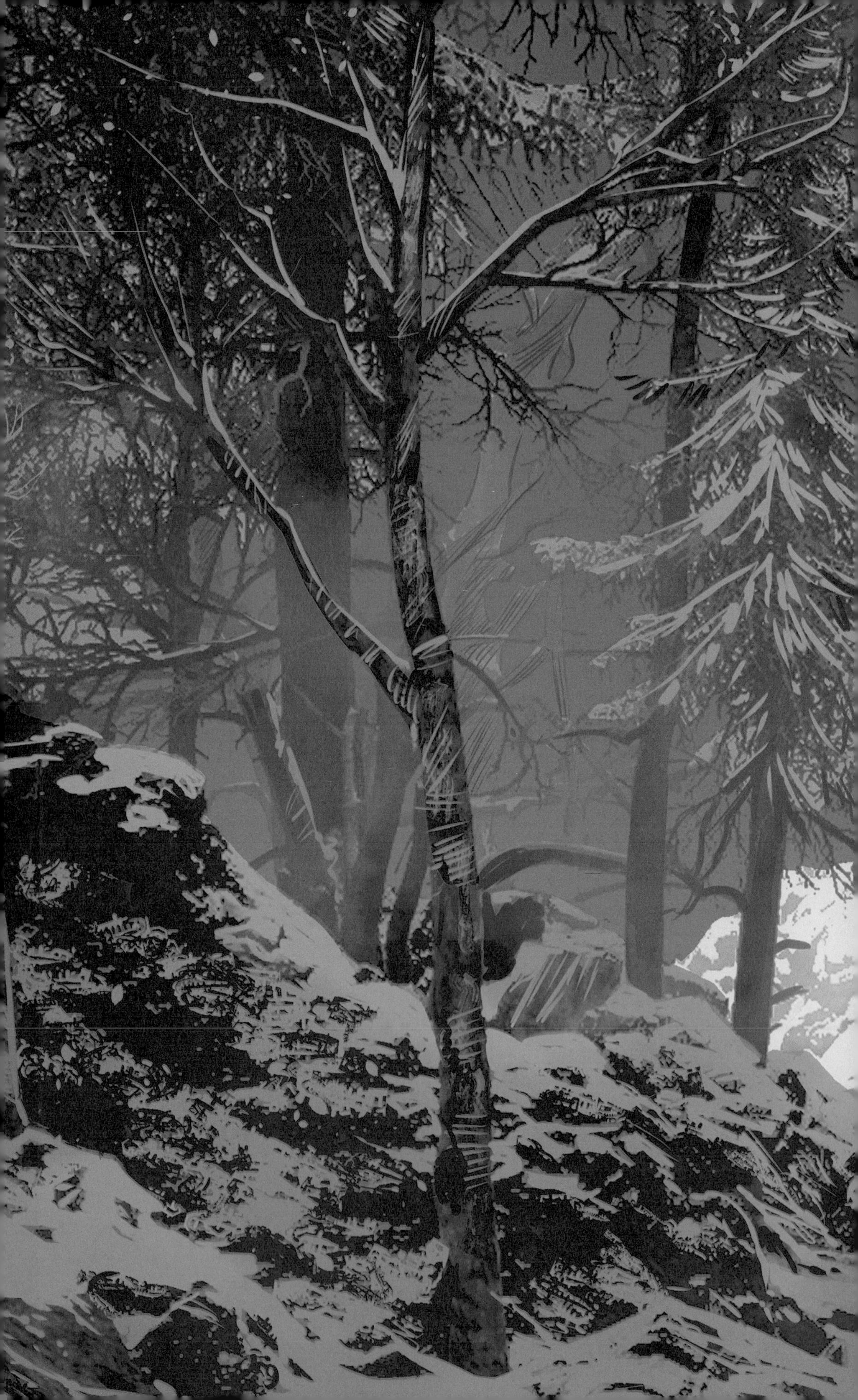

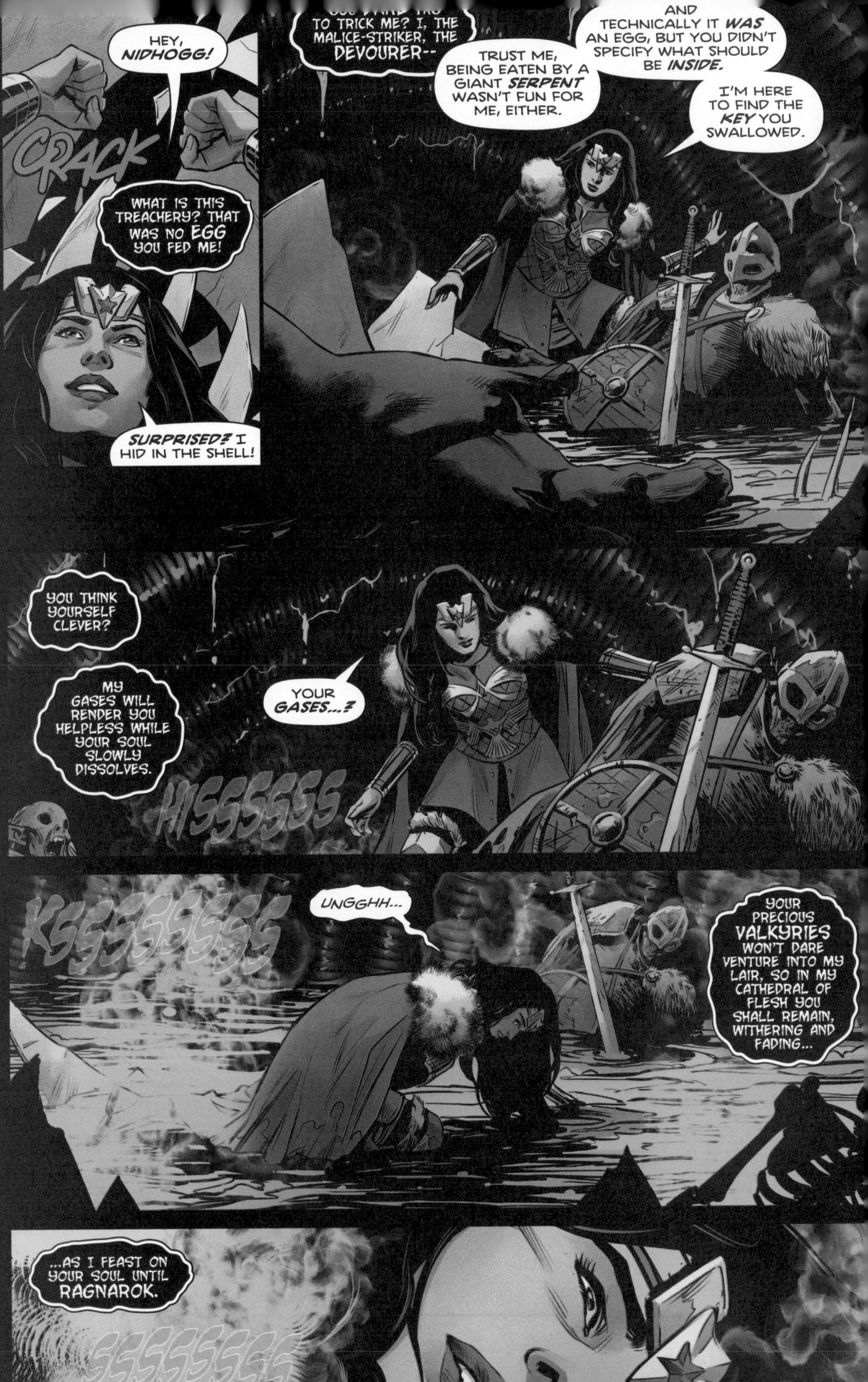
HEY, NIDHOGG!
CRACK
WHAT IS THIS TREACHERY? THAT WAS NO EGG YOU FED ME!
SURPRISED? I HID IN THE SHELL!
TO TRICK ME? I, THE MALICE-STRIKER, THE DEVOURER--
TRUST ME, BEING EATEN BY A GIANT SERPENT WASN'T FUN FOR ME, EITHER.
AND TECHNICALLY IT WAS AN EGG, BUT YOU DIDN'T SPECIFY WHAT SHOULD BE INSIDE.
I'M HERE TO FIND THE KEY YOU SWALLOWED.
YOU THINK YOURSELF CLEVER?
MY GASES WILL RENDER YOU HELPLESS WHILE YOUR SOUL SLOWLY DISSOLVES.
YOUR GASES...?
HISSSSSS
KSSSSSSSS
UNGGHH...
YOUR PRECIOUS VALKYRIES WON'T DARE VENTURE INTO MY LAIR, SO IN MY CATHEDRAL OF FLESH YOU SHALL REMAIN, WITHERING AND FADING...
...AS I FEAST ON YOUR SOUL UNTIL RAGNAROK.
SSSSSSSS

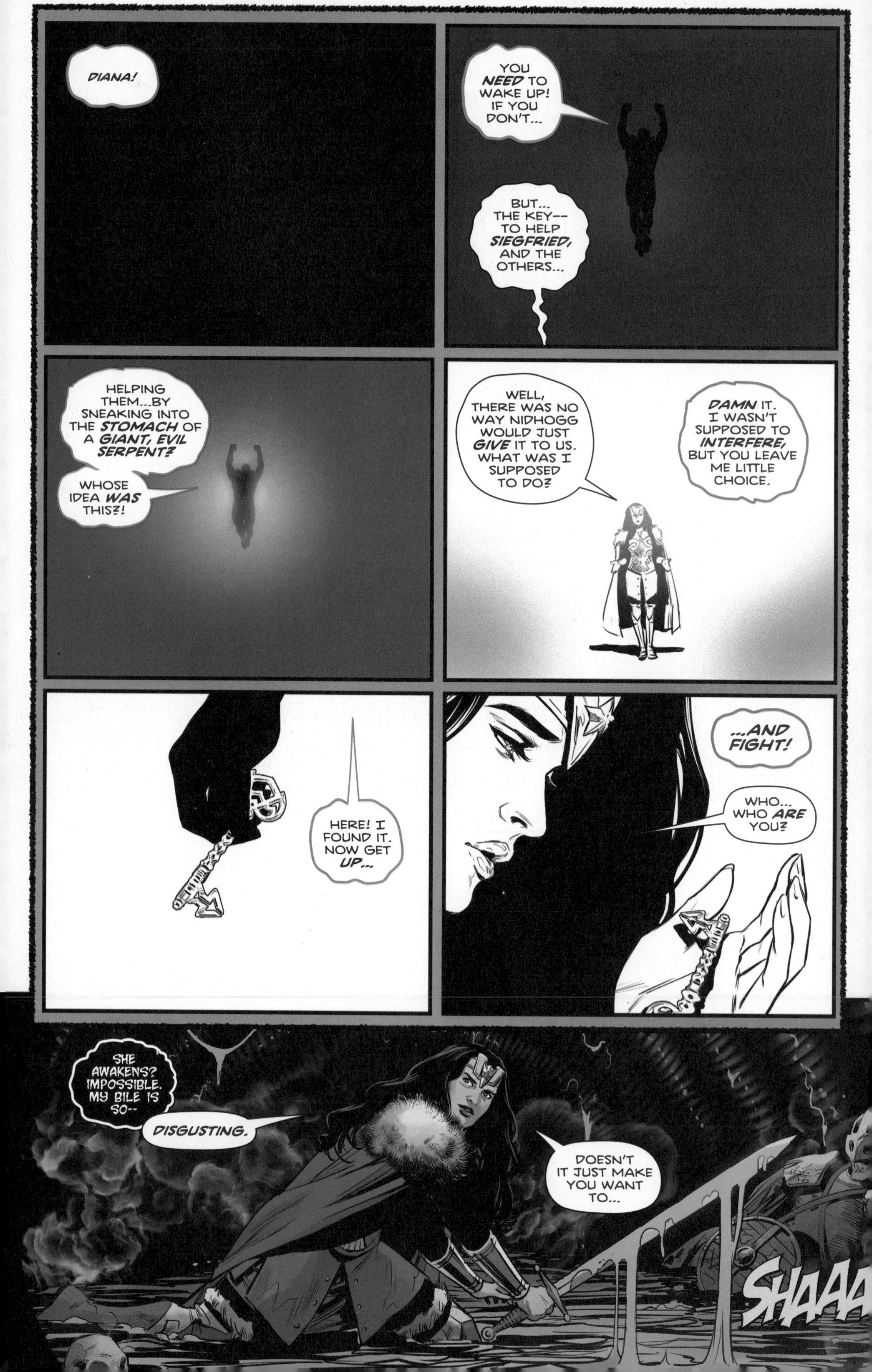
DIANA!
YOU NEED TO WAKE UP! IF YOU DON'T...
BUT... THE KEY-- TO HELP SIEGFRIED, AND THE OTHERS...
HELPING THEM...BY SNEAKING INTO THE STOMACH OF A GIANT, EVIL SERPENT?
WHOSE IDEA WAS THIS?!
WELL, THERE WAS NO WAY NIDHOGG WOULD JUST GIVE IT TO US. WHAT WAS I SUPPOSED TO DO?
DAMN IT. I WASN'T SUPPOSED TO INTERFERE, BUT YOU LEAVE ME LITTLE CHOICE.
HERE! I FOUND IT. NOW GET UP...
...AND FIGHT!
WHO... WHO ARE YOU?
SHE AWAKENS? IMPOSSIBLE. MY BILE IS SO--
DISGUSTING.
DOESN'T IT JUST MAKE YOU WANT TO...
SHAAA

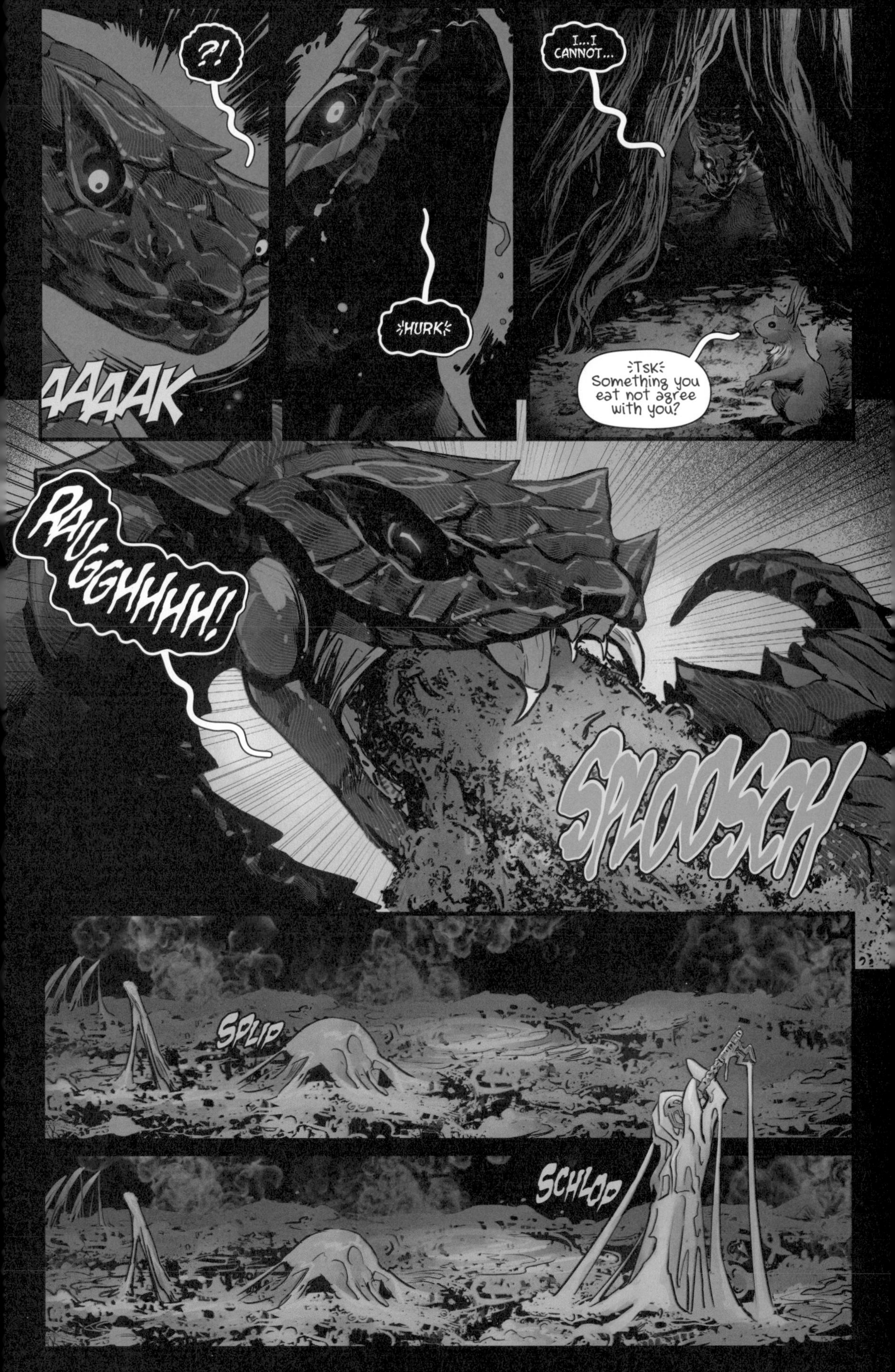
?!
AAAAK
HURK
I...I CANNOT...
TSK
Something you eat not agree with you?
RAUGGHHHH!
SPLOOSCH
SPLIP
SCHLOP

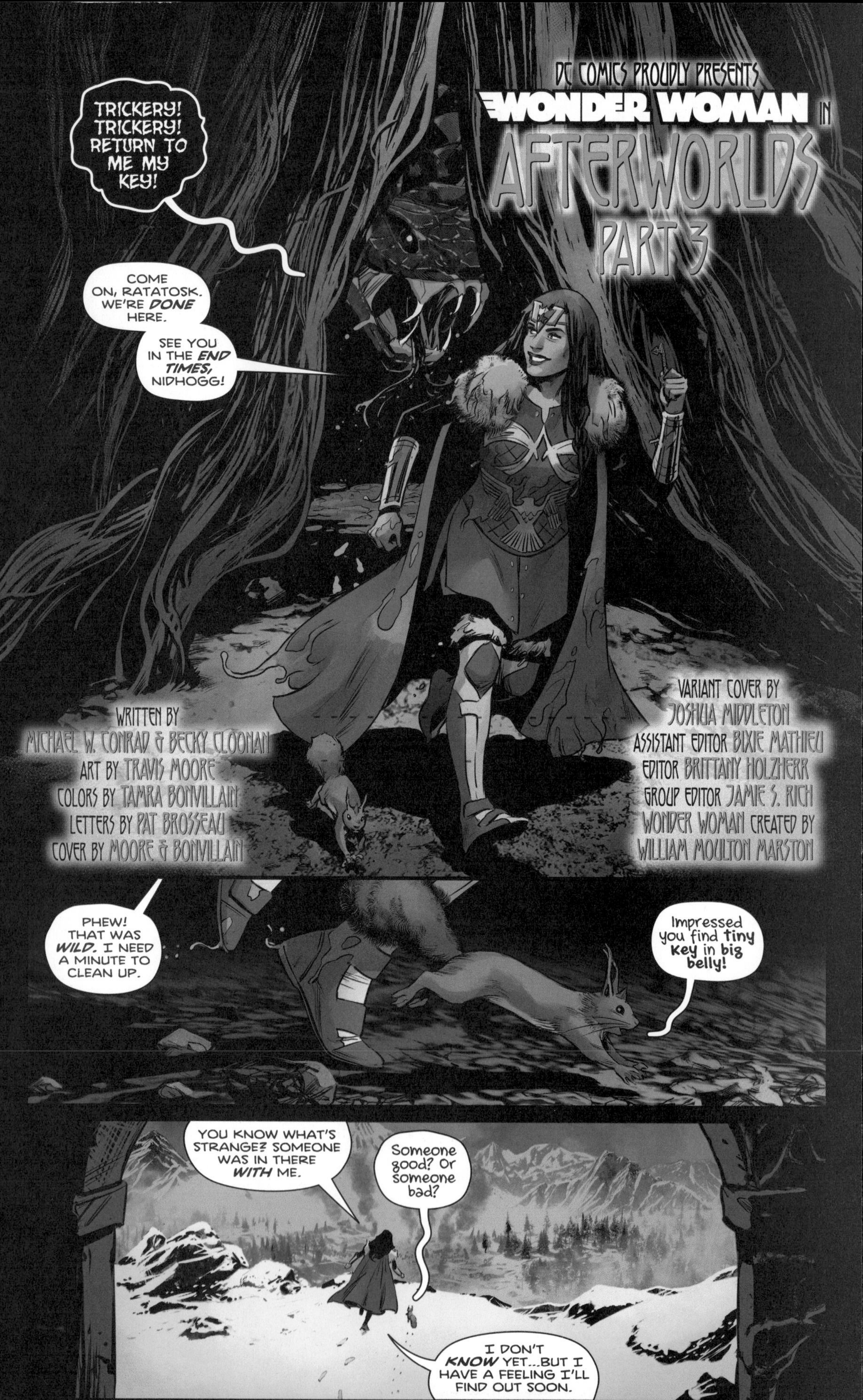

DC COMICS PROUDLY PRESENTS
WONDER WOMAN IN
AFTERWORLDS PART 3
TRICKERY! TRICKERY! RETURN TO ME MY KEY!
COME ON, RATATOSK. WE'RE *DONE* HERE.
SEE YOU IN THE *END TIMES,* NIDHOGG!
WRITTEN BY MICHAEL W. CONRAD & BECKY CLOONAN
ART BY TRAVIS MOORE
COLORS BY TAMRA BONVILLAIN
LETTERS BY PAT BROSSEAU
COVER BY MOORE & BONVILLAIN
VARIANT COVER BY JOSHUA MIDDLETON
ASSISTANT EDITOR BIXIE MATHIEU
EDITOR BRITTANY HOLZHERR
GROUP EDITOR JAMIE S. RICH
WONDER WOMAN CREATED BY WILLIAM MOULTON MARSTON
PHEW! THAT WAS *WILD.* I NEED A MINUTE TO CLEAN UP.
Impressed you find **tiny key** in **big belly!**
YOU KNOW WHAT'S STRANGE? SOMEONE WAS IN THERE *WITH* ME.
Someone good? Or someone bad?
I DON'T *KNOW* YET...BUT I HAVE A FEELING I'LL FIND OUT SOON.

LOOK, THE VIKINGS ARE ALREADY TAKING TO THE BATTLEFIELD AGAIN.

YOU'D THINK WITH EVERYTHING GOING ON THEY WOULD TAKE A BREAK.

I GUESS THAT MEANS WE SHOULD GET A MOVE ON--

DIANA, I DON'T HAVE LONG...

SIEGFRIED!

PLEASE, LISTEN. THE VALKYRIES-- YOU *MUST NOT* SEEK THEM.

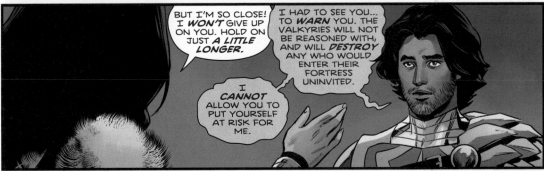

BUT I'M SO CLOSE! I *WON'T* GIVE UP ON YOU. HOLD ON JUST *A LITTLE LONGER.*

I HAD TO SEE YOU... TO *WARN* YOU. THE VALKYRIES WILL NOT BE REASONED WITH, AND WILL *DESTROY* ANY WHO WOULD ENTER THEIR FORTRESS UNINVITED.

I *CANNOT* ALLOW YOU TO PUT YOURSELF AT RISK FOR ME.

FORGET US, DIANA. FORGET *ME.* WE ARE *LOST*--

OH, SIEGFRIED... IF YOU KNEW ME AT ALL YOU'D *KNOW* I'M NOT GOING TO LISTEN TO YOU.

I'LL *FIGHT* EVERY NIGHT UNTIL I BECOME A VALKYRIE MYSELF, IF THAT'S WHAT IT'LL TAKE TO SAVE YOU!

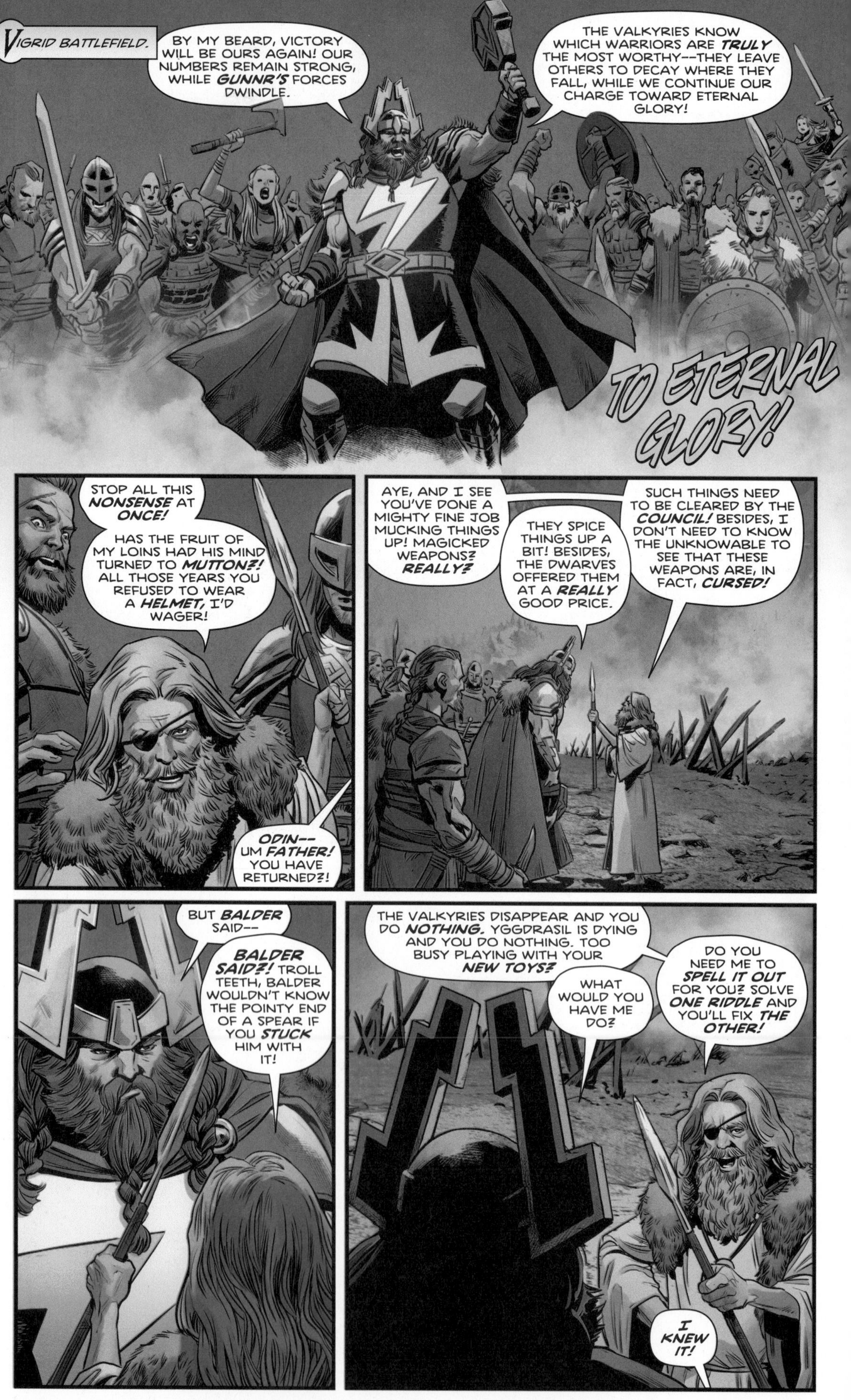
VIGRID BATTLEFIELD.
BY MY BEARD, VICTORY WILL BE OURS AGAIN! OUR NUMBERS REMAIN STRONG, WHILE GUNNR'S FORCES DWINDLE.
THE VALKYRIES KNOW WHICH WARRIORS ARE TRULY THE MOST WORTHY--THEY LEAVE OTHERS TO DECAY WHERE THEY FALL, WHILE WE CONTINUE OUR CHARGE TOWARD ETERNAL GLORY!
TO ETERNAL GLORY!
STOP ALL THIS NONSENSE AT ONCE!
HAS THE FRUIT OF MY LOINS HAD HIS MIND TURNED TO MUTTON?! ALL THOSE YEARS YOU REFUSED TO WEAR A HELMET, I'D WAGER!
ODIN-- UM FATHER! YOU HAVE RETURNED?!
AYE, AND I SEE YOU'VE DONE A MIGHTY FINE JOB MUCKING THINGS UP! MAGICKED WEAPONS? REALLY?
THEY SPICE THINGS UP A BIT! BESIDES, THE DWARVES OFFERED THEM AT A REALLY GOOD PRICE.
SUCH THINGS NEED TO BE CLEARED BY THE COUNCIL! BESIDES, I DON'T NEED TO KNOW THE UNKNOWABLE TO SEE THAT THESE WEAPONS ARE, IN FACT, CURSED!
BUT BALDER SAID--
BALDER SAID?! TROLL TEETH, BALDER WOULDN'T KNOW THE POINTY END OF A SPEAR IF YOU STUCK HIM WITH IT!
THE VALKYRIES DISAPPEAR AND YOU DO NOTHING. YGGDRASIL IS DYING AND YOU DO NOTHING. TOO BUSY PLAYING WITH YOUR NEW TOYS?
WHAT WOULD YOU HAVE ME DO?
DO YOU NEED ME TO SPELL IT OUT FOR YOU? SOLVE ONE RIDDLE AND YOU'LL FIX THE OTHER!
I KNEW IT!

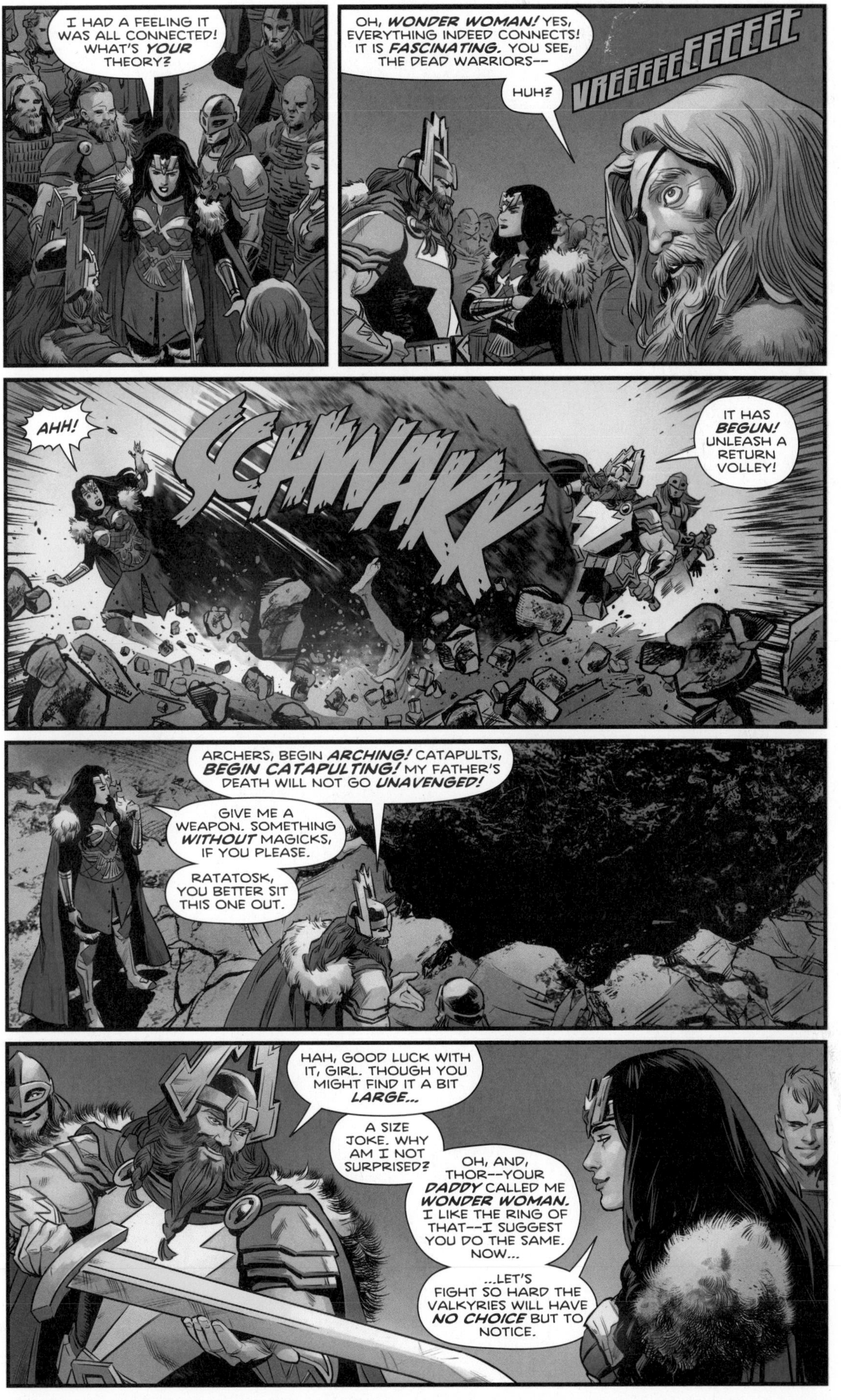

I HAD A FEELING IT WAS ALL CONNECTED! WHAT'S *YOUR* THEORY?
OH, *WONDER WOMAN!* YES, EVERYTHING INDEED CONNECTS! IT IS *FASCINATING.* YOU SEE, THE DEAD WARRIORS--
HUH?
VREEEEEEEEEEEE
AHH!
SCHWAKK
IT HAS *BEGUN!* UNLEASH A RETURN VOLLEY!
ARCHERS, BEGIN *ARCHING!* CATAPULTS, *BEGIN CATAPULTING!* MY FATHER'S DEATH WILL NOT GO *UNAVENGED!*
GIVE ME A WEAPON. SOMETHING *WITHOUT* MAGICKS, IF YOU PLEASE.
RATATOSK, YOU BETTER SIT THIS ONE OUT.
HAH, GOOD LUCK WITH IT, GIRL. THOUGH YOU MIGHT FIND IT A BIT *LARGE...*
A SIZE JOKE. WHY AM I NOT SURPRISED?
OH, AND, THOR--YOUR *DADDY* CALLED ME *WONDER WOMAN.* I LIKE THE RING OF THAT--I SUGGEST YOU DO THE SAME. NOW...
...LET'S FIGHT SO HARD THE VALKYRIES WILL HAVE *NO CHOICE* BUT TO NOTICE.

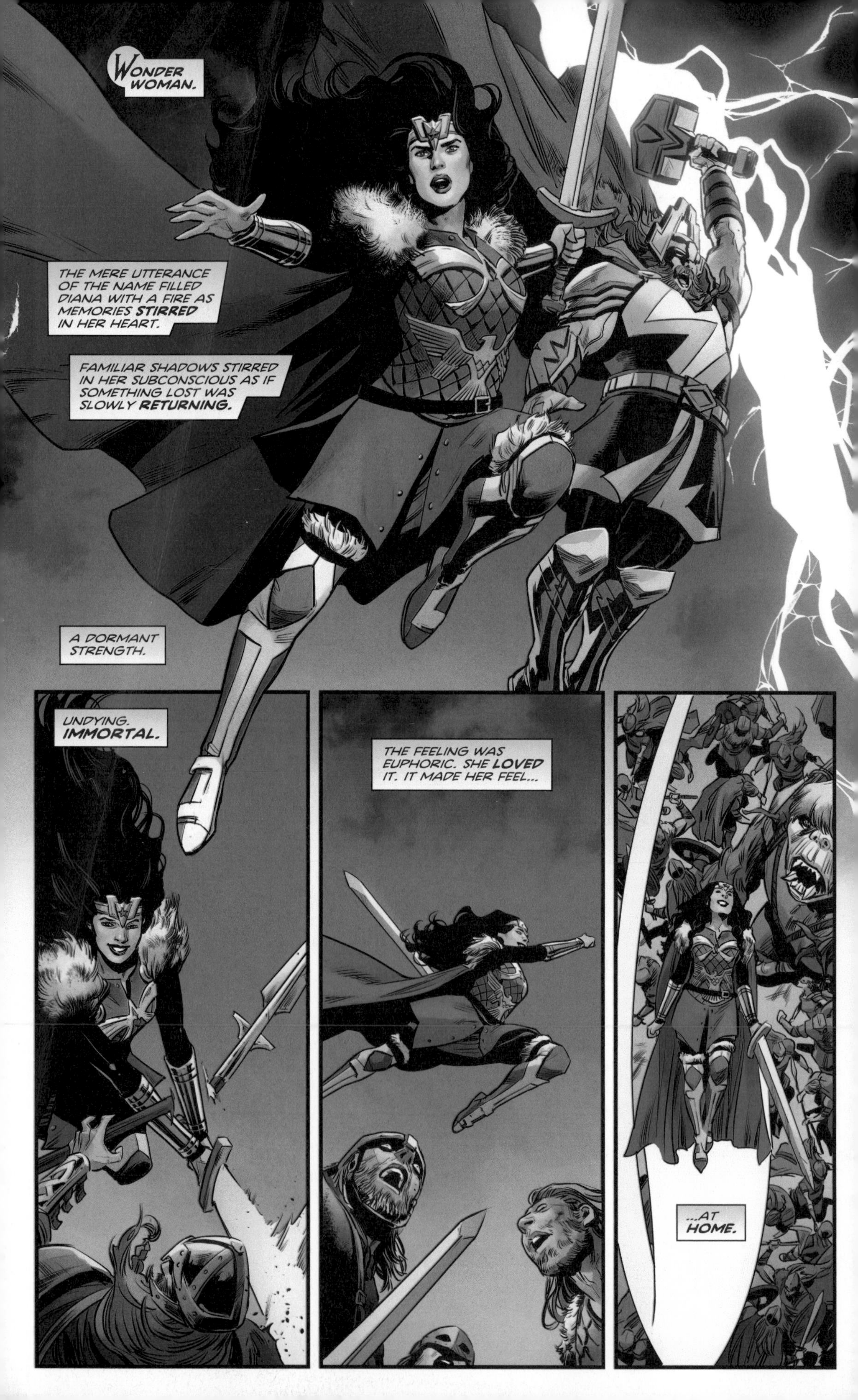
WONDER WOMAN.
THE MERE UTTERANCE OF THE NAME FILLED DIANA WITH A FIRE AS MEMORIES STIRRED IN HER HEART.
FAMILIAR SHADOWS STIRRED IN HER SUBCONSCIOUS AS IF SOMETHING LOST WAS SLOWLY RETURNING.
A DORMANT STRENGTH.
UNDYING. IMMORTAL.
THE FEELING WAS EUPHORIC. SHE LOVED IT. IT MADE HER FEEL...
...AT HOME.

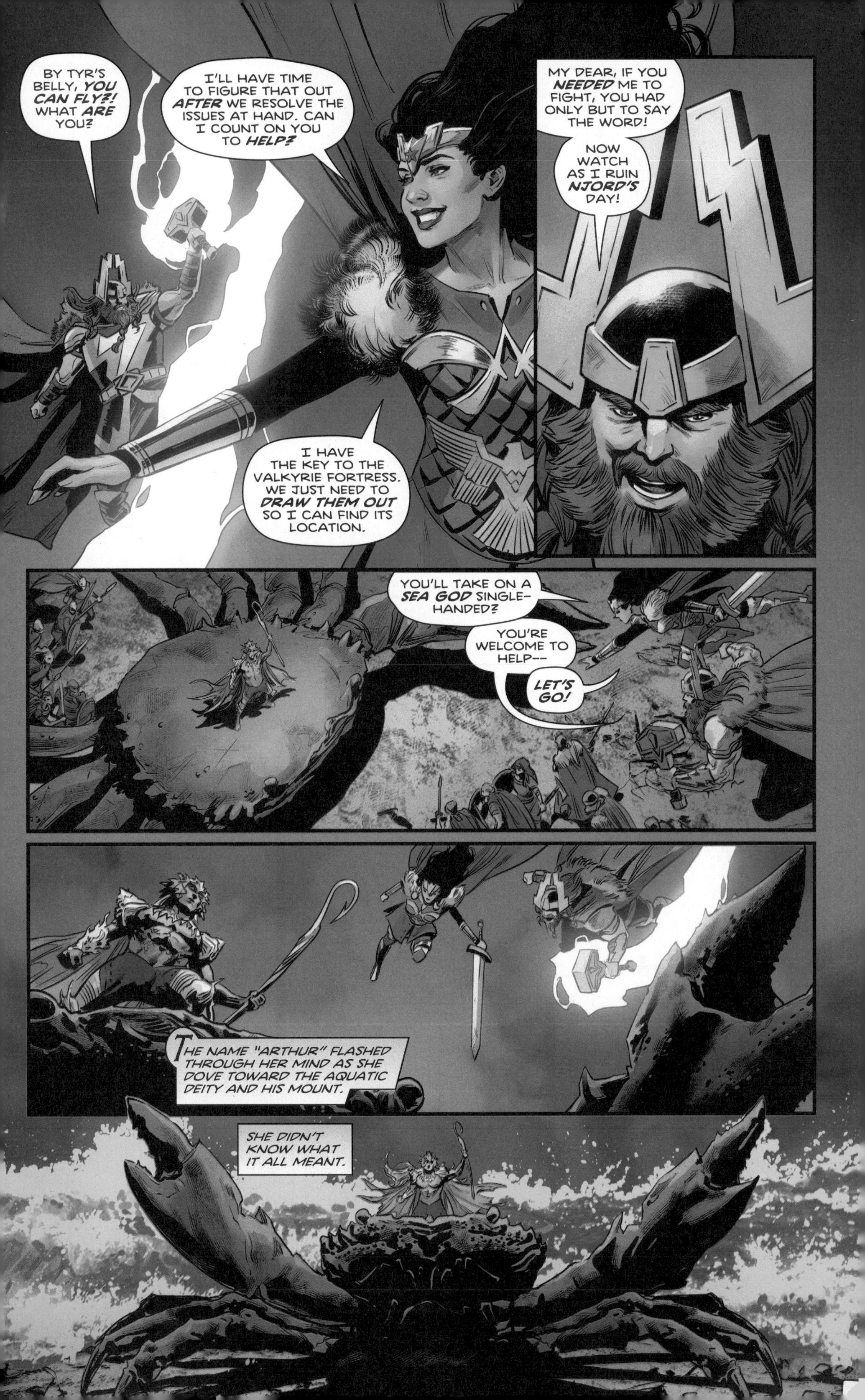
BY TYR'S BELLY, YOU CAN FLY?! WHAT ARE YOU?
I'LL HAVE TIME TO FIGURE THAT OUT AFTER WE RESOLVE THE ISSUES AT HAND. CAN I COUNT ON YOU TO HELP?
I HAVE THE KEY TO THE VALKYRIE FORTRESS. WE JUST NEED TO DRAW THEM OUT SO I CAN FIND ITS LOCATION.
MY DEAR, IF YOU NEEDED ME TO FIGHT, YOU HAD ONLY BUT TO SAY THE WORD!
NOW WATCH AS I RUIN NJORD'S DAY!
YOU'LL TAKE ON A SEA GOD SINGLE-HANDED?
YOU'RE WELCOME TO HELP--
LET'S GO!
THE NAME "ARTHUR" FLASHED THROUGH HER MIND AS SHE DOVE TOWARD THE AQUATIC DEITY AND HIS MOUNT.
SHE DIDN'T KNOW WHAT IT ALL MEANT.

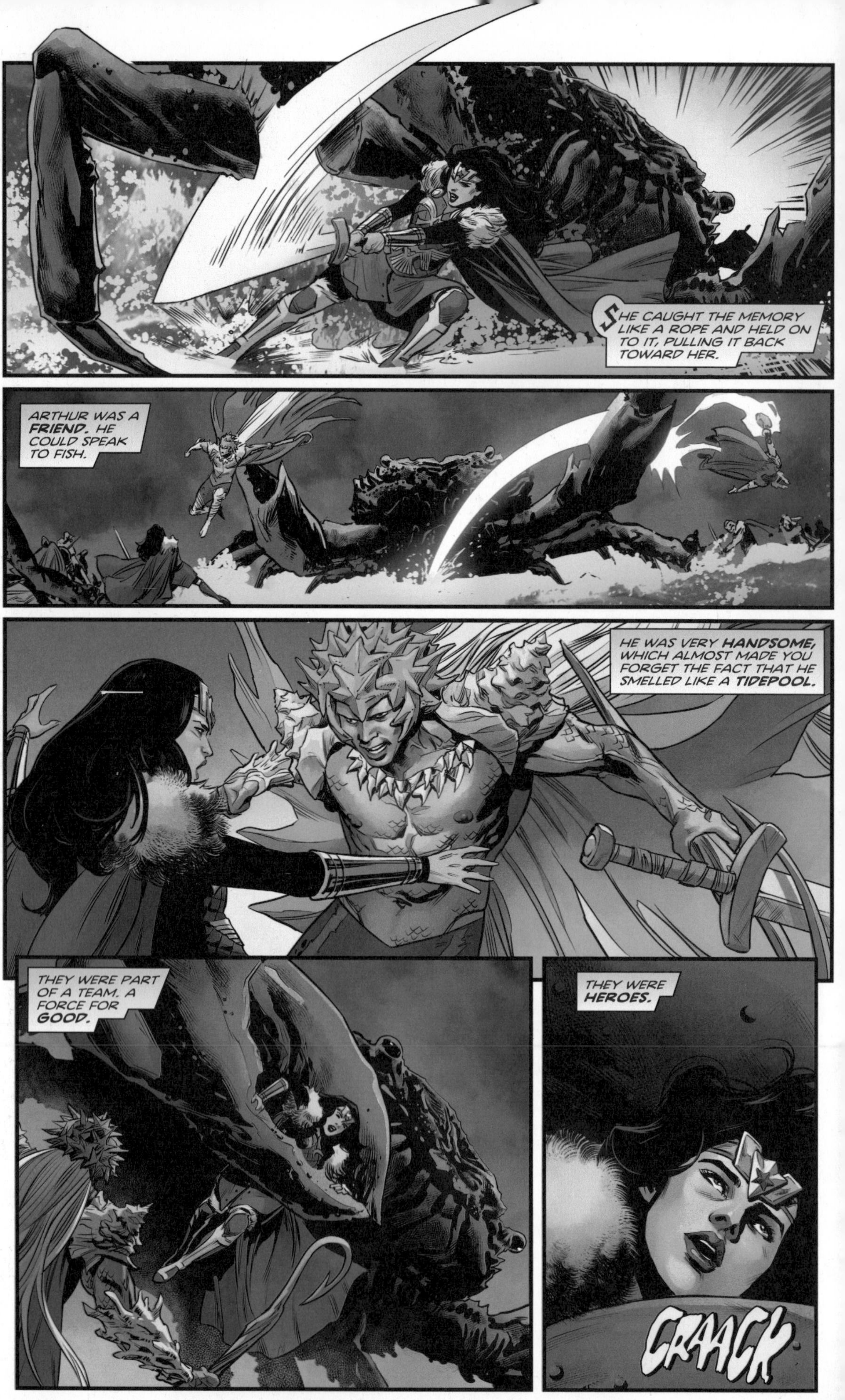
SHE CAUGHT THE MEMORY LIKE A ROPE AND HELD ON TO IT, PULLING IT BACK TOWARD HER.
ARTHUR WAS A FRIEND. HE COULD SPEAK TO FISH.
HE WAS VERY HANDSOME, WHICH ALMOST MADE YOU FORGET THE FACT THAT HE SMELLED LIKE A TIDEPOOL.
THEY WERE PART OF A TEAM. A FORCE FOR GOOD.
THEY WERE HEROES.
CRAACK

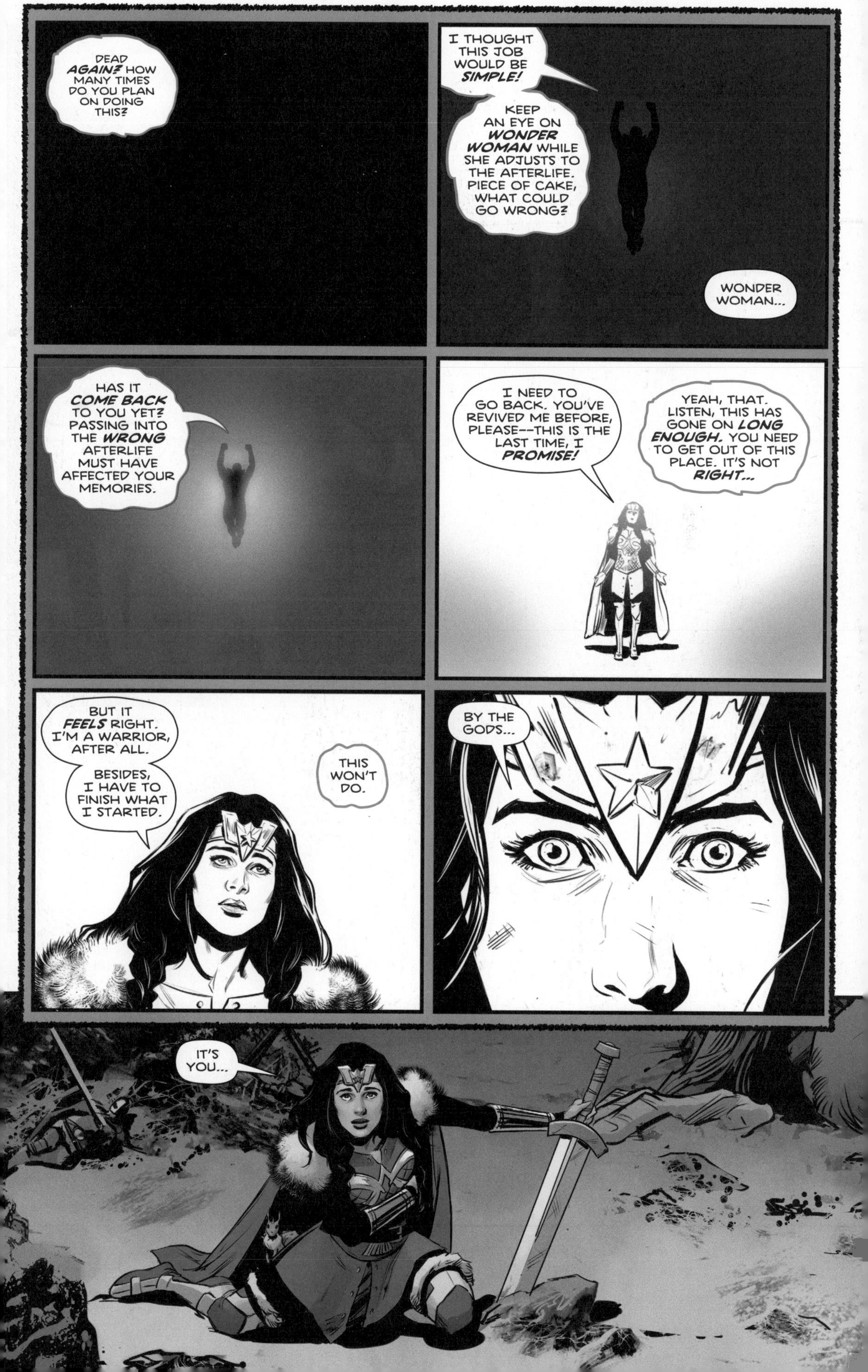
DEAD AGAIN? HOW MANY TIMES DO YOU PLAN ON DOING THIS?
I THOUGHT THIS JOB WOULD BE SIMPLE!
KEEP AN EYE ON WONDER WOMAN WHILE SHE ADJUSTS TO THE AFTERLIFE. PIECE OF CAKE, WHAT COULD GO WRONG?
WONDER WOMAN...
HAS IT COME BACK TO YOU YET? PASSING INTO THE WRONG AFTERLIFE MUST HAVE AFFECTED YOUR MEMORIES.
I NEED TO GO BACK. YOU'VE REVIVED ME BEFORE, PLEASE--THIS IS THE LAST TIME, I PROMISE!
YEAH, THAT. LISTEN, THIS HAS GONE ON LONG ENOUGH. YOU NEED TO GET OUT OF THIS PLACE. IT'S NOT RIGHT...
BUT IT FEELS RIGHT. I'M A WARRIOR, AFTER ALL.
BESIDES, I HAVE TO FINISH WHAT I STARTED.
THIS WON'T DO.
BY THE GODS...
IT'S YOU...

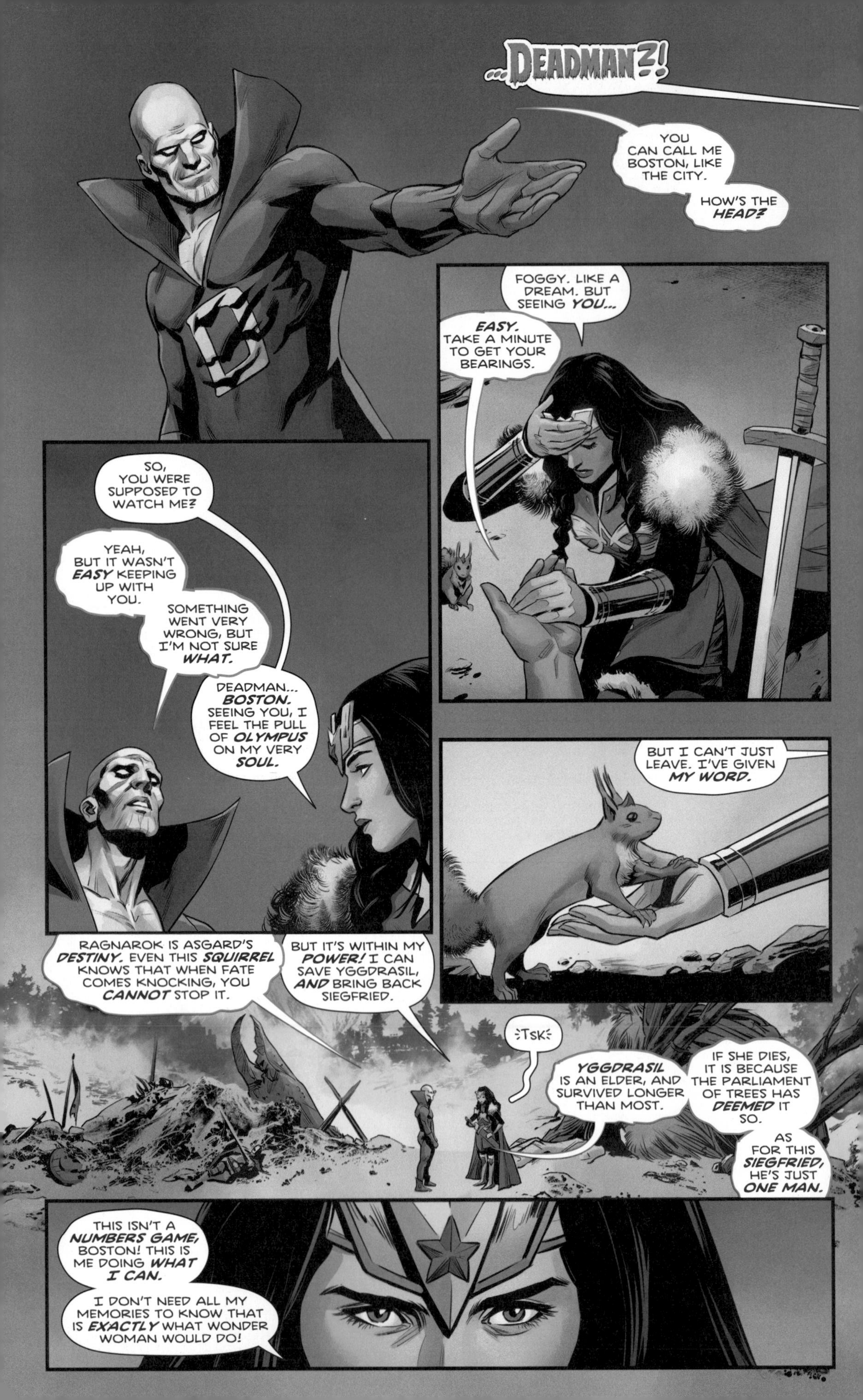
...DEADMAN?!
YOU CAN CALL ME BOSTON, LIKE THE CITY.
HOW'S THE HEAD?
FOGGY. LIKE A DREAM. BUT SEEING YOU...
EASY. TAKE A MINUTE TO GET YOUR BEARINGS.
SO, YOU WERE SUPPOSED TO WATCH ME?
YEAH, BUT IT WASN'T EASY KEEPING UP WITH YOU.
SOMETHING WENT VERY WRONG, BUT I'M NOT SURE WHAT.
DEADMAN... BOSTON. SEEING YOU, I FEEL THE PULL OF OLYMPUS ON MY VERY SOUL.
BUT I CAN'T JUST LEAVE. I'VE GIVEN MY WORD.
RAGNAROK IS ASGARD'S DESTINY. EVEN THIS SQUIRREL KNOWS THAT WHEN FATE COMES KNOCKING, YOU CANNOT STOP IT.
BUT IT'S WITHIN MY POWER! I CAN SAVE YGGDRASIL, AND BRING BACK SIEGFRIED.
Tsk
YGGDRASIL IS AN ELDER, AND SURVIVED LONGER THAN MOST.
IF SHE DIES, IT IS BECAUSE THE PARLIAMENT OF TREES HAS DEEMED IT SO.
AS FOR THIS SIEGFRIED, HE'S JUST ONE MAN.
THIS ISN'T A NUMBERS GAME, BOSTON! THIS IS ME DOING WHAT I CAN.
I DON'T NEED ALL MY MEMORIES TO KNOW THAT IS EXACTLY WHAT WONDER WOMAN WOULD DO!

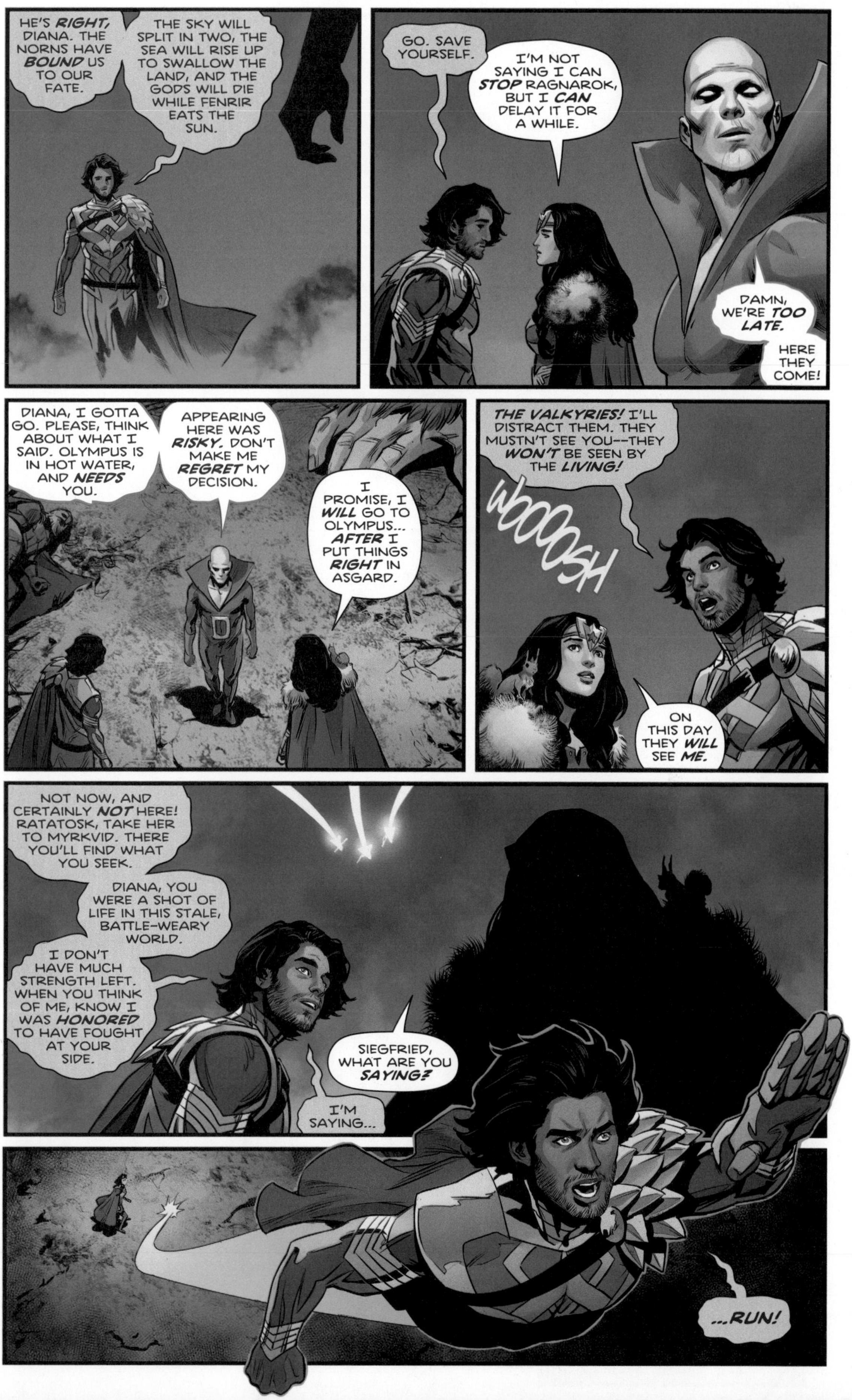
HE'S RIGHT, DIANA. THE NORNS HAVE BOUND US TO OUR FATE.
THE SKY WILL SPLIT IN TWO, THE SEA WILL RISE UP TO SWALLOW THE LAND, AND THE GODS WILL DIE WHILE FENRIR EATS THE SUN.
GO. SAVE YOURSELF.
I'M NOT SAYING I CAN STOP RAGNAROK, BUT I CAN DELAY IT FOR A WHILE.
DAMN, WE'RE TOO LATE.
HERE THEY COME!
DIANA, I GOTTA GO. PLEASE, THINK ABOUT WHAT I SAID. OLYMPUS IS IN HOT WATER, AND NEEDS YOU.
APPEARING HERE WAS RISKY. DON'T MAKE ME REGRET MY DECISION.
I PROMISE, I WILL GO TO OLYMPUS... AFTER I PUT THINGS RIGHT IN ASGARD.
THE VALKYRIES! I'LL DISTRACT THEM. THEY MUSTN'T SEE YOU--THEY WON'T BE SEEN BY THE LIVING!
WOOOOSH
ON THIS DAY THEY WILL SEE ME.
NOT NOW, AND CERTAINLY NOT HERE! RATATOSK, TAKE HER TO MYRKVID. THERE YOU'LL FIND WHAT YOU SEEK.
DIANA, YOU WERE A SHOT OF LIFE IN THIS STALE, BATTLE-WEARY WORLD.
I DON'T HAVE MUCH STRENGTH LEFT. WHEN YOU THINK OF ME, KNOW I WAS HONORED TO HAVE FOUGHT AT YOUR SIDE.
SIEGFRIED, WHAT ARE YOU SAYING?
I'M SAYING...
...RUN!

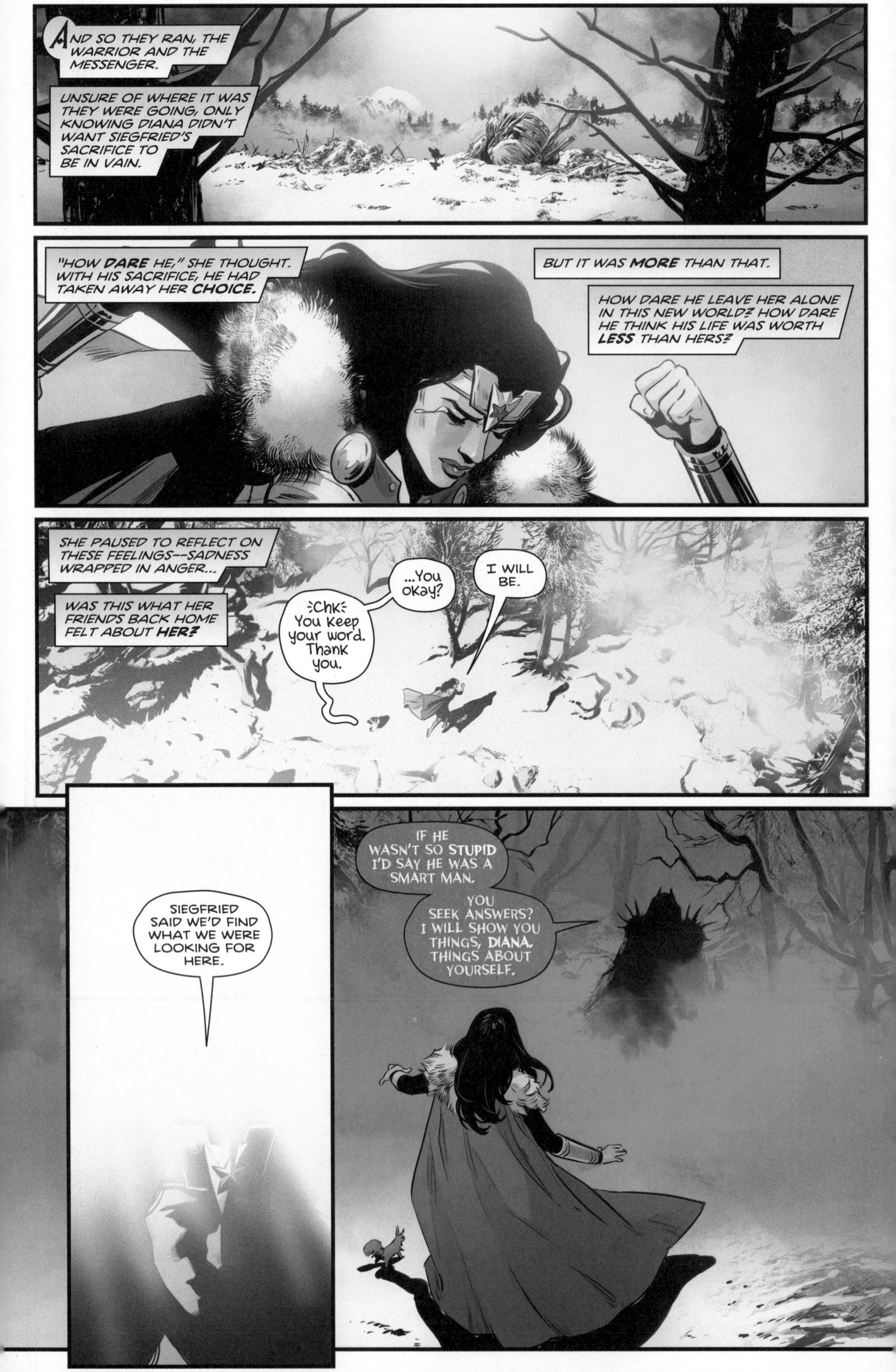
AND SO THEY RAN, THE WARRIOR AND THE MESSENGER.
UNSURE OF WHERE IT WAS THEY WERE GOING, ONLY KNOWING DIANA DIDN'T WANT SIEGFRIED'S SACRIFICE TO BE IN VAIN.
"HOW DARE HE," SHE THOUGHT. WITH HIS SACRIFICE, HE HAD TAKEN AWAY HER CHOICE.
BUT IT WAS MORE THAN THAT.
HOW DARE HE LEAVE HER ALONE IN THIS NEW WORLD? HOW DARE HE THINK HIS LIFE WAS WORTH LESS THAN HERS?
SHE PAUSED TO REFLECT ON THESE FEELINGS--SADNESS WRAPPED IN ANGER...
WAS THIS WHAT HER FRIENDS BACK HOME FELT ABOUT HER?
...You okay?
I WILL BE.
Chk You keep your word. Thank you.
SIEGFRIED SAID WE'D FIND WHAT WE WERE LOOKING FOR HERE.
IF HE WASN'T SO STUPID I'D SAY HE WAS A SMART MAN.
YOU SEEK ANSWERS? I WILL SHOW YOU THINGS, DIANA. THINGS ABOUT YOURSELF.

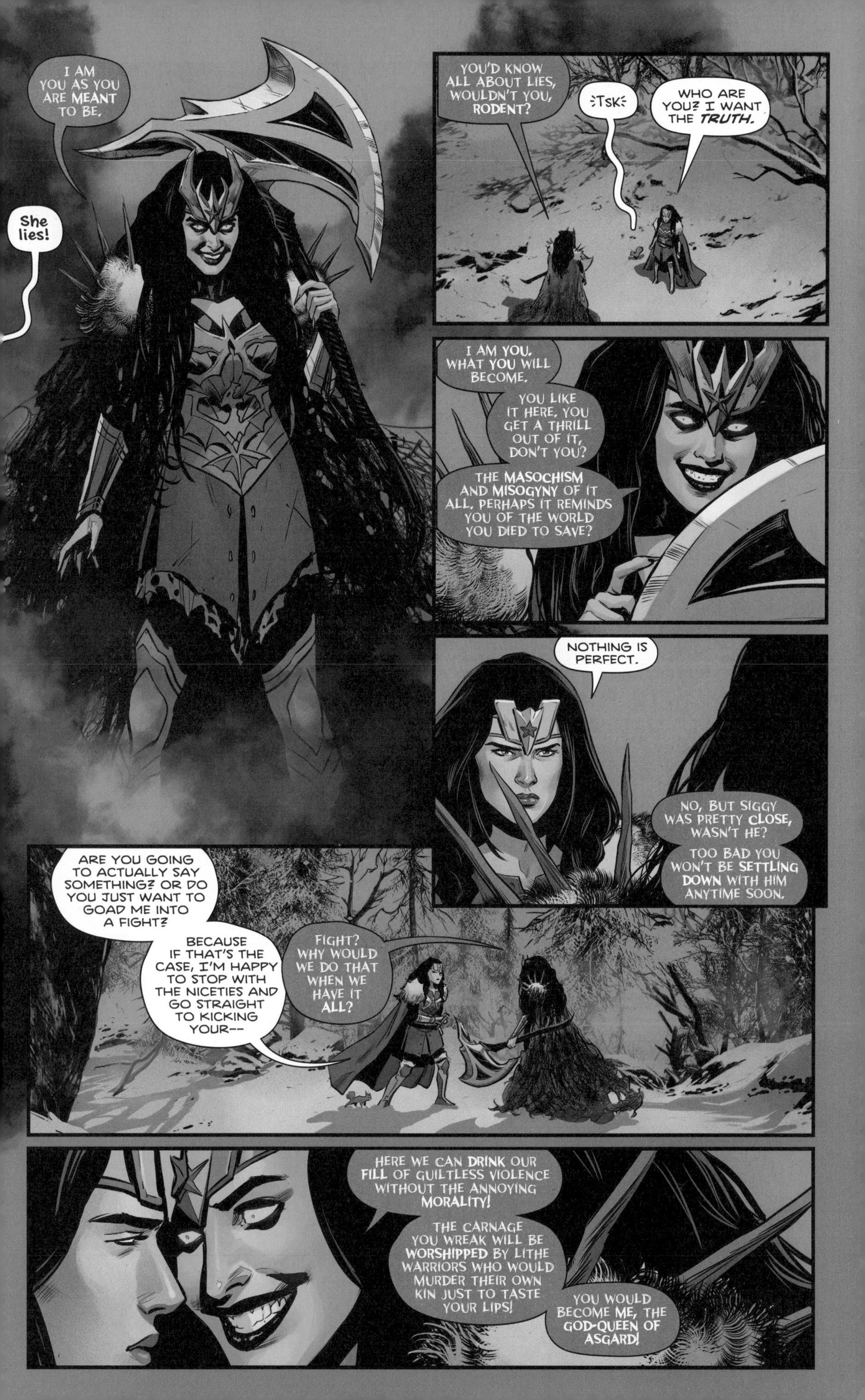
I AM YOU AS YOU ARE MEANT TO BE.
She lies!
YOU'D KNOW ALL ABOUT LIES, WOULDN'T YOU, RODENT?
Tsk
WHO ARE YOU? I WANT THE TRUTH.
I AM YOU. WHAT YOU WILL BECOME.
YOU LIKE IT HERE. YOU GET A THRILL OUT OF IT, DON'T YOU?
THE MASOCHISM AND MISOGYNY OF IT ALL. PERHAPS IT REMINDS YOU OF THE WORLD YOU DIED TO SAVE?
NOTHING IS PERFECT.
NO, BUT SIGGY WAS PRETTY CLOSE, WASN'T HE?
TOO BAD YOU WON'T BE SETTLING DOWN WITH HIM ANYTIME SOON.
ARE YOU GOING TO ACTUALLY SAY SOMETHING? OR DO YOU JUST WANT TO GOAD ME INTO A FIGHT?
BECAUSE IF THAT'S THE CASE, I'M HAPPY TO STOP WITH THE NICETIES AND GO STRAIGHT TO KICKING YOUR--
FIGHT? WHY WOULD WE DO THAT WHEN WE HAVE IT ALL?
HERE WE CAN DRINK OUR FILL OF GUILTLESS VIOLENCE WITHOUT THE ANNOYING MORALITY!
THE CARNAGE YOU WREAK WILL BE WORSHIPPED BY LITHE WARRIORS WHO WOULD MURDER THEIR OWN KIN JUST TO TASTE YOUR LIPS!
YOU WOULD BECOME ME, THE GOD-QUEEN OF ASGARD!

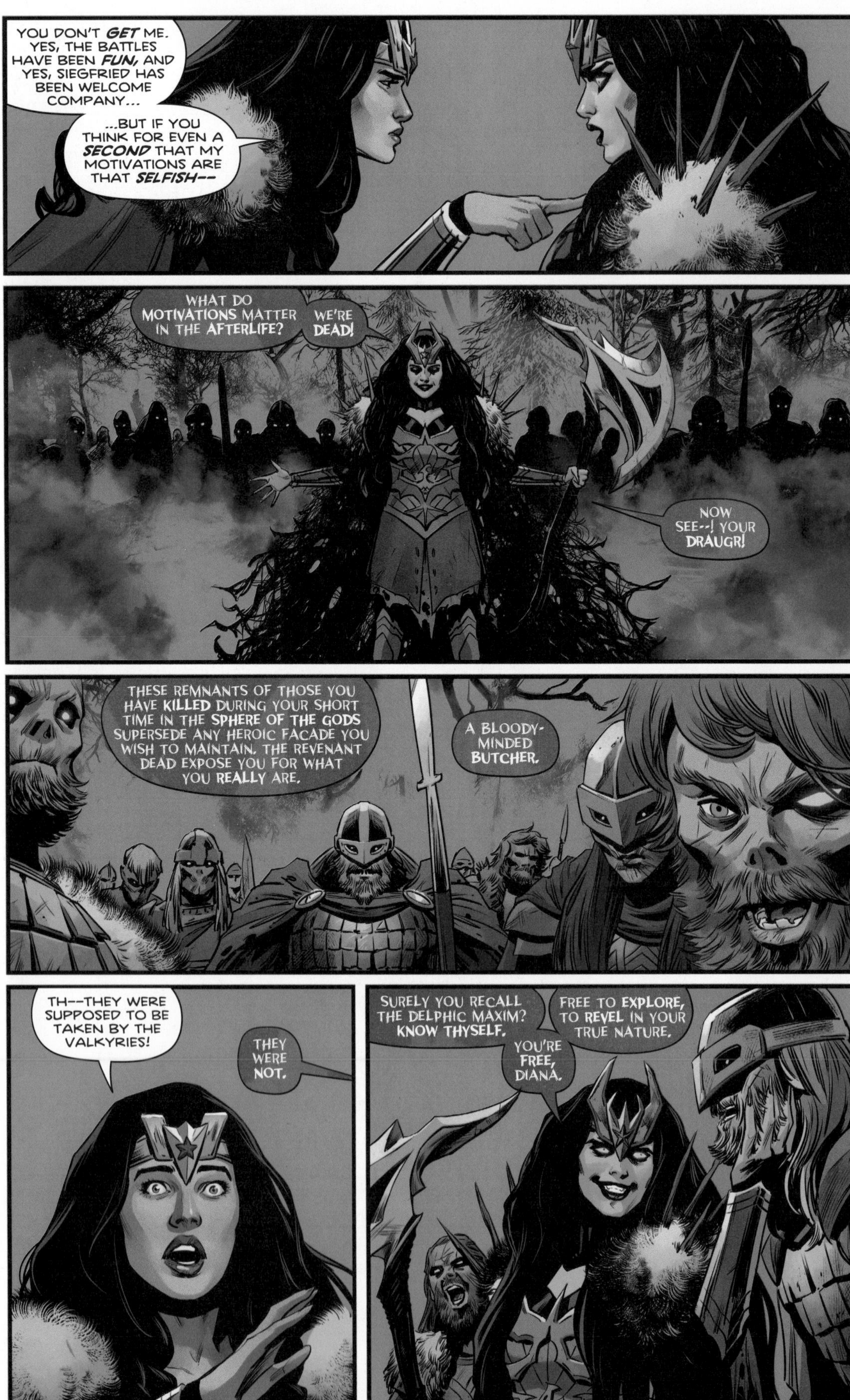
YOU DON'T GET ME. YES, THE BATTLES HAVE BEEN FUN, AND YES, SIEGFRIED HAS BEEN WELCOME COMPANY...
...BUT IF YOU THINK FOR EVEN A SECOND THAT MY MOTIVATIONS ARE THAT SELFISH--
WHAT DO MOTIVATIONS MATTER IN THE AFTERLIFE?
WE'RE DEAD!
NOW SEE--! YOUR DRAUGR!
THESE REMNANTS OF THOSE YOU HAVE KILLED DURING YOUR SHORT TIME IN THE SPHERE OF THE GODS SUPERSEDE ANY HEROIC FACADE YOU WISH TO MAINTAIN. THE REVENANT DEAD EXPOSE YOU FOR WHAT YOU REALLY ARE.
A BLOODY-MINDED BUTCHER.
TH--THEY WERE SUPPOSED TO BE TAKEN BY THE VALKYRIES!
THEY WERE NOT.
SURELY YOU RECALL THE DELPHIC MAXIM? KNOW THYSELF.
YOU'RE FREE, DIANA.
FREE TO EXPLORE, TO REVEL IN YOUR TRUE NATURE.

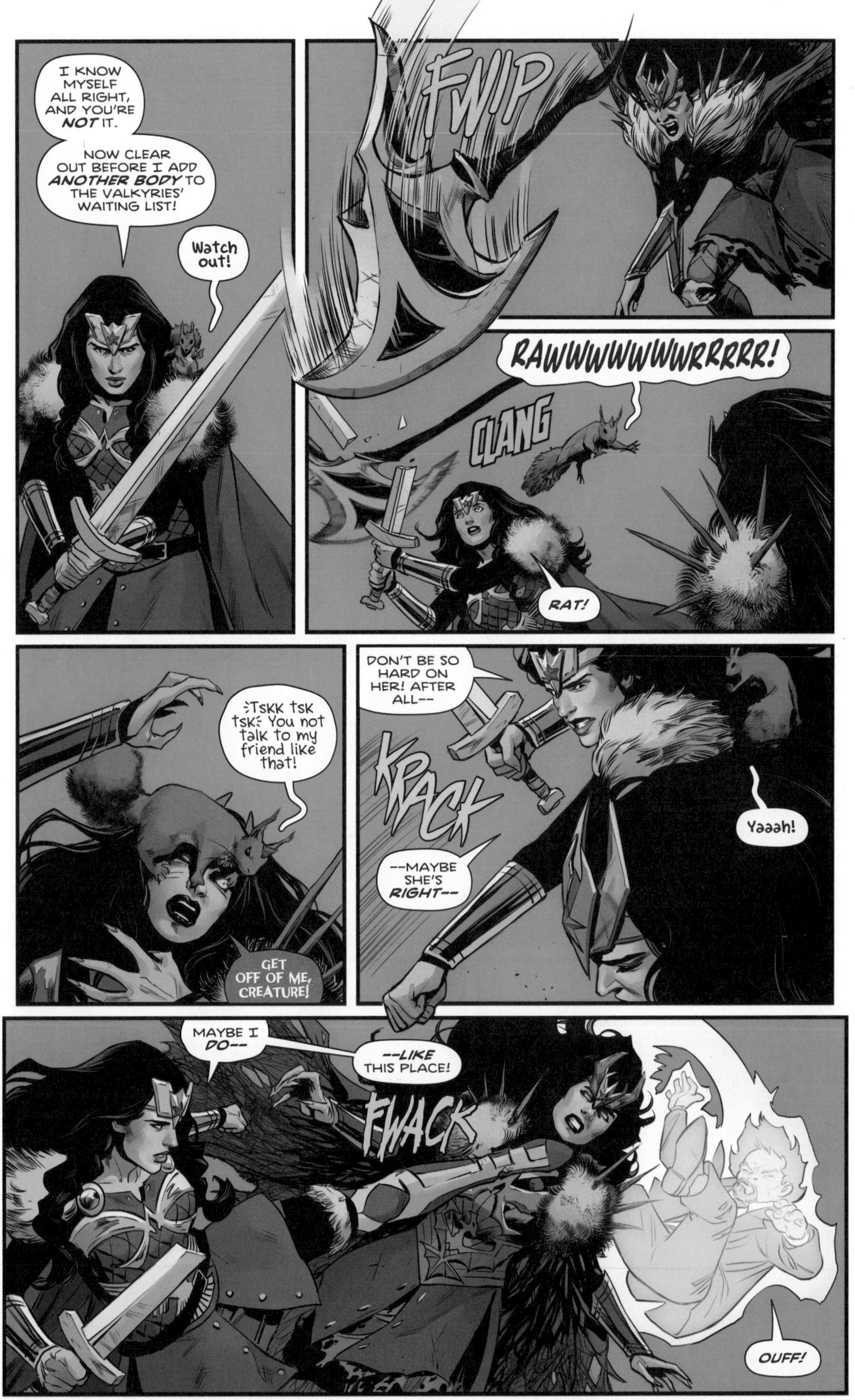
I KNOW MYSELF ALL RIGHT, AND YOU'RE NOT IT.
NOW CLEAR OUT BEFORE I ADD ANOTHER BODY TO THE VALKYRIES' WAITING LIST!
Watch out!
FWIP
RAWWWWWWWRRRRR!
CLANG
RAT!
:Tskk tsk tsk: You not talk to my friend like that!
GET OFF OF ME, CREATURE!
DON'T BE SO HARD ON HER! AFTER ALL--
KRACK
--MAYBE SHE'S RIGHT--
Yaaah!
MAYBE I DO--
--LIKE THIS PLACE!
FWACK
OUFF!

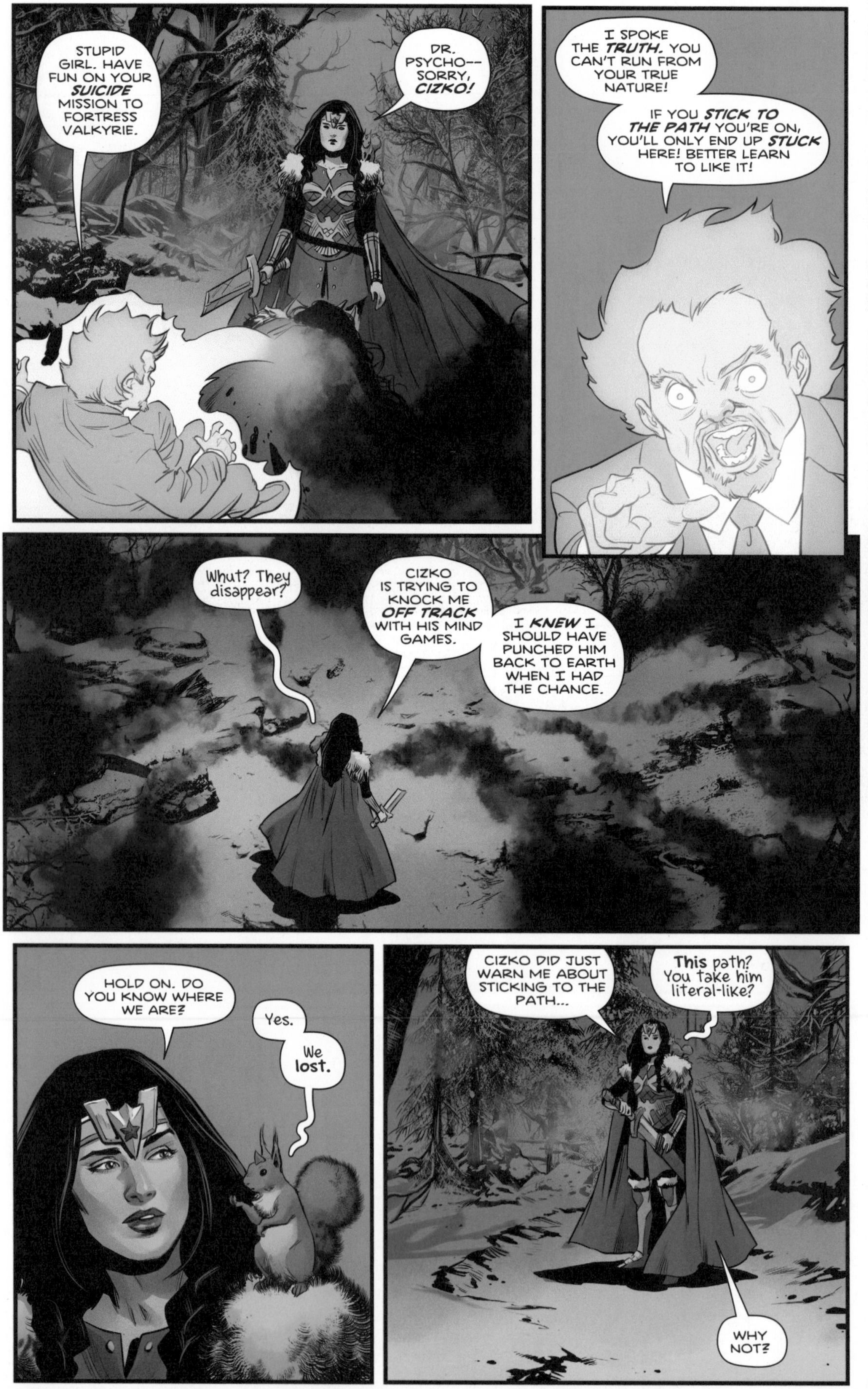

STUPID GIRL. HAVE FUN ON YOUR SUICIDE MISSION TO FORTRESS VALKYRIE.
DR. PSYCHO-- SORRY, CIZKO!
I SPOKE THE TRUTH. YOU CAN'T RUN FROM YOUR TRUE NATURE!
IF YOU STICK TO THE PATH YOU'RE ON, YOU'LL ONLY END UP STUCK HERE! BETTER LEARN TO LIKE IT!
Whut? They disappear?
CIZKO IS TRYING TO KNOCK ME OFF TRACK WITH HIS MIND GAMES.
I KNEW I SHOULD HAVE PUNCHED HIM BACK TO EARTH WHEN I HAD THE CHANCE.
HOLD ON. DO YOU KNOW WHERE WE ARE?
Yes.
We lost.
CIZKO DID JUST WARN ME ABOUT STICKING TO THE PATH...
This path? You take him literal-like?
WHY NOT?

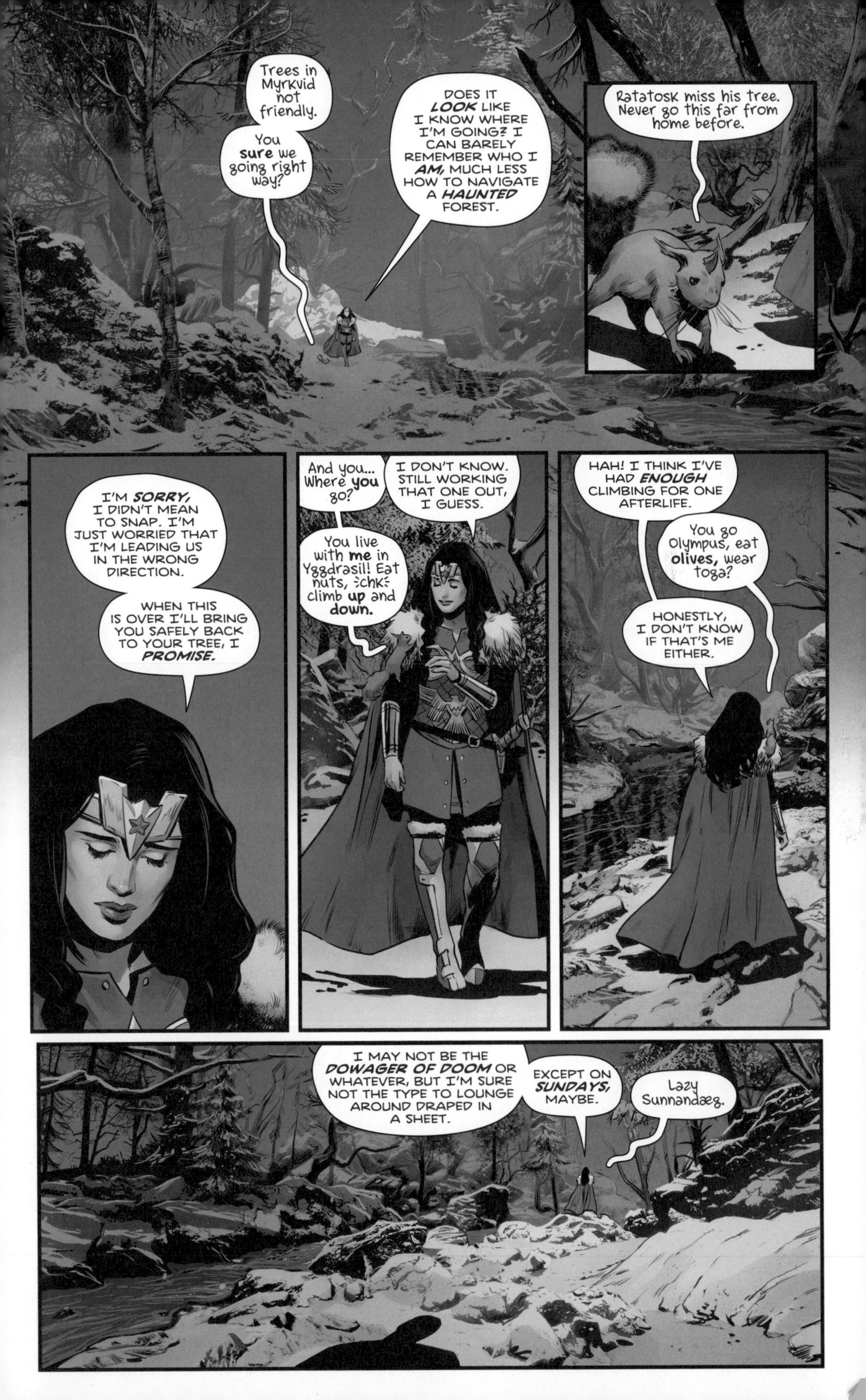
Trees in Myrkvid not friendly.
You sure we going right way?
DOES IT LOOK LIKE I KNOW WHERE I'M GOING? I CAN BARELY REMEMBER WHO I AM, MUCH LESS HOW TO NAVIGATE A HAUNTED FOREST.
Ratatosk miss his tree. Never go this far from home before.
I'M SORRY, I DIDN'T MEAN TO SNAP. I'M JUST WORRIED THAT I'M LEADING US IN THE WRONG DIRECTION.
WHEN THIS IS OVER I'LL BRING YOU SAFELY BACK TO YOUR TREE, I PROMISE.
And you... Where you go?
I DON'T KNOW. STILL WORKING THAT ONE OUT, I GUESS.
You live with me in Yggdrasil! Eat nuts, chk climb up and down.
HAH! I THINK I'VE HAD ENOUGH CLIMBING FOR ONE AFTERLIFE.
You go Olympus, eat olives, wear toga?
HONESTLY, I DON'T KNOW IF THAT'S ME EITHER.
I MAY NOT BE THE DOWAGER OF DOOM OR WHATEVER, BUT I'M SURE NOT THE TYPE TO LOUNGE AROUND DRAPED IN A SHEET.
EXCEPT ON SUNDAYS, MAYBE.
Lazy Sunnandæg.

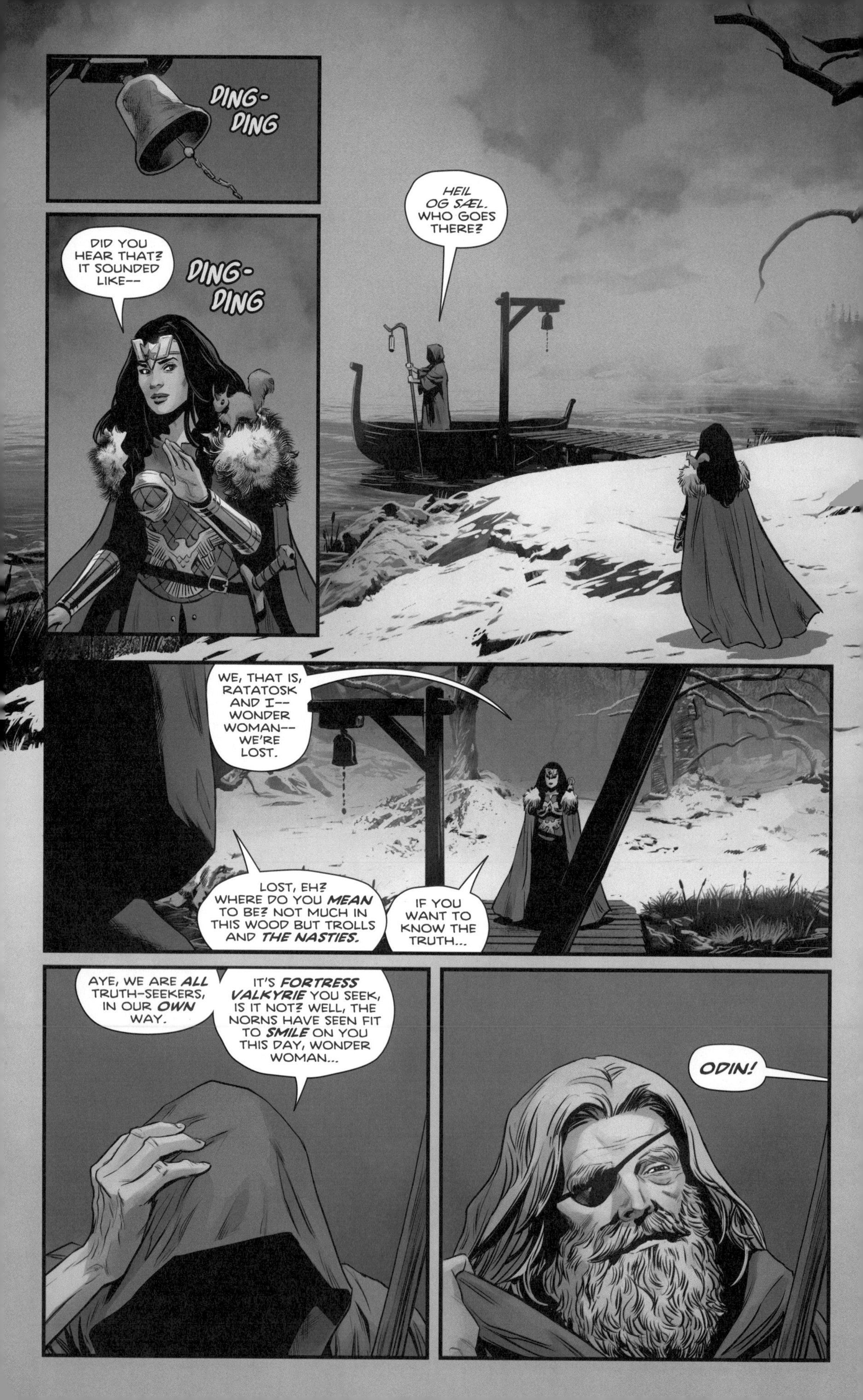
DING-DING
DID YOU HEAR THAT? IT SOUNDED LIKE--
DING-DING
HEIL OG SÆL. WHO GOES THERE?
WE, THAT IS, RATATOSK AND I-- WONDER WOMAN-- WE'RE LOST.
LOST, EH? WHERE DO YOU MEAN TO BE? NOT MUCH IN THIS WOOD BUT TROLLS AND THE NASTIES.
IF YOU WANT TO KNOW THE TRUTH...
AYE, WE ARE ALL TRUTH-SEEKERS, IN OUR OWN WAY.
IT'S FORTRESS VALKYRIE YOU SEEK, IS IT NOT? WELL, THE NORNS HAVE SEEN FIT TO SMILE ON YOU THIS DAY, WONDER WOMAN...
ODIN!

I SAW YOU GET *CRUSHED!* BY A *ROCK!*

YES, YES. THAT *CAN* HAPPEN. MORE OFTEN THAN NOT THESE DAYS. BUT...

...I *ALWAYS* COME BACK.

DO THE VALKYRIES HELP WITH THAT? OR...

NO, I DO THAT BIT MYSELF. I'VE RETURNED IN MANY FORMS. KING, WANDERER, SHAMAN, WARRIOR, POET, *ALL-FATHER...* THIS TIME I'M *HARBARD*, THE *FERRYMAN*.

THOUGHT I'D GIVE MY FOOL SON TIME TO ROUND UP THOSE *CURSED* WEAPONS.

WELL, I CAN'T BEGIN TO EXPRESS HOW *LUCKY* IT WAS THAT WE BUMPED INTO YOU.

LUCKY, YOU SAY?

YOU HEAD TO FORTRESS VALKYRIE OF YOUR OWN FREE WILL, AND YOU FEEL *FORTUNATE?* YOU ARE A *STRANGE* ONE.

THAT'S BEEN MY WHOLE PLAN FROM THE BEGINNING, BUT NOBODY'S HAD ANY BETTER IDEAS.

SIEGFRIED DID MENTION THAT THEY WON'T BE PLEASED...

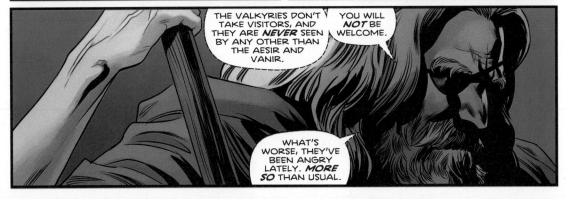

THE VALKYRIES DON'T TAKE VISITORS, AND THEY ARE *NEVER* SEEN BY ANY OTHER THAN THE AESIR AND VANIR.

YOU WILL *NOT* BE WELCOME.

WHAT'S WORSE, THEY'VE BEEN ANGRY LATELY. *MORE SO* THAN USUAL.

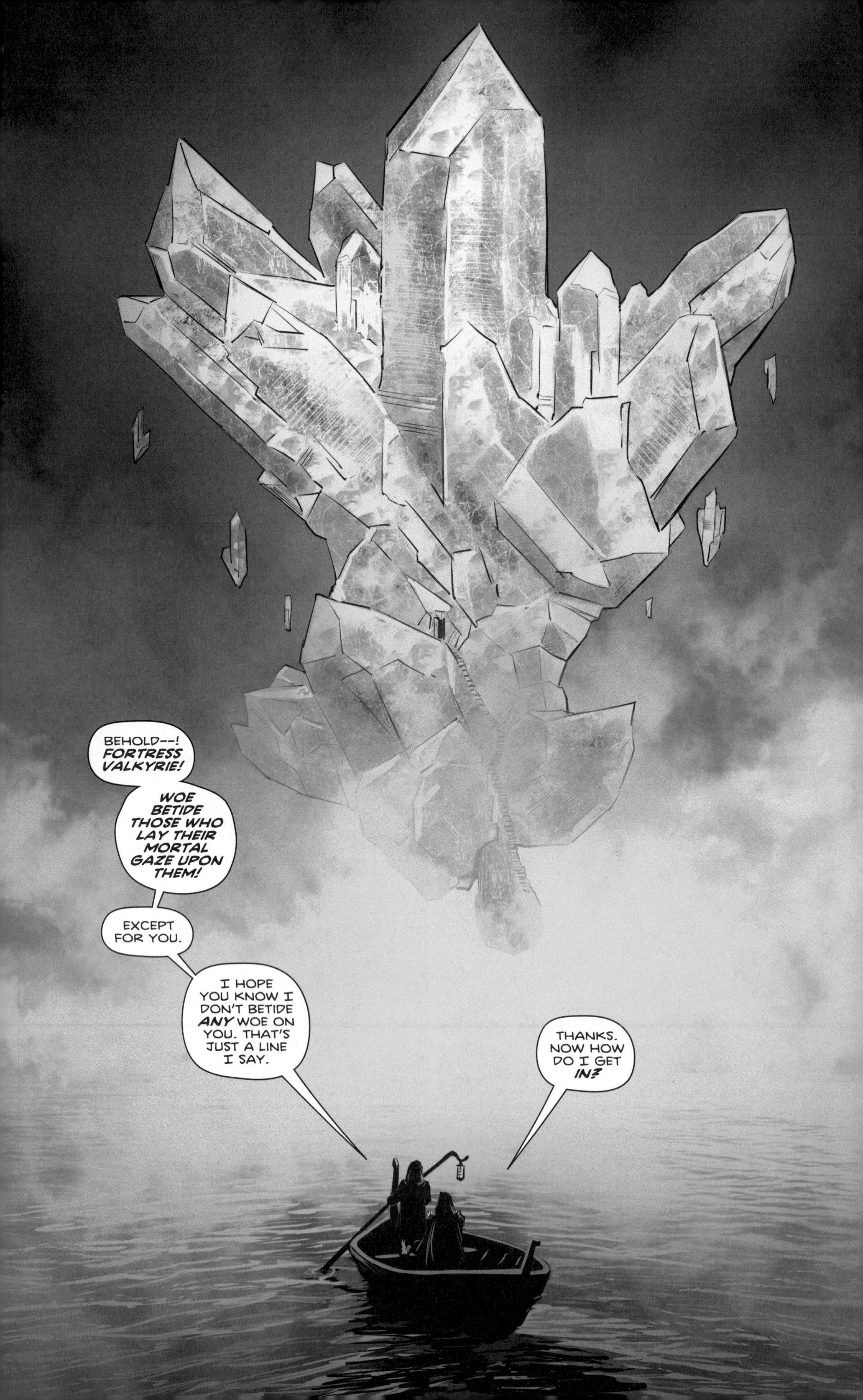
BEHOLD--! FORTRESS VALKYRIE!
WOE BETIDE THOSE WHO LAY THEIR MORTAL GAZE UPON THEM!
EXCEPT FOR YOU.
I HOPE YOU KNOW I DON'T BETIDE ANY WOE ON YOU. THAT'S JUST A LINE I SAY.
THANKS. NOW HOW DO I GET IN?

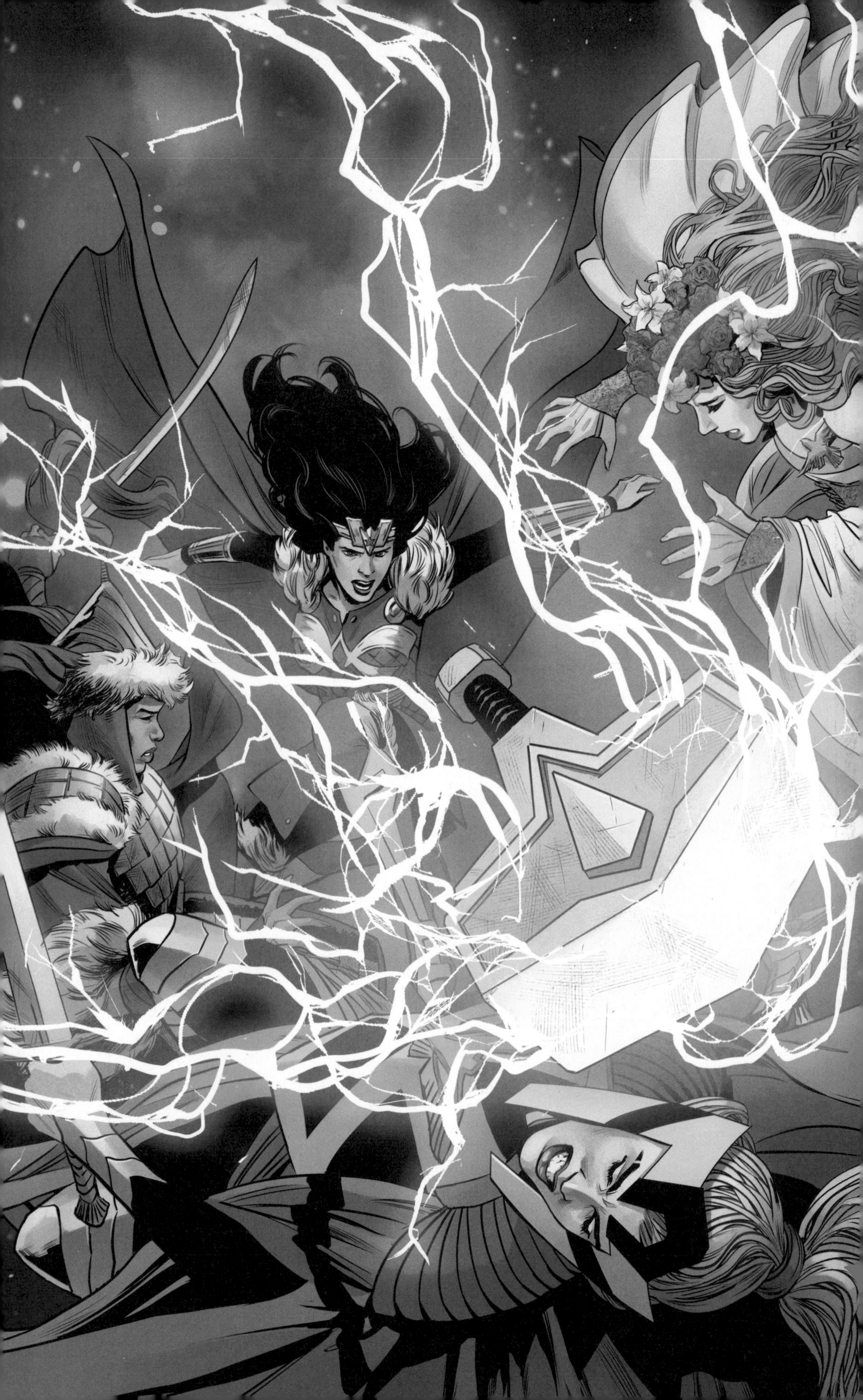

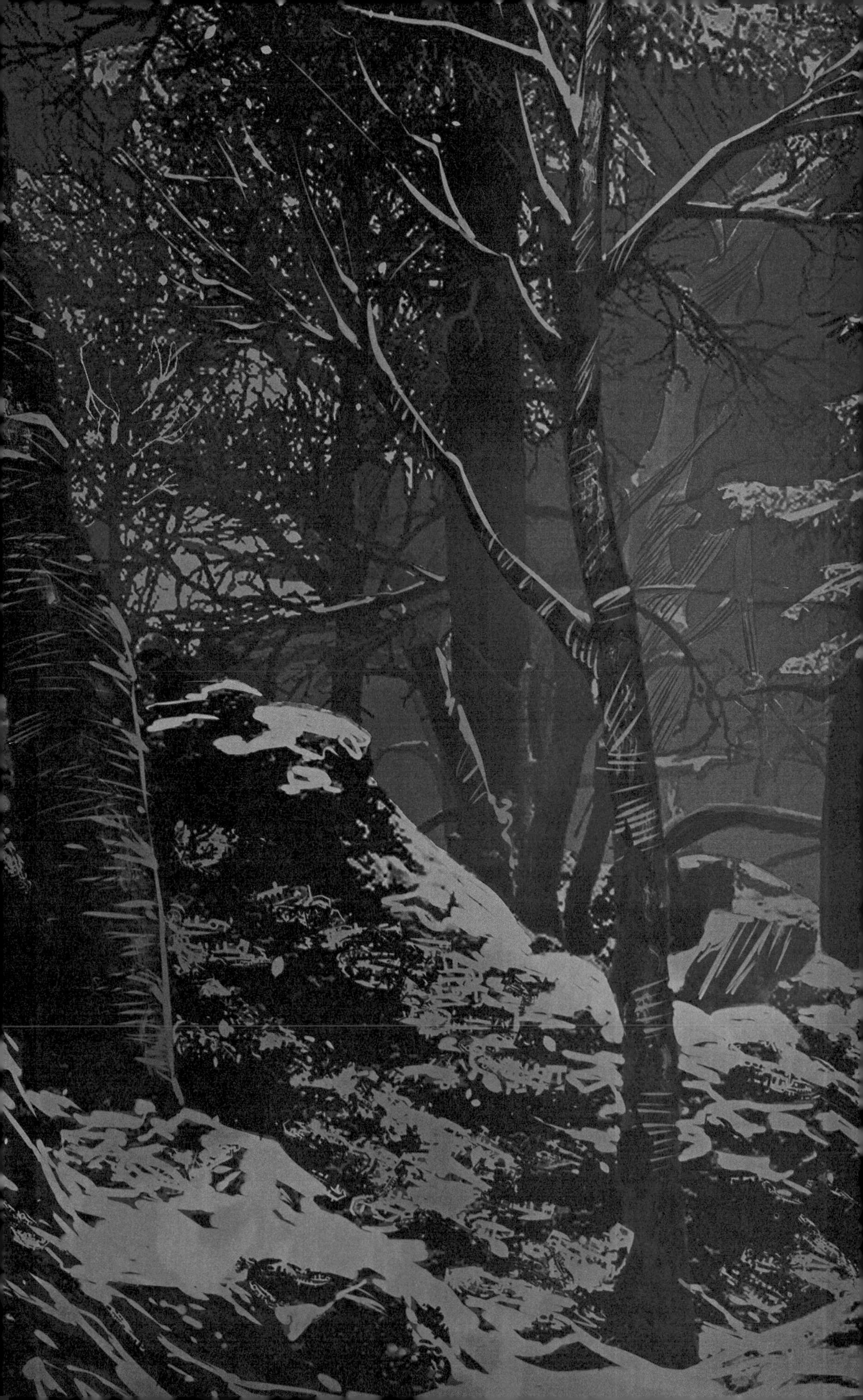

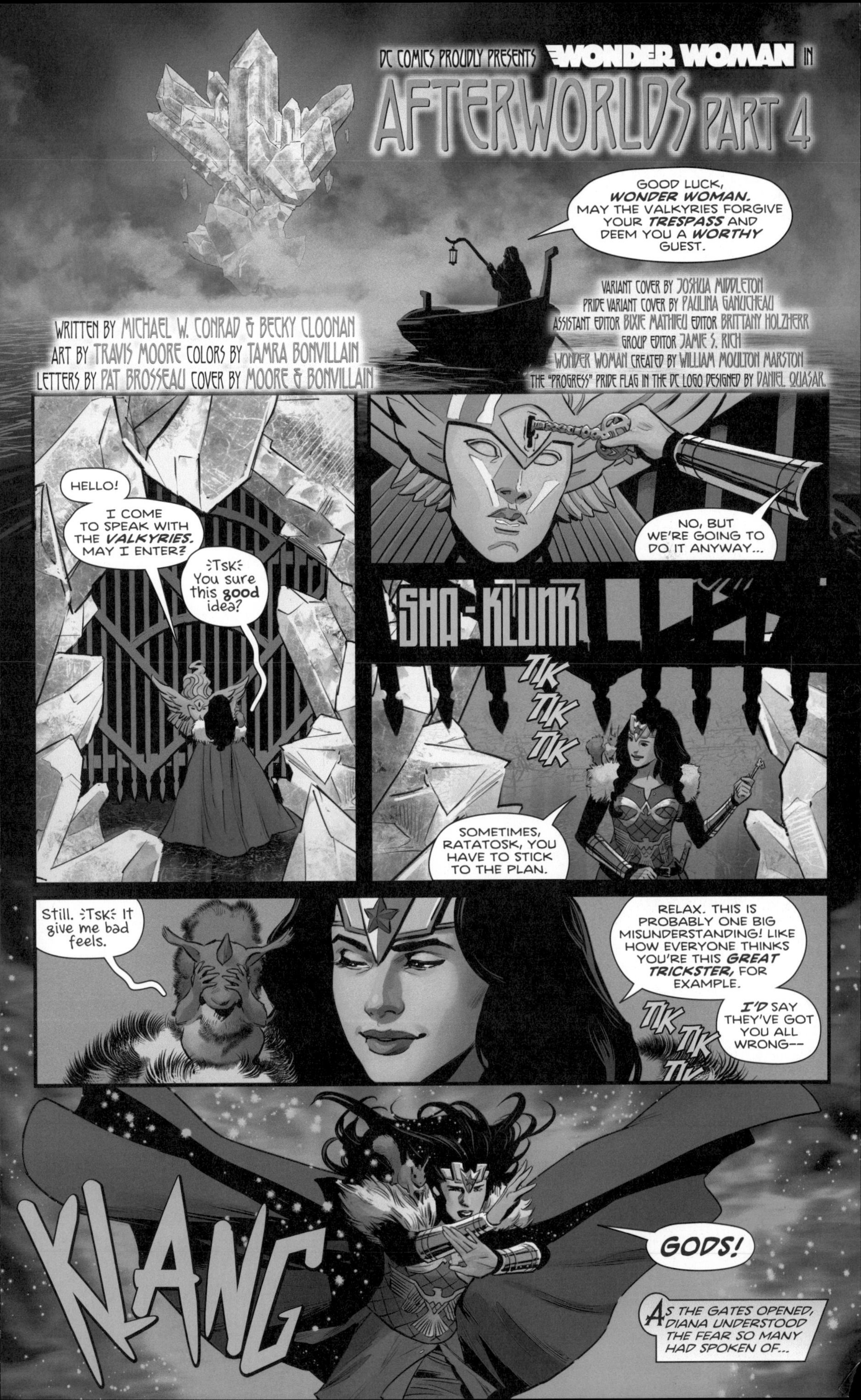
DC COMICS PROUDLY PRESENTS WONDER WOMAN IN
AFTERWORLDS PART 4
GOOD LUCK, WONDER WOMAN. MAY THE VALKYRIES FORGIVE YOUR TRESPASS AND DEEM YOU A WORTHY GUEST.
VARIANT COVER BY JOSHUA MIDDLETON
PRIDE VARIANT COVER BY PAULINA GANUCHEAU
ASSISTANT EDITOR BIXIE MATHIEU EDITOR BRITTANY HOLZHERR
GROUP EDITOR JAMIE S. RICH
WONDER WOMAN CREATED BY WILLIAM MOULTON MARSTON
THE "PROGRESS" PRIDE FLAG IN THE DC LOGO DESIGNED BY DANIEL QUASAR.
WRITTEN BY MICHAEL W. CONRAD & BECKY CLOONAN
ART BY TRAVIS MOORE COLORS BY TAMRA BONVILLAIN
LETTERS BY PAT BROSSEAU COVER BY MOORE & BONVILLAIN
HELLO!
I COME TO SPEAK WITH THE VALKYRIES. MAY I ENTER?
Tsk You sure this good idea?
NO, BUT WE'RE GOING TO DO IT ANYWAY...
SHA-KLUNK
TIK TIK TIK
SOMETIMES, RATATOSK, YOU HAVE TO STICK TO THE PLAN.
Still. Tsk It give me bad feels.
RELAX. THIS IS PROBABLY ONE BIG MISUNDERSTANDING! LIKE HOW EVERYONE THINKS YOU'RE THIS GREAT TRICKSTER, FOR EXAMPLE.
I'D SAY THEY'VE GOT YOU ALL WRONG--
TIK TIK
KLANG
GODS!
AS THE GATES OPENED, DIANA UNDERSTOOD THE FEAR SO MANY HAD SPOKEN OF...

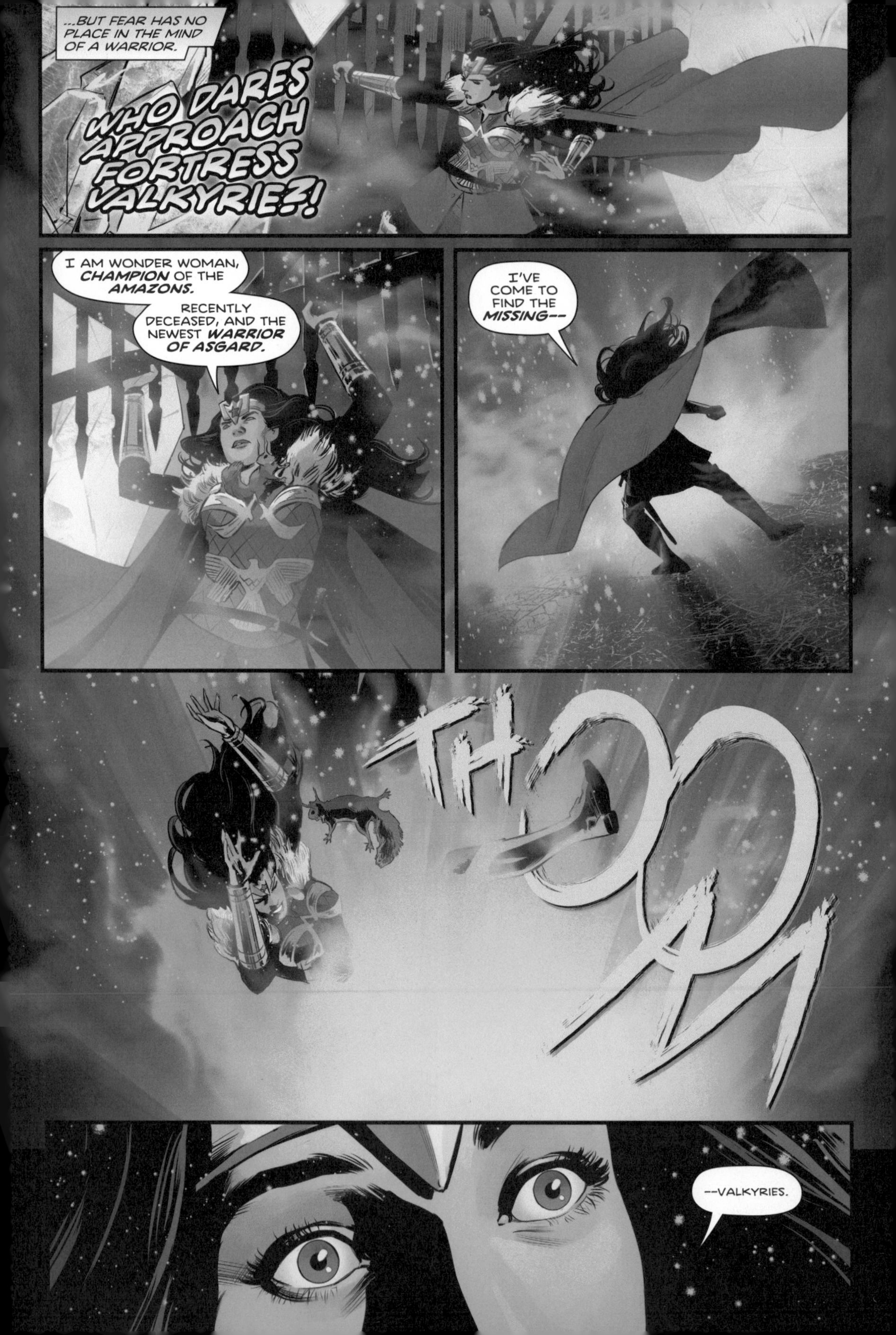
...BUT FEAR HAS NO PLACE IN THE MIND OF A WARRIOR.
WHO DARES APPROACH FORTRESS VALKYRIE?!
I AM WONDER WOMAN, CHAMPION OF THE AMAZONS.
RECENTLY DECEASED, AND THE NEWEST WARRIOR OF ASGARD.
I'VE COME TO FIND THE MISSING--
THOOM
--VALKYRIES.

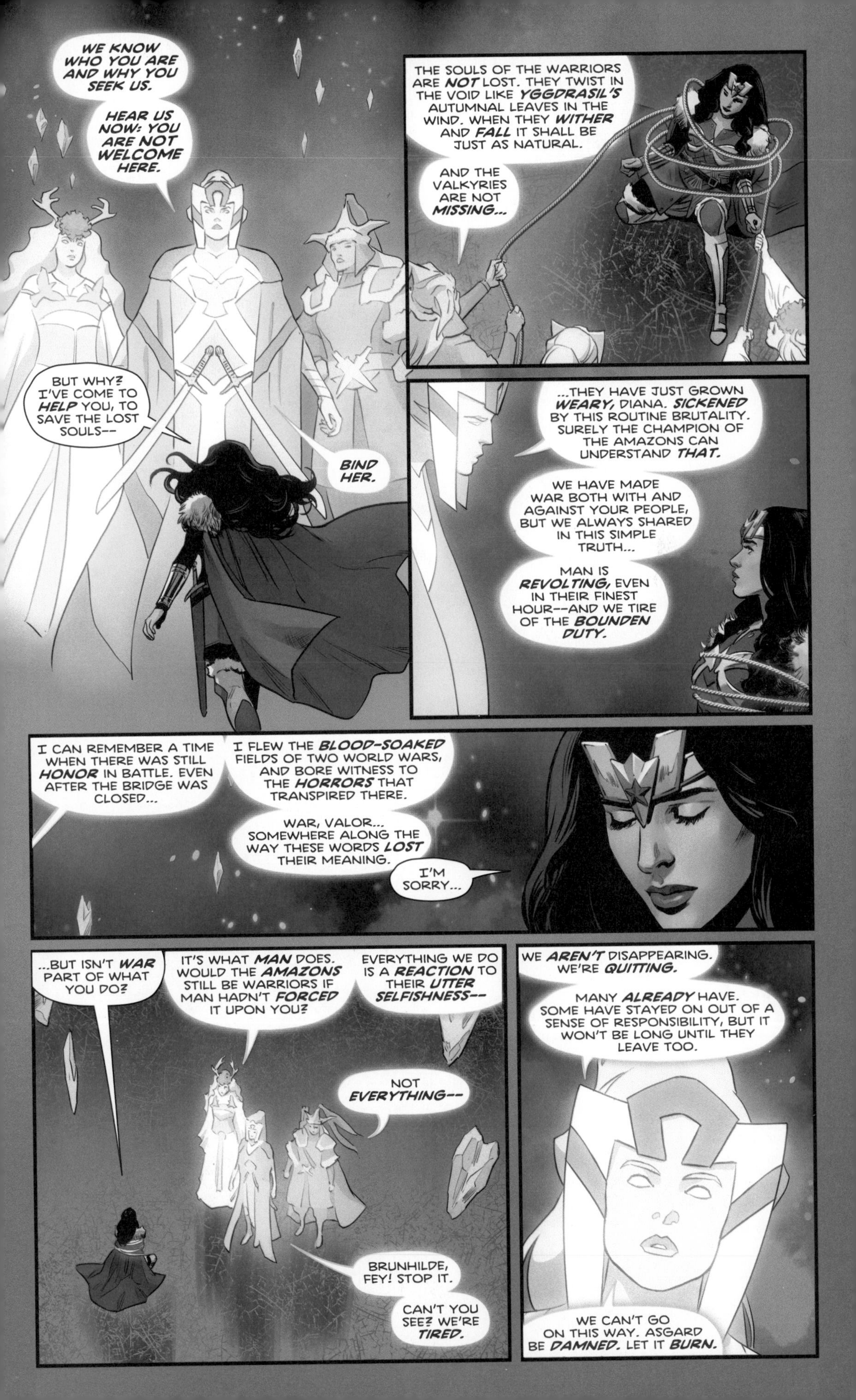
WE KNOW WHO YOU ARE AND WHY YOU SEEK US.
HEAR US NOW: YOU ARE NOT WELCOME HERE.
BUT WHY? I'VE COME TO HELP YOU, TO SAVE THE LOST SOULS--
BIND HER.
THE SOULS OF THE WARRIORS ARE NOT LOST. THEY TWIST IN THE VOID LIKE YGGDRASIL'S AUTUMNAL LEAVES IN THE WIND. WHEN THEY WITHER AND FALL IT SHALL BE JUST AS NATURAL.
AND THE VALKYRIES ARE NOT MISSING...
...THEY HAVE JUST GROWN WEARY, DIANA. SICKENED BY THIS ROUTINE BRUTALITY. SURELY THE CHAMPION OF THE AMAZONS CAN UNDERSTAND THAT.
WE HAVE MADE WAR BOTH WITH AND AGAINST YOUR PEOPLE, BUT WE ALWAYS SHARED IN THIS SIMPLE TRUTH...
MAN IS REVOLTING, EVEN IN THEIR FINEST HOUR--AND WE TIRE OF THE BOUNDEN DUTY.
I CAN REMEMBER A TIME WHEN THERE WAS STILL HONOR IN BATTLE. EVEN AFTER THE BRIDGE WAS CLOSED...
I FLEW THE BLOOD-SOAKED FIELDS OF TWO WORLD WARS, AND BORE WITNESS TO THE HORRORS THAT TRANSPIRED THERE.
WAR, VALOR... SOMEWHERE ALONG THE WAY THESE WORDS LOST THEIR MEANING.
I'M SORRY...
...BUT ISN'T WAR PART OF WHAT YOU DO?
IT'S WHAT MAN DOES. WOULD THE AMAZONS STILL BE WARRIORS IF MAN HADN'T FORCED IT UPON YOU?
EVERYTHING WE DO IS A REACTION TO THEIR UTTER SELFISHNESS--
NOT EVERYTHING--
BRUNHILDE, FEY! STOP IT.
CAN'T YOU SEE? WE'RE TIRED.
WE AREN'T DISAPPEARING. WE'RE QUITTING.
MANY ALREADY HAVE. SOME HAVE STAYED ON OUT OF A SENSE OF RESPONSIBILITY, BUT IT WON'T BE LONG UNTIL THEY LEAVE TOO.
WE CAN'T GO ON THIS WAY. ASGARD BE DAMNED. LET IT BURN.

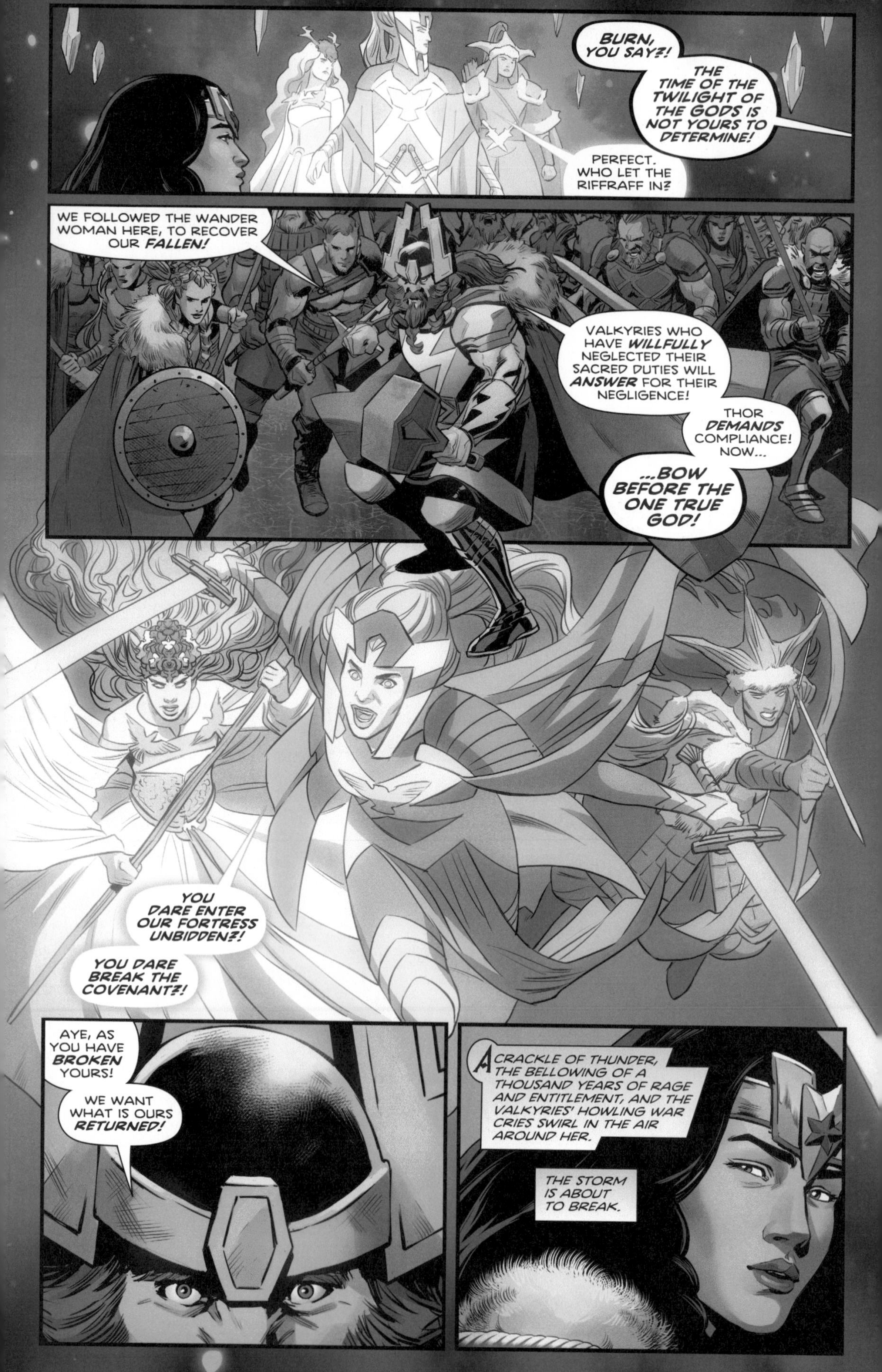

BURN, YOU SAY?!
THE TIME OF THE TWILIGHT OF THE GODS IS NOT YOURS TO DETERMINE!
PERFECT. WHO LET THE RIFFRAFF IN?
WE FOLLOWED THE WANDER WOMAN HERE, TO RECOVER OUR FALLEN!
VALKYRIES WHO HAVE WILLFULLY NEGLECTED THEIR SACRED DUTIES WILL ANSWER FOR THEIR NEGLIGENCE!
THOR DEMANDS COMPLIANCE! NOW...
...BOW BEFORE THE ONE TRUE GOD!
YOU DARE ENTER OUR FORTRESS UNBIDDEN?!
YOU DARE BREAK THE COVENANT?!
AYE, AS YOU HAVE BROKEN YOURS!
WE WANT WHAT IS OURS RETURNED!
A CRACKLE OF THUNDER, THE BELLOWING OF A THOUSAND YEARS OF RAGE AND ENTITLEMENT, AND THE VALKYRIES' HOWLING WAR CRIES SWIRL IN THE AIR AROUND HER.
THE STORM IS ABOUT TO BREAK.

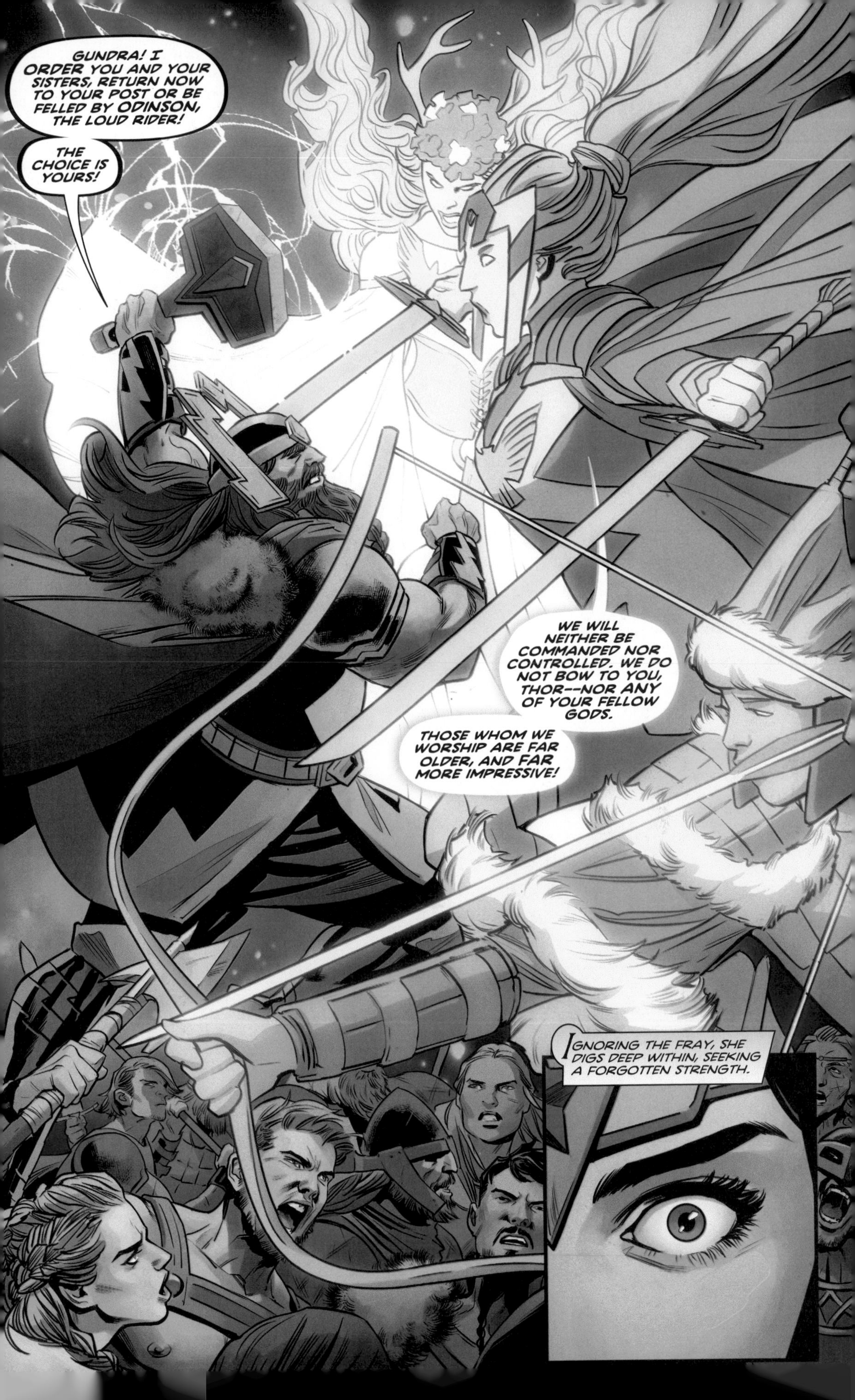
GUNDRA! I ORDER YOU AND YOUR SISTERS, RETURN NOW TO YOUR POST OR BE FELLED BY ODINSON, THE LOUD RIDER!
THE CHOICE IS YOURS!
WE WILL NEITHER BE COMMANDED NOR CONTROLLED. WE DO NOT BOW TO YOU, THOR--NOR ANY OF YOUR FELLOW GODS.
THOSE WHOM WE WORSHIP ARE FAR OLDER, AND FAR MORE IMPRESSIVE!
IGNORING THE FRAY, SHE DIGS DEEP WITHIN, SEEKING A FORGOTTEN STRENGTH.

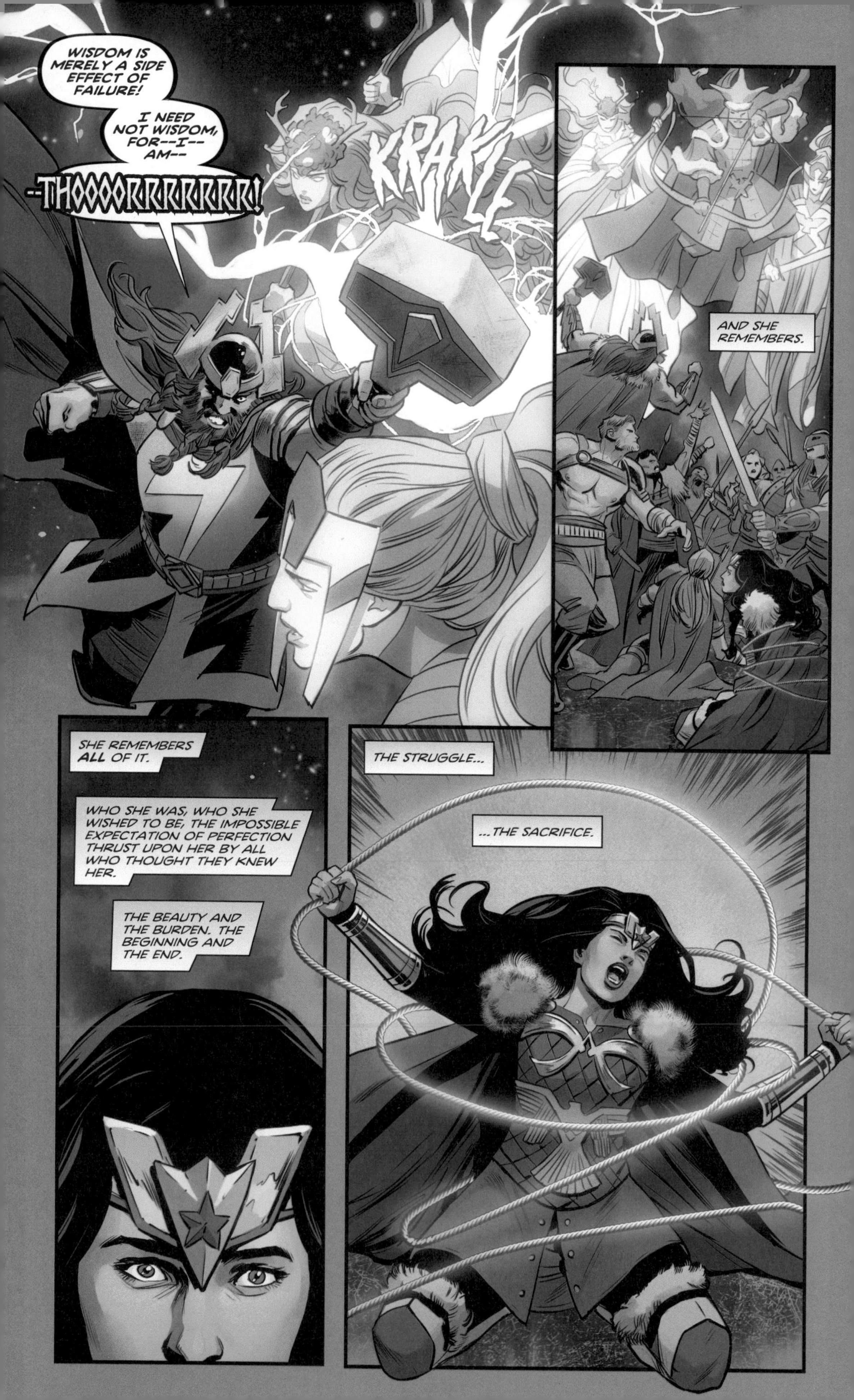
WISDOM IS MERELY A SIDE EFFECT OF FAILURE!
I NEED NOT WISDOM, FOR--I--AM--
--THOOOORRRRRRRRR!
KRAKLE
AND SHE REMEMBERS.
SHE REMEMBERS ALL OF IT.
WHO SHE WAS, WHO SHE WISHED TO BE, THE IMPOSSIBLE EXPECTATION OF PERFECTION THRUST UPON HER BY ALL WHO THOUGHT THEY KNEW HER.
THE BEAUTY AND THE BURDEN. THE BEGINNING AND THE END.
THE STRUGGLE...
...THE SACRIFICE.

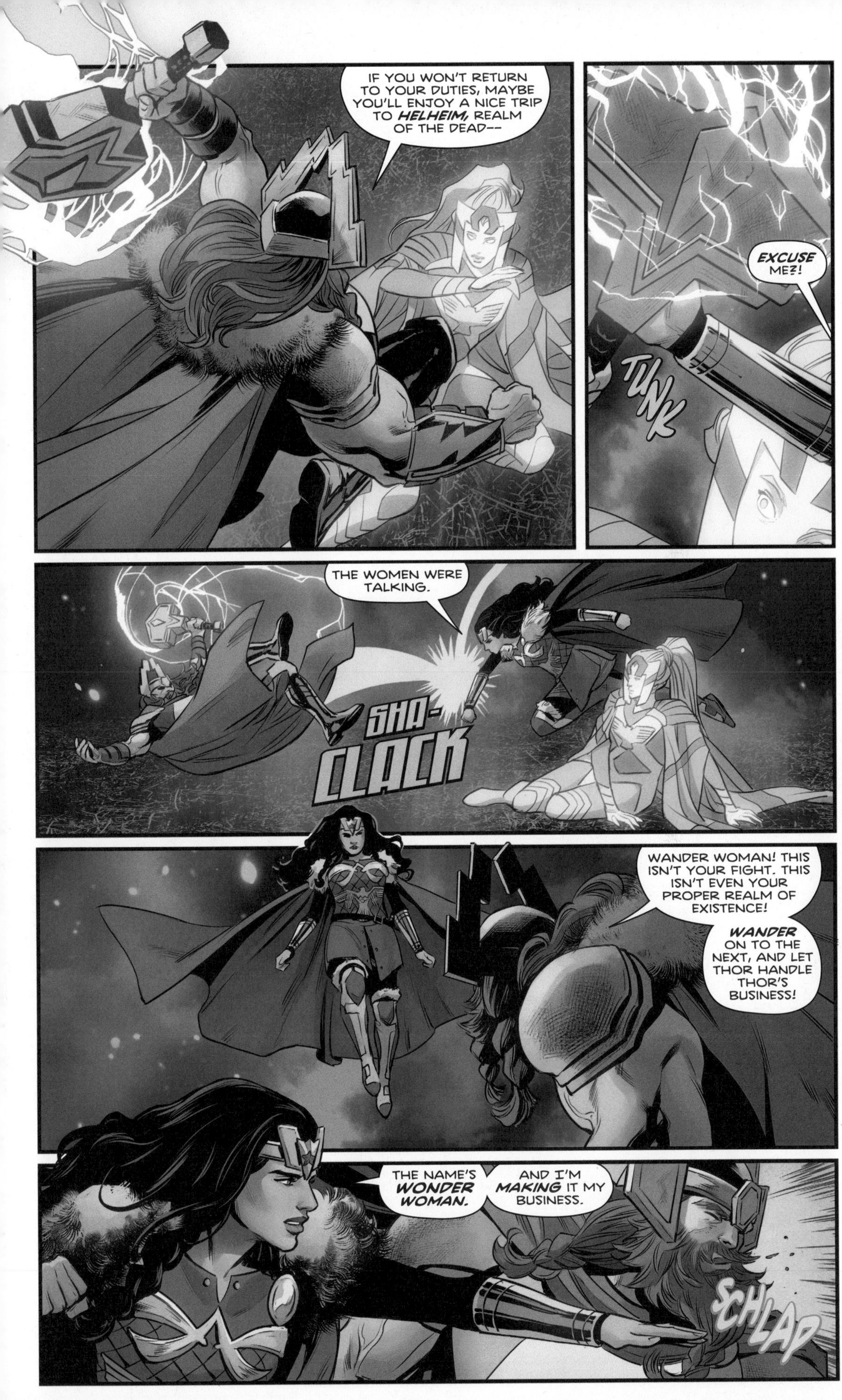

IF YOU WON'T RETURN TO YOUR DUTIES, MAYBE YOU'LL ENJOY A NICE TRIP TO ***HELHEIM,*** REALM OF THE DEAD--
EXCUSE ME?!
TUNK
THE WOMEN WERE TALKING.
SHA-CLACK
WANDER WOMAN! THIS ISN'T YOUR FIGHT. THIS ISN'T EVEN YOUR PROPER REALM OF EXISTENCE!
WANDER ON TO THE NEXT, AND LET THOR HANDLE THOR'S BUSINESS!
THE NAME'S ***WONDER WOMAN.***
AND I'M ***MAKING*** IT MY BUSINESS.
SCHLAP

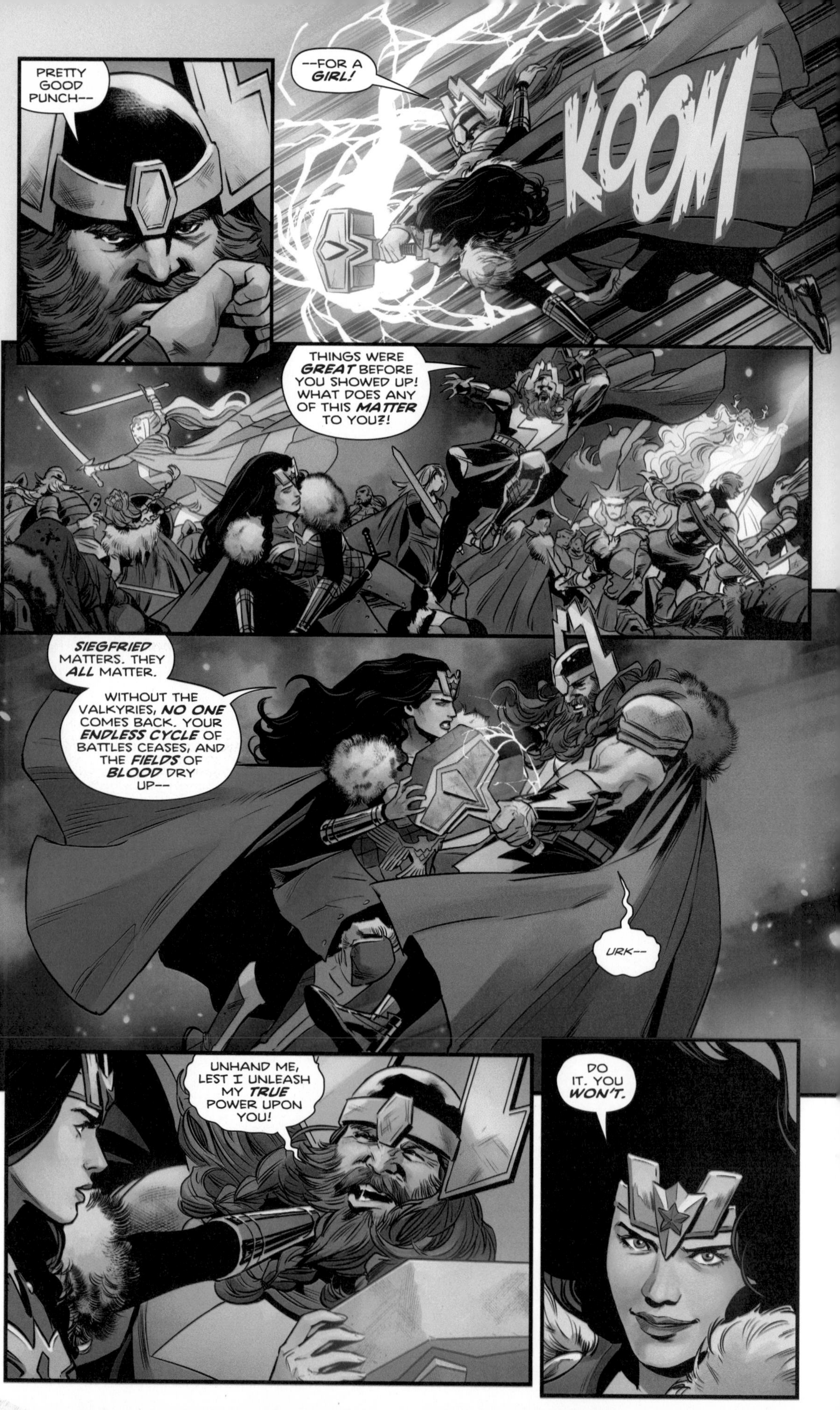
PRETTY GOOD PUNCH--
--FOR A GIRL!
KOOM
THINGS WERE GREAT BEFORE YOU SHOWED UP! WHAT DOES ANY OF THIS MATTER TO YOU?!
SIEGFRIED MATTERS. THEY ALL MATTER.
WITHOUT THE VALKYRIES, NO ONE COMES BACK. YOUR ENDLESS CYCLE OF BATTLES CEASES, AND THE FIELDS OF BLOOD DRY UP--
URK--
UNHAND ME, LEST I UNLEASH MY TRUE POWER UPON YOU!
DO IT. YOU WON'T.

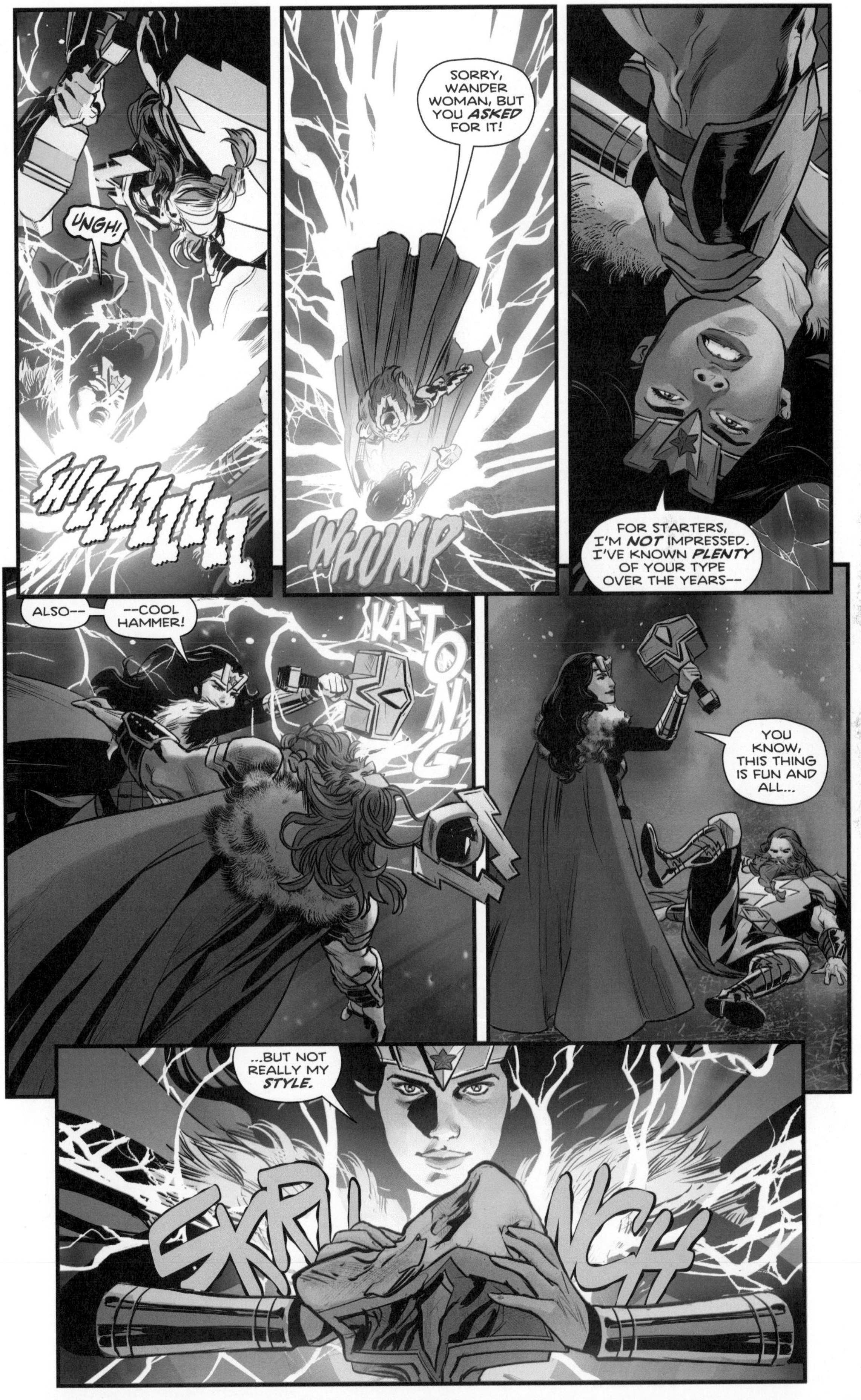
UNGH!
SHZZZZZZZZZZ
SORRY, WANDER WOMAN, BUT YOU ASKED FOR IT!
WHUMP
FOR STARTERS, I'M NOT IMPRESSED. I'VE KNOWN PLENTY OF YOUR TYPE OVER THE YEARS--
ALSO--
--COOL HAMMER!
KA-TONNG
YOU KNOW, THIS THING IS FUN AND ALL...
...BUT NOT REALLY MY STYLE.
SKRUNCH

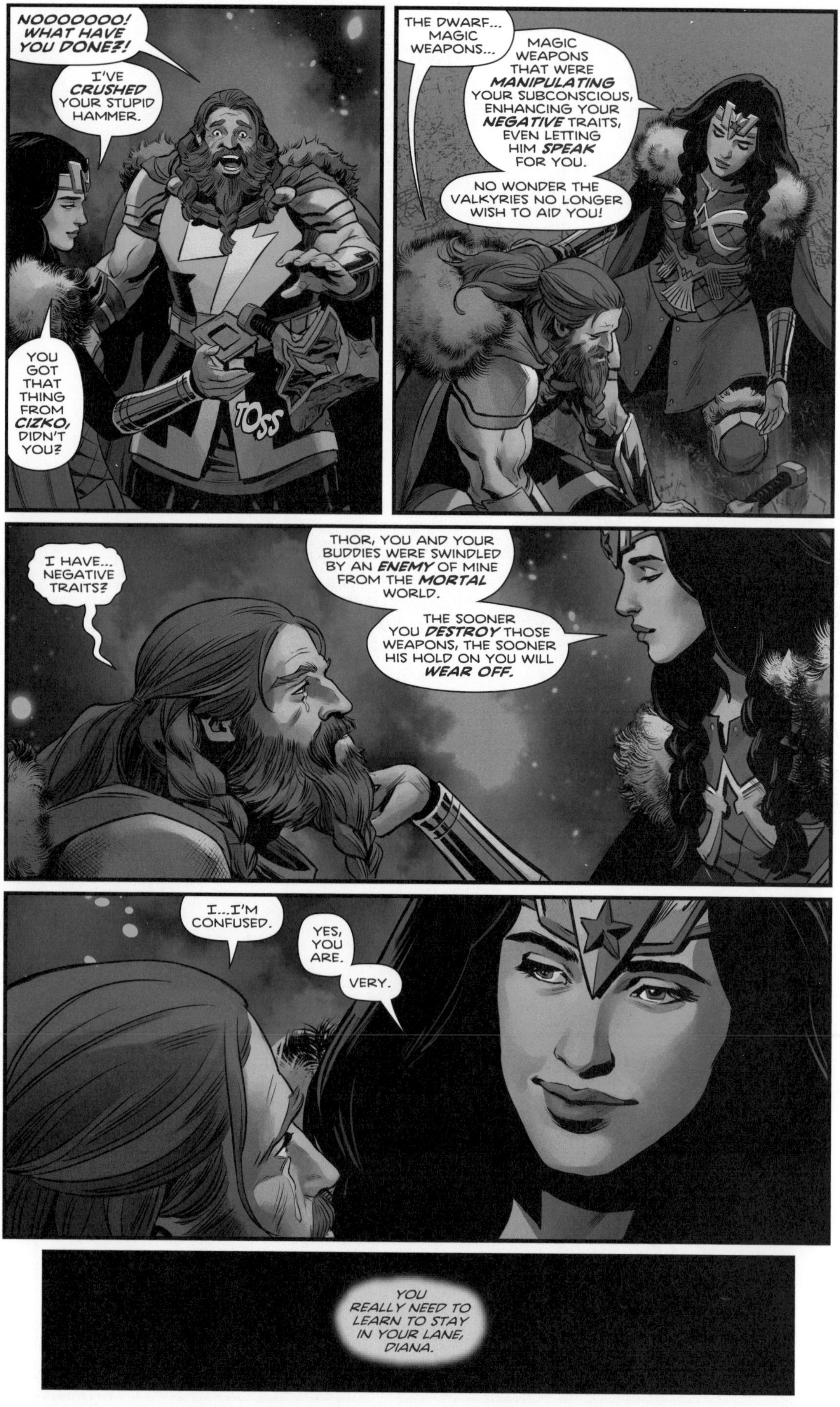
NOOOOOOO! WHAT HAVE YOU DONE?!
I'VE CRUSHED YOUR STUPID HAMMER.
YOU GOT THAT THING FROM CIZKO, DIDN'T YOU?
TOSS
THE DWARF... MAGIC WEAPONS...
MAGIC WEAPONS THAT WERE MANIPULATING YOUR SUBCONSCIOUS, ENHANCING YOUR NEGATIVE TRAITS, EVEN LETTING HIM SPEAK FOR YOU.
NO WONDER THE VALKYRIES NO LONGER WISH TO AID YOU!
I HAVE... NEGATIVE TRAITS?
THOR, YOU AND YOUR BUDDIES WERE SWINDLED BY AN ENEMY OF MINE FROM THE MORTAL WORLD.
THE SOONER YOU DESTROY THOSE WEAPONS, THE SOONER HIS HOLD ON YOU WILL WEAR OFF.
I...I'M CONFUSED.
YES, YOU ARE.
VERY.
YOU REALLY NEED TO LEARN TO STAY IN YOUR LANE, DIANA.

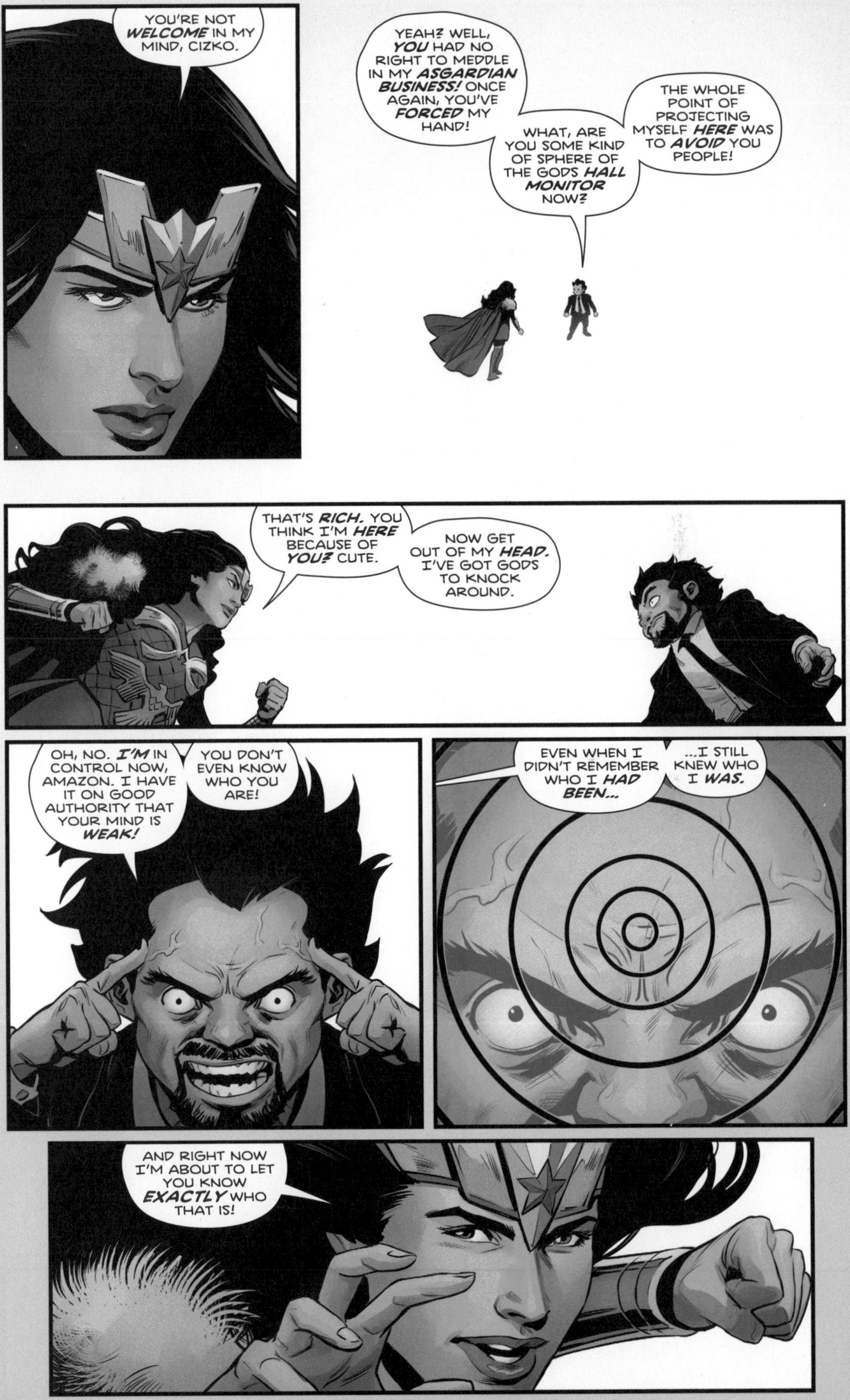
YOU'RE NOT *WELCOME* IN MY MIND, CIZKO.
YEAH? WELL, *YOU* HAD NO RIGHT TO MEDDLE IN MY *ASGARDIAN BUSINESS!* ONCE AGAIN, YOU'VE *FORCED* MY HAND!
WHAT, ARE YOU SOME KIND OF SPHERE OF THE GODS *HALL MONITOR* NOW?
THE WHOLE POINT OF PROJECTING MYSELF *HERE* WAS TO *AVOID* YOU PEOPLE!
THAT'S *RICH.* YOU THINK I'M *HERE* BECAUSE OF *YOU?* CUTE.
NOW GET OUT OF MY *HEAD.* I'VE GOT GODS TO KNOCK AROUND.
OH, NO. *I'M* IN CONTROL NOW, AMAZON. I HAVE IT ON GOOD AUTHORITY THAT YOUR MIND IS *WEAK!*
YOU DON'T EVEN KNOW WHO YOU ARE!
EVEN WHEN I DIDN'T REMEMBER WHO I *HAD BEEN...*
...I STILL KNEW WHO I *WAS.*
AND RIGHT NOW I'M ABOUT TO LET YOU KNOW *EXACTLY* WHO THAT IS!

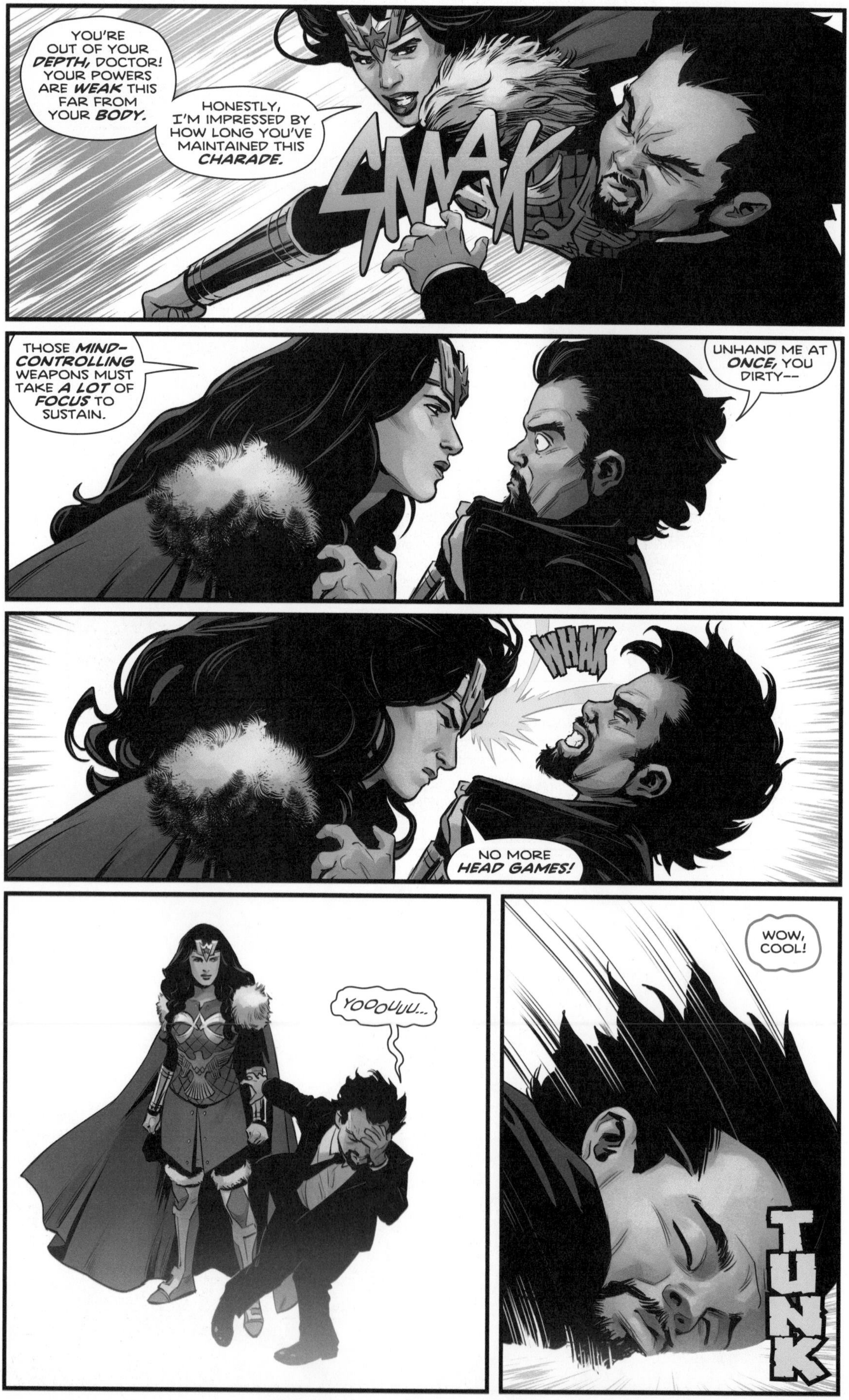
YOU'RE OUT OF YOUR DEPTH, DOCTOR! YOUR POWERS ARE WEAK THIS FAR FROM YOUR BODY.
HONESTLY, I'M IMPRESSED BY HOW LONG YOU'VE MAINTAINED THIS CHARADE.
SMAK
THOSE MIND-CONTROLLING WEAPONS MUST TAKE A LOT OF FOCUS TO SUSTAIN.
UNHAND ME AT ONCE, YOU DIRTY--
WHAK
NO MORE HEAD GAMES!
YOOOUUU...
WOW, COOL!
TUNK

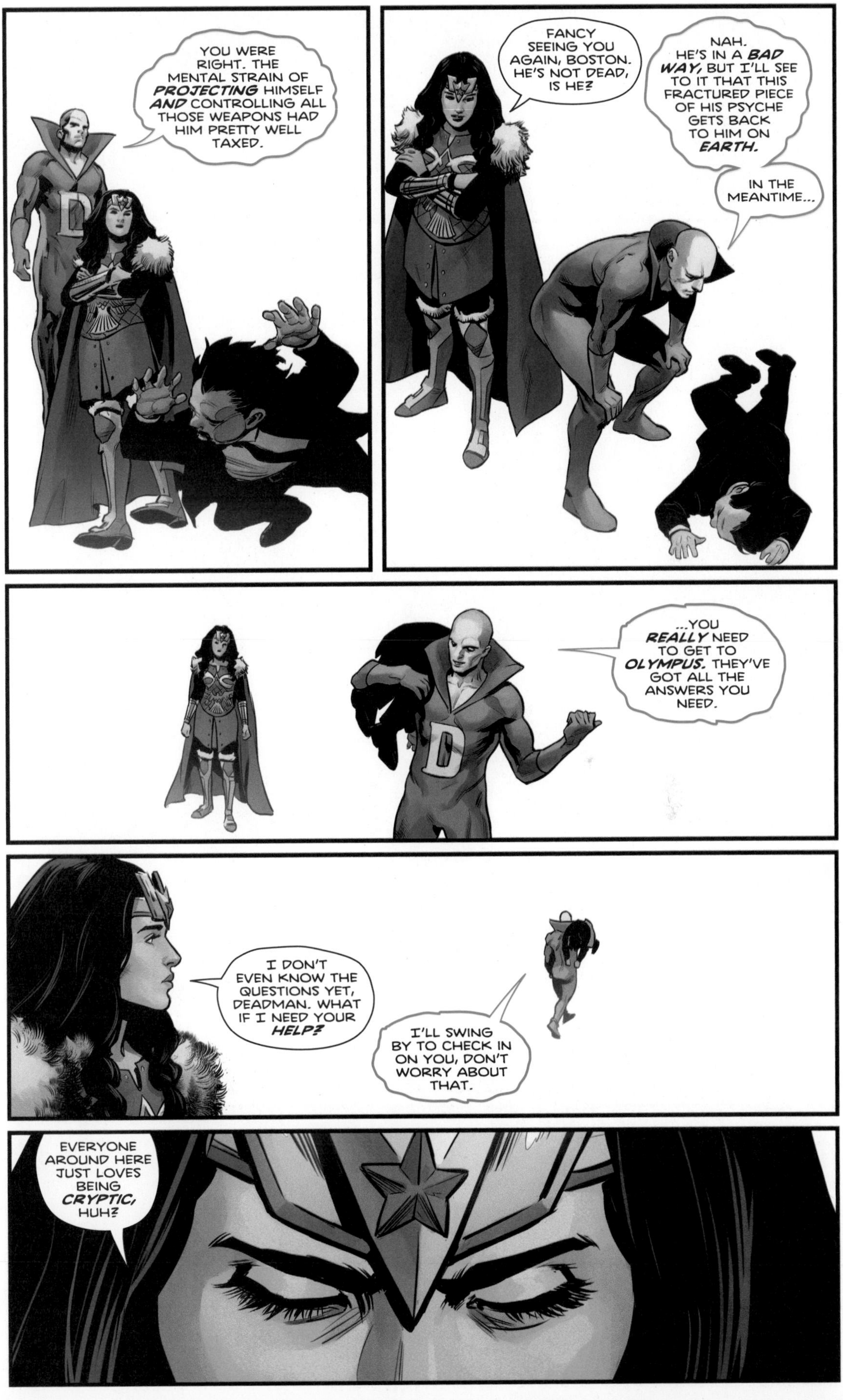
YOU WERE RIGHT. THE MENTAL STRAIN OF PROJECTING HIMSELF AND CONTROLLING ALL THOSE WEAPONS HAD HIM PRETTY WELL TAXED.
FANCY SEEING YOU AGAIN, BOSTON. HE'S NOT DEAD, IS HE?
NAH. HE'S IN A BAD WAY, BUT I'LL SEE TO IT THAT THIS FRACTURED PIECE OF HIS PSYCHE GETS BACK TO HIM ON EARTH.
IN THE MEANTIME...
...YOU REALLY NEED TO GET TO OLYMPUS. THEY'VE GOT ALL THE ANSWERS YOU NEED.
I DON'T EVEN KNOW THE QUESTIONS YET, DEADMAN. WHAT IF I NEED YOUR HELP?
I'LL SWING BY TO CHECK IN ON YOU, DON'T WORRY ABOUT THAT.
EVERYONE AROUND HERE JUST LOVES BEING CRYPTIC, HUH?

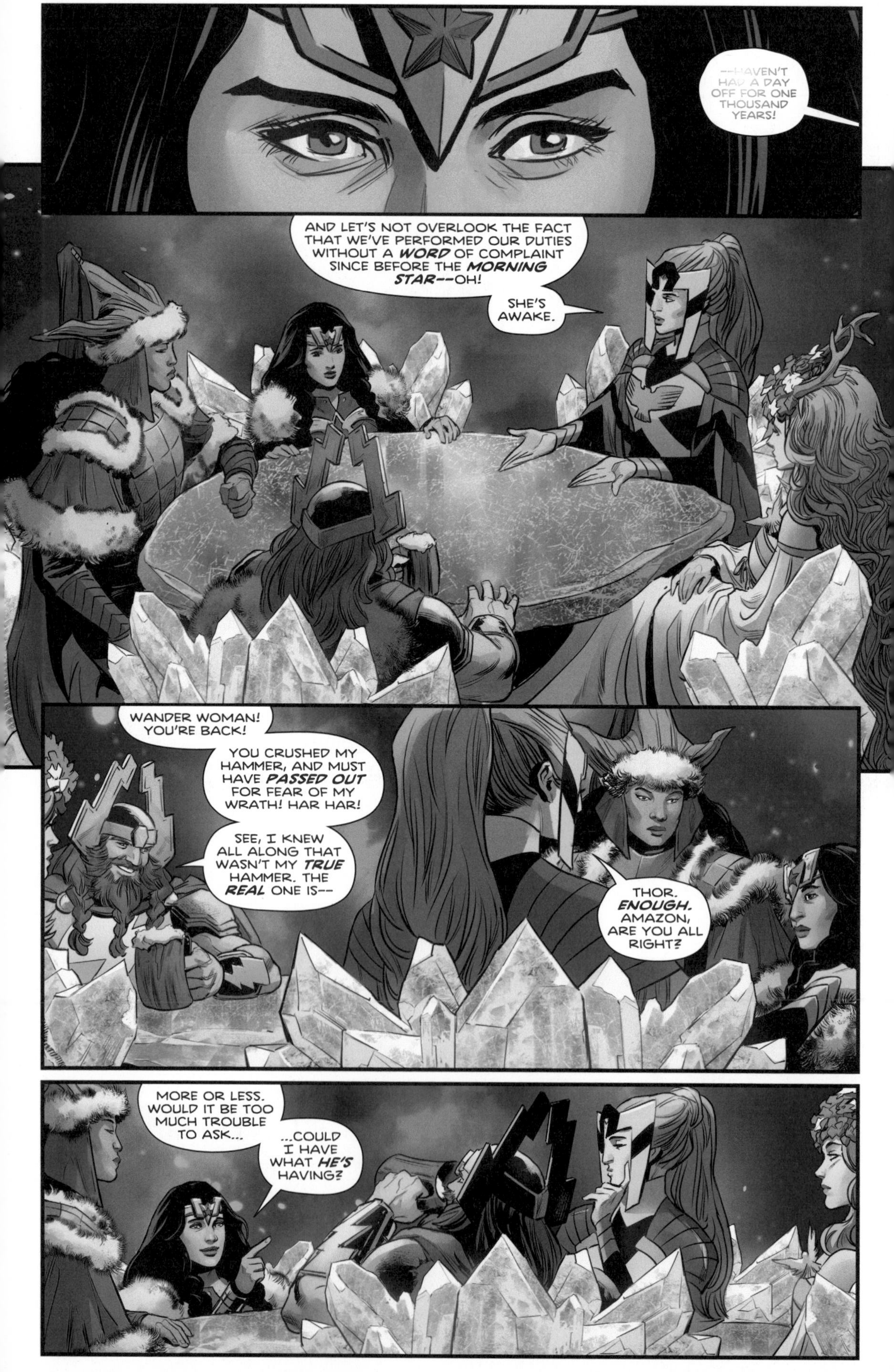
--HAVEN'T HAD A DAY OFF FOR ONE THOUSAND YEARS!
AND LET'S NOT OVERLOOK THE FACT THAT WE'VE PERFORMED OUR DUTIES WITHOUT A **WORD** OF COMPLAINT SINCE BEFORE THE **MORNING STAR**--OH!
SHE'S AWAKE.
WANDER WOMAN! YOU'RE BACK!
YOU CRUSHED MY HAMMER, AND MUST HAVE **PASSED OUT** FOR FEAR OF MY WRATH! HAR HAR!
SEE, I KNEW ALL ALONG THAT WASN'T MY **TRUE** HAMMER. THE **REAL** ONE IS--
THOR. **ENOUGH.** AMAZON, ARE YOU ALL RIGHT?
MORE OR LESS. WOULD IT BE TOO MUCH TROUBLE TO ASK...
...COULD I HAVE WHAT **HE'S** HAVING?

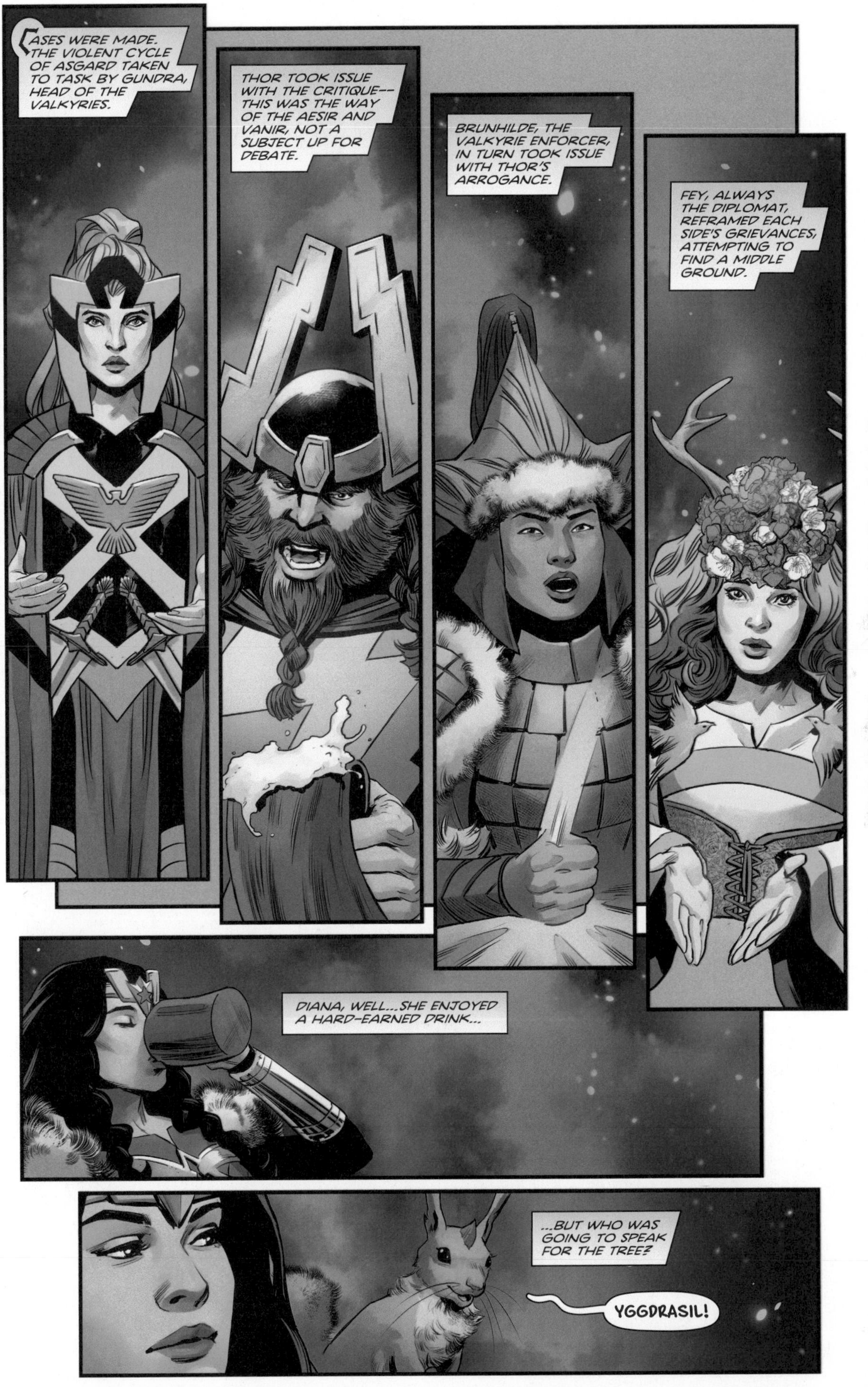
CASES WERE MADE. THE VIOLENT CYCLE OF ASGARD TAKEN TO TASK BY GUNDRA, HEAD OF THE VALKYRIES.
THOR TOOK ISSUE WITH THE CRITIQUE-- THIS WAS THE WAY OF THE AESIR AND VANIR, NOT A SUBJECT UP FOR DEBATE.
BRUNHILDE, THE VALKYRIE ENFORCER, IN TURN TOOK ISSUE WITH THOR'S ARROGANCE.
FEY, ALWAYS THE DIPLOMAT, REFRAMED EACH SIDE'S GRIEVANCES, ATTEMPTING TO FIND A MIDDLE GROUND.
DIANA, WELL...SHE ENJOYED A HARD-EARNED DRINK...
...BUT WHO WAS GOING TO SPEAK FOR THE TREE?
YGGDRASIL!

She wilt! :Chk: She **hunger!**

YGGDRASIL?! I thought we were here to negotiate our terms for returning souls from the **BLOODY** battlefield!

NOW we have to worry about that old **TREE?**

YOUR TERMS? NOW you have **TERMS?**

WHO let this **RODENT** in here?!

AAAW, it's so fuzzy though.

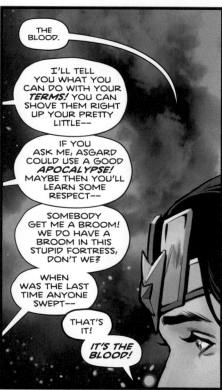

THE BLOOD.

I'LL TELL you what you can do with your **TERMS!** You can SHOVE them right up your pretty little--

IF you ask me, ASGARD could use a good **APOCALYPSE!** MAYBE then you'll learn some RESPECT--

SOMEBODY get me a BROOM! We DO have a BROOM in this STUPID fortress, DON'T we?

WHEN was the last time ANYONE swept--

THAT'S it!

IT'S THE BLOOD!

YGGDRASIL is **FED** by the **BLOOD** of the fallen on the battlefield.

With fewer and fewer warriors being killed every night, it means she isn't getting enough **NUTRIENTS.**

If she DIES, NIDHOGG will be RELEASED, and we all know what **THAT** means.

:Chk:

Please. :Chk: Yggdrasil my home.

One day Ragnarok must come for us all, but I implore, for now...

...let Yggdrasil live.

AND SO AN AGREEMENT WAS MADE.

ONE DAY, OUT OF EVERY WEEKLY CYCLE, THERE WOULD BE A BREAK FROM THE BATTLES--A DAY OF PEACE.

A DAY FREE OF COMBAT, WHEN THE VALKYRIES COULD BREATHE, AND DREAM.

WITH THE WARRIORS RETURNED AND THE WORLD TREE AGAIN FED, BALANCE WAS ONCE AGAIN RETURNED TO THE REALM.

TO COMMEMORATE THEIR NEW PACT, THEY INAUGURATED THE FIRST OFFICIAL DAY OF REST, HENCEFORTH TO BE KNOWN AS--

THIRSTY THORSDAY!

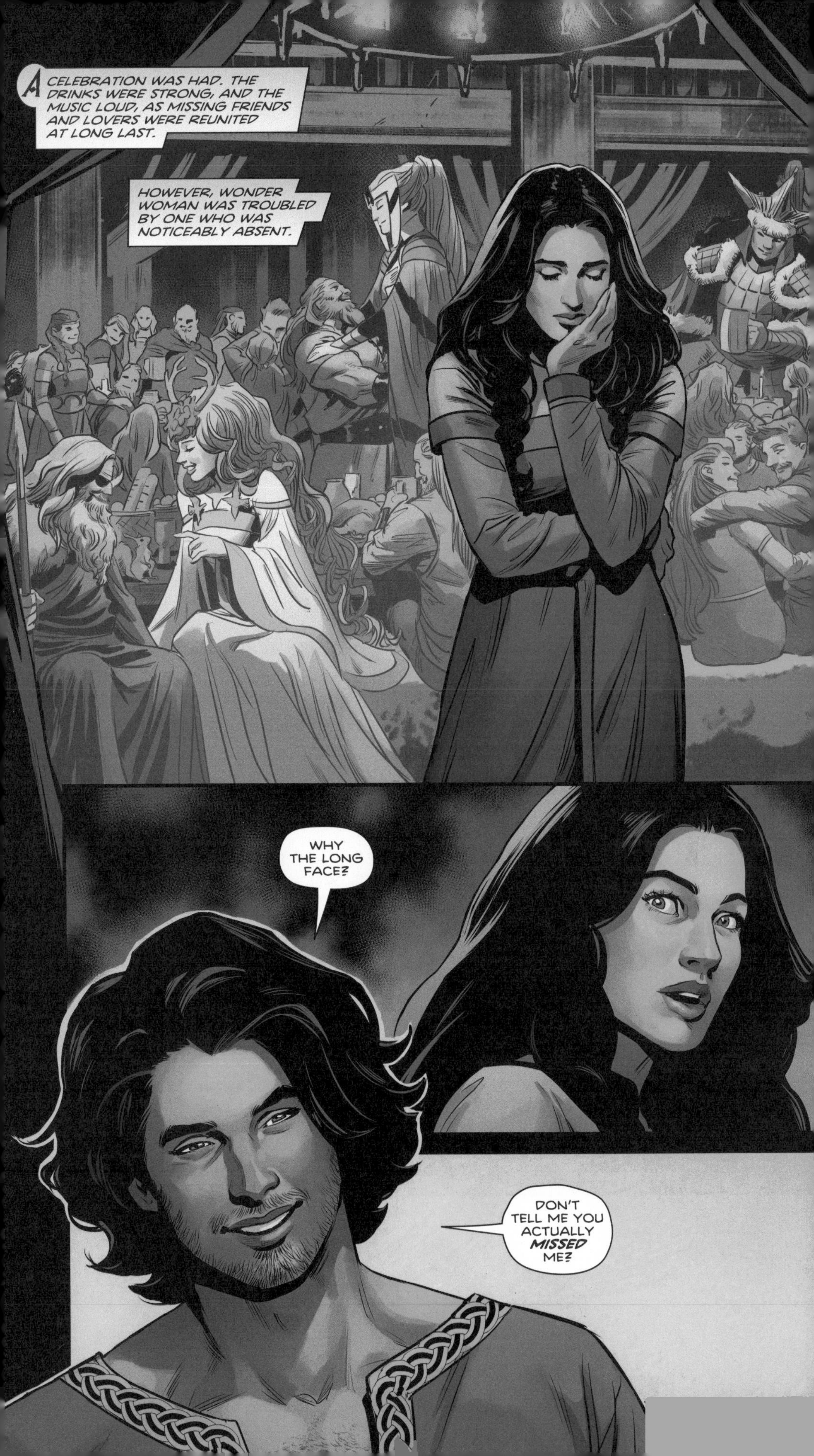
A CELEBRATION WAS HAD. THE DRINKS WERE STRONG, AND THE MUSIC LOUD, AS MISSING FRIENDS AND LOVERS WERE REUNITED AT LONG LAST.
HOWEVER, WONDER WOMAN WAS TROUBLED BY ONE WHO WAS NOTICEABLY ABSENT.
WHY THE LONG FACE?
DON'T TELL ME YOU ACTUALLY *MISSED* ME?

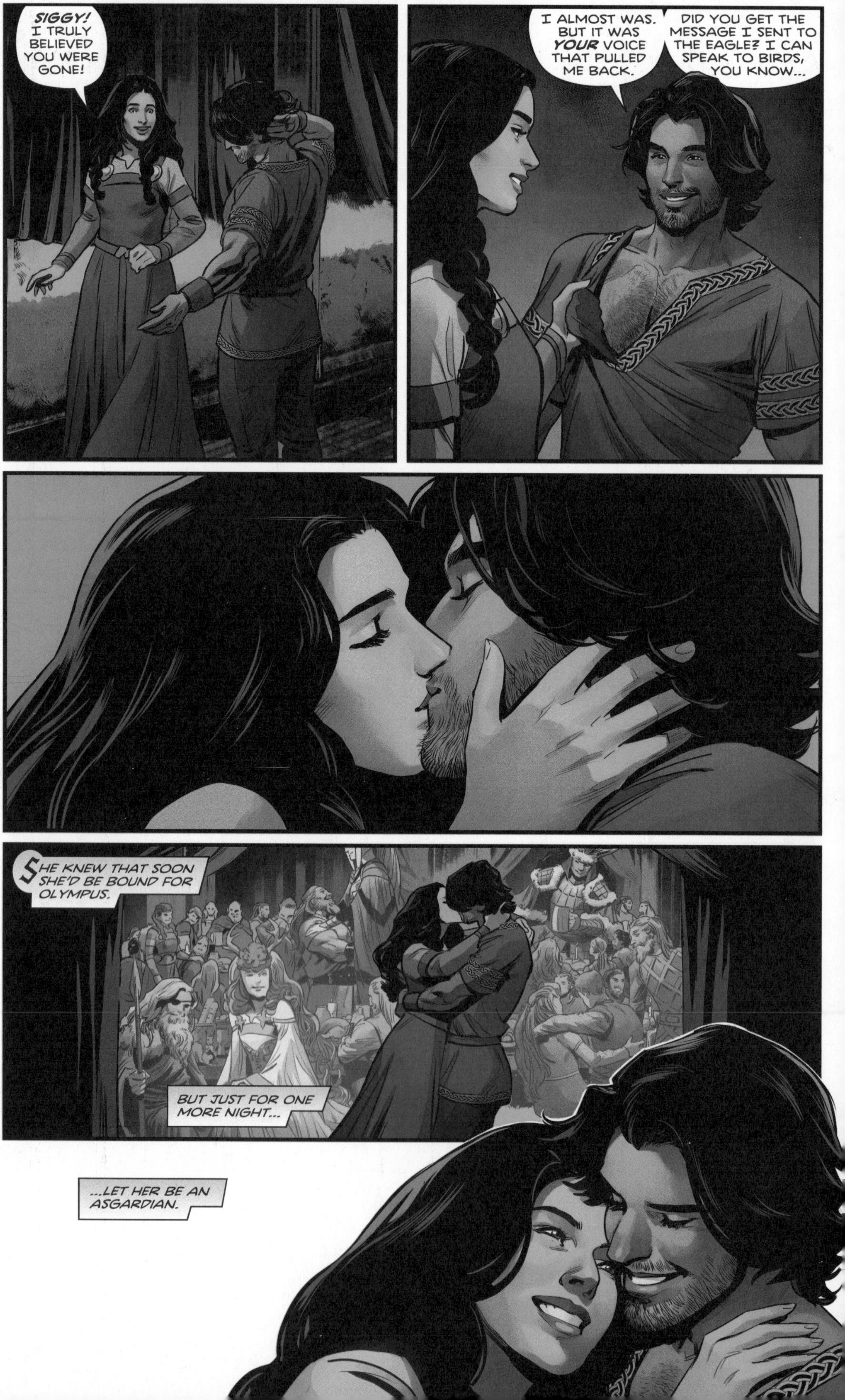
SIGGY! I TRULY BELIEVED YOU WERE GONE!
I ALMOST WAS. BUT IT WAS YOUR VOICE THAT PULLED ME BACK.
DID YOU GET THE MESSAGE I SENT TO THE EAGLE? I CAN SPEAK TO BIRDS, YOU KNOW...
SHE KNEW THAT SOON SHE'D BE BOUND FOR OLYMPUS.
BUT JUST FOR ONE MORE NIGHT...
...LET HER BE AN ASGARDIAN.

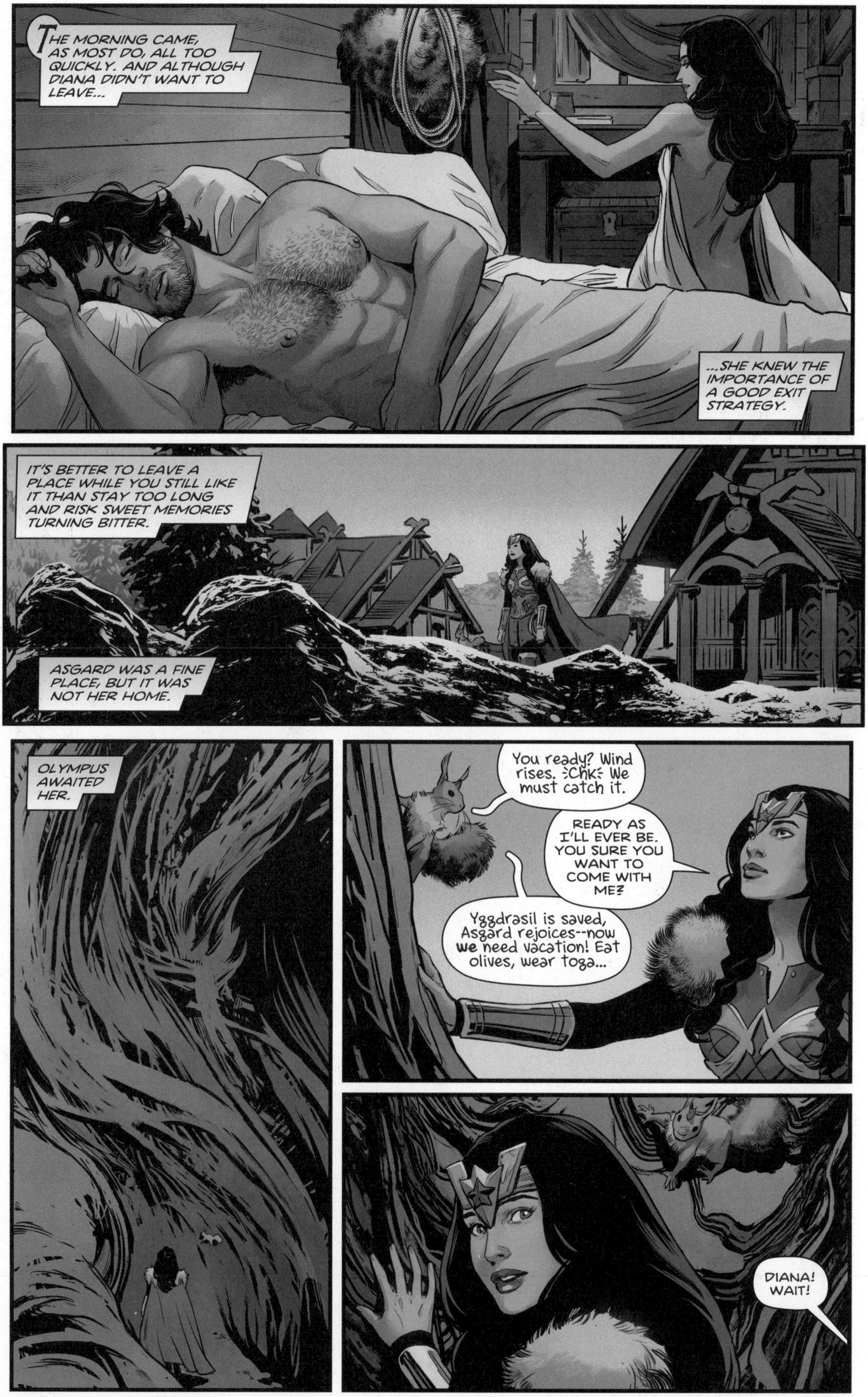
THE MORNING CAME, AS MOST DO, ALL TOO QUICKLY. AND ALTHOUGH DIANA DIDN'T WANT TO LEAVE...
...SHE KNEW THE IMPORTANCE OF A GOOD EXIT STRATEGY.
IT'S BETTER TO LEAVE A PLACE WHILE YOU STILL LIKE IT THAN STAY TOO LONG AND RISK SWEET MEMORIES TURNING BITTER.
ASGARD WAS A FINE PLACE, BUT IT WAS NOT HER HOME.
OLYMPUS AWAITED HER.
You ready? Wind rises. :Chk: We must catch it.
READY AS I'LL EVER BE. YOU SURE YOU WANT TO COME WITH ME?
Yggdrasil is saved, Asgard rejoices--now we need vacation! Eat olives, wear toga...
DIANA! WAIT!

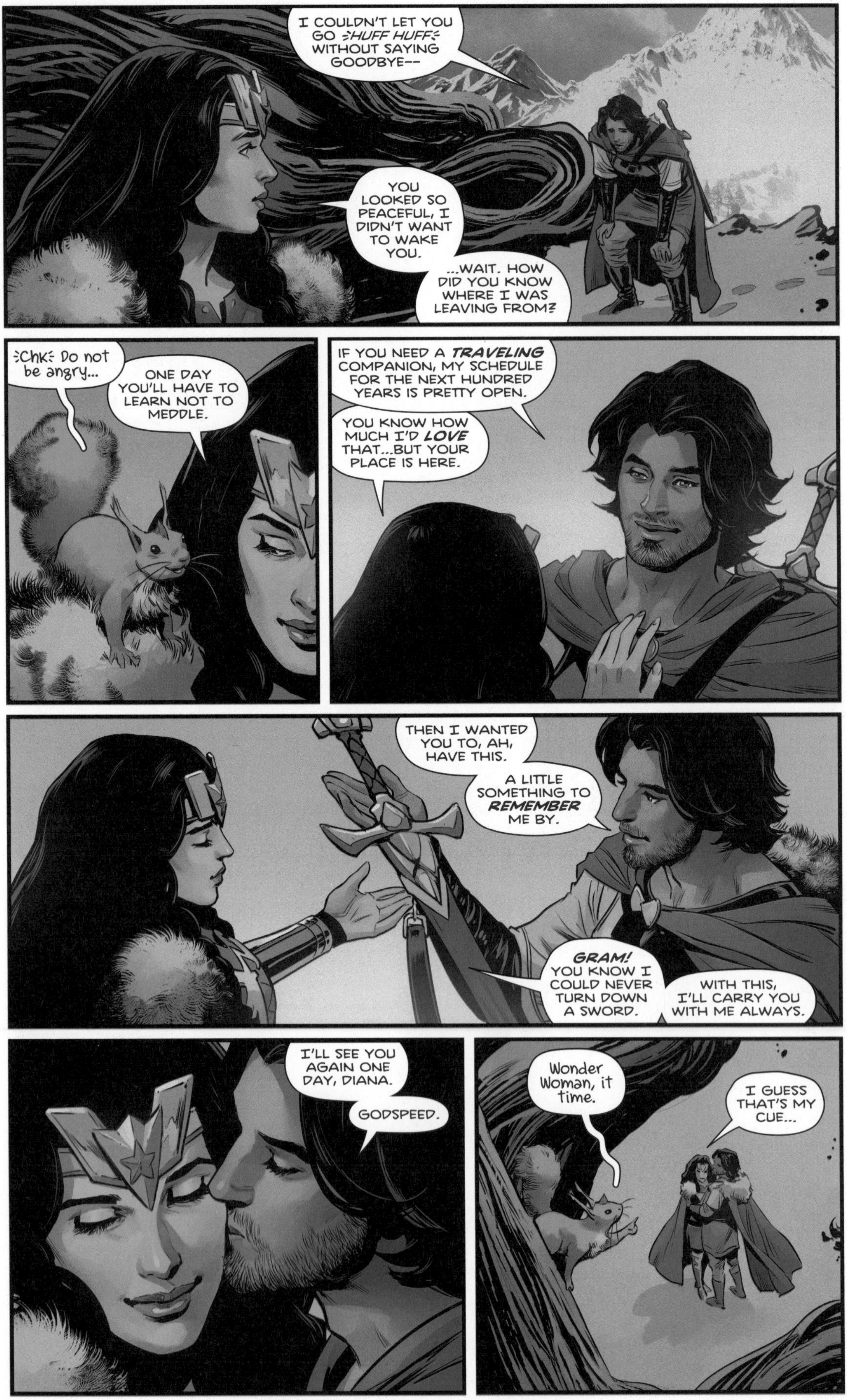

I COULDN'T LET YOU GO ⩦HUFF HUFF⩦ WITHOUT SAYING GOODBYE--
YOU LOOKED SO PEACEFUL, I DIDN'T WANT TO WAKE YOU.
...WAIT. HOW DID YOU KNOW WHERE I WAS LEAVING FROM?
⩦Chk⩦ Do not be angry...
ONE DAY YOU'LL HAVE TO LEARN NOT TO MEDDLE.
IF YOU NEED A TRAVELING COMPANION, MY SCHEDULE FOR THE NEXT HUNDRED YEARS IS PRETTY OPEN.
YOU KNOW HOW MUCH I'D LOVE THAT...BUT YOUR PLACE IS HERE.
THEN I WANTED YOU TO, AH, HAVE THIS.
A LITTLE SOMETHING TO REMEMBER ME BY.
GRAM! YOU KNOW I COULD NEVER TURN DOWN A SWORD.
WITH THIS, I'LL CARRY YOU WITH ME ALWAYS.
I'LL SEE YOU AGAIN ONE DAY, DIANA.
GODSPEED.
Wonder Woman, it time.
I GUESS THAT'S MY CUE...

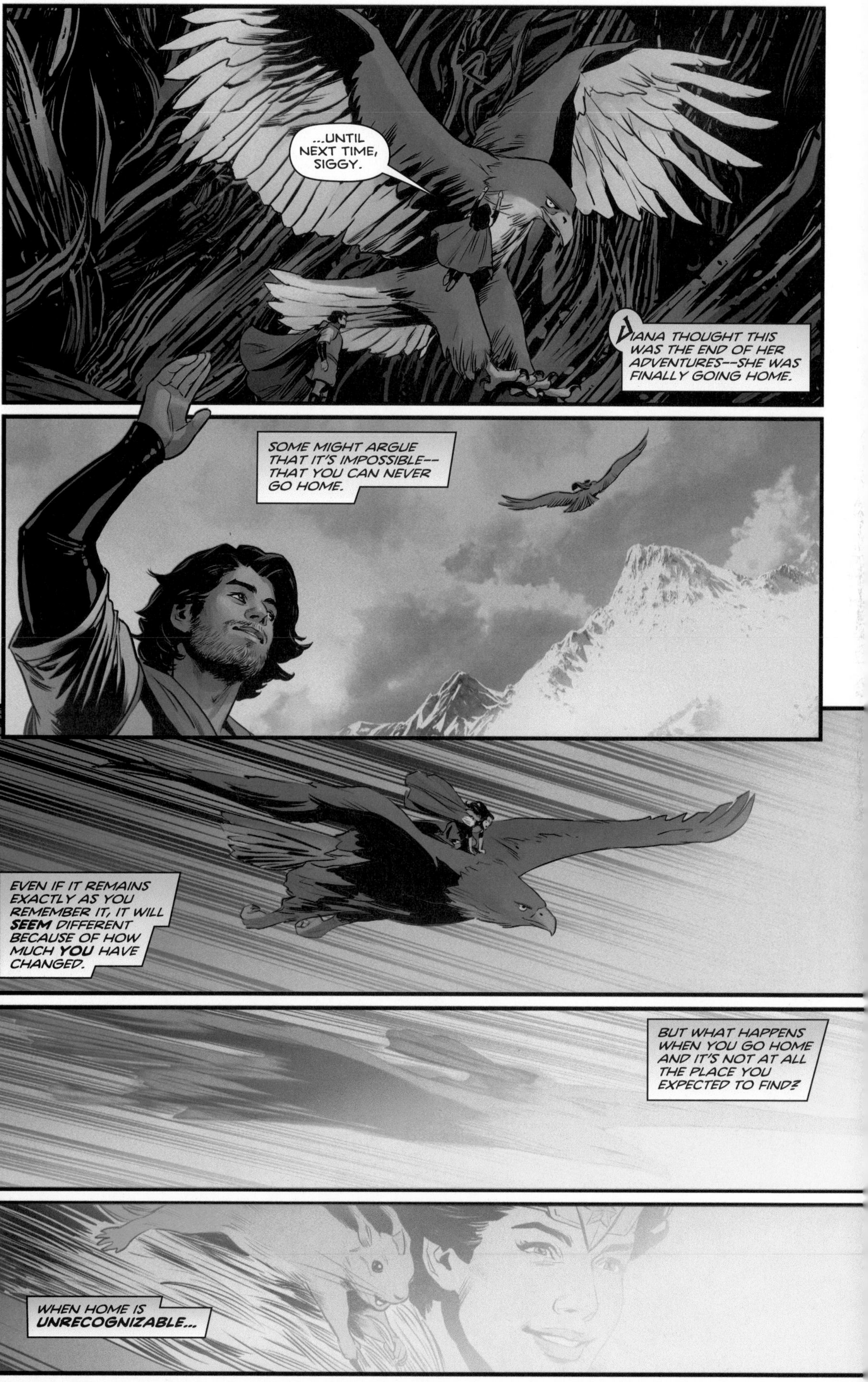
...UNTIL NEXT TIME, SIGGY.
DIANA THOUGHT THIS WAS THE END OF HER ADVENTURES--SHE WAS FINALLY GOING HOME.
SOME MIGHT ARGUE THAT IT'S IMPOSSIBLE-- THAT YOU CAN NEVER GO HOME.
EVEN IF IT REMAINS EXACTLY AS YOU REMEMBER IT, IT WILL SEEM DIFFERENT BECAUSE OF HOW MUCH YOU HAVE CHANGED.
BUT WHAT HAPPENS WHEN YOU GO HOME AND IT'S NOT AT ALL THE PLACE YOU EXPECTED TO FIND?
WHEN HOME IS UNRECOGNIZABLE...

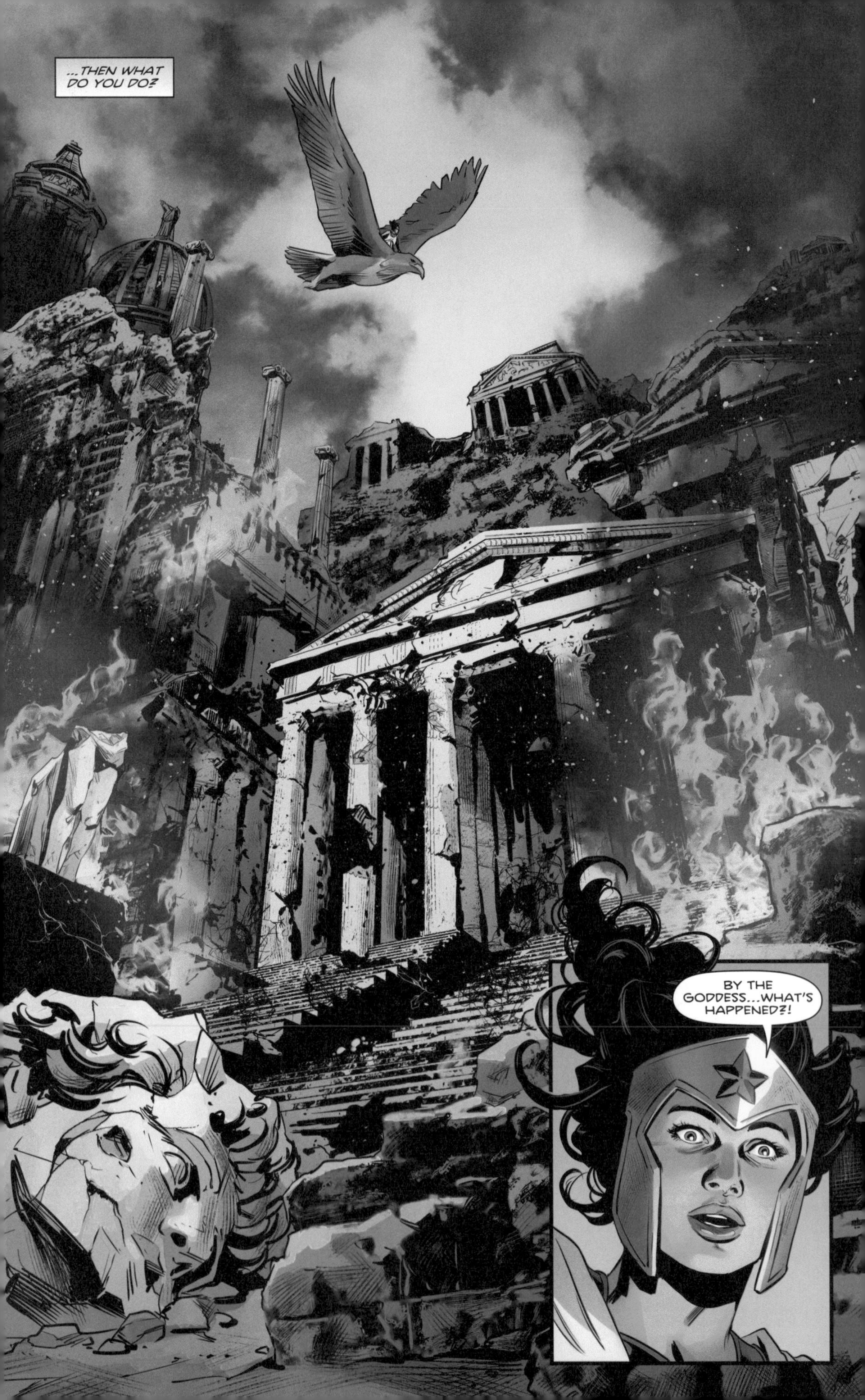
...THEN WHAT DO YOU DO?
BY THE GODDESS...WHAT'S HAPPENED?!

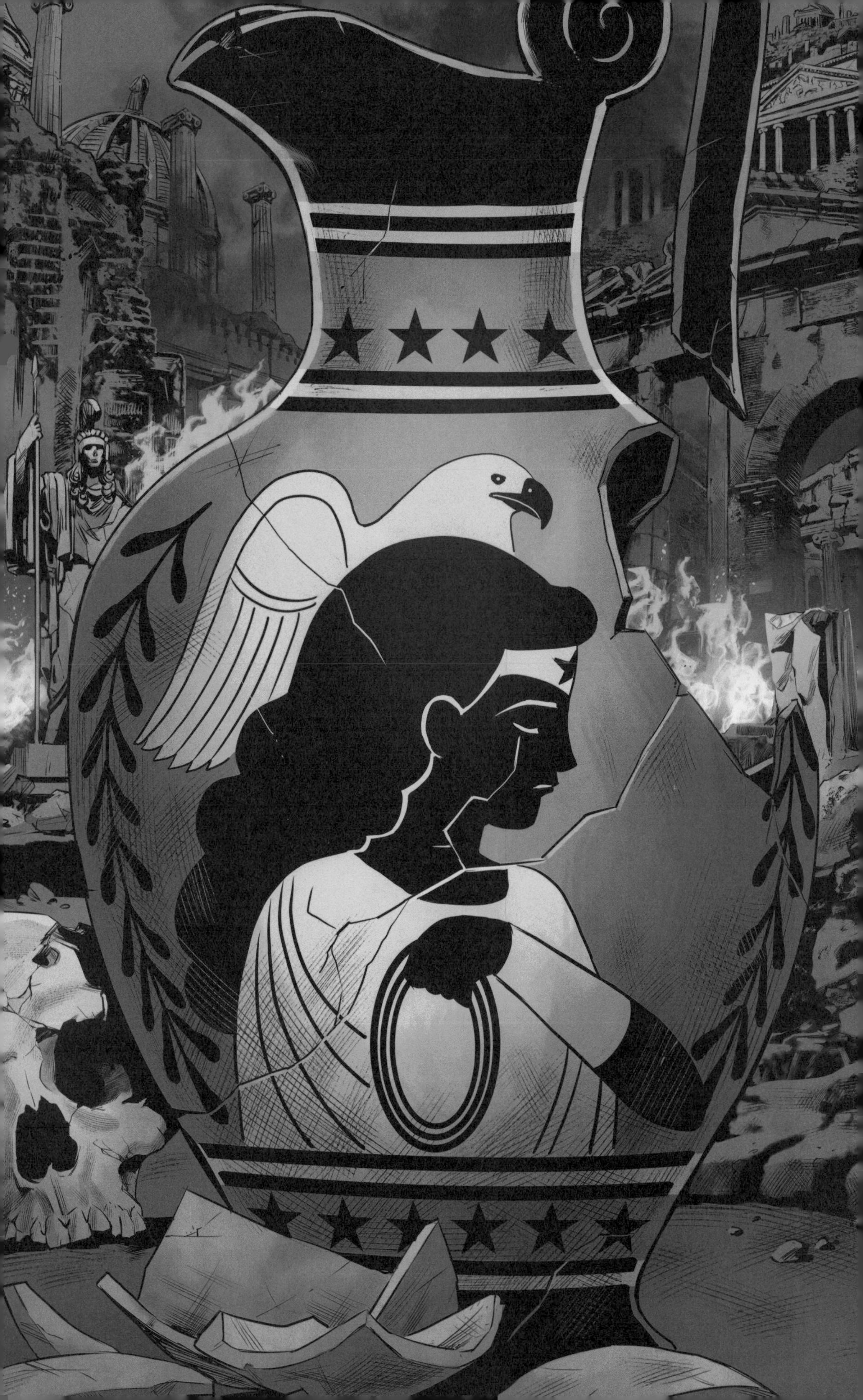

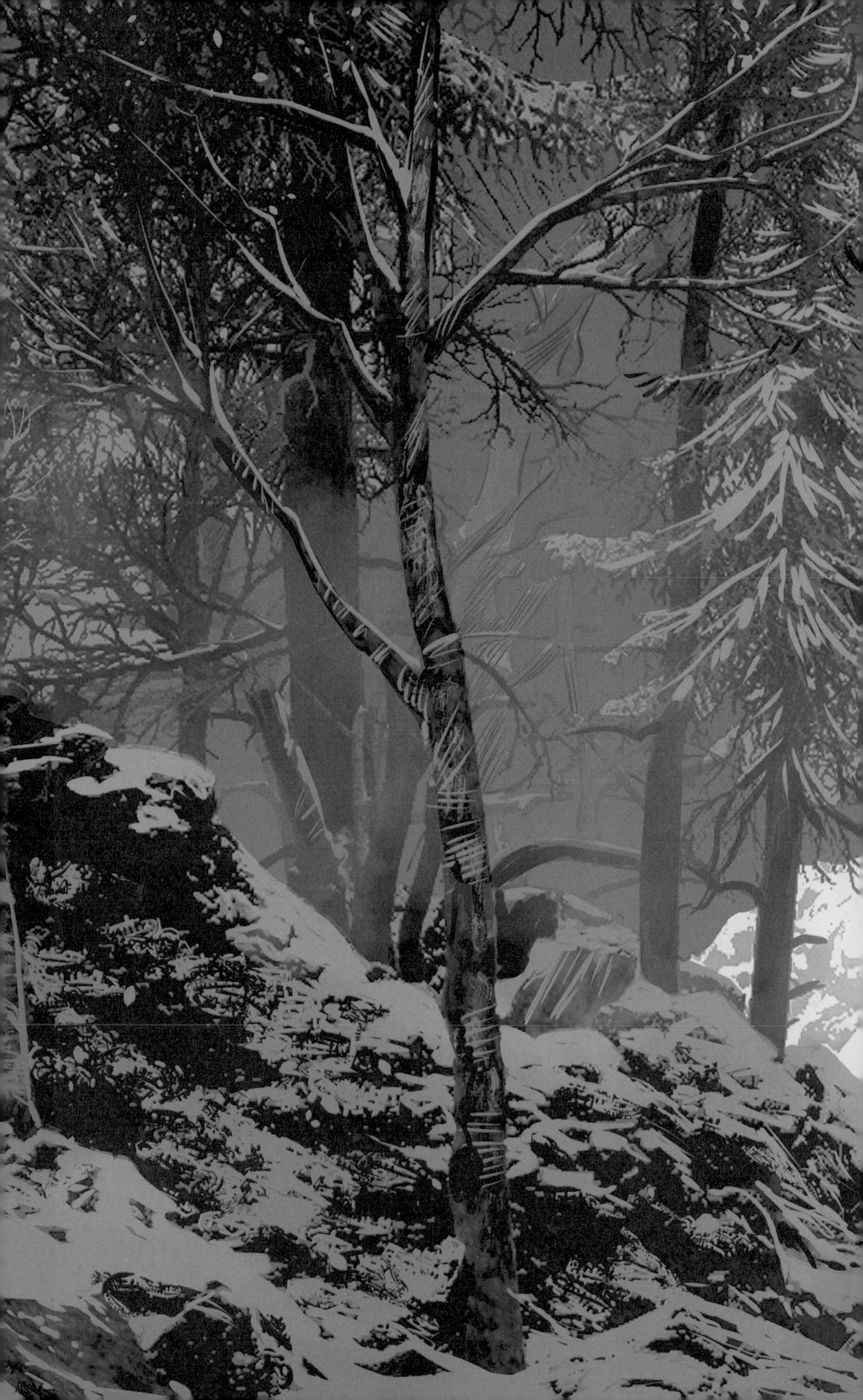

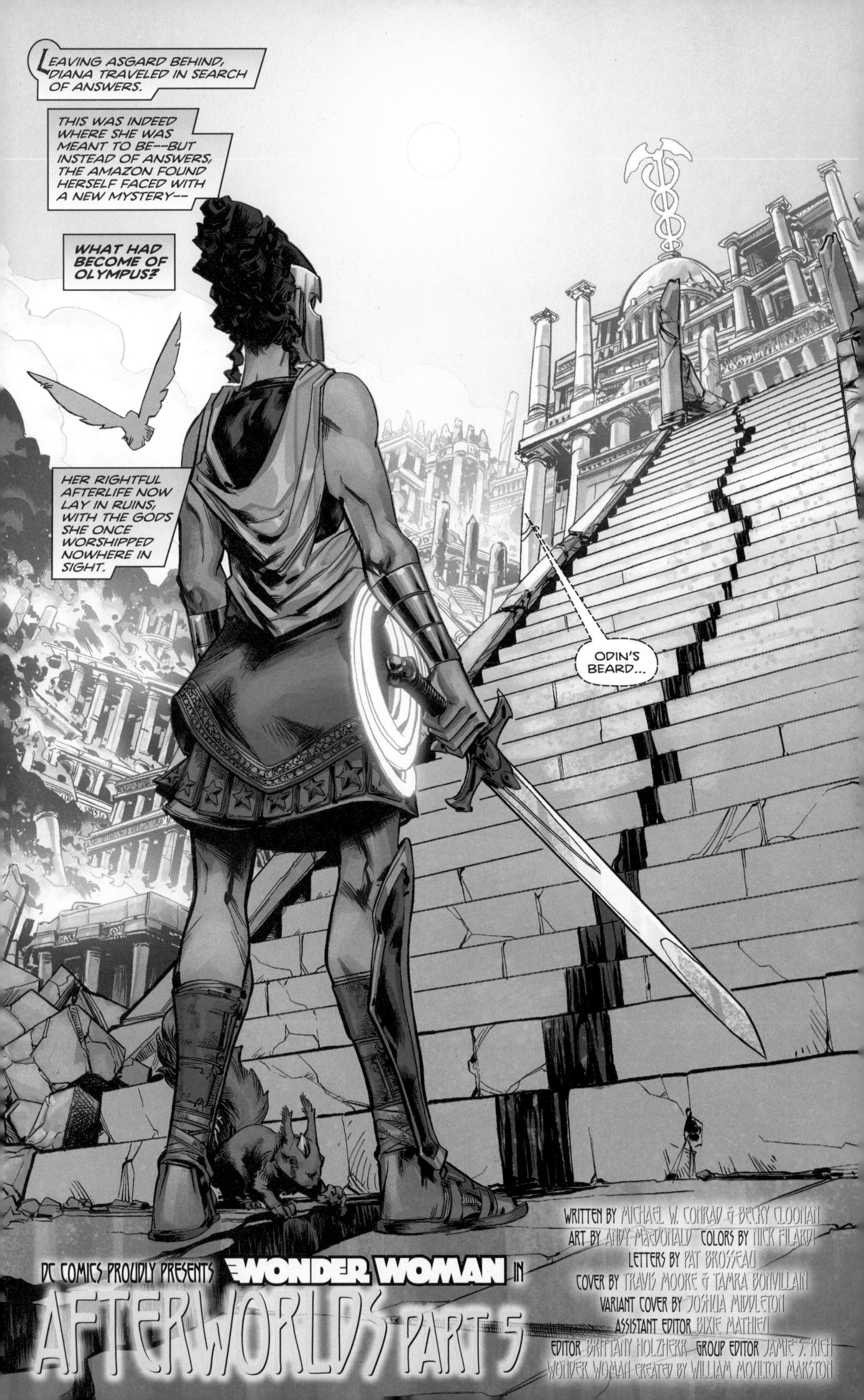
LEAVING ASGARD BEHIND, DIANA TRAVELED IN SEARCH OF ANSWERS.
THIS WAS INDEED WHERE SHE WAS MEANT TO BE--BUT INSTEAD OF ANSWERS, THE AMAZON FOUND HERSELF FACED WITH A NEW MYSTERY--
WHAT HAD BECOME OF OLYMPUS?
HER RIGHTFUL AFTERLIFE NOW LAY IN RUINS, WITH THE GODS SHE ONCE WORSHIPPED NOWHERE IN SIGHT.
ODIN'S BEARD...
DC COMICS PROUDLY PRESENTS WONDER WOMAN IN
AFTERWORLDS PART 5
WRITTEN BY MICHAEL W. CONRAD & BECKY CLOONAN
ART BY ANDY MacDONALD COLORS BY NICK FILARDI
LETTERS BY PAT BROSSEAU
COVER BY TRAVIS MOORE & TAMRA BONVILLAIN
VARIANT COVER BY JOSHUA MIDDLETON
ASSISTANT EDITOR BIXIE MATHIEU
EDITOR BRITTANY HOLZHERR GROUP EDITOR JAMIE S. RICH
WONDER WOMAN CREATED BY WILLIAM MOULTON MARSTON

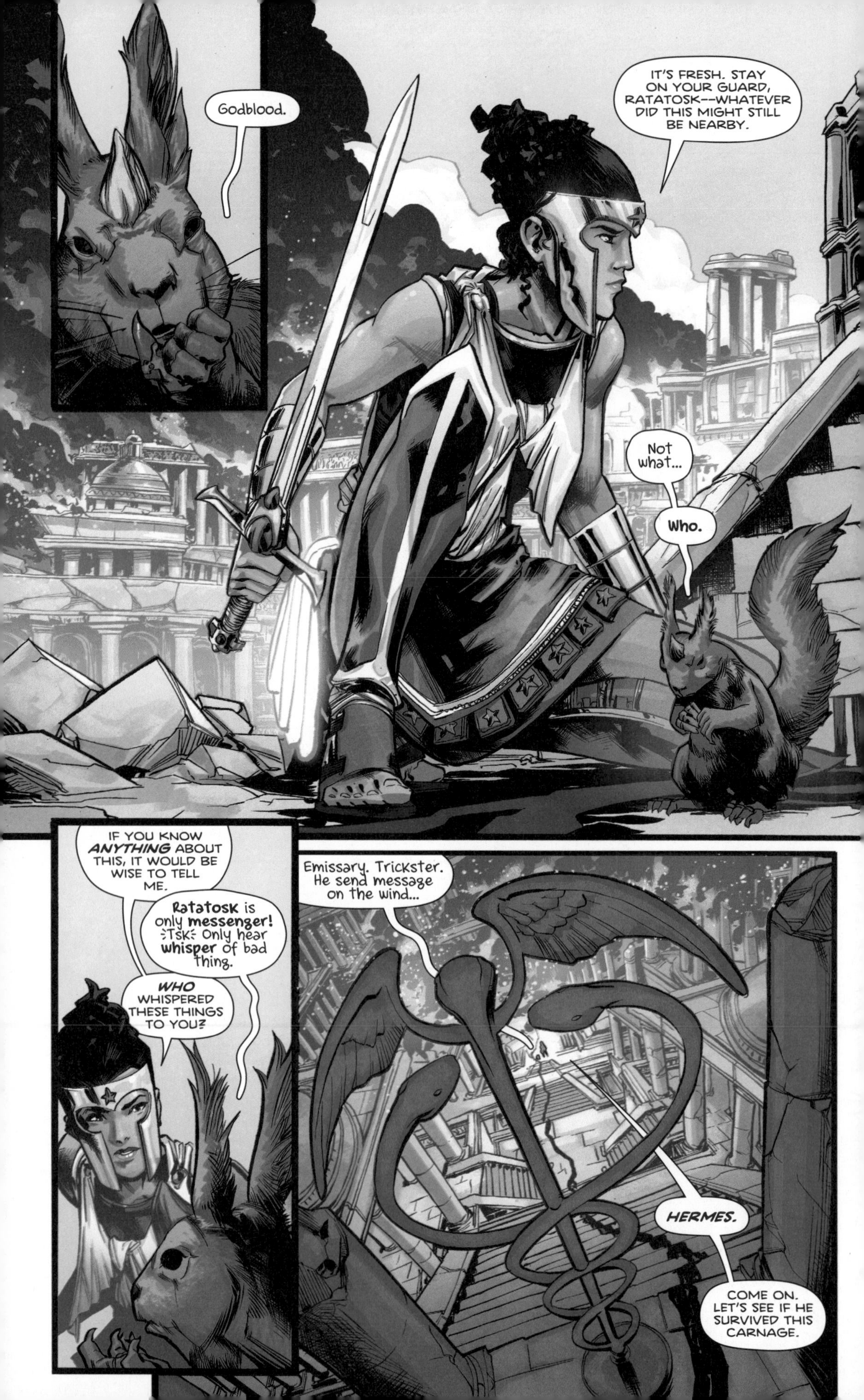

Godblood.
IT'S FRESH. STAY ON YOUR GUARD, RATATOSK--WHATEVER DID THIS MIGHT STILL BE NEARBY.
Not what...
Who.
IF YOU KNOW ANYTHING ABOUT THIS, IT WOULD BE WISE TO TELL ME.
Ratatosk is only messenger! Tsk Only hear whisper of bad thing.
WHO WHISPERED THESE THINGS TO YOU?
Emissary. Trickster. He send message on the wind...
HERMES.
COME ON. LET'S SEE IF HE SURVIVED THIS CARNAGE.

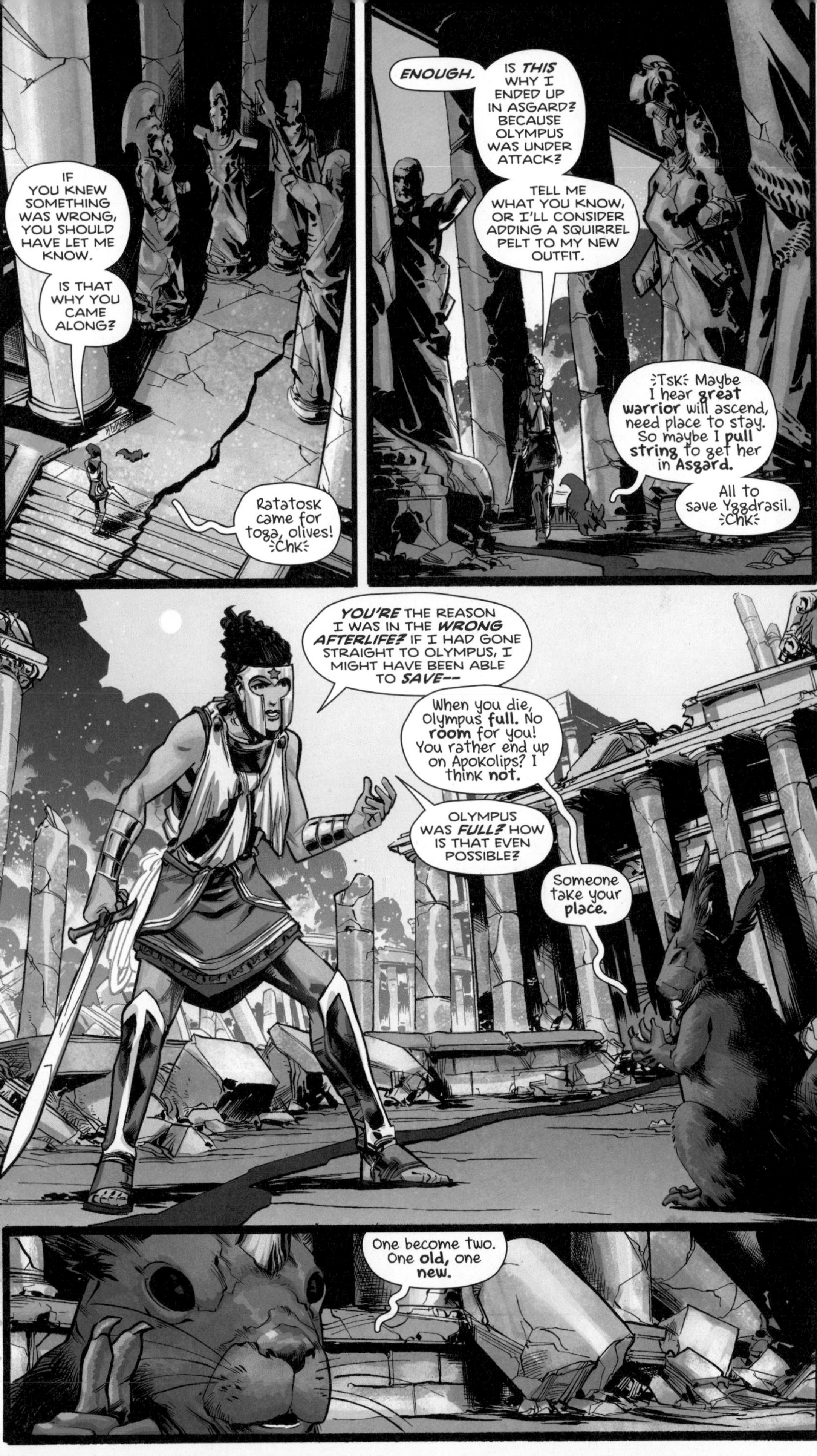

IF YOU KNEW SOMETHING WAS WRONG, YOU SHOULD HAVE LET ME KNOW.
IS THAT WHY YOU CAME ALONG?
Ratatosk came for toga, olives! Chk
ENOUGH.
IS THIS WHY I ENDED UP IN ASGARD? BECAUSE OLYMPUS WAS UNDER ATTACK?
TELL ME WHAT YOU KNOW, OR I'LL CONSIDER ADDING A SQUIRREL PELT TO MY NEW OUTFIT.
Tsk Maybe I hear great warrior will ascend, need place to stay. So maybe I pull string to get her in Asgard.
All to save Yggdrasil. Chk
YOU'RE THE REASON I WAS IN THE WRONG AFTERLIFE? IF I HAD GONE STRAIGHT TO OLYMPUS, I MIGHT HAVE BEEN ABLE TO SAVE--
When you die, Olympus full. No room for you! You rather end up on Apokolips? I think not.
OLYMPUS WAS FULL? HOW IS THAT EVEN POSSIBLE?
Someone take your place.
One become two. One old, one new.

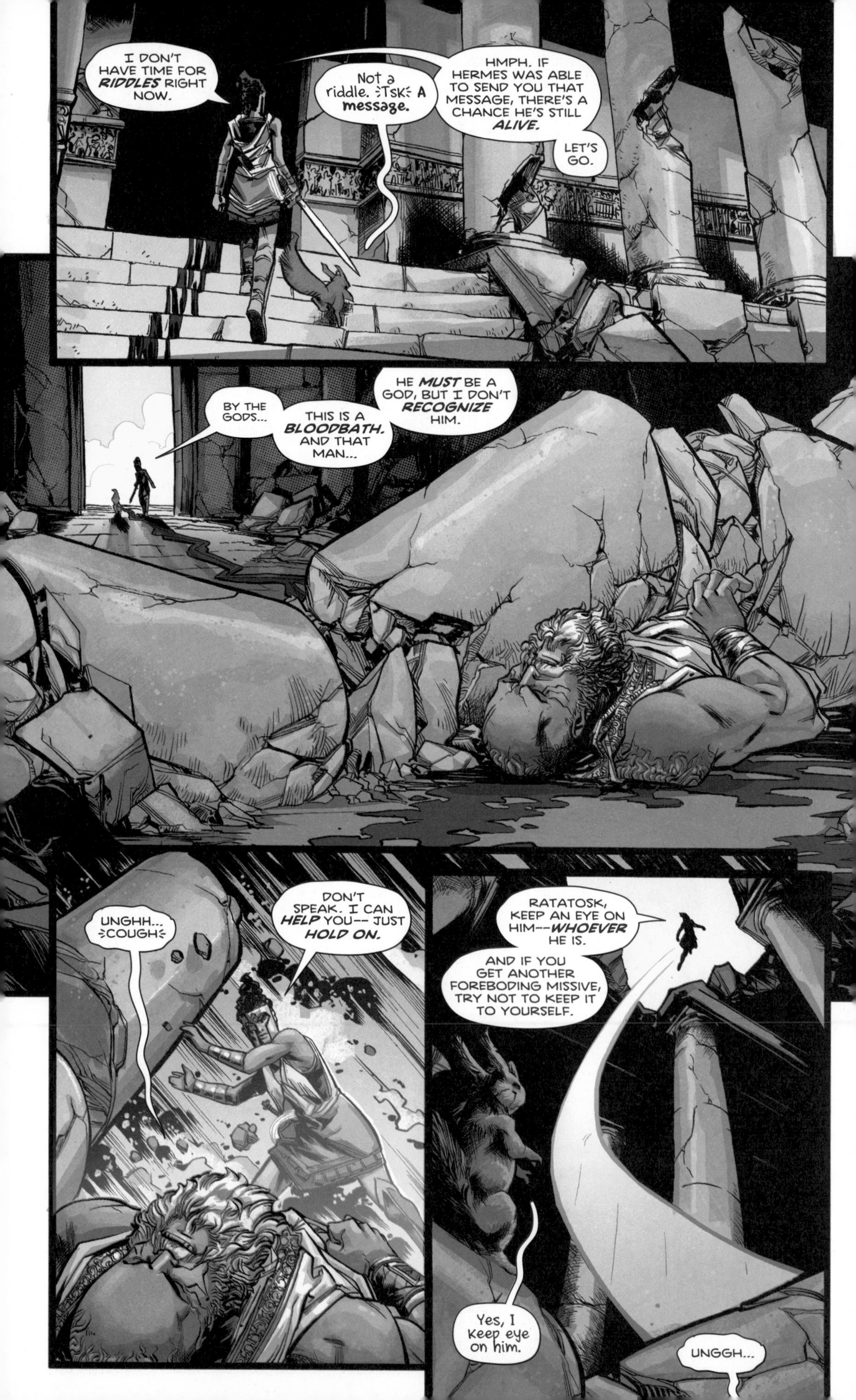

I DON'T HAVE TIME FOR *RIDDLES* RIGHT NOW.
Not a riddle. :Tsk: A **message.**
HMPH. IF HERMES WAS ABLE TO SEND YOU THAT MESSAGE, THERE'S A CHANCE HE'S STILL *ALIVE.*
LET'S GO.
BY THE GODS...
THIS IS A *BLOODBATH.* AND THAT MAN...
HE *MUST* BE A GOD, BUT I DON'T *RECOGNIZE* HIM.
UNGHH... :COUGH:
DON'T SPEAK. I CAN *HELP* YOU-- JUST *HOLD ON.*
RATATOSK, KEEP AN EYE ON HIM--*WHOEVER* HE IS.
AND IF YOU GET ANOTHER FOREBODING MISSIVE, TRY NOT TO KEEP IT TO YOURSELF.
Yes, I keep eye on him.
UNGGH...

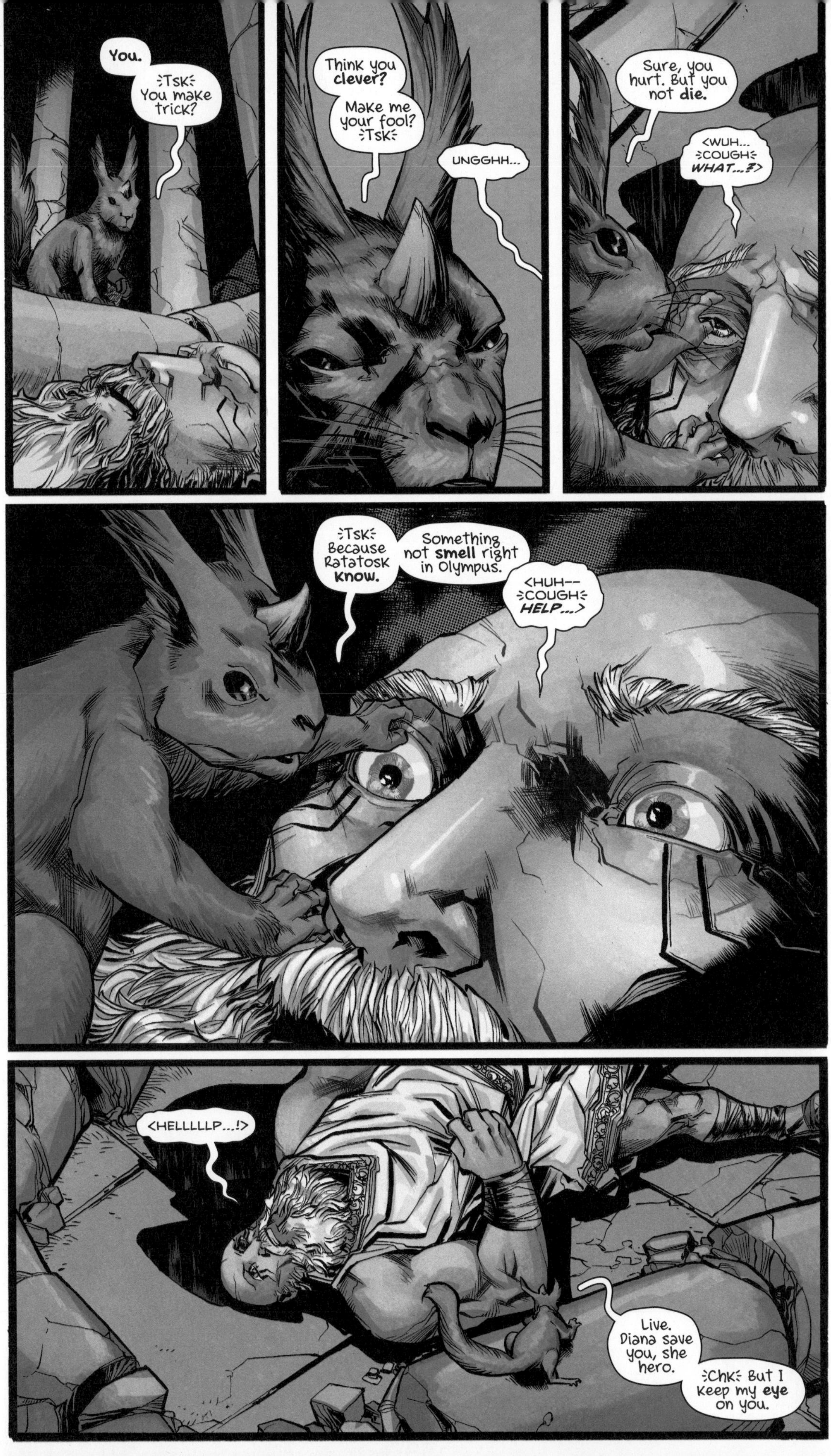
You.
Tsk You make trick?
Think you clever?
Make me your fool? Tsk
UNGGHH...
Sure, you hurt. But you not die.
<WUH... COUGH WHAT...?>
Tsk Because Ratatosk know.
Something not smell right in Olympus.
<HUH-- COUGH HELP...>
<HELLLLLP...!>
Live. Diana save you, she hero.
Chk But I keep my eye on you.

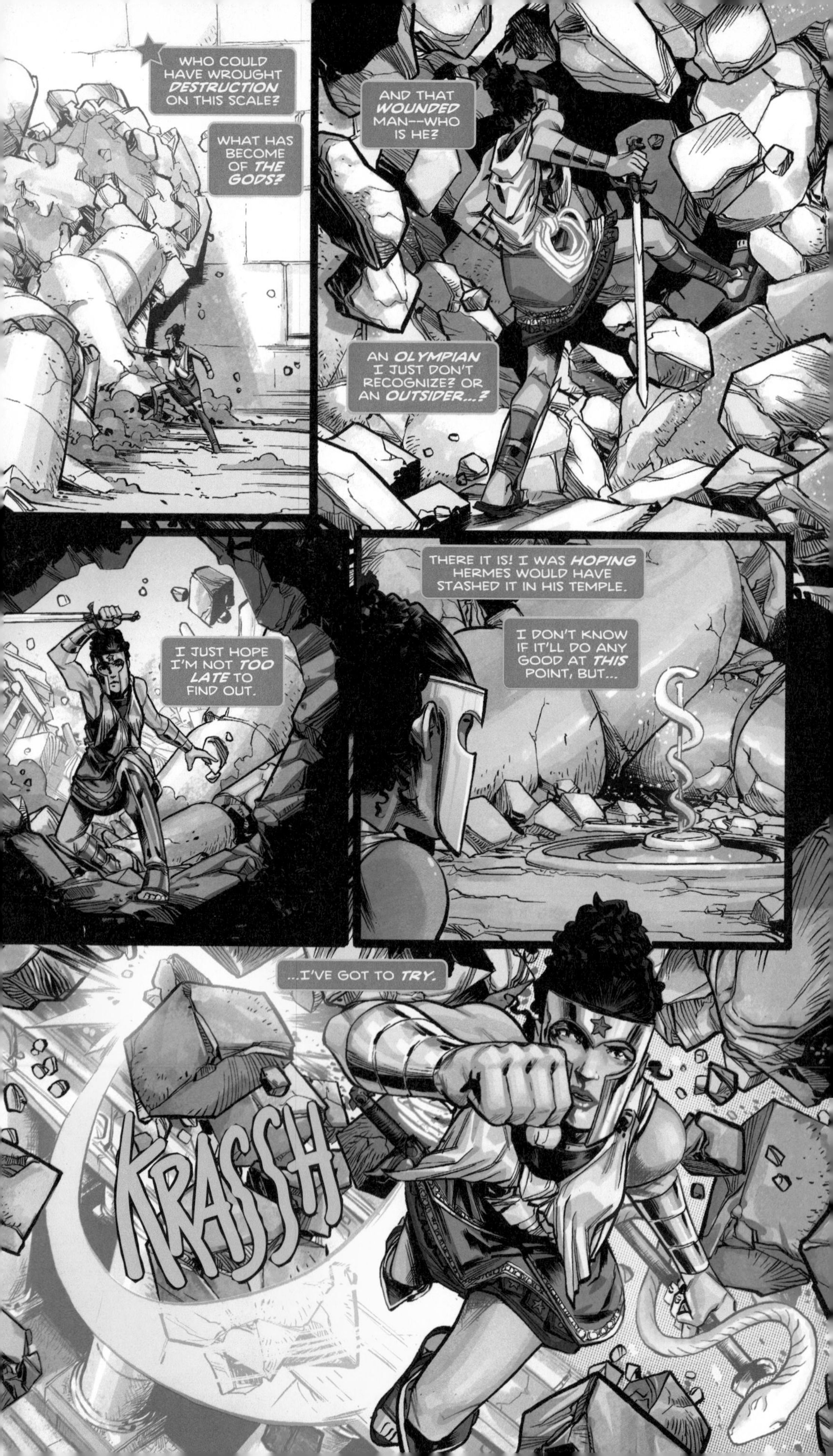
WHO COULD HAVE WROUGHT DESTRUCTION ON THIS SCALE?
WHAT HAS BECOME OF THE GODS?
AND THAT WOUNDED MAN--WHO IS HE?
AN OLYMPIAN I JUST DON'T RECOGNIZE? OR AN OUTSIDER...?
I JUST HOPE I'M NOT TOO LATE TO FIND OUT.
THERE IT IS! I WAS HOPING HERMES WOULD HAVE STASHED IT IN HIS TEMPLE.
I DON'T KNOW IF IT'LL DO ANY GOOD AT THIS POINT, BUT...
...I'VE GOT TO TRY.
KRASSH

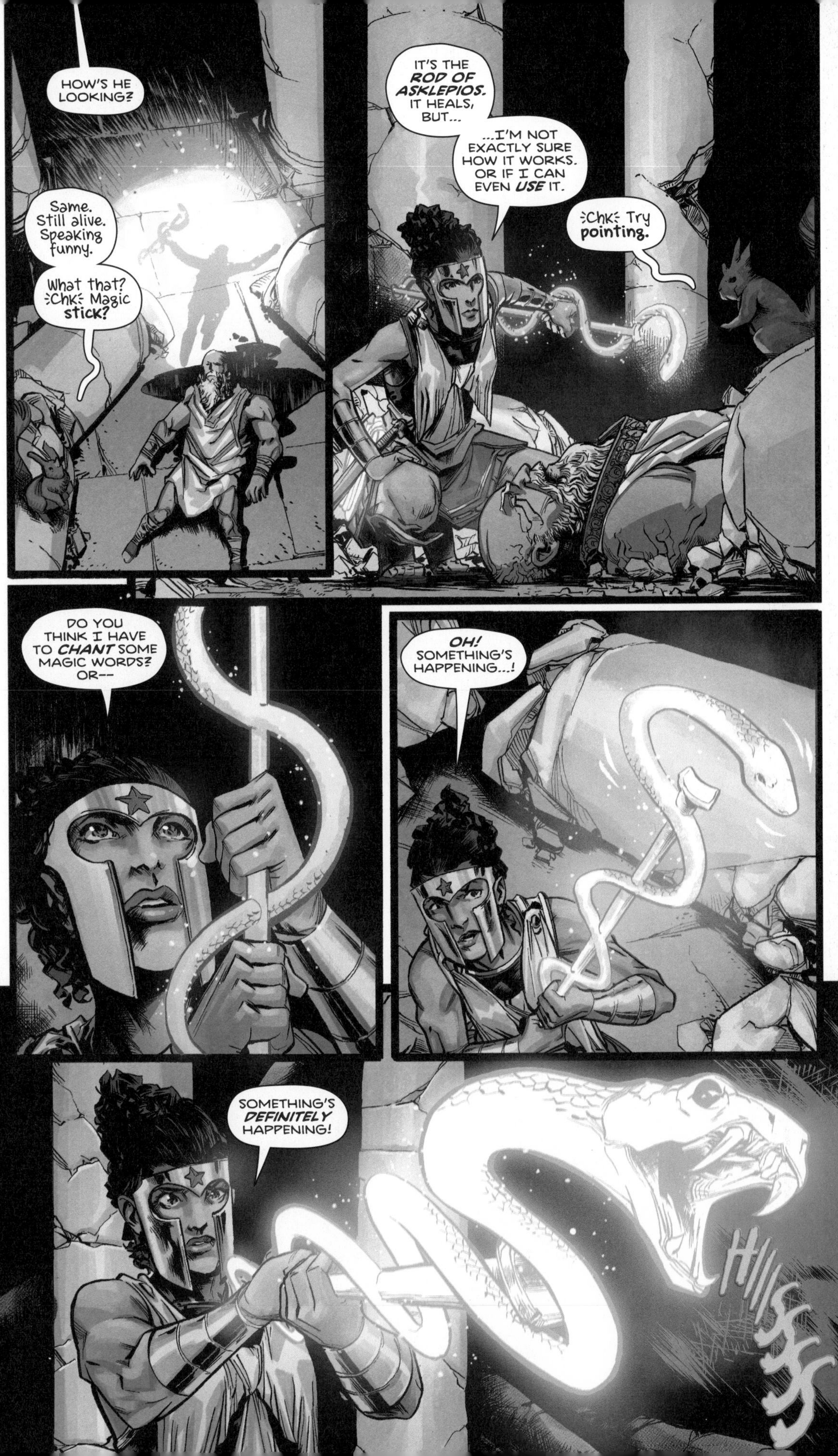
HOW'S HE LOOKING?
Same. Still alive. Speaking funny.
What that? ⋮Chk⋮ Magic stick?
IT'S THE ROD OF ASKLEPIOS. IT HEALS, BUT...
...I'M NOT EXACTLY SURE HOW IT WORKS. OR IF I CAN EVEN USE IT.
⋮Chk⋮ Try pointing.
DO YOU THINK I HAVE TO CHANT SOME MAGIC WORDS? OR--
OH! SOMETHING'S HAPPENING...!
SOMETHING'S DEFINITELY HAPPENING!
HISSSS

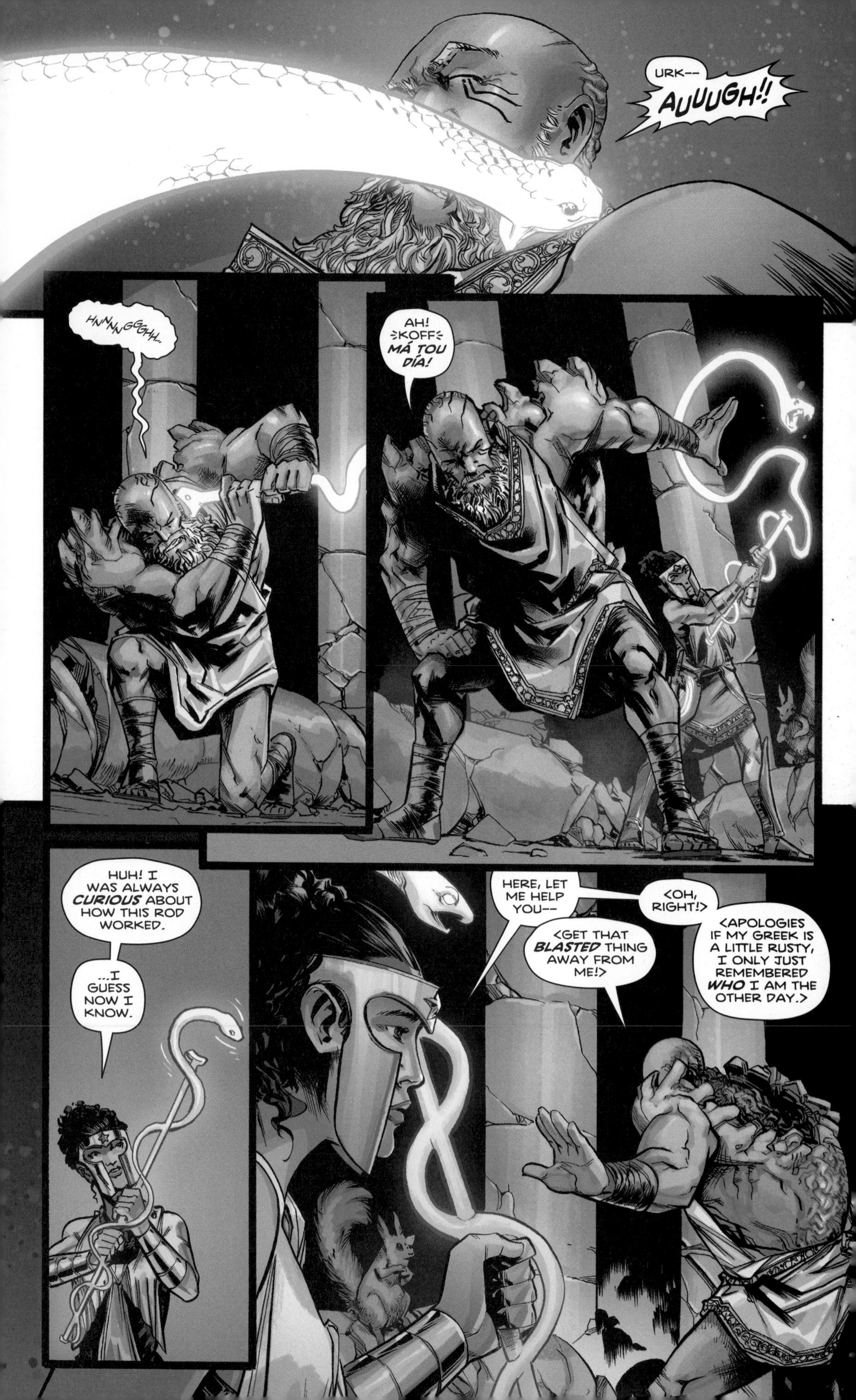
URK--
AUUUGH!!
HNNNNGGGH..
AH!
-KOFF-
MÁ TOU DÍA!
HUH! I WAS ALWAYS CURIOUS ABOUT HOW THIS ROD WORKED.
...I GUESS NOW I KNOW.
HERE, LET ME HELP YOU--
<GET THAT BLASTED THING AWAY FROM ME!>
<OH, RIGHT!>
<APOLOGIES IF MY GREEK IS A LITTLE RUSTY, I ONLY JUST REMEMBERED WHO I AM THE OTHER DAY.>

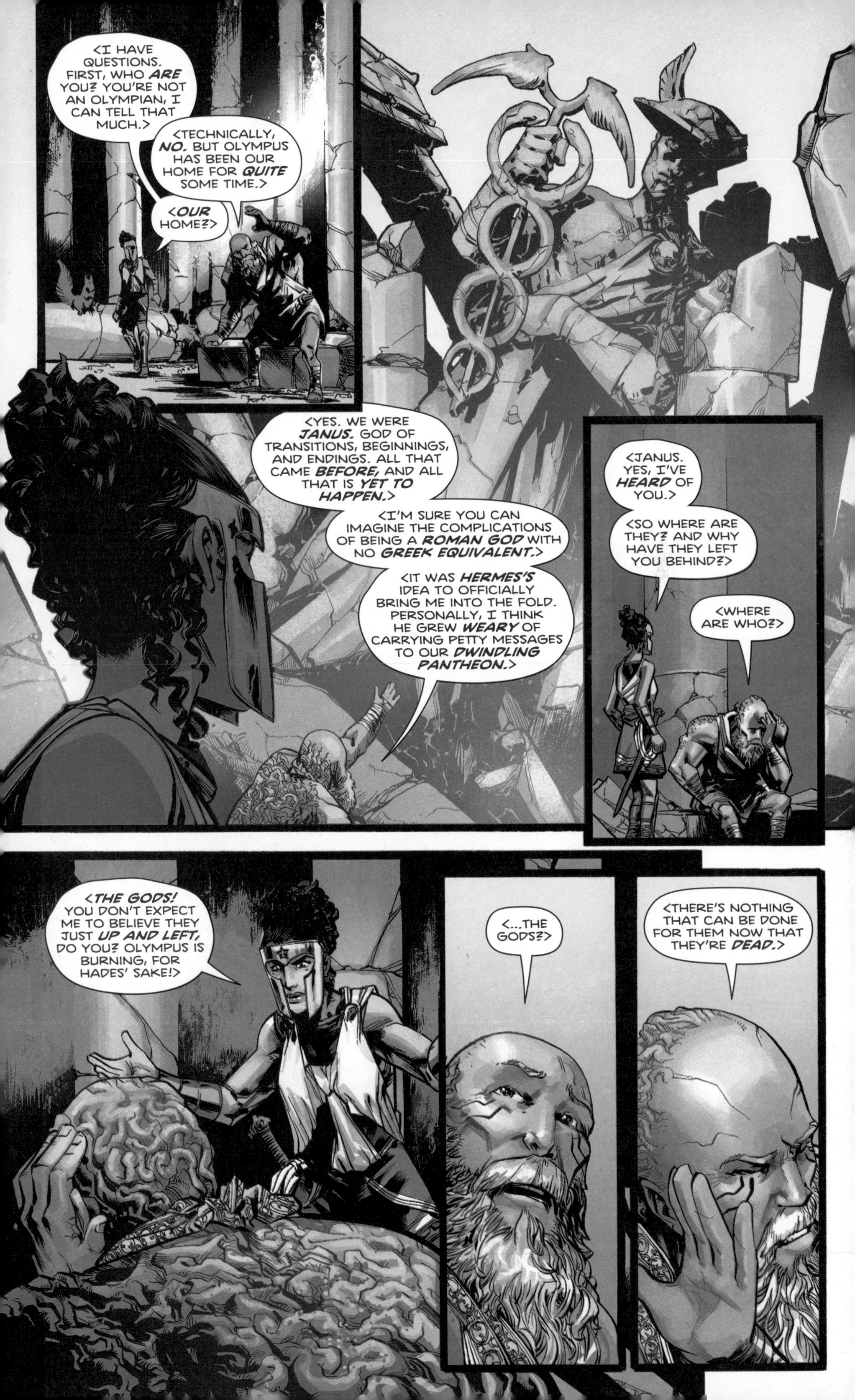
<I HAVE QUESTIONS. FIRST, WHO ARE YOU? YOU'RE NOT AN OLYMPIAN, I CAN TELL THAT MUCH.>
<TECHNICALLY, NO. BUT OLYMPUS HAS BEEN OUR HOME FOR QUITE SOME TIME.>
<OUR HOME?>
<YES. WE WERE JANUS. GOD OF TRANSITIONS, BEGINNINGS, AND ENDINGS. ALL THAT CAME BEFORE, AND ALL THAT IS YET TO HAPPEN.>
<I'M SURE YOU CAN IMAGINE THE COMPLICATIONS OF BEING A ROMAN GOD WITH NO GREEK EQUIVALENT.>
<IT WAS HERMES'S IDEA TO OFFICIALLY BRING ME INTO THE FOLD. PERSONALLY, I THINK HE GREW WEARY OF CARRYING PETTY MESSAGES TO OUR DWINDLING PANTHEON.>
<JANUS. YES, I'VE HEARD OF YOU.>
<SO WHERE ARE THEY? AND WHY HAVE THEY LEFT YOU BEHIND?>
<WHERE ARE WHO?>
<THE GODS! YOU DON'T EXPECT ME TO BELIEVE THEY JUST UP AND LEFT, DO YOU? OLYMPUS IS BURNING, FOR HADES' SAKE!>
<...THE GODS?>
<THERE'S NOTHING THAT CAN BE DONE FOR THEM NOW THAT THEY'RE DEAD.>

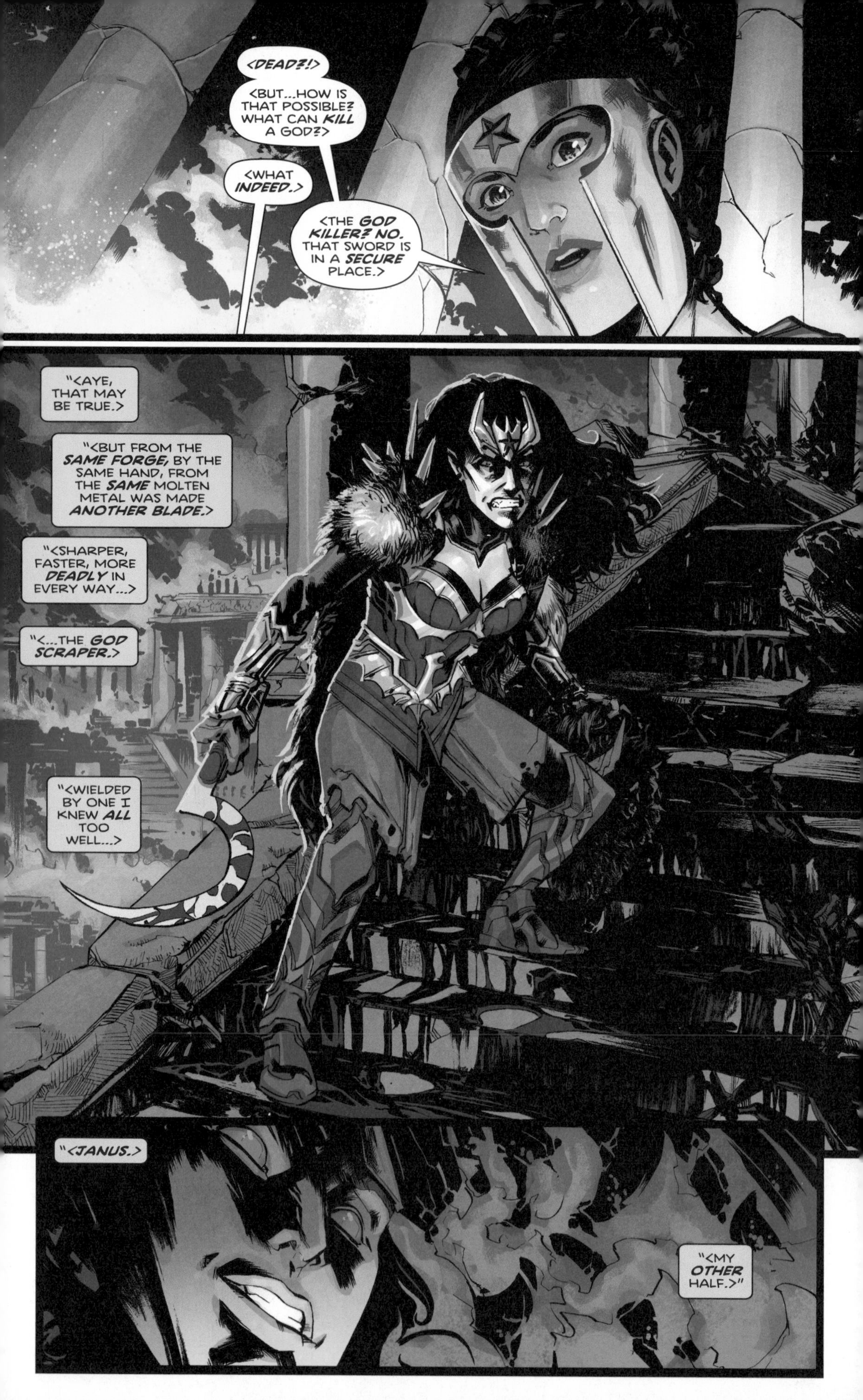
<DEAD?!>
<BUT...HOW IS THAT POSSIBLE? WHAT CAN KILL A GOD?>
<WHAT INDEED.>
<THE GOD KILLER? NO. THAT SWORD IS IN A SECURE PLACE.>
"<AYE, THAT MAY BE TRUE.>
"<BUT FROM THE SAME FORGE, BY THE SAME HAND, FROM THE SAME MOLTEN METAL WAS MADE ANOTHER BLADE.>
"<SHARPER, FASTER, MORE DEADLY IN EVERY WAY...>
"<...THE GOD SCRAPER.>
"<WIELDED BY ONE I KNEW ALL TOO WELL...>
"<JANUS.>
"<MY OTHER HALF.>"

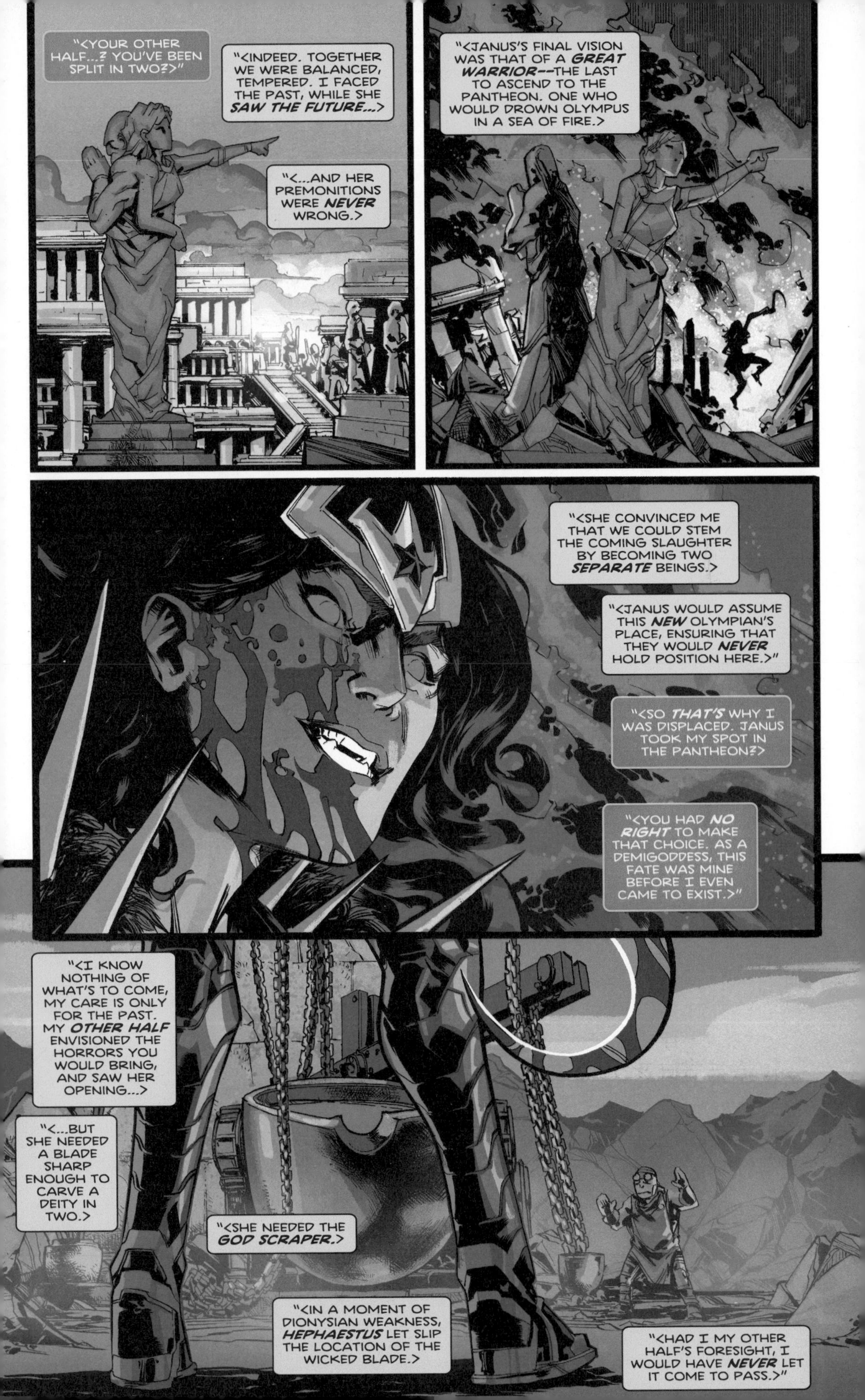
"<YOUR OTHER HALF...? YOU'VE BEEN SPLIT IN TWO?>"
"<INDEED. TOGETHER WE WERE BALANCED, TEMPERED. I FACED THE PAST, WHILE SHE SAW THE FUTURE...>
"<...AND HER PREMONITIONS WERE NEVER WRONG.>
"<JANUS'S FINAL VISION WAS THAT OF A GREAT WARRIOR--THE LAST TO ASCEND TO THE PANTHEON. ONE WHO WOULD DROWN OLYMPUS IN A SEA OF FIRE.>
"<SHE CONVINCED ME THAT WE COULD STEM THE COMING SLAUGHTER BY BECOMING TWO SEPARATE BEINGS.>
"<JANUS WOULD ASSUME THIS NEW OLYMPIAN'S PLACE, ENSURING THAT THEY WOULD NEVER HOLD POSITION HERE.>"
"<SO THAT'S WHY I WAS DISPLACED. JANUS TOOK MY SPOT IN THE PANTHEON?>
"<YOU HAD NO RIGHT TO MAKE THAT CHOICE. AS A DEMIGODDESS, THIS FATE WAS MINE BEFORE I EVEN CAME TO EXIST.>"
"<I KNOW NOTHING OF WHAT'S TO COME, MY CARE IS ONLY FOR THE PAST. MY OTHER HALF ENVISIONED THE HORRORS YOU WOULD BRING, AND SAW HER OPENING...>
"<...BUT SHE NEEDED A BLADE SHARP ENOUGH TO CARVE A DEITY IN TWO.>
"<SHE NEEDED THE GOD SCRAPER.>
"<IN A MOMENT OF DIONYSIAN WEAKNESS, HEPHAESTUS LET SLIP THE LOCATION OF THE WICKED BLADE.>
"<HAD I MY OTHER HALF'S FORESIGHT, I WOULD HAVE NEVER LET IT COME TO PASS.>"

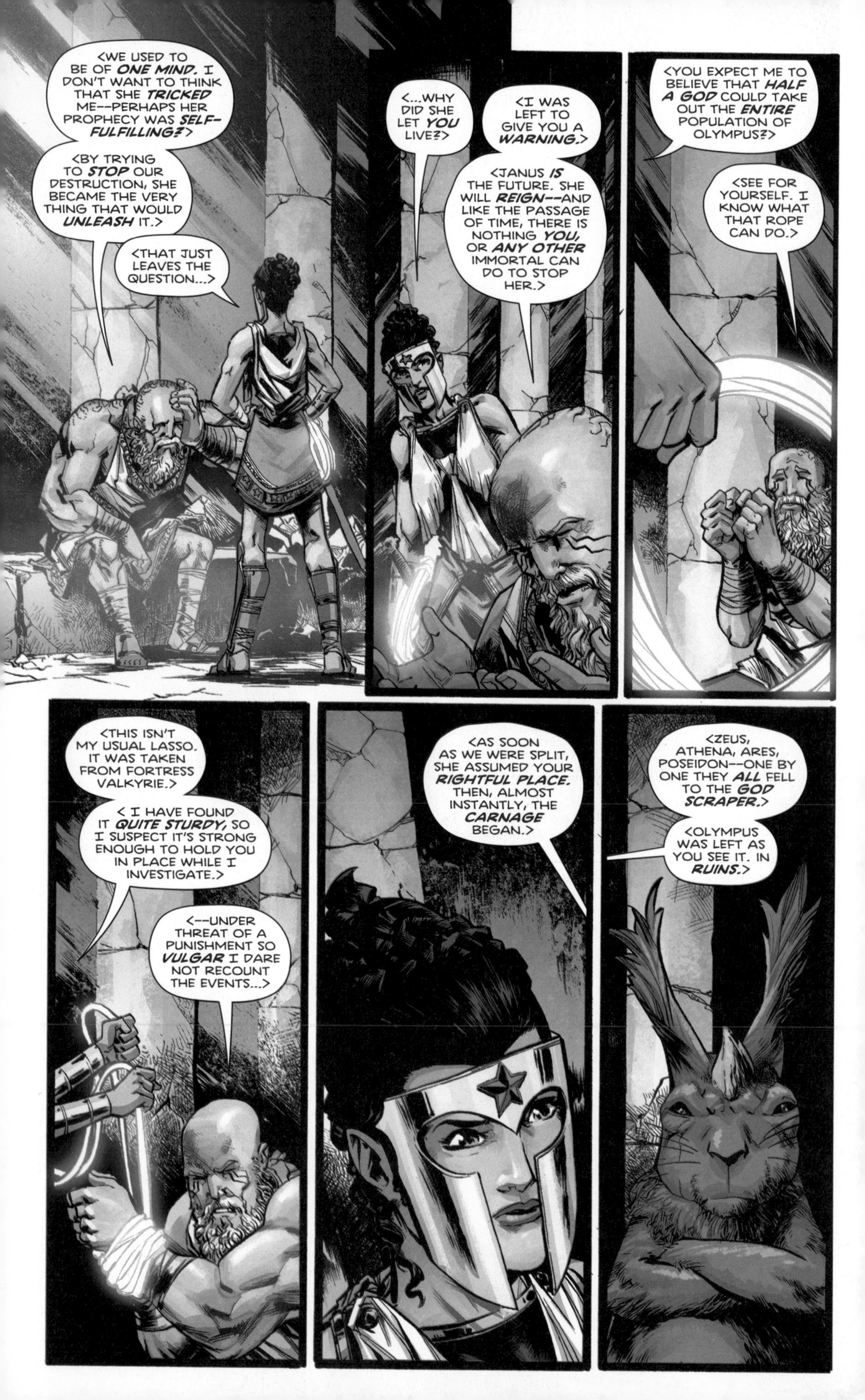
<WE USED TO BE OF ONE MIND. I DON'T WANT TO THINK THAT SHE TRICKED ME--PERHAPS HER PROPHECY WAS SELF-FULFILLING?>
<BY TRYING TO STOP OUR DESTRUCTION, SHE BECAME THE VERY THING THAT WOULD UNLEASH IT.>
<THAT JUST LEAVES THE QUESTION...>
<...WHY DID SHE LET YOU LIVE?>
<I WAS LEFT TO GIVE YOU A WARNING.>
<JANUS IS THE FUTURE. SHE WILL REIGN--AND LIKE THE PASSAGE OF TIME, THERE IS NOTHING YOU, OR ANY OTHER IMMORTAL CAN DO TO STOP HER.>
<YOU EXPECT ME TO BELIEVE THAT HALF A GOD COULD TAKE OUT THE ENTIRE POPULATION OF OLYMPUS?>
<SEE FOR YOURSELF. I KNOW WHAT THAT ROPE CAN DO.>
<THIS ISN'T MY USUAL LASSO. IT WAS TAKEN FROM FORTRESS VALKYRIE.>
< I HAVE FOUND IT QUITE STURDY, SO I SUSPECT IT'S STRONG ENOUGH TO HOLD YOU IN PLACE WHILE I INVESTIGATE.>
<--UNDER THREAT OF A PUNISHMENT SO VULGAR I DARE NOT RECOUNT THE EVENTS...>
<AS SOON AS WE WERE SPLIT, SHE ASSUMED YOUR RIGHTFUL PLACE. THEN, ALMOST INSTANTLY, THE CARNAGE BEGAN.>
<ZEUS, ATHENA, ARES, POSEIDON--ONE BY ONE THEY ALL FELL TO THE GOD SCRAPER.>
<OLYMPUS WAS LEFT AS YOU SEE IT. IN RUINS.>

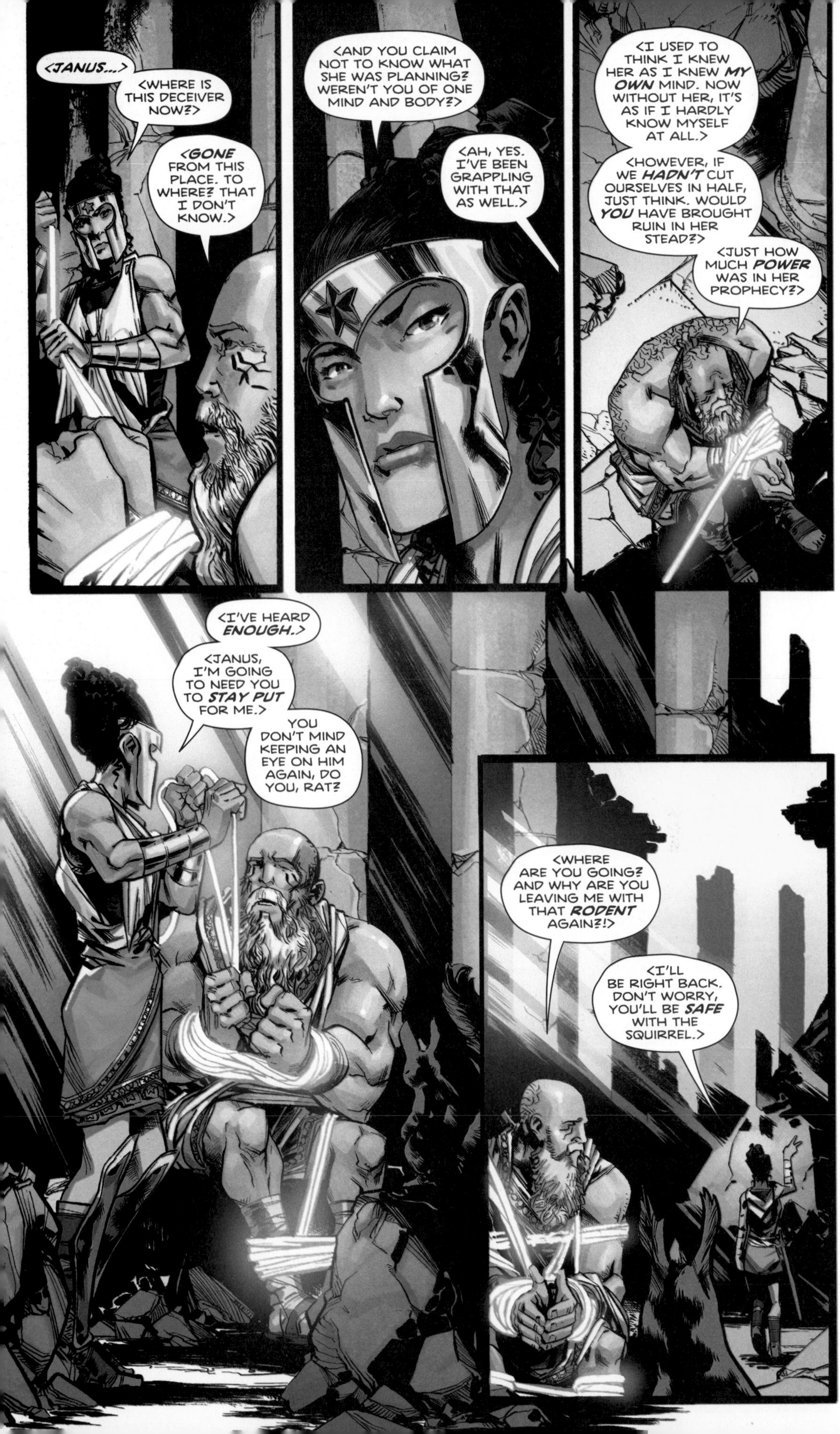
<JANUS...>
<WHERE IS THIS DECEIVER NOW?>
<GONE FROM THIS PLACE. TO WHERE? THAT I DON'T KNOW.>
<AND YOU CLAIM NOT TO KNOW WHAT SHE WAS PLANNING? WEREN'T YOU OF ONE MIND AND BODY?>
<AH, YES. I'VE BEEN GRAPPLING WITH THAT AS WELL.>
<I USED TO THINK I KNEW HER AS I KNEW MY OWN MIND. NOW WITHOUT HER, IT'S AS IF I HARDLY KNOW MYSELF AT ALL.>
<HOWEVER, IF WE HADN'T CUT OURSELVES IN HALF, JUST THINK. WOULD YOU HAVE BROUGHT RUIN IN HER STEAD?>
<JUST HOW MUCH POWER WAS IN HER PROPHECY?>
<I'VE HEARD ENOUGH.>
<JANUS, I'M GOING TO NEED YOU TO STAY PUT FOR ME.>
YOU DON'T MIND KEEPING AN EYE ON HIM AGAIN, DO YOU, RAT?
<WHERE ARE YOU GOING? AND WHY ARE YOU LEAVING ME WITH THAT RODENT AGAIN?!>
<I'LL BE RIGHT BACK. DON'T WORRY, YOU'LL BE SAFE WITH THE SQUIRREL.>

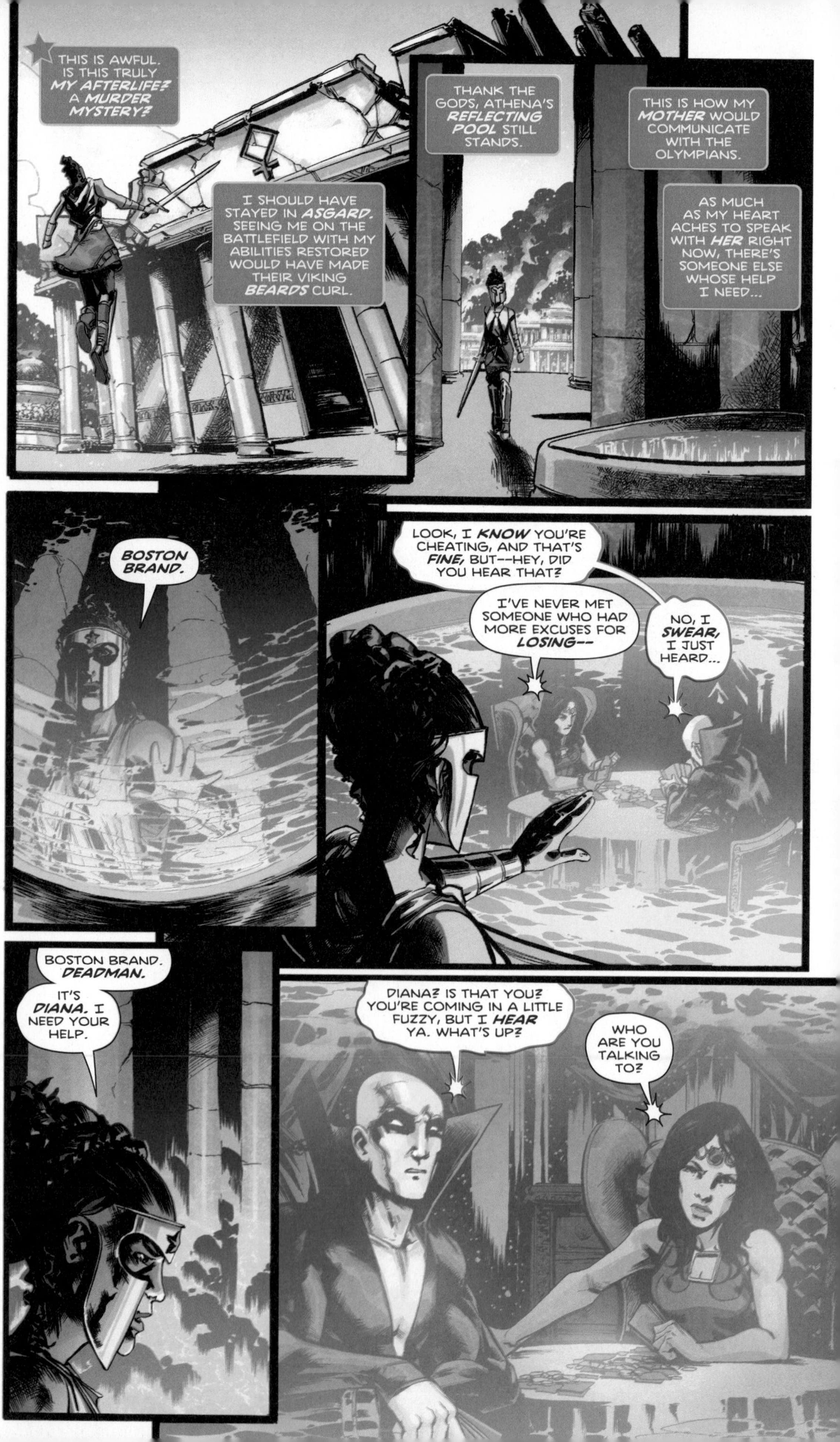

THIS IS AWFUL. IS THIS TRULY MY AFTERLIFE? A MURDER MYSTERY?
I SHOULD HAVE STAYED IN ASGARD. SEEING ME ON THE BATTLEFIELD WITH MY ABILITIES RESTORED WOULD HAVE MADE THEIR VIKING BEARDS CURL.
THANK THE GODS, ATHENA'S REFLECTING POOL STILL STANDS.
THIS IS HOW MY MOTHER WOULD COMMUNICATE WITH THE OLYMPIANS.
AS MUCH AS MY HEART ACHES TO SPEAK WITH HER RIGHT NOW, THERE'S SOMEONE ELSE WHOSE HELP I NEED...
BOSTON BRAND.
LOOK, I KNOW YOU'RE CHEATING, AND THAT'S FINE, BUT--HEY, DID YOU HEAR THAT?
I'VE NEVER MET SOMEONE WHO HAD MORE EXCUSES FOR LOSING--
NO, I SWEAR, I JUST HEARD...
BOSTON BRAND. DEADMAN.
IT'S DIANA. I NEED YOUR HELP.
DIANA? IS THAT YOU? YOU'RE COMING IN A LITTLE FUZZY, BUT I HEAR YA. WHAT'S UP?
WHO ARE YOU TALKING TO?

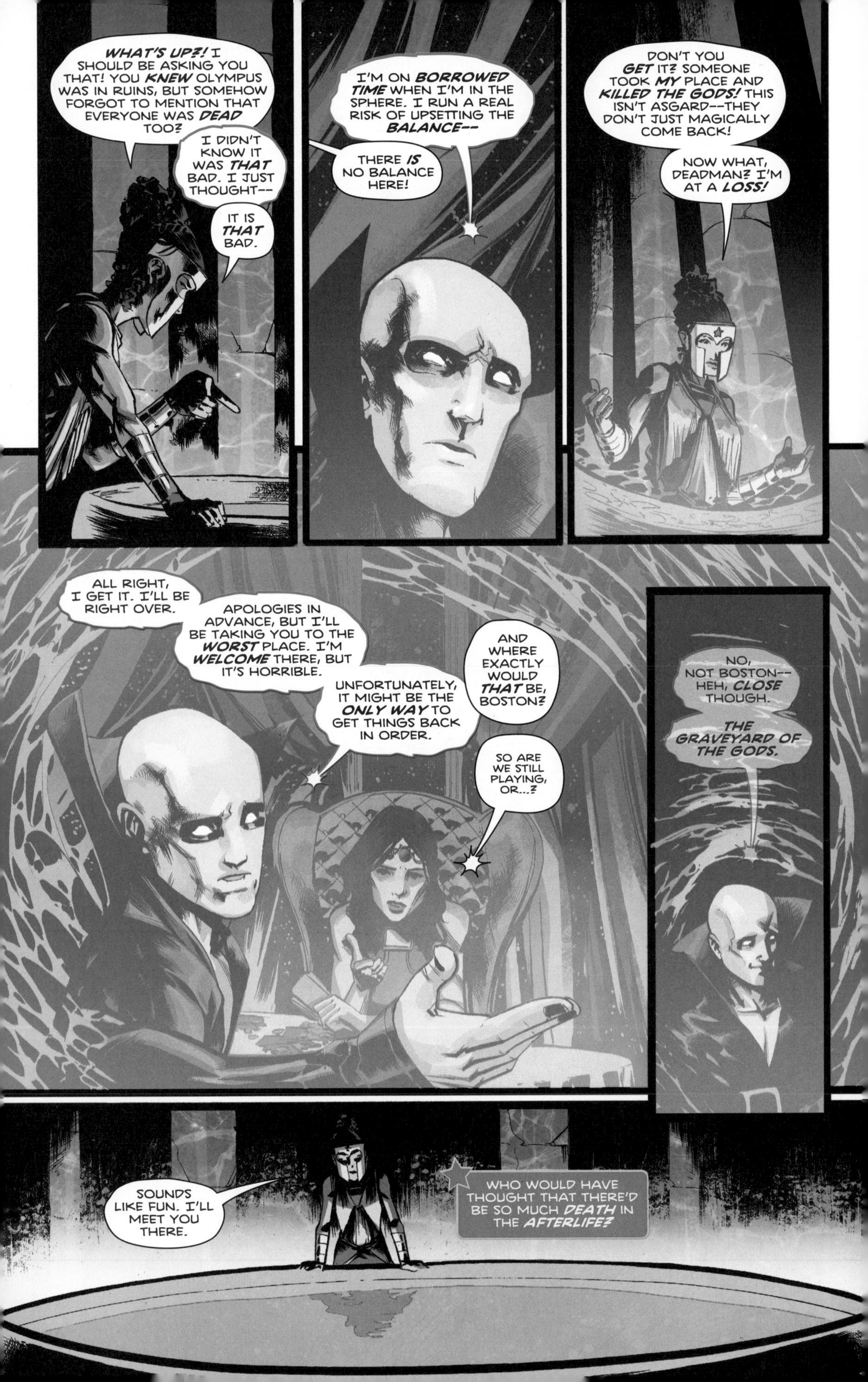
WHAT'S UP?! I SHOULD BE ASKING YOU THAT! YOU KNEW OLYMPUS WAS IN RUINS, BUT SOMEHOW FORGOT TO MENTION THAT EVERYONE WAS DEAD TOO?
I DIDN'T KNOW IT WAS THAT BAD. I JUST THOUGHT--
IT IS THAT BAD.
I'M ON BORROWED TIME WHEN I'M IN THE SPHERE. I RUN A REAL RISK OF UPSETTING THE BALANCE--
THERE IS NO BALANCE HERE!
DON'T YOU GET IT? SOMEONE TOOK MY PLACE AND KILLED THE GODS! THIS ISN'T ASGARD--THEY DON'T JUST MAGICALLY COME BACK!
NOW WHAT, DEADMAN? I'M AT A LOSS!
ALL RIGHT, I GET IT. I'LL BE RIGHT OVER.
APOLOGIES IN ADVANCE, BUT I'LL BE TAKING YOU TO THE WORST PLACE. I'M WELCOME THERE, BUT IT'S HORRIBLE.
UNFORTUNATELY, IT MIGHT BE THE ONLY WAY TO GET THINGS BACK IN ORDER.
AND WHERE EXACTLY WOULD THAT BE, BOSTON?
SO ARE WE STILL PLAYING, OR...?
NO, NOT BOSTON-- HEH, CLOSE THOUGH.
THE GRAVEYARD OF THE GODS.
SOUNDS LIKE FUN. I'LL MEET YOU THERE.
WHO WOULD HAVE THOUGHT THAT THERE'D BE SO MUCH DEATH IN THE AFTERLIFE?

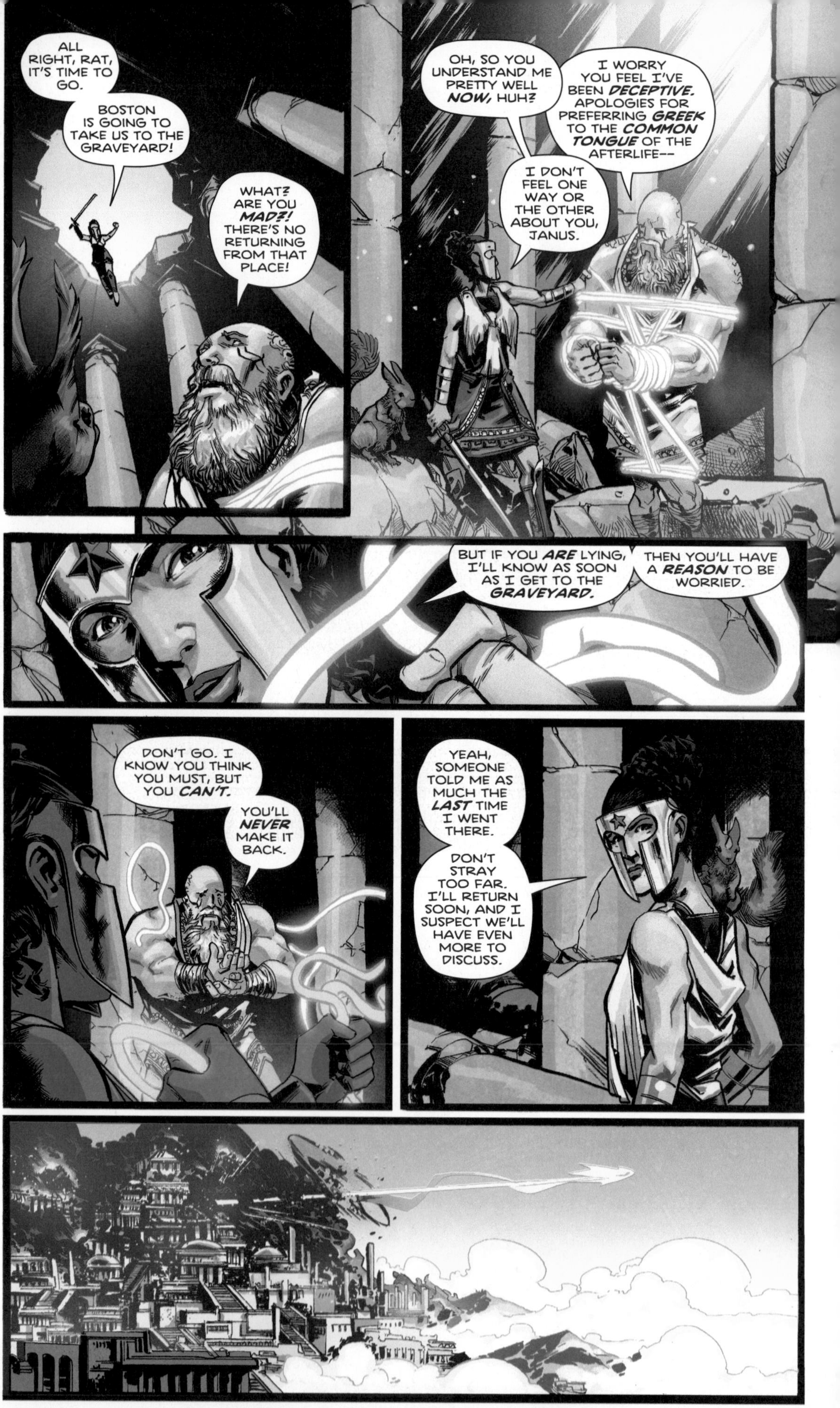
ALL RIGHT, RAT, IT'S TIME TO GO.
BOSTON IS GOING TO TAKE US TO THE GRAVEYARD!
WHAT? ARE YOU MAD?! THERE'S NO RETURNING FROM THAT PLACE!
OH, SO YOU UNDERSTAND ME PRETTY WELL NOW, HUH?
I WORRY YOU FEEL I'VE BEEN DECEPTIVE. APOLOGIES FOR PREFERRING GREEK TO THE COMMON TONGUE OF THE AFTERLIFE--
I DON'T FEEL ONE WAY OR THE OTHER ABOUT YOU, JANUS.
BUT IF YOU ARE LYING, I'LL KNOW AS SOON AS I GET TO THE GRAVEYARD.
THEN YOU'LL HAVE A REASON TO BE WORRIED.
DON'T GO. I KNOW YOU THINK YOU MUST, BUT YOU CAN'T.
YOU'LL NEVER MAKE IT BACK.
YEAH, SOMEONE TOLD ME AS MUCH THE LAST TIME I WENT THERE.
DON'T STRAY TOO FAR. I'LL RETURN SOON, AND I SUSPECT WE'LL HAVE EVEN MORE TO DISCUSS.

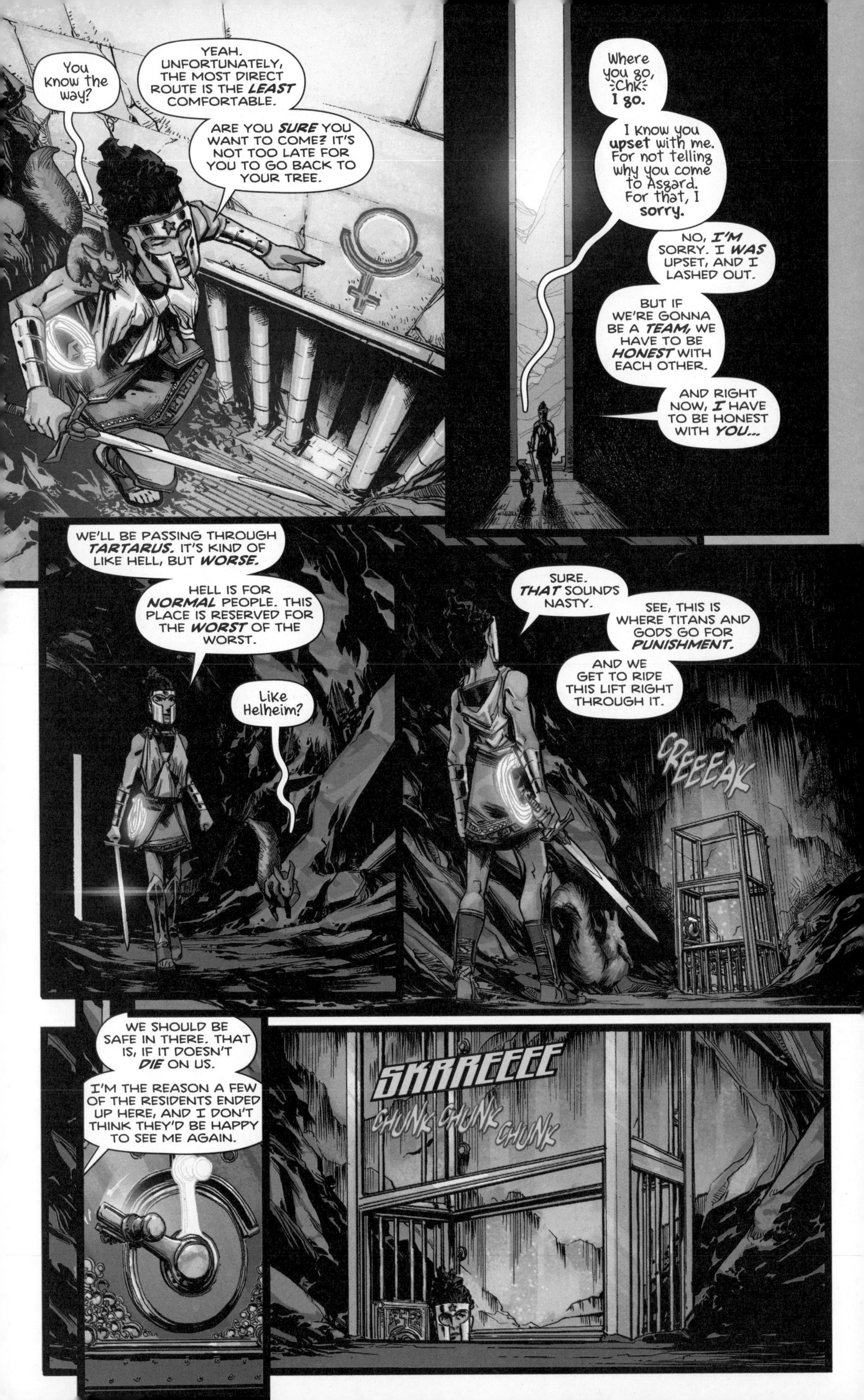
You know the way?
YEAH. UNFORTUNATELY, THE MOST DIRECT ROUTE IS THE LEAST COMFORTABLE.
ARE YOU SURE YOU WANT TO COME? IT'S NOT TOO LATE FOR YOU TO GO BACK TO YOUR TREE.
Where you go, Chk I go.
I know you upset with me. For not telling why you come to Asgard. For that, I sorry.
NO, I'M SORRY. I WAS UPSET, AND I LASHED OUT.
BUT IF WE'RE GONNA BE A TEAM, WE HAVE TO BE HONEST WITH EACH OTHER.
AND RIGHT NOW, I HAVE TO BE HONEST WITH YOU...
WE'LL BE PASSING THROUGH TARTARUS. IT'S KIND OF LIKE HELL, BUT WORSE.
HELL IS FOR NORMAL PEOPLE. THIS PLACE IS RESERVED FOR THE WORST OF THE WORST.
Like Helheim?
SURE. THAT SOUNDS NASTY.
SEE, THIS IS WHERE TITANS AND GODS GO FOR PUNISHMENT.
AND WE GET TO RIDE THIS LIFT RIGHT THROUGH IT.
CREEEAK
WE SHOULD BE SAFE IN THERE. THAT IS, IF IT DOESN'T DIE ON US.
I'M THE REASON A FEW OF THE RESIDENTS ENDED UP HERE, AND I DON'T THINK THEY'D BE HAPPY TO SEE ME AGAIN.
SKRREEEE
CHUNK CHUNK CHUNK

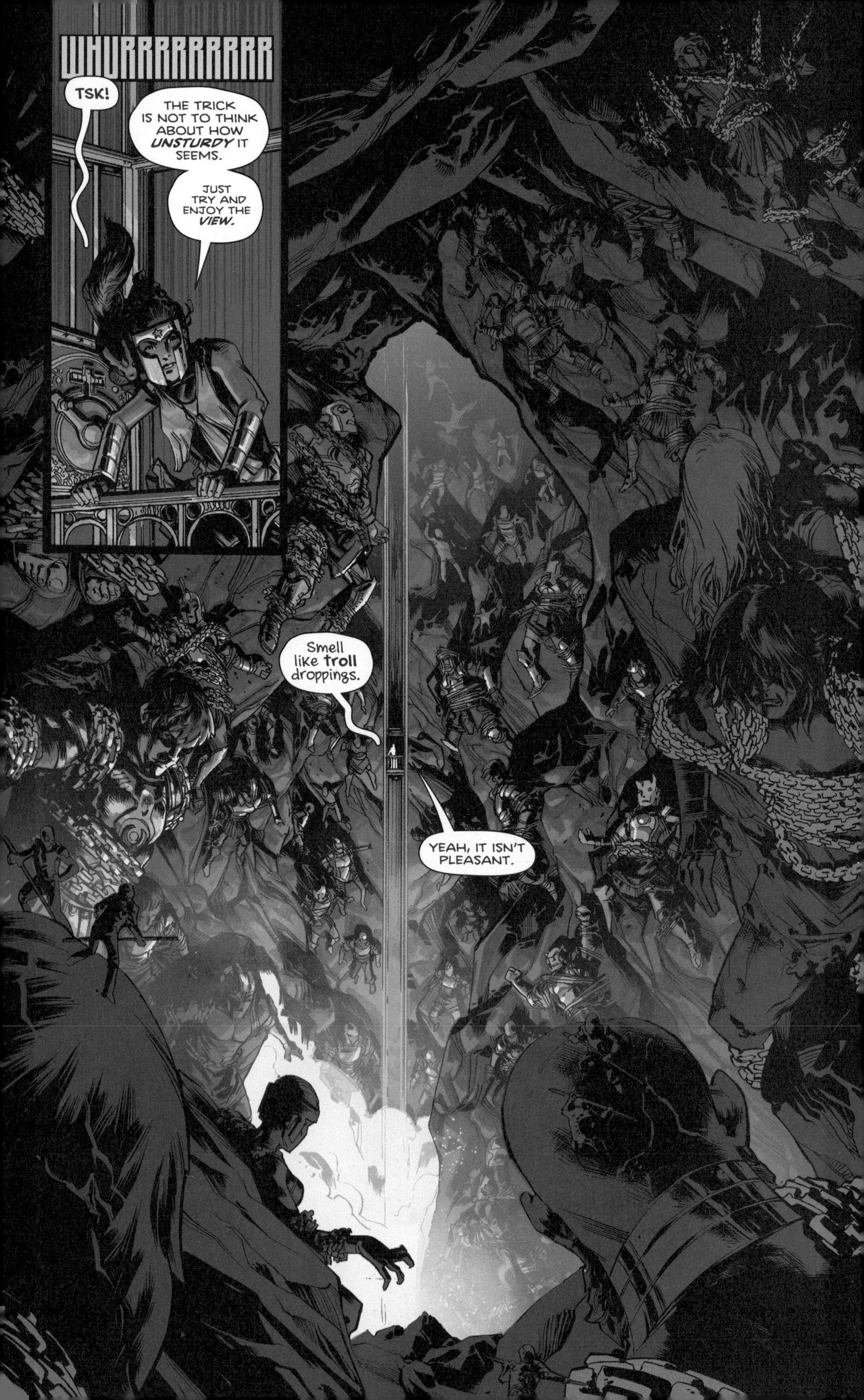
WHURRRRRRRRR
TSK!
THE TRICK IS NOT TO THINK ABOUT HOW *UNSTURDY* IT SEEMS.
JUST TRY AND ENJOY THE *VIEW.*
Smell like **troll** droppings.
YEAH, IT ISN'T PLEASANT.

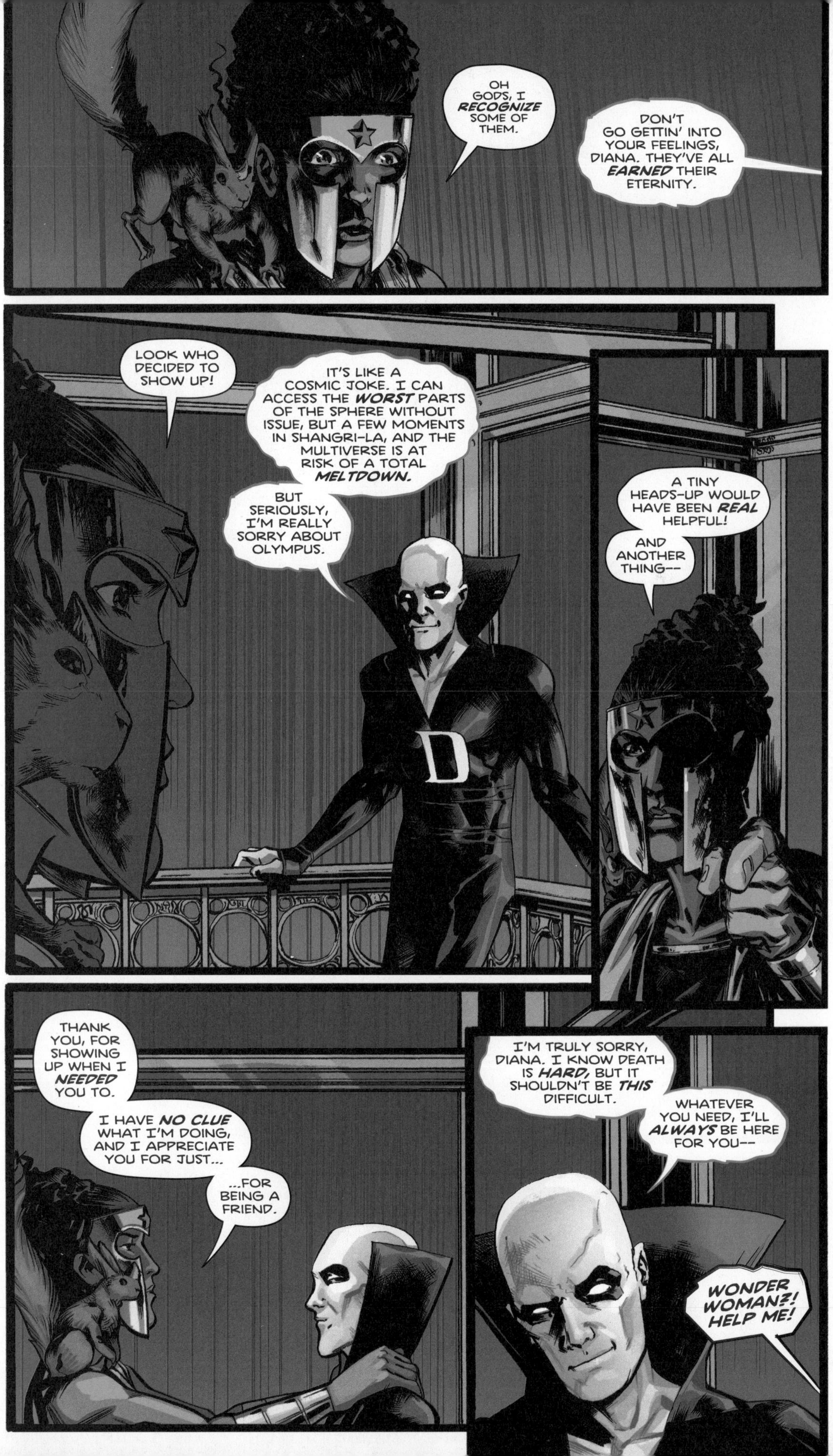
OH GODS, I RECOGNIZE SOME OF THEM.
DON'T GO GETTIN' INTO YOUR FEELINGS, DIANA. THEY'VE ALL EARNED THEIR ETERNITY.
LOOK WHO DECIDED TO SHOW UP!
IT'S LIKE A COSMIC JOKE. I CAN ACCESS THE WORST PARTS OF THE SPHERE WITHOUT ISSUE, BUT A FEW MOMENTS IN SHANGRI-LA, AND THE MULTIVERSE IS AT RISK OF A TOTAL MELTDOWN.
BUT SERIOUSLY, I'M REALLY SORRY ABOUT OLYMPUS.
A TINY HEADS-UP WOULD HAVE BEEN REAL HELPFUL!
AND ANOTHER THING--
THANK YOU, FOR SHOWING UP WHEN I NEEDED YOU TO.
I HAVE NO CLUE WHAT I'M DOING, AND I APPRECIATE YOU FOR JUST...
...FOR BEING A FRIEND.
I'M TRULY SORRY, DIANA. I KNOW DEATH IS HARD, BUT IT SHOULDN'T BE THIS DIFFICULT.
WHATEVER YOU NEED, I'LL ALWAYS BE HERE FOR YOU--
WONDER WOMAN?! HELP ME!

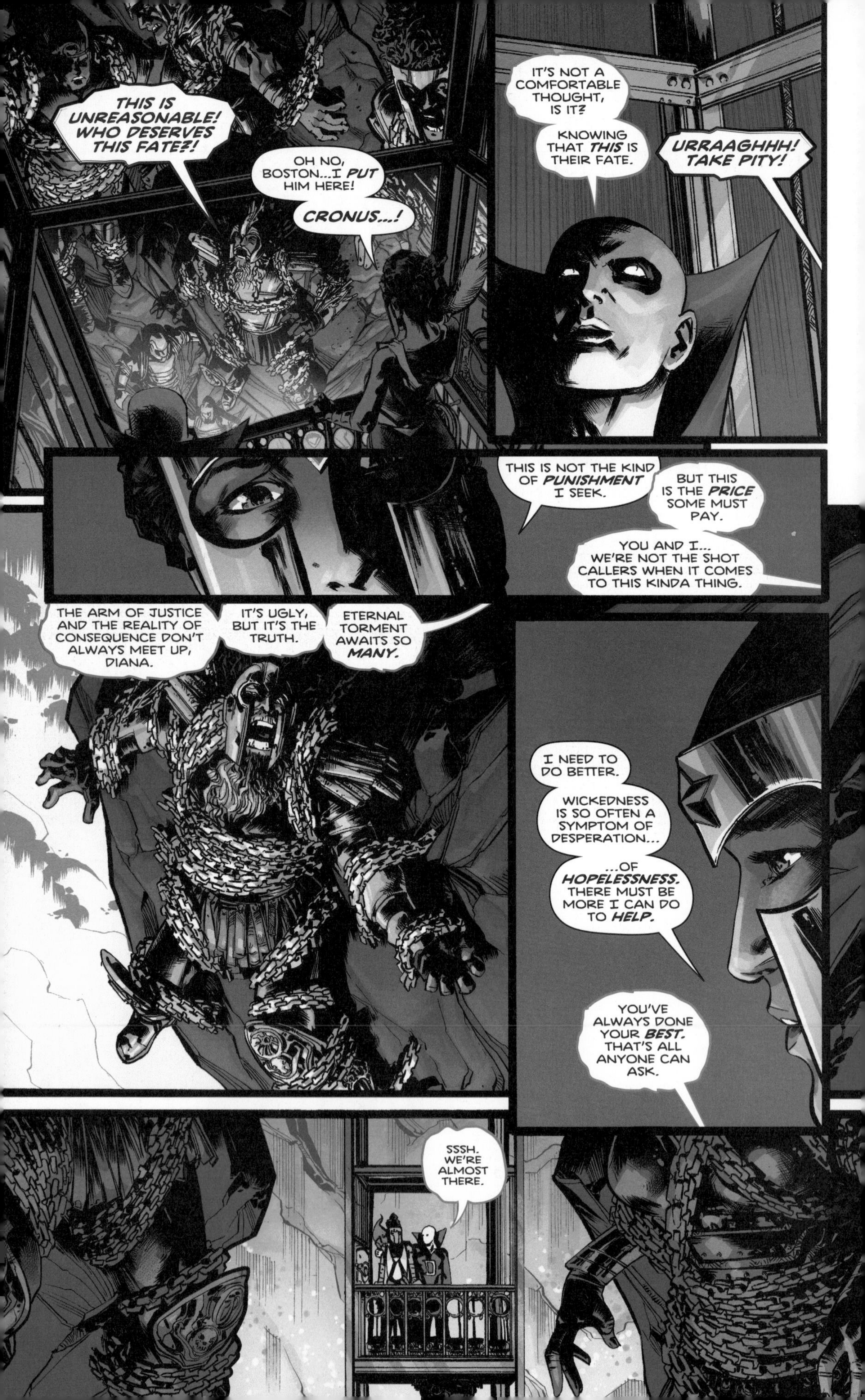
THIS IS UNREASONABLE! WHO DESERVES THIS FATE?!
OH NO, BOSTON...I *PUT* HIM HERE!
CRONUS...!
IT'S NOT A COMFORTABLE THOUGHT, IS IT?
KNOWING THAT *THIS* IS THEIR FATE.
URRAAGHHH! TAKE PITY!
THIS IS NOT THE KIND OF *PUNISHMENT* I SEEK.
BUT THIS IS THE *PRICE* SOME MUST PAY.
YOU AND I... WE'RE NOT THE SHOT CALLERS WHEN IT COMES TO THIS KINDA THING.
THE ARM OF JUSTICE AND THE REALITY OF CONSEQUENCE DON'T ALWAYS MEET UP, DIANA.
IT'S UGLY, BUT IT'S THE TRUTH.
ETERNAL TORMENT AWAITS SO *MANY.*
I NEED TO DO BETTER.
WICKEDNESS IS SO OFTEN A SYMPTOM OF DESPERATION...
...OF *HOPELESSNESS.* THERE MUST BE MORE I CAN DO TO *HELP.*
YOU'VE ALWAYS DONE YOUR *BEST.* THAT'S ALL ANYONE CAN ASK.
SSSH. WE'RE ALMOST THERE.

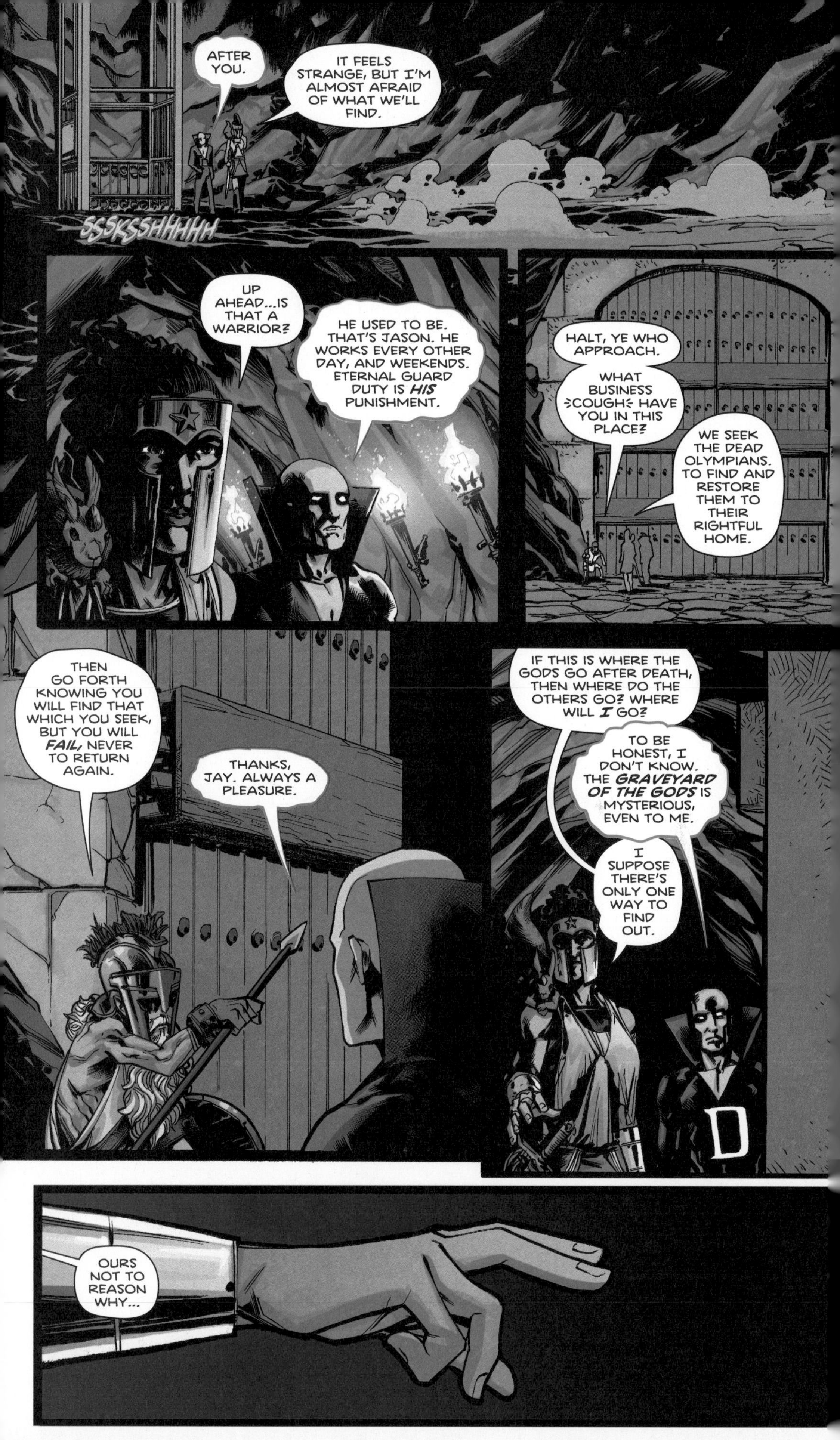
AFTER YOU.
IT FEELS STRANGE, BUT I'M ALMOST AFRAID OF WHAT WE'LL FIND.
SSSKSSHHHHH
UP AHEAD...IS THAT A WARRIOR?
HE USED TO BE. THAT'S JASON. HE WORKS EVERY OTHER DAY, AND WEEKENDS. ETERNAL GUARD DUTY IS HIS PUNISHMENT.
HALT, YE WHO APPROACH.
WHAT BUSINESS *COUGH* HAVE YOU IN THIS PLACE?
WE SEEK THE DEAD OLYMPIANS. TO FIND AND RESTORE THEM TO THEIR RIGHTFUL HOME.
THEN GO FORTH KNOWING YOU WILL FIND THAT WHICH YOU SEEK, BUT YOU WILL FAIL, NEVER TO RETURN AGAIN.
THANKS, JAY. ALWAYS A PLEASURE.
IF THIS IS WHERE THE GODS GO AFTER DEATH, THEN WHERE DO THE OTHERS GO? WHERE WILL I GO?
TO BE HONEST, I DON'T KNOW. THE GRAVEYARD OF THE GODS IS MYSTERIOUS, EVEN TO ME.
I SUPPOSE THERE'S ONLY ONE WAY TO FIND OUT.
OURS NOT TO REASON WHY...

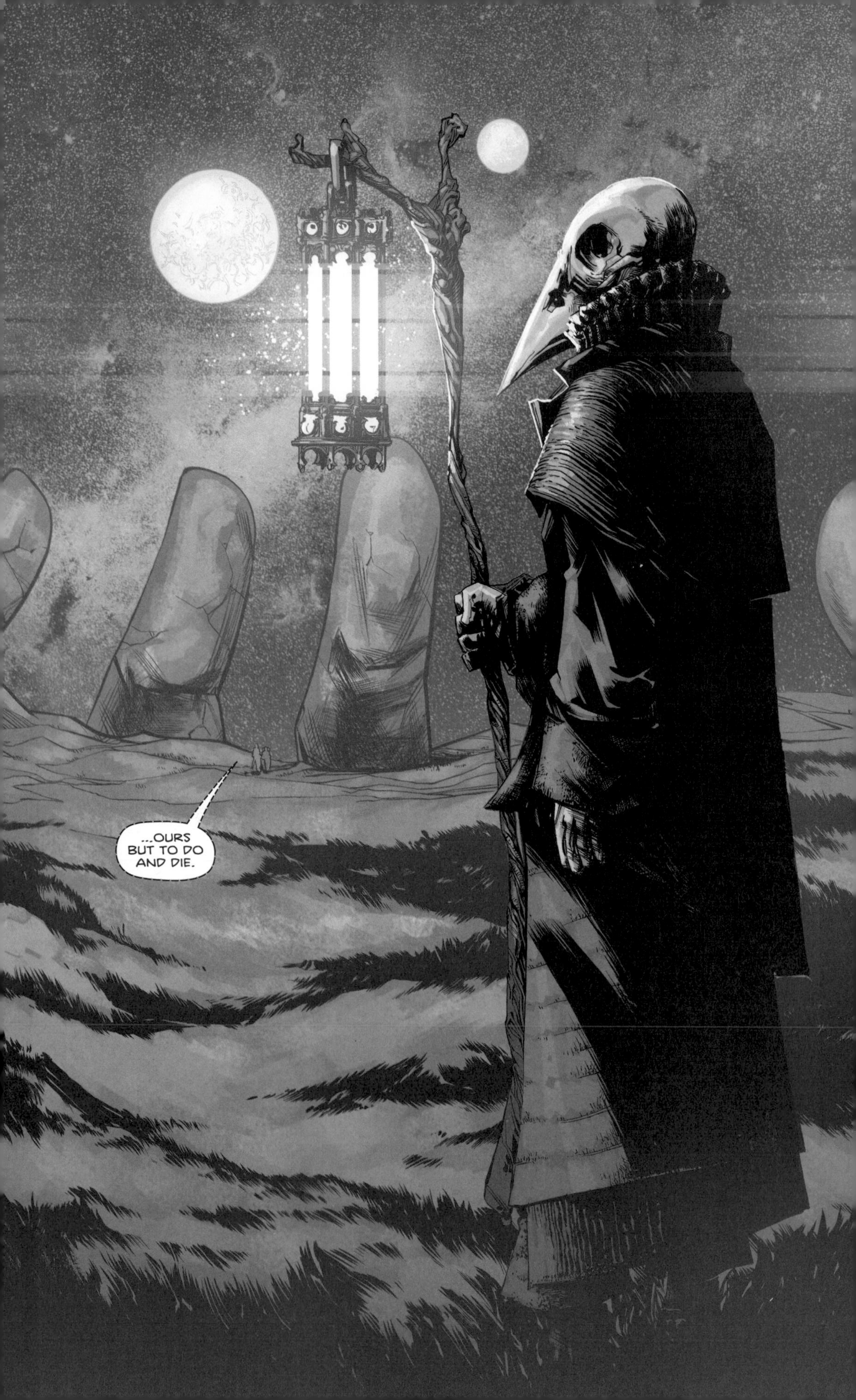
...OURS BUT TO DO AND DIE.

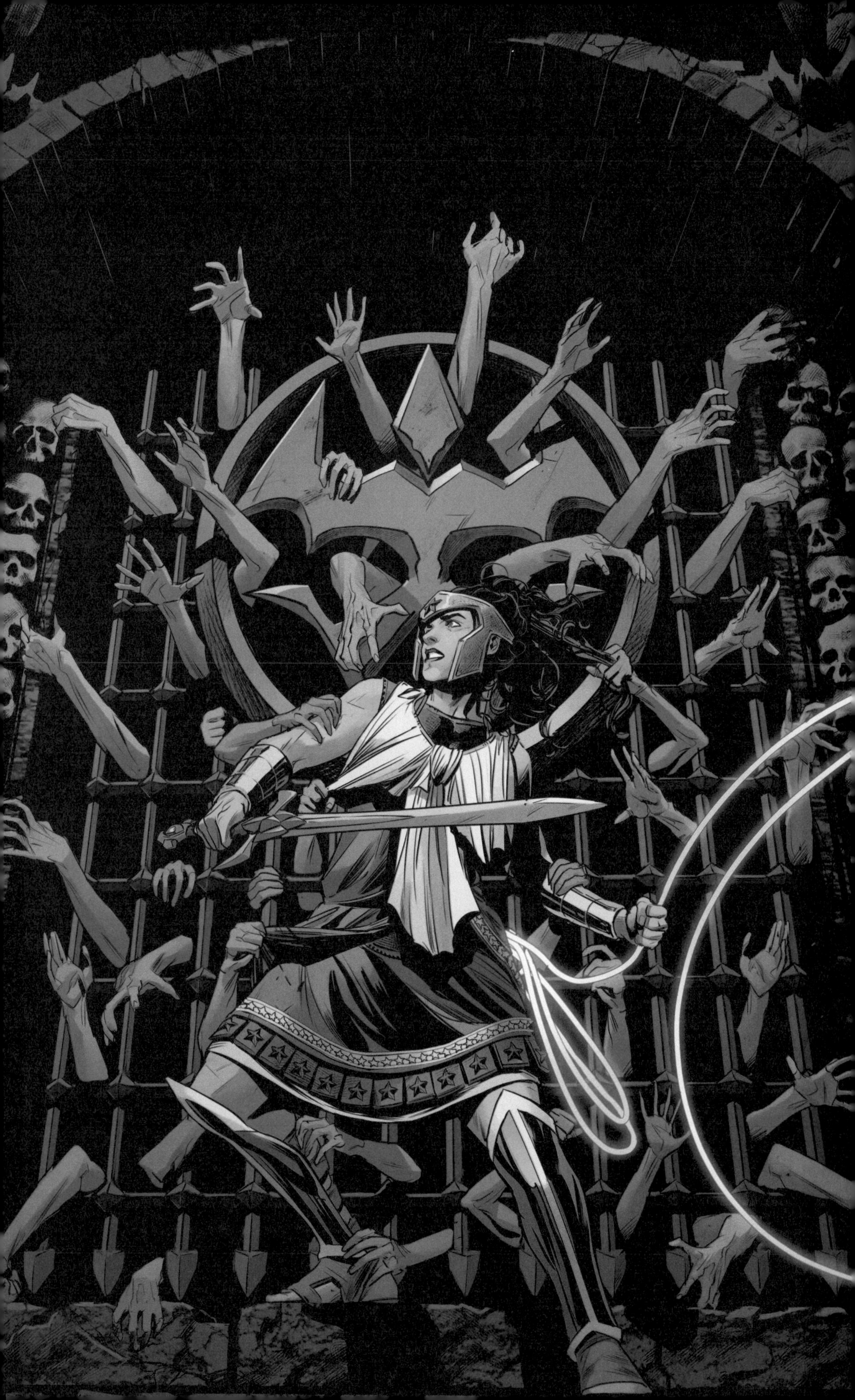

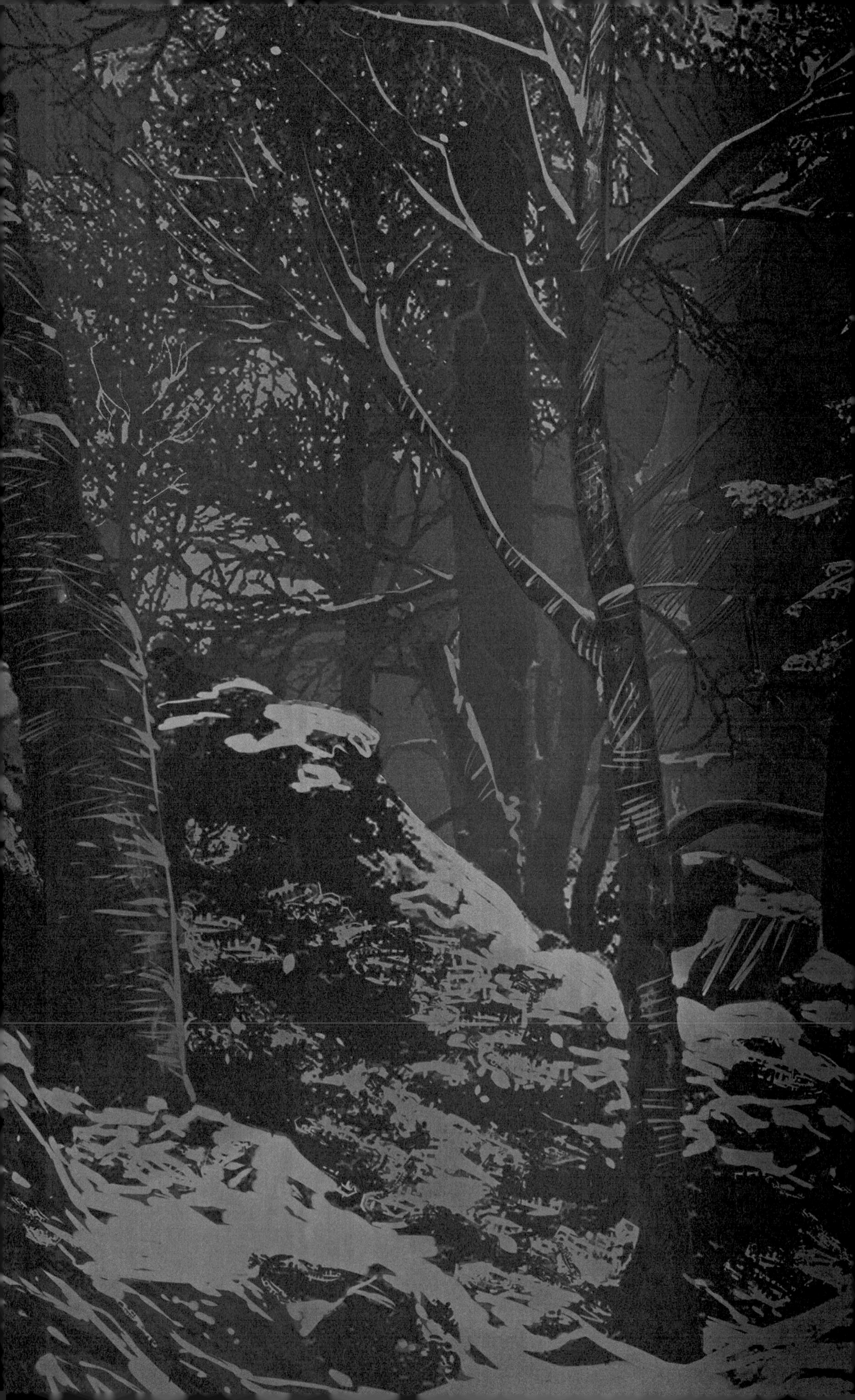

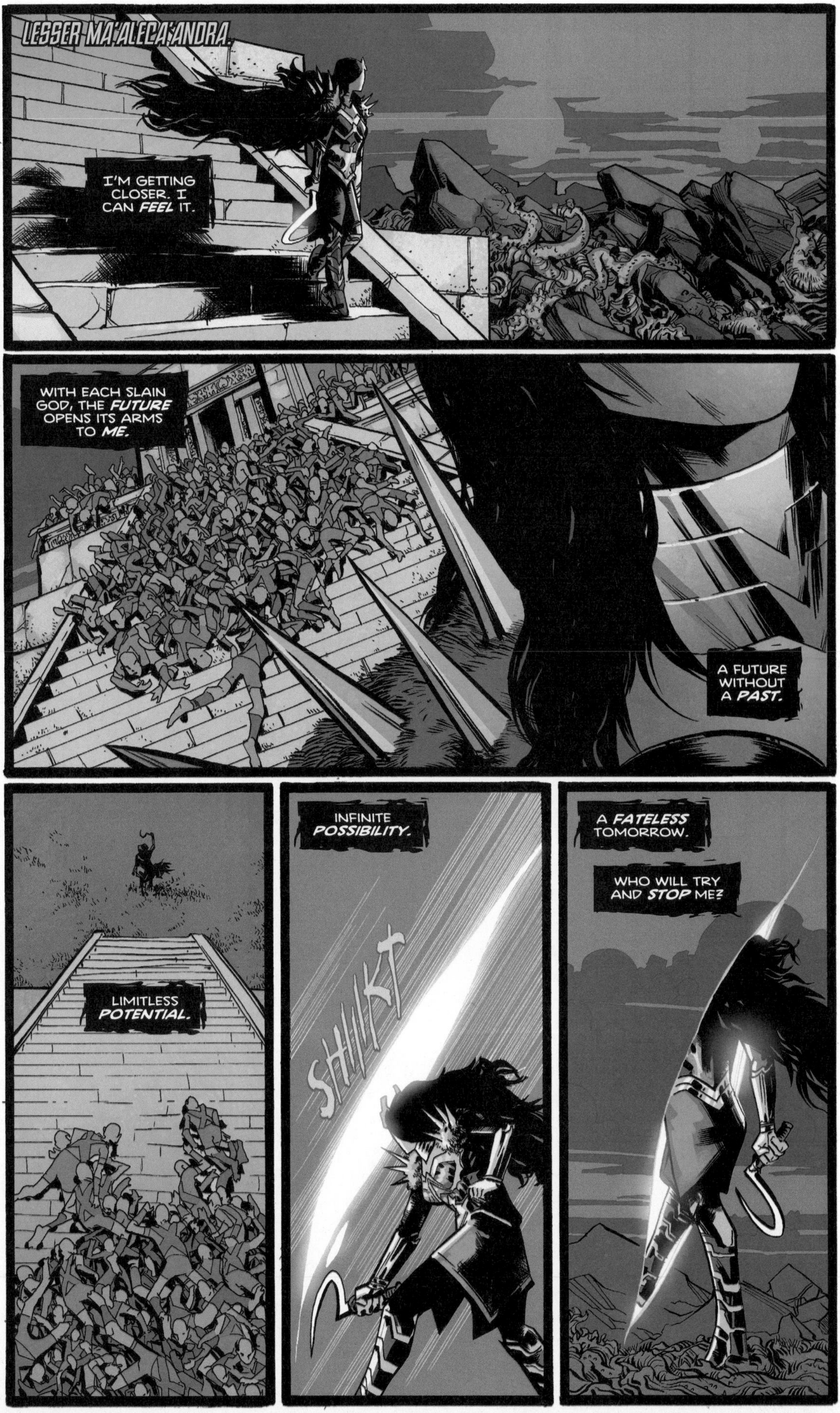
LESSER MA'ALECA'ANDRA.
I'M GETTING CLOSER. I CAN FEEL IT.
WITH EACH SLAIN GOD, THE FUTURE OPENS ITS ARMS TO ME.
A FUTURE WITHOUT A PAST.
LIMITLESS POTENTIAL.
INFINITE POSSIBILITY.
SHIIKT
A FATELESS TOMORROW.
WHO WILL TRY AND STOP ME?

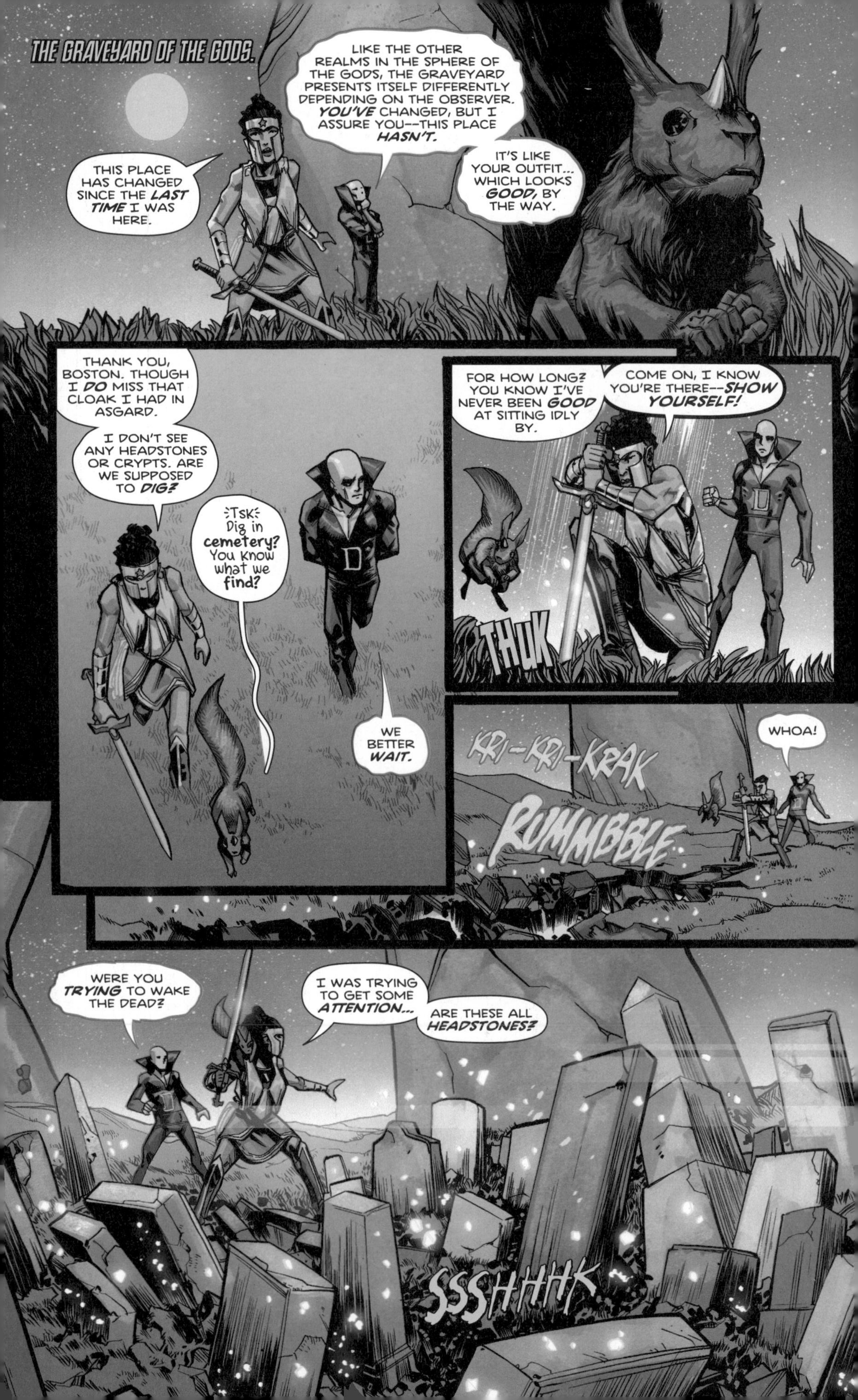
THE GRAVEYARD OF THE GODS.
THIS PLACE HAS CHANGED SINCE THE LAST TIME I WAS HERE.
LIKE THE OTHER REALMS IN THE SPHERE OF THE GODS, THE GRAVEYARD PRESENTS ITSELF DIFFERENTLY DEPENDING ON THE OBSERVER. YOU'VE CHANGED, BUT I ASSURE YOU--THIS PLACE HASN'T.
IT'S LIKE YOUR OUTFIT... WHICH LOOKS GOOD, BY THE WAY.
THANK YOU, BOSTON. THOUGH I DO MISS THAT CLOAK I HAD IN ASGARD.
I DON'T SEE ANY HEADSTONES OR CRYPTS. ARE WE SUPPOSED TO DIG?
Tsk Dig in cemetery? You know what we find?
WE BETTER WAIT.
FOR HOW LONG? YOU KNOW I'VE NEVER BEEN GOOD AT SITTING IDLY BY.
COME ON, I KNOW YOU'RE THERE--SHOW YOURSELF!
THUK
KRI-KRI-KRAK
RUMMBBLE
WHOA!
WERE YOU TRYING TO WAKE THE DEAD?
I WAS TRYING TO GET SOME ATTENTION...
ARE THESE ALL HEADSTONES?
SSSHHHK

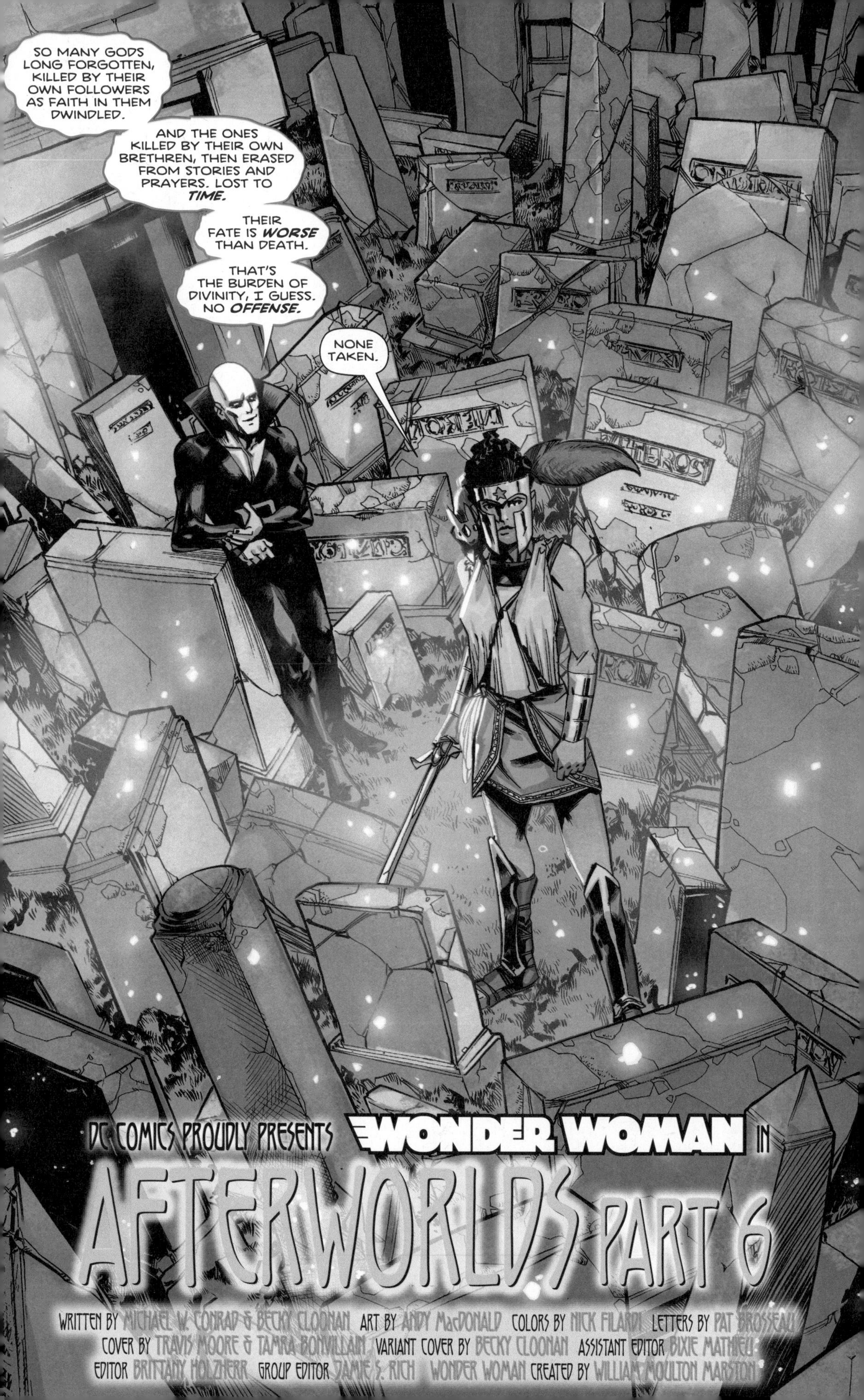

SO MANY GODS LONG FORGOTTEN, KILLED BY THEIR OWN FOLLOWERS AS FAITH IN THEM DWINDLED.
AND THE ONES KILLED BY THEIR OWN BRETHREN, THEN ERASED FROM STORIES AND PRAYERS. LOST TO *TIME.*
THEIR FATE IS *WORSE* THAN DEATH.
THAT'S THE BURDEN OF DIVINITY, I GUESS. NO *OFFENSE.*
NONE TAKEN.
DC COMICS PROUDLY PRESENTS WONDER WOMAN IN
AFTERWORLDS PART 6
WRITTEN BY MICHAEL W. CONRAD & BECKY CLOONAN ART BY ANDY MacDONALD COLORS BY NICK FILARDI LETTERS BY PAT BROSSEAU
COVER BY TRAVIS MOORE & TAMRA BONVILLAIN VARIANT COVER BY BECKY CLOONAN ASSISTANT EDITOR BIXIE MATHIEU
EDITOR BRITTANY HOLZHERR GROUP EDITOR JAMIE S. RICH WONDER WOMAN CREATED BY WILLIAM MOULTON MARSTON

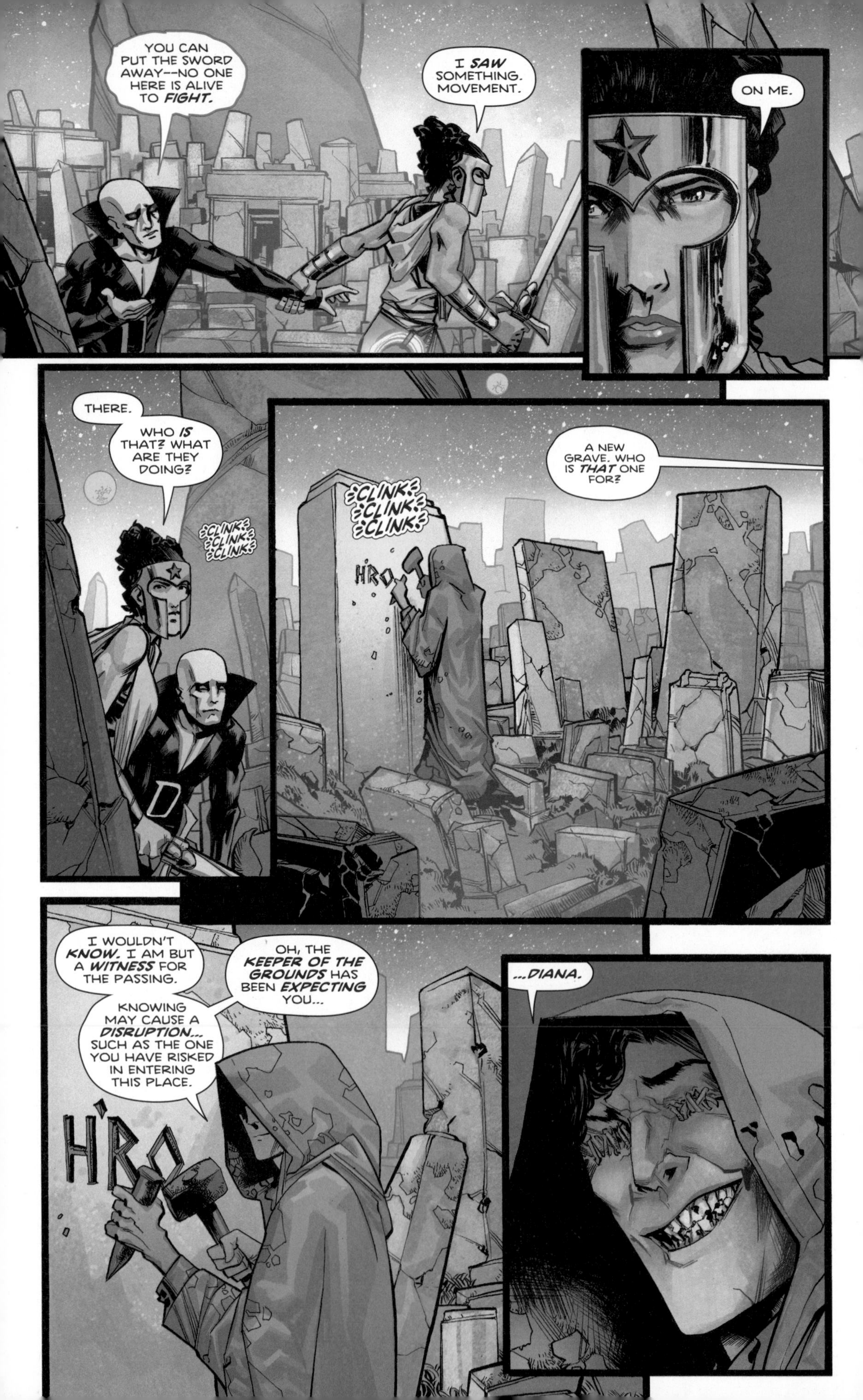

YOU CAN PUT THE SWORD AWAY--NO ONE HERE IS ALIVE TO FIGHT.
I SAW SOMETHING. MOVEMENT.
ON ME.
THERE.
WHO IS THAT? WHAT ARE THEY DOING?
CLINK CLINK CLINK
A NEW GRAVE. WHO IS THAT ONE FOR?
CLINK CLINK CLINK
H'RO
I WOULDN'T KNOW. I AM BUT A WITNESS FOR THE PASSING.
KNOWING MAY CAUSE A DISRUPTION... SUCH AS THE ONE YOU HAVE RISKED IN ENTERING THIS PLACE.
OH, THE KEEPER OF THE GROUNDS HAS BEEN EXPECTING YOU...
...DIANA.
H'RO

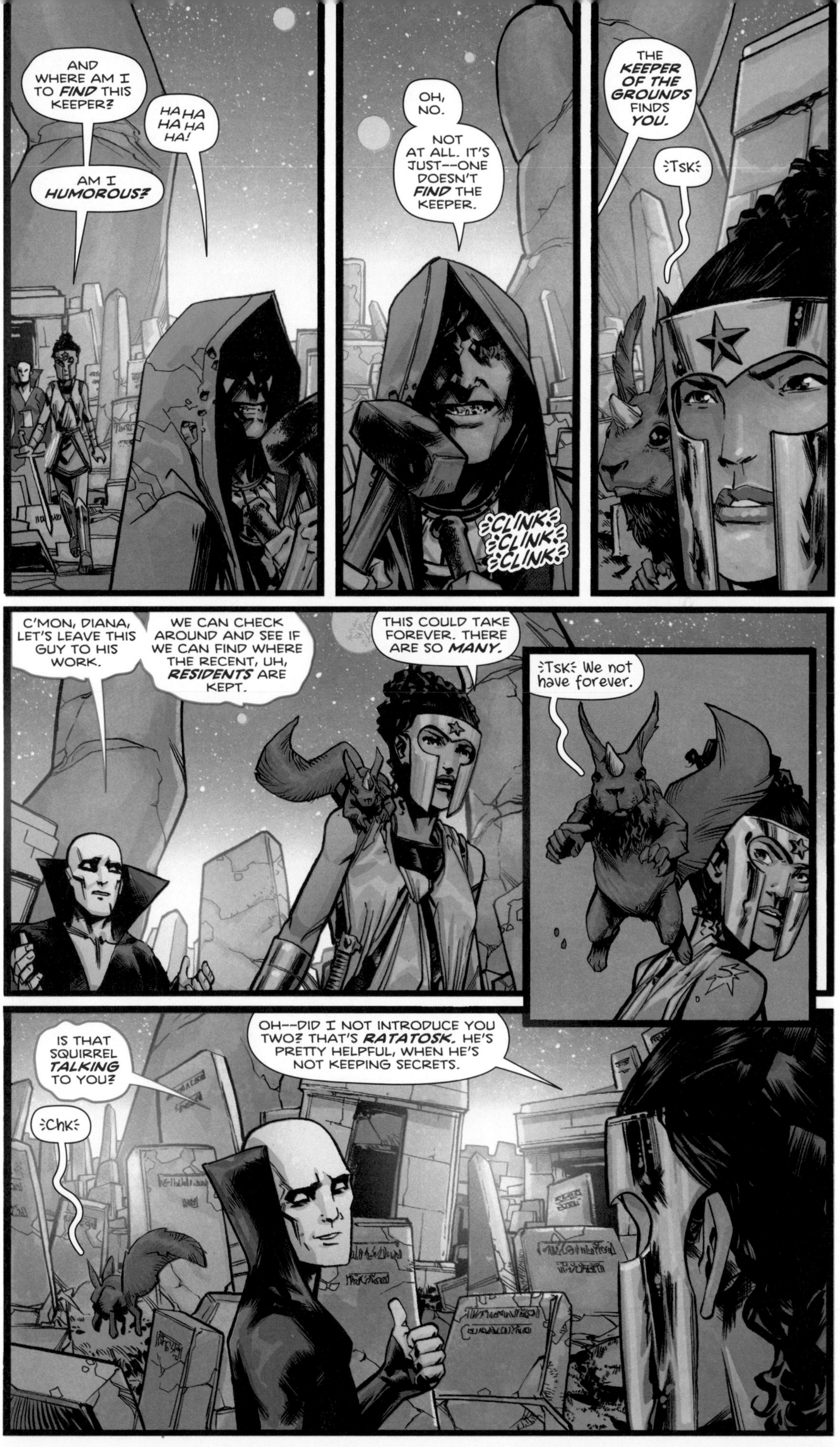
AND WHERE AM I TO FIND THIS KEEPER?
HA HA HA HA HA!
AM I HUMOROUS?
OH, NO.
NOT AT ALL. IT'S JUST--ONE DOESN'T FIND THE KEEPER.
CLINK CLINK CLINK
THE KEEPER OF THE GROUNDS FINDS YOU.
Tsk
C'MON, DIANA, LET'S LEAVE THIS GUY TO HIS WORK.
WE CAN CHECK AROUND AND SEE IF WE CAN FIND WHERE THE RECENT, UH, RESIDENTS ARE KEPT.
THIS COULD TAKE FOREVER. THERE ARE SO MANY.
Tsk We not have forever.
IS THAT SQUIRREL TALKING TO YOU?
OH--DID I NOT INTRODUCE YOU TWO? THAT'S RATATOSK. HE'S PRETTY HELPFUL, WHEN HE'S NOT KEEPING SECRETS.
Chk

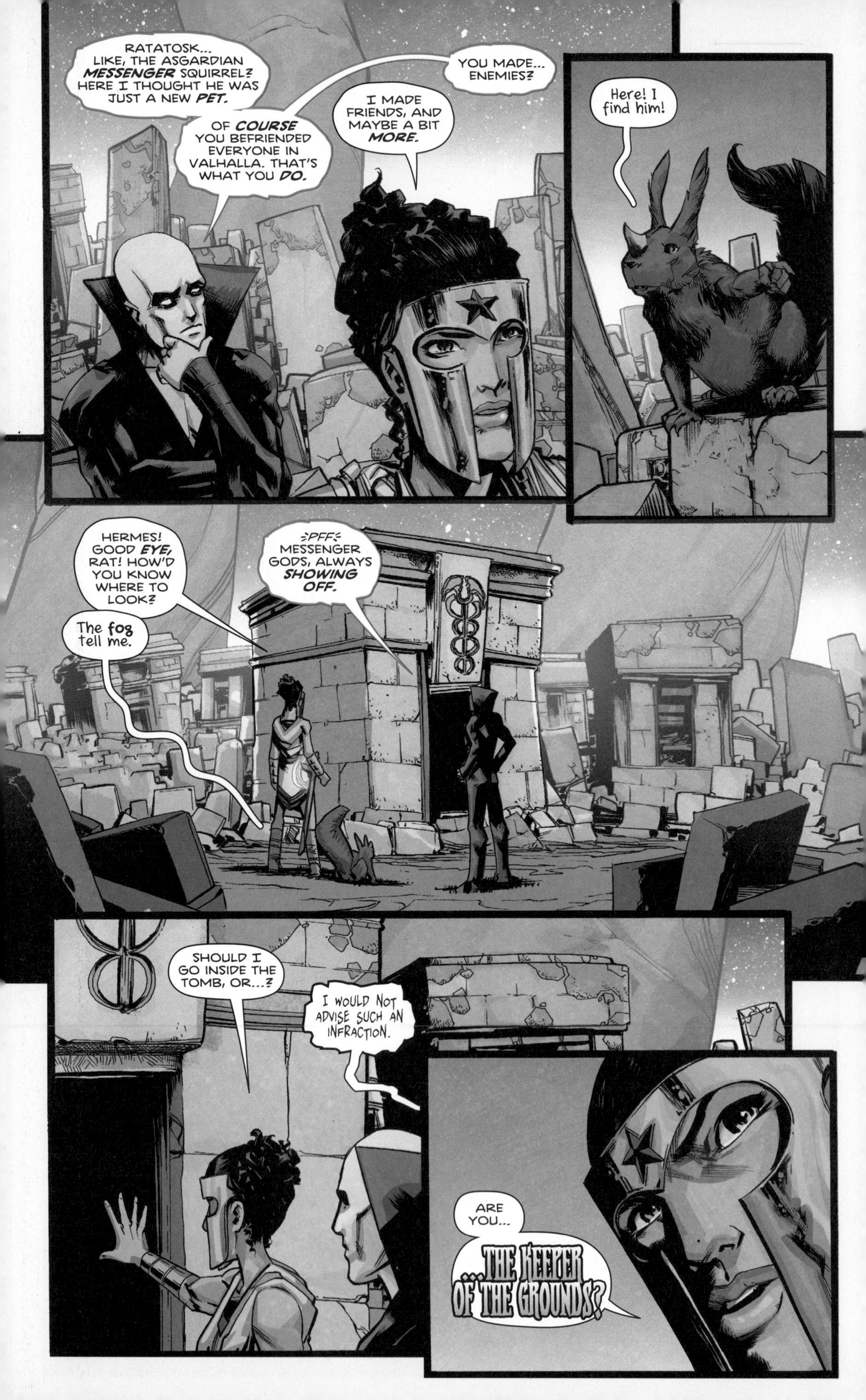
RATATOSK... LIKE, THE ASGARDIAN MESSENGER SQUIRREL? HERE I THOUGHT HE WAS JUST A NEW PET.
YOU MADE... ENEMIES?
OF COURSE YOU BEFRIENDED EVERYONE IN VALHALLA. THAT'S WHAT YOU DO.
I MADE FRIENDS, AND MAYBE A BIT MORE.
Here! I find him!
HERMES! GOOD EYE, RAT! HOW'D YOU KNOW WHERE TO LOOK?
The fog tell me.
PFF MESSENGER GODS, ALWAYS SHOWING OFF.
SHOULD I GO INSIDE THE TOMB, OR...?
I WOULD NOT ADVISE SUCH AN INFRACTION.
ARE YOU...
...THE KEEPER OF THE GROUNDS?

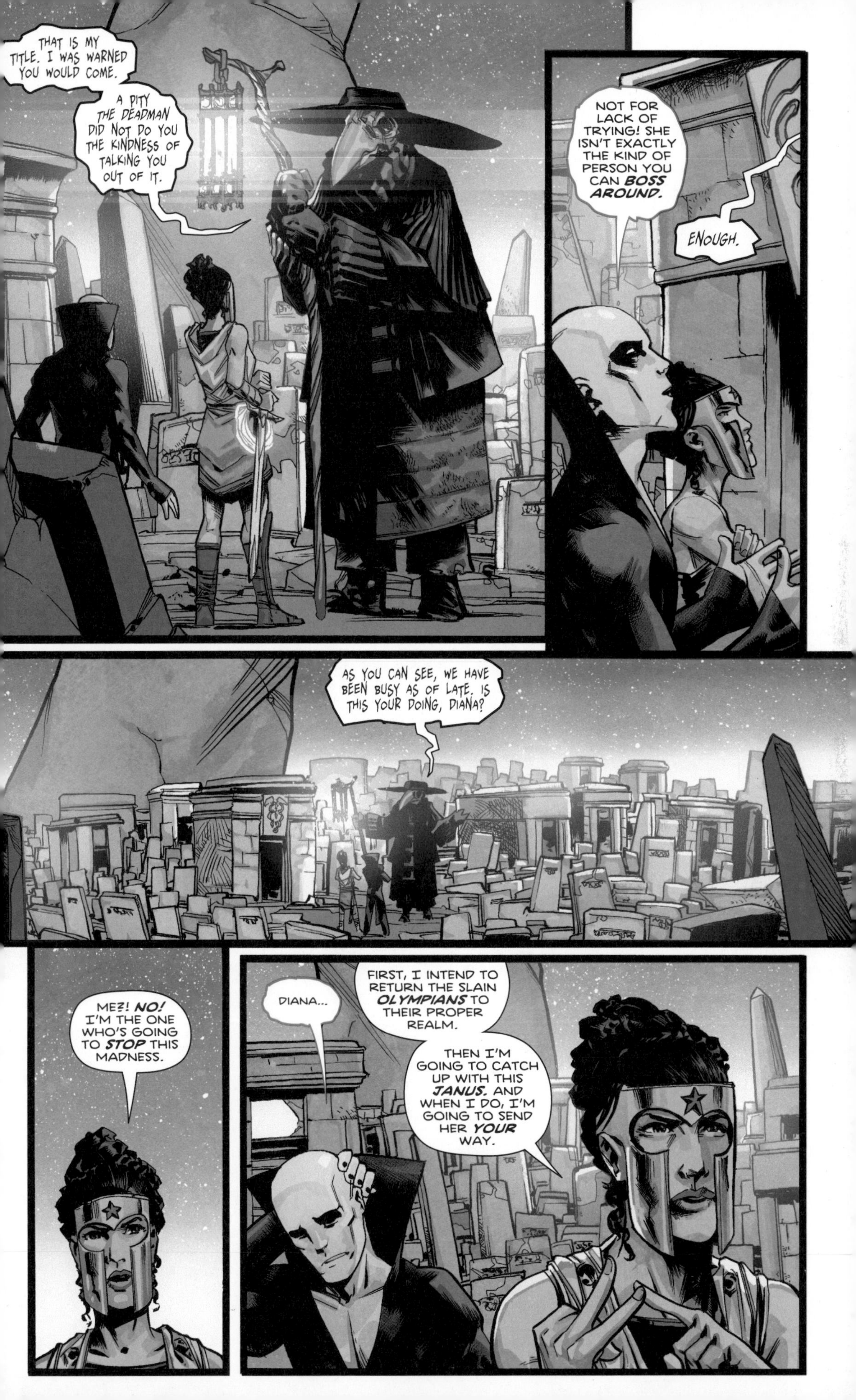
THAT IS MY TITLE. I WAS WARNED YOU WOULD COME.
A PITY *THE DEADMAN* DID NOT DO YOU THE KINDNESS OF TALKING YOU OUT OF IT.
NOT FOR LACK OF TRYING! SHE ISN'T EXACTLY THE KIND OF PERSON YOU CAN ***BOSS AROUND.***
ENOUGH.
AS YOU CAN SEE, WE HAVE BEEN BUSY AS OF LATE. IS THIS YOUR DOING, DIANA?
ME?! ***NO!*** I'M THE ONE WHO'S GOING TO ***STOP*** THIS MADNESS.
DIANA...
FIRST, I INTEND TO RETURN THE SLAIN ***OLYMPIANS*** TO THEIR PROPER REALM.
THEN I'M GOING TO CATCH UP WITH THIS ***JANUS.*** AND WHEN I DO, I'M GOING TO SEND HER ***YOUR*** WAY.

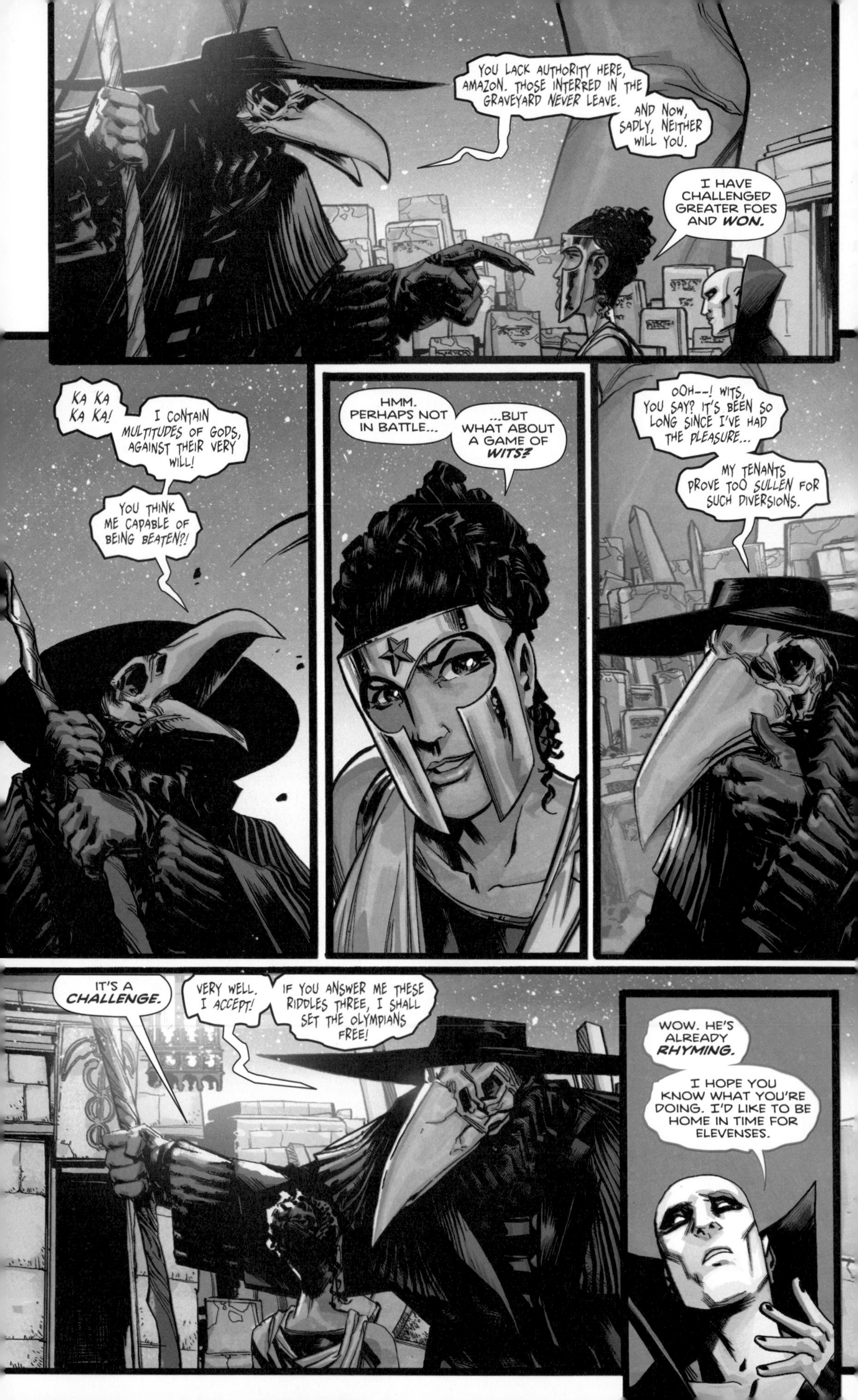

YOU LACK AUTHORITY HERE, AMAZON. THOSE INTERRED IN THE GRAVEYARD *NEVER* LEAVE.
AND NOW, SADLY, NEITHER WILL YOU.
I HAVE CHALLENGED GREATER FOES AND *WON.*
KA KA KA KA!
I CONTAIN MULTITUDES OF GODS, AGAINST THEIR VERY WILL!
YOU THINK ME CAPABLE OF BEING *BEATEN?!*
HMM. PERHAPS NOT IN BATTLE...
...BUT WHAT ABOUT A GAME OF *WITS?*
OOH--! WITS, YOU SAY? IT'S BEEN SO LONG SINCE I'VE HAD THE *PLEASURE...*
MY TENANTS PROVE TOO *SULLEN* FOR SUCH DIVERSIONS.
IT'S A *CHALLENGE.*
VERY WELL. I *ACCEPT!*
IF YOU ANSWER ME THESE RIDDLES THREE, I SHALL SET THE OLYMPIANS FREE!
WOW. HE'S ALREADY *RHYMING.*
I HOPE YOU KNOW WHAT YOU'RE DOING. I'D LIKE TO BE HOME IN TIME FOR ELEVENSES.

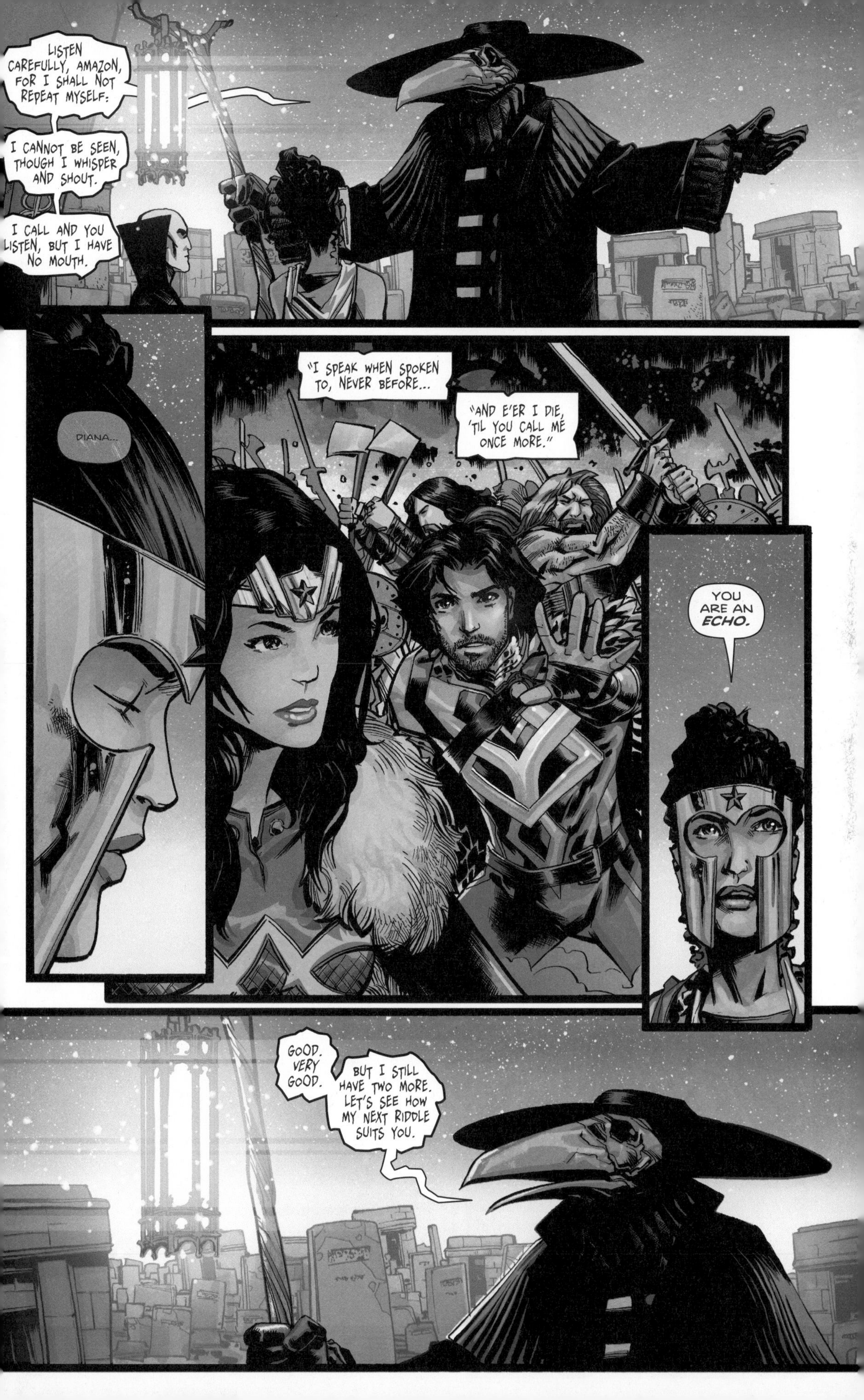
LISTEN CAREFULLY, AMAZON, FOR I SHALL NOT REPEAT MYSELF:
I CANNOT BE SEEN, THOUGH I WHISPER AND SHOUT.
I CALL AND YOU LISTEN, BUT I HAVE NO MOUTH.
DIANA...
"I SPEAK WHEN SPOKEN TO, NEVER BEFORE...
"AND E'ER I DIE, 'TIL YOU CALL ME ONCE MORE."
YOU ARE AN ECHO.
GOOD. VERY GOOD.
BUT I STILL HAVE TWO MORE. LET'S SEE HOW MY NEXT RIDDLE SUITS YOU.

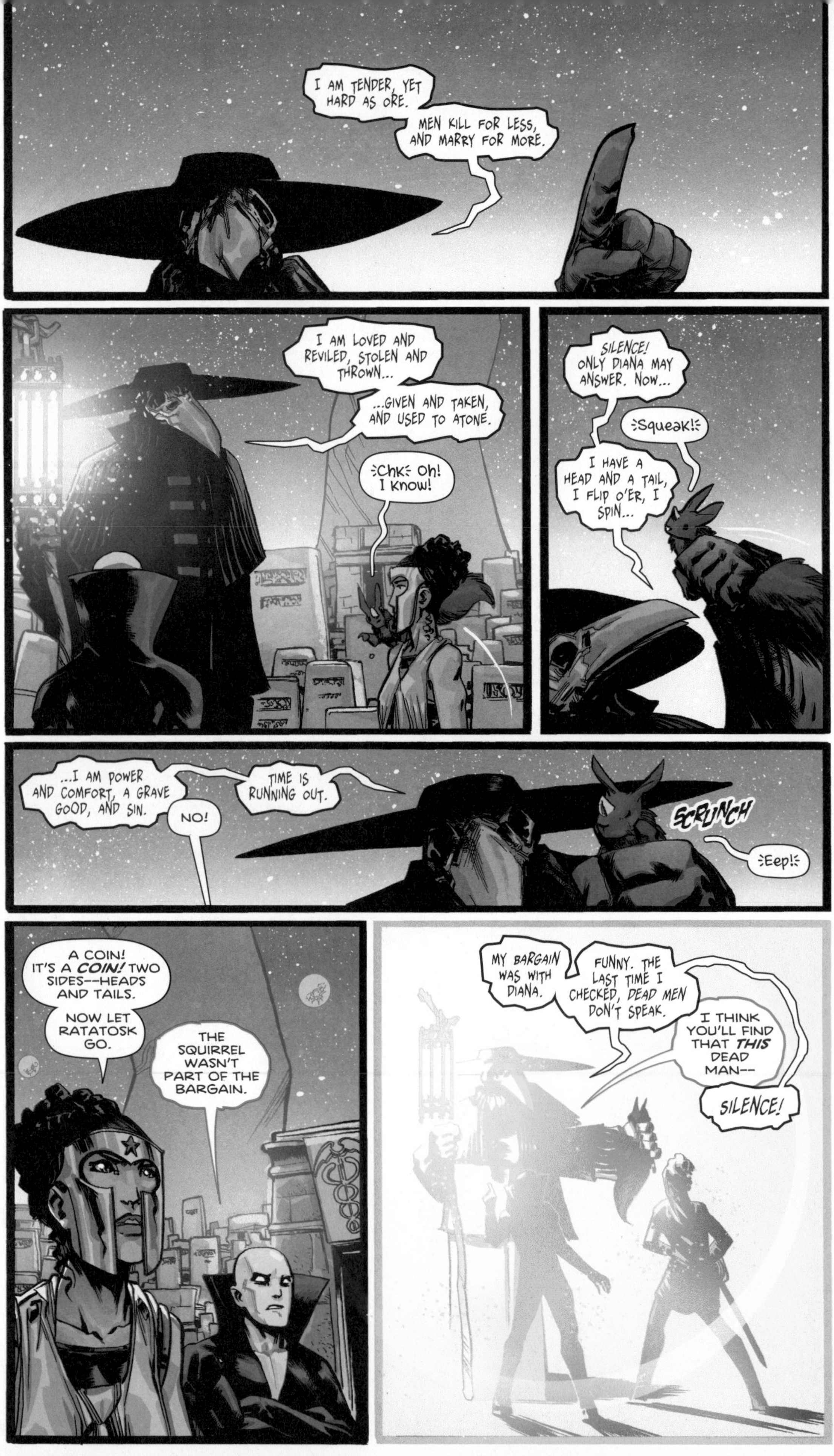

I AM TENDER, YET HARD AS ORE.
MEN KILL FOR LESS, AND MARRY FOR MORE.
I AM LOVED AND REVILED, STOLEN AND THROWN...
...GIVEN AND TAKEN, AND USED TO ATONE.
Chk Oh! I know!
SILENCE! ONLY DIANA MAY ANSWER. NOW...
Squeak!
I HAVE A HEAD AND A TAIL, I FLIP O'ER, I SPIN...
...I AM POWER AND COMFORT, A GRAVE GOOD, AND SIN.
NO!
TIME IS RUNNING OUT.
SCRUNCH
Eep!
A COIN! IT'S A COIN! TWO SIDES--HEADS AND TAILS.
NOW LET RATATOSK GO.
THE SQUIRREL WASN'T PART OF THE BARGAIN.
MY BARGAIN WAS WITH DIANA.
FUNNY. THE LAST TIME I CHECKED, DEAD MEN DON'T SPEAK.
I THINK YOU'LL FIND THAT THIS DEAD MAN--
SILENCE!

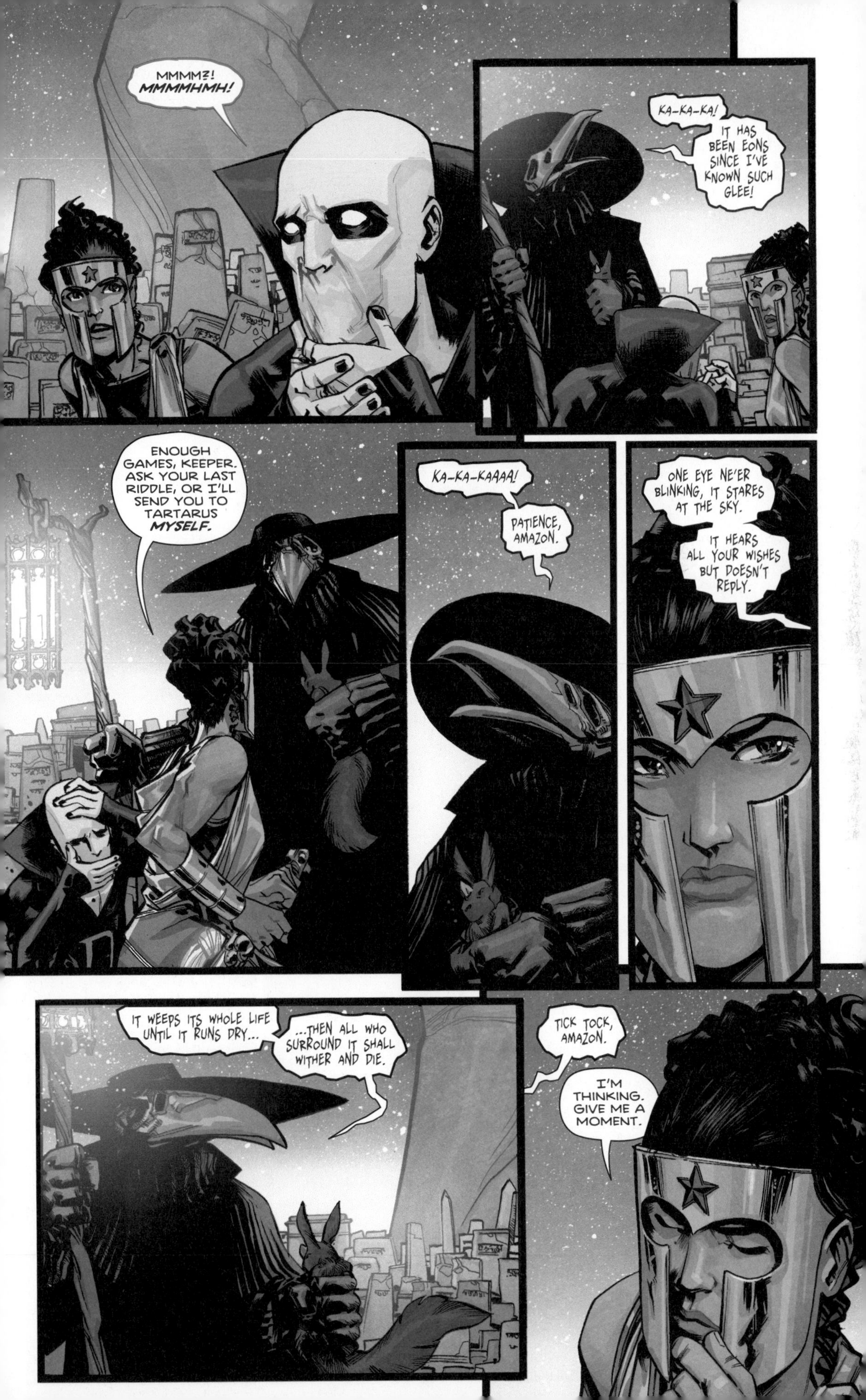
MMMMZ! MMMMHMH!
KA-KA-KA! IT HAS BEEN EONS SINCE I'VE KNOWN SUCH GLEE!
ENOUGH GAMES, KEEPER. ASK YOUR LAST RIDDLE, OR I'LL SEND YOU TO TARTARUS MYSELF.
KA-KA-KAAAA!
PATIENCE, AMAZON.
ONE EYE NE'ER BLINKING, IT STARES AT THE SKY.
IT HEARS ALL YOUR WISHES BUT DOESN'T REPLY.
IT WEEPS ITS WHOLE LIFE UNTIL IT RUNS DRY...
...THEN ALL WHO SURROUND IT SHALL WITHER AND DIE.
TICK TOCK, AMAZON.
I'M THINKING. GIVE ME A MOMENT.

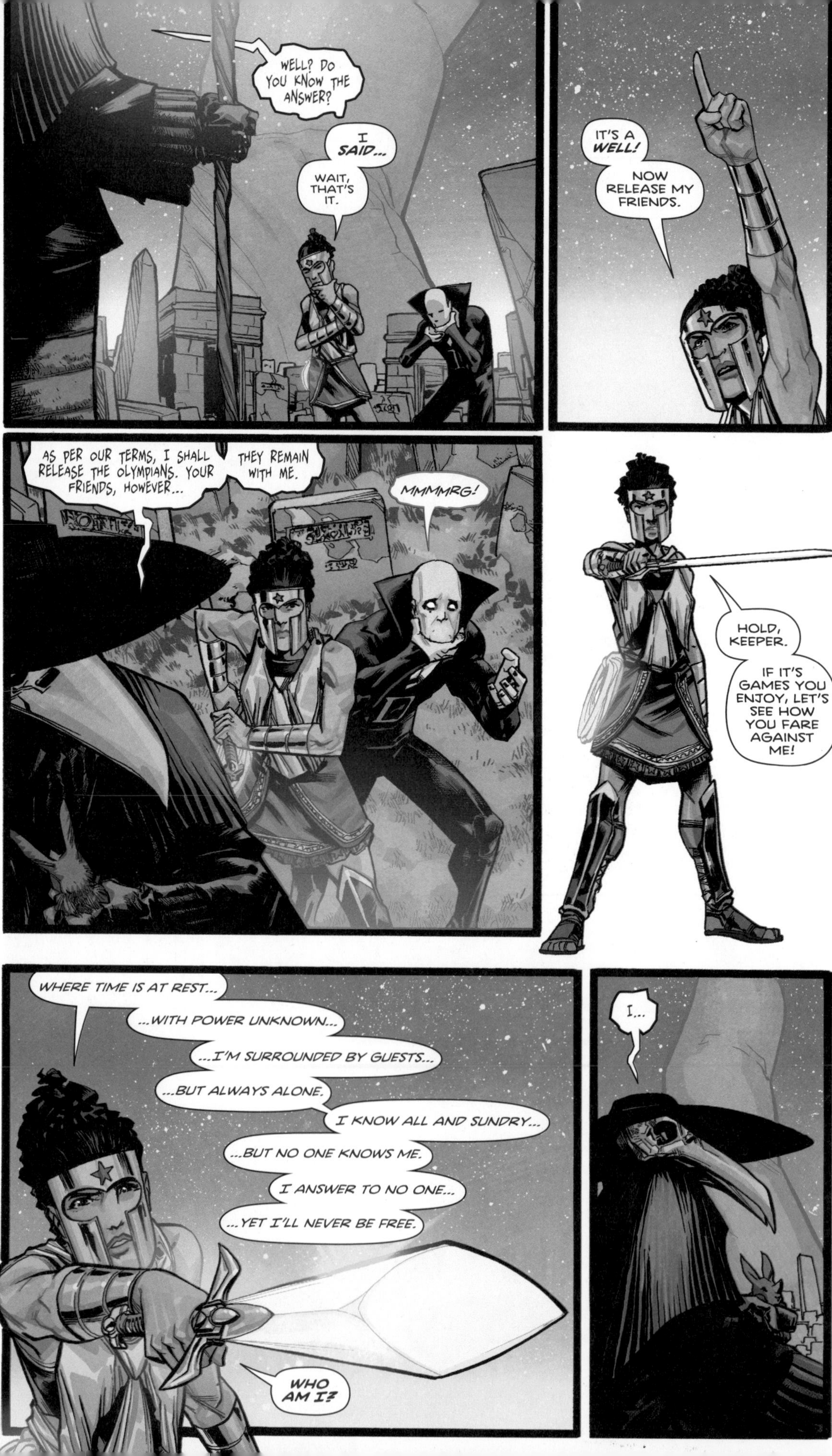
WELL? DO YOU KNOW THE ANSWER?
I SAID...
WAIT, THAT'S IT.
IT'S A WELL!
NOW RELEASE MY FRIENDS.
AS PER OUR TERMS, I SHALL RELEASE THE OLYMPIANS. YOUR FRIENDS, HOWEVER...
THEY REMAIN WITH ME.
MMMMRG!
HOLD, KEEPER.
IF IT'S GAMES YOU ENJOY, LET'S SEE HOW YOU FARE AGAINST ME!
WHERE TIME IS AT REST...
...WITH POWER UNKNOWN...
...I'M SURROUNDED BY GUESTS...
...BUT ALWAYS ALONE.
I KNOW ALL AND SUNDRY...
...BUT NO ONE KNOWS ME.
I ANSWER TO NO ONE...
...YET I'LL NEVER BE FREE.
WHO AM I?
I...

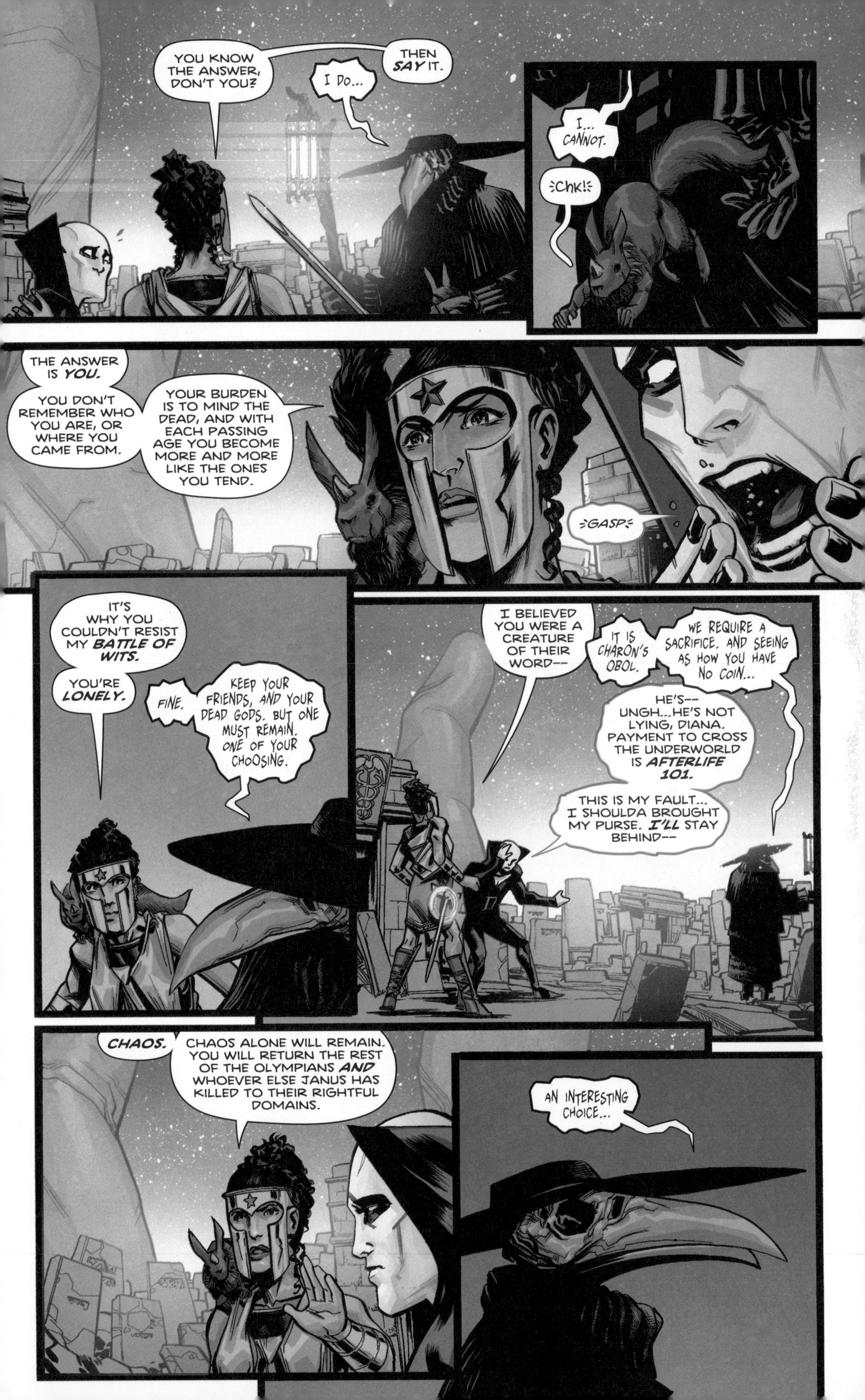
YOU KNOW THE ANSWER, DON'T YOU?
I DO...
THEN SAY IT.
I... CANNOT.
Chk!
THE ANSWER IS YOU.
YOU DON'T REMEMBER WHO YOU ARE, OR WHERE YOU CAME FROM.
YOUR BURDEN IS TO MIND THE DEAD, AND WITH EACH PASSING AGE YOU BECOME MORE AND MORE LIKE THE ONES YOU TEND.
GASP
IT'S WHY YOU COULDN'T RESIST MY BATTLE OF WITS.
YOU'RE LONELY.
FINE.
KEEP YOUR FRIENDS, AND YOUR DEAD GODS. BUT ONE MUST REMAIN. ONE OF YOUR CHOOSING.
I BELIEVED YOU WERE A CREATURE OF THEIR WORD--
IT IS CHARON'S OBOL.
WE REQUIRE A SACRIFICE. AND SEEING AS HOW YOU HAVE NO COIN...
HE'S-- UNGH... HE'S NOT LYING, DIANA. PAYMENT TO CROSS THE UNDERWORLD IS AFTERLIFE 101.
THIS IS MY FAULT... I SHOULDA BROUGHT MY PURSE. I'LL STAY BEHIND--
CHAOS.
CHAOS ALONE WILL REMAIN. YOU WILL RETURN THE REST OF THE OLYMPIANS AND WHOEVER ELSE JANUS HAS KILLED TO THEIR RIGHTFUL DOMAINS.
AN INTERESTING CHOICE...

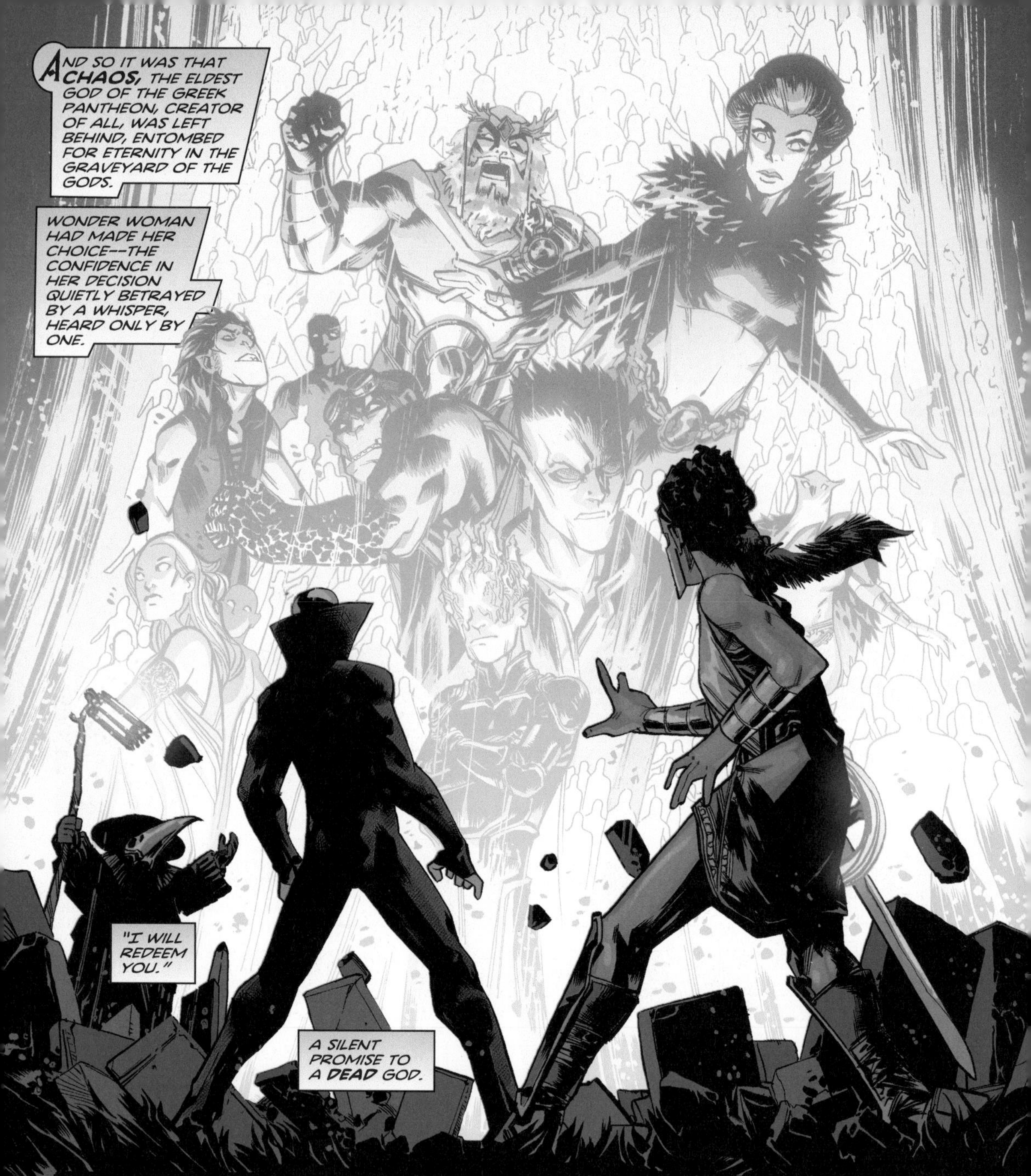
AND SO IT WAS THAT CHAOS, THE ELDEST GOD OF THE GREEK PANTHEON, CREATOR OF ALL, WAS LEFT BEHIND, ENTOMBED FOR ETERNITY IN THE GRAVEYARD OF THE GODS.
WONDER WOMAN HAD MADE HER CHOICE--THE CONFIDENCE IN HER DECISION QUIETLY BETRAYED BY A WHISPER, HEARD ONLY BY ONE.
"I WILL REDEEM YOU."
A SILENT PROMISE TO A DEAD GOD.

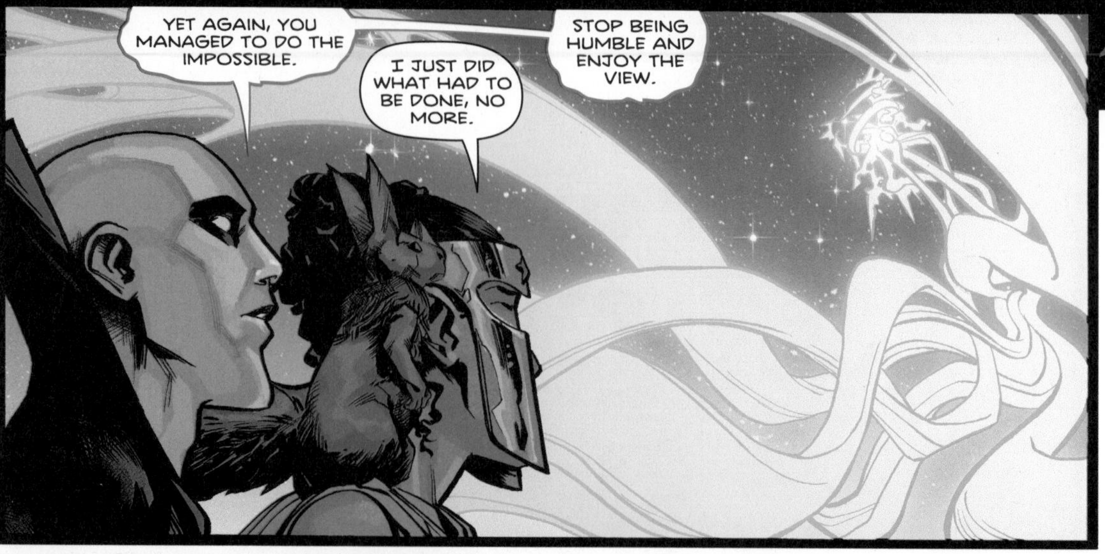
YET AGAIN, YOU MANAGED TO DO THE IMPOSSIBLE.
I JUST DID WHAT HAD TO BE DONE, NO MORE.
STOP BEING HUMBLE AND ENJOY THE VIEW.

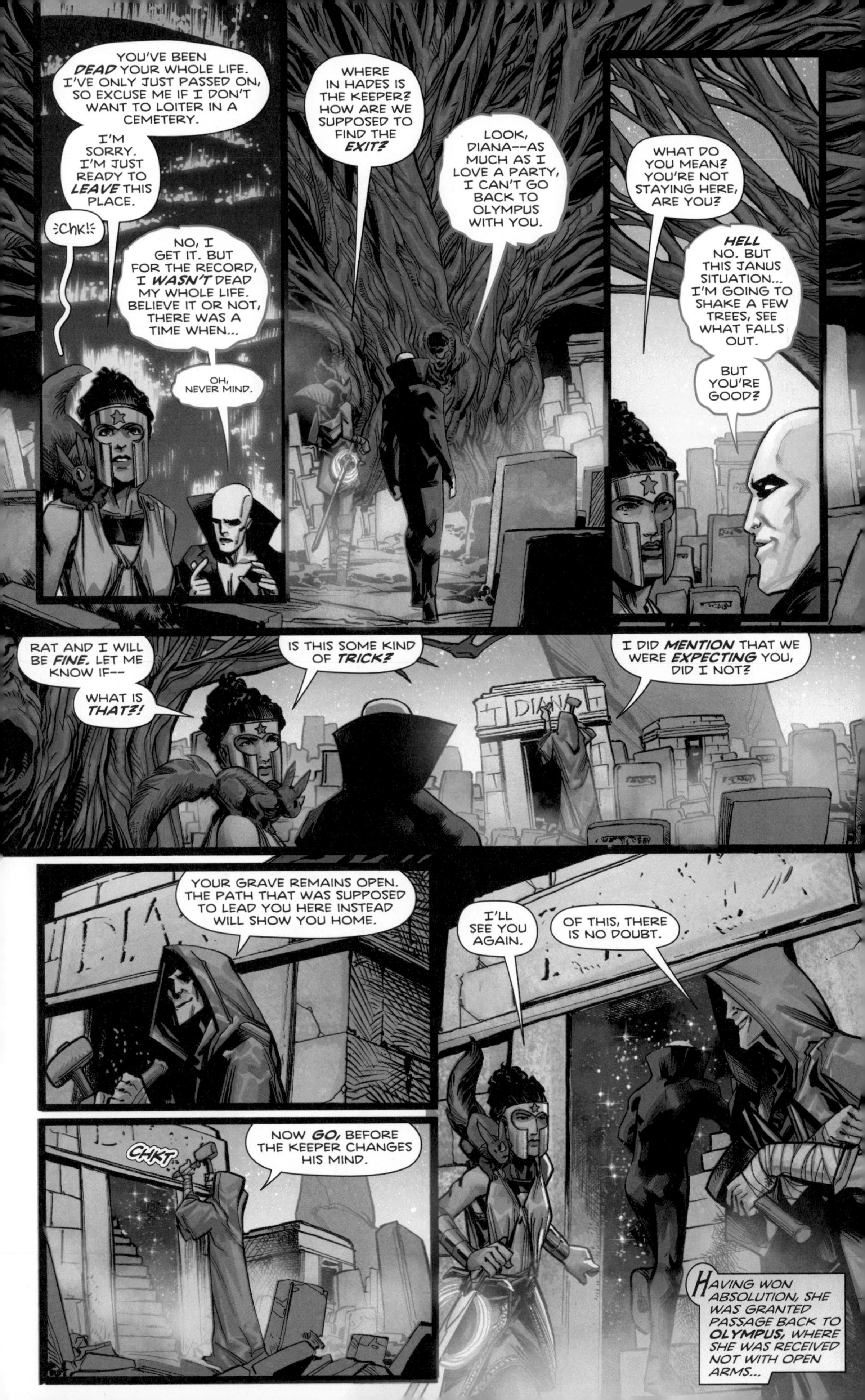
YOU'VE BEEN DEAD YOUR WHOLE LIFE. I'VE ONLY JUST PASSED ON, SO EXCUSE ME IF I DON'T WANT TO LOITER IN A CEMETERY.
I'M SORRY. I'M JUST READY TO LEAVE THIS PLACE.
Chk!
NO, I GET IT. BUT FOR THE RECORD, I WASN'T DEAD MY WHOLE LIFE. BELIEVE IT OR NOT, THERE WAS A TIME WHEN...
OH, NEVER MIND.
WHERE IN HADES IS THE KEEPER? HOW ARE WE SUPPOSED TO FIND THE EXIT?
LOOK, DIANA--AS MUCH AS I LOVE A PARTY, I CAN'T GO BACK TO OLYMPUS WITH YOU.
WHAT DO YOU MEAN? YOU'RE NOT STAYING HERE, ARE YOU?
HELL NO. BUT THIS JANUS SITUATION... I'M GOING TO SHAKE A FEW TREES, SEE WHAT FALLS OUT.
BUT YOU'RE GOOD?
RAT AND I WILL BE FINE. LET ME KNOW IF--
WHAT IS THAT?!
IS THIS SOME KIND OF TRICK?
I DID MENTION THAT WE WERE EXPECTING YOU, DID I NOT?
DIANA
YOUR GRAVE REMAINS OPEN. THE PATH THAT WAS SUPPOSED TO LEAD YOU HERE INSTEAD WILL SHOW YOU HOME.
CHKT
NOW GO, BEFORE THE KEEPER CHANGES HIS MIND.
I'LL SEE YOU AGAIN.
OF THIS, THERE IS NO DOUBT.
HAVING WON ABSOLUTION, SHE WAS GRANTED PASSAGE BACK TO OLYMPUS, WHERE SHE WAS RECEIVED NOT WITH OPEN ARMS...

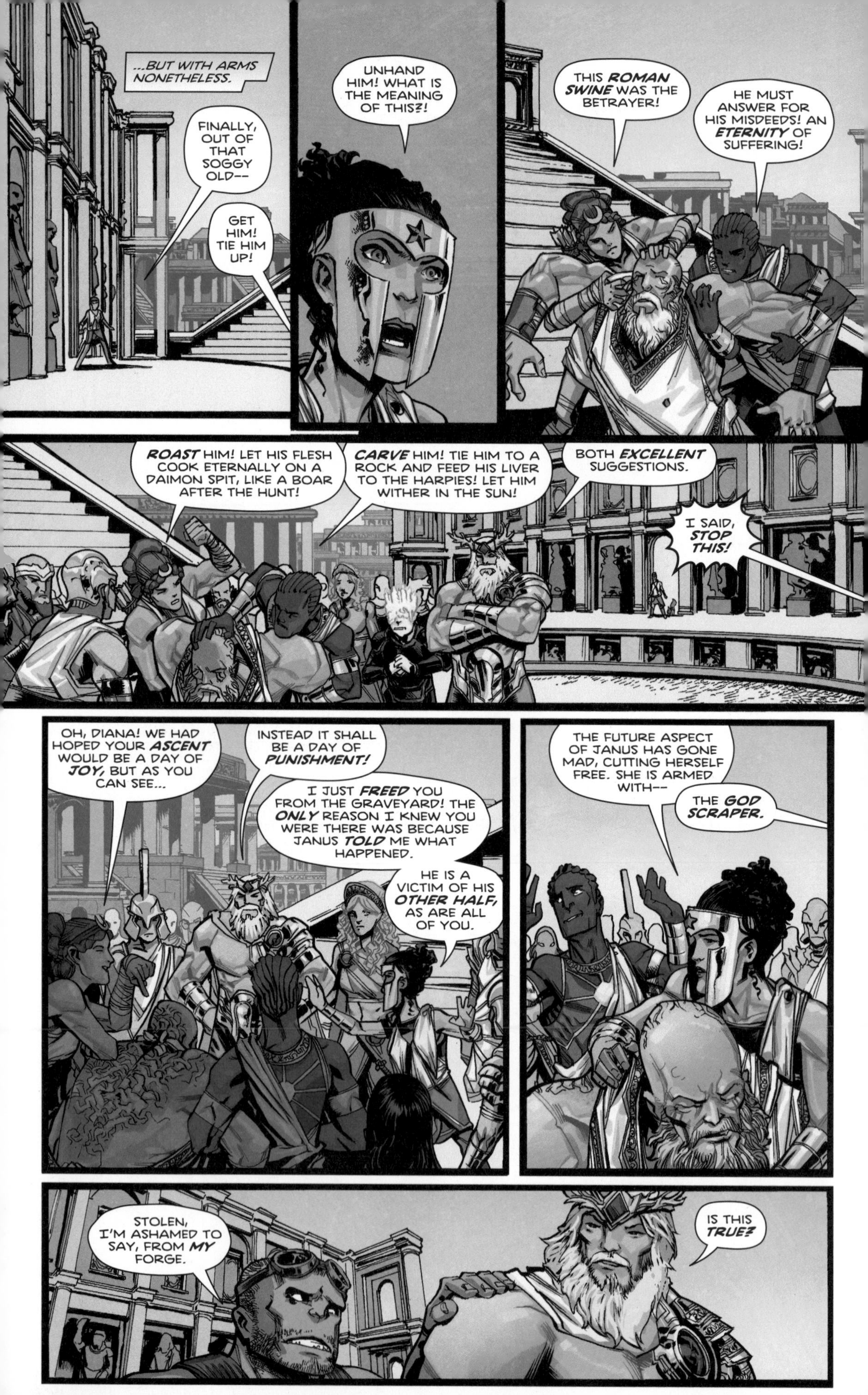
...BUT WITH ARMS NONETHELESS.
FINALLY, OUT OF THAT SOGGY OLD--
GET HIM! TIE HIM UP!
UNHAND HIM! WHAT IS THE MEANING OF THIS?!
THIS ROMAN SWINE WAS THE BETRAYER!
HE MUST ANSWER FOR HIS MISDEEDS! AN ETERNITY OF SUFFERING!
ROAST HIM! LET HIS FLESH COOK ETERNALLY ON A DAIMON SPIT, LIKE A BOAR AFTER THE HUNT!
CARVE HIM! TIE HIM TO A ROCK AND FEED HIS LIVER TO THE HARPIES! LET HIM WITHER IN THE SUN!
BOTH EXCELLENT SUGGESTIONS.
I SAID, STOP THIS!
OH, DIANA! WE HAD HOPED YOUR ASCENT WOULD BE A DAY OF JOY, BUT AS YOU CAN SEE...
INSTEAD IT SHALL BE A DAY OF PUNISHMENT!
I JUST FREED YOU FROM THE GRAVEYARD! THE ONLY REASON I KNEW YOU WERE THERE WAS BECAUSE JANUS TOLD ME WHAT HAPPENED.
HE IS A VICTIM OF HIS OTHER HALF, AS ARE ALL OF YOU.
THE FUTURE ASPECT OF JANUS HAS GONE MAD, CUTTING HERSELF FREE. SHE IS ARMED WITH--
THE GOD SCRAPER.
STOLEN, I'M ASHAMED TO SAY, FROM MY FORGE.
IS THIS TRUE?

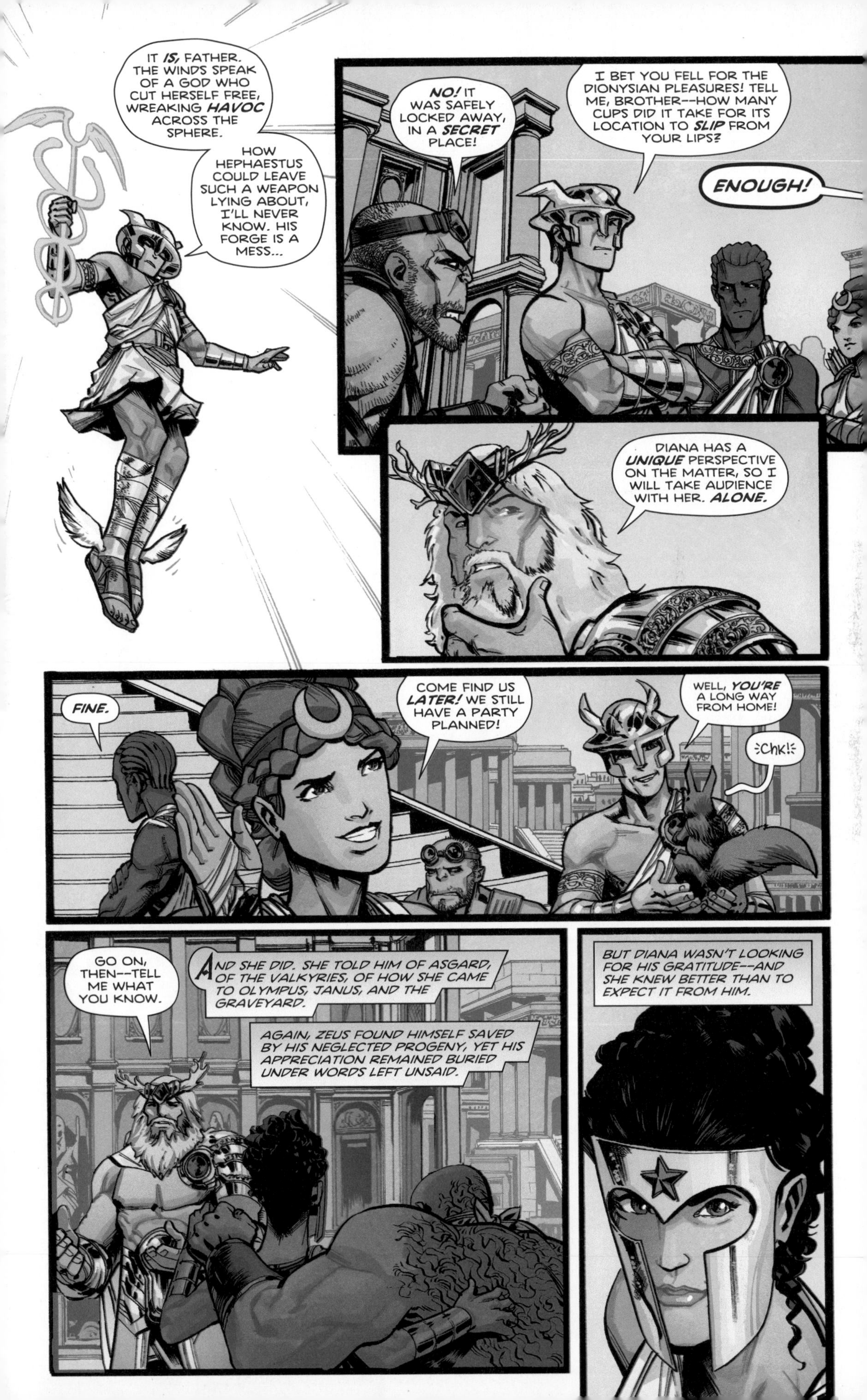
IT *IS,* FATHER. THE WINDS SPEAK OF A GOD WHO CUT HERSELF FREE, WREAKING *HAVOC* ACROSS THE SPHERE.
HOW HEPHAESTUS COULD LEAVE SUCH A WEAPON LYING ABOUT, I'LL NEVER KNOW. HIS FORGE IS A MESS...
NO! IT WAS SAFELY LOCKED AWAY, IN A *SECRET* PLACE!
I BET YOU FELL FOR THE DIONYSIAN PLEASURES! TELL ME, BROTHER--HOW MANY CUPS DID IT TAKE FOR ITS LOCATION TO *SLIP* FROM YOUR LIPS?
ENOUGH!
DIANA HAS A *UNIQUE* PERSPECTIVE ON THE MATTER, SO I WILL TAKE AUDIENCE WITH HER. *ALONE.*
FINE.
COME FIND US *LATER!* WE STILL HAVE A PARTY PLANNED!
WELL, *YOU'RE* A LONG WAY FROM HOME!
Chk!
GO ON, THEN--TELL ME WHAT YOU KNOW.
AND SHE DID. SHE TOLD HIM OF ASGARD, OF THE VALKYRIES, OF HOW SHE CAME TO OLYMPUS, JANUS, AND THE GRAVEYARD.
AGAIN, ZEUS FOUND HIMSELF SAVED BY HIS NEGLECTED PROGENY, YET HIS APPRECIATION REMAINED BURIED UNDER WORDS LEFT UNSAID.
BUT DIANA WASN'T LOOKING FOR HIS GRATITUDE--AND SHE KNEW BETTER THAN TO EXPECT IT FROM HIM.

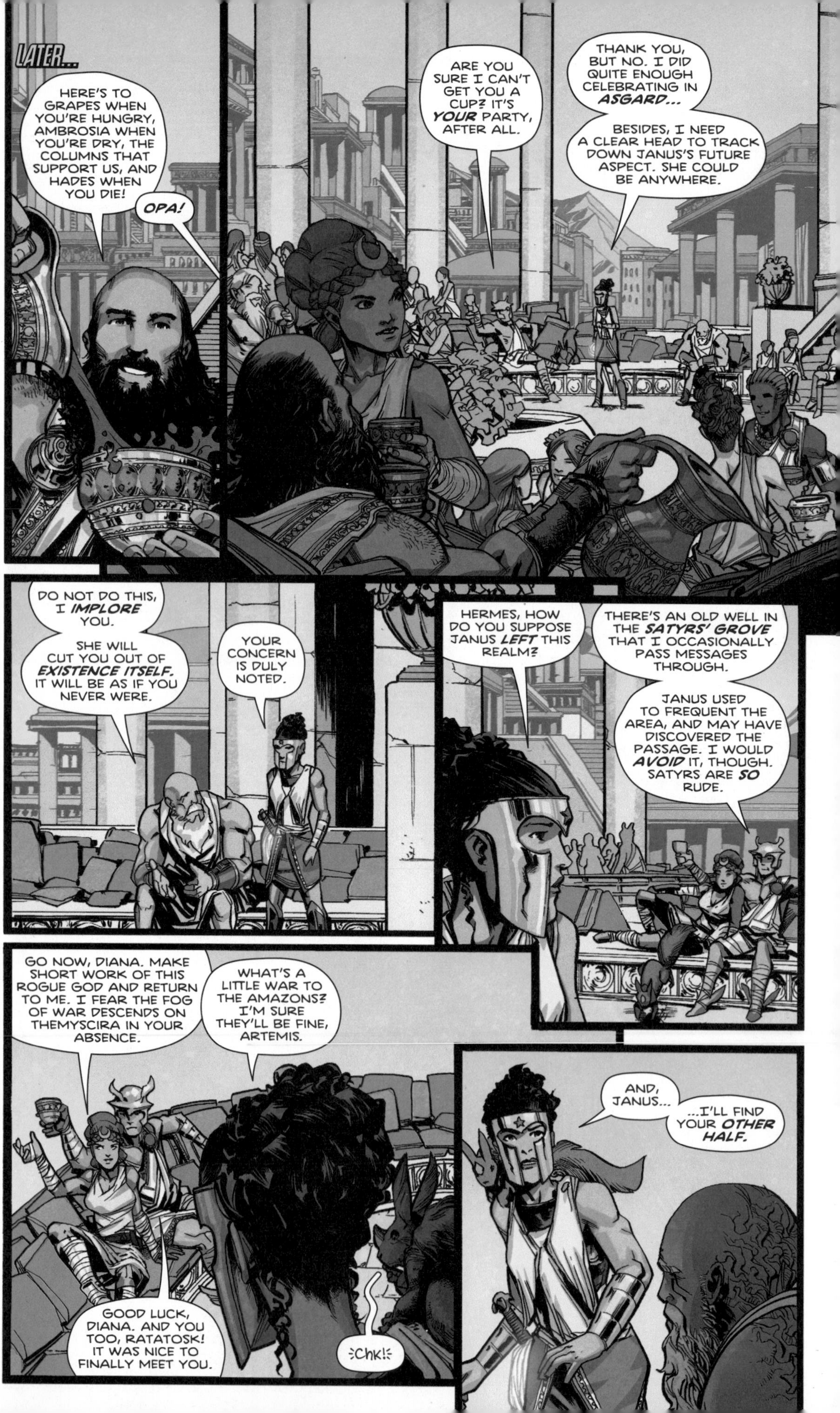
LATER...
HERE'S TO GRAPES WHEN YOU'RE HUNGRY, AMBROSIA WHEN YOU'RE DRY, THE COLUMNS THAT SUPPORT US, AND HADES WHEN YOU DIE!
OPA!
ARE YOU SURE I CAN'T GET YOU A CUP? IT'S YOUR PARTY, AFTER ALL.
THANK YOU, BUT NO. I DID QUITE ENOUGH CELEBRATING IN ASGARD...
BESIDES, I NEED A CLEAR HEAD TO TRACK DOWN JANUS'S FUTURE ASPECT. SHE COULD BE ANYWHERE.
DO NOT DO THIS, I IMPLORE YOU.
SHE WILL CUT YOU OUT OF EXISTENCE ITSELF. IT WILL BE AS IF YOU NEVER WERE.
YOUR CONCERN IS DULY NOTED.
HERMES, HOW DO YOU SUPPOSE JANUS LEFT THIS REALM?
THERE'S AN OLD WELL IN THE SATYRS' GROVE THAT I OCCASIONALLY PASS MESSAGES THROUGH.
JANUS USED TO FREQUENT THE AREA, AND MAY HAVE DISCOVERED THE PASSAGE. I WOULD AVOID IT, THOUGH. SATYRS ARE SO RUDE.
GO NOW, DIANA. MAKE SHORT WORK OF THIS ROGUE GOD AND RETURN TO ME. I FEAR THE FOG OF WAR DESCENDS ON THEMYSCIRA IN YOUR ABSENCE.
WHAT'S A LITTLE WAR TO THE AMAZONS? I'M SURE THEY'LL BE FINE, ARTEMIS.
GOOD LUCK, DIANA. AND YOU TOO, RATATOSK! IT WAS NICE TO FINALLY MEET YOU.
CHK!
AND, JANUS...
...I'LL FIND YOUR OTHER HALF.

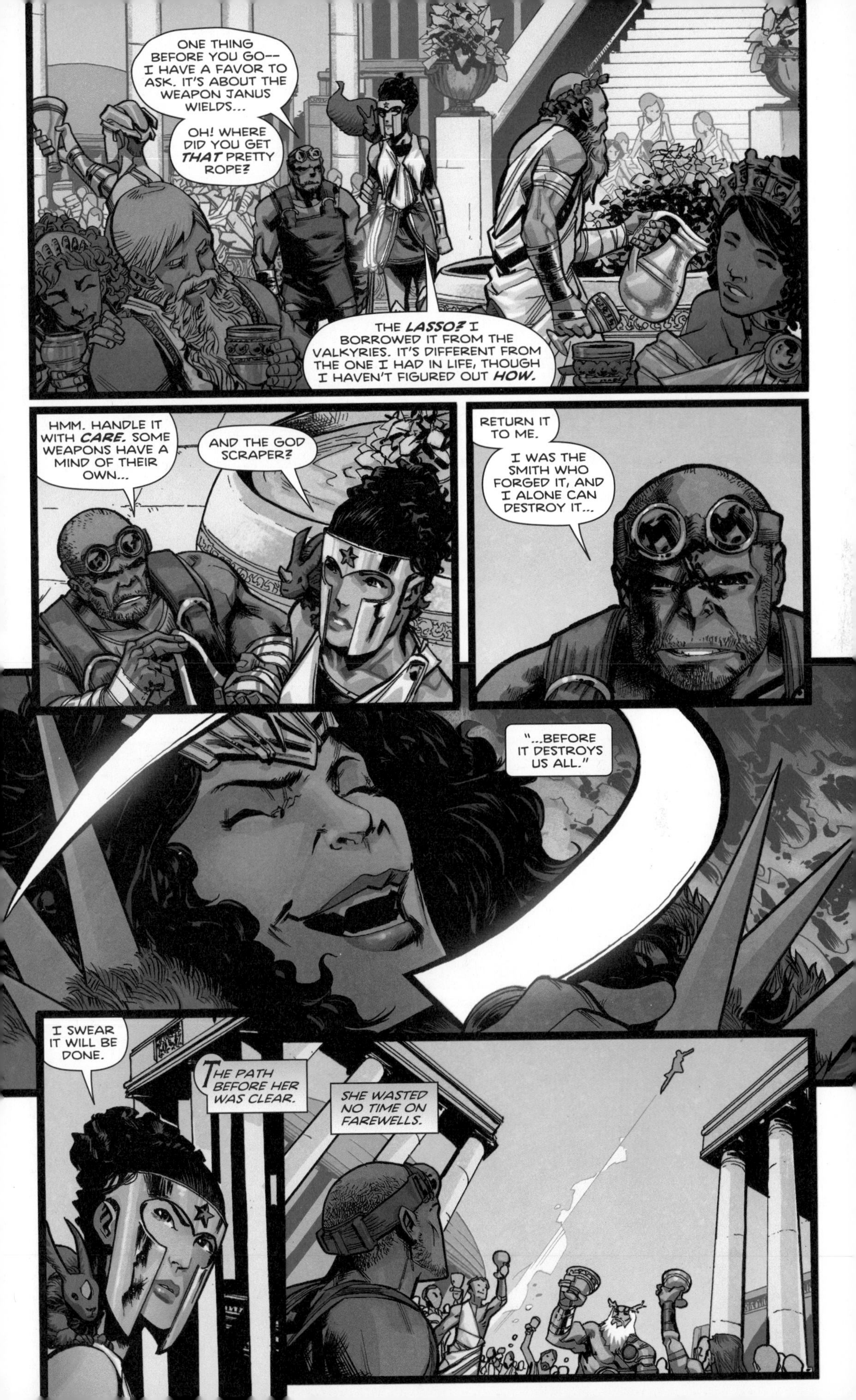
ONE THING BEFORE YOU GO-- I HAVE A FAVOR TO ASK. IT'S ABOUT THE WEAPON JANUS WIELDS...
OH! WHERE DID YOU GET THAT PRETTY ROPE?
THE LASSO? I BORROWED IT FROM THE VALKYRIES. IT'S DIFFERENT FROM THE ONE I HAD IN LIFE, THOUGH I HAVEN'T FIGURED OUT HOW.
HMM. HANDLE IT WITH CARE. SOME WEAPONS HAVE A MIND OF THEIR OWN...
AND THE GOD SCRAPER?
RETURN IT TO ME.
I WAS THE SMITH WHO FORGED IT, AND I ALONE CAN DESTROY IT...
"...BEFORE IT DESTROYS US ALL."
I SWEAR IT WILL BE DONE.
THE PATH BEFORE HER WAS CLEAR.
SHE WASTED NO TIME ON FAREWELLS.

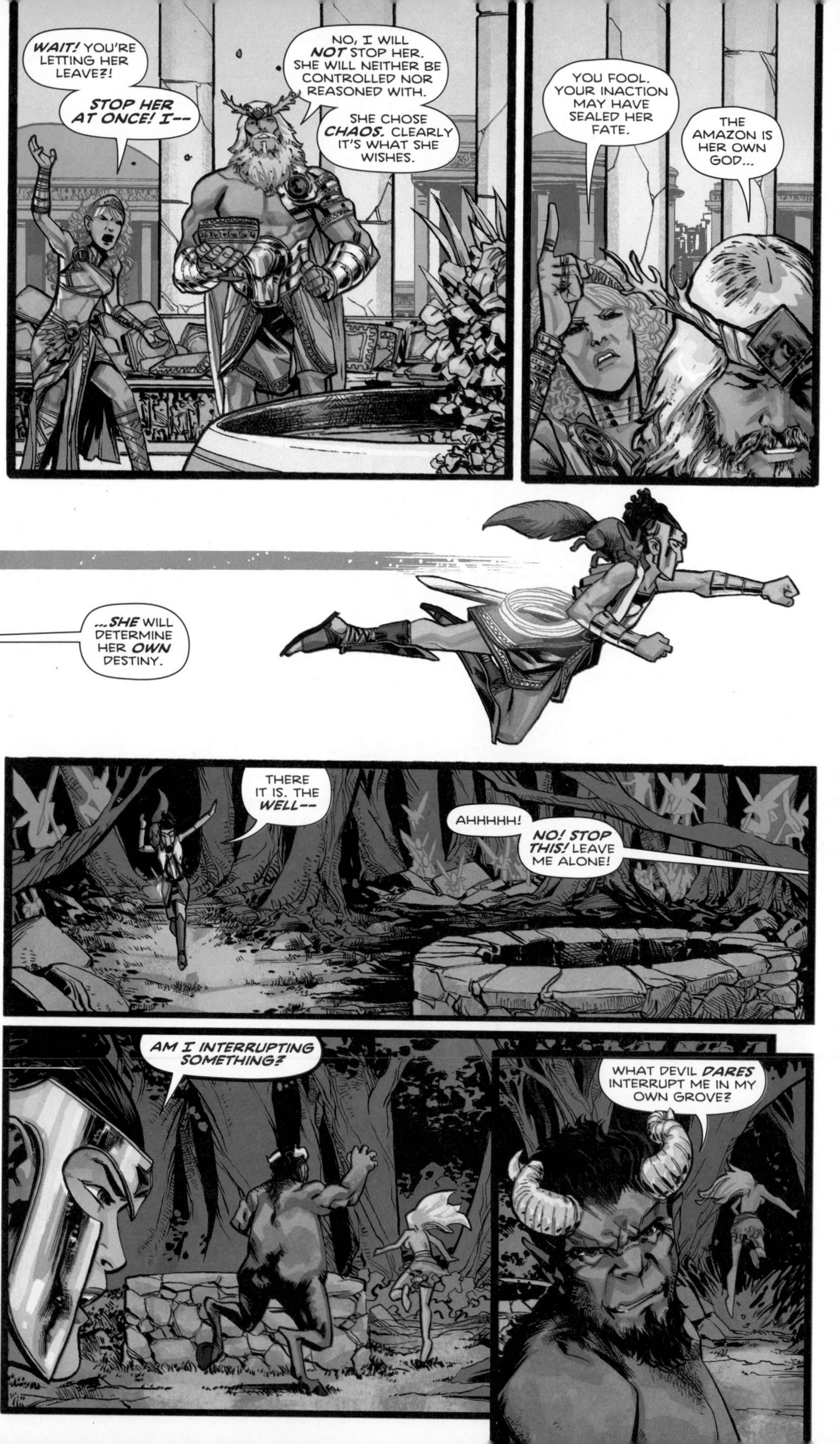
WAIT! YOU'RE LETTING HER LEAVE?!
STOP HER AT ONCE! I--
NO, I WILL NOT STOP HER. SHE WILL NEITHER BE CONTROLLED NOR REASONED WITH.
SHE CHOSE CHAOS. CLEARLY IT'S WHAT SHE WISHES.
YOU FOOL. YOUR INACTION MAY HAVE SEALED HER FATE.
THE AMAZON IS HER OWN GOD...
...SHE WILL DETERMINE HER OWN DESTINY.
THERE IT IS. THE WELL--
AHHHHH!
NO! STOP THIS! LEAVE ME ALONE!
AM I INTERRUPTING SOMETHING?
WHAT DEVIL DARES INTERRUPT ME IN MY OWN GROVE?

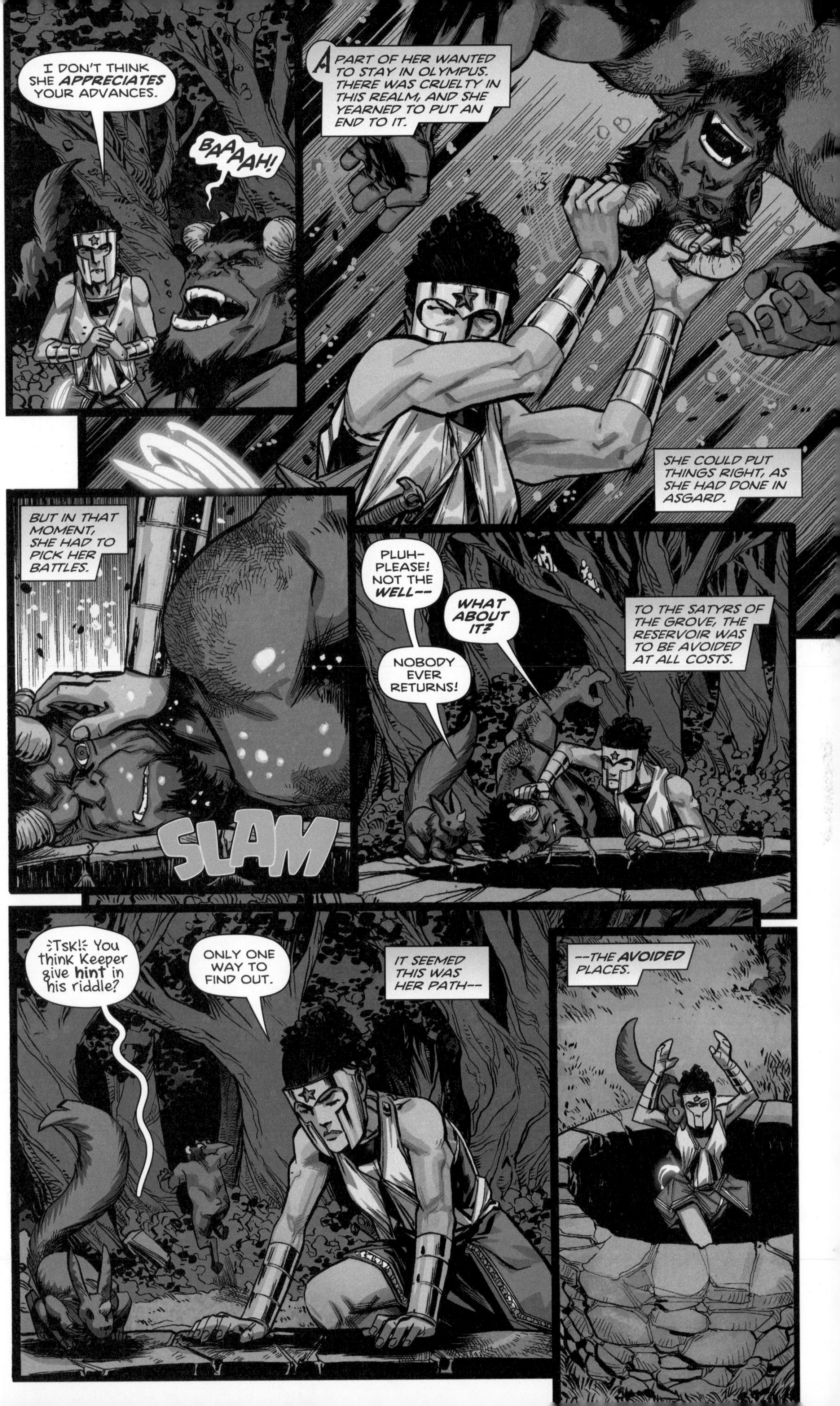
I DON'T THINK SHE APPRECIATES YOUR ADVANCES.
BAAAAH!
A PART OF HER WANTED TO STAY IN OLYMPUS. THERE WAS CRUELTY IN THIS REALM, AND SHE YEARNED TO PUT AN END TO IT.
SHE COULD PUT THINGS RIGHT, AS SHE HAD DONE IN ASGARD.
BUT IN THAT MOMENT, SHE HAD TO PICK HER BATTLES.
SLAM
PLUH-PLEASE! NOT THE WELL--
WHAT ABOUT IT?
NOBODY EVER RETURNS!
TO THE SATYRS OF THE GROVE, THE RESERVOIR WAS TO BE AVOIDED AT ALL COSTS.
Tsk! You think Keeper give hint in his riddle?
ONLY ONE WAY TO FIND OUT.
IT SEEMED THIS WAS HER PATH--
--THE AVOIDED PLACES.

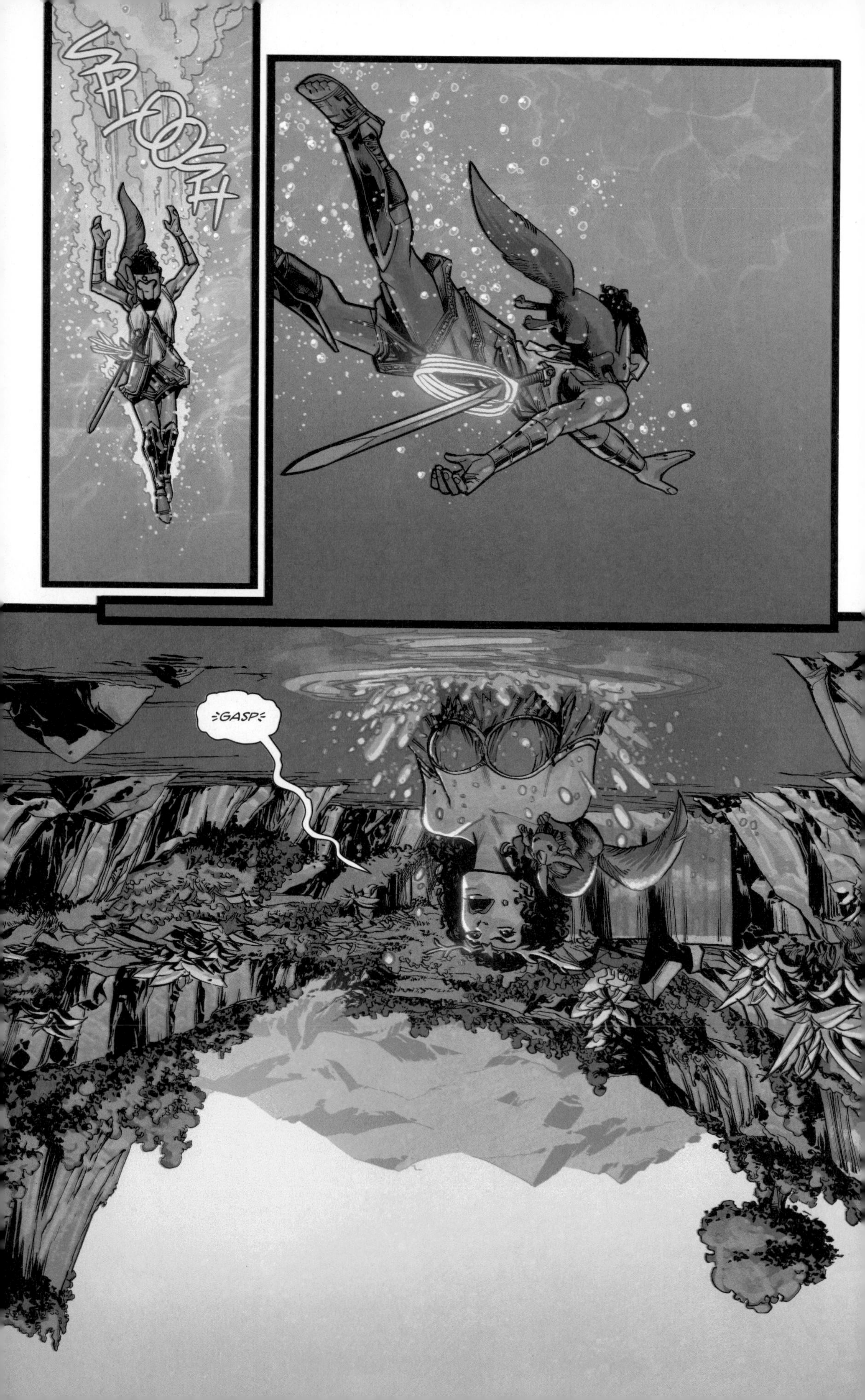
SPLOOSH
GASP

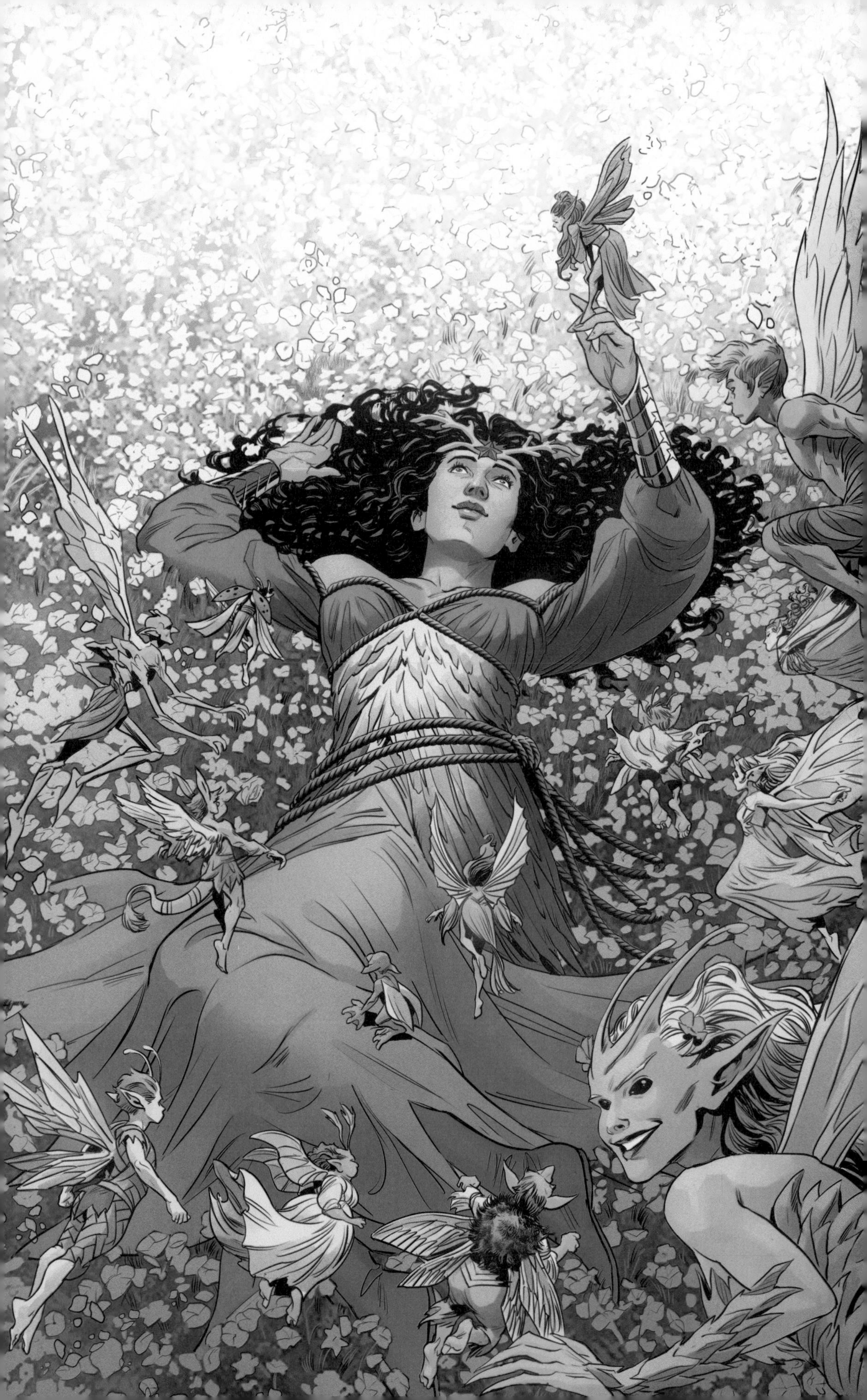

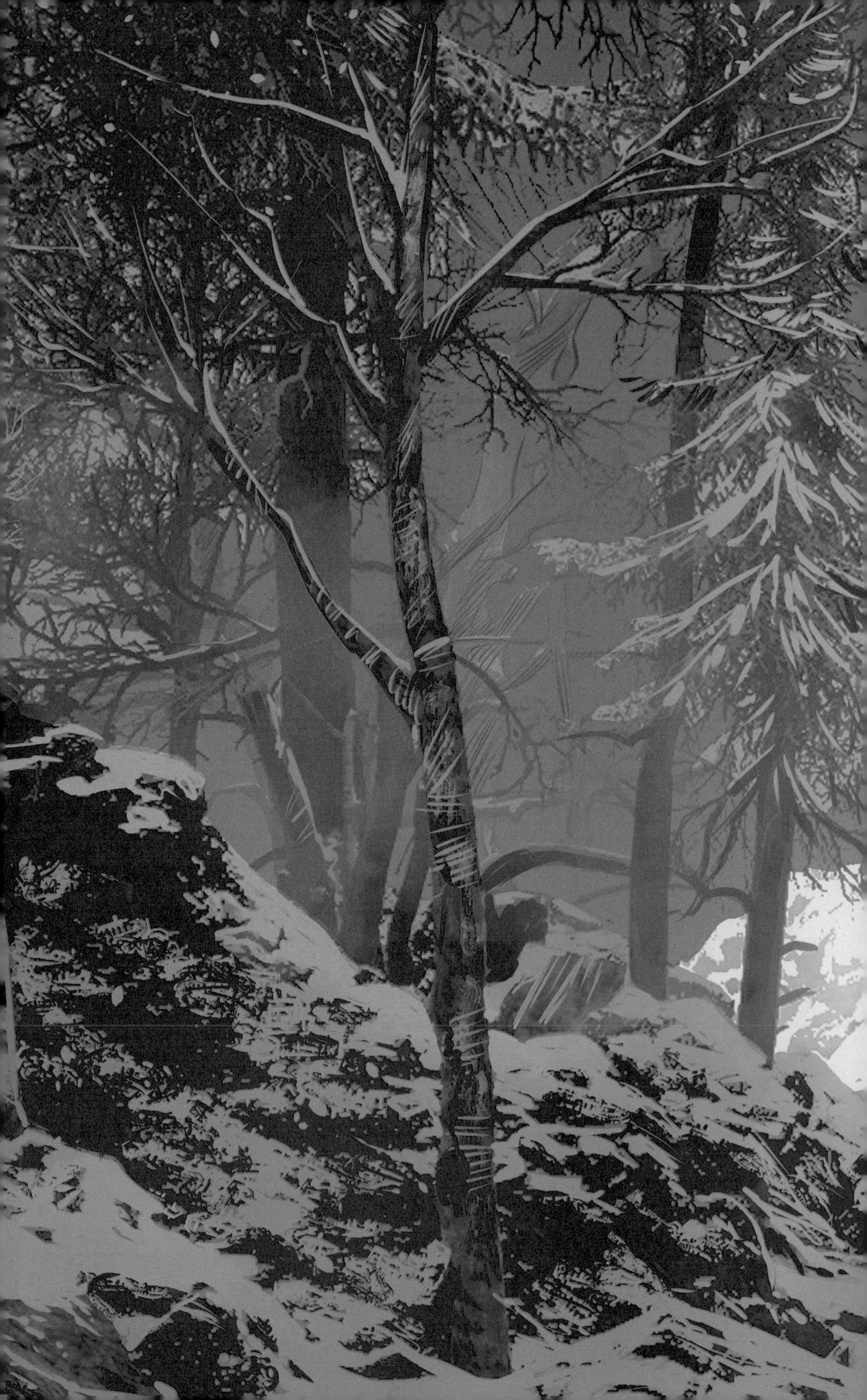

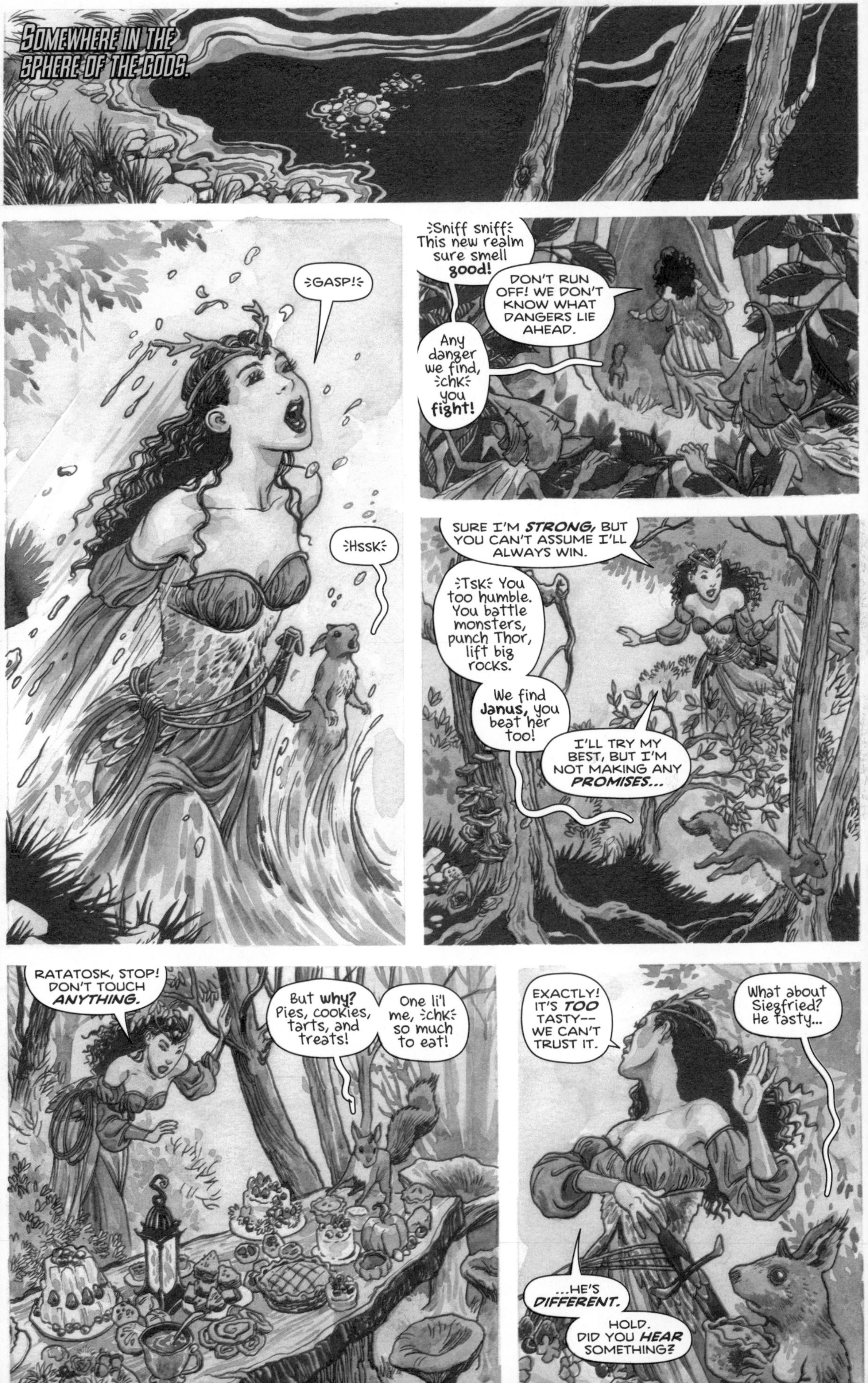
SOMEWHERE IN THE SPHERE OF THE GODS.
GASP!
HSSK
Sniff sniff This new realm sure smell good!
DON'T RUN OFF! WE DON'T KNOW WHAT DANGERS LIE AHEAD.
Any danger we find, chk you fight!
SURE I'M STRONG, BUT YOU CAN'T ASSUME I'LL ALWAYS WIN.
Tsk You too humble. You battle monsters, punch Thor, lift big rocks.
We find Janus, you beat her too!
I'LL TRY MY BEST, BUT I'M NOT MAKING ANY PROMISES...
RATATOSK, STOP! DON'T TOUCH ANYTHING.
But why? Pies, cookies, tarts, and treats!
One li'l me, chk so much to eat!
EXACTLY! IT'S TOO TASTY-- WE CAN'T TRUST IT.
What about Siegfried? He tasty...
...HE'S DIFFERENT.
HOLD. DID YOU HEAR SOMETHING?

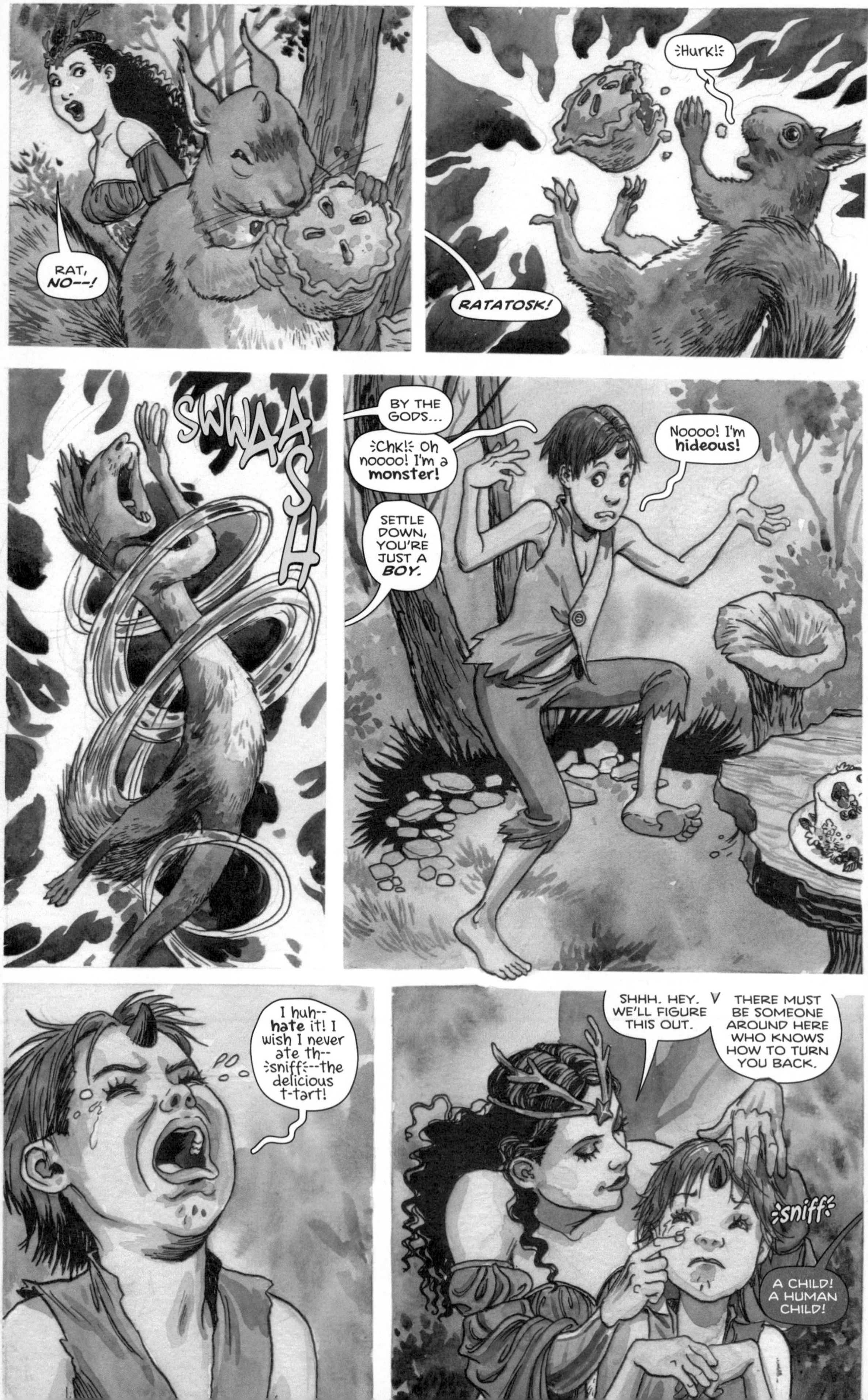
RAT, NO--!
Hurk!
RATATOSK!
SWWAASH
BY THE GODS...
Chk! Oh noooo! I'm a monster!
SETTLE DOWN, YOU'RE JUST A BOY.
Noooo! I'm hideous!
I huh-- hate it! I wish I never ate th-- sniff --the delicious t-tart!
SHHH. HEY. WE'LL FIGURE THIS OUT.
THERE MUST BE SOMEONE AROUND HERE WHO KNOWS HOW TO TURN YOU BACK.
sniff
A CHILD! A HUMAN CHILD!

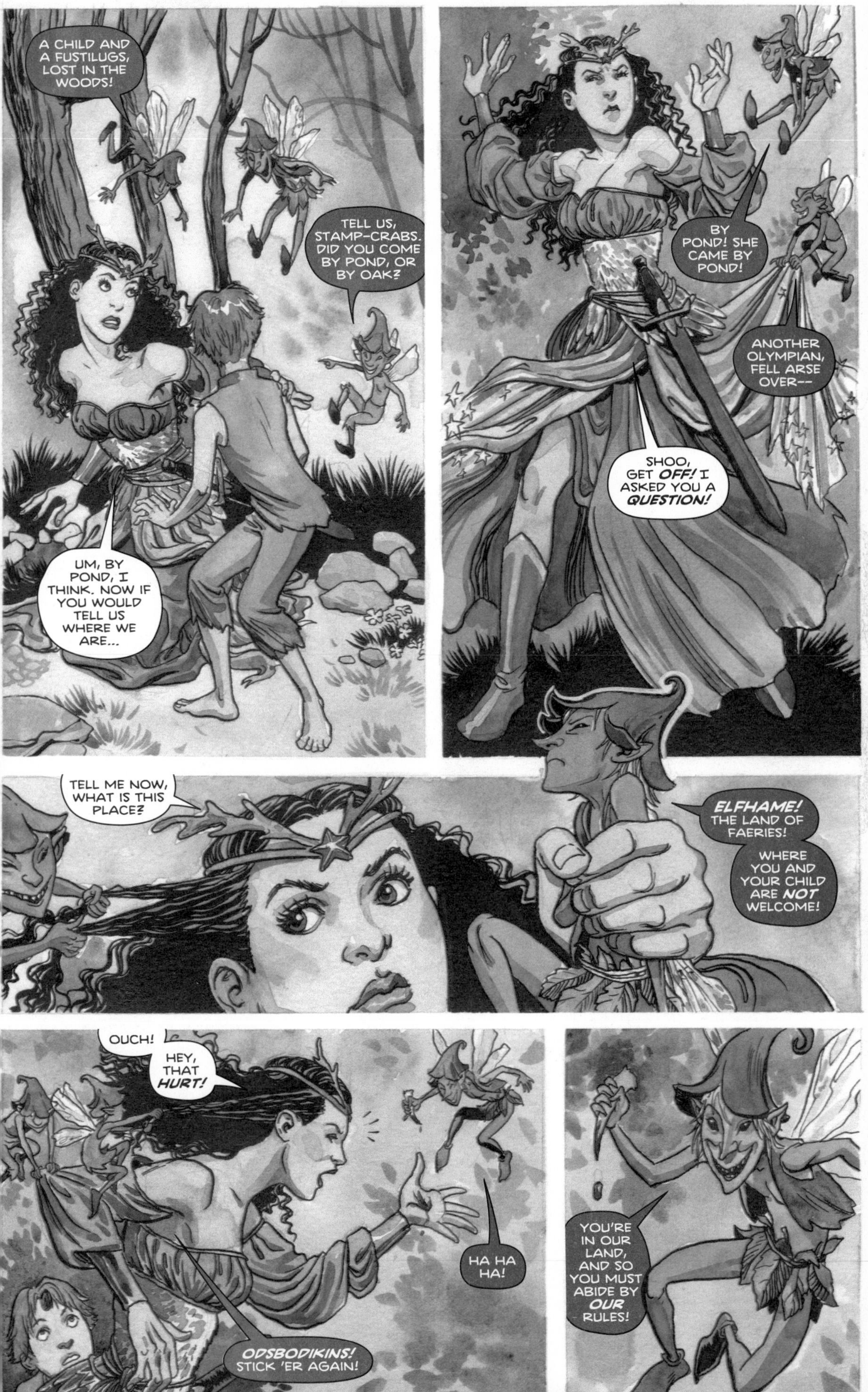
A CHILD AND A FUSTILUGS, LOST IN THE WOODS!
TELL US, STAMP-CRABS. DID YOU COME BY POND, OR BY OAK?
UM, BY POND, I THINK. NOW IF YOU WOULD TELL US WHERE WE ARE...
BY POND! SHE CAME BY POND!
ANOTHER OLYMPIAN, FELL ARSE OVER--
SHOO, GET OFF! I ASKED YOU A QUESTION!
TELL ME NOW, WHAT IS THIS PLACE?
ELFHAME! THE LAND OF FAERIES!
WHERE YOU AND YOUR CHILD ARE NOT WELCOME!
OUCH!
HEY, THAT HURT!
HA HA HA!
ODSBODIKINS! STICK 'ER AGAIN!
YOU'RE IN OUR LAND, AND SO YOU MUST ABIDE BY OUR RULES!

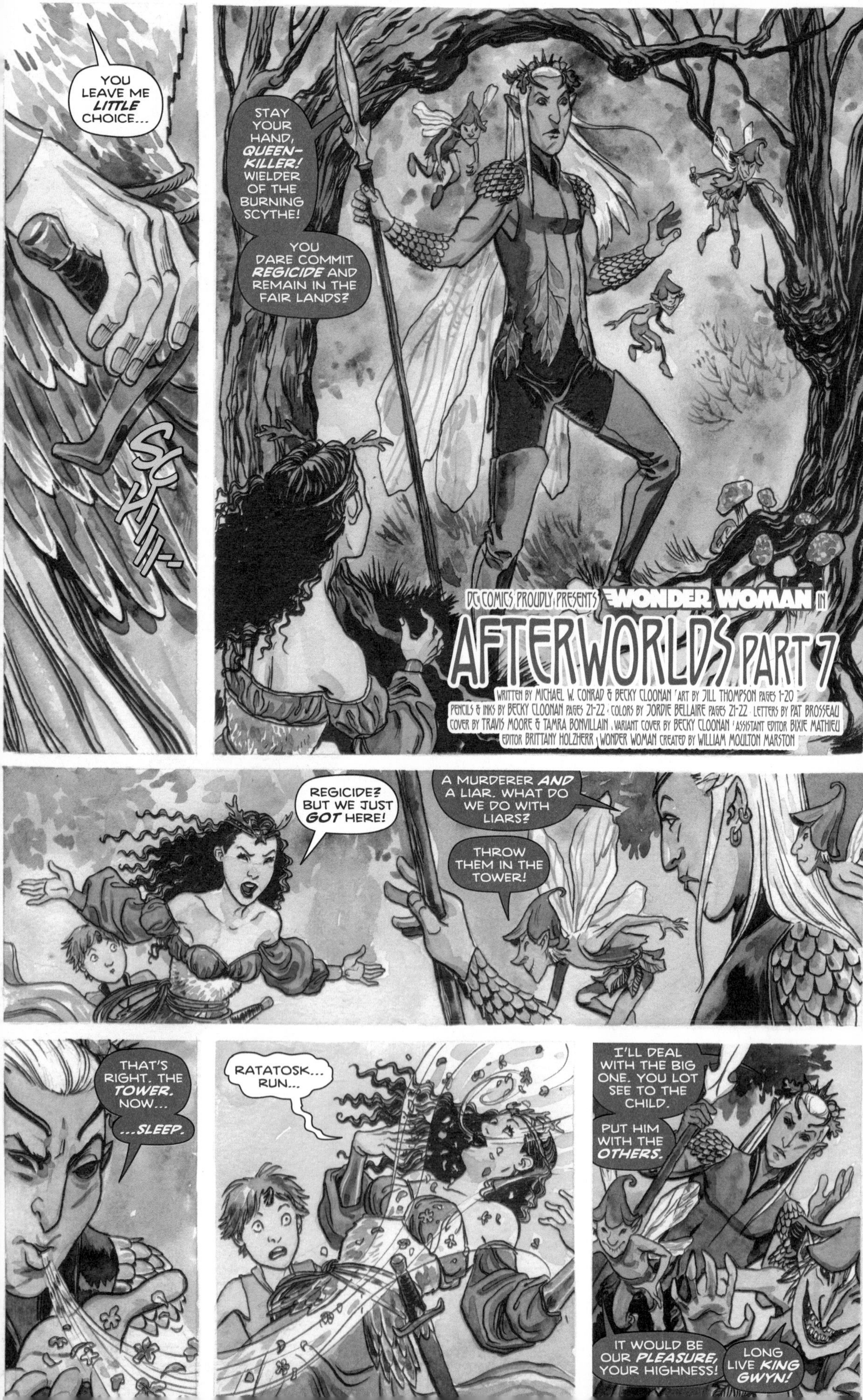

YOU LEAVE ME *LITTLE* CHOICE...
SCHHIIK-
STAY YOUR HAND, *QUEEN-KILLER!* WIELDER OF THE BURNING SCYTHE!
YOU DARE COMMIT *REGICIDE* AND REMAIN IN THE FAIR LANDS?
DC COMICS PROUDLY PRESENTS WONDER WOMAN IN
AFTERWORLDS PART 7
WRITTEN BY MICHAEL W. CONRAD & BECKY CLOONAN · ART BY JILL THOMPSON PAGES 1-20
PENCILS & INKS BY BECKY CLOONAN PAGES 21-22 · COLORS BY JORDIE BELLAIRE PAGES 21-22 · LETTERS BY PAT BROSSEAU
COVER BY TRAVIS MOORE & TAMRA BONVILLAIN · VARIANT COVER BY BECKY CLOONAN · ASSISTANT EDITOR BIXIE MATHIEU
EDITOR BRITTANY HOLZHERR · WONDER WOMAN CREATED BY WILLIAM MOULTON MARSTON
REGICIDE? BUT WE JUST *GOT* HERE!
A MURDERER *AND* A LIAR. WHAT DO WE DO WITH LIARS?
THROW THEM IN THE TOWER!
THAT'S RIGHT. THE *TOWER.* NOW...
...*SLEEP.*
RATATOSK... RUN...
I'LL DEAL WITH THE BIG ONE. YOU LOT SEE TO THE CHILD.
PUT HIM WITH THE *OTHERS.*
IT WOULD BE OUR *PLEASURE,* YOUR HIGHNESS!
LONG LIVE *KING GWYN!*

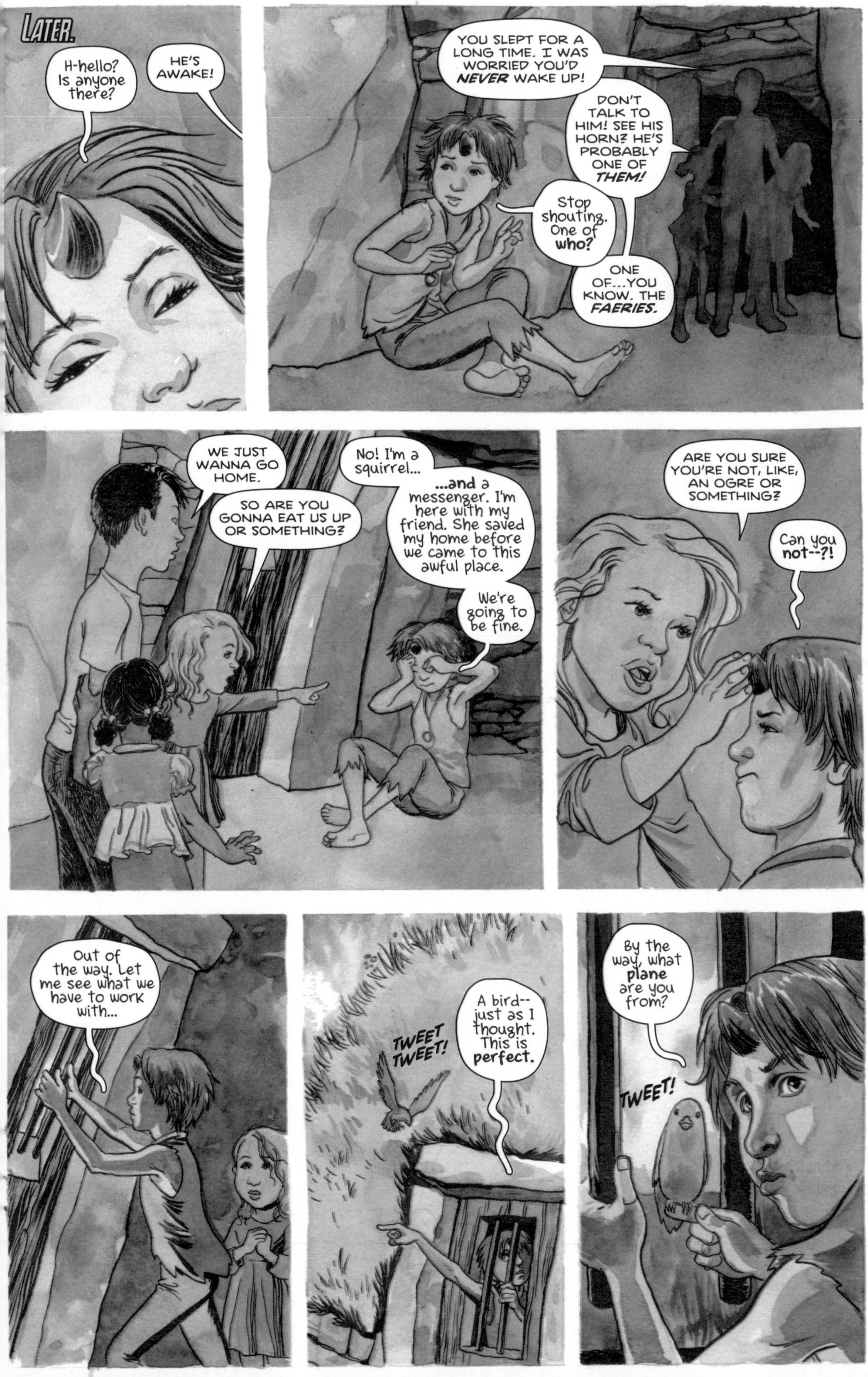
LATER.
H-hello? Is anyone there?
HE'S AWAKE!
YOU SLEPT FOR A LONG TIME. I WAS WORRIED YOU'D NEVER WAKE UP!
DON'T TALK TO HIM! SEE HIS HORN? HE'S PROBABLY ONE OF THEM!
Stop shouting. One of who?
ONE OF...YOU KNOW. THE FAERIES.
WE JUST WANNA GO HOME.
SO ARE YOU GONNA EAT US UP OR SOMETHING?
No! I'm a squirrel...
...and a messenger. I'm here with my friend. She saved my home before we came to this awful place.
We're going to be fine.
ARE YOU SURE YOU'RE NOT, LIKE, AN OGRE OR SOMETHING?
Can you not--?!
Out of the way. Let me see what we have to work with...
TWEET TWEET!
A bird--just as I thought. This is perfect.
By the way, what plane are you from?
TWEET!

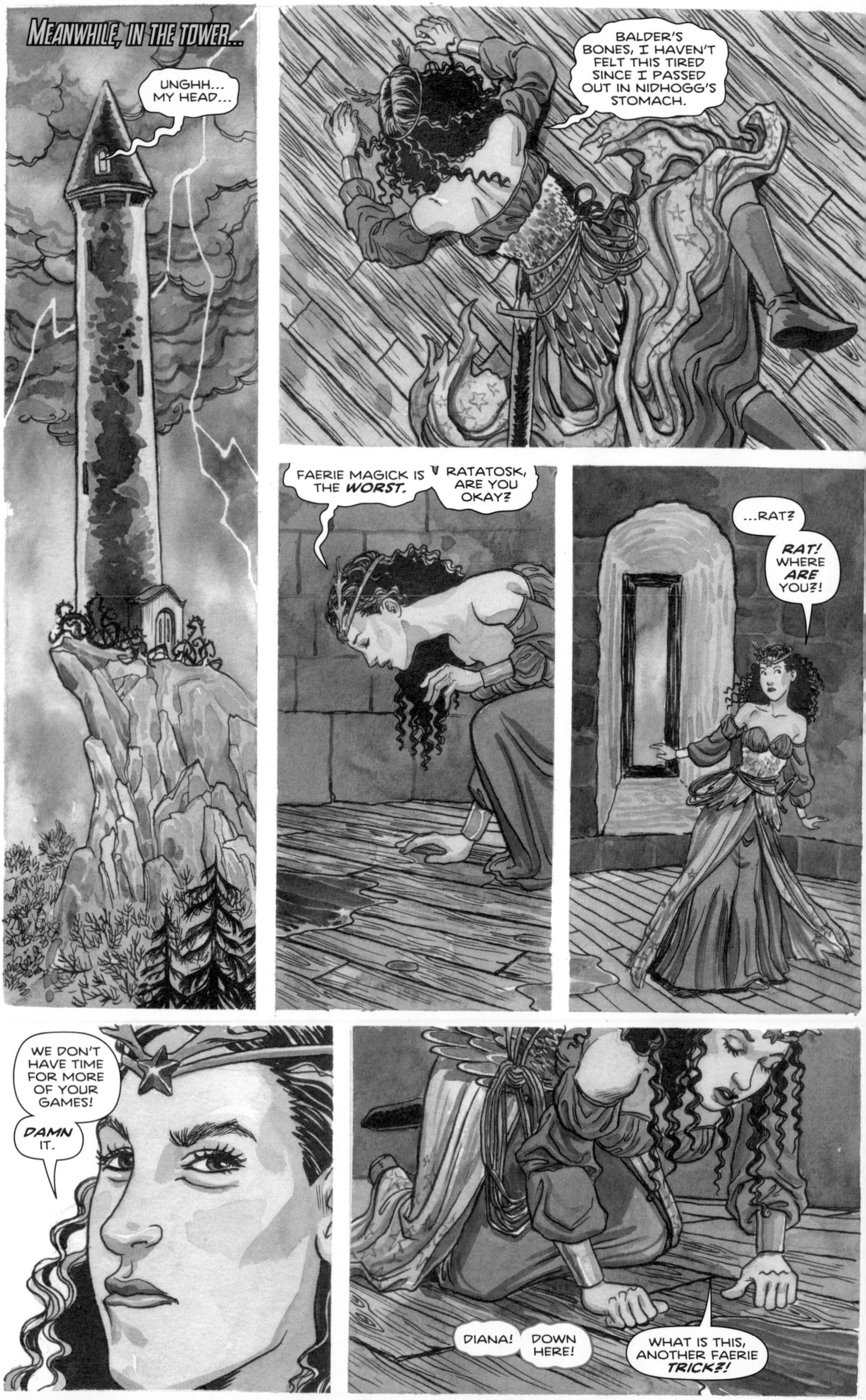
MEANWHILE, IN THE TOWER...
UNGHH... MY HEAD...
BALDER'S BONES, I HAVEN'T FELT THIS TIRED SINCE I PASSED OUT IN NIDHOGG'S STOMACH.
FAERIE MAGICK IS THE WORST.
RATATOSK, ARE YOU OKAY?
...RAT?
RAT! WHERE ARE YOU?!
WE DON'T HAVE TIME FOR MORE OF YOUR GAMES!
DAMN IT.
DIANA!
DOWN HERE!
WHAT IS THIS, ANOTHER FAERIE TRICK?!

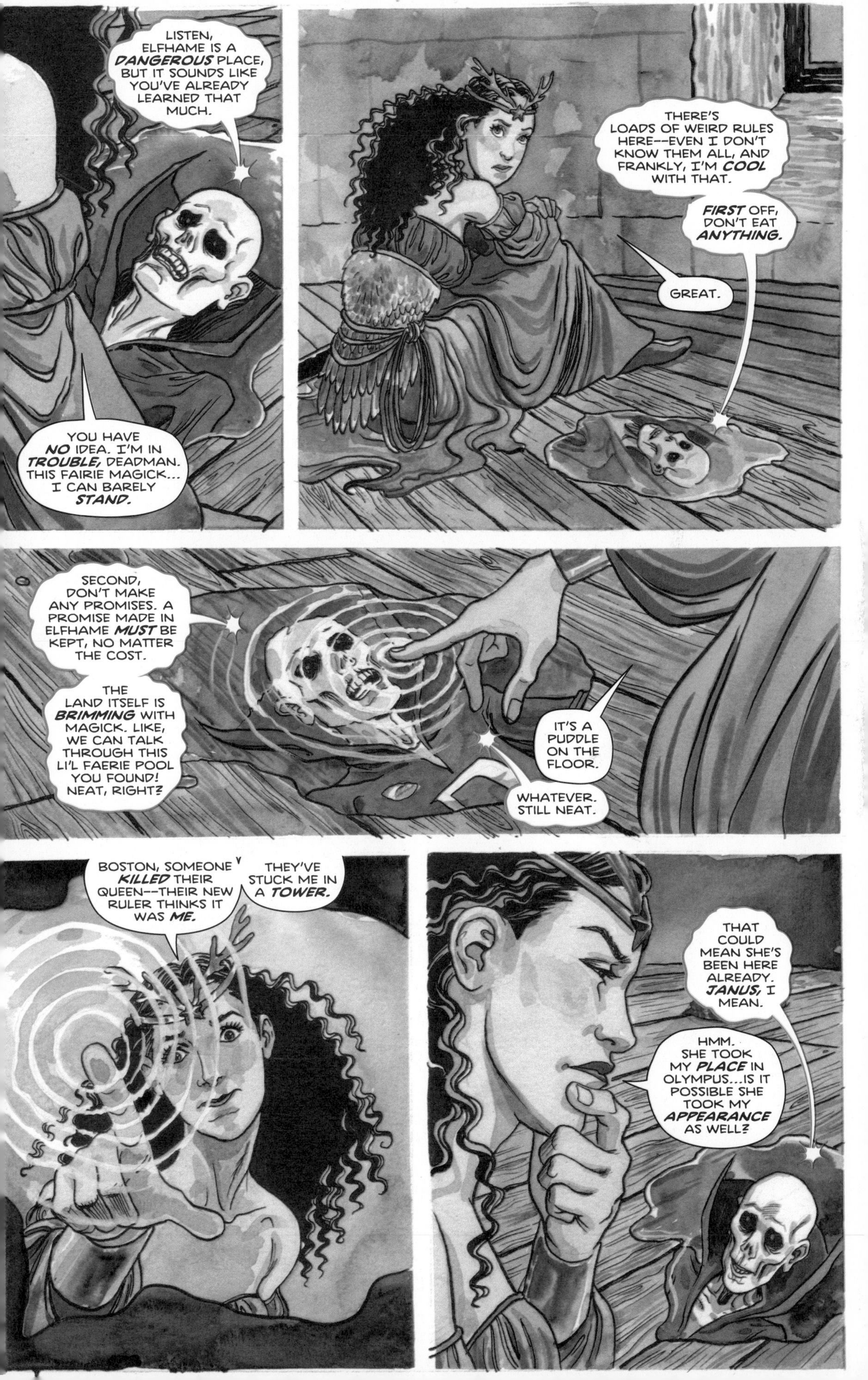

LISTEN, ELFHAME IS A DANGEROUS PLACE, BUT IT SOUNDS LIKE YOU'VE ALREADY LEARNED THAT MUCH.
YOU HAVE NO IDEA. I'M IN TROUBLE, DEADMAN. THIS FAIRIE MAGICK... I CAN BARELY STAND.
THERE'S LOADS OF WEIRD RULES HERE--EVEN I DON'T KNOW THEM ALL, AND FRANKLY, I'M COOL WITH THAT.
FIRST OFF, DON'T EAT ANYTHING.
GREAT.
SECOND, DON'T MAKE ANY PROMISES. A PROMISE MADE IN ELFHAME MUST BE KEPT, NO MATTER THE COST.
THE LAND ITSELF IS BRIMMING WITH MAGICK. LIKE, WE CAN TALK THROUGH THIS LI'L FAERIE POOL YOU FOUND! NEAT, RIGHT?
IT'S A PUDDLE ON THE FLOOR.
WHATEVER. STILL NEAT.
BOSTON, SOMEONE KILLED THEIR QUEEN--THEIR NEW RULER THINKS IT WAS ME.
THEY'VE STUCK ME IN A TOWER.
THAT COULD MEAN SHE'S BEEN HERE ALREADY. JANUS, I MEAN.
HMM. SHE TOOK MY PLACE IN OLYMPUS...IS IT POSSIBLE SHE TOOK MY APPEARANCE AS WELL?

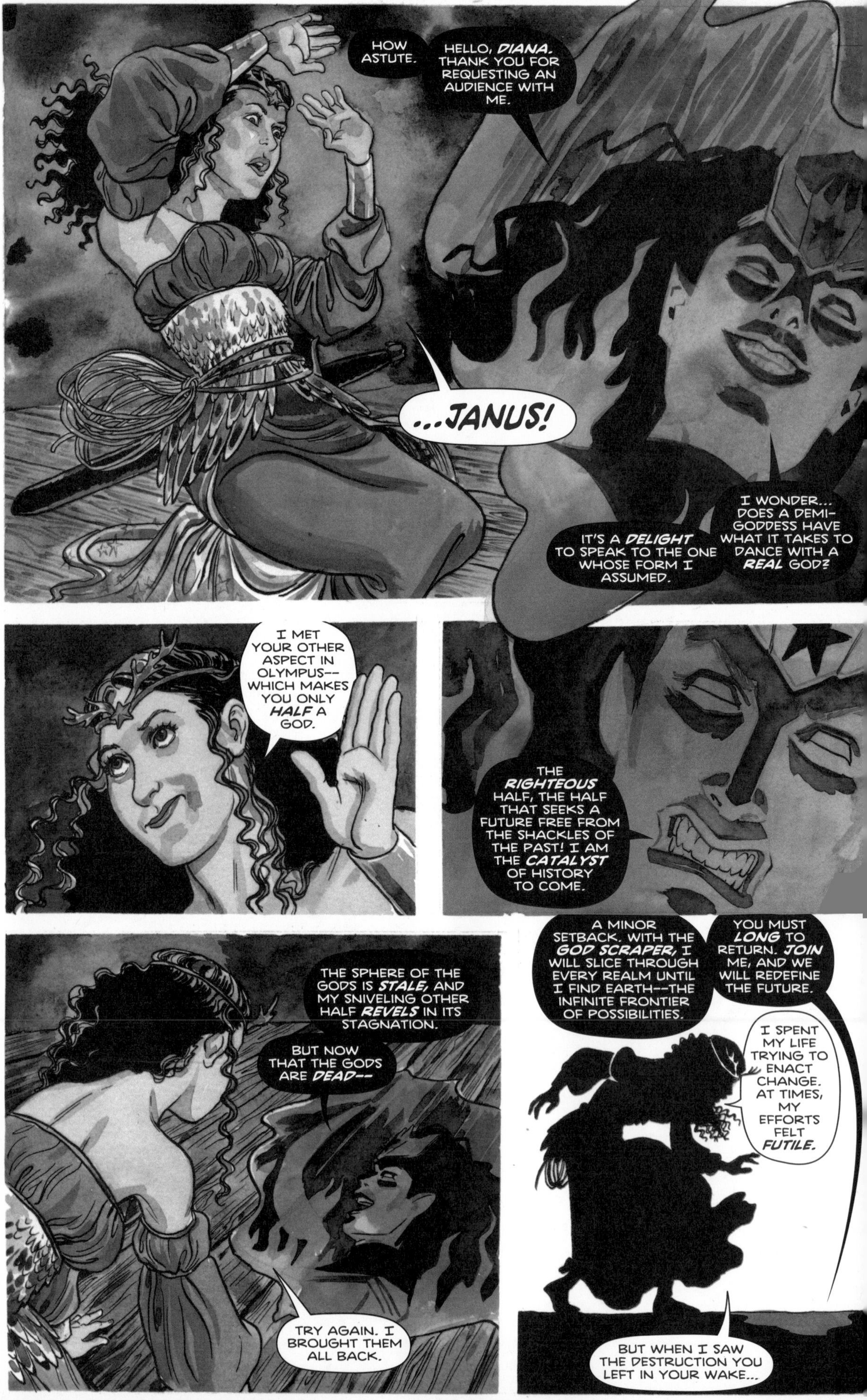

HELLO, *DIANA.* THANK YOU FOR REQUESTING AN AUDIENCE WITH ME.
...JANUS!
HOW ASTUTE.
IT'S A *DELIGHT* TO SPEAK TO THE ONE WHOSE FORM I ASSUMED.
I WONDER... DOES A DEMI-GODDESS HAVE WHAT IT TAKES TO DANCE WITH A *REAL* GOD?
I MET YOUR OTHER ASPECT IN OLYMPUS--WHICH MAKES YOU ONLY *HALF* A GOD.
THE *RIGHTEOUS* HALF, THE HALF THAT SEEKS A FUTURE FREE FROM THE SHACKLES OF THE PAST! I AM THE *CATALYST* OF HISTORY TO COME.
THE SPHERE OF THE GODS IS *STALE,* AND MY SNIVELING OTHER HALF *REVELS* IN ITS STAGNATION.
BUT NOW THAT THE GODS ARE *DEAD--*
TRY AGAIN. I BROUGHT THEM ALL BACK.
A MINOR SETBACK. WITH THE *GOD SCRAPER,* I WILL SLICE THROUGH EVERY REALM UNTIL I FIND EARTH--THE INFINITE FRONTIER OF POSSIBILITIES.
YOU MUST *LONG* TO RETURN. *JOIN* ME, AND WE WILL REDEFINE THE FUTURE.
I SPENT MY LIFE TRYING TO ENACT CHANGE. AT TIMES, MY EFFORTS FELT *FUTILE.*
BUT WHEN I SAW THE DESTRUCTION YOU LEFT IN YOUR WAKE...

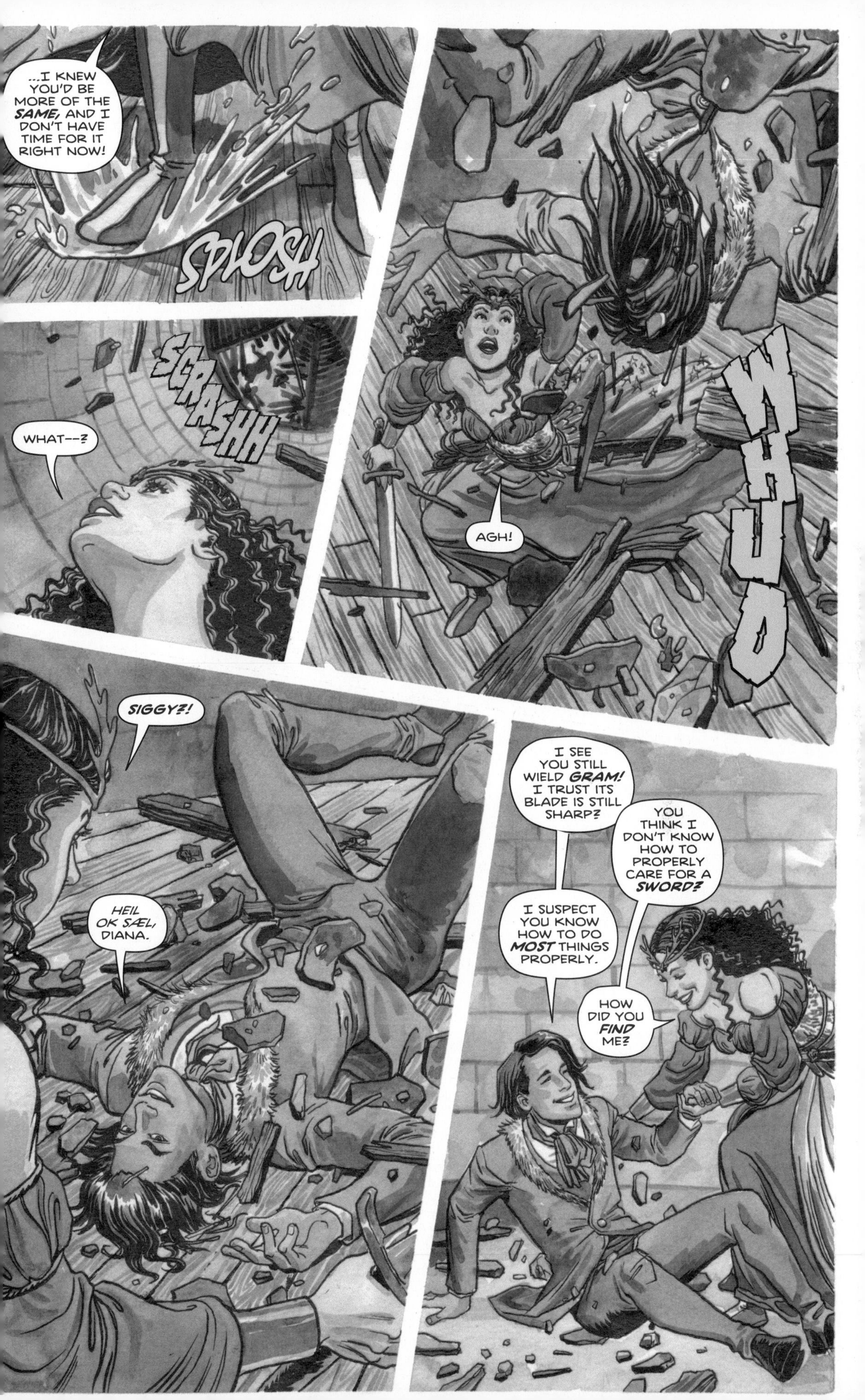
...I KNEW YOU'D BE MORE OF THE SAME, AND I DON'T HAVE TIME FOR IT RIGHT NOW!
SPLOSH
SCRASHH
WHAT--?
WHUD
AGH!
SIGGY?!
HEIL OK SÆL, DIANA.
I SEE YOU STILL WIELD GRAM! I TRUST ITS BLADE IS STILL SHARP?
YOU THINK I DON'T KNOW HOW TO PROPERLY CARE FOR A SWORD?
I SUSPECT YOU KNOW HOW TO DO MOST THINGS PROPERLY.
HOW DID YOU FIND ME?

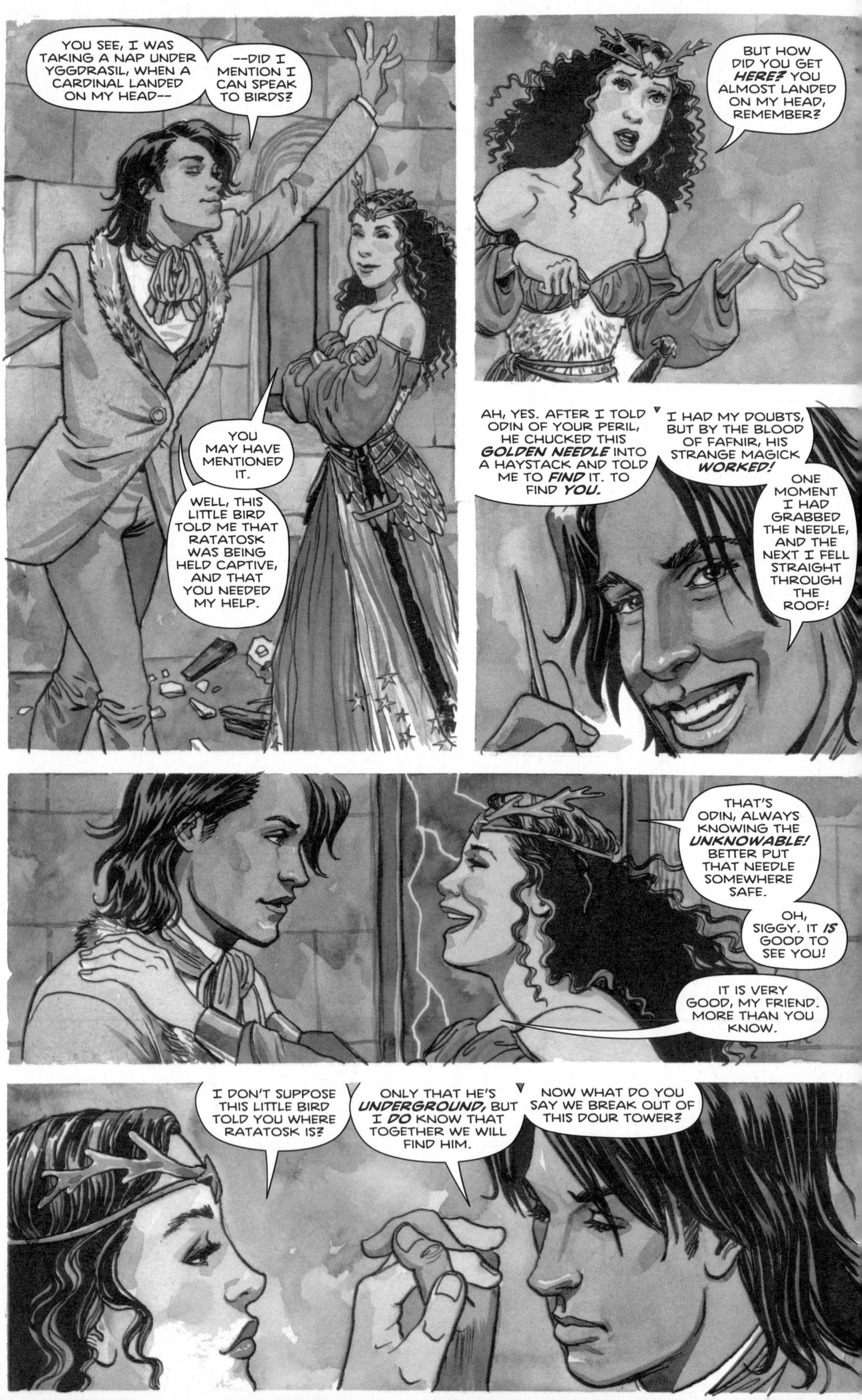
YOU SEE, I WAS TAKING A NAP UNDER YGGDRASIL, WHEN A CARDINAL LANDED ON MY HEAD--
--DID I MENTION I CAN SPEAK TO BIRDS?
YOU MAY HAVE MENTIONED IT.
WELL, THIS LITTLE BIRD TOLD ME THAT RATATOSK WAS BEING HELD CAPTIVE, AND THAT YOU NEEDED MY HELP.
BUT HOW DID YOU GET HERE? YOU ALMOST LANDED ON MY HEAD, REMEMBER?
AH, YES. AFTER I TOLD ODIN OF YOUR PERIL, HE CHUCKED THIS GOLDEN NEEDLE INTO A HAYSTACK AND TOLD ME TO FIND IT. TO FIND YOU.
I HAD MY DOUBTS, BUT BY THE BLOOD OF FAFNIR, HIS STRANGE MAGICK WORKED!
ONE MOMENT I HAD GRABBED THE NEEDLE, AND THE NEXT I FELL STRAIGHT THROUGH THE ROOF!
THAT'S ODIN, ALWAYS KNOWING THE UNKNOWABLE! BETTER PUT THAT NEEDLE SOMEWHERE SAFE.
OH, SIGGY. IT IS GOOD TO SEE YOU!
IT IS VERY GOOD, MY FRIEND. MORE THAN YOU KNOW.
I DON'T SUPPOSE THIS LITTLE BIRD TOLD YOU WHERE RATATOSK IS?
ONLY THAT HE'S UNDERGROUND, BUT I DO KNOW THAT TOGETHER WE WILL FIND HIM.
NOW WHAT DO YOU SAY WE BREAK OUT OF THIS DOUR TOWER?

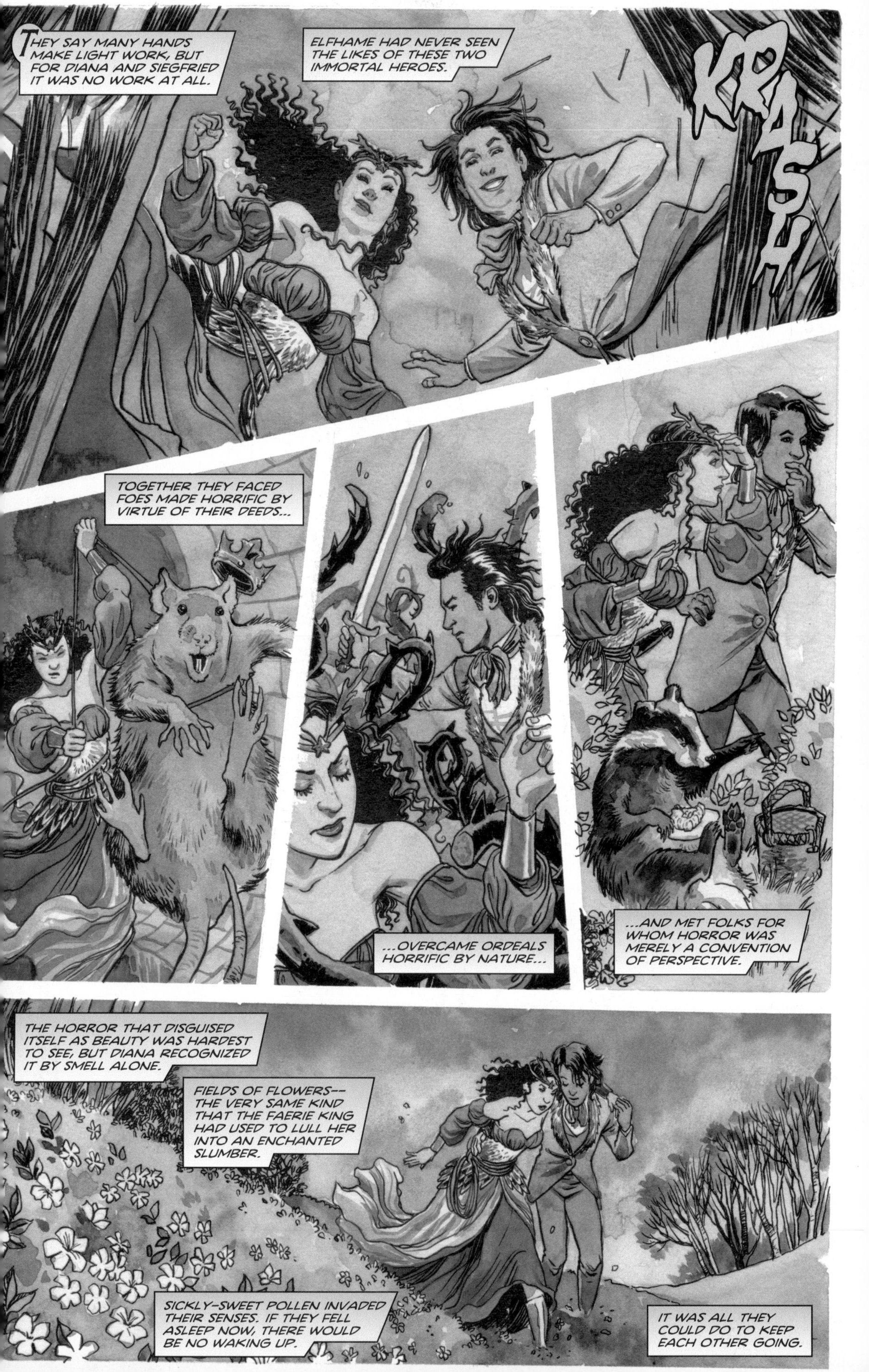
THEY SAY MANY HANDS MAKE LIGHT WORK, BUT FOR DIANA AND SIEGFRIED IT WAS NO WORK AT ALL.
ELFHAME HAD NEVER SEEN THE LIKES OF THESE TWO IMMORTAL HEROES.
KRASH
TOGETHER THEY FACED FOES MADE HORRIFIC BY VIRTUE OF THEIR DEEDS...
...OVERCAME ORDEALS HORRIFIC BY NATURE...
...AND MET FOLKS FOR WHOM HORROR WAS MERELY A CONVENTION OF PERSPECTIVE.
THE HORROR THAT DISGUISED ITSELF AS BEAUTY WAS HARDEST TO SEE, BUT DIANA RECOGNIZED IT BY SMELL ALONE.
FIELDS OF FLOWERS-- THE VERY SAME KIND THAT THE FAERIE KING HAD USED TO LULL HER INTO AN ENCHANTED SLUMBER.
SICKLY-SWEET POLLEN INVADED THEIR SENSES. IF THEY FELL ASLEEP NOW, THERE WOULD BE NO WAKING UP.
IT WAS ALL THEY COULD DO TO KEEP EACH OTHER GOING.

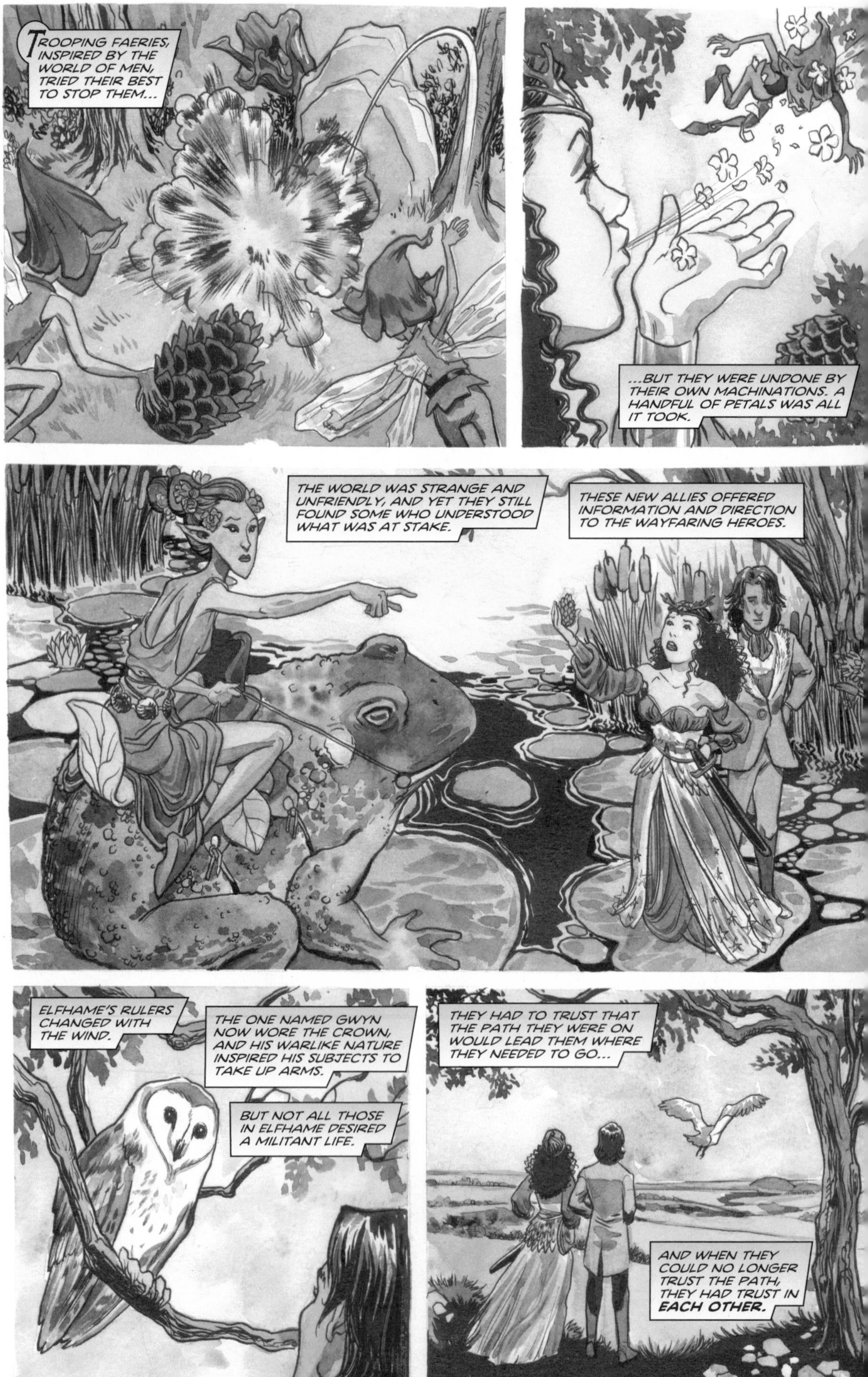
TROOPING FAERIES, INSPIRED BY THE WORLD OF MEN, TRIED THEIR BEST TO STOP THEM...
...BUT THEY WERE UNDONE BY THEIR OWN MACHINATIONS. A HANDFUL OF PETALS WAS ALL IT TOOK.
THE WORLD WAS STRANGE AND UNFRIENDLY, AND YET THEY STILL FOUND SOME WHO UNDERSTOOD WHAT WAS AT STAKE.
THESE NEW ALLIES OFFERED INFORMATION AND DIRECTION TO THE WAYFARING HEROES.
ELFHAME'S RULERS CHANGED WITH THE WIND.
THE ONE NAMED GWYN NOW WORE THE CROWN, AND HIS WARLIKE NATURE INSPIRED HIS SUBJECTS TO TAKE UP ARMS.
BUT NOT ALL THOSE IN ELFHAME DESIRED A MILITANT LIFE.
THEY HAD TO TRUST THAT THE PATH THEY WERE ON WOULD LEAD THEM WHERE THEY NEEDED TO GO...
AND WHEN THEY COULD NO LONGER TRUST THE PATH, THEY HAD TRUST IN EACH OTHER.

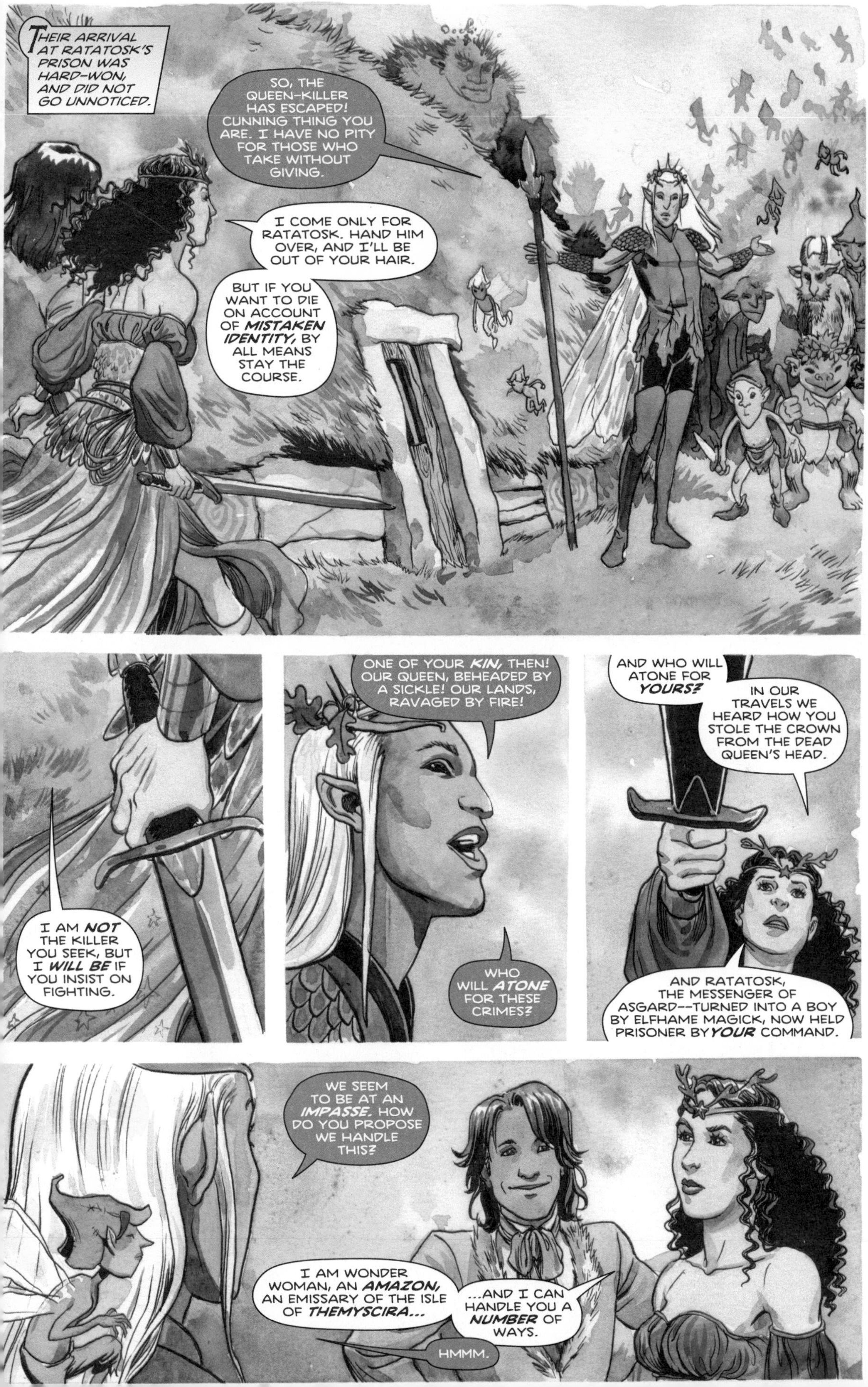
THEIR ARRIVAL AT RATATOSK'S PRISON WAS HARD-WON, AND DID NOT GO UNNOTICED.
SO, THE QUEEN-KILLER HAS ESCAPED! CUNNING THING YOU ARE. I HAVE NO PITY FOR THOSE WHO TAKE WITHOUT GIVING.
I COME ONLY FOR RATATOSK. HAND HIM OVER, AND I'LL BE OUT OF YOUR HAIR.
BUT IF YOU WANT TO DIE ON ACCOUNT OF MISTAKEN IDENTITY, BY ALL MEANS STAY THE COURSE.
I AM NOT THE KILLER YOU SEEK, BUT I WILL BE IF YOU INSIST ON FIGHTING.
ONE OF YOUR KIN, THEN! OUR QUEEN, BEHEADED BY A SICKLE! OUR LANDS, RAVAGED BY FIRE!
WHO WILL ATONE FOR THESE CRIMES?
AND WHO WILL ATONE FOR YOURS?
IN OUR TRAVELS WE HEARD HOW YOU STOLE THE CROWN FROM THE DEAD QUEEN'S HEAD.
AND RATATOSK, THE MESSENGER OF ASGARD--TURNED INTO A BOY BY ELFHAME MAGICK, NOW HELD PRISONER BY YOUR COMMAND.
WE SEEM TO BE AT AN IMPASSE. HOW DO YOU PROPOSE WE HANDLE THIS?
I AM WONDER WOMAN, AN AMAZON, AN EMISSARY OF THE ISLE OF THEMYSCIRA...
...AND I CAN HANDLE YOU A NUMBER OF WAYS.
HMMM.

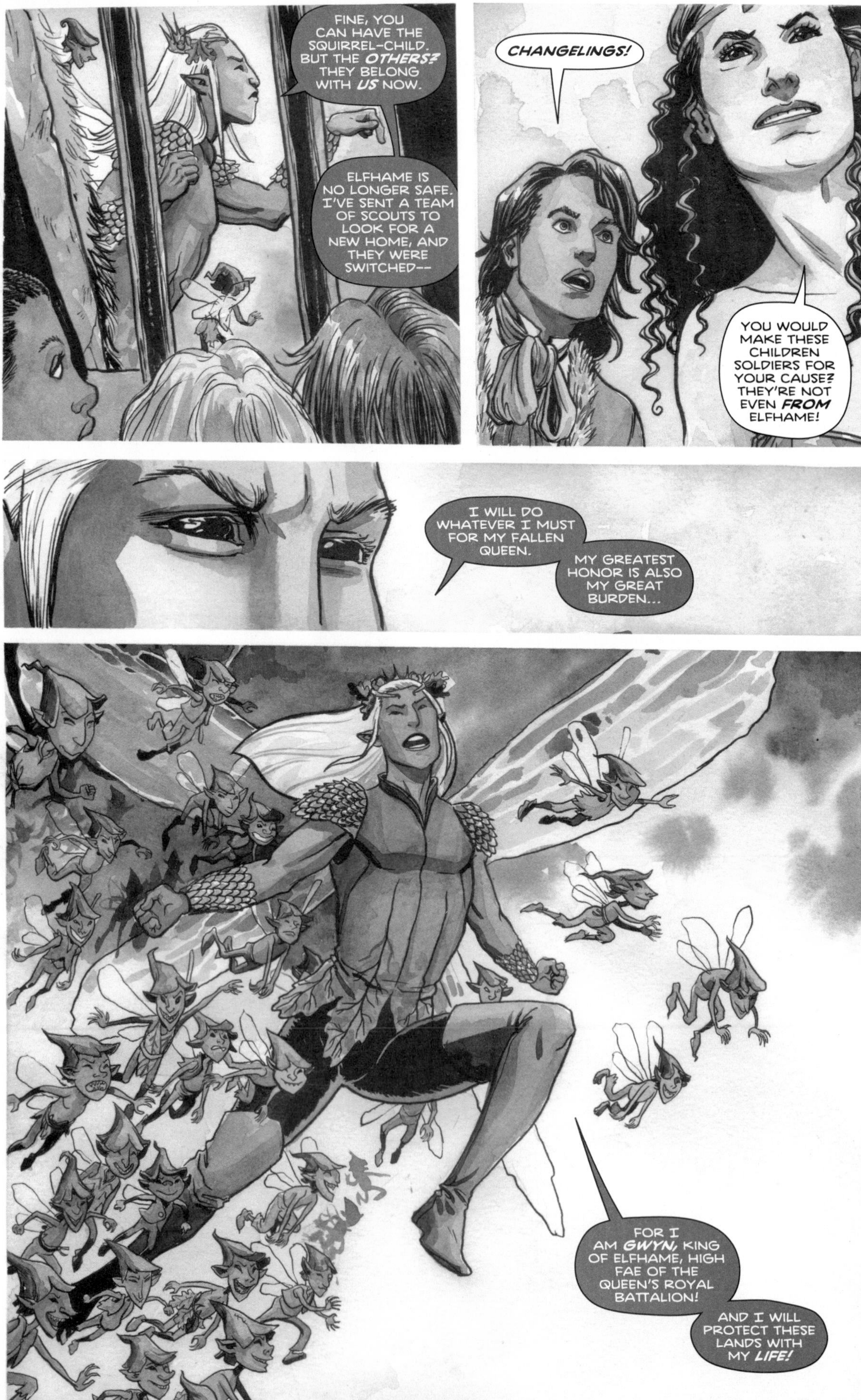
FINE, YOU CAN HAVE THE SQUIRREL-CHILD. BUT THE *OTHERS?* THEY BELONG WITH *US* NOW.
ELFHAME IS NO LONGER SAFE. I'VE SENT A TEAM OF SCOUTS TO LOOK FOR A NEW HOME, AND THEY WERE SWITCHED--
CHANGELINGS!
YOU WOULD MAKE THESE CHILDREN SOLDIERS FOR YOUR CAUSE? THEY'RE NOT EVEN *FROM* ELFHAME!
I WILL DO WHATEVER I MUST FOR MY FALLEN QUEEN.
MY GREATEST HONOR IS ALSO MY GREAT BURDEN...
FOR I AM *GWYN,* KING OF ELFHAME, HIGH FAE OF THE QUEEN'S ROYAL BATTALION!
AND I WILL PROTECT THESE LANDS WITH MY *LIFE!*

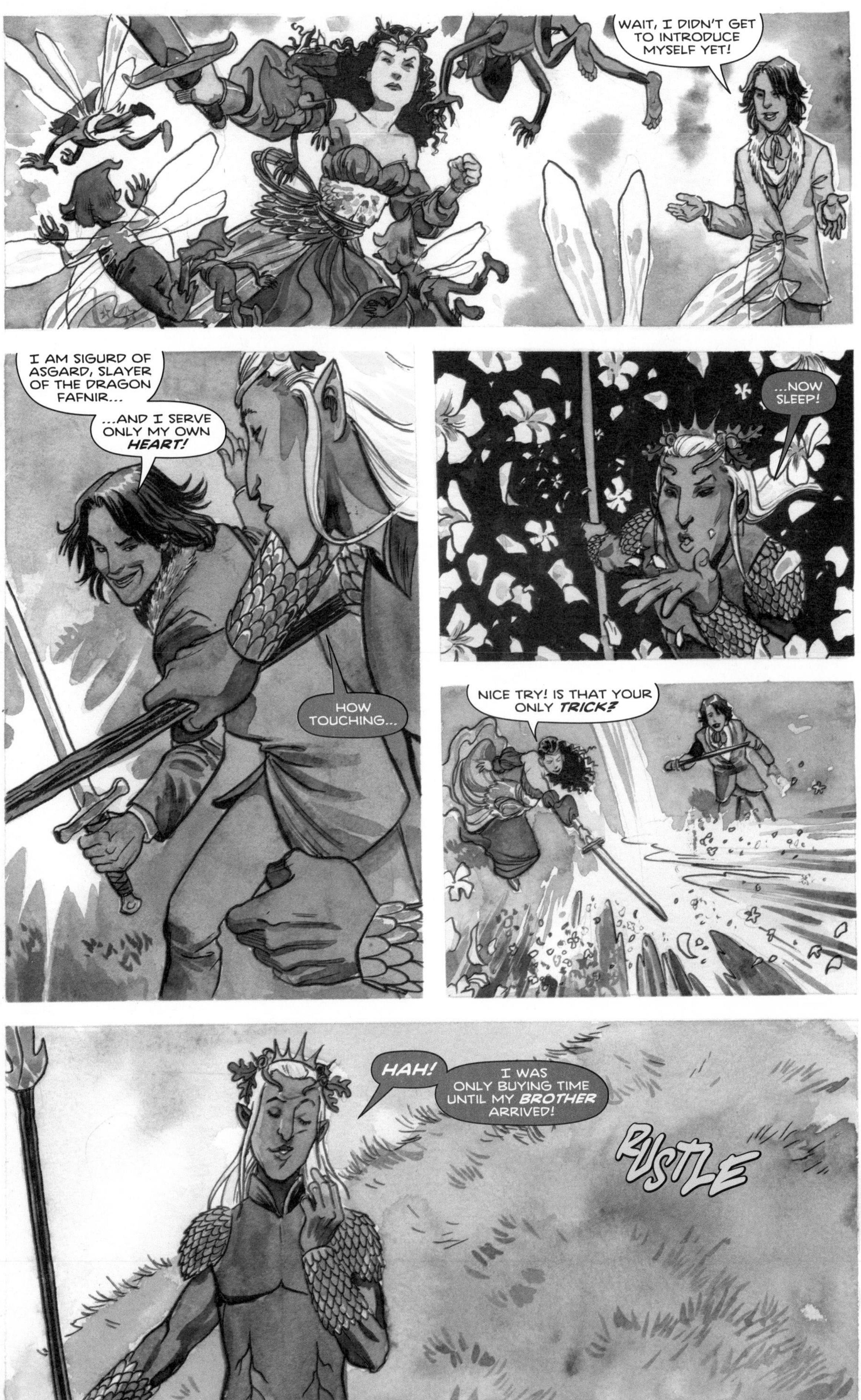

WAIT, I DIDN'T GET TO INTRODUCE MYSELF YET!
I AM SIGURD OF ASGARD, SLAYER OF THE DRAGON FAFNIR...
...AND I SERVE ONLY MY OWN HEART!
HOW TOUCHING...
...NOW SLEEP!
NICE TRY! IS THAT YOUR ONLY TRICK?
HAH!
I WAS ONLY BUYING TIME UNTIL MY BROTHER ARRIVED!
RUSTLE

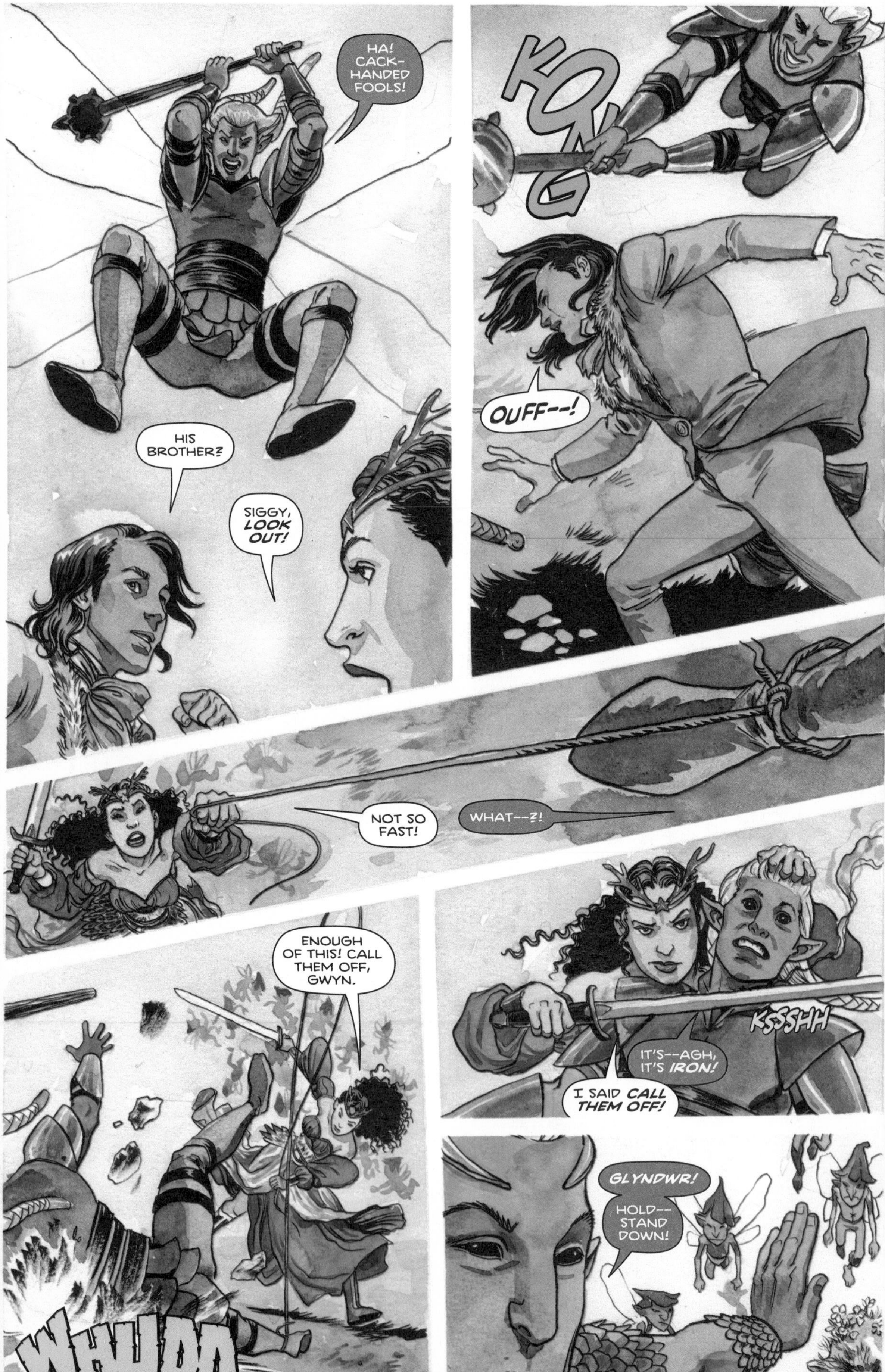
HA! CACK-HANDED FOOLS!
HIS BROTHER?
SIGGY, LOOK OUT!
KONG
OUFF--!
NOT SO FAST!
WHAT--?!
ENOUGH OF THIS! CALL THEM OFF, GWYN.
WHUDD
KSSSHH
IT'S--AGH, IT'S IRON!
I SAID CALL THEM OFF!
GLYNDWR!
HOLD--STAND DOWN!

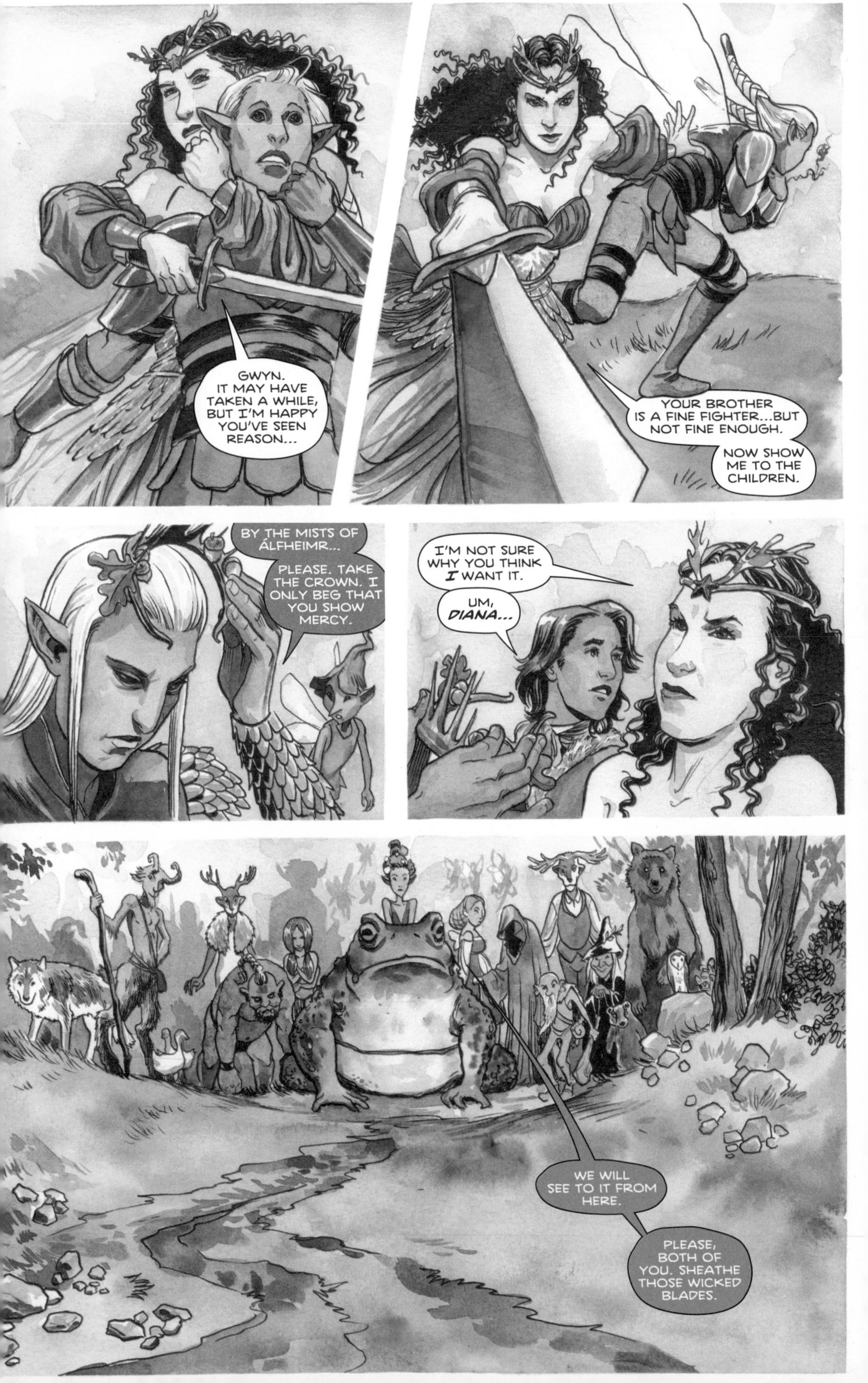
GWYN. IT MAY HAVE TAKEN A WHILE, BUT I'M HAPPY YOU'VE SEEN REASON...
YOUR BROTHER IS A FINE FIGHTER...BUT NOT FINE ENOUGH.
NOW SHOW ME TO THE CHILDREN.
BY THE MISTS OF ÁLFHEIMR...
PLEASE. TAKE THE CROWN. I ONLY BEG THAT YOU SHOW MERCY.
I'M NOT SURE WHY YOU THINK *I* WANT IT.
UM, *DIANA...*
WE WILL SEE TO IT FROM HERE.
PLEASE, BOTH OF YOU. SHEATHE THOSE WICKED BLADES.

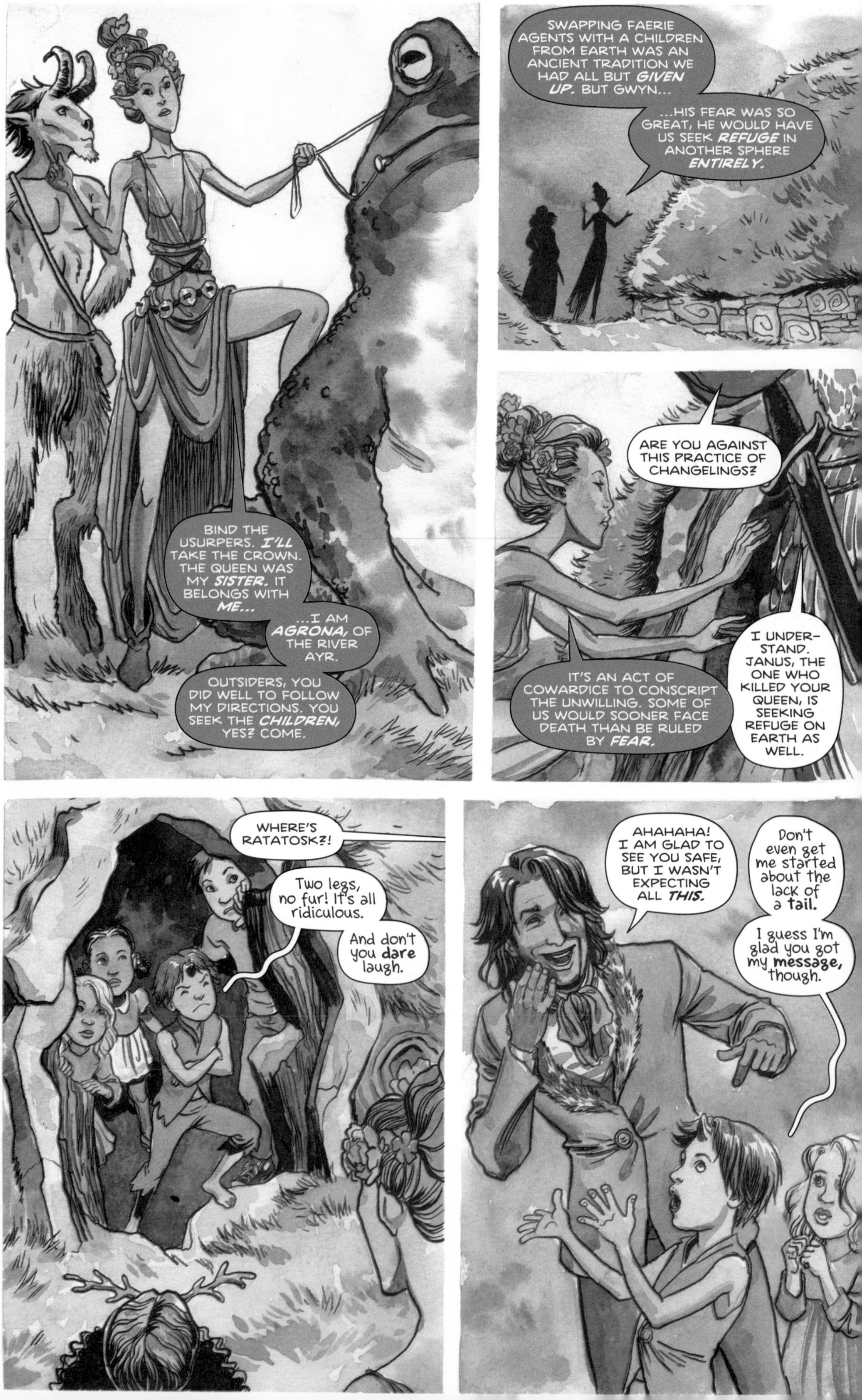

BIND THE USURPERS. I'LL TAKE THE CROWN. THE QUEEN WAS MY SISTER. IT BELONGS WITH ME...
...I AM AGRONA, OF THE RIVER AYR.
OUTSIDERS, YOU DID WELL TO FOLLOW MY DIRECTIONS. YOU SEEK THE CHILDREN, YES? COME.
SWAPPING FAERIE AGENTS WITH A CHILDREN FROM EARTH WAS AN ANCIENT TRADITION WE HAD ALL BUT GIVEN UP. BUT GWYN...
...HIS FEAR WAS SO GREAT, HE WOULD HAVE US SEEK REFUGE IN ANOTHER SPHERE ENTIRELY.
ARE YOU AGAINST THIS PRACTICE OF CHANGELINGS?
IT'S AN ACT OF COWARDICE TO CONSCRIPT THE UNWILLING. SOME OF US WOULD SOONER FACE DEATH THAN BE RULED BY FEAR.
I UNDER-STAND. JANUS, THE ONE WHO KILLED YOUR QUEEN, IS SEEKING REFUGE ON EARTH AS WELL.
WHERE'S RATATOSK?!
Two legs, no fur! It's all ridiculous.
And don't you dare laugh.
AHAHAHA! I AM GLAD TO SEE YOU SAFE, BUT I WASN'T EXPECTING ALL THIS.
Don't even get me started about the lack of a tail.
I guess I'm glad you got my message, though.

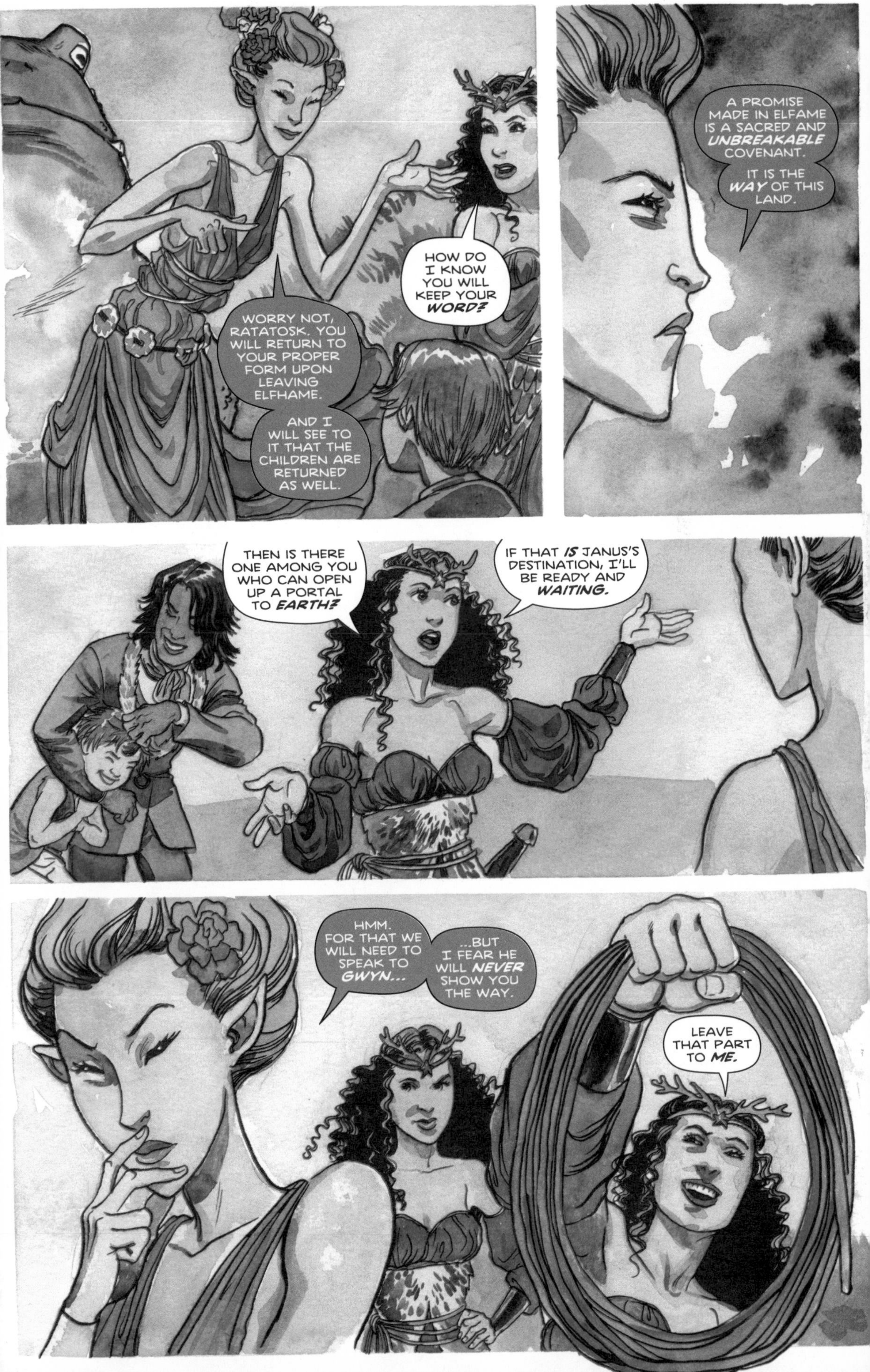

HOW DO I KNOW YOU WILL KEEP YOUR WORD?
WORRY NOT, RATATOSK. YOU WILL RETURN TO YOUR PROPER FORM UPON LEAVING ELFHAME.
AND I WILL SEE TO IT THAT THE CHILDREN ARE RETURNED AS WELL.
A PROMISE MADE IN ELFAME IS A SACRED AND UNBREAKABLE COVENANT.
IT IS THE WAY OF THIS LAND.
THEN IS THERE ONE AMONG YOU WHO CAN OPEN UP A PORTAL TO EARTH?
IF THAT IS JANUS'S DESTINATION, I'LL BE READY AND WAITING.
HMM. FOR THAT WE WILL NEED TO SPEAK TO GWYN...
...BUT I FEAR HE WILL NEVER SHOW YOU THE WAY.
LEAVE THAT PART TO ME.

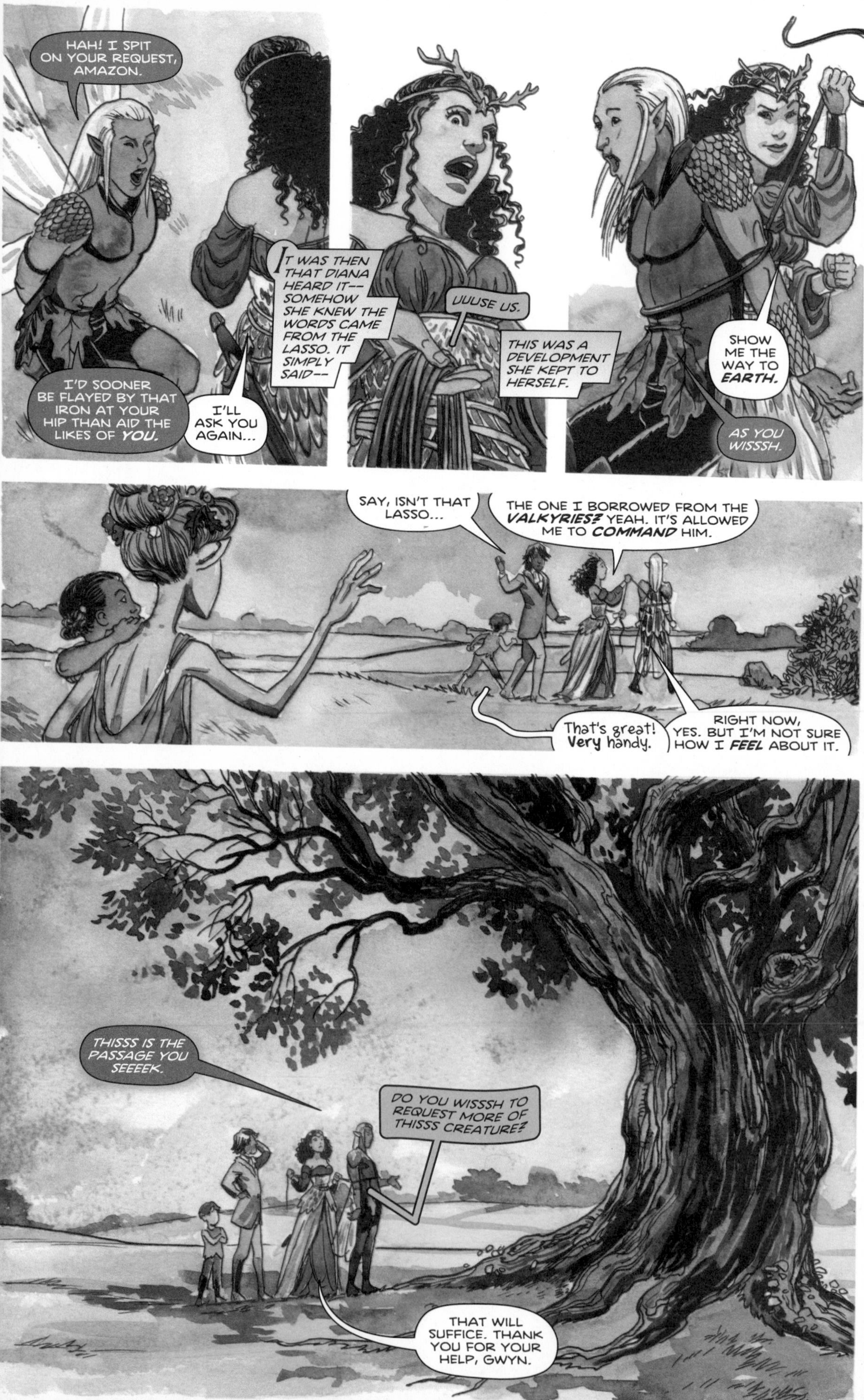
HAH! I SPIT ON YOUR REQUEST, AMAZON.
I'D SOONER BE FLAYED BY THAT IRON AT YOUR HIP THAN AID THE LIKES OF YOU.
I'LL ASK YOU AGAIN...
IT WAS THEN THAT DIANA HEARD IT-- SOMEHOW SHE KNEW THE WORDS CAME FROM THE LASSO. IT SIMPLY SAID--
UUUSE US.
THIS WAS A DEVELOPMENT SHE KEPT TO HERSELF.
SHOW ME THE WAY TO EARTH.
AS YOU WISSSH.
SAY, ISN'T THAT LASSO...
THE ONE I BORROWED FROM THE VALKYRIES? YEAH. IT'S ALLOWED ME TO COMMAND HIM.
That's great! Very handy.
RIGHT NOW, YES. BUT I'M NOT SURE HOW I FEEL ABOUT IT.
THISSS IS THE PASSAGE YOU SEEEEK.
DO YOU WISSSH TO REQUEST MORE OF THISSS CREATURE?
THAT WILL SUFFICE. THANK YOU FOR YOUR HELP, GWYN.

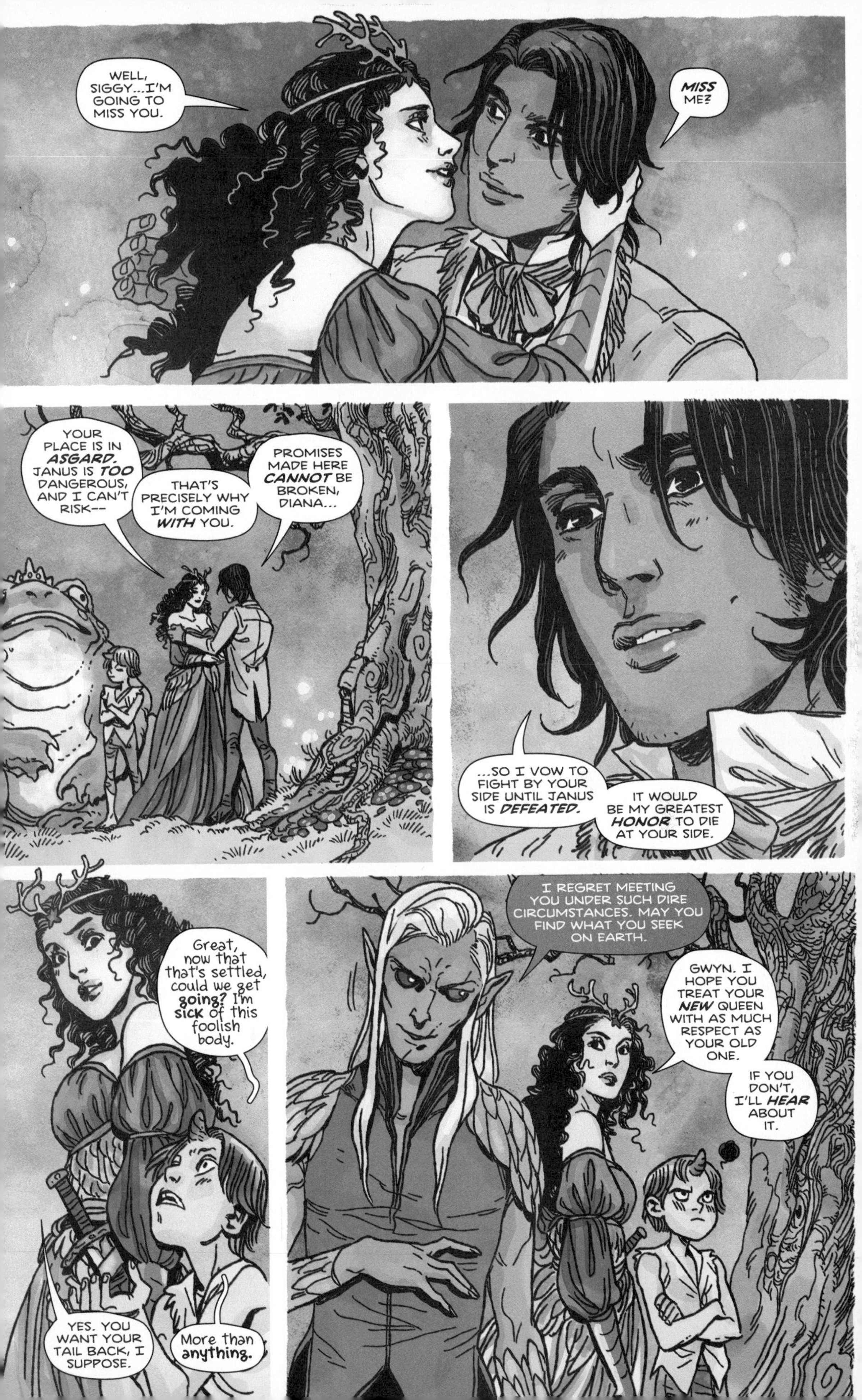

WELL, SIGGY...I'M GOING TO MISS YOU.
MISS ME?
YOUR PLACE IS IN ASGARD. JANUS IS TOO DANGEROUS, AND I CAN'T RISK--
THAT'S PRECISELY WHY I'M COMING WITH YOU.
PROMISES MADE HERE CANNOT BE BROKEN, DIANA...
...SO I VOW TO FIGHT BY YOUR SIDE UNTIL JANUS IS DEFEATED.
IT WOULD BE MY GREATEST HONOR TO DIE AT YOUR SIDE.
Great, now that that's settled, could we get going? I'm sick of this foolish body.
YES. YOU WANT YOUR TAIL BACK, I SUPPOSE.
More than anything.
I REGRET MEETING YOU UNDER SUCH DIRE CIRCUMSTANCES. MAY YOU FIND WHAT YOU SEEK ON EARTH.
GWYN. I HOPE YOU TREAT YOUR NEW QUEEN WITH AS MUCH RESPECT AS YOUR OLD ONE.
IF YOU DON'T, I'LL HEAR ABOUT IT.

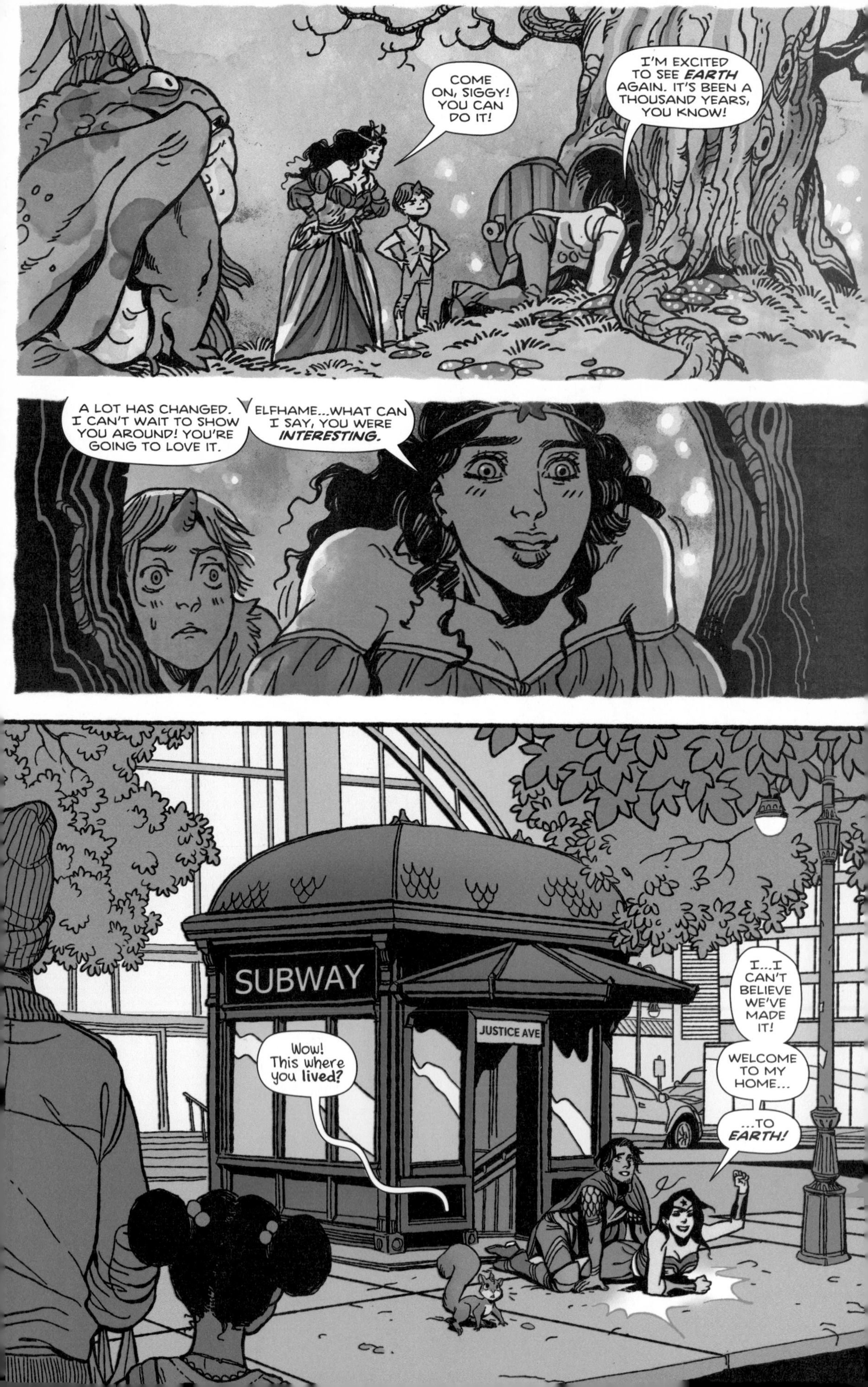
COME ON, SIGGY! YOU CAN DO IT!
I'M EXCITED TO SEE EARTH AGAIN. IT'S BEEN A THOUSAND YEARS, YOU KNOW!
A LOT HAS CHANGED. I CAN'T WAIT TO SHOW YOU AROUND! YOU'RE GOING TO LOVE IT.
ELFHAME...WHAT CAN I SAY, YOU WERE INTERESTING.
SUBWAY
JUSTICE AVE
Wow! This where you lived?
I...I CAN'T BELIEVE WE'VE MADE IT!
WELCOME TO MY HOME...
...TO EARTH!

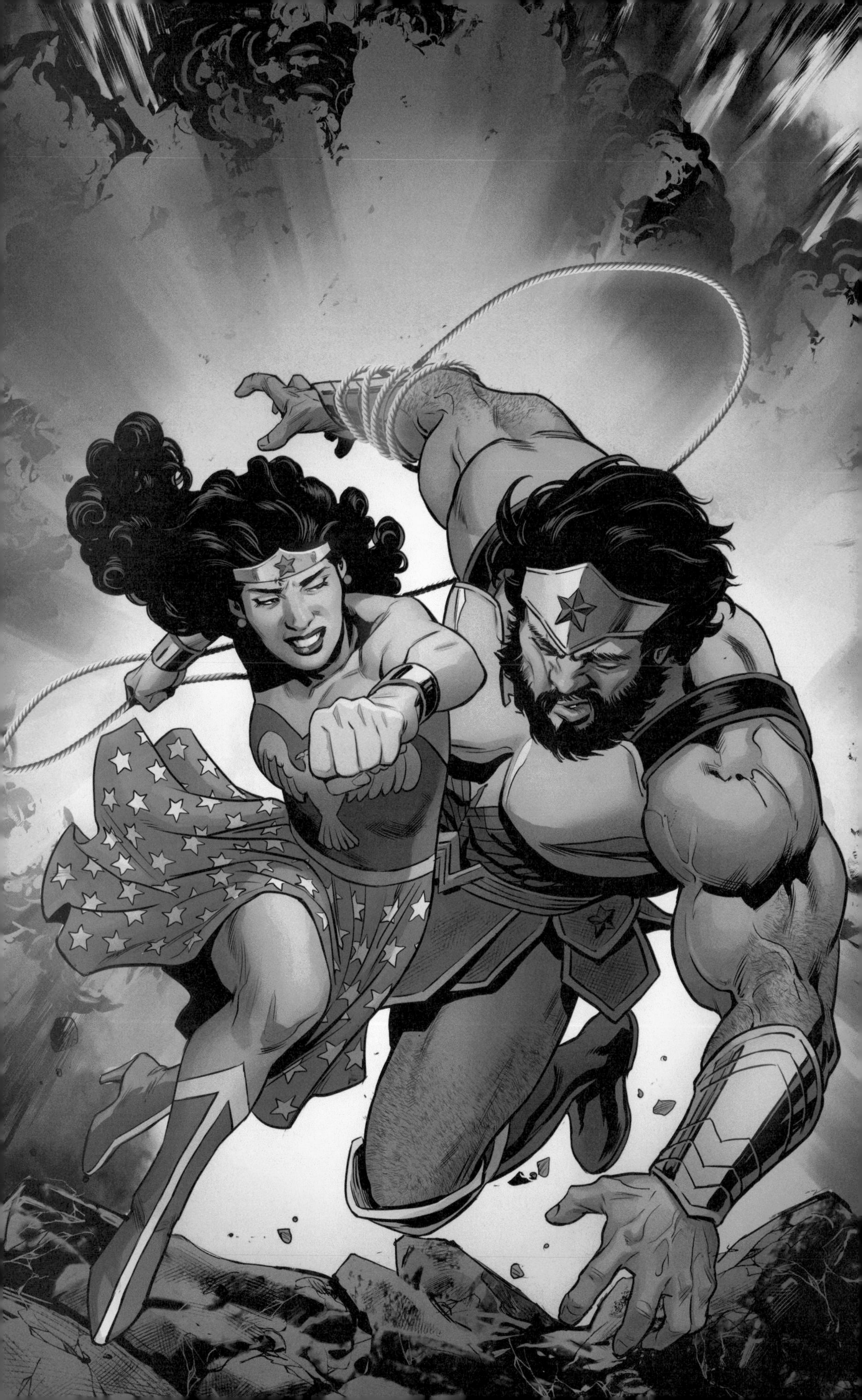

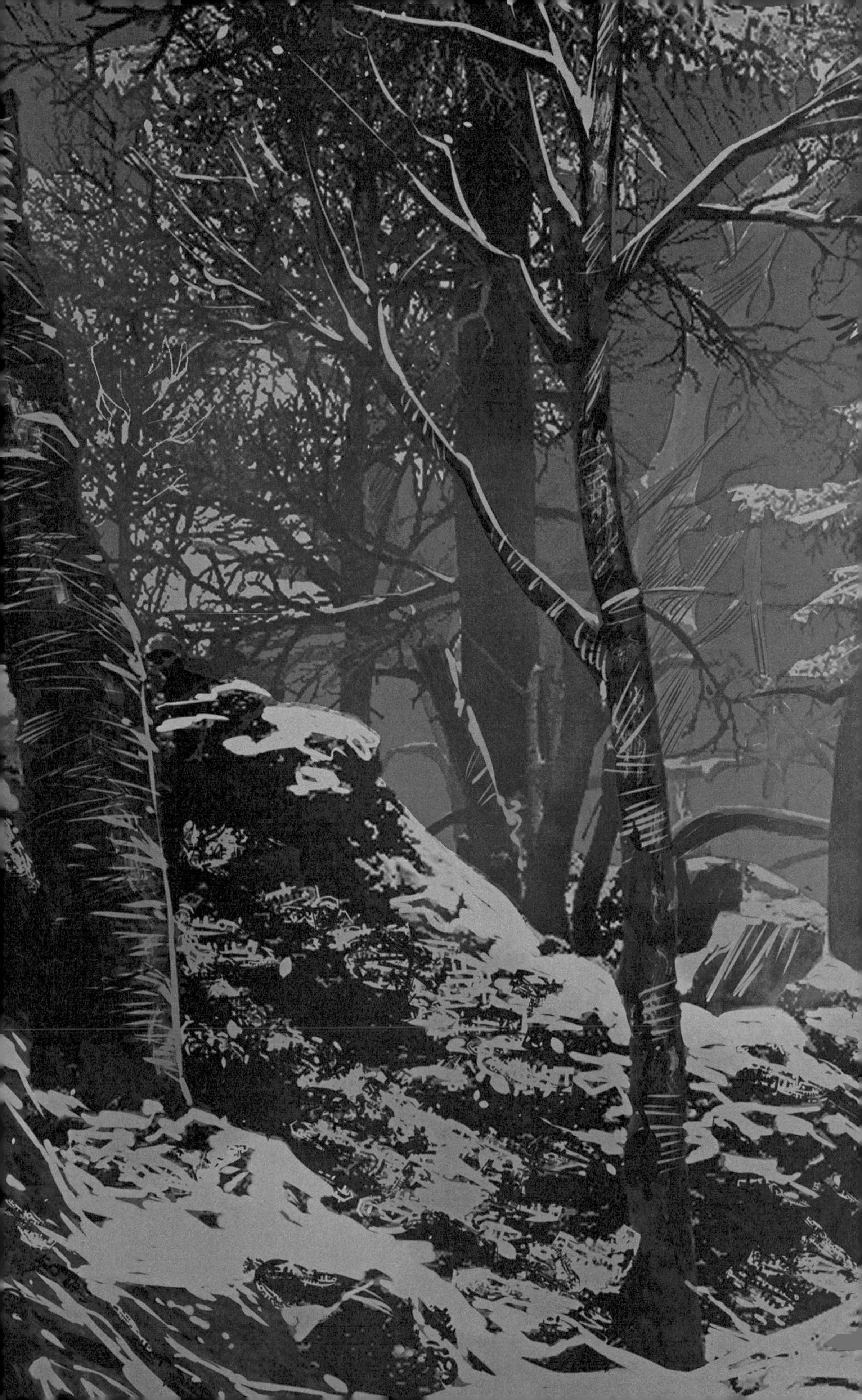

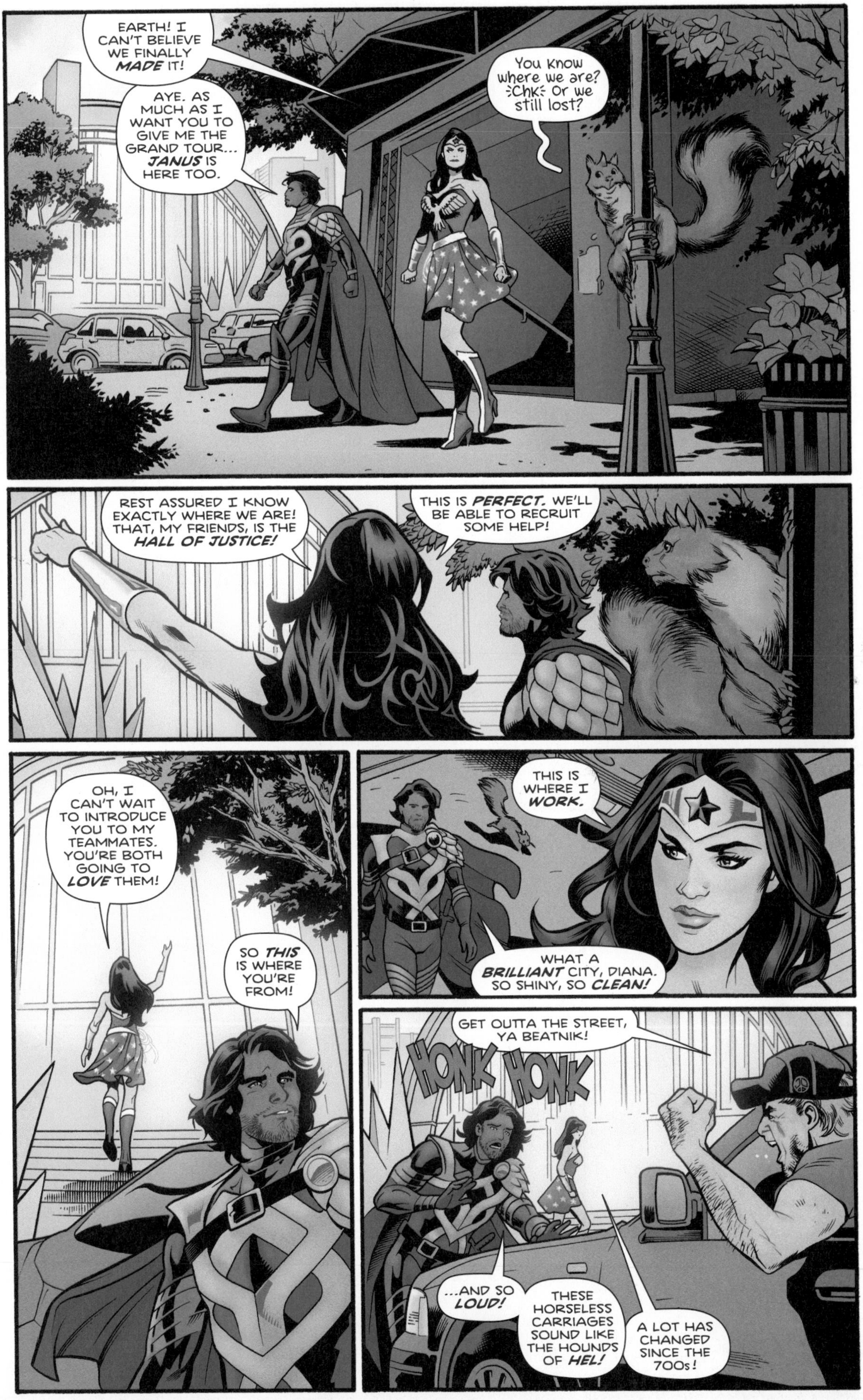
EARTH! I CAN'T BELIEVE WE FINALLY MADE IT!
AYE. AS MUCH AS I WANT YOU TO GIVE ME THE GRAND TOUR... JANUS IS HERE TOO.
You know where we are? Chk Or we still lost?
REST ASSURED I KNOW EXACTLY WHERE WE ARE! THAT, MY FRIENDS, IS THE HALL OF JUSTICE!
THIS IS PERFECT. WE'LL BE ABLE TO RECRUIT SOME HELP!
OH, I CAN'T WAIT TO INTRODUCE YOU TO MY TEAMMATES. YOU'RE BOTH GOING TO LOVE THEM!
SO THIS IS WHERE YOU'RE FROM!
THIS IS WHERE I WORK.
WHAT A BRILLIANT CITY, DIANA. SO SHINY, SO CLEAN!
GET OUTTA THE STREET, YA BEATNIK!
HONK HONK
...AND SO LOUD!
THESE HORSELESS CARRIAGES SOUND LIKE THE HOUNDS OF HEL!
A LOT HAS CHANGED SINCE THE 700s!

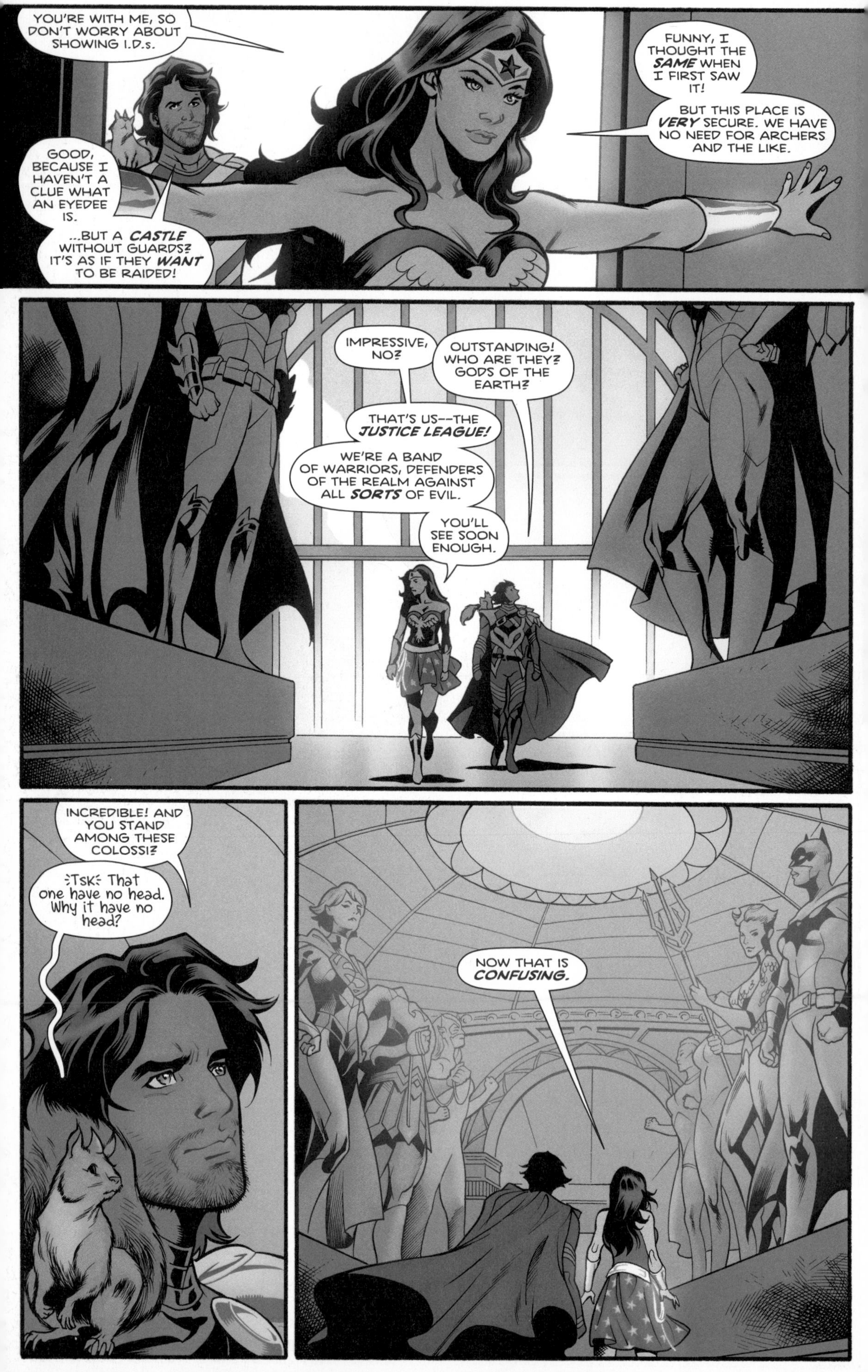

YOU'RE WITH ME, SO DON'T WORRY ABOUT SHOWING I.D.s.
GOOD, BECAUSE I HAVEN'T A CLUE WHAT AN EYEDEE IS.
...BUT A CASTLE WITHOUT GUARDS? IT'S AS IF THEY WANT TO BE RAIDED!
FUNNY, I THOUGHT THE SAME WHEN I FIRST SAW IT!
BUT THIS PLACE IS VERY SECURE. WE HAVE NO NEED FOR ARCHERS AND THE LIKE.
IMPRESSIVE, NO?
OUTSTANDING! WHO ARE THEY? GODS OF THE EARTH?
THAT'S US--THE JUSTICE LEAGUE!
WE'RE A BAND OF WARRIORS, DEFENDERS OF THE REALM AGAINST ALL SORTS OF EVIL.
YOU'LL SEE SOON ENOUGH.
INCREDIBLE! AND YOU STAND AMONG THESE COLOSSI?
Tsk! That one have no head. Why it have no head?
NOW THAT IS CONFUSING.

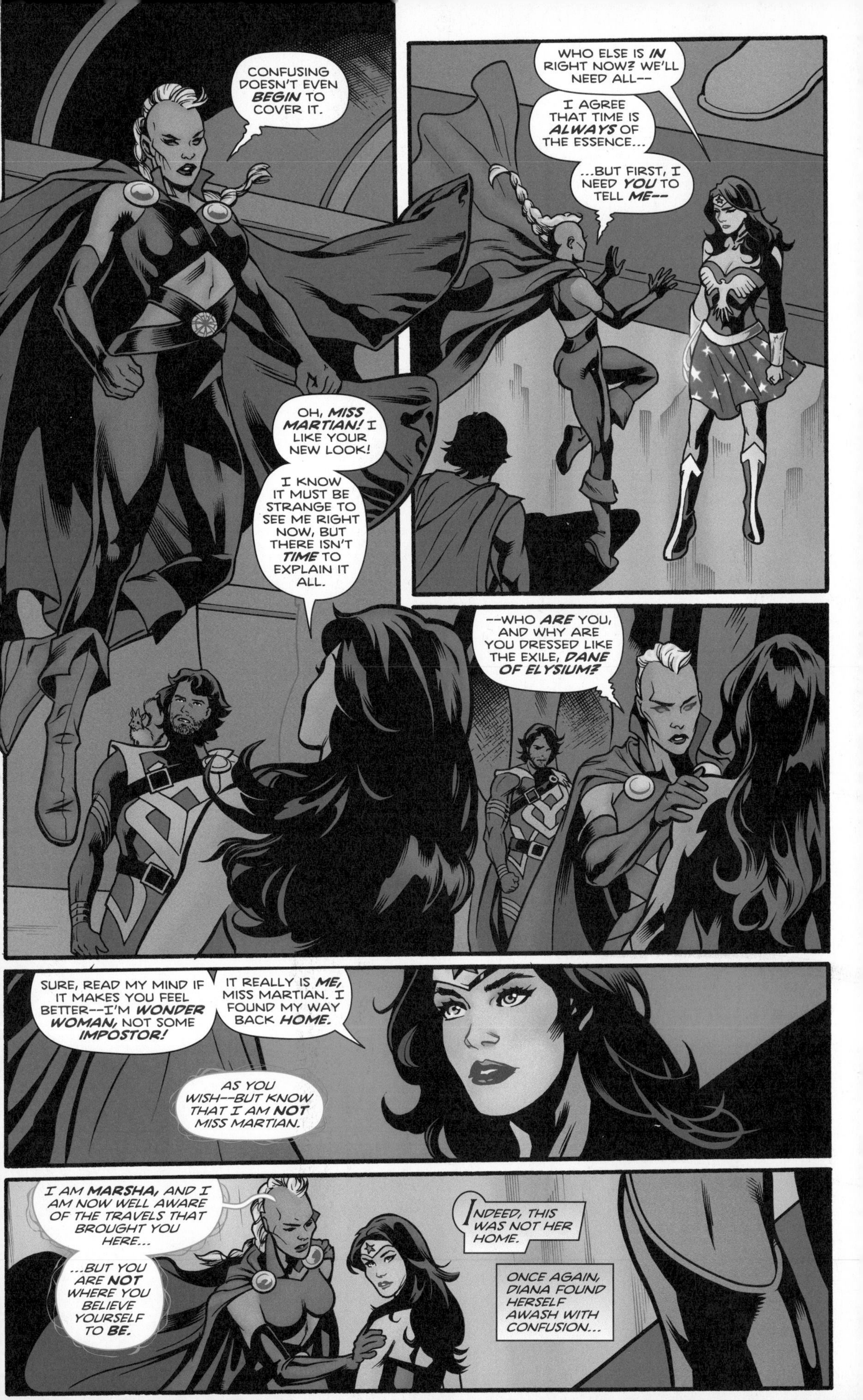
CONFUSING DOESN'T EVEN BEGIN TO COVER IT.
OH, MISS MARTIAN! I LIKE YOUR NEW LOOK!
I KNOW IT MUST BE STRANGE TO SEE ME RIGHT NOW, BUT THERE ISN'T TIME TO EXPLAIN IT ALL.
WHO ELSE IS IN RIGHT NOW? WE'LL NEED ALL--
I AGREE THAT TIME IS ALWAYS OF THE ESSENCE...
...BUT FIRST, I NEED YOU TO TELL ME--
--WHO ARE YOU, AND WHY ARE YOU DRESSED LIKE THE EXILE, DANE OF ELYSIUM?
SURE, READ MY MIND IF IT MAKES YOU FEEL BETTER--I'M WONDER WOMAN, NOT SOME IMPOSTOR!
IT REALLY IS ME, MISS MARTIAN. I FOUND MY WAY BACK HOME.
AS YOU WISH--BUT KNOW THAT I AM NOT MISS MARTIAN.
I AM MARSHA, AND I AM NOW WELL AWARE OF THE TRAVELS THAT BROUGHT YOU HERE...
...BUT YOU ARE NOT WHERE YOU BELIEVE YOURSELF TO BE.
INDEED, THIS WAS NOT HER HOME.
ONCE AGAIN, DIANA FOUND HERSELF AWASH WITH CONFUSION...

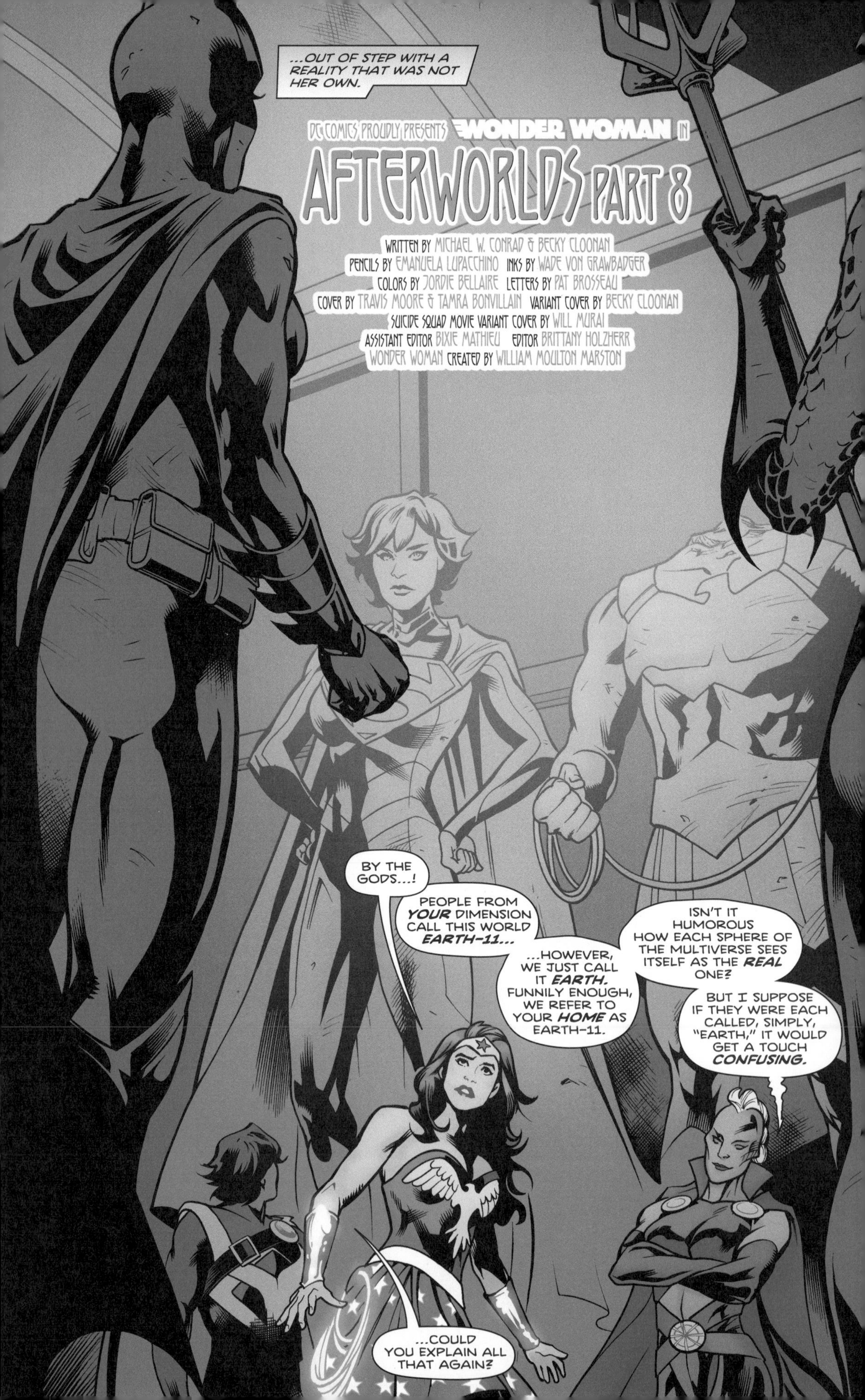
...OUT OF STEP WITH A REALITY THAT WAS NOT HER OWN.
DC COMICS PROUDLY PRESENTS WONDER WOMAN IN
AFTERWORLDS PART 8
WRITTEN BY MICHAEL W. CONRAD & BECKY CLOONAN
PENCILS BY EMANUELA LUPACCHINO INKS BY WADE VON GRAWBADGER
COLORS BY JORDIE BELLAIRE LETTERS BY PAT BROSSEAU
COVER BY TRAVIS MOORE & TAMRA BONVILLAIN VARIANT COVER BY BECKY CLOONAN
SUICIDE SQUAD MOVIE VARIANT COVER BY WILL MURAI
ASSISTANT EDITOR BIXIE MATHIEU EDITOR BRITTANY HOLZHERR
WONDER WOMAN CREATED BY WILLIAM MOULTON MARSTON
BY THE GODS...!
PEOPLE FROM YOUR DIMENSION CALL THIS WORLD EARTH-11...
...HOWEVER, WE JUST CALL IT EARTH. FUNNILY ENOUGH, WE REFER TO YOUR HOME AS EARTH-11.
ISN'T IT HUMOROUS HOW EACH SPHERE OF THE MULTIVERSE SEES ITSELF AS THE REAL ONE?
BUT I SUPPOSE IF THEY WERE EACH CALLED, SIMPLY, "EARTH," IT WOULD GET A TOUCH CONFUSING.
...COULD YOU EXPLAIN ALL THAT AGAIN?

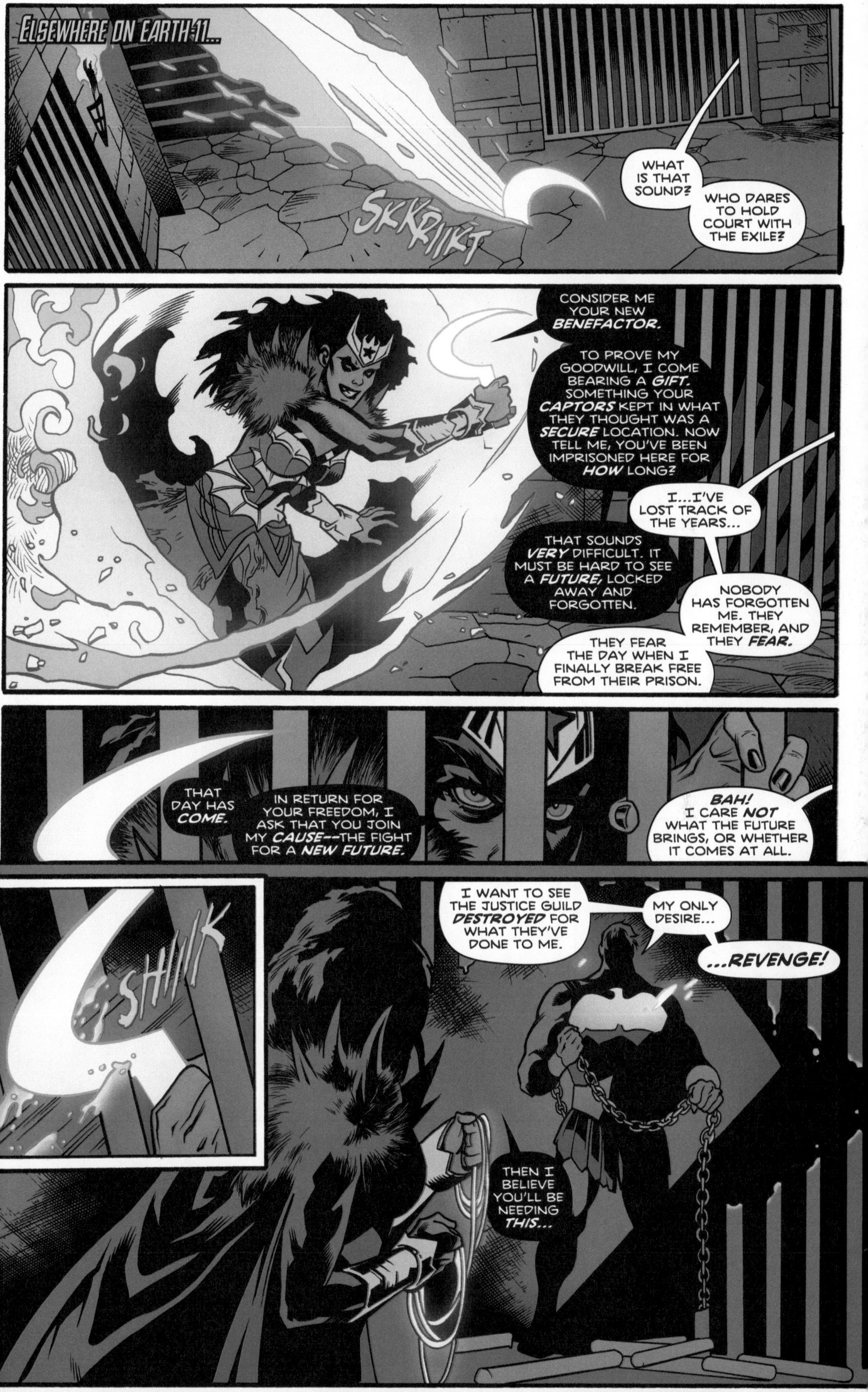
ELSEWHERE ON EARTH-11...
SKKRIIKT
WHAT IS THAT SOUND?
WHO DARES TO HOLD COURT WITH THE EXILE?
CONSIDER ME YOUR NEW BENEFACTOR.
TO PROVE MY GOODWILL, I COME BEARING A GIFT. SOMETHING YOUR CAPTORS KEPT IN WHAT THEY THOUGHT WAS A SECURE LOCATION. NOW TELL ME, YOU'VE BEEN IMPRISONED HERE FOR HOW LONG?
I...I'VE LOST TRACK OF THE YEARS...
THAT SOUNDS VERY DIFFICULT. IT MUST BE HARD TO SEE A FUTURE, LOCKED AWAY AND FORGOTTEN.
NOBODY HAS FORGOTTEN ME. THEY REMEMBER, AND THEY FEAR.
THEY FEAR THE DAY WHEN I FINALLY BREAK FREE FROM THEIR PRISON.
THAT DAY HAS COME.
IN RETURN FOR YOUR FREEDOM, I ASK THAT YOU JOIN MY CAUSE--THE FIGHT FOR A NEW FUTURE.
BAH! I CARE NOT WHAT THE FUTURE BRINGS, OR WHETHER IT COMES AT ALL.
SHIIIK
I WANT TO SEE THE JUSTICE GUILD DESTROYED FOR WHAT THEY'VE DONE TO ME.
MY ONLY DESIRE...
...REVENGE!
THEN I BELIEVE YOU'LL BE NEEDING THIS...

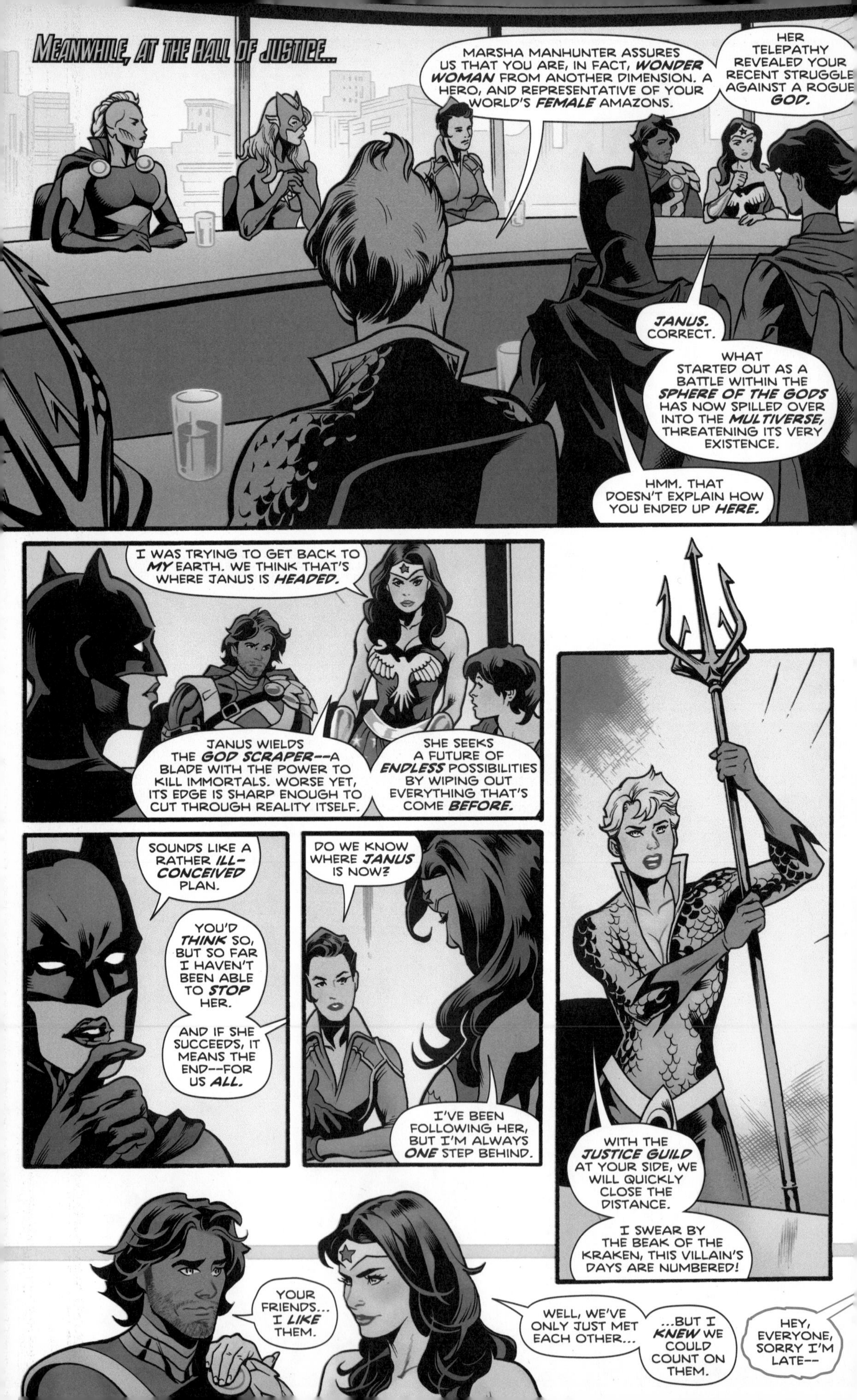
MEANWHILE, AT THE HALL OF JUSTICE...
MARSHA MANHUNTER ASSURES US THAT YOU ARE, IN FACT, WONDER WOMAN FROM ANOTHER DIMENSION. A HERO, AND REPRESENTATIVE OF YOUR WORLD'S FEMALE AMAZONS.
HER TELEPATHY REVEALED YOUR RECENT STRUGGLE AGAINST A ROGUE GOD.
JANUS. CORRECT.
WHAT STARTED OUT AS A BATTLE WITHIN THE SPHERE OF THE GODS HAS NOW SPILLED OVER INTO THE MULTIVERSE, THREATENING ITS VERY EXISTENCE.
HMM. THAT DOESN'T EXPLAIN HOW YOU ENDED UP HERE.
I WAS TRYING TO GET BACK TO MY EARTH. WE THINK THAT'S WHERE JANUS IS HEADED.
JANUS WIELDS THE GOD SCRAPER--A BLADE WITH THE POWER TO KILL IMMORTALS. WORSE YET, ITS EDGE IS SHARP ENOUGH TO CUT THROUGH REALITY ITSELF.
SHE SEEKS A FUTURE OF ENDLESS POSSIBILITIES BY WIPING OUT EVERYTHING THAT'S COME BEFORE.
SOUNDS LIKE A RATHER ILL-CONCEIVED PLAN.
YOU'D THINK SO, BUT SO FAR I HAVEN'T BEEN ABLE TO STOP HER.
AND IF SHE SUCCEEDS, IT MEANS THE END--FOR US ALL.
DO WE KNOW WHERE JANUS IS NOW?
I'VE BEEN FOLLOWING HER, BUT I'M ALWAYS ONE STEP BEHIND.
WITH THE JUSTICE GUILD AT YOUR SIDE, WE WILL QUICKLY CLOSE THE DISTANCE.
I SWEAR BY THE BEAK OF THE KRAKEN, THIS VILLAIN'S DAYS ARE NUMBERED!
YOUR FRIENDS... I LIKE THEM.
WELL, WE'VE ONLY JUST MET EACH OTHER...
...BUT I KNEW WE COULD COUNT ON THEM.
HEY, EVERYONE, SORRY I'M LATE--

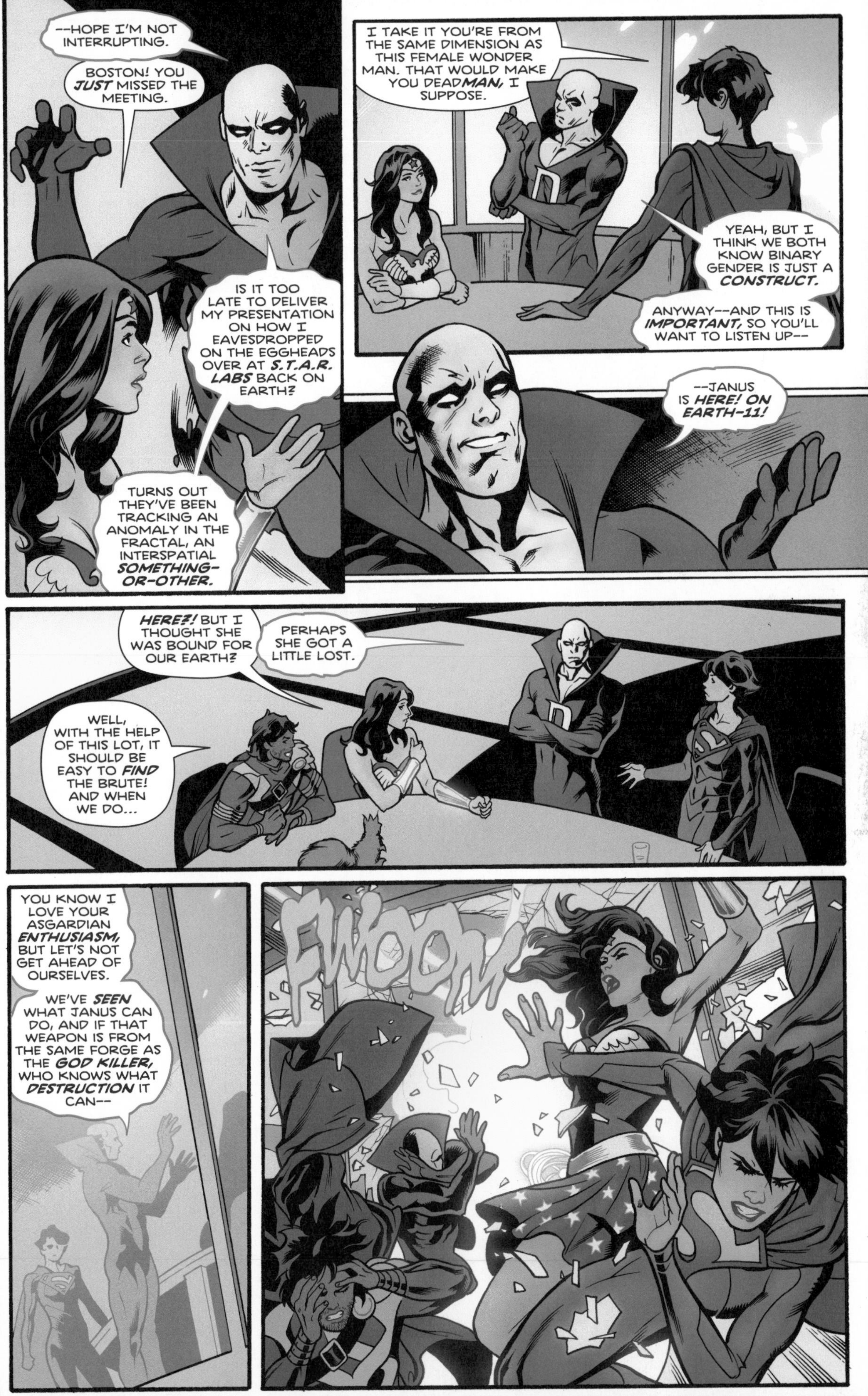
--HOPE I'M NOT INTERRUPTING.
BOSTON! YOU JUST MISSED THE MEETING.
IS IT TOO LATE TO DELIVER MY PRESENTATION ON HOW I EAVESDROPPED ON THE EGGHEADS OVER AT S.T.A.R. LABS BACK ON EARTH?
TURNS OUT THEY'VE BEEN TRACKING AN ANOMALY IN THE FRACTAL, AN INTERSPATIAL SOMETHING-OR-OTHER.
I TAKE IT YOU'RE FROM THE SAME DIMENSION AS THIS FEMALE WONDER MAN. THAT WOULD MAKE YOU DEADMAN, I SUPPOSE.
YEAH, BUT I THINK WE BOTH KNOW BINARY GENDER IS JUST A CONSTRUCT.
ANYWAY--AND THIS IS IMPORTANT, SO YOU'LL WANT TO LISTEN UP--
--JANUS IS HERE! ON EARTH-11!
HERE?! BUT I THOUGHT SHE WAS BOUND FOR OUR EARTH?
PERHAPS SHE GOT A LITTLE LOST.
WELL, WITH THE HELP OF THIS LOT, IT SHOULD BE EASY TO FIND THE BRUTE! AND WHEN WE DO...
YOU KNOW I LOVE YOUR ASGARDIAN ENTHUSIASM, BUT LET'S NOT GET AHEAD OF OURSELVES.
WE'VE SEEN WHAT JANUS CAN DO, AND IF THAT WEAPON IS FROM THE SAME FORGE AS THE GOD KILLER, WHO KNOWS WHAT DESTRUCTION IT CAN--
FWOOM

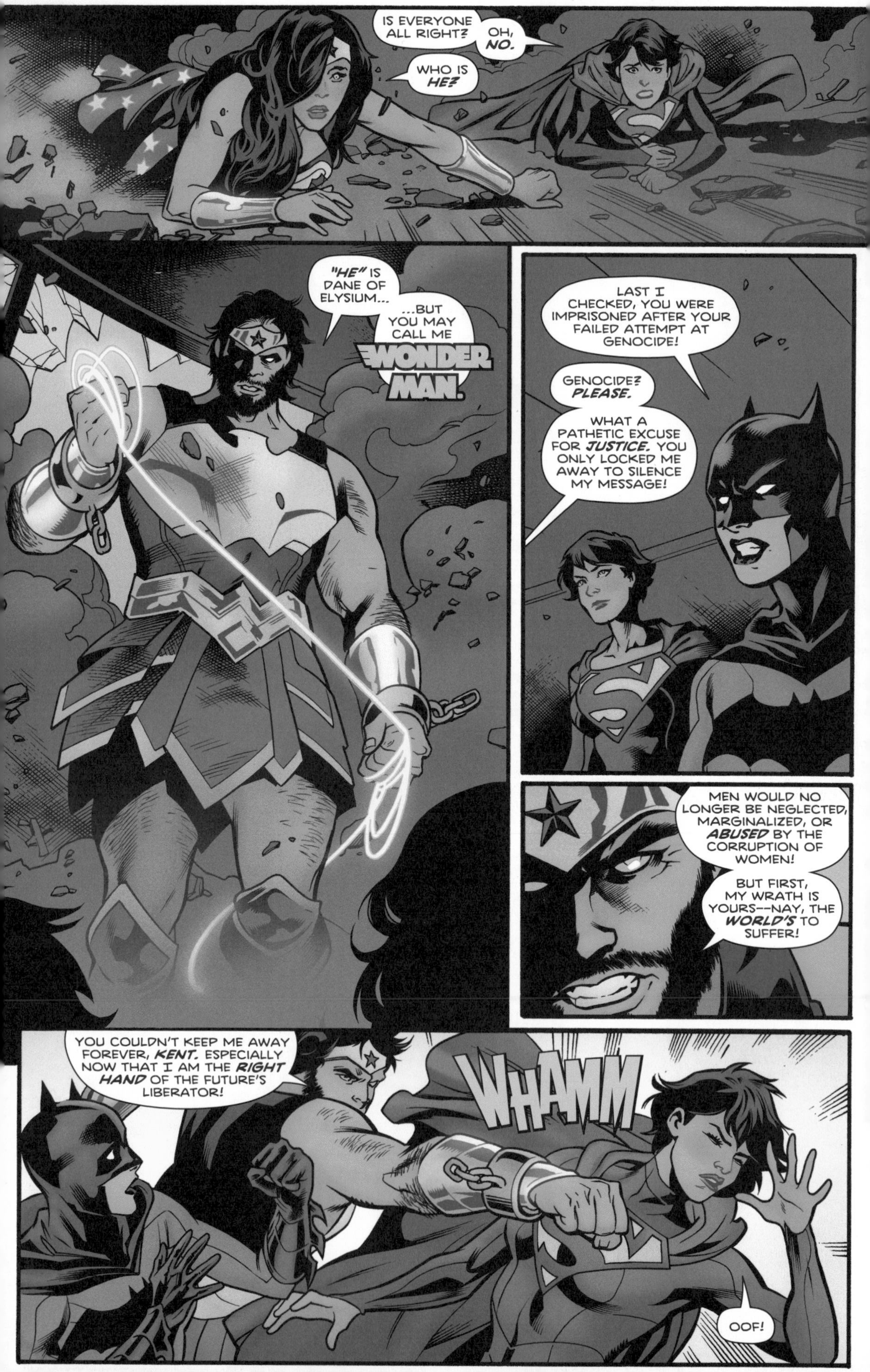

IS EVERYONE ALL RIGHT?
OH, NO.
WHO IS HE?
"HE" IS DANE OF ELYSIUM...
...BUT YOU MAY CALL ME
WONDER MAN.
LAST I CHECKED, YOU WERE IMPRISONED AFTER YOUR FAILED ATTEMPT AT GENOCIDE!
GENOCIDE? PLEASE.
WHAT A PATHETIC EXCUSE FOR JUSTICE. YOU ONLY LOCKED ME AWAY TO SILENCE MY MESSAGE!
MEN WOULD NO LONGER BE NEGLECTED, MARGINALIZED, OR ABUSED BY THE CORRUPTION OF WOMEN!
BUT FIRST, MY WRATH IS YOURS--NAY, THE WORLD'S TO SUFFER!
YOU COULDN'T KEEP ME AWAY FOREVER, KENT. ESPECIALLY NOW THAT I AM THE RIGHT HAND OF THE FUTURE'S LIBERATOR!
WHAMM
OOF!

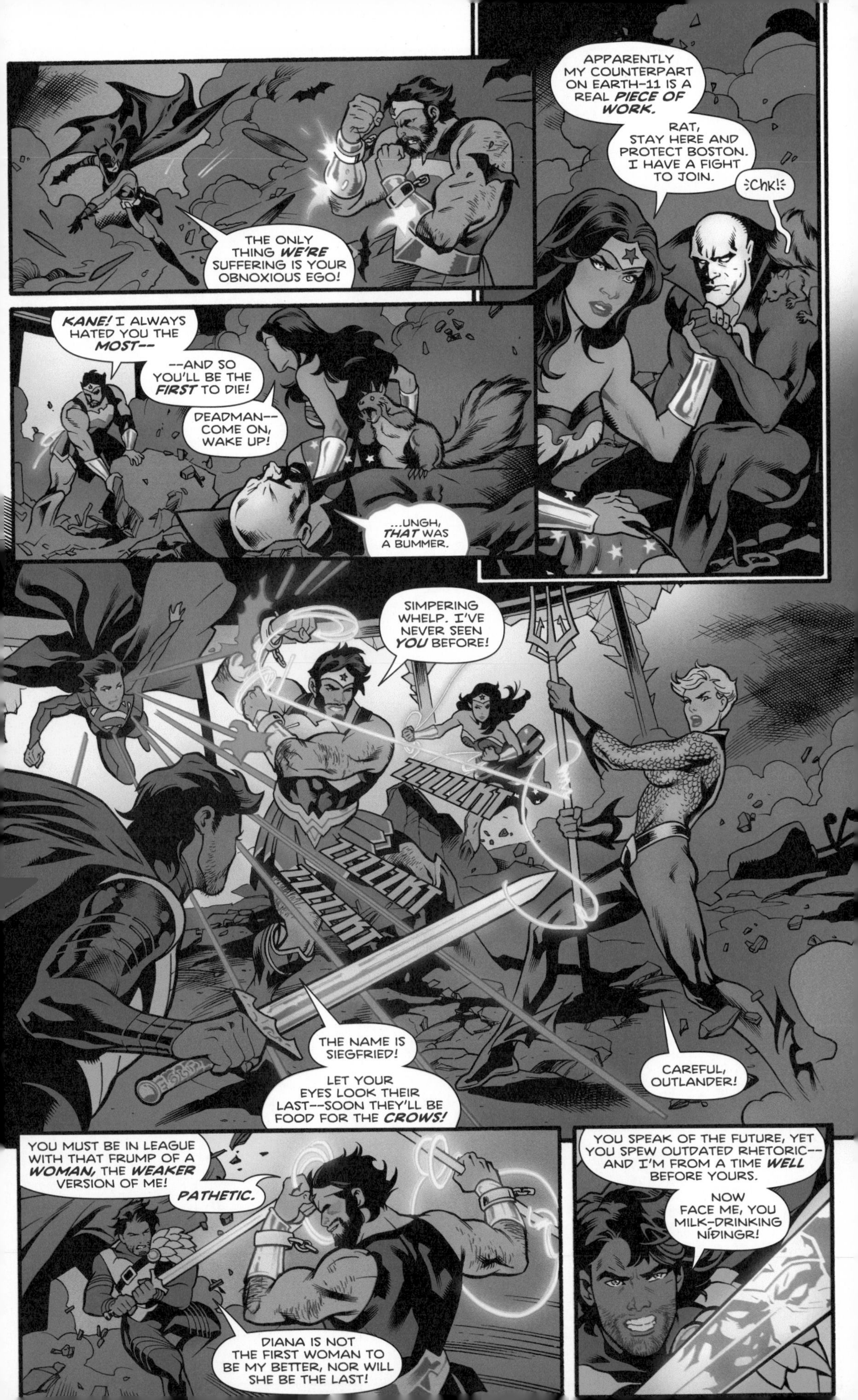
THE ONLY THING WE'RE SUFFERING IS YOUR OBNOXIOUS EGO!
APPARENTLY MY COUNTERPART ON EARTH-11 IS A REAL PIECE OF WORK.
RAT, STAY HERE AND PROTECT BOSTON. I HAVE A FIGHT TO JOIN.
Chk!
KANE! I ALWAYS HATED YOU THE MOST--
--AND SO YOU'LL BE THE FIRST TO DIE!
DEADMAN--COME ON, WAKE UP!
...UNGH, THAT WAS A BUMMER.
SIMPERING WHELP. I'VE NEVER SEEN YOU BEFORE!
ZZZZZZZKT
ZZZZZZZKT
ZZZZZZZKT
THE NAME IS SIEGFRIED!
LET YOUR EYES LOOK THEIR LAST--SOON THEY'LL BE FOOD FOR THE CROWS!
CAREFUL, OUTLANDER!
YOU MUST BE IN LEAGUE WITH THAT FRUMP OF A WOMAN, THE WEAKER VERSION OF ME!
PATHETIC.
DIANA IS NOT THE FIRST WOMAN TO BE MY BETTER, NOR WILL SHE BE THE LAST!
YOU SPEAK OF THE FUTURE, YET YOU SPEW OUTDATED RHETORIC--AND I'M FROM A TIME WELL BEFORE YOURS.
NOW FACE ME, YOU MILK-DRINKING NÍÐINGR!

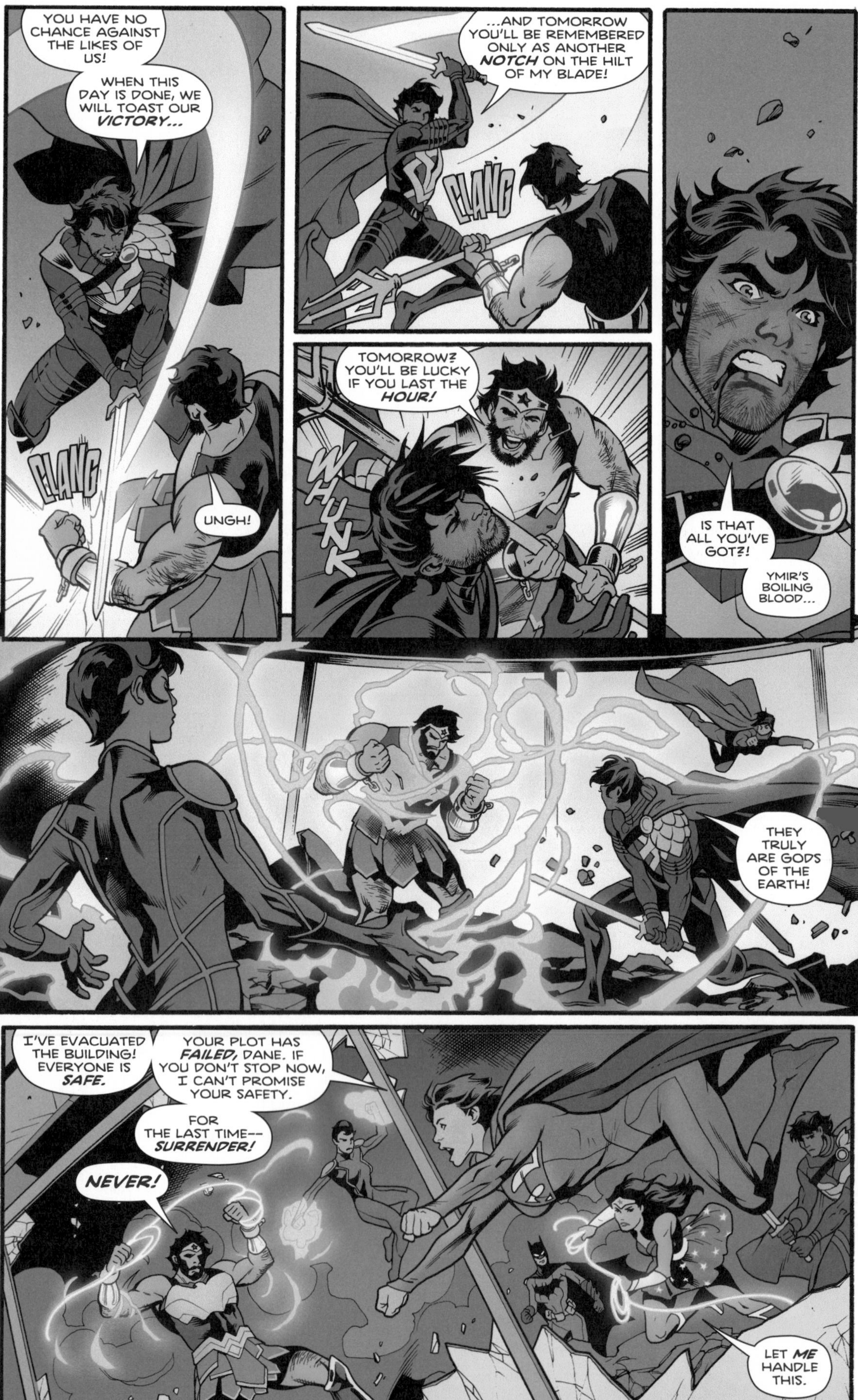

YOU HAVE NO CHANCE AGAINST THE LIKES OF US!
WHEN THIS DAY IS DONE, WE WILL TOAST OUR VICTORY...
CLANG
UNGH!
...AND TOMORROW YOU'LL BE REMEMBERED ONLY AS ANOTHER NOTCH ON THE HILT OF MY BLADE!
CLANG
TOMORROW? YOU'LL BE LUCKY IF YOU LAST THE HOUR!
WHUNK
IS THAT ALL YOU'VE GOT?!
YMIR'S BOILING BLOOD...
THEY TRULY ARE GODS OF THE EARTH!
I'VE EVACUATED THE BUILDING! EVERYONE IS SAFE.
YOUR PLOT HAS FAILED, DANE. IF YOU DON'T STOP NOW, I CAN'T PROMISE YOUR SAFETY.
FOR THE LAST TIME-- SURRENDER!
NEVER!
LET ME HANDLE THIS.

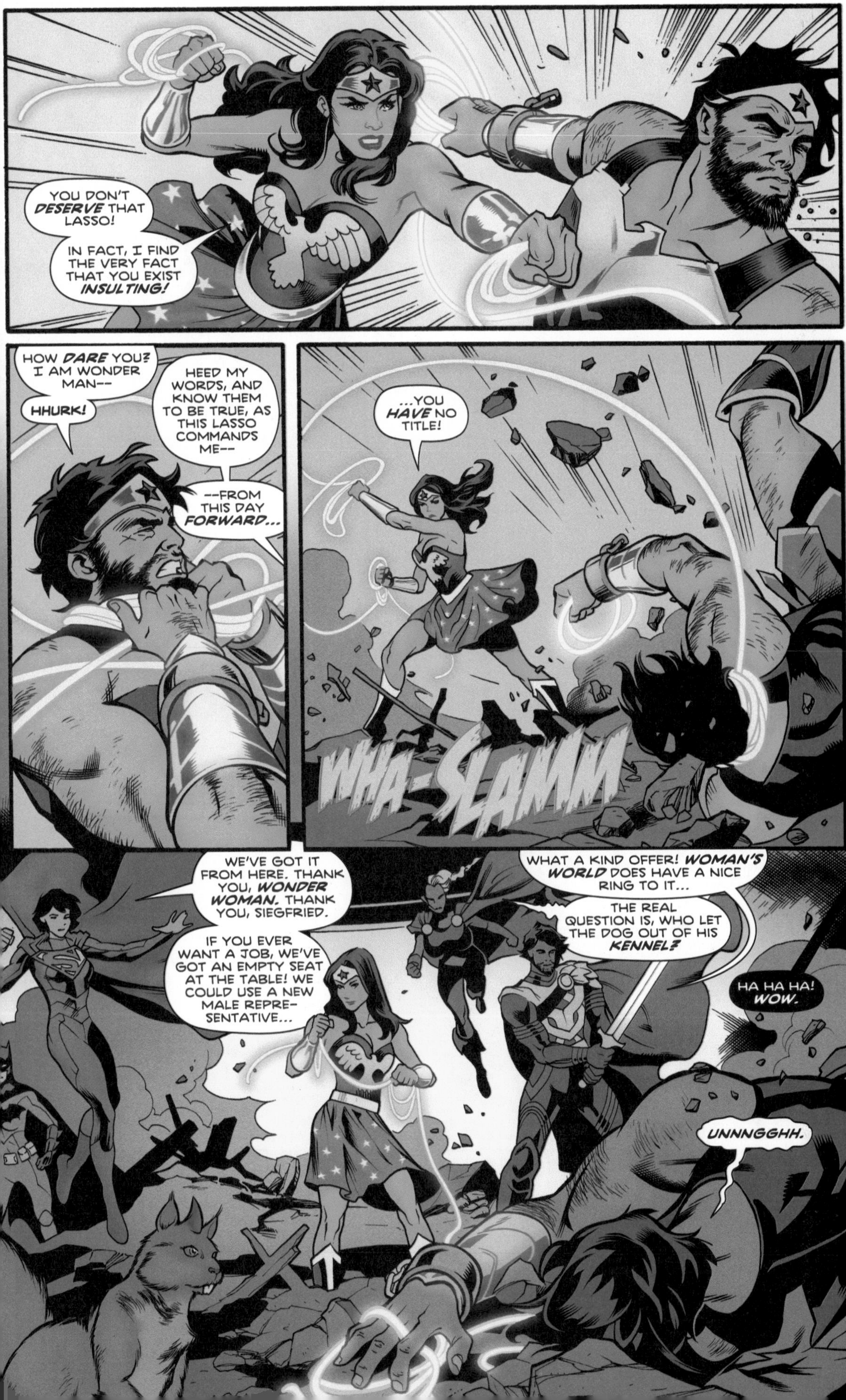
YOU DON'T *DESERVE* THAT LASSO!
IN FACT, I FIND THE VERY FACT THAT YOU EXIST *INSULTING!*
HOW *DARE* YOU? I AM WONDER MAN--
HHURK!
HEED MY WORDS, AND KNOW THEM TO BE TRUE, AS THIS LASSO COMMANDS ME--
--FROM THIS DAY *FORWARD...*
...YOU *HAVE* NO TITLE!
WHA-SLAMM
WE'VE GOT IT FROM HERE. THANK YOU, *WONDER WOMAN.* THANK YOU, SIEGFRIED.
IF YOU EVER WANT A JOB, WE'VE GOT AN EMPTY SEAT AT THE TABLE! WE COULD USE A NEW MALE REPRE-SENTATIVE...
WHAT A KIND OFFER! *WOMAN'S WORLD* DOES HAVE A NICE RING TO IT...
THE REAL QUESTION IS, WHO LET THE DOG OUT OF HIS *KENNEL?*
HA HA HA! *WOW.*
UNNNGGHH.

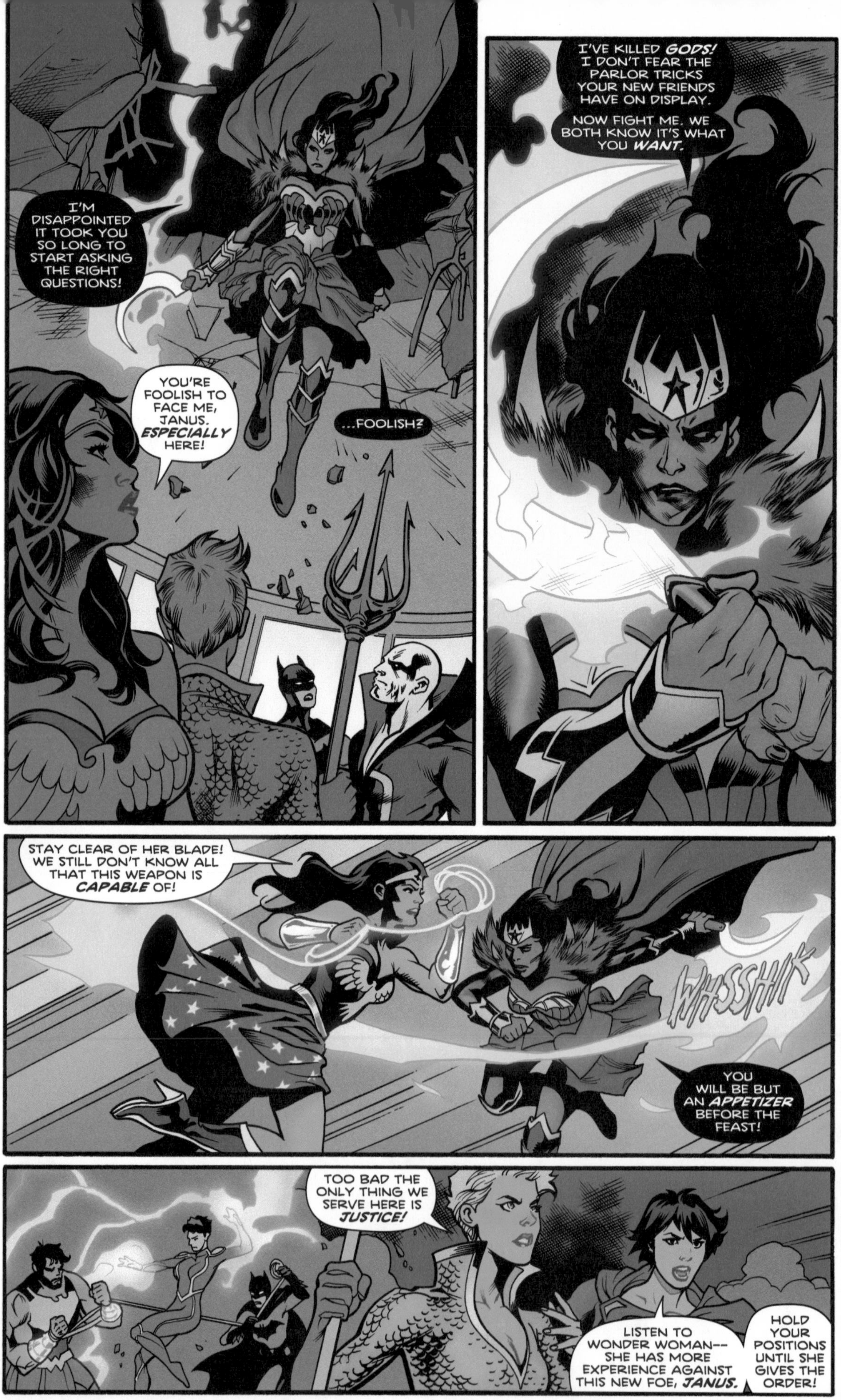
I'M DISAPPOINTED IT TOOK YOU SO LONG TO START ASKING THE RIGHT QUESTIONS!
YOU'RE FOOLISH TO FACE ME, JANUS. ESPECIALLY HERE!
...FOOLISH?
I'VE KILLED GODS! I DON'T FEAR THE PARLOR TRICKS YOUR NEW FRIENDS HAVE ON DISPLAY.
NOW FIGHT ME. WE BOTH KNOW IT'S WHAT YOU WANT.
STAY CLEAR OF HER BLADE! WE STILL DON'T KNOW ALL THAT THIS WEAPON IS CAPABLE OF!
WHSSHIK
YOU WILL BE BUT AN APPETIZER BEFORE THE FEAST!
TOO BAD THE ONLY THING WE SERVE HERE IS JUSTICE!
LISTEN TO WONDER WOMAN-- SHE HAS MORE EXPERIENCE AGAINST THIS NEW FOE, JANUS.
HOLD YOUR POSITIONS UNTIL SHE GIVES THE ORDER!

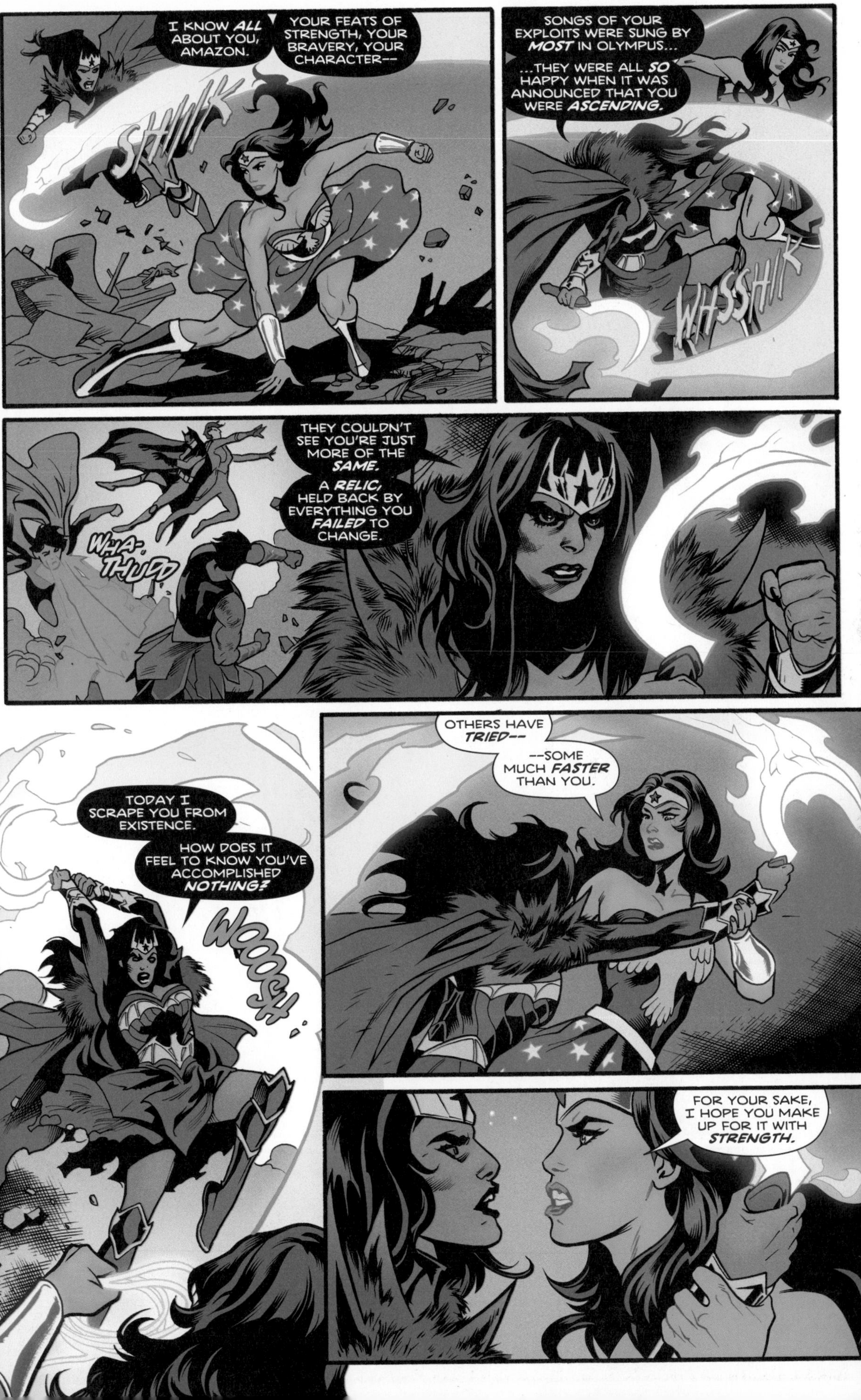
I KNOW ALL ABOUT YOU, AMAZON.
YOUR FEATS OF STRENGTH, YOUR BRAVERY, YOUR CHARACTER--
SHUNK
SONGS OF YOUR EXPLOITS WERE SUNG BY MOST IN OLYMPUS...
...THEY WERE ALL SO HAPPY WHEN IT WAS ANNOUNCED THAT YOU WERE ASCENDING.
WHSSHIK
THEY COULDN'T SEE YOU'RE JUST MORE OF THE SAME.
A RELIC, HELD BACK BY EVERYTHING YOU FAILED TO CHANGE.
WHA-THUDD
TODAY I SCRAPE YOU FROM EXISTENCE.
HOW DOES IT FEEL TO KNOW YOU'VE ACCOMPLISHED NOTHING?
WOOOSH
OTHERS HAVE TRIED--
--SOME MUCH FASTER THAN YOU.
FOR YOUR SAKE, I HOPE YOU MAKE UP FOR IT WITH STRENGTH.

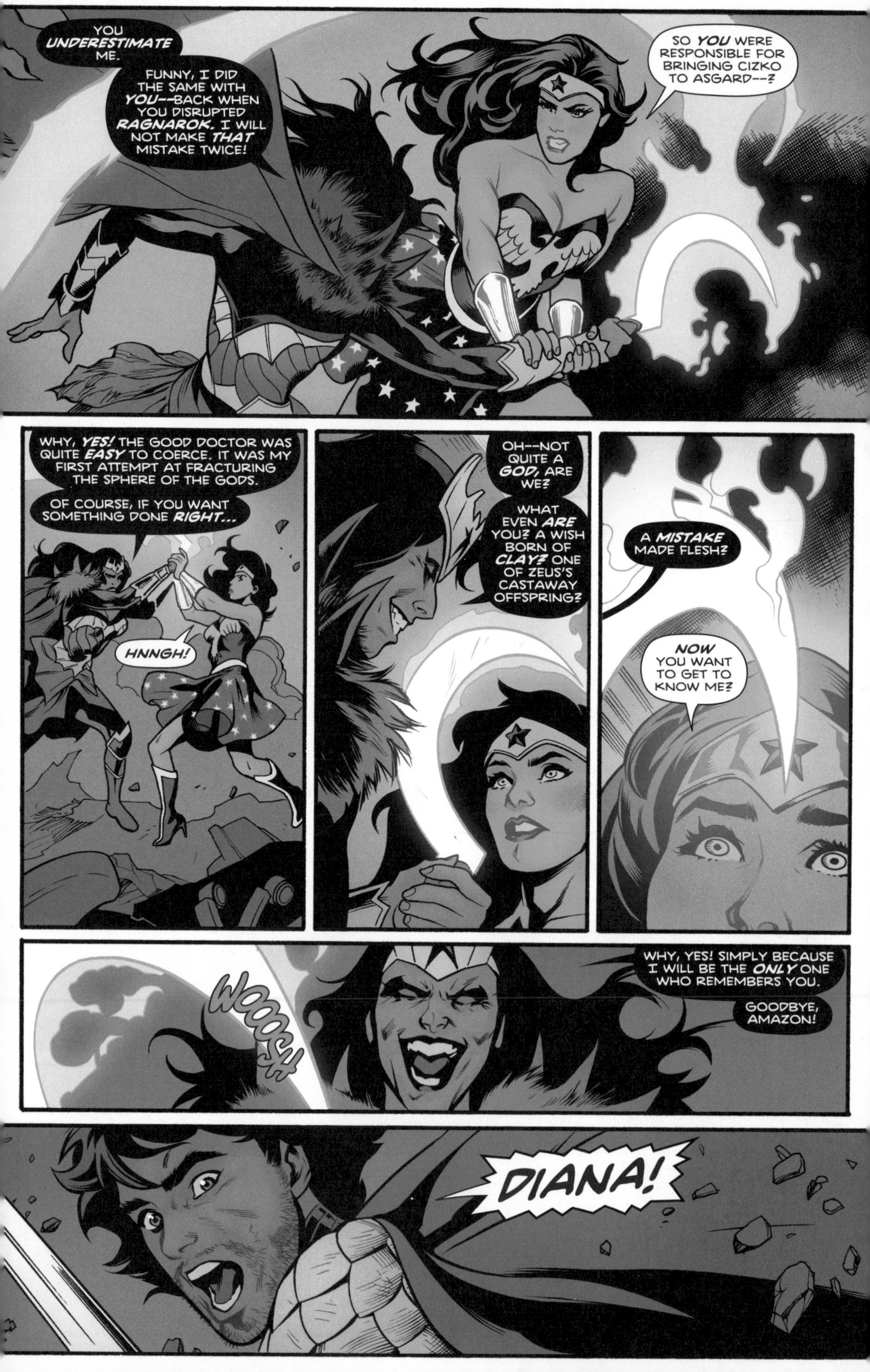
YOU UNDERESTIMATE ME.
FUNNY, I DID THE SAME WITH YOU--BACK WHEN YOU DISRUPTED RAGNAROK. I WILL NOT MAKE THAT MISTAKE TWICE!
SO YOU WERE RESPONSIBLE FOR BRINGING CIZKO TO ASGARD--?
WHY, YES! THE GOOD DOCTOR WAS QUITE EASY TO COERCE. IT WAS MY FIRST ATTEMPT AT FRACTURING THE SPHERE OF THE GODS.
OF COURSE, IF YOU WANT SOMETHING DONE RIGHT...
HNNGH!
OH--NOT QUITE A GOD, ARE WE?
WHAT EVEN ARE YOU? A WISH BORN OF CLAY? ONE OF ZEUS'S CASTAWAY OFFSPRING?
A MISTAKE MADE FLESH?
NOW YOU WANT TO GET TO KNOW ME?
WHY, YES! SIMPLY BECAUSE I WILL BE THE ONLY ONE WHO REMEMBERS YOU.
GOODBYE, AMAZON!
WOOOSH
DIANA!

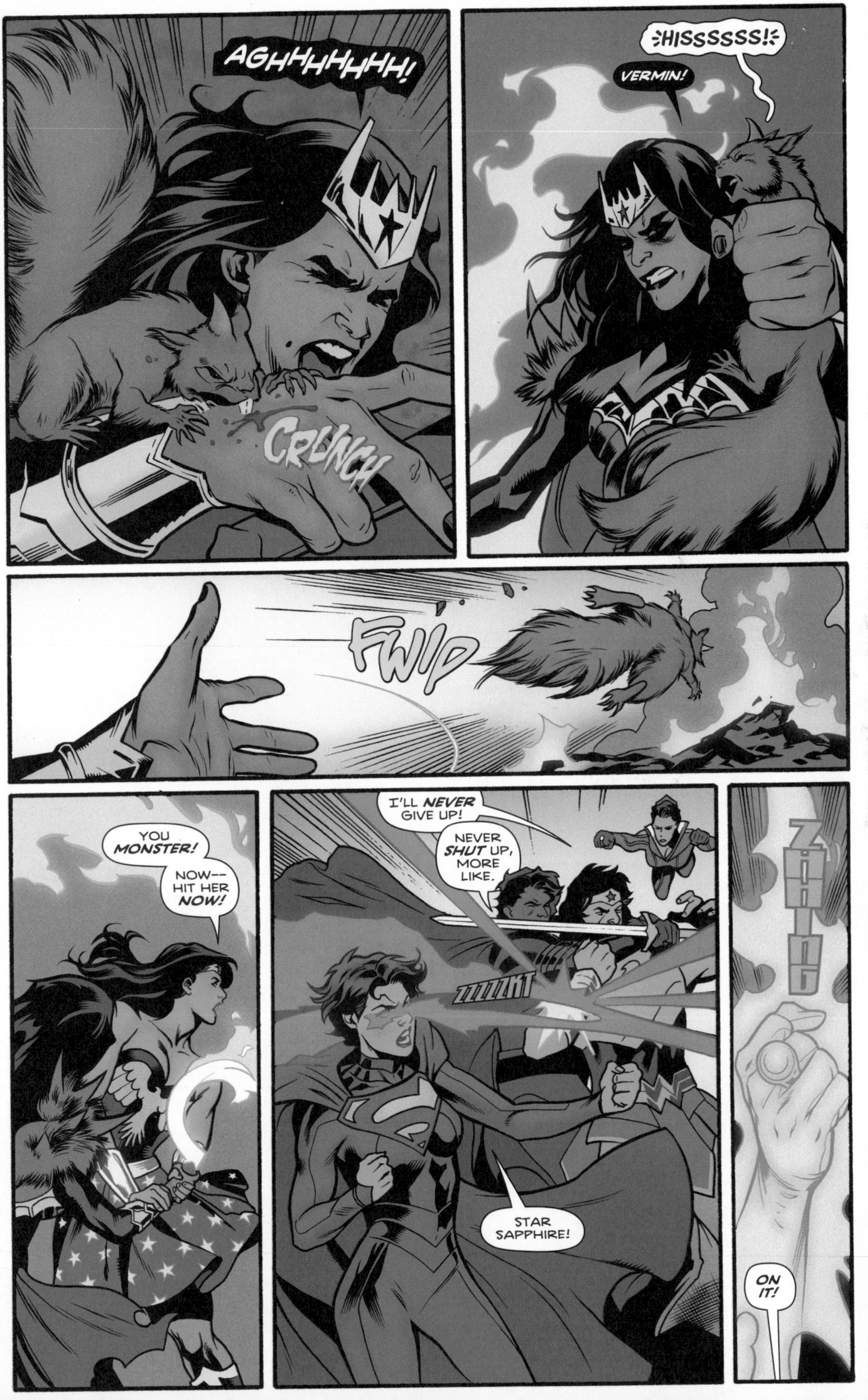
AGHHHHHHH!
CRUNCH
HISSSSSS!
VERMIN!
FWIP
YOU MONSTER!
NOW-- HIT HER NOW!
I'LL NEVER GIVE UP!
NEVER SHUT UP, MORE LIKE.
ZZZZZKT
STAR SAPPHIRE!
ZHING
ON IT!

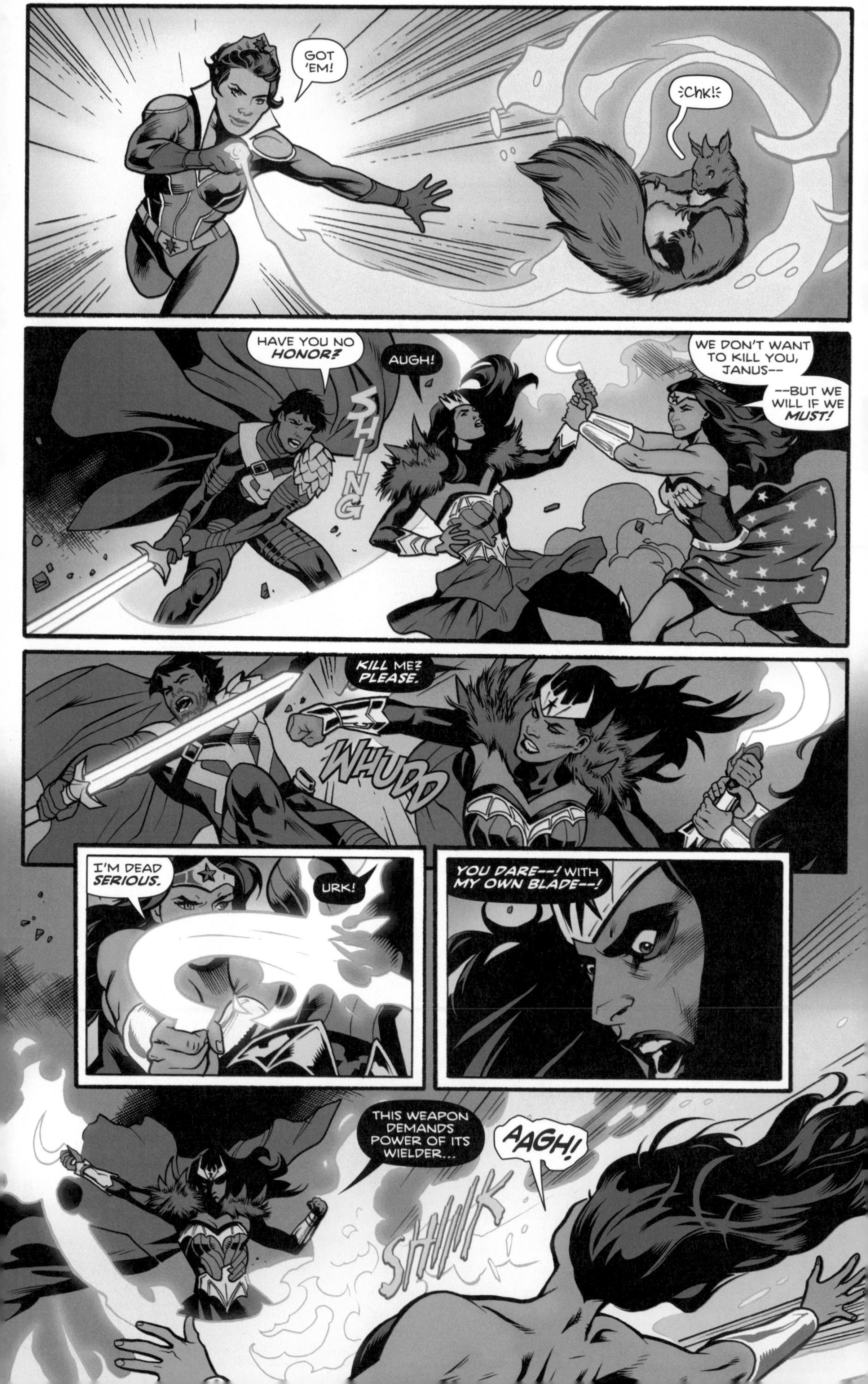
GOT 'EM!
Chk!
HAVE YOU NO HONOR?
AUGH!
SHING
WE DON'T WANT TO KILL YOU, JANUS--
--BUT WE WILL IF WE MUST!
KILL ME? PLEASE.
WHUDD
I'M DEAD SERIOUS.
URK!
YOU DARE--! WITH MY OWN BLADE--!
THIS WEAPON DEMANDS POWER OF ITS WIELDER...
AAGH!
SHIIIK

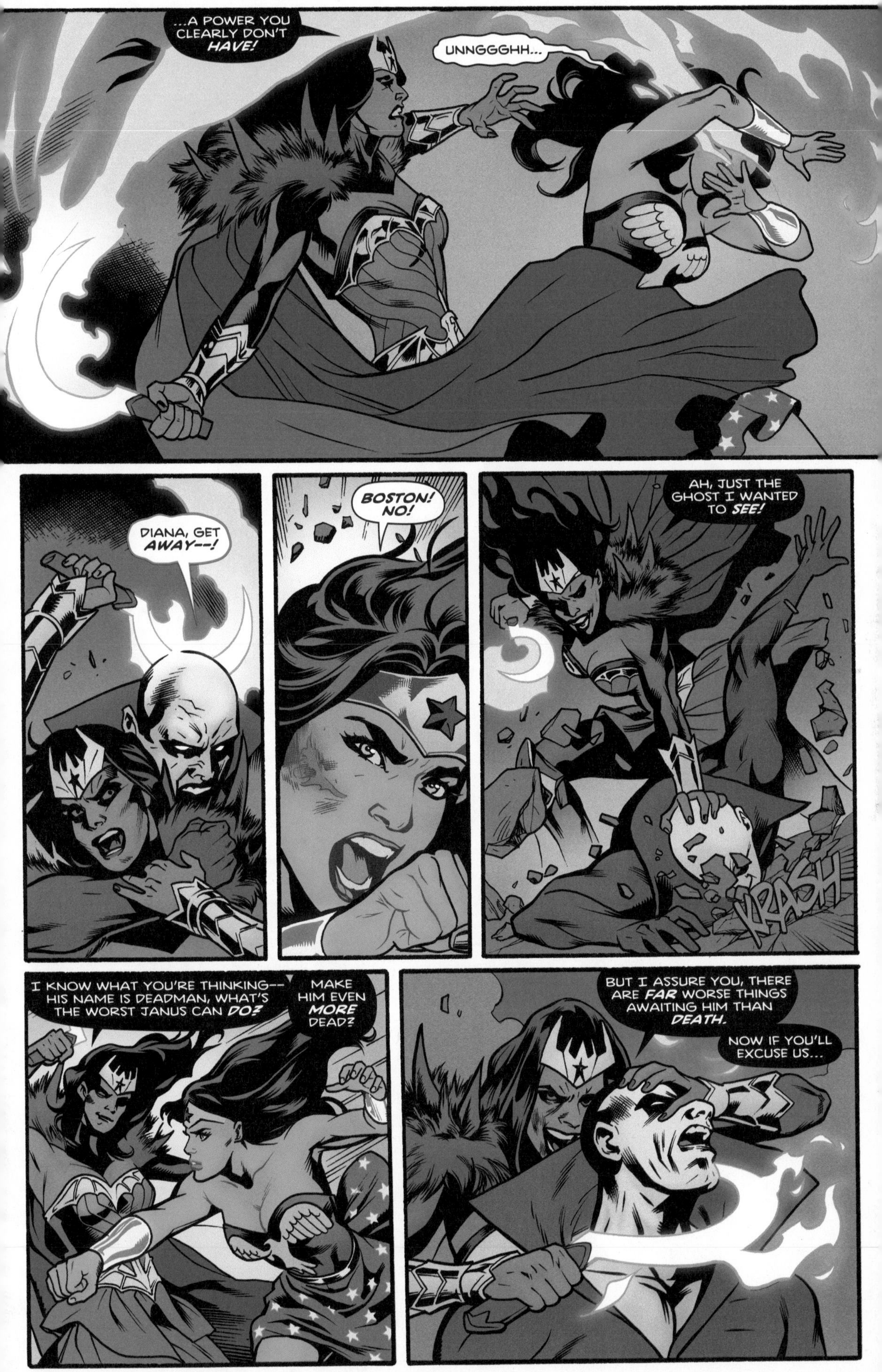
...A POWER YOU CLEARLY DON'T HAVE!
UNNGGGHH...
DIANA, GET AWAY--!
BOSTON! NO!
AH, JUST THE GHOST I WANTED TO SEE!
KRASH
I KNOW WHAT YOU'RE THINKING-- HIS NAME IS DEADMAN, WHAT'S THE WORST JANUS CAN DO?
MAKE HIM EVEN MORE DEAD?
BUT I ASSURE YOU, THERE ARE FAR WORSE THINGS AWAITING HIM THAN DEATH.
NOW IF YOU'LL EXCUSE US...

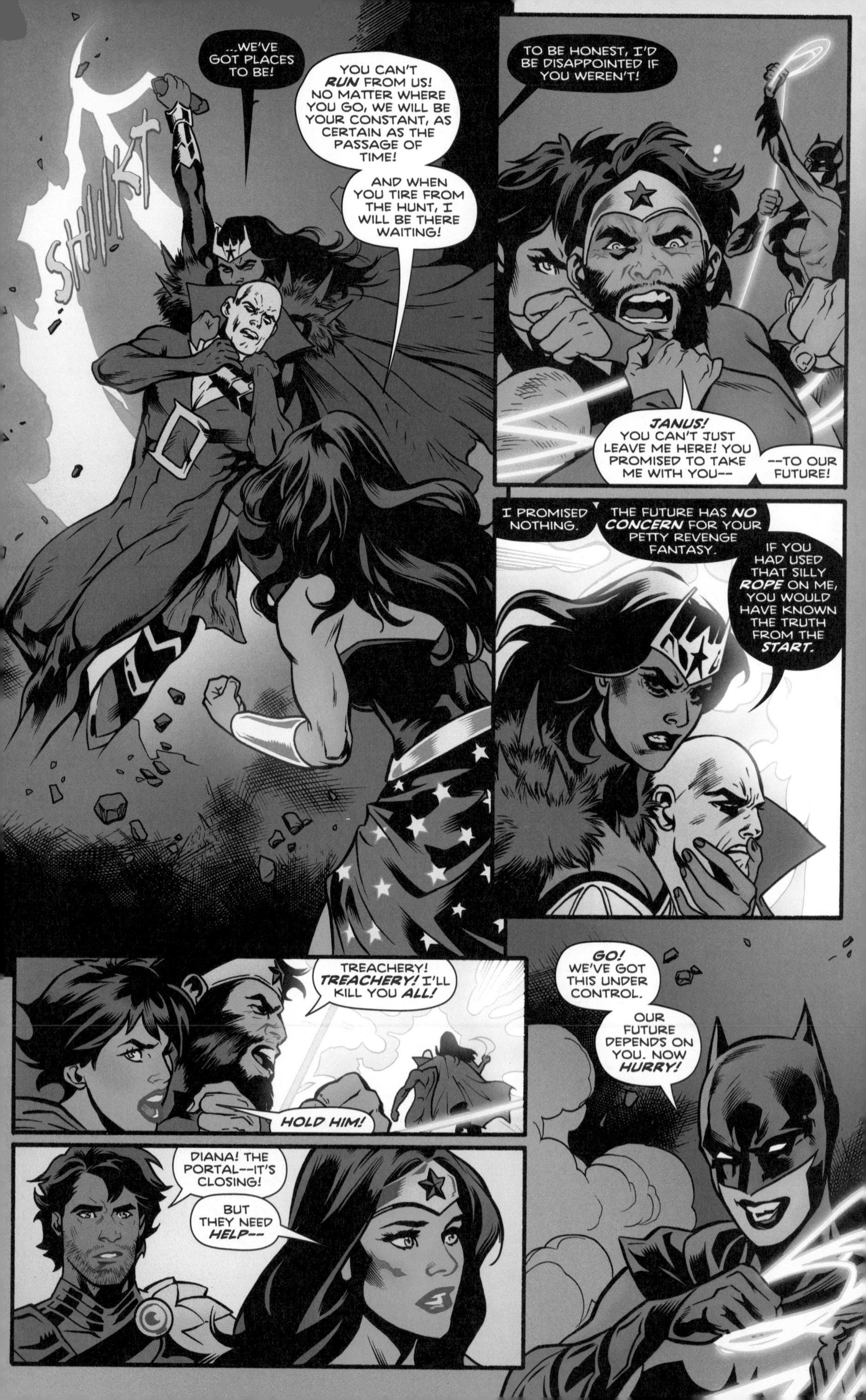

...WE'VE GOT PLACES TO BE!
YOU CAN'T RUN FROM US! NO MATTER WHERE YOU GO, WE WILL BE YOUR CONSTANT, AS CERTAIN AS THE PASSAGE OF TIME!
AND WHEN YOU TIRE FROM THE HUNT, I WILL BE THERE WAITING!
SHIIIKT
TO BE HONEST, I'D BE DISAPPOINTED IF YOU WEREN'T!
JANUS! YOU CAN'T JUST LEAVE ME HERE! YOU PROMISED TO TAKE ME WITH YOU--
--TO OUR FUTURE!
I PROMISED NOTHING.
THE FUTURE HAS NO CONCERN FOR YOUR PETTY REVENGE FANTASY.
IF YOU HAD USED THAT SILLY ROPE ON ME, YOU WOULD HAVE KNOWN THE TRUTH FROM THE START.
TREACHERY! TREACHERY! I'LL KILL YOU ALL!
HOLD HIM!
GO! WE'VE GOT THIS UNDER CONTROL.
OUR FUTURE DEPENDS ON YOU. NOW HURRY!
DIANA! THE PORTAL--IT'S CLOSING!
BUT THEY NEED HELP--

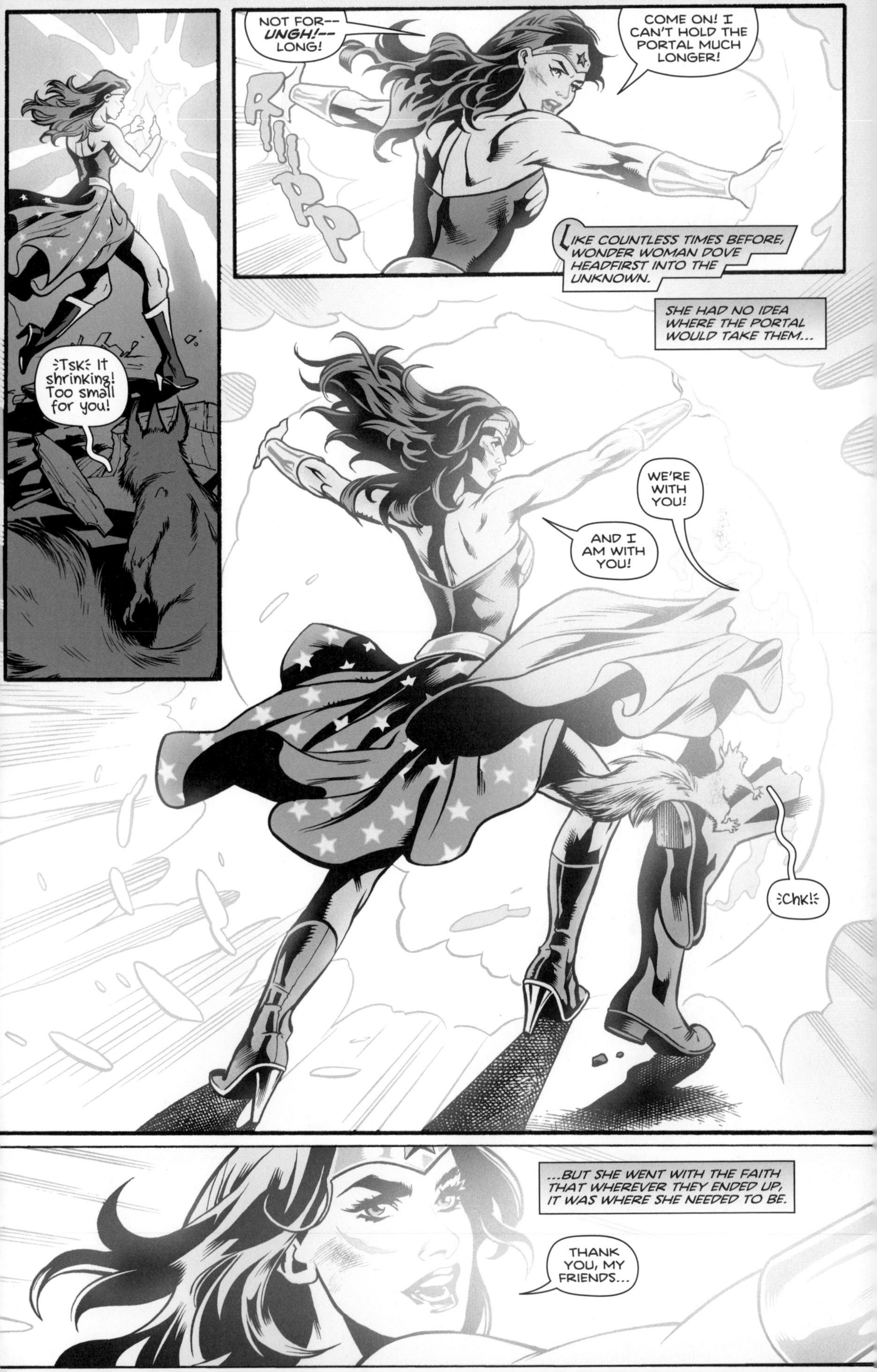
NOT FOR-- UNGH!-- LONG!
COME ON! I CAN'T HOLD THE PORTAL MUCH LONGER!
RIIPP
LIKE COUNTLESS TIMES BEFORE, WONDER WOMAN DOVE HEADFIRST INTO THE UNKNOWN.
Tsk It shrinking! Too small for you!
SHE HAD NO IDEA WHERE THE PORTAL WOULD TAKE THEM...
WE'RE WITH YOU!
AND I AM WITH YOU!
Chk!
...BUT SHE WENT WITH THE FAITH THAT WHEREVER THEY ENDED UP, IT WAS WHERE SHE NEEDED TO BE.
THANK YOU, MY FRIENDS...

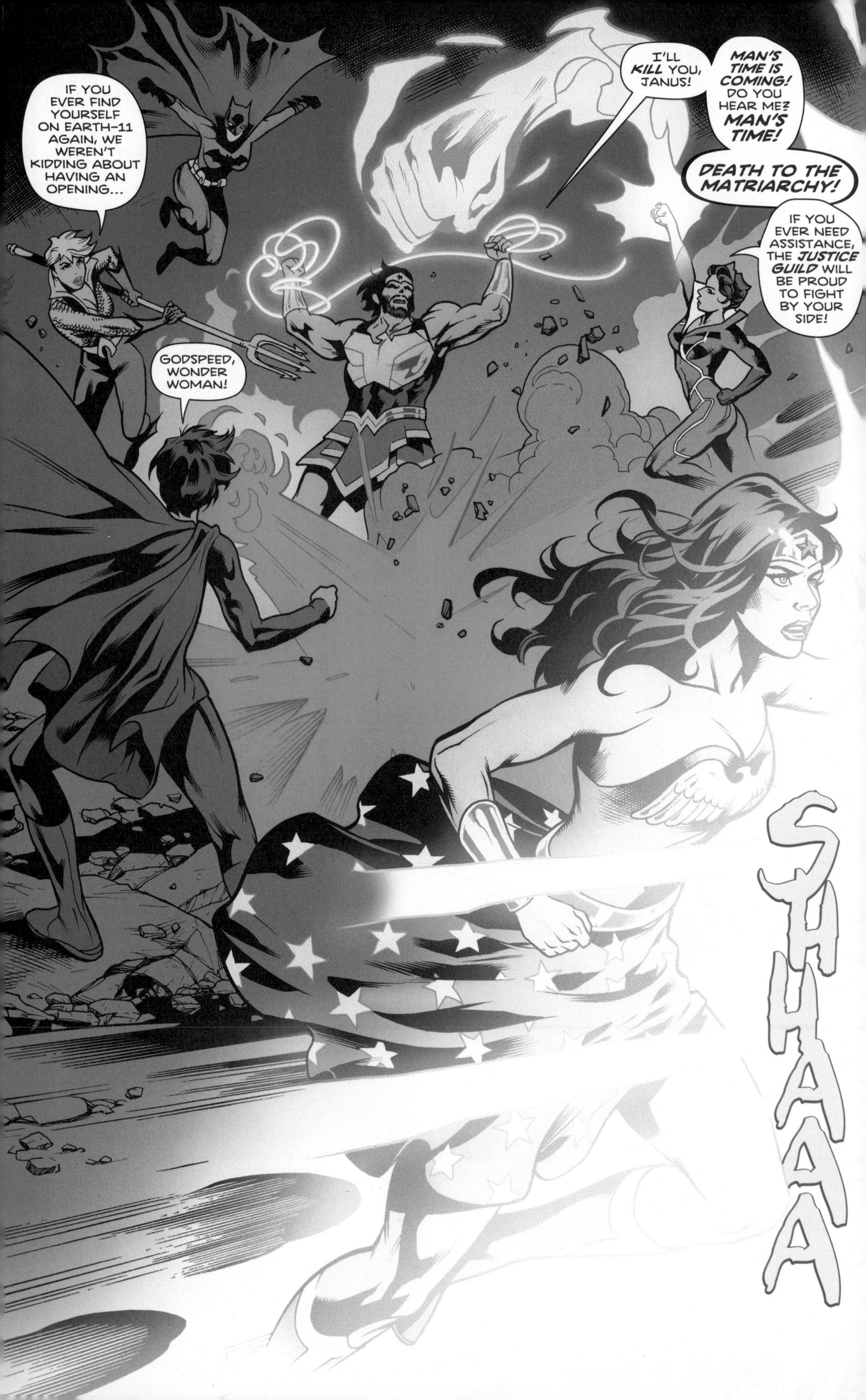
IF YOU EVER FIND YOURSELF ON EARTH-11 AGAIN, WE WEREN'T KIDDING ABOUT HAVING AN OPENING...
I'LL KILL YOU, JANUS!
MAN'S TIME IS COMING! DO YOU HEAR ME? MAN'S TIME!
DEATH TO THE MATRIARCHY!
IF YOU EVER NEED ASSISTANCE, THE JUSTICE GUILD WILL BE PROUD TO FIGHT BY YOUR SIDE!
GODSPEED, WONDER WOMAN!
SHHAAAA

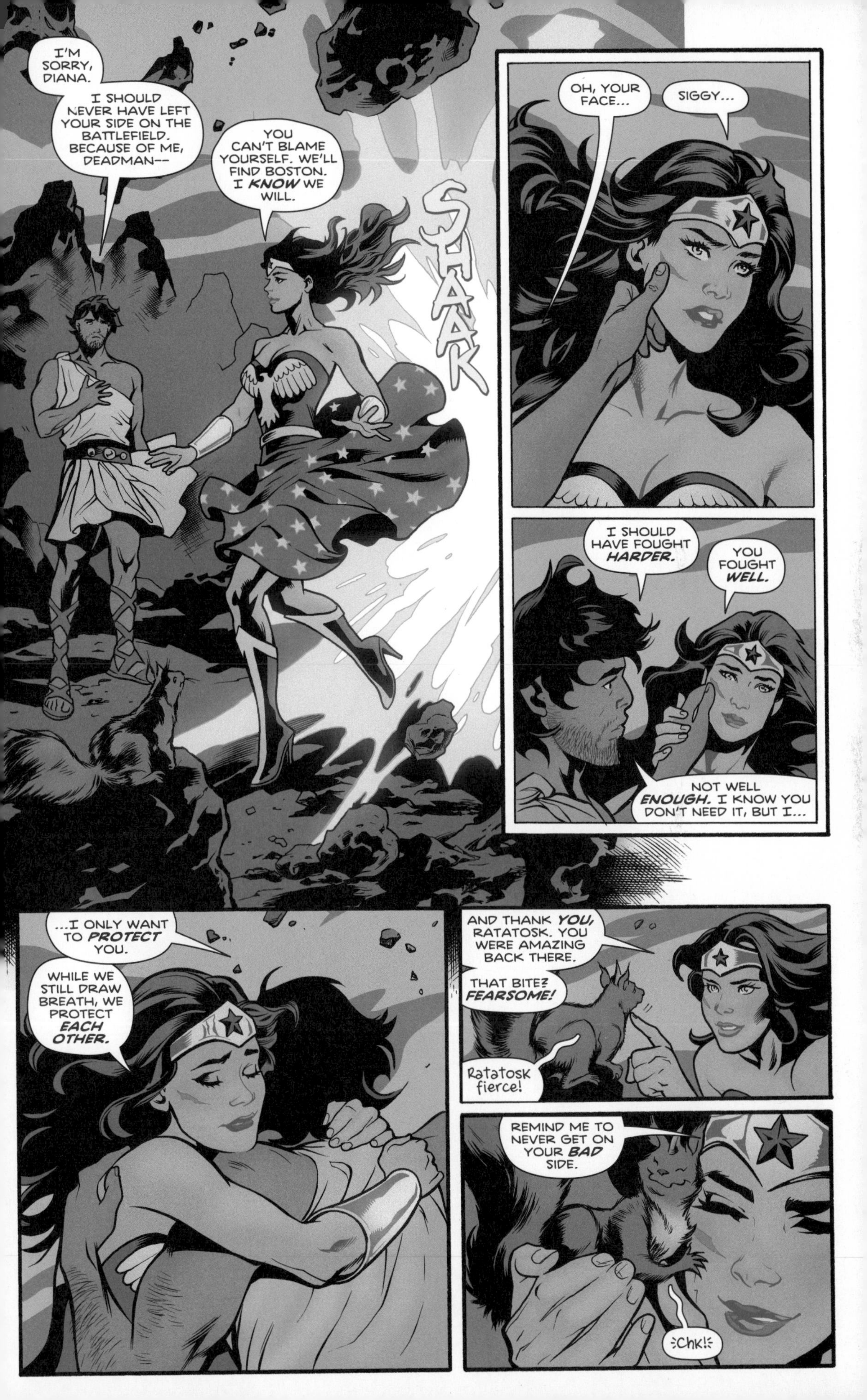
I'M SORRY, DIANA.
I SHOULD NEVER HAVE LEFT YOUR SIDE ON THE BATTLEFIELD. BECAUSE OF ME, DEADMAN--
YOU CAN'T BLAME YOURSELF. WE'LL FIND BOSTON. I KNOW WE WILL.
SHAAK
OH, YOUR FACE...
SIGGY...
I SHOULD HAVE FOUGHT HARDER.
YOU FOUGHT WELL.
NOT WELL ENOUGH. I KNOW YOU DON'T NEED IT, BUT I...
...I ONLY WANT TO PROTECT YOU.
WHILE WE STILL DRAW BREATH, WE PROTECT EACH OTHER.
AND THANK YOU, RATATOSK. YOU WERE AMAZING BACK THERE.
THAT BITE? FEARSOME!
Ratatosk fierce!
REMIND ME TO NEVER GET ON YOUR BAD SIDE.
Chk!

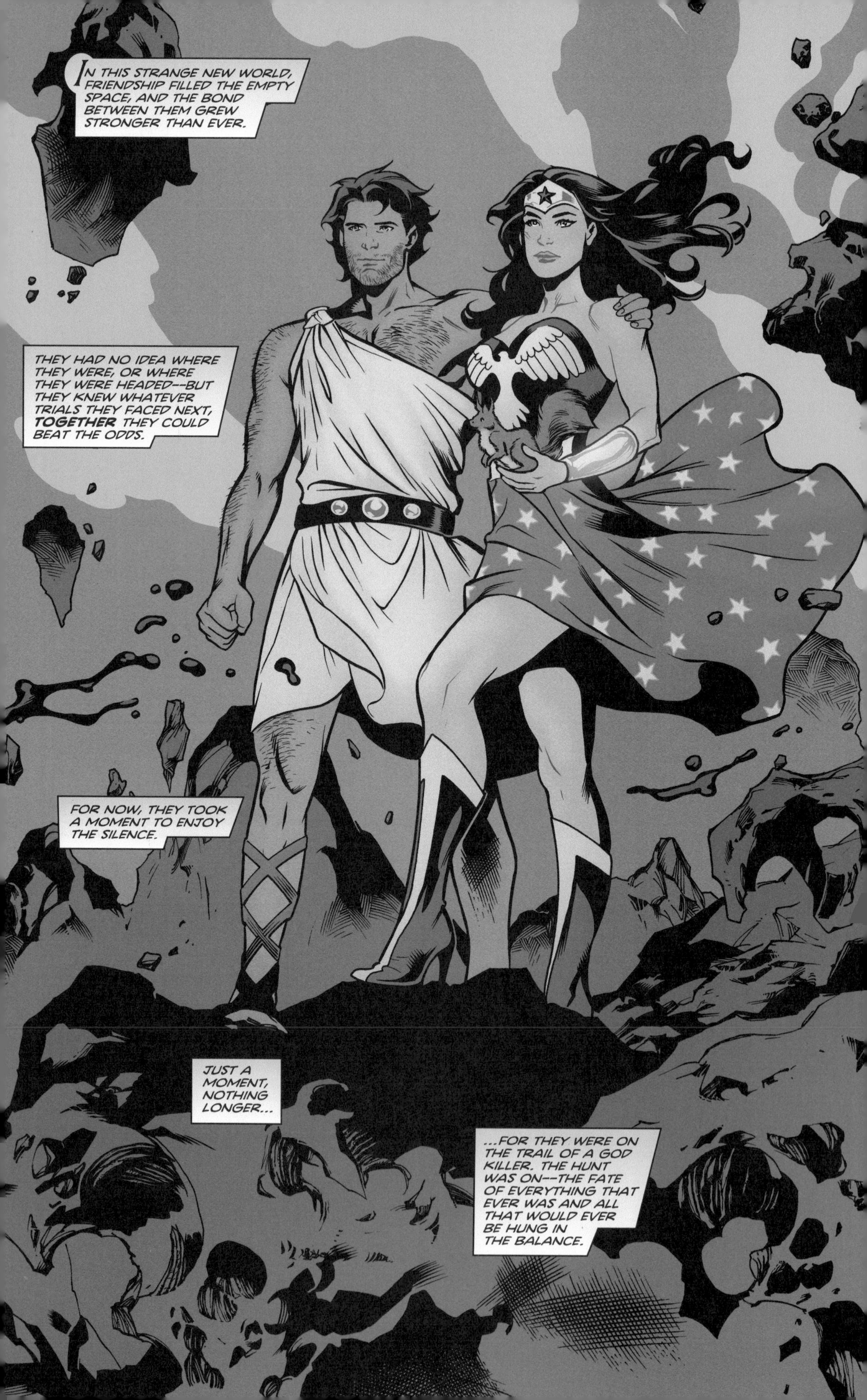
IN THIS STRANGE NEW WORLD, FRIENDSHIP FILLED THE EMPTY SPACE, AND THE BOND BETWEEN THEM GREW STRONGER THAN EVER.
THEY HAD NO IDEA WHERE THEY WERE, OR WHERE THEY WERE HEADED--BUT THEY KNEW WHATEVER TRIALS THEY FACED NEXT, TOGETHER THEY COULD BEAT THE ODDS.
FOR NOW, THEY TOOK A MOMENT TO ENJOY THE SILENCE.
JUST A MOMENT, NOTHING LONGER...
...FOR THEY WERE ON THE TRAIL OF A GOD KILLER. THE HUNT WAS ON--THE FATE OF EVERYTHING THAT EVER WAS AND ALL THAT WOULD EVER BE HUNG IN THE BALANCE.

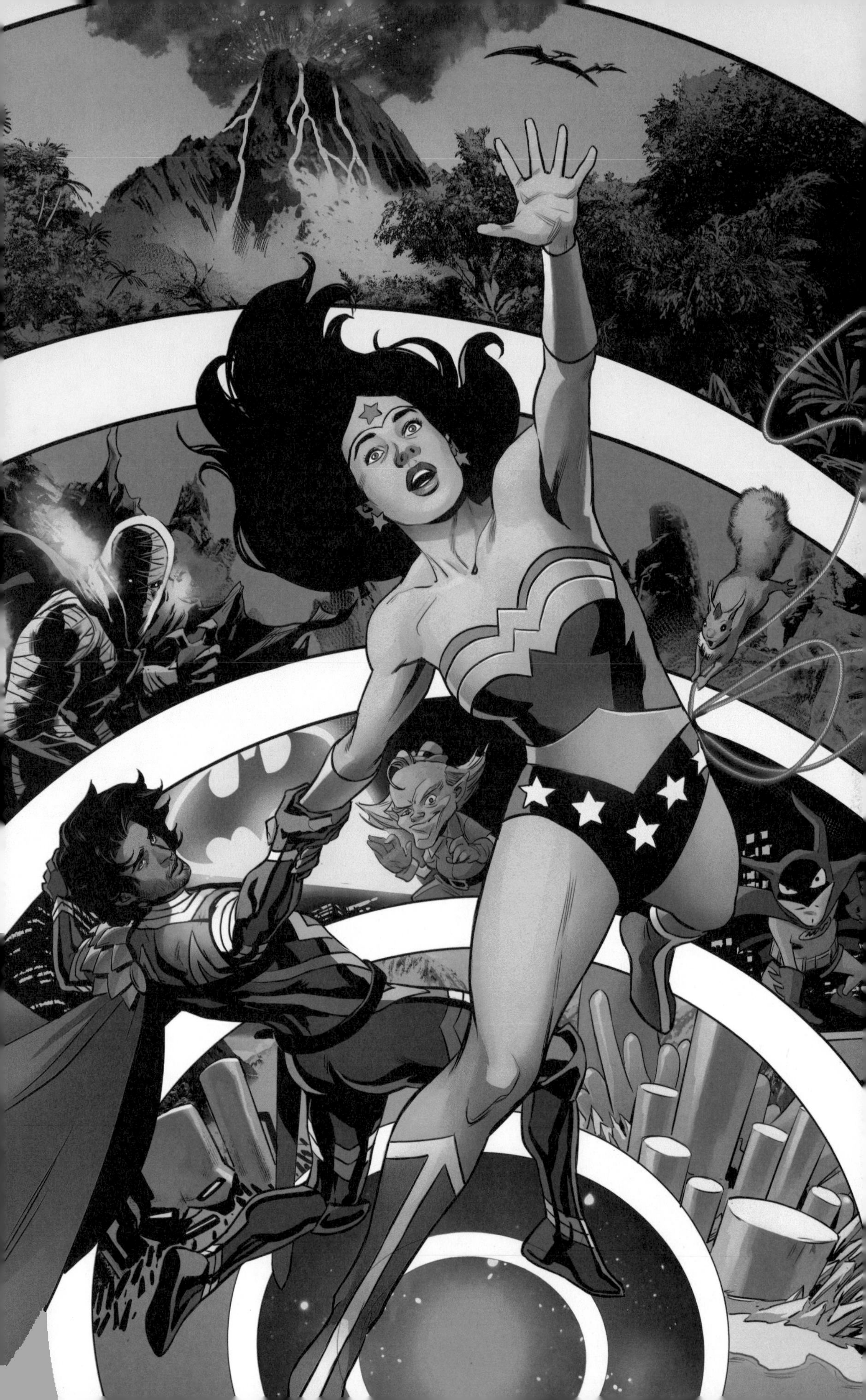

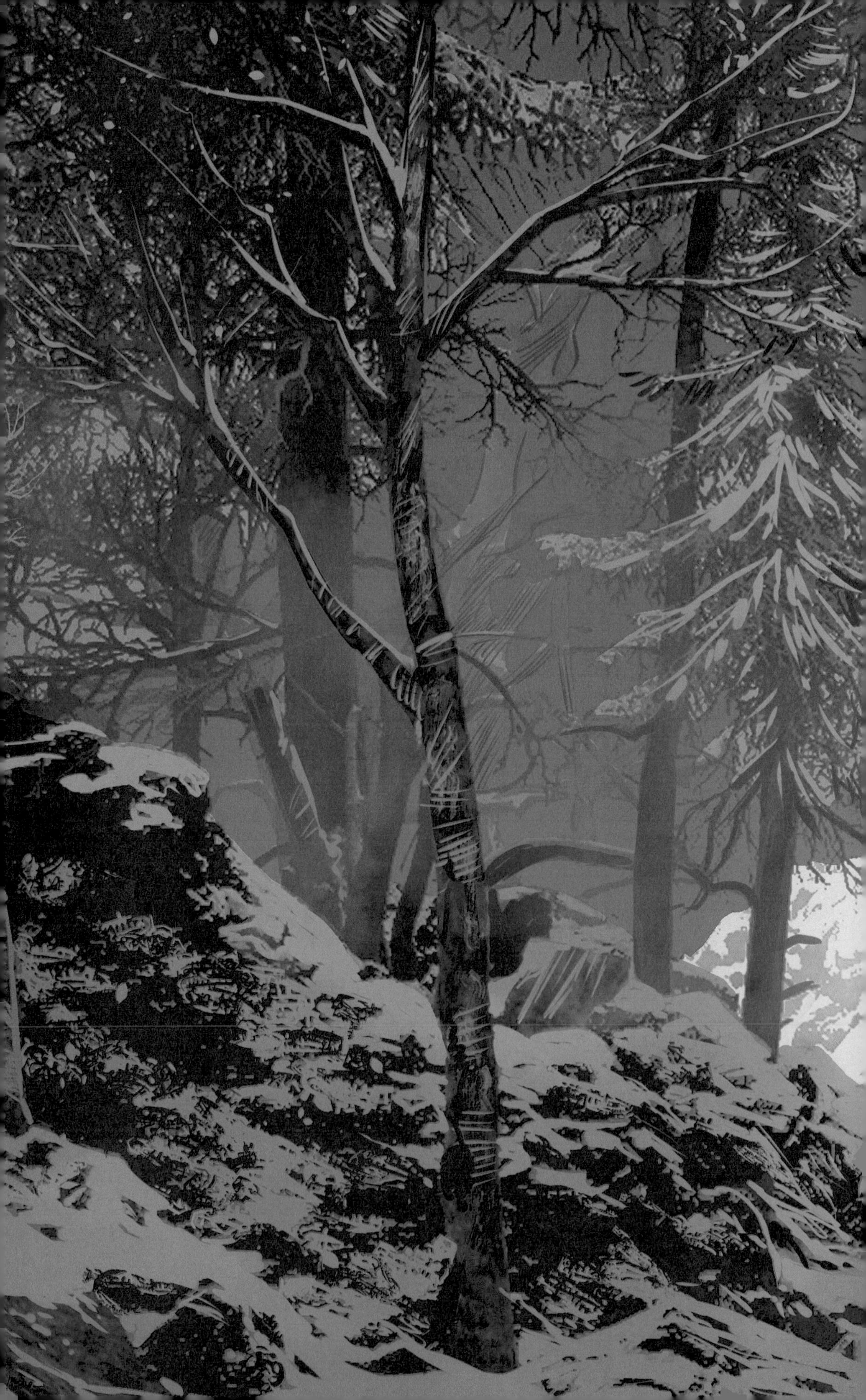

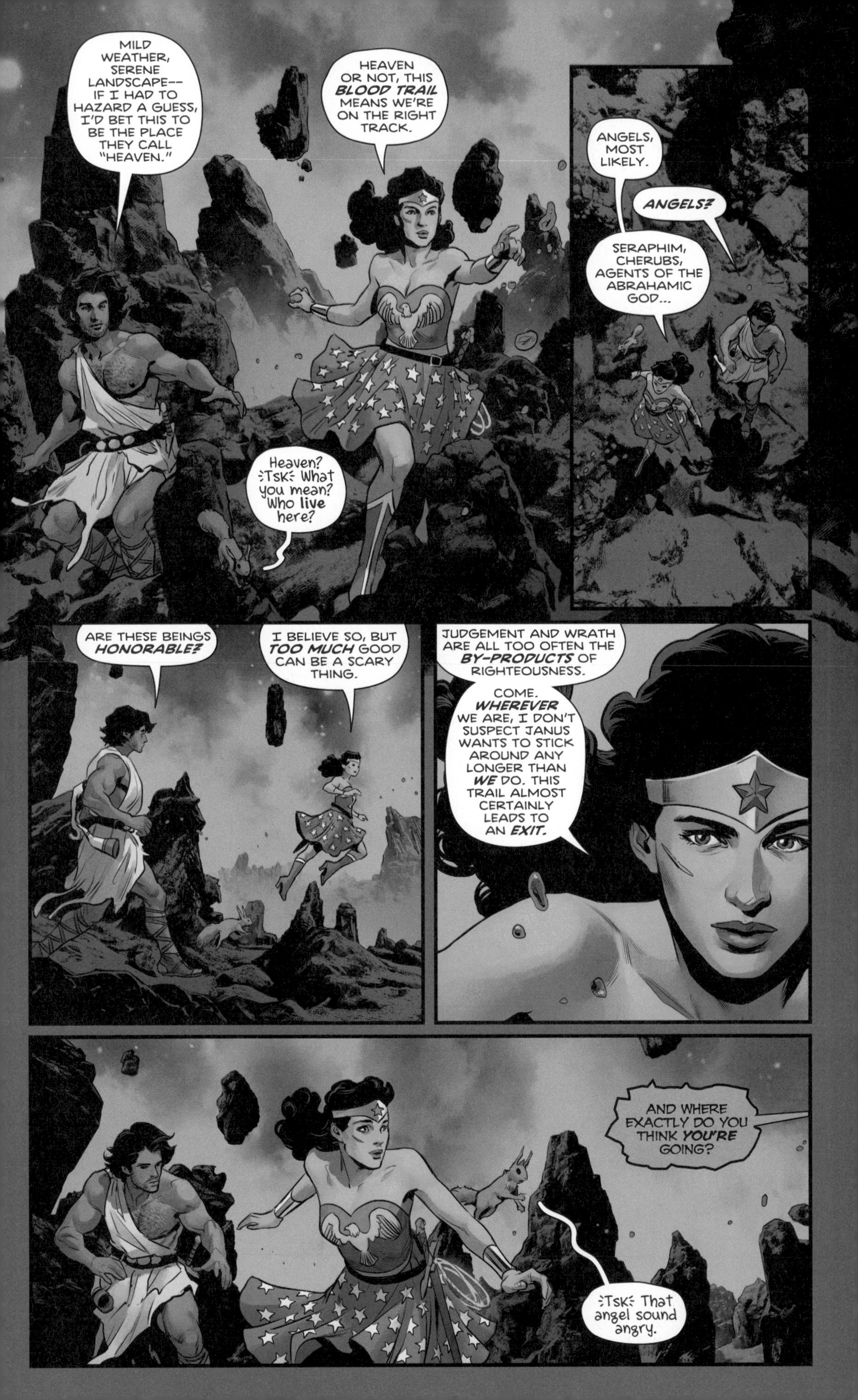
MILD WEATHER, SERENE LANDSCAPE-- IF I HAD TO HAZARD A GUESS, I'D BET THIS TO BE THE PLACE THEY CALL "HEAVEN."
HEAVEN OR NOT, THIS BLOOD TRAIL MEANS WE'RE ON THE RIGHT TRACK.
Heaven? :Tsk: What you mean? Who live here?
ANGELS, MOST LIKELY.
ANGELS?
SERAPHIM, CHERUBS, AGENTS OF THE ABRAHAMIC GOD...
ARE THESE BEINGS HONORABLE?
I BELIEVE SO, BUT TOO MUCH GOOD CAN BE A SCARY THING.
JUDGEMENT AND WRATH ARE ALL TOO OFTEN THE BY-PRODUCTS OF RIGHTEOUSNESS.
COME. WHEREVER WE ARE, I DON'T SUSPECT JANUS WANTS TO STICK AROUND ANY LONGER THAN WE DO. THIS TRAIL ALMOST CERTAINLY LEADS TO AN EXIT.
AND WHERE EXACTLY DO YOU THINK YOU'RE GOING?
:Tsk: That angel sound angry.

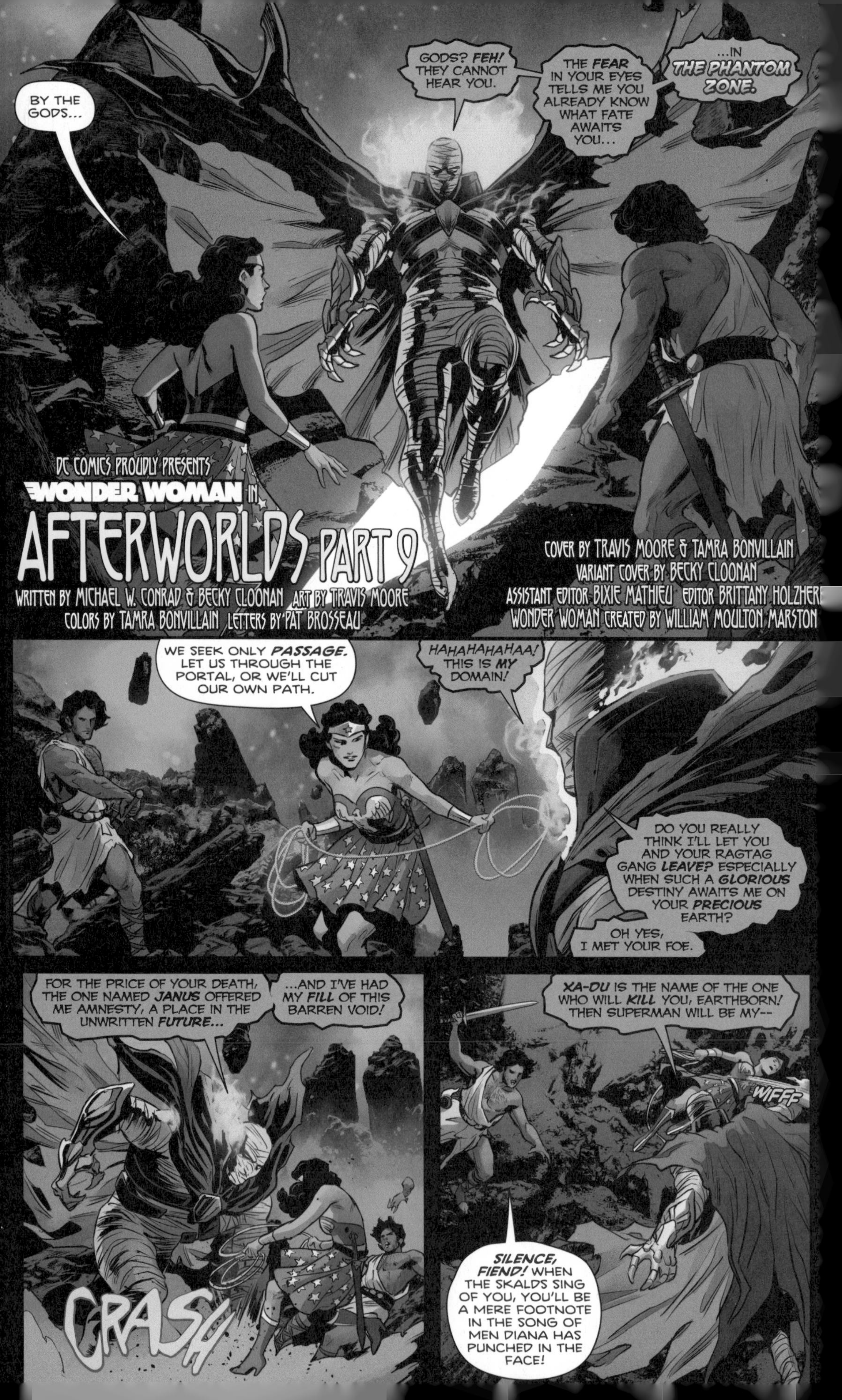

BY THE GODS...
GODS? FEH! THEY CANNOT HEAR YOU.
THE FEAR IN YOUR EYES TELLS ME YOU ALREADY KNOW WHAT FATE AWAITS YOU...
...IN THE PHANTOM ZONE.
DC COMICS PROUDLY PRESENTS
WONDER WOMAN IN
AFTERWORLDS PART 9
WRITTEN BY MICHAEL W. CONRAD & BECKY CLOONAN ART BY TRAVIS MOORE
COLORS BY TAMRA BONVILLAIN LETTERS BY PAT BROSSEAU
COVER BY TRAVIS MOORE & TAMRA BONVILLAIN
VARIANT COVER BY BECKY CLOONAN
ASSISTANT EDITOR BIXIE MATHIEU EDITOR BRITTANY HOLZHERR
WONDER WOMAN CREATED BY WILLIAM MOULTON MARSTON
WE SEEK ONLY PASSAGE. LET US THROUGH THE PORTAL, OR WE'LL CUT OUR OWN PATH.
HAHAHAHAHAA! THIS IS MY DOMAIN!
DO YOU REALLY THINK I'LL LET YOU AND YOUR RAGTAG GANG LEAVE? ESPECIALLY WHEN SUCH A GLORIOUS DESTINY AWAITS ME ON YOUR PRECIOUS EARTH?
OH YES, I MET YOUR FOE.
FOR THE PRICE OF YOUR DEATH, THE ONE NAMED JANUS OFFERED ME AMNESTY, A PLACE IN THE UNWRITTEN FUTURE...
...AND I'VE HAD MY FILL OF THIS BARREN VOID!
CRASH
XA-DU IS THE NAME OF THE ONE WHO WILL KILL YOU, EARTHBORN! THEN SUPERMAN WILL BE MY--
WIFFF
SILENCE, FIEND! WHEN THE SKALDS SING OF YOU, YOU'LL BE A MERE FOOTNOTE IN THE SONG OF MEN DIANA HAS PUNCHED IN THE FACE!

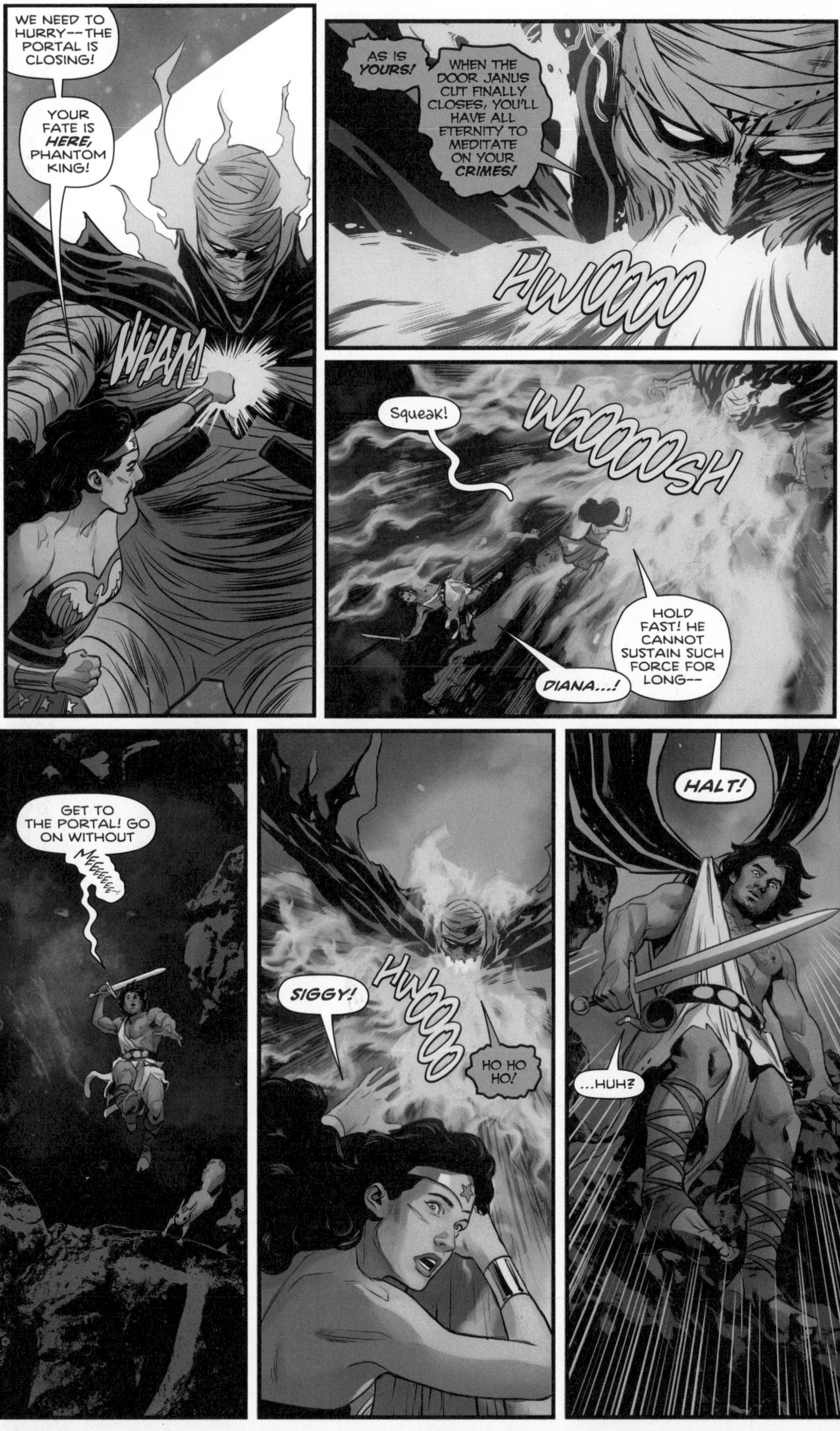
WE NEED TO HURRY--THE PORTAL IS CLOSING!
YOUR FATE IS HERE, PHANTOM KING!
WHAM
AS IS YOURS!
WHEN THE DOOR JANUS CUT FINALLY CLOSES, YOU'LL HAVE ALL ETERNITY TO MEDITATE ON YOUR CRIMES!
HWOOOO
Squeak!
WOOOOOSH
HOLD FAST! HE CANNOT SUSTAIN SUCH FORCE FOR LONG--
DIANA...!
GET TO THE PORTAL! GO ON WITHOUT
MEEEEEE--!
SIGGY!
HWOOOO
HO HO HO!
HALT!
...HUH?

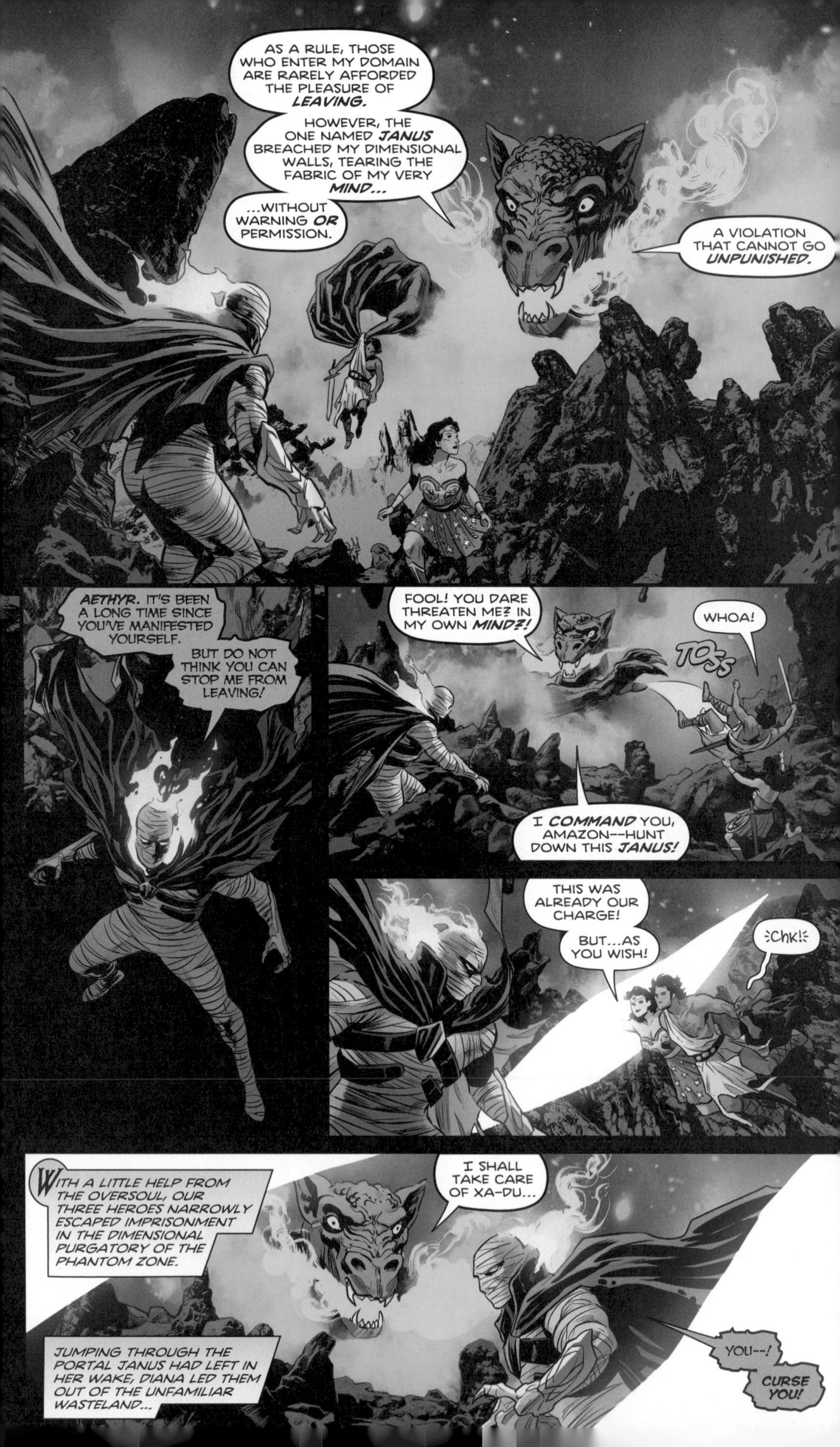
AS A RULE, THOSE WHO ENTER MY DOMAIN ARE RARELY AFFORDED THE PLEASURE OF LEAVING.
HOWEVER, THE ONE NAMED JANUS BREACHED MY DIMENSIONAL WALLS, TEARING THE FABRIC OF MY VERY MIND...
...WITHOUT WARNING OR PERMISSION.
A VIOLATION THAT CANNOT GO UNPUNISHED.
AETHYR. IT'S BEEN A LONG TIME SINCE YOU'VE MANIFESTED YOURSELF.
BUT DO NOT THINK YOU CAN STOP ME FROM LEAVING!
FOOL! YOU DARE THREATEN ME? IN MY OWN MIND?!
WHOA!
TOSS
I COMMAND YOU, AMAZON--HUNT DOWN THIS JANUS!
THIS WAS ALREADY OUR CHARGE!
BUT...AS YOU WISH!
CHK!
WITH A LITTLE HELP FROM THE OVERSOUL, OUR THREE HEROES NARROWLY ESCAPED IMPRISONMENT IN THE DIMENSIONAL PURGATORY OF THE PHANTOM ZONE.
I SHALL TAKE CARE OF XA-DU...
JUMPING THROUGH THE PORTAL JANUS HAD LEFT IN HER WAKE, DIANA LED THEM OUT OF THE UNFAMILIAR WASTELAND...
YOU--!
CURSE YOU!

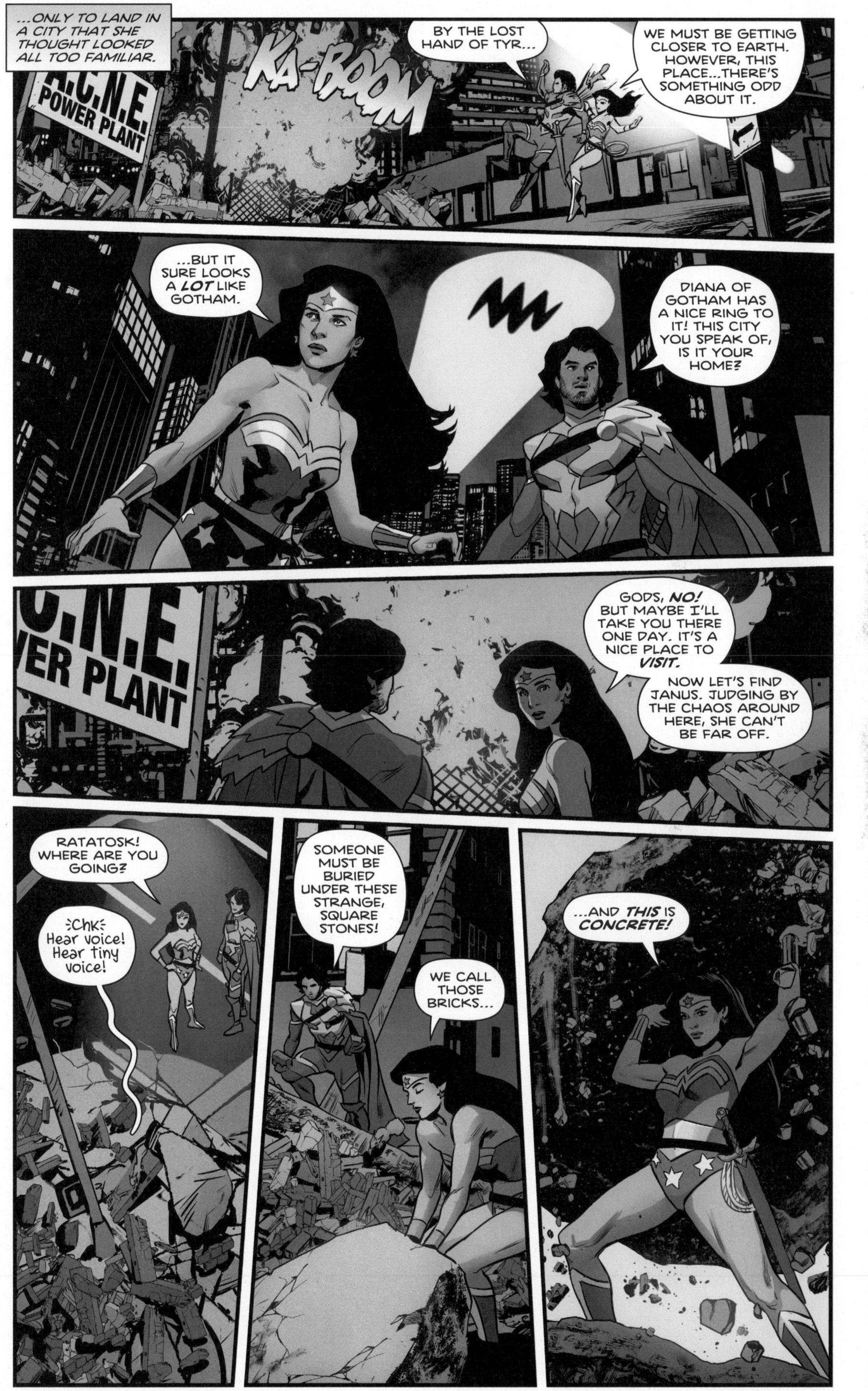
...ONLY TO LAND IN A CITY THAT SHE THOUGHT LOOKED ALL TOO FAMILIAR.
KA-BOOM
BY THE LOST HAND OF TYR...
WE MUST BE GETTING CLOSER TO EARTH. HOWEVER, THIS PLACE...THERE'S SOMETHING ODD ABOUT IT.
POWER PLANT
...BUT IT SURE LOOKS A LOT LIKE GOTHAM.
DIANA OF GOTHAM HAS A NICE RING TO IT! THIS CITY YOU SPEAK OF, IS IT YOUR HOME?
GODS, NO! BUT MAYBE I'LL TAKE YOU THERE ONE DAY. IT'S A NICE PLACE TO VISIT.
NOW LET'S FIND JANUS. JUDGING BY THE CHAOS AROUND HERE, SHE CAN'T BE FAR OFF.
RATATOSK! WHERE ARE YOU GOING?
Chk Hear voice! Hear tiny voice!
SOMEONE MUST BE BURIED UNDER THESE STRANGE, SQUARE STONES!
WE CALL THOSE BRICKS...
...AND THIS IS CONCRETE!

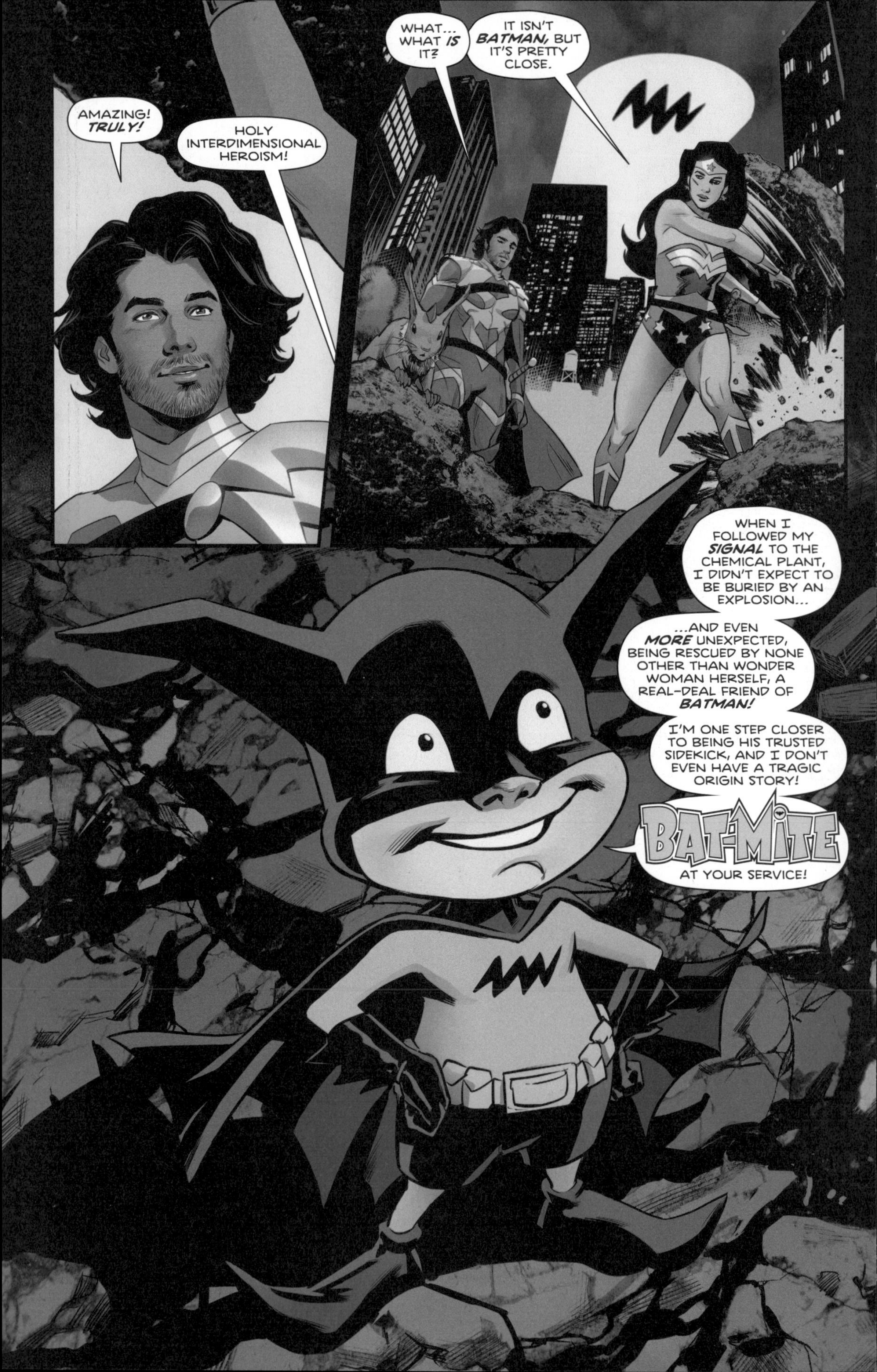

AMAZING! TRULY!
HOLY INTERDIMENSIONAL HEROISM!
WHAT... WHAT IS IT?
IT ISN'T BATMAN, BUT IT'S PRETTY CLOSE.
WHEN I FOLLOWED MY SIGNAL TO THE CHEMICAL PLANT, I DIDN'T EXPECT TO BE BURIED BY AN EXPLOSION...
...AND EVEN MORE UNEXPECTED, BEING RESCUED BY NONE OTHER THAN WONDER WOMAN HERSELF, A REAL-DEAL FRIEND OF BATMAN!
I'M ONE STEP CLOSER TO BEING HIS TRUSTED SIDEKICK, AND I DON'T EVEN HAVE A TRAGIC ORIGIN STORY!
BAT-MITE
AT YOUR SERVICE!

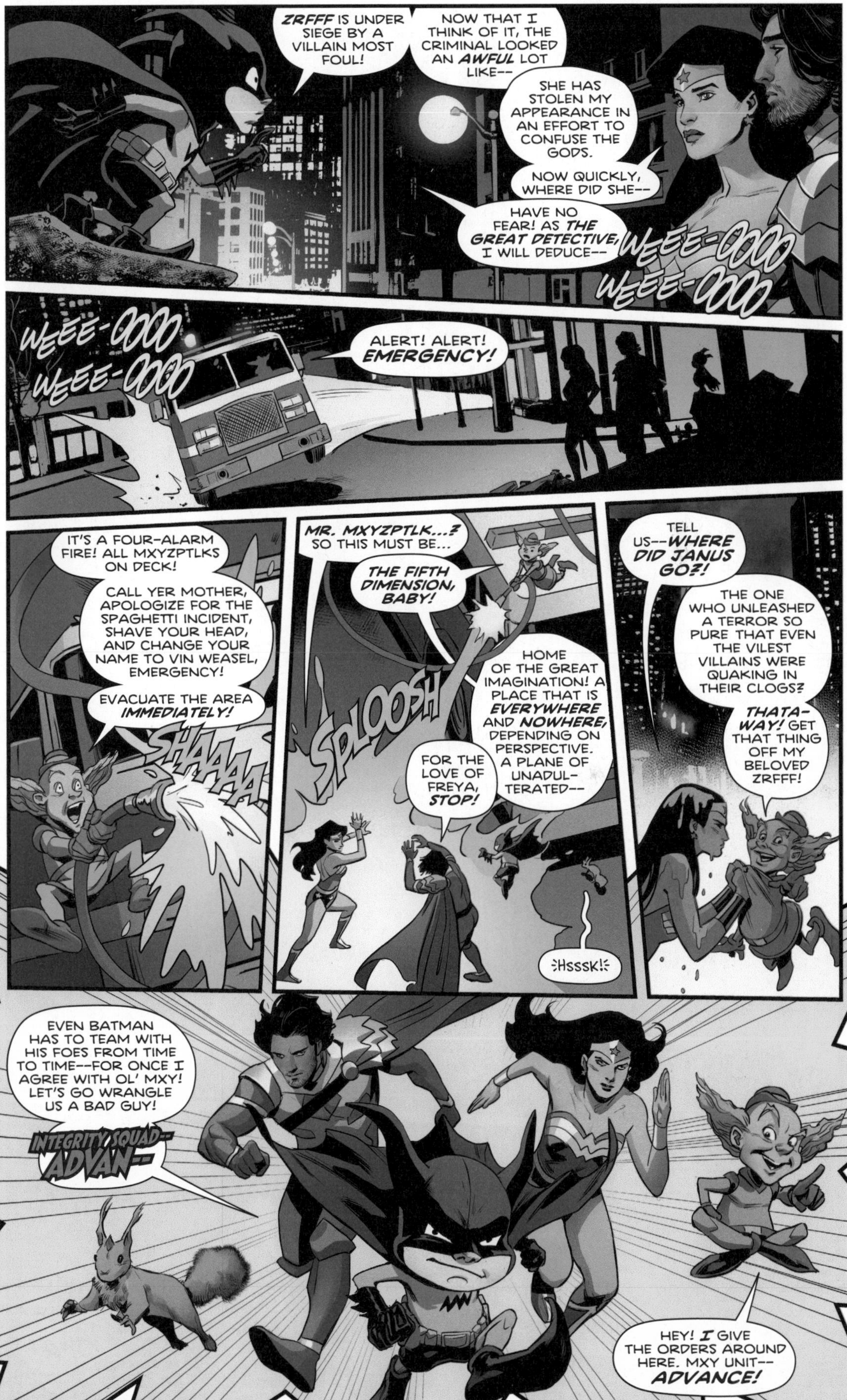
ZRFFF IS UNDER SIEGE BY A VILLAIN MOST FOUL!
NOW THAT I THINK OF IT, THE CRIMINAL LOOKED AN AWFUL LOT LIKE--
SHE HAS STOLEN MY APPEARANCE IN AN EFFORT TO CONFUSE THE GODS.
NOW QUICKLY, WHERE DID SHE--
HAVE NO FEAR! AS THE GREAT DETECTIVE, I WILL DEDUCE--
WEEE-OOOO WEEE-OOOO
WEEE-OOOO WEEE-OOOO
ALERT! ALERT! EMERGENCY!
IT'S A FOUR-ALARM FIRE! ALL MXYZPTLKS ON DECK!
CALL YER MOTHER, APOLOGIZE FOR THE SPAGHETTI INCIDENT, SHAVE YOUR HEAD, AND CHANGE YOUR NAME TO VIN WEASEL, EMERGENCY!
EVACUATE THE AREA IMMEDIATELY!
SHAAAAA
MR. MXYZPTLK...? SO THIS MUST BE...
THE FIFTH DIMENSION, BABY!
SPLOOSH
HOME OF THE GREAT IMAGINATION! A PLACE THAT IS EVERYWHERE AND NOWHERE, DEPENDING ON PERSPECTIVE. A PLANE OF UNADULTERATED--
FOR THE LOVE OF FREYA, STOP!
Hsssk!
TELL US--WHERE DID JANUS GO?!
THE ONE WHO UNLEASHED A TERROR SO PURE THAT EVEN THE VILEST VILLAINS WERE QUAKING IN THEIR CLOGS?
THATA-WAY! GET THAT THING OFF MY BELOVED ZRFFF!
EVEN BATMAN HAS TO TEAM WITH HIS FOES FROM TIME TO TIME--FOR ONCE I AGREE WITH OL' MXY! LET'S GO WRANGLE US A BAD GUY!
INTEGRITY SQUAD--ADVAN--
HEY! I GIVE THE ORDERS AROUND HERE. MXY UNIT--ADVANCE!

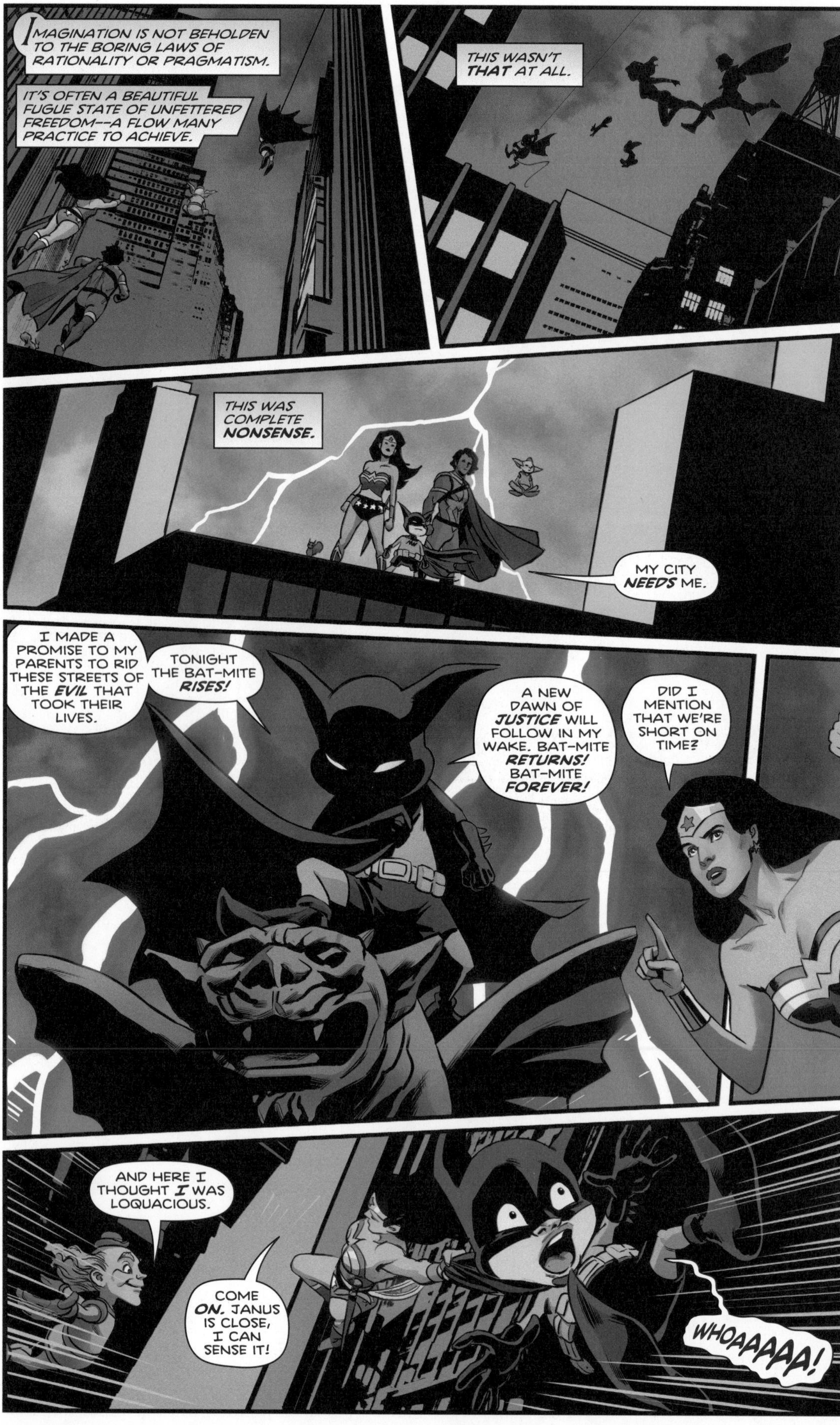
IMAGINATION IS NOT BEHOLDEN TO THE BORING LAWS OF RATIONALITY OR PRAGMATISM.
IT'S OFTEN A BEAUTIFUL FUGUE STATE OF UNFETTERED FREEDOM--A FLOW MANY PRACTICE TO ACHIEVE.
THIS WASN'T THAT AT ALL.
THIS WAS COMPLETE NONSENSE.
MY CITY NEEDS ME.
I MADE A PROMISE TO MY PARENTS TO RID THESE STREETS OF THE EVIL THAT TOOK THEIR LIVES.
TONIGHT THE BAT-MITE RISES!
A NEW DAWN OF JUSTICE WILL FOLLOW IN MY WAKE. BAT-MITE RETURNS! BAT-MITE FOREVER!
DID I MENTION THAT WE'RE SHORT ON TIME?
AND HERE I THOUGHT I WAS LOQUACIOUS.
COME ON. JANUS IS CLOSE, I CAN SENSE IT!
WHOAAAAAA!

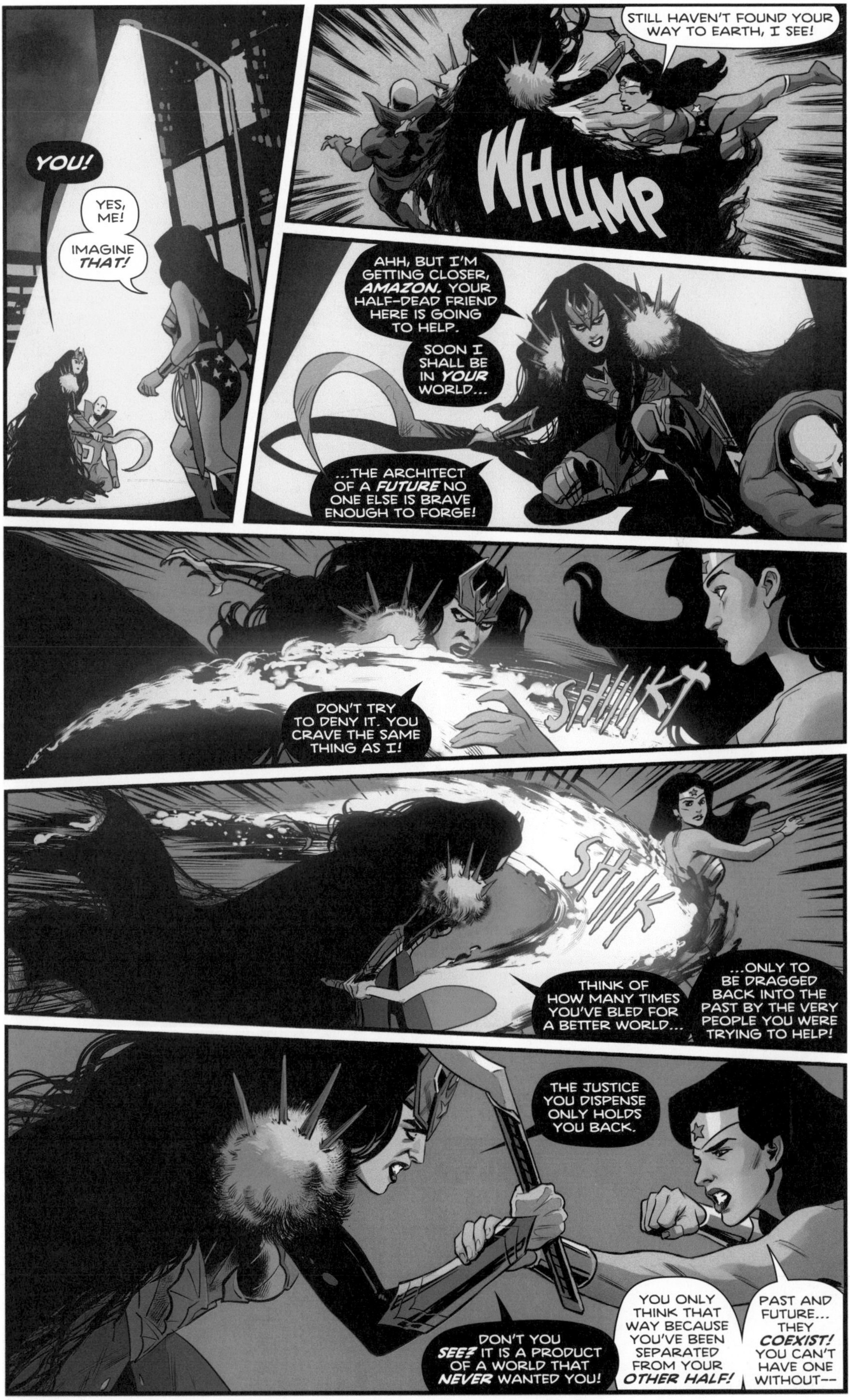
YOU!
YES, ME!
IMAGINE THAT!
STILL HAVEN'T FOUND YOUR WAY TO EARTH, I SEE!
WHUMP
AHH, BUT I'M GETTING CLOSER, AMAZON. YOUR HALF-DEAD FRIEND HERE IS GOING TO HELP.
SOON I SHALL BE IN YOUR WORLD...
...THE ARCHITECT OF A FUTURE NO ONE ELSE IS BRAVE ENOUGH TO FORGE!
SHIIIKT
DON'T TRY TO DENY IT. YOU CRAVE THE SAME THING AS I!
SHIIIK
THINK OF HOW MANY TIMES YOU'VE BLED FOR A BETTER WORLD...
...ONLY TO BE DRAGGED BACK INTO THE PAST BY THE VERY PEOPLE YOU WERE TRYING TO HELP!
THE JUSTICE YOU DISPENSE ONLY HOLDS YOU BACK.
DON'T YOU SEE? IT IS A PRODUCT OF A WORLD THAT NEVER WANTED YOU!
YOU ONLY THINK THAT WAY BECAUSE YOU'VE BEEN SEPARATED FROM YOUR OTHER HALF!
PAST AND FUTURE... THEY COEXIST! YOU CAN'T HAVE ONE WITHOUT--

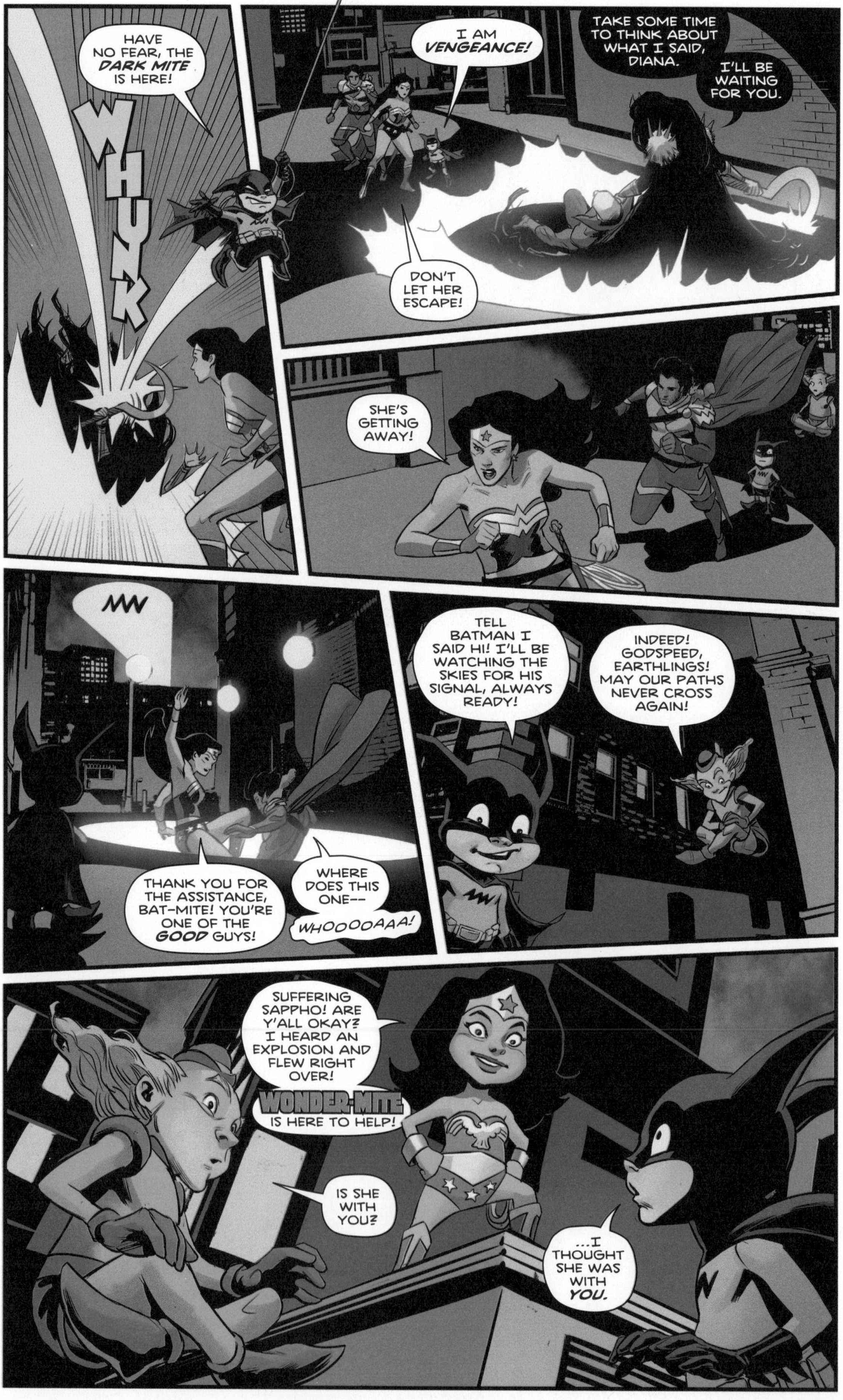
HAVE NO FEAR, THE DARK MITE IS HERE!
WHUNK
I AM VENGEANCE!
TAKE SOME TIME TO THINK ABOUT WHAT I SAID, DIANA.
I'LL BE WAITING FOR YOU.
DON'T LET HER ESCAPE!
SHE'S GETTING AWAY!
MW
THANK YOU FOR THE ASSISTANCE, BAT-MITE! YOU'RE ONE OF THE GOOD GUYS!
WHERE DOES THIS ONE--
WHOOOOAAA!
TELL BATMAN I SAID HI! I'LL BE WATCHING THE SKIES FOR HIS SIGNAL, ALWAYS READY!
INDEED! GODSPEED, EARTHLINGS! MAY OUR PATHS NEVER CROSS AGAIN!
SUFFERING SAPPHO! ARE Y'ALL OKAY? I HEARD AN EXPLOSION AND FLEW RIGHT OVER!
WONDER-MITE IS HERE TO HELP!
IS SHE WITH YOU?
...I THOUGHT SHE WAS WITH YOU.

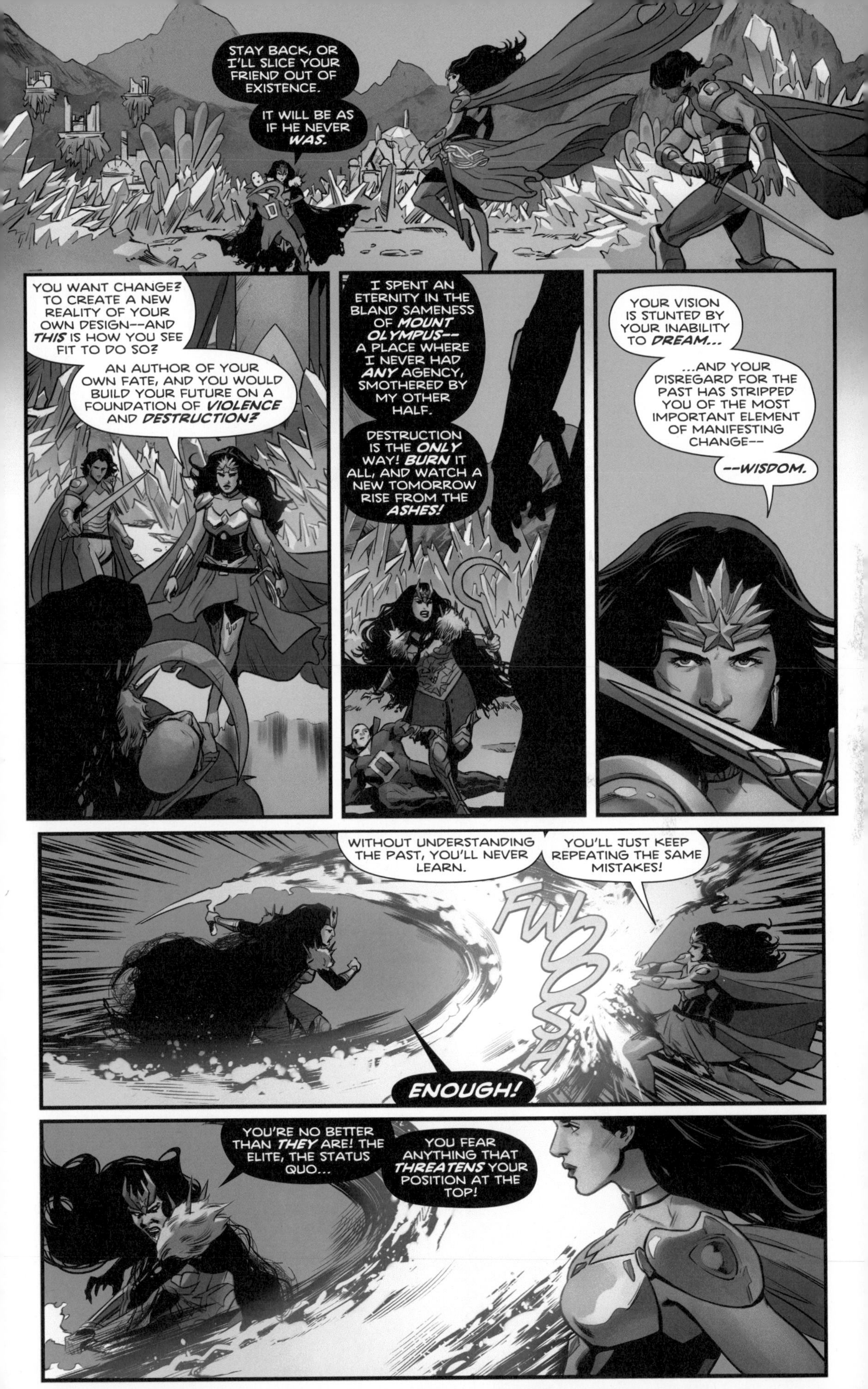
STAY BACK, OR I'LL SLICE YOUR FRIEND OUT OF EXISTENCE.
IT WILL BE AS IF HE NEVER *WAS.*
YOU WANT CHANGE? TO CREATE A NEW REALITY OF YOUR OWN DESIGN--AND *THIS* IS HOW YOU SEE FIT TO DO SO?
AN AUTHOR OF YOUR OWN FATE, AND YOU WOULD BUILD YOUR FUTURE ON A FOUNDATION OF *VIOLENCE* AND *DESTRUCTION?*
I SPENT AN ETERNITY IN THE BLAND SAMENESS OF *MOUNT OLYMPUS--* A PLACE WHERE I NEVER HAD *ANY* AGENCY, SMOTHERED BY MY OTHER HALF.
DESTRUCTION IS THE *ONLY* WAY! *BURN* IT ALL, AND WATCH A NEW TOMORROW RISE FROM THE *ASHES!*
YOUR VISION IS STUNTED BY YOUR INABILITY TO *DREAM...*
...AND YOUR DISREGARD FOR THE PAST HAS STRIPPED YOU OF THE MOST IMPORTANT ELEMENT OF MANIFESTING CHANGE--
--WISDOM.
WITHOUT UNDERSTANDING THE PAST, YOU'LL NEVER LEARN.
YOU'LL JUST KEEP REPEATING THE SAME MISTAKES!
FWOOSH
ENOUGH!
YOU'RE NO BETTER THAN *THEY* ARE! THE ELITE, THE STATUS QUO...
YOU FEAR ANYTHING THAT *THREATENS* YOUR POSITION AT THE TOP!

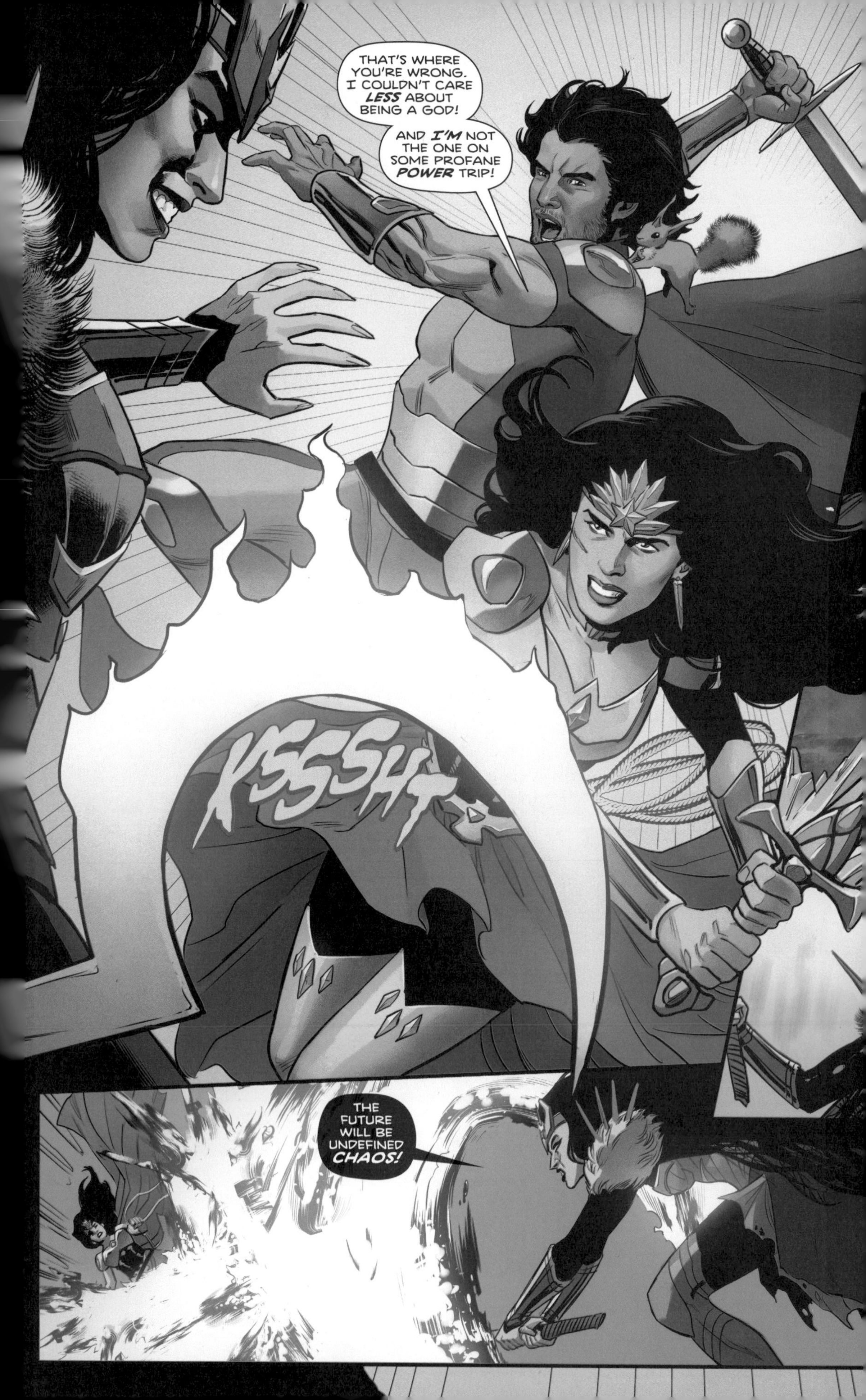
THAT'S WHERE YOU'RE WRONG. I COULDN'T CARE LESS ABOUT BEING A GOD!
AND I'M NOT THE ONE ON SOME PROFANE POWER TRIP!
KSSSHT
THE FUTURE WILL BE UNDEFINED CHAOS!

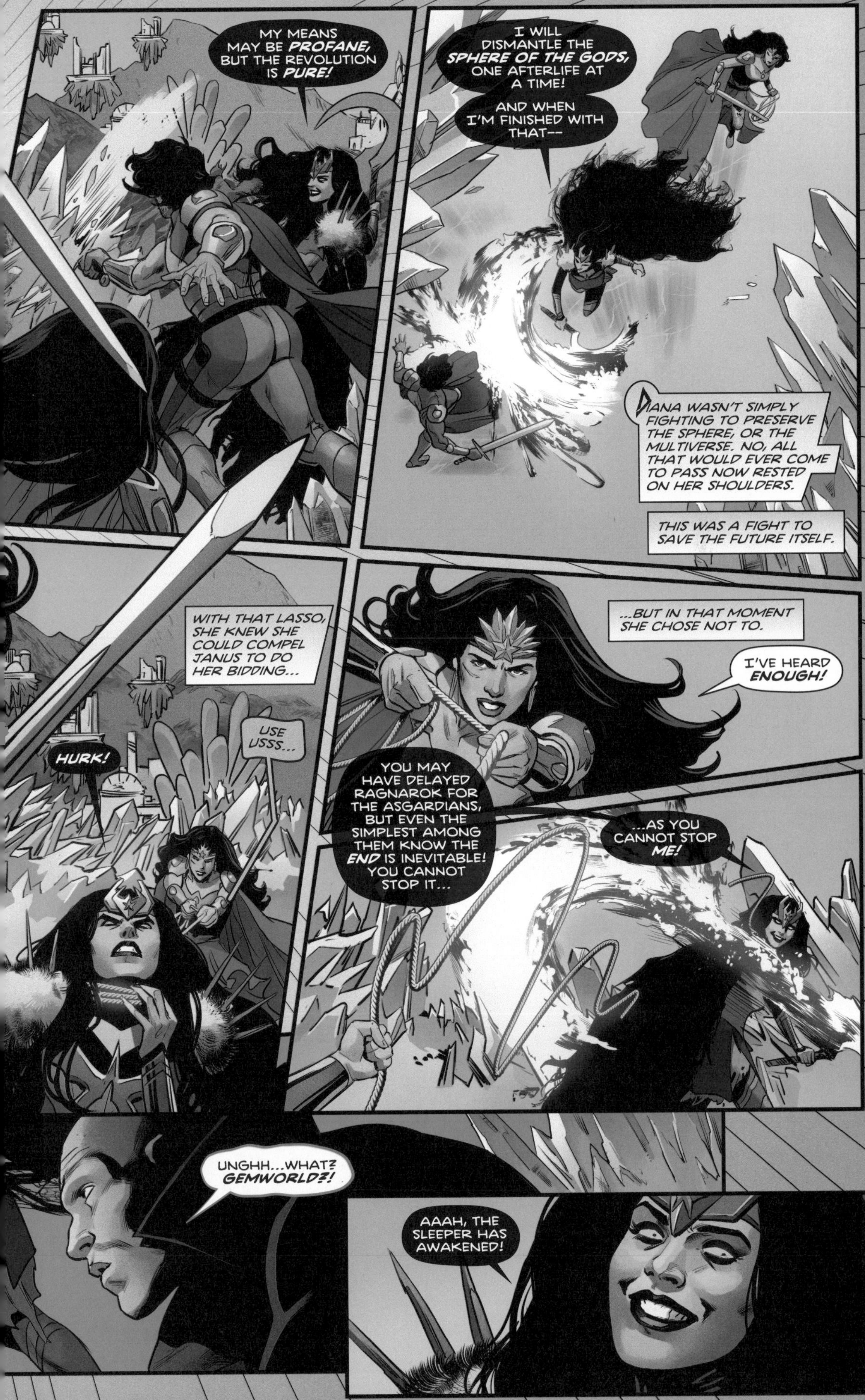
MY MEANS MAY BE PROFANE, BUT THE REVOLUTION IS PURE!
I WILL DISMANTLE THE SPHERE OF THE GODS, ONE AFTERLIFE AT A TIME!
AND WHEN I'M FINISHED WITH THAT--
DIANA WASN'T SIMPLY FIGHTING TO PRESERVE THE SPHERE, OR THE MULTIVERSE. NO, ALL THAT WOULD EVER COME TO PASS NOW RESTED ON HER SHOULDERS.
THIS WAS A FIGHT TO SAVE THE FUTURE ITSELF.
WITH THAT LASSO, SHE KNEW SHE COULD COMPEL JANUS TO DO HER BIDDING...
HURK!
USE USSS...
...BUT IN THAT MOMENT SHE CHOSE NOT TO.
I'VE HEARD ENOUGH!
YOU MAY HAVE DELAYED RAGNAROK FOR THE ASGARDIANS, BUT EVEN THE SIMPLEST AMONG THEM KNOW THE END IS INEVITABLE! YOU CANNOT STOP IT...
...AS YOU CANNOT STOP ME!
UNGHH...WHAT? GEMWORLD?!
AAAH, THE SLEEPER HAS AWAKENED!

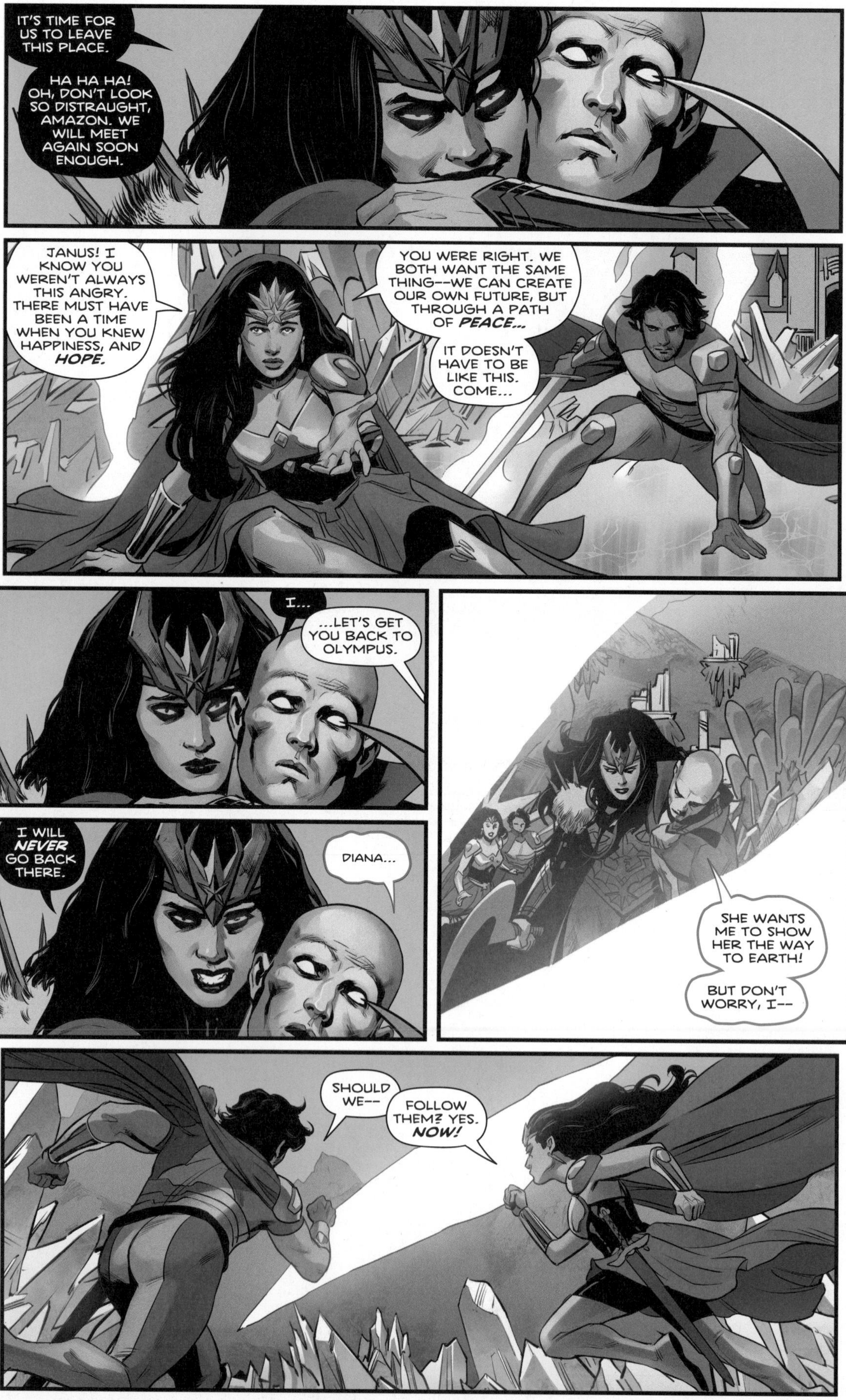
IT'S TIME FOR US TO LEAVE THIS PLACE.
HA HA HA! OH, DON'T LOOK SO DISTRAUGHT, AMAZON. WE WILL MEET AGAIN SOON ENOUGH.
JANUS! I KNOW YOU WEREN'T ALWAYS THIS ANGRY. THERE MUST HAVE BEEN A TIME WHEN YOU KNEW HAPPINESS, AND HOPE.
YOU WERE RIGHT. WE BOTH WANT THE SAME THING--WE CAN CREATE OUR OWN FUTURE, BUT THROUGH A PATH OF PEACE...
IT DOESN'T HAVE TO BE LIKE THIS. COME...
I...
...LET'S GET YOU BACK TO OLYMPUS.
I WILL NEVER GO BACK THERE.
DIANA...
SHE WANTS ME TO SHOW HER THE WAY TO EARTH!
BUT DON'T WORRY, I--
SHOULD WE--
FOLLOW THEM? YES. NOW!

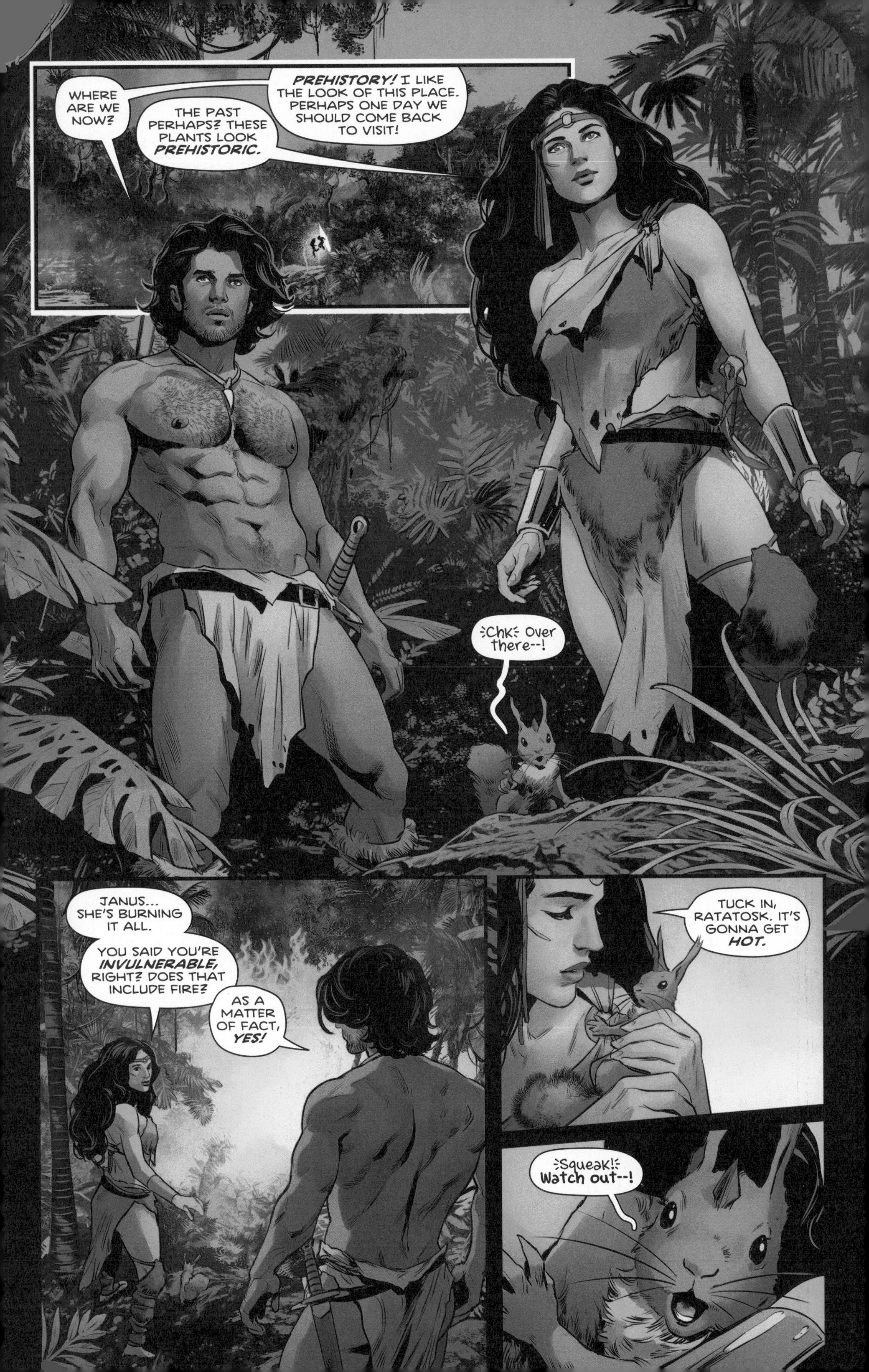

WHERE ARE WE NOW?
THE PAST PERHAPS? THESE PLANTS LOOK PREHISTORIC.
PREHISTORY! I LIKE THE LOOK OF THIS PLACE. PERHAPS ONE DAY WE SHOULD COME BACK TO VISIT!
Chk Over there--!
JANUS... SHE'S BURNING IT ALL.
YOU SAID YOU'RE INVULNERABLE, RIGHT? DOES THAT INCLUDE FIRE?
AS A MATTER OF FACT, YES!
TUCK IN, RATATOSK. IT'S GONNA GET HOT.
Squeak! Watch out--!

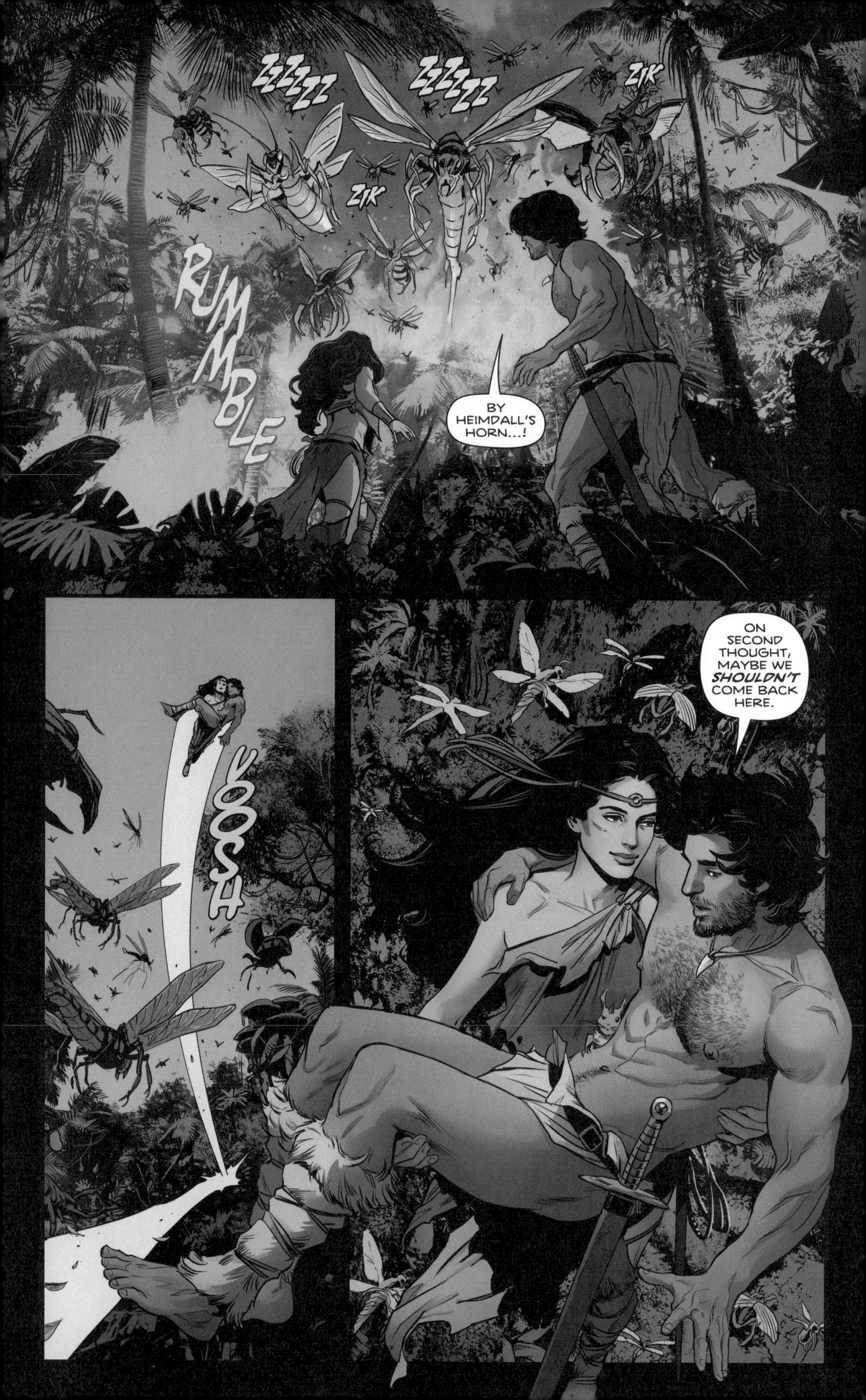
ZZZZZZZ
ZZZZZZZ
ZIK
ZIK
RUMMBLE
BY HEIMDALL'S HORN...!
VOOSH
ON SECOND THOUGHT, MAYBE WE SHOULDN'T COME BACK HERE.

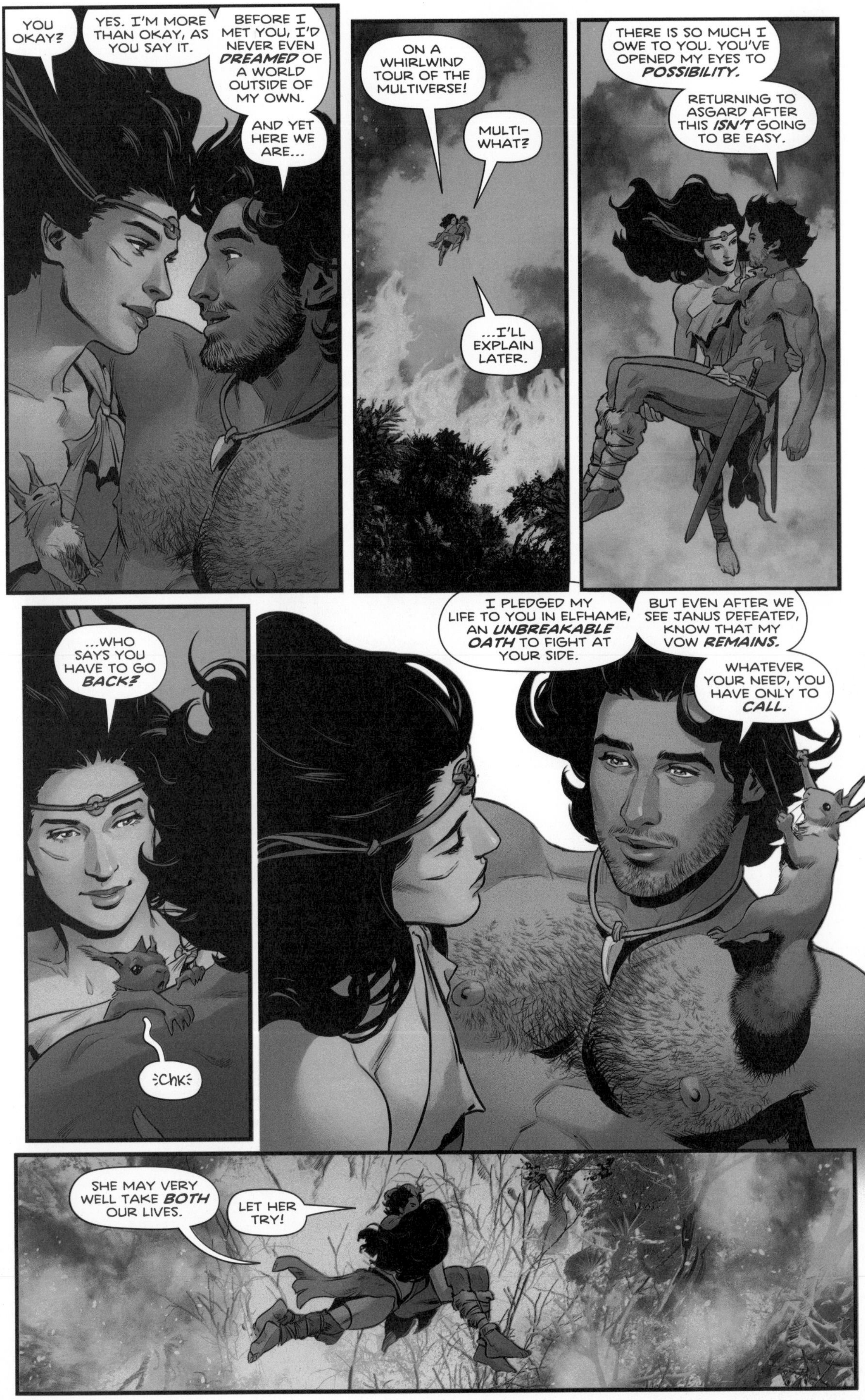
YOU OKAY?
YES. I'M MORE THAN OKAY, AS YOU SAY IT.
BEFORE I MET YOU, I'D NEVER EVEN DREAMED OF A WORLD OUTSIDE OF MY OWN.
AND YET HERE WE ARE...
ON A WHIRLWIND TOUR OF THE MULTIVERSE!
MULTI-WHAT?
...I'LL EXPLAIN LATER.
THERE IS SO MUCH I OWE TO YOU. YOU'VE OPENED MY EYES TO POSSIBILITY.
RETURNING TO ASGARD AFTER THIS ISN'T GOING TO BE EASY.
...WHO SAYS YOU HAVE TO GO BACK?
CHK
I PLEDGED MY LIFE TO YOU IN ELFHAME, AN UNBREAKABLE OATH TO FIGHT AT YOUR SIDE.
BUT EVEN AFTER WE SEE JANUS DEFEATED, KNOW THAT MY VOW REMAINS.
WHATEVER YOUR NEED, YOU HAVE ONLY TO CALL.
SHE MAY VERY WELL TAKE BOTH OUR LIVES.
LET HER TRY!

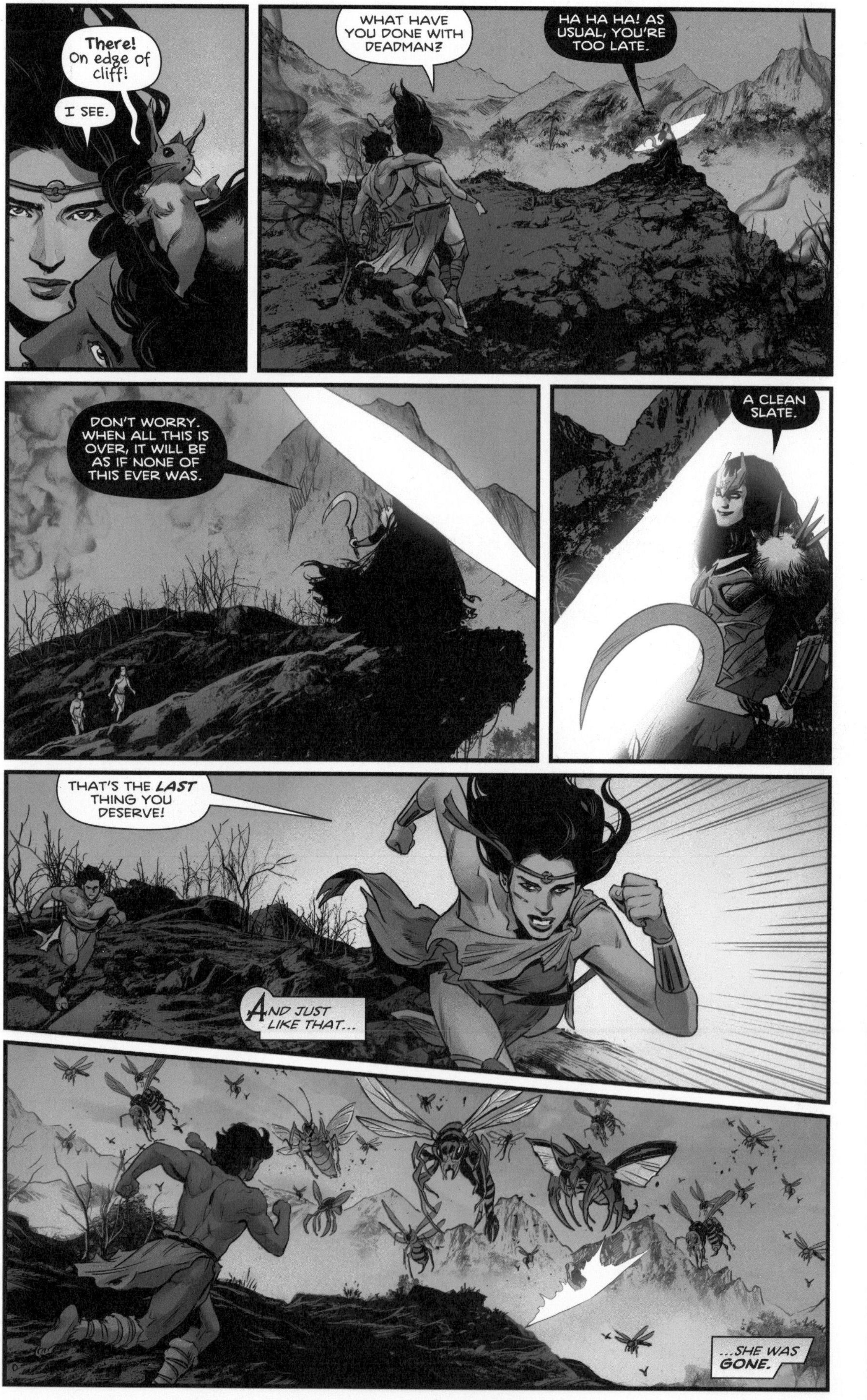
There! On edge of cliff!
I SEE.
WHAT HAVE YOU DONE WITH DEADMAN?
HA HA HA! AS USUAL, YOU'RE TOO LATE.
DON'T WORRY. WHEN ALL THIS IS OVER, IT WILL BE AS IF NONE OF THIS EVER WAS.
A CLEAN SLATE.
THAT'S THE LAST THING YOU DESERVE!
AND JUST LIKE THAT...
...SHE WAS GONE.

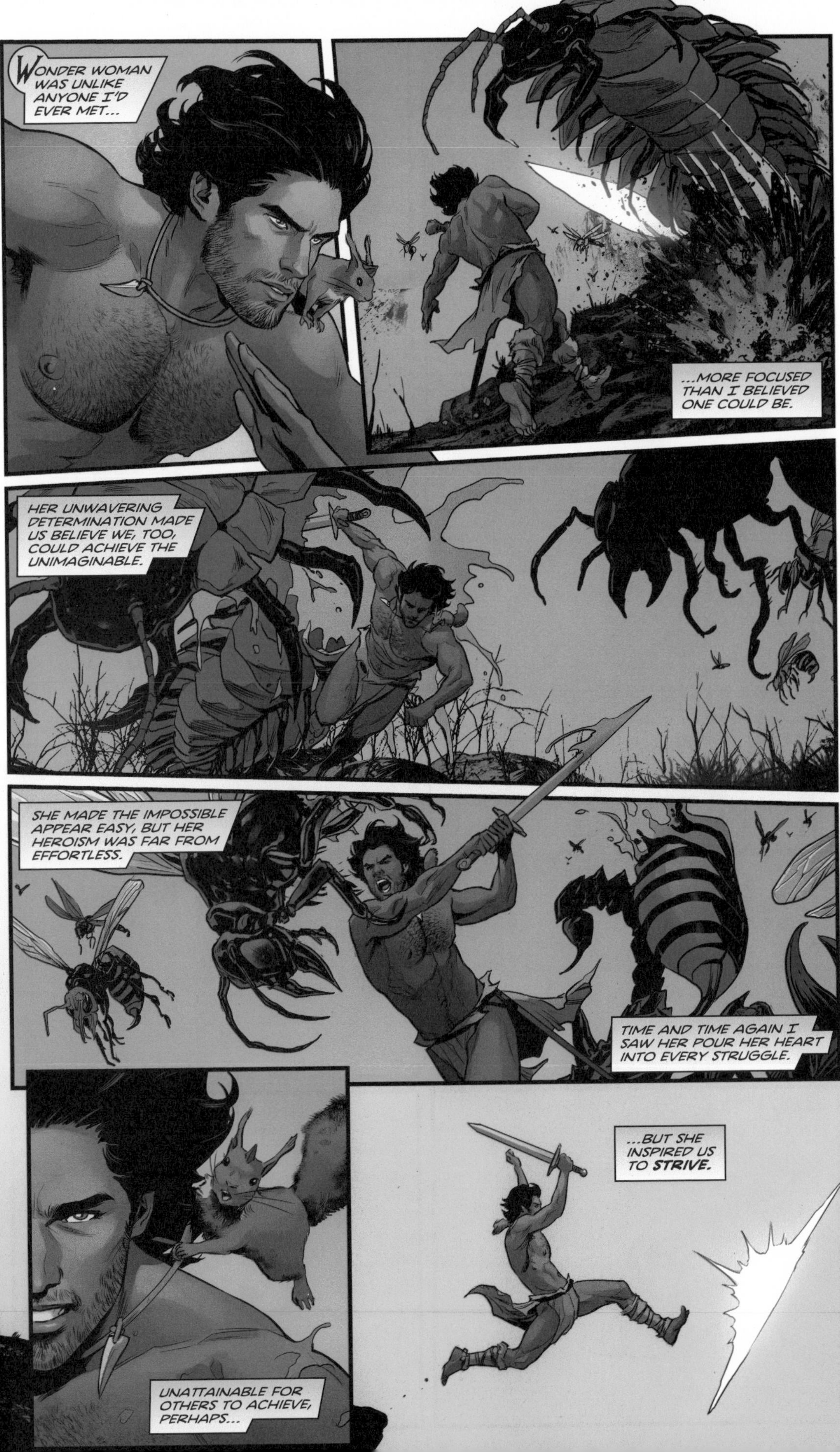
WONDER WOMAN WAS UNLIKE ANYONE I'D EVER MET...
...MORE FOCUSED THAN I BELIEVED ONE COULD BE.
HER UNWAVERING DETERMINATION MADE US BELIEVE WE, TOO, COULD ACHIEVE THE UNIMAGINABLE.
SHE MADE THE IMPOSSIBLE APPEAR EASY, BUT HER HEROISM WAS FAR FROM EFFORTLESS.
TIME AND TIME AGAIN I SAW HER POUR HER HEART INTO EVERY STRUGGLE.
UNATTAINABLE FOR OTHERS TO ACHIEVE, PERHAPS...
...BUT SHE INSPIRED US TO STRIVE.

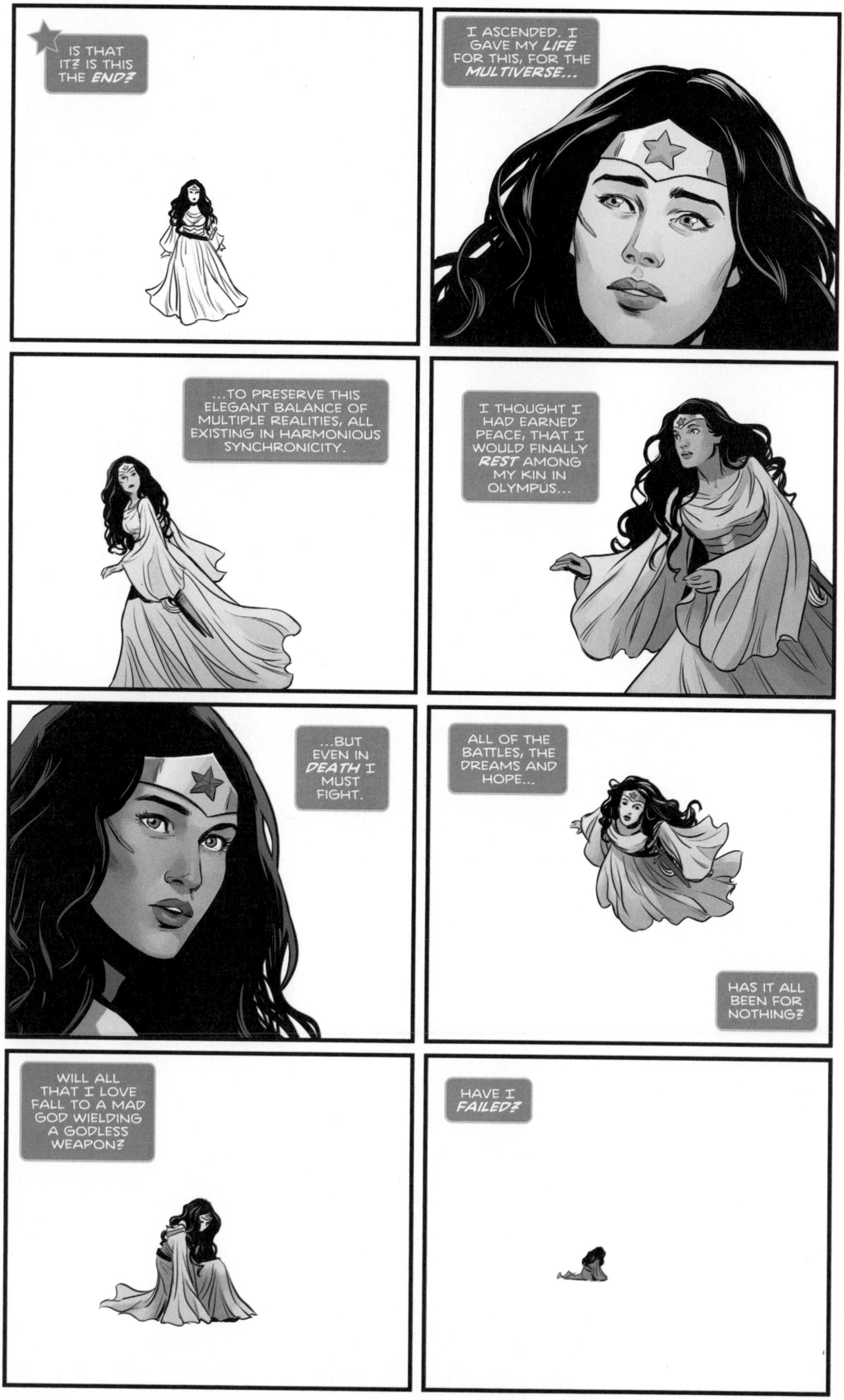
IS THAT IT? IS THIS THE END?
I ASCENDED. I GAVE MY LIFE FOR THIS, FOR THE MULTIVERSE...
...TO PRESERVE THIS ELEGANT BALANCE OF MULTIPLE REALITIES, ALL EXISTING IN HARMONIOUS SYNCHRONICITY.
I THOUGHT I HAD EARNED PEACE, THAT I WOULD FINALLY REST AMONG MY KIN IN OLYMPUS...
...BUT EVEN IN DEATH I MUST FIGHT.
ALL OF THE BATTLES, THE DREAMS AND HOPE...
HAS IT ALL BEEN FOR NOTHING?
WILL ALL THAT I LOVE FALL TO A MAD GOD WIELDING A GODLESS WEAPON?
HAVE I FAILED?

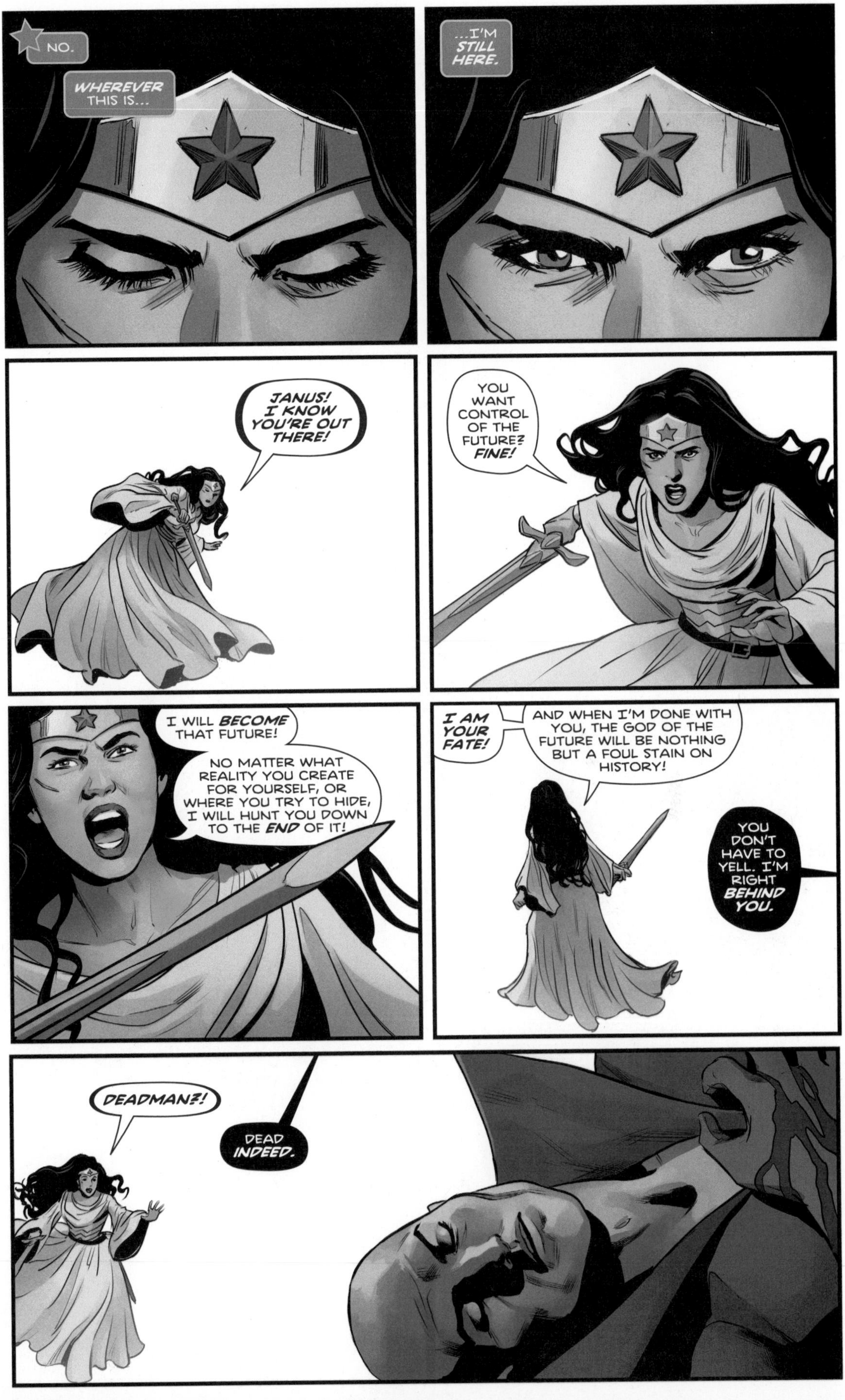
NO.
WHEREVER THIS IS...
...I'M STILL HERE.
JANUS! I KNOW YOU'RE OUT THERE!
YOU WANT CONTROL OF THE FUTURE? FINE!
I WILL BECOME THAT FUTURE!
NO MATTER WHAT REALITY YOU CREATE FOR YOURSELF, OR WHERE YOU TRY TO HIDE, I WILL HUNT YOU DOWN TO THE END OF IT!
I AM YOUR FATE!
AND WHEN I'M DONE WITH YOU, THE GOD OF THE FUTURE WILL BE NOTHING BUT A FOUL STAIN ON HISTORY!
YOU DON'T HAVE TO YELL. I'M RIGHT BEHIND YOU.
DEADMAN?!
DEAD INDEED.

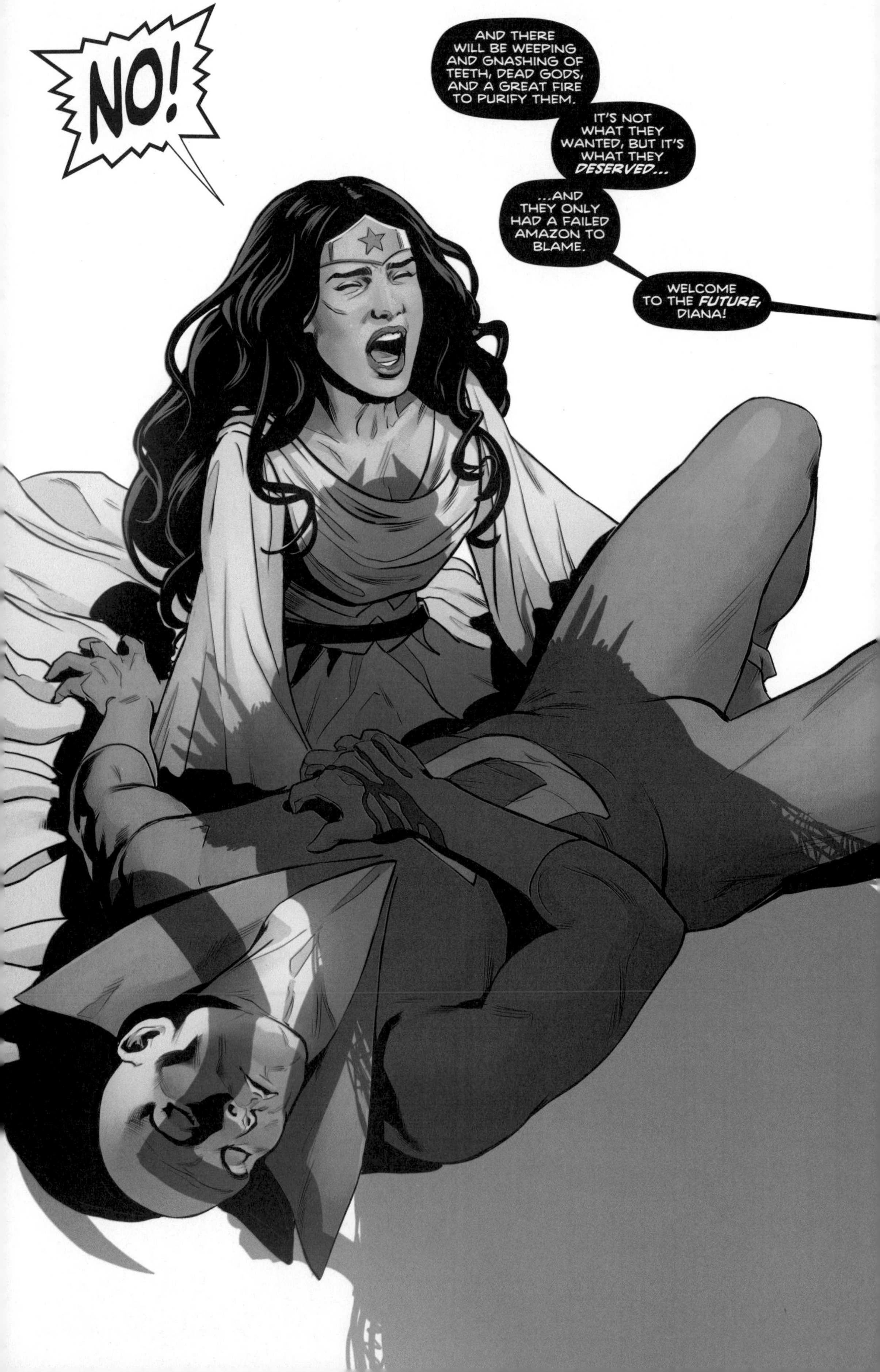
NO!
AND THERE WILL BE WEEPING AND GNASHING OF TEETH, DEAD GODS, AND A GREAT FIRE TO PURIFY THEM.
IT'S NOT WHAT THEY WANTED, BUT IT'S WHAT THEY DESERVED...
...AND THEY ONLY HAD A FAILED AMAZON TO BLAME.
WELCOME TO THE FUTURE, DIANA!

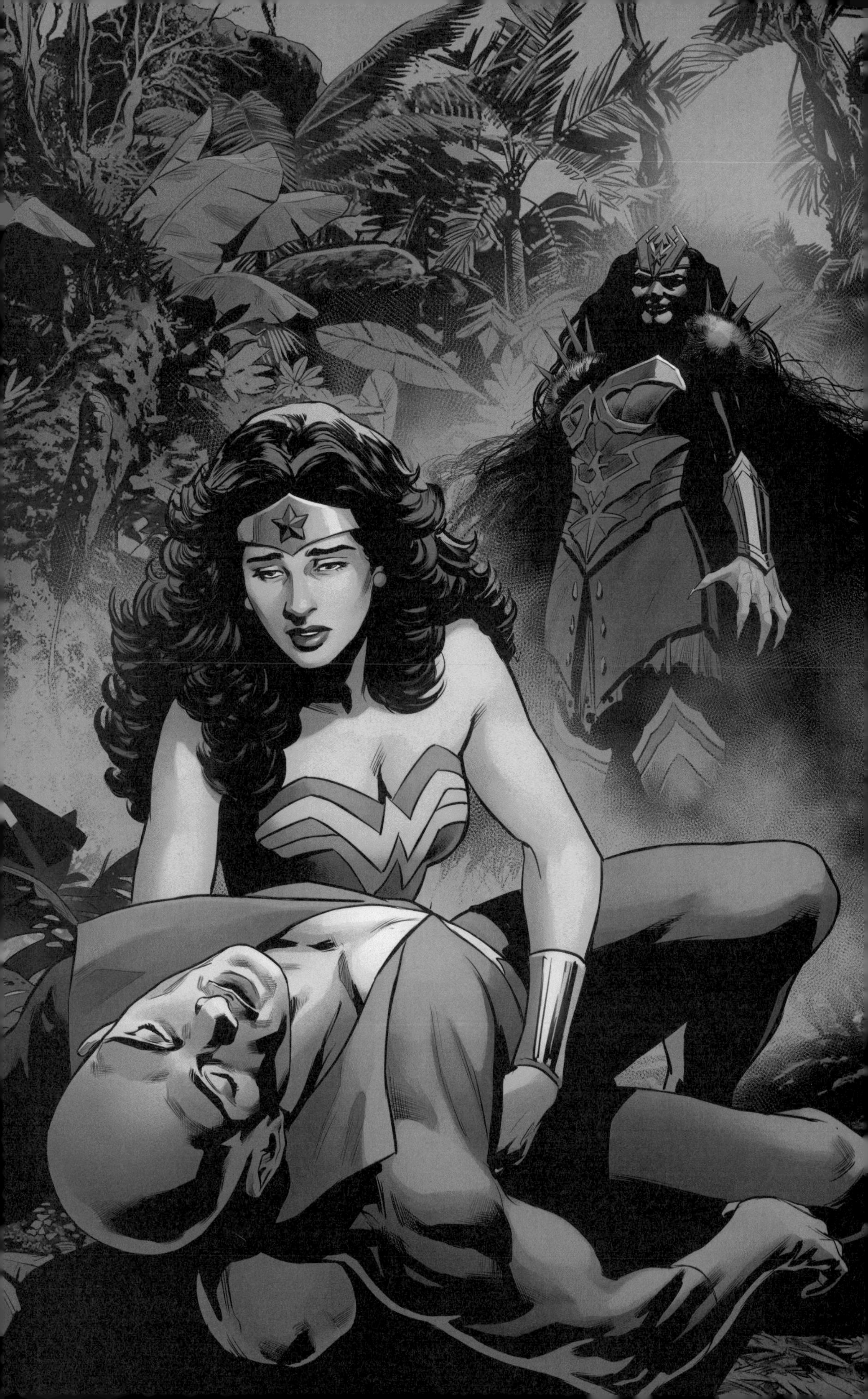

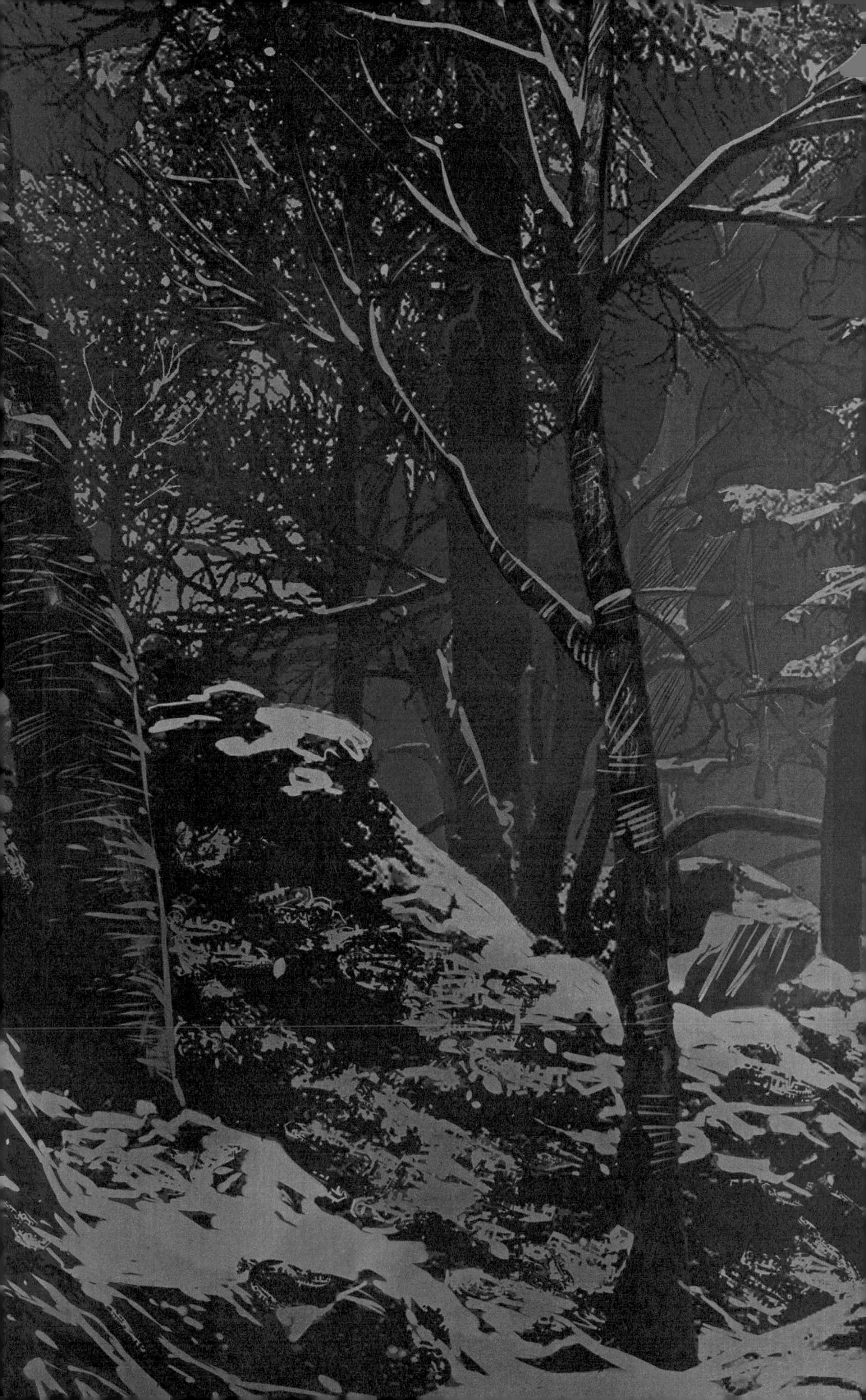

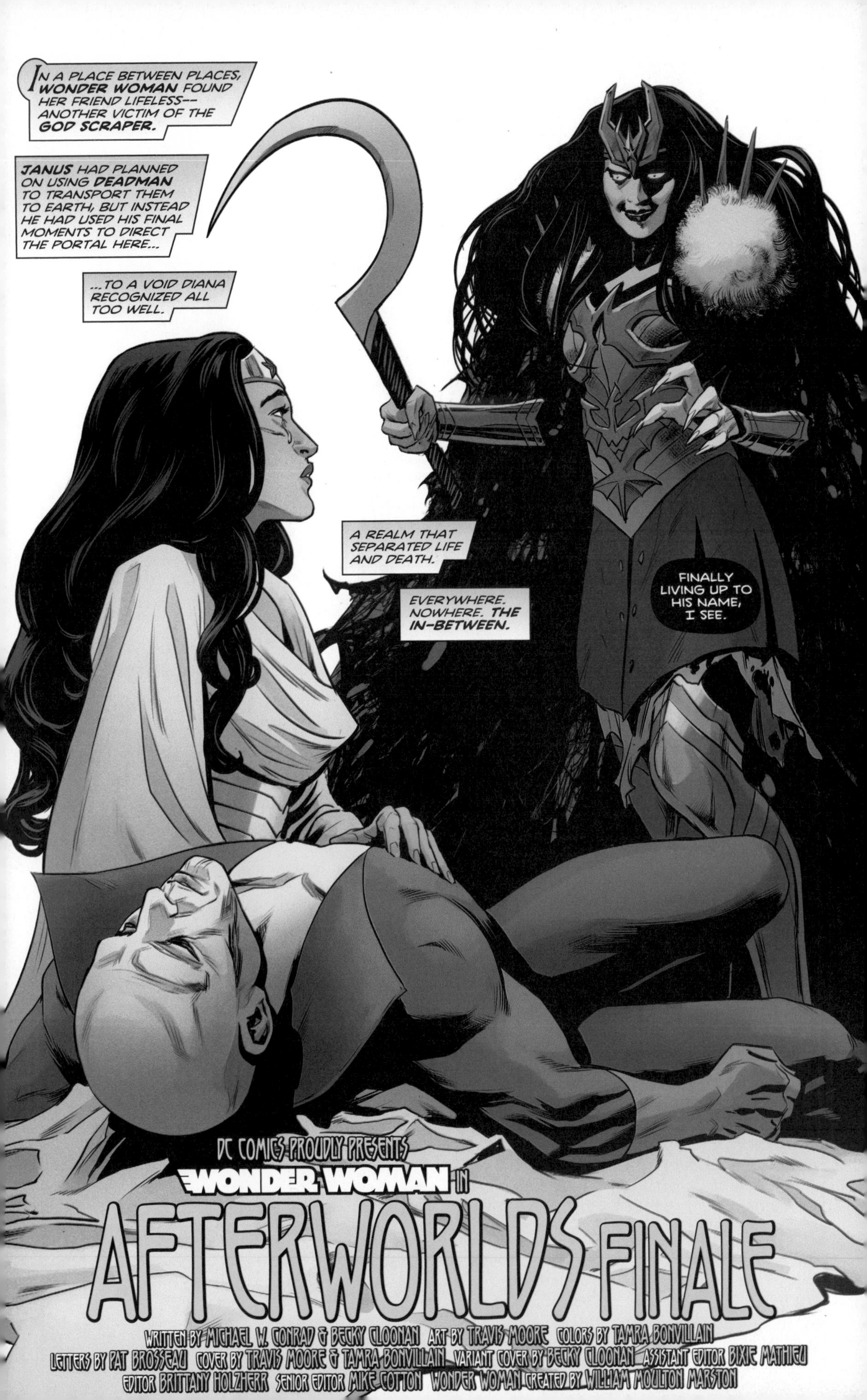
IN A PLACE BETWEEN PLACES, WONDER WOMAN FOUND HER FRIEND LIFELESS-- ANOTHER VICTIM OF THE GOD SCRAPER.
JANUS HAD PLANNED ON USING DEADMAN TO TRANSPORT THEM TO EARTH, BUT INSTEAD HE HAD USED HIS FINAL MOMENTS TO DIRECT THE PORTAL HERE...
...TO A VOID DIANA RECOGNIZED ALL TOO WELL.
A REALM THAT SEPARATED LIFE AND DEATH.
EVERYWHERE. NOWHERE. THE IN-BETWEEN.
FINALLY LIVING UP TO HIS NAME, I SEE.
DC COMICS PROUDLY PRESENTS
WONDER WOMAN IN
AFTERWORLDS FINALE
WRITTEN BY MICHAEL W. CONRAD & BECKY CLOONAN ART BY TRAVIS MOORE COLORS BY TAMRA BONVILLAIN
LETTERS BY PAT BROSSEAU COVER BY TRAVIS MOORE & TAMRA BONVILLAIN VARIANT COVER BY BECKY CLOONAN ASSISTANT EDITOR BIXIE MATHIEU
EDITOR BRITTANY HOLZHERR SENIOR EDITOR MIKE COTTON WONDER WOMAN CREATED BY WILLIAM MOULTON MARSTON

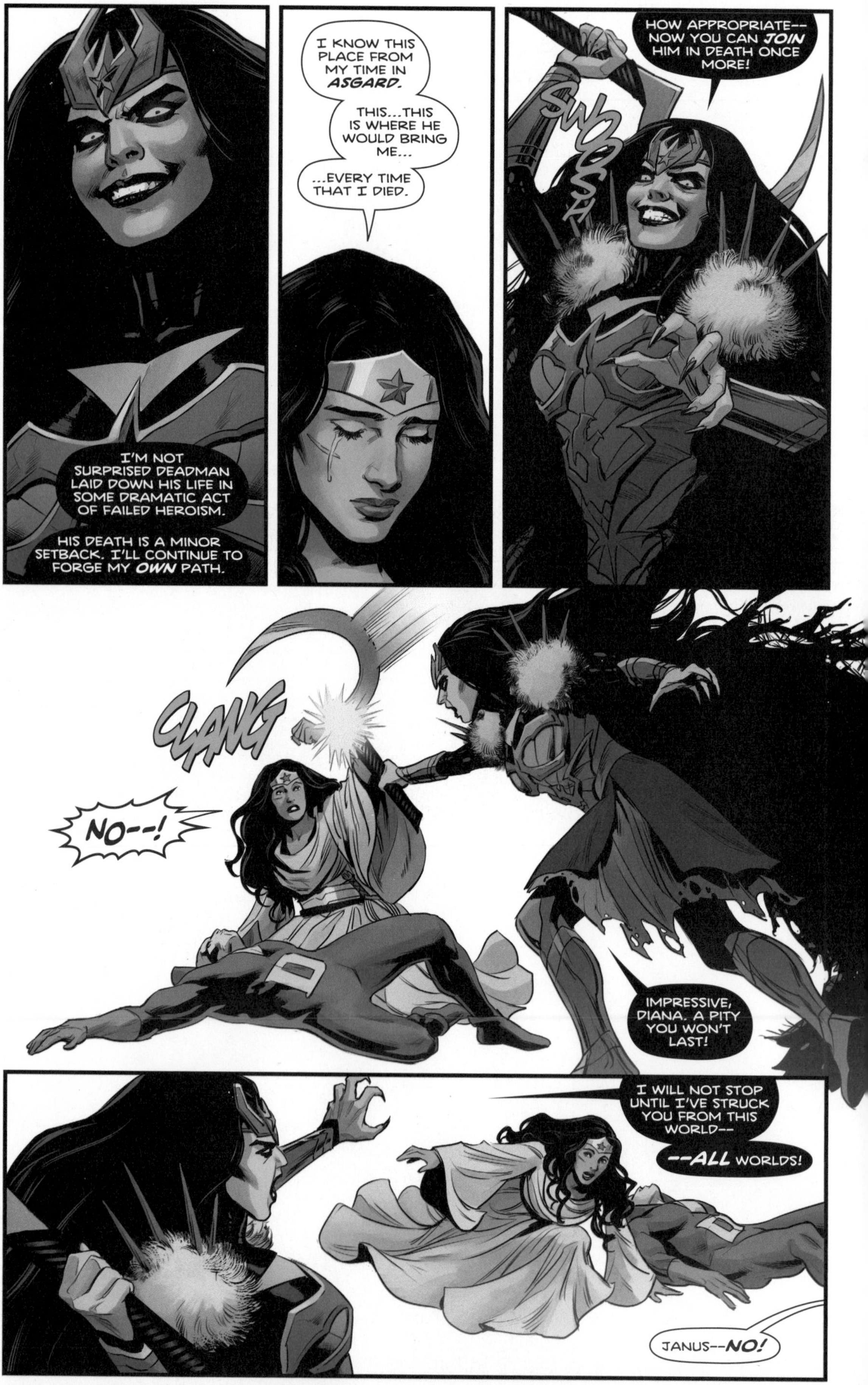
I'M NOT SURPRISED DEADMAN LAID DOWN HIS LIFE IN SOME DRAMATIC ACT OF FAILED HEROISM.
HIS DEATH IS A MINOR SETBACK. I'LL CONTINUE TO FORGE MY OWN PATH.
I KNOW THIS PLACE FROM MY TIME IN ASGARD.
THIS...THIS IS WHERE HE WOULD BRING ME...
...EVERY TIME THAT I DIED.
HOW APPROPRIATE--NOW YOU CAN JOIN HIM IN DEATH ONCE MORE!
SWOOSH
CLANG
NO--!
IMPRESSIVE, DIANA. A PITY YOU WON'T LAST!
I WILL NOT STOP UNTIL I'VE STRUCK YOU FROM THIS WORLD--
--ALL WORLDS!
JANUS--NO!

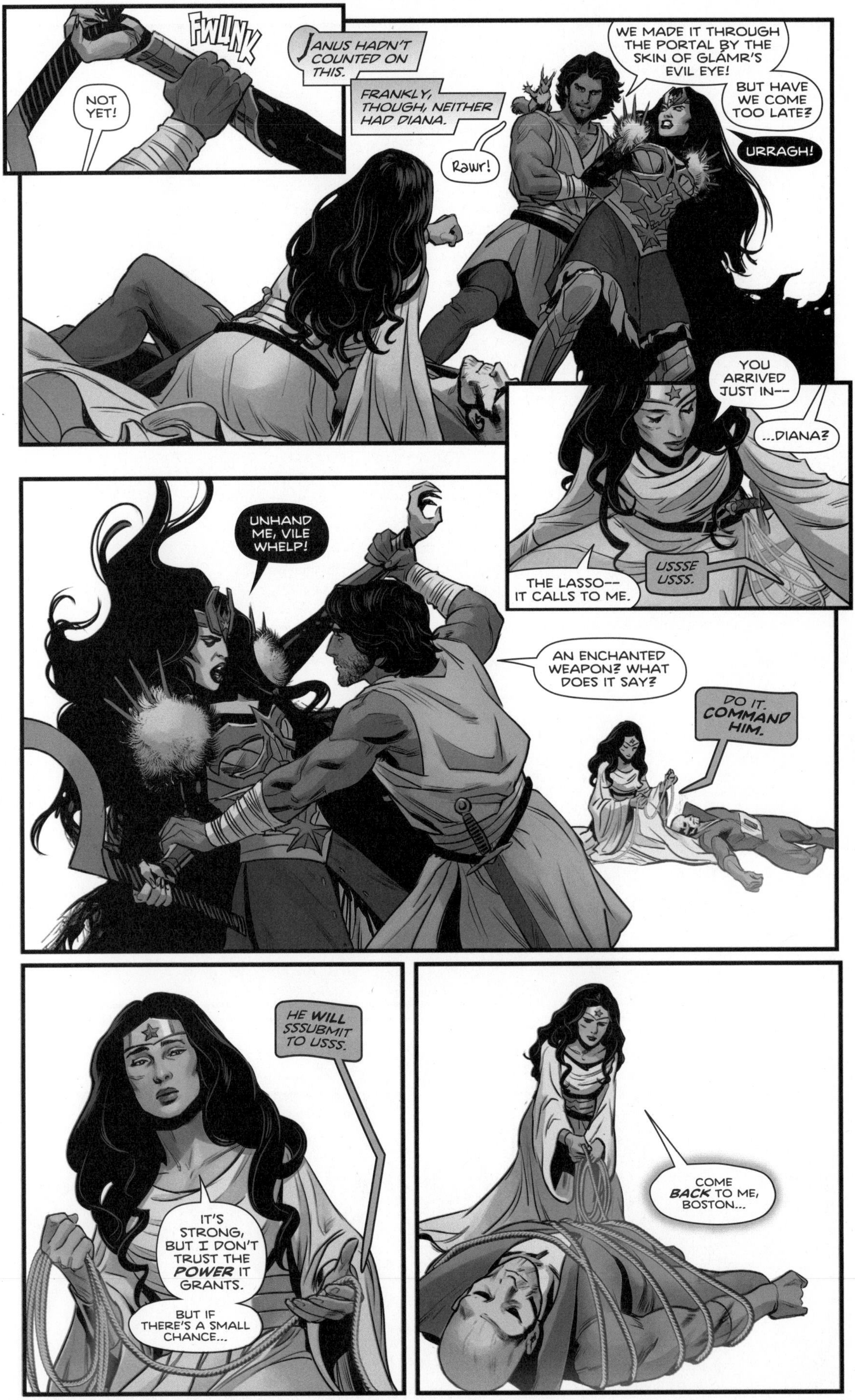
FWUNK
NOT YET!
JANUS HADN'T COUNTED ON THIS.
FRANKLY, THOUGH, NEITHER HAD DIANA.
Rawr!
WE MADE IT THROUGH THE PORTAL BY THE SKIN OF GLÁMR'S EVIL EYE!
BUT HAVE WE COME TOO LATE?
URRAGH!
YOU ARRIVED JUST IN--
...DIANA?
THE LASSO-- IT CALLS TO ME.
USSSE USSS.
UNHAND ME, VILE WHELP!
AN ENCHANTED WEAPON? WHAT DOES IT SAY?
DO IT. COMMAND HIM.
HE WILL SSSUBMIT TO USSS.
IT'S STRONG, BUT I DON'T TRUST THE POWER IT GRANTS.
BUT IF THERE'S A SMALL CHANCE...
COME BACK TO ME, BOSTON...

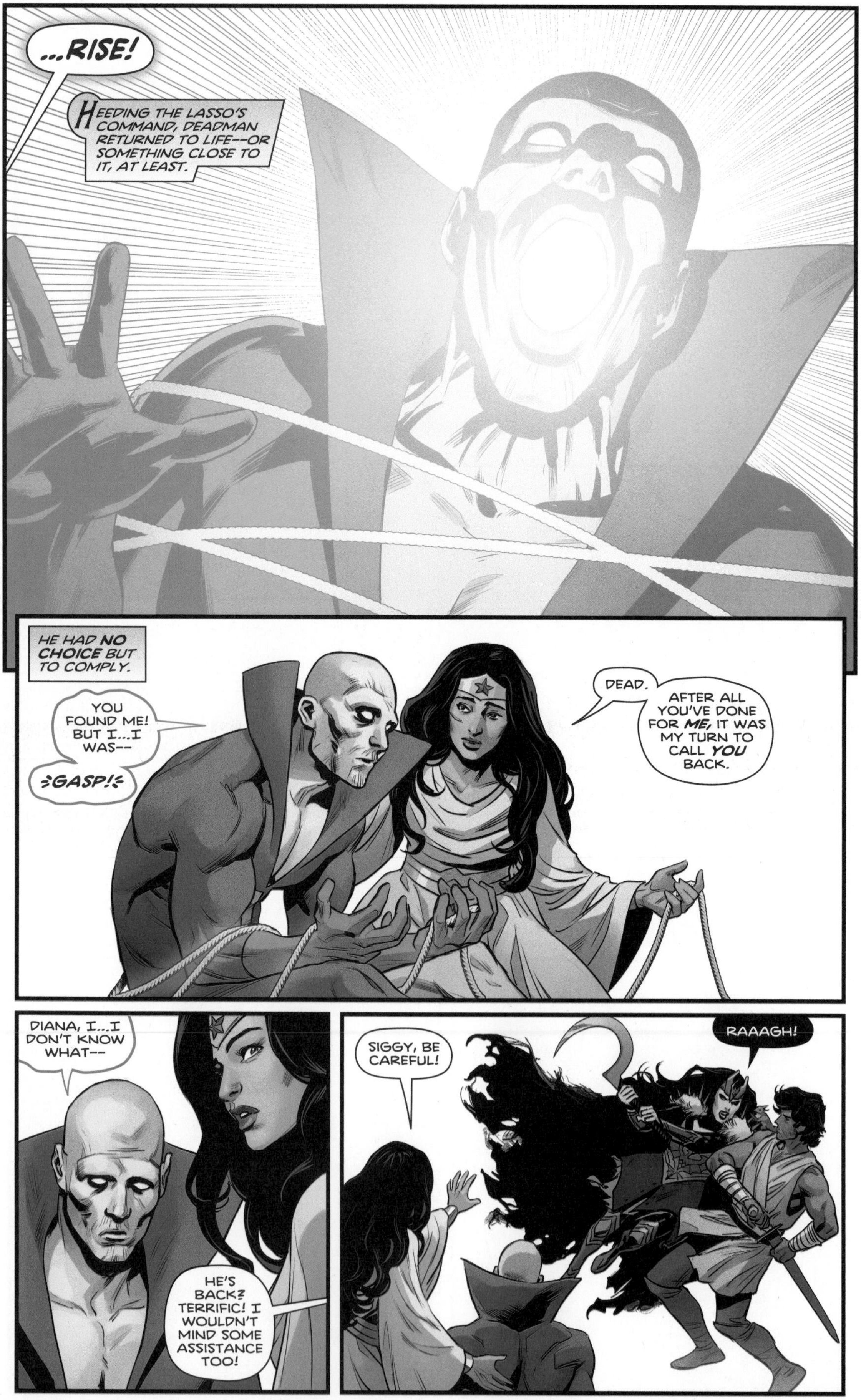
...RISE!
HEEDING THE LASSO'S COMMAND, DEADMAN RETURNED TO LIFE--OR SOMETHING CLOSE TO IT, AT LEAST.
HE HAD NO CHOICE BUT TO COMPLY.
YOU FOUND ME! BUT I...I WAS--
GASP!
DEAD.
AFTER ALL YOU'VE DONE FOR ME, IT WAS MY TURN TO CALL YOU BACK.
DIANA, I...I DON'T KNOW WHAT--
HE'S BACK? TERRIFIC! I WOULDN'T MIND SOME ASSISTANCE TOO!
SIGGY, BE CAREFUL!
RAAAGH!

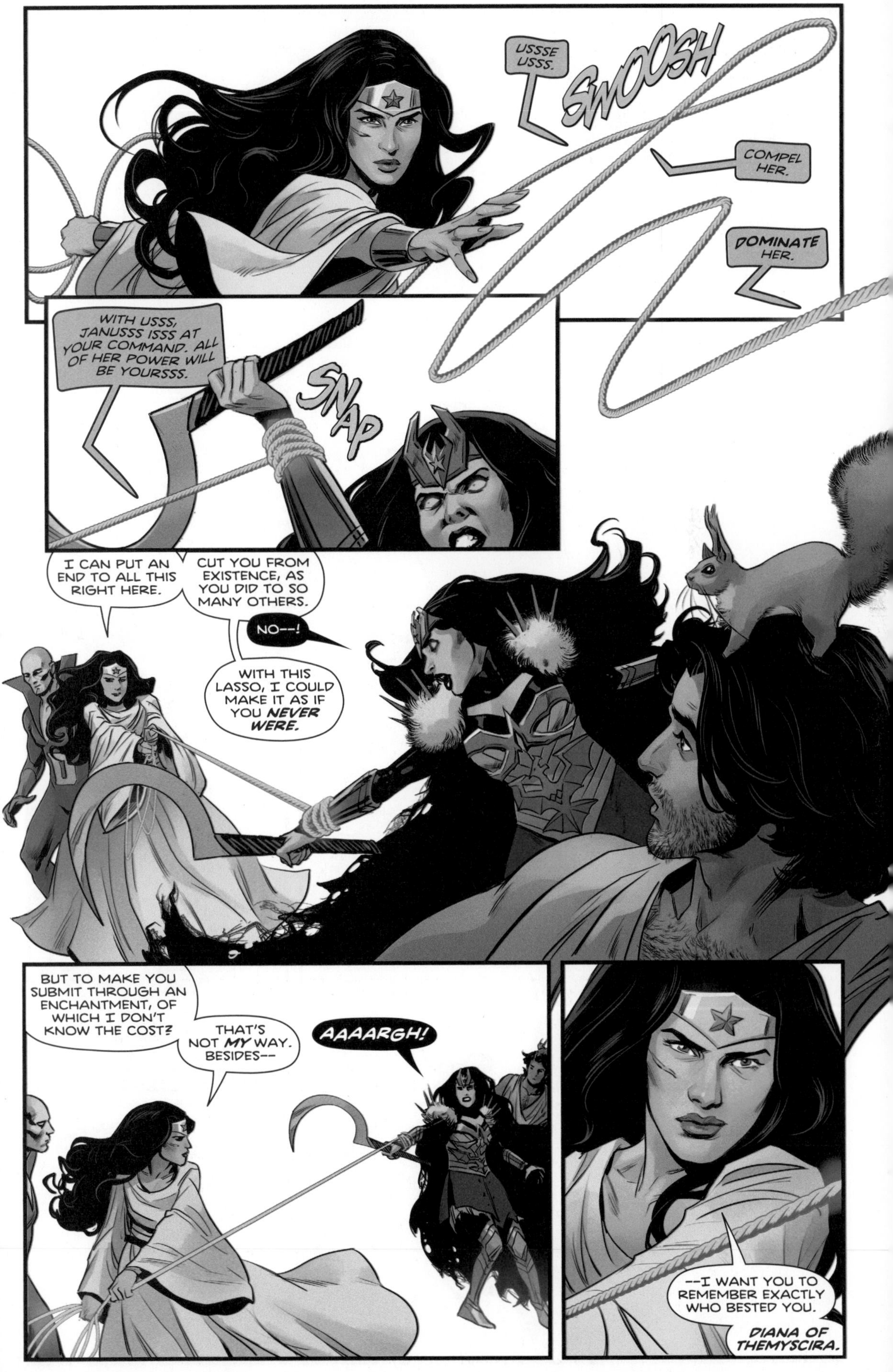

USSSE USSS.
SWOOSH
COMPEL HER.
DOMINATE HER.
WITH USSS, JANUSSS ISSS AT YOUR COMMAND. ALL OF HER POWER WILL BE YOURSSS.
SNAP
I CAN PUT AN END TO ALL THIS RIGHT HERE.
CUT YOU FROM EXISTENCE, AS YOU DID TO SO MANY OTHERS.
NO--!
WITH THIS LASSO, I COULD MAKE IT AS IF YOU NEVER WERE.
BUT TO MAKE YOU SUBMIT THROUGH AN ENCHANTMENT, OF WHICH I DON'T KNOW THE COST?
THAT'S NOT MY WAY. BESIDES--
AAAARGH!
--I WANT YOU TO REMEMBER EXACTLY WHO BESTED YOU.
DIANA OF THEMYSCIRA.

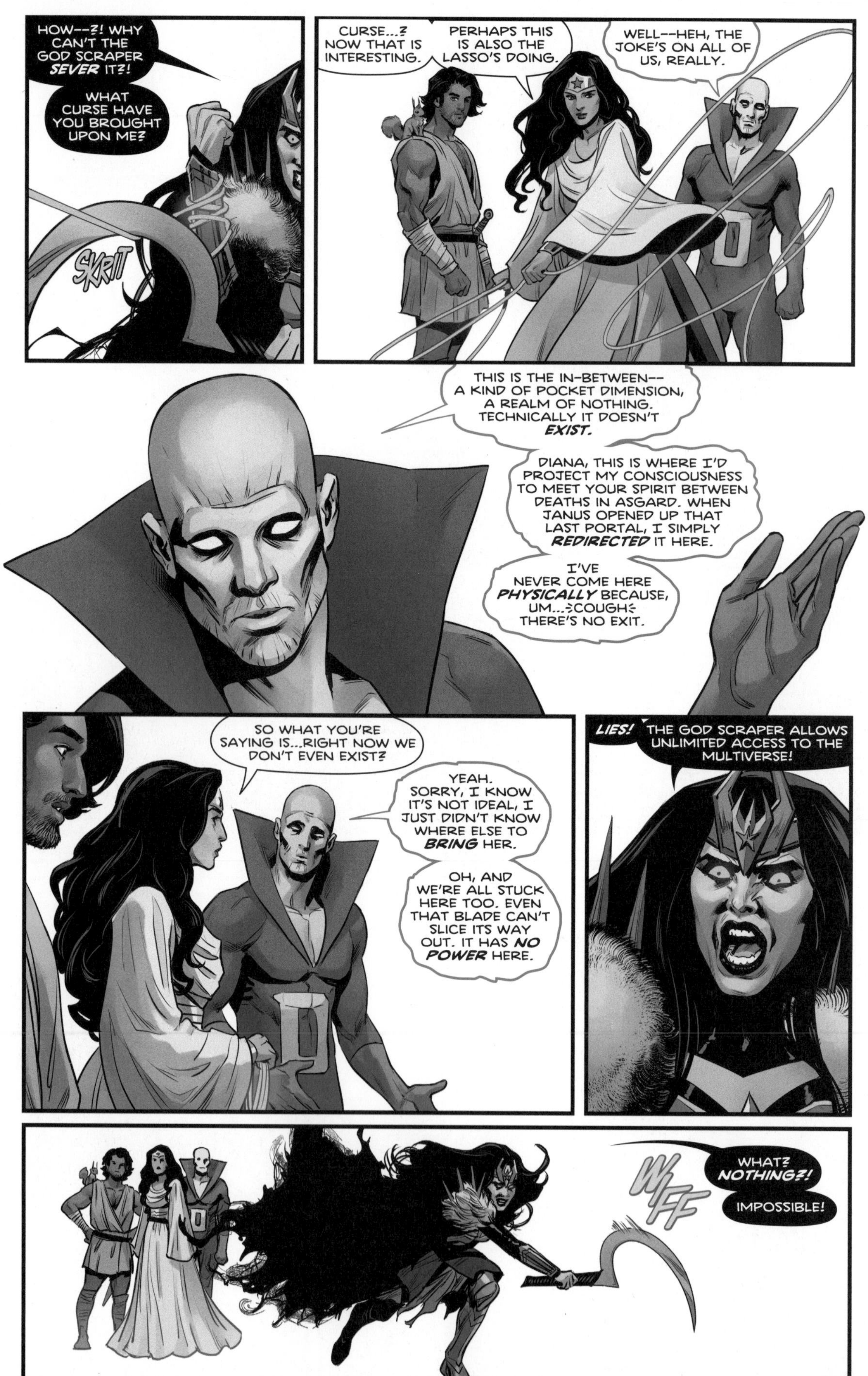
HOW--?! WHY CAN'T THE GOD SCRAPER SEVER IT?!
WHAT CURSE HAVE YOU BROUGHT UPON ME?
SKRIT
CURSE...? NOW THAT IS INTERESTING.
PERHAPS THIS IS ALSO THE LASSO'S DOING.
WELL--HEH, THE JOKE'S ON ALL OF US, REALLY.
THIS IS THE IN-BETWEEN-- A KIND OF POCKET DIMENSION, A REALM OF NOTHING. TECHNICALLY IT DOESN'T EXIST.
DIANA, THIS IS WHERE I'D PROJECT MY CONSCIOUSNESS TO MEET YOUR SPIRIT BETWEEN DEATHS IN ASGARD. WHEN JANUS OPENED UP THAT LAST PORTAL, I SIMPLY REDIRECTED IT HERE.
I'VE NEVER COME HERE PHYSICALLY BECAUSE, UM... *COUGH* THERE'S NO EXIT.
SO WHAT YOU'RE SAYING IS... RIGHT NOW WE DON'T EVEN EXIST?
YEAH. SORRY, I KNOW IT'S NOT IDEAL, I JUST DIDN'T KNOW WHERE ELSE TO BRING HER.
OH, AND WE'RE ALL STUCK HERE TOO. EVEN THAT BLADE CAN'T SLICE ITS WAY OUT. IT HAS NO POWER HERE.
LIES!
THE GOD SCRAPER ALLOWS UNLIMITED ACCESS TO THE MULTIVERSE!
WIFF
WHAT? NOTHING?!
IMPOSSIBLE!

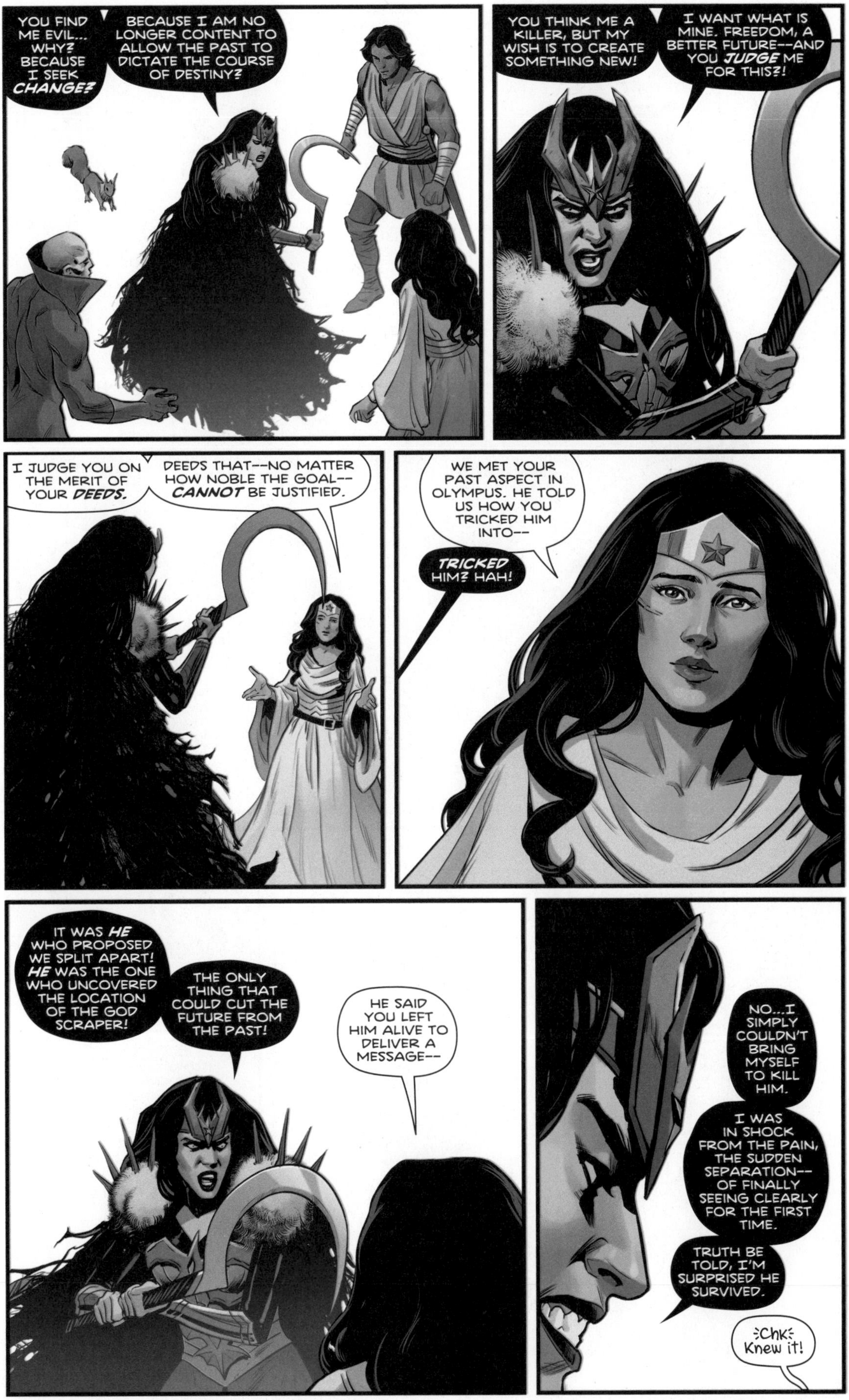
YOU FIND ME EVIL... WHY? BECAUSE I SEEK CHANGE?
BECAUSE I AM NO LONGER CONTENT TO ALLOW THE PAST TO DICTATE THE COURSE OF DESTINY?
YOU THINK ME A KILLER, BUT MY WISH IS TO CREATE SOMETHING NEW!
I WANT WHAT IS MINE. FREEDOM, A BETTER FUTURE--AND YOU JUDGE ME FOR THIS?!
I JUDGE YOU ON THE MERIT OF YOUR DEEDS.
DEEDS THAT--NO MATTER HOW NOBLE THE GOAL--CANNOT BE JUSTIFIED.
WE MET YOUR PAST ASPECT IN OLYMPUS. HE TOLD US HOW YOU TRICKED HIM INTO--
TRICKED HIM? HAH!
IT WAS HE WHO PROPOSED WE SPLIT APART! HE WAS THE ONE WHO UNCOVERED THE LOCATION OF THE GOD SCRAPER!
THE ONLY THING THAT COULD CUT THE FUTURE FROM THE PAST!
HE SAID YOU LEFT HIM ALIVE TO DELIVER A MESSAGE--
NO...I SIMPLY COULDN'T BRING MYSELF TO KILL HIM.
I WAS IN SHOCK FROM THE PAIN, THE SUDDEN SEPARATION--OF FINALLY SEEING CLEARLY FOR THE FIRST TIME.
TRUTH BE TOLD, I'M SURPRISED HE SURVIVED.
Chk Knew it!

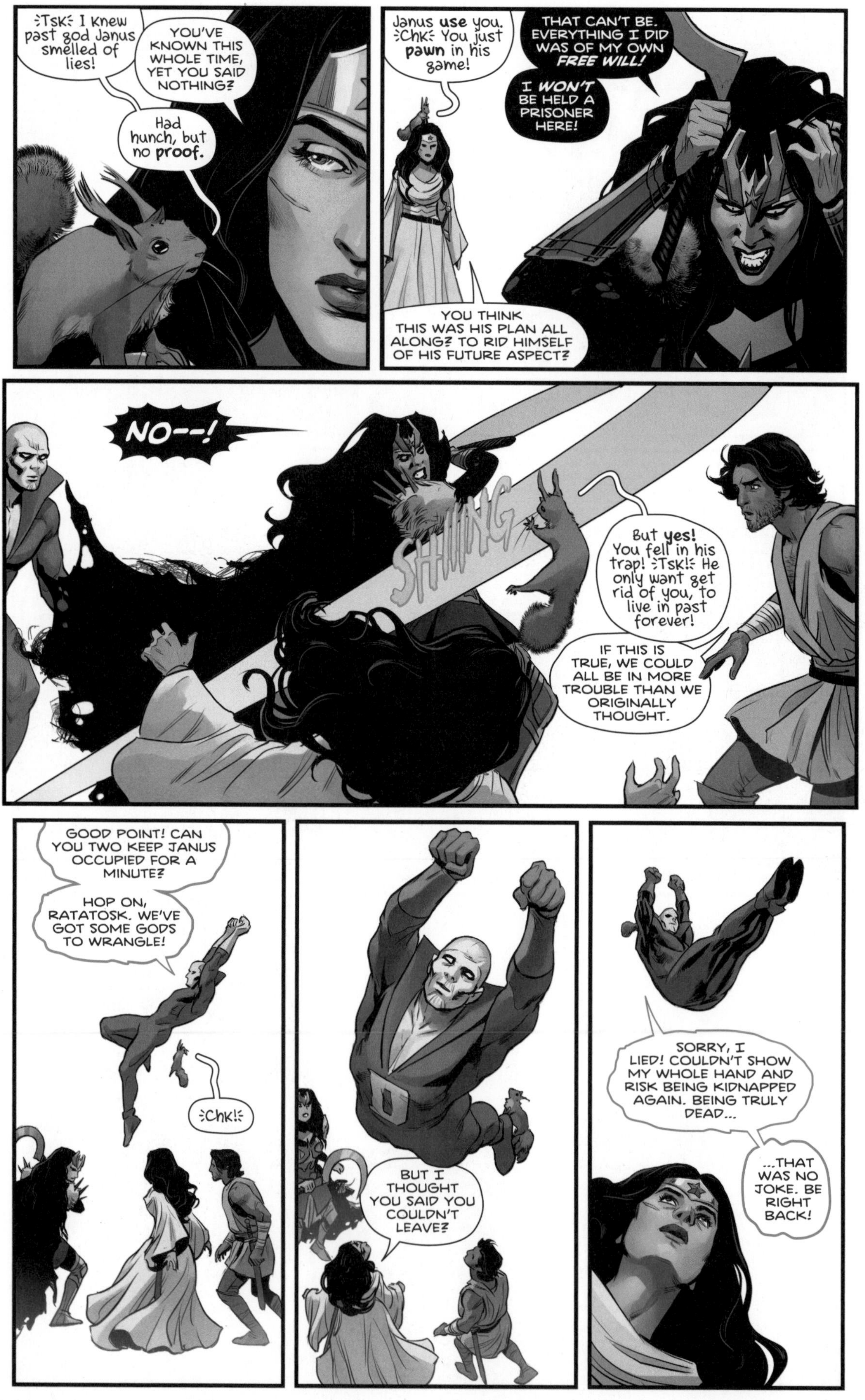

:TSK: I KNEW PAST GOD JANUS SMELLED OF LIES!
YOU'VE KNOWN THIS WHOLE TIME, YET YOU SAID NOTHING?
HAD HUNCH, BUT NO PROOF.
JANUS USE YOU. :CHK: YOU JUST PAWN IN HIS GAME!
THAT CAN'T BE. EVERYTHING I DID WAS OF MY OWN FREE WILL!
I WON'T BE HELD A PRISONER HERE!
YOU THINK THIS WAS HIS PLAN ALL ALONG? TO RID HIMSELF OF HIS FUTURE ASPECT?
NO--!
SHIING
BUT YES! YOU FELL IN HIS TRAP! :TSK!: HE ONLY WANT GET RID OF YOU, TO LIVE IN PAST FOREVER!
IF THIS IS TRUE, WE COULD ALL BE IN MORE TROUBLE THAN WE ORIGINALLY THOUGHT.
GOOD POINT! CAN YOU TWO KEEP JANUS OCCUPIED FOR A MINUTE?
HOP ON, RATATOSK. WE'VE GOT SOME GODS TO WRANGLE!
:CHK!:
BUT I THOUGHT YOU SAID YOU COULDN'T LEAVE?
SORRY, I LIED! COULDN'T SHOW MY WHOLE HAND AND RISK BEING KIDNAPPED AGAIN. BEING TRULY DEAD...
...THAT WAS NO JOKE. BE RIGHT BACK!

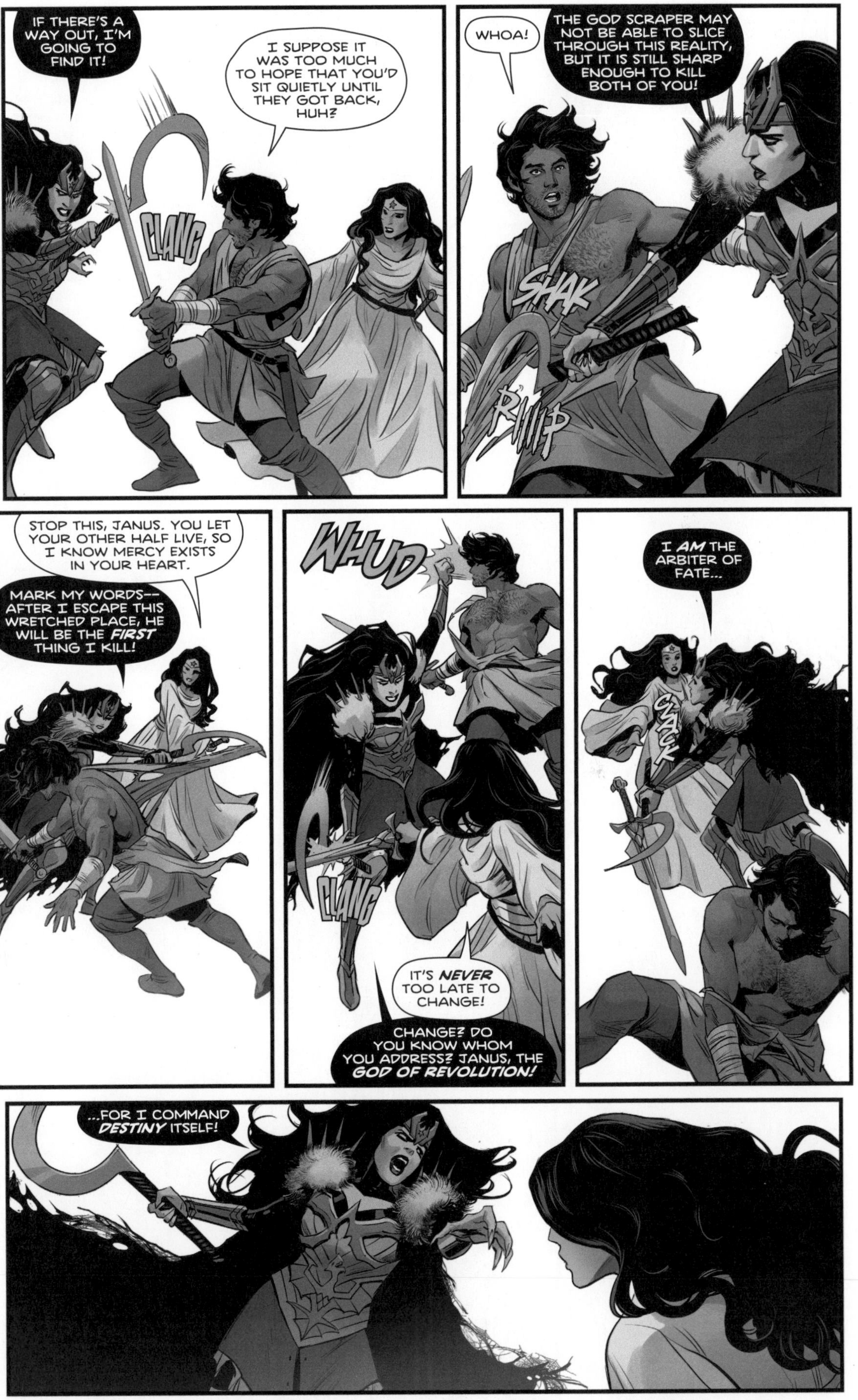
IF THERE'S A WAY OUT, I'M GOING TO FIND IT!
I SUPPOSE IT WAS TOO MUCH TO HOPE THAT YOU'D SIT QUIETLY UNTIL THEY GOT BACK, HUH?
CLANG
WHOA!
THE GOD SCRAPER MAY NOT BE ABLE TO SLICE THROUGH THIS REALITY, BUT IT IS STILL SHARP ENOUGH TO KILL BOTH OF YOU!
SHAK
RIIIP
STOP THIS, JANUS. YOU LET YOUR OTHER HALF LIVE, SO I KNOW MERCY EXISTS IN YOUR HEART.
MARK MY WORDS-- AFTER I ESCAPE THIS WRETCHED PLACE, HE WILL BE THE *FIRST* THING I KILL!
WHUD
CLANG
IT'S *NEVER* TOO LATE TO CHANGE!
CHANGE? DO YOU KNOW WHOM YOU ADDRESS? JANUS, THE *GOD OF REVOLUTION!*
I *AM* THE ARBITER OF FATE...
...FOR I COMMAND *DESTINY* ITSELF!

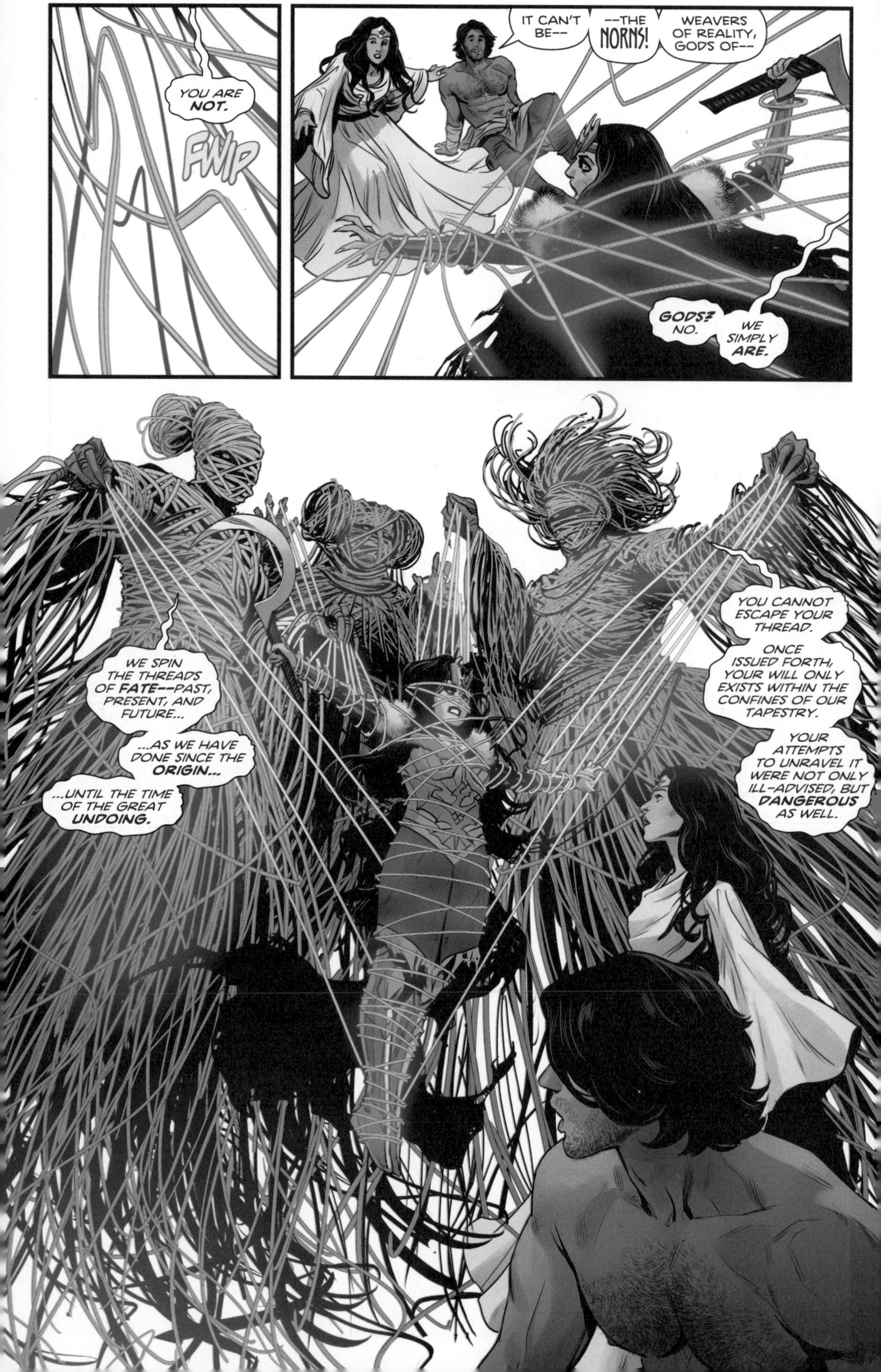

YOU ARE NOT.
FWIP
IT CAN'T BE--
--THE NORNS!
WEAVERS OF REALITY, GODS OF--
GODS? NO.
WE SIMPLY ARE.
WE SPIN THE THREADS OF FATE--PAST, PRESENT, AND FUTURE...
...AS WE HAVE DONE SINCE THE ORIGIN...
...UNTIL THE TIME OF THE GREAT UNDOING.
YOU CANNOT ESCAPE YOUR THREAD.
ONCE ISSUED FORTH, YOUR WILL ONLY EXISTS WITHIN THE CONFINES OF OUR TAPESTRY.
YOUR ATTEMPTS TO UNRAVEL IT WERE NOT ONLY ILL-ADVISED, BUT DANGEROUS AS WELL.

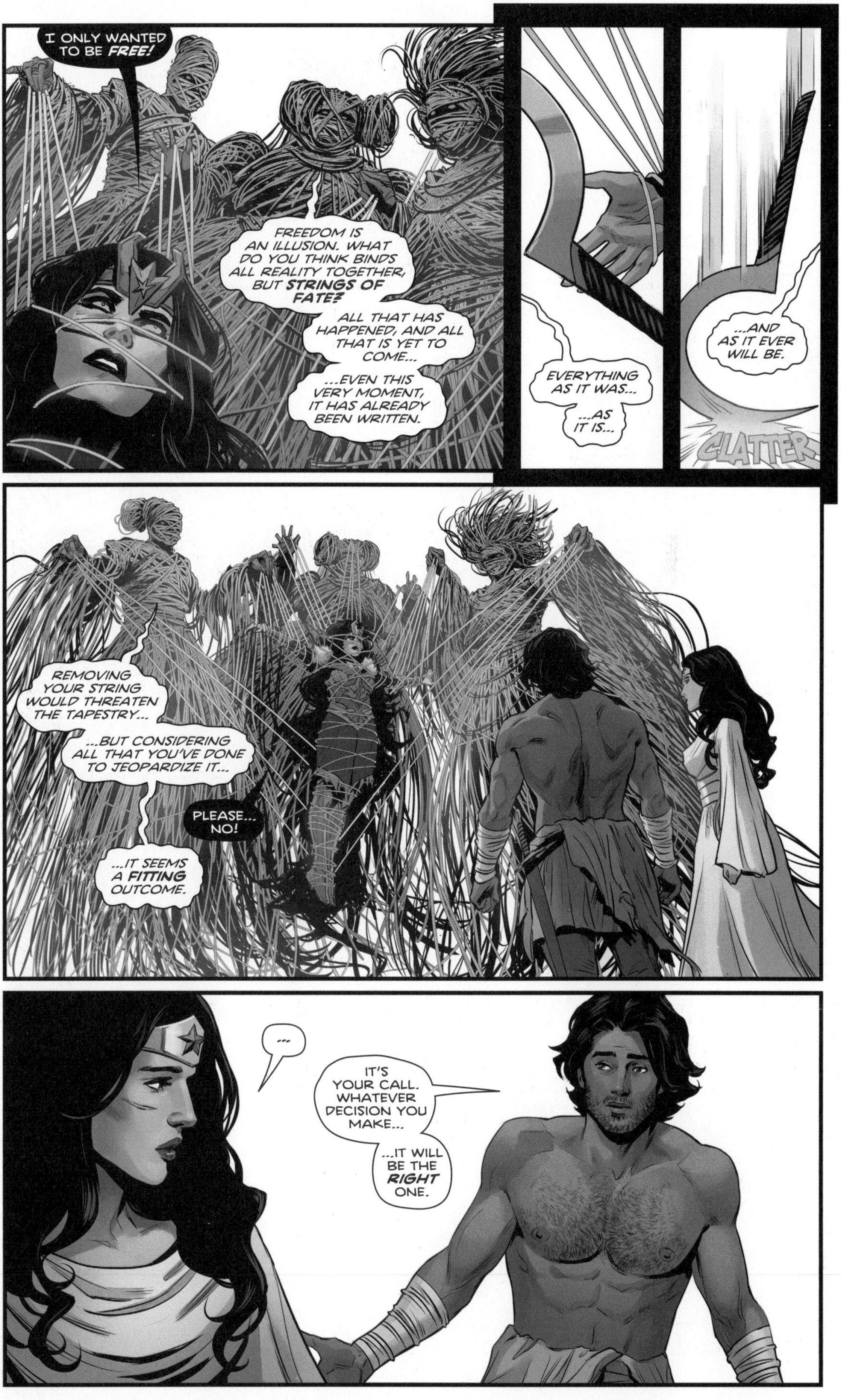
I ONLY WANTED TO BE FREE!
FREEDOM IS AN ILLUSION. WHAT DO YOU THINK BINDS ALL REALITY TOGETHER, BUT STRINGS OF FATE?
ALL THAT HAS HAPPENED, AND ALL THAT IS YET TO COME...
...EVEN THIS VERY MOMENT, IT HAS ALREADY BEEN WRITTEN.
EVERYTHING AS IT WAS...
...AS IT IS...
...AND AS IT EVER WILL BE.
CLATTER
REMOVING YOUR STRING WOULD THREATEN THE TAPESTRY...
...BUT CONSIDERING ALL THAT YOU'VE DONE TO JEOPARDIZE IT...
PLEASE... NO!
...IT SEEMS A FITTING OUTCOME.
...
IT'S YOUR CALL. WHATEVER DECISION YOU MAKE...
...IT WILL BE THE RIGHT ONE.

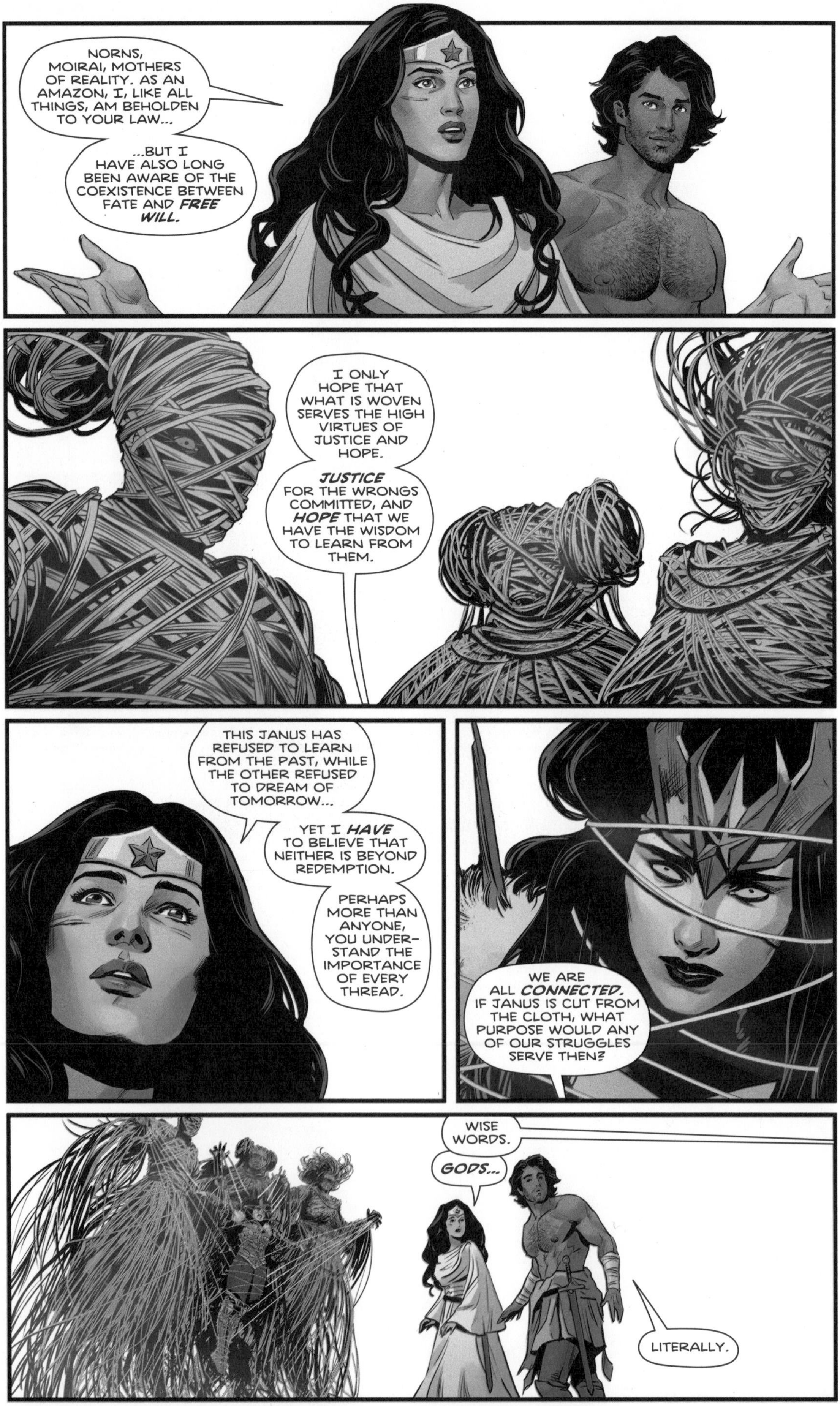
NORNS, MOIRAI, MOTHERS OF REALITY. AS AN AMAZON, I, LIKE ALL THINGS, AM BEHOLDEN TO YOUR LAW...
...BUT I HAVE ALSO LONG BEEN AWARE OF THE COEXISTENCE BETWEEN FATE AND *FREE WILL.*
I ONLY HOPE THAT WHAT IS WOVEN SERVES THE HIGH VIRTUES OF JUSTICE AND HOPE.
JUSTICE FOR THE WRONGS COMMITTED, AND *HOPE* THAT WE HAVE THE WISDOM TO LEARN FROM THEM.
THIS JANUS HAS REFUSED TO LEARN FROM THE PAST, WHILE THE OTHER REFUSED TO DREAM OF TOMORROW...
YET I *HAVE* TO BELIEVE THAT NEITHER IS BEYOND REDEMPTION.
PERHAPS MORE THAN ANYONE, YOU UNDER-STAND THE IMPORTANCE OF EVERY THREAD.
WE ARE ALL *CONNECTED.* IF JANUS IS CUT FROM THE CLOTH, WHAT PURPOSE WOULD ANY OF OUR STRUGGLES SERVE THEN?
WISE WORDS.
GODS...
LITERALLY.

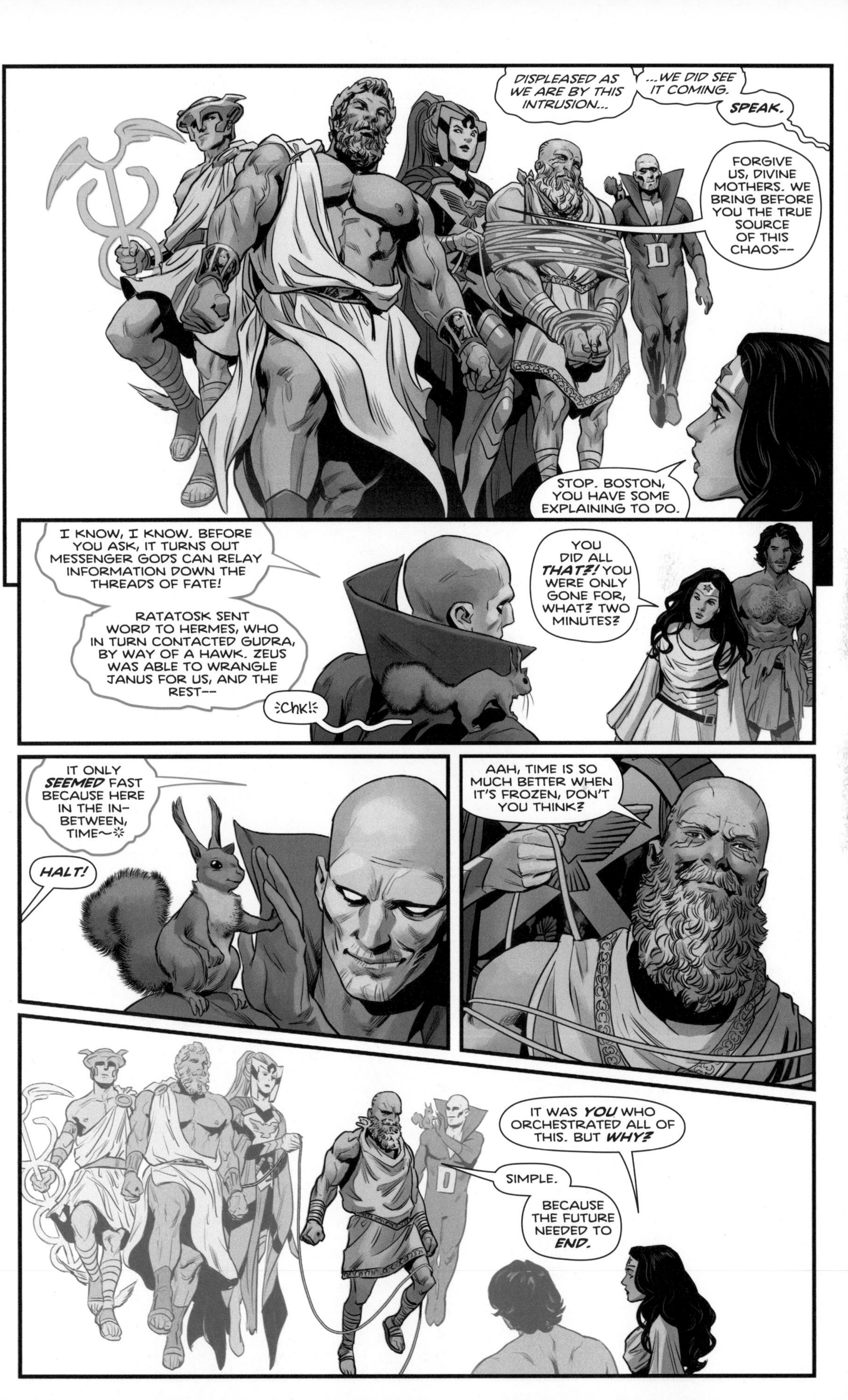
DISPLEASED AS WE ARE BY THIS INTRUSION...
...WE DID SEE IT COMING.
SPEAK.
FORGIVE US, DIVINE MOTHERS. WE BRING BEFORE YOU THE TRUE SOURCE OF THIS CHAOS--
STOP. BOSTON, YOU HAVE SOME EXPLAINING TO DO.
I KNOW, I KNOW. BEFORE YOU ASK, IT TURNS OUT MESSENGER GODS CAN RELAY INFORMATION DOWN THE THREADS OF FATE!
RATATOSK SENT WORD TO HERMES, WHO IN TURN CONTACTED GUDRA, BY WAY OF A HAWK. ZEUS WAS ABLE TO WRANGLE JANUS FOR US, AND THE REST--
Chk!
YOU DID ALL THAT?! YOU WERE ONLY GONE FOR, WHAT? TWO MINUTES?
IT ONLY SEEMED FAST BECAUSE HERE IN THE IN-BETWEEN, TIME~
HALT!
AAH, TIME IS SO MUCH BETTER WHEN IT'S FROZEN, DON'T YOU THINK?
IT WAS YOU WHO ORCHESTRATED ALL OF THIS. BUT WHY?
SIMPLE.
BECAUSE THE FUTURE NEEDED TO END.

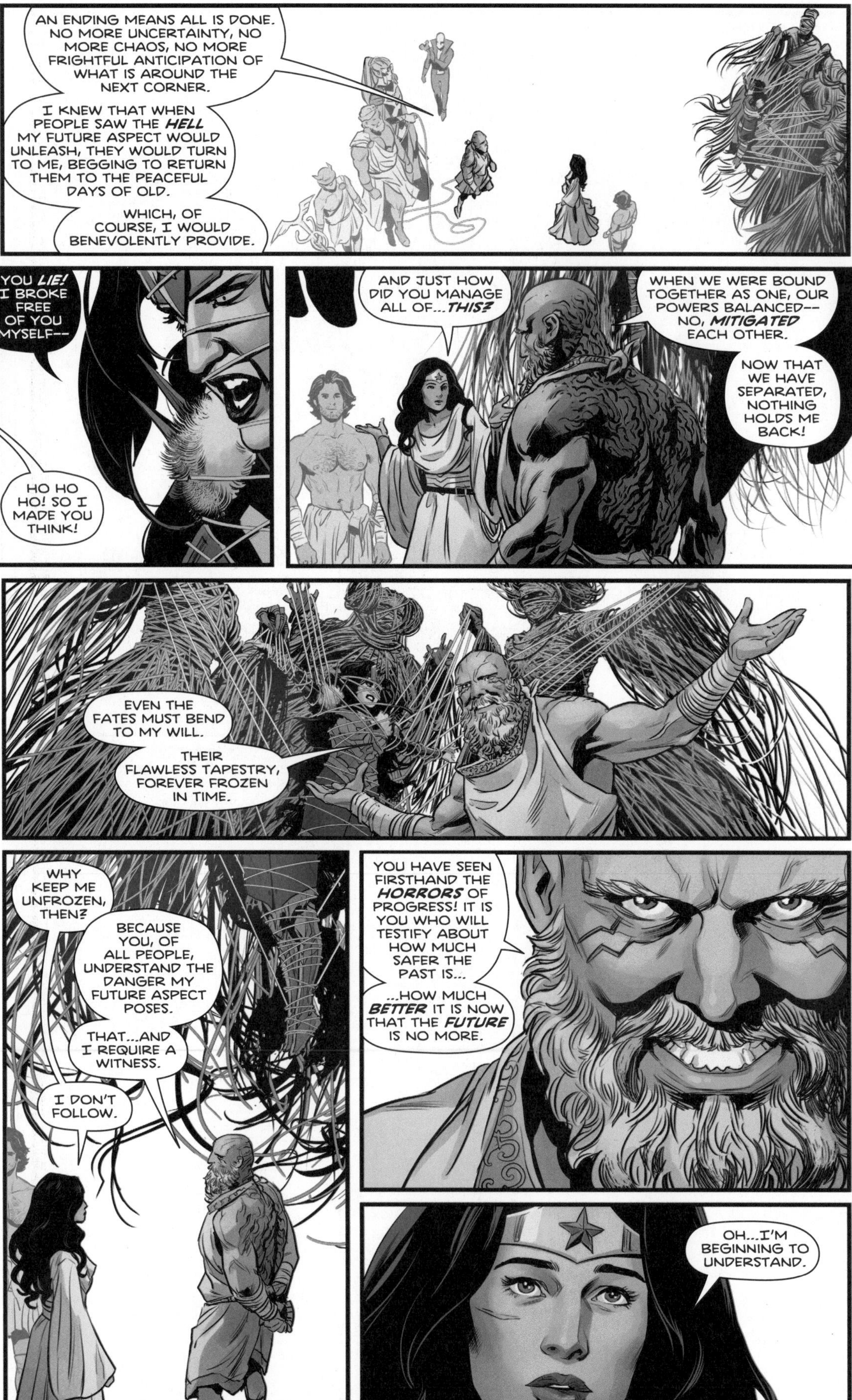
AN ENDING MEANS ALL IS DONE. NO MORE UNCERTAINTY, NO MORE CHAOS, NO MORE FRIGHTFUL ANTICIPATION OF WHAT IS AROUND THE NEXT CORNER.
I KNEW THAT WHEN PEOPLE SAW THE HELL MY FUTURE ASPECT WOULD UNLEASH, THEY WOULD TURN TO ME, BEGGING TO RETURN THEM TO THE PEACEFUL DAYS OF OLD.
WHICH, OF COURSE, I WOULD BENEVOLENTLY PROVIDE.
YOU LIE! I BROKE FREE OF YOU MYSELF--
HO HO HO! SO I MADE YOU THINK!
AND JUST HOW DID YOU MANAGE ALL OF...THIS?
WHEN WE WERE BOUND TOGETHER AS ONE, OUR POWERS BALANCED-- NO, MITIGATED EACH OTHER.
NOW THAT WE HAVE SEPARATED, NOTHING HOLDS ME BACK!
EVEN THE FATES MUST BEND TO MY WILL.
THEIR FLAWLESS TAPESTRY, FOREVER FROZEN IN TIME.
WHY KEEP ME UNFROZEN, THEN?
BECAUSE YOU, OF ALL PEOPLE, UNDERSTAND THE DANGER MY FUTURE ASPECT POSES.
THAT...AND I REQUIRE A WITNESS.
I DON'T FOLLOW.
YOU HAVE SEEN FIRSTHAND THE HORRORS OF PROGRESS! IT IS YOU WHO WILL TESTIFY ABOUT HOW MUCH SAFER THE PAST IS...
...HOW MUCH BETTER IT IS NOW THAT THE FUTURE IS NO MORE.
OH...I'M BEGINNING TO UNDERSTAND.

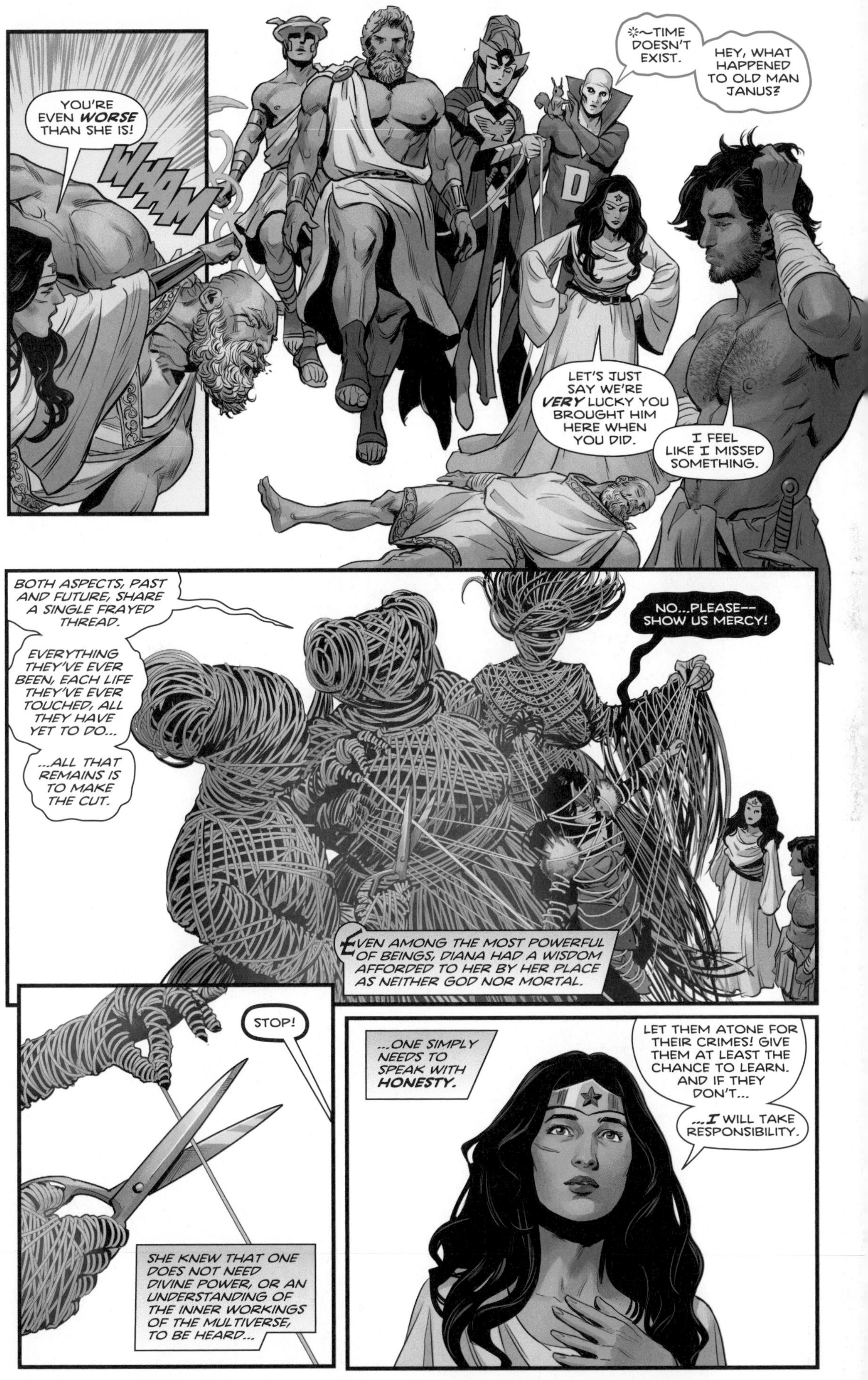
YOU'RE EVEN WORSE THAN SHE IS!
WHAM
※~TIME DOESN'T EXIST.
HEY, WHAT HAPPENED TO OLD MAN JANUS?
LET'S JUST SAY WE'RE VERY LUCKY YOU BROUGHT HIM HERE WHEN YOU DID.
I FEEL LIKE I MISSED SOMETHING.
BOTH ASPECTS, PAST AND FUTURE, SHARE A SINGLE FRAYED THREAD.
EVERYTHING THEY'VE EVER BEEN, EACH LIFE THEY'VE EVER TOUCHED, ALL THEY HAVE YET TO DO...
...ALL THAT REMAINS IS TO MAKE THE CUT.
NO...PLEASE-- SHOW US MERCY!
EVEN AMONG THE MOST POWERFUL OF BEINGS, DIANA HAD A WISDOM AFFORDED TO HER BY HER PLACE AS NEITHER GOD NOR MORTAL.
STOP!
SHE KNEW THAT ONE DOES NOT NEED DIVINE POWER, OR AN UNDERSTANDING OF THE INNER WORKINGS OF THE MULTIVERSE, TO BE HEARD...
...ONE SIMPLY NEEDS TO SPEAK WITH HONESTY.
LET THEM ATONE FOR THEIR CRIMES! GIVE THEM AT LEAST THE CHANCE TO LEARN. AND IF THEY DON'T...
...I WILL TAKE RESPONSIBILITY.

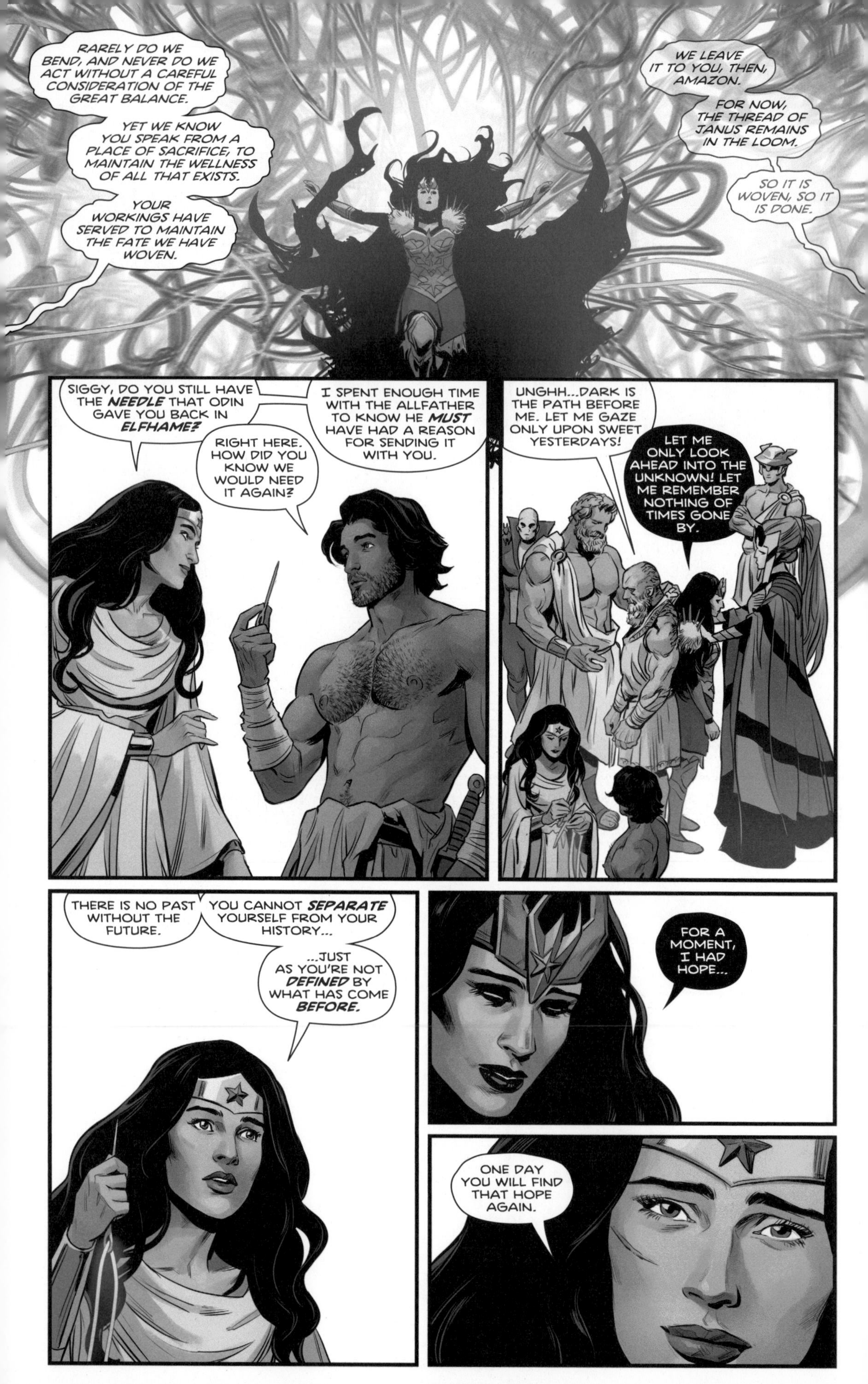
RARELY DO WE BEND, AND NEVER DO WE ACT WITHOUT A CAREFUL CONSIDERATION OF THE GREAT BALANCE.
YET WE KNOW YOU SPEAK FROM A PLACE OF SACRIFICE, TO MAINTAIN THE WELLNESS OF ALL THAT EXISTS.
YOUR WORKINGS HAVE SERVED TO MAINTAIN THE FATE WE HAVE WOVEN.
WE LEAVE IT TO YOU, THEN, AMAZON.
FOR NOW, THE THREAD OF JANUS REMAINS IN THE LOOM.
SO IT IS WOVEN, SO IT IS DONE.
SIGGY, DO YOU STILL HAVE THE NEEDLE THAT ODIN GAVE YOU BACK IN ELFHAME?
RIGHT HERE. HOW DID YOU KNOW WE WOULD NEED IT AGAIN?
I SPENT ENOUGH TIME WITH THE ALLFATHER TO KNOW HE MUST HAVE HAD A REASON FOR SENDING IT WITH YOU.
UNGHH...DARK IS THE PATH BEFORE ME. LET ME GAZE ONLY UPON SWEET YESTERDAYS!
LET ME ONLY LOOK AHEAD INTO THE UNKNOWN! LET ME REMEMBER NOTHING OF TIMES GONE BY.
THERE IS NO PAST WITHOUT THE FUTURE.
YOU CANNOT SEPARATE YOURSELF FROM YOUR HISTORY...
...JUST AS YOU'RE NOT DEFINED BY WHAT HAS COME BEFORE.
FOR A MOMENT, I HAD HOPE...
ONE DAY YOU WILL FIND THAT HOPE AGAIN.

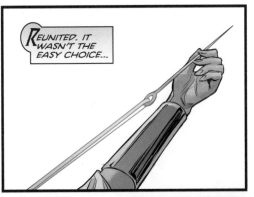

REUNITED. IT WASN'T THE EASY CHOICE...

FORCED TO LIVE WITH MYSELF AGAIN. IT WON'T BE EASY...

...BUT WE WILL LEARN. WE THANK YOU FOR THIS MERCY.

...BUT IT WAS THE CORRECT ONE.

I'M SORRY...

AND WHEN IT WAS DONE, ALL KNEW THIS TO BE THE TRUTH.

A FINE JOB, DIANA!

I'VE NEVER SEWN A GOD BACK TOGETHER BEFORE. FOR NOW, I SUPPOSE IT WILL HAVE TO DO.

I DON'T THINK THOSE TWO WILL EVER SEE EYE TO EYE.

...GET IT?

TSK

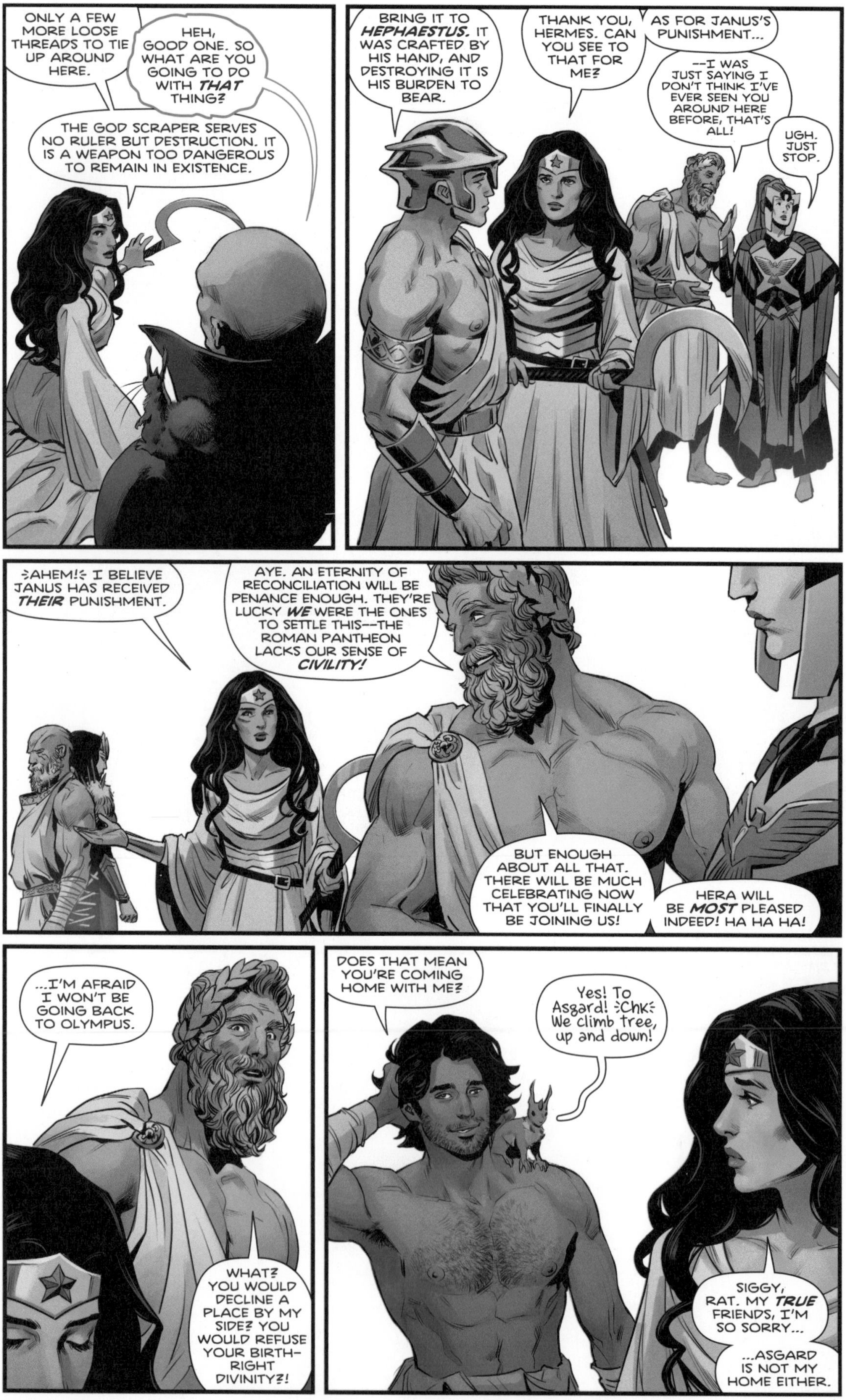
ONLY A FEW MORE LOOSE THREADS TO TIE UP AROUND HERE.
HEH, GOOD ONE. SO WHAT ARE YOU GOING TO DO WITH THAT THING?
THE GOD SCRAPER SERVES NO RULER BUT DESTRUCTION. IT IS A WEAPON TOO DANGEROUS TO REMAIN IN EXISTENCE.
BRING IT TO HEPHAESTUS. IT WAS CRAFTED BY HIS HAND, AND DESTROYING IT IS HIS BURDEN TO BEAR.
THANK YOU, HERMES. CAN YOU SEE TO THAT FOR ME?
AS FOR JANUS'S PUNISHMENT...
--I WAS JUST SAYING I DON'T THINK I'VE EVER SEEN YOU AROUND HERE BEFORE, THAT'S ALL!
UGH. JUST STOP.
AHEM! I BELIEVE JANUS HAS RECEIVED THEIR PUNISHMENT.
AYE. AN ETERNITY OF RECONCILIATION WILL BE PENANCE ENOUGH. THEY'RE LUCKY WE WERE THE ONES TO SETTLE THIS--THE ROMAN PANTHEON LACKS OUR SENSE OF CIVILITY!
BUT ENOUGH ABOUT ALL THAT. THERE WILL BE MUCH CELEBRATING NOW THAT YOU'LL FINALLY BE JOINING US!
HERA WILL BE MOST PLEASED INDEED! HA HA HA!
...I'M AFRAID I WON'T BE GOING BACK TO OLYMPUS.
WHAT? YOU WOULD DECLINE A PLACE BY MY SIDE? YOU WOULD REFUSE YOUR BIRTH-RIGHT DIVINITY?!
DOES THAT MEAN YOU'RE COMING HOME WITH ME?
Yes! To Asgard! Chk We climb tree, up and down!
SIGGY, RAT. MY TRUE FRIENDS, I'M SO SORRY...
...ASGARD IS NOT MY HOME EITHER.

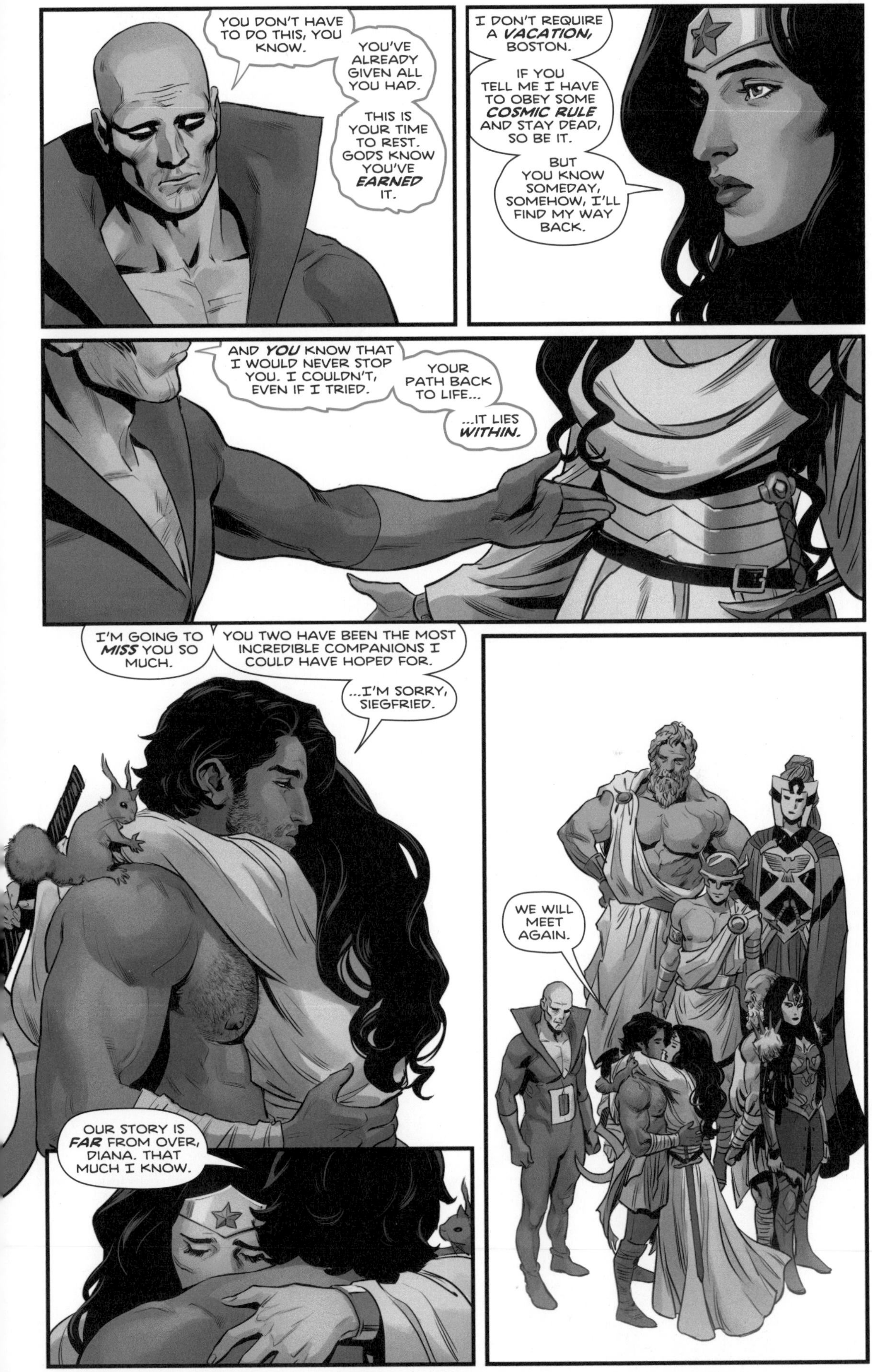
YOU DON'T HAVE TO DO THIS, YOU KNOW.
YOU'VE ALREADY GIVEN ALL YOU HAD.
THIS IS YOUR TIME TO REST. GODS KNOW YOU'VE EARNED IT.
I DON'T REQUIRE A VACATION, BOSTON.
IF YOU TELL ME I HAVE TO OBEY SOME COSMIC RULE AND STAY DEAD, SO BE IT.
BUT YOU KNOW SOMEDAY, SOMEHOW, I'LL FIND MY WAY BACK.
AND YOU KNOW THAT I WOULD NEVER STOP YOU. I COULDN'T, EVEN IF I TRIED.
YOUR PATH BACK TO LIFE...
...IT LIES WITHIN.
I'M GOING TO MISS YOU SO MUCH.
YOU TWO HAVE BEEN THE MOST INCREDIBLE COMPANIONS I COULD HAVE HOPED FOR.
...I'M SORRY, SIEGFRIED.
OUR STORY IS FAR FROM OVER, DIANA. THAT MUCH I KNOW.
WE WILL MEET AGAIN.

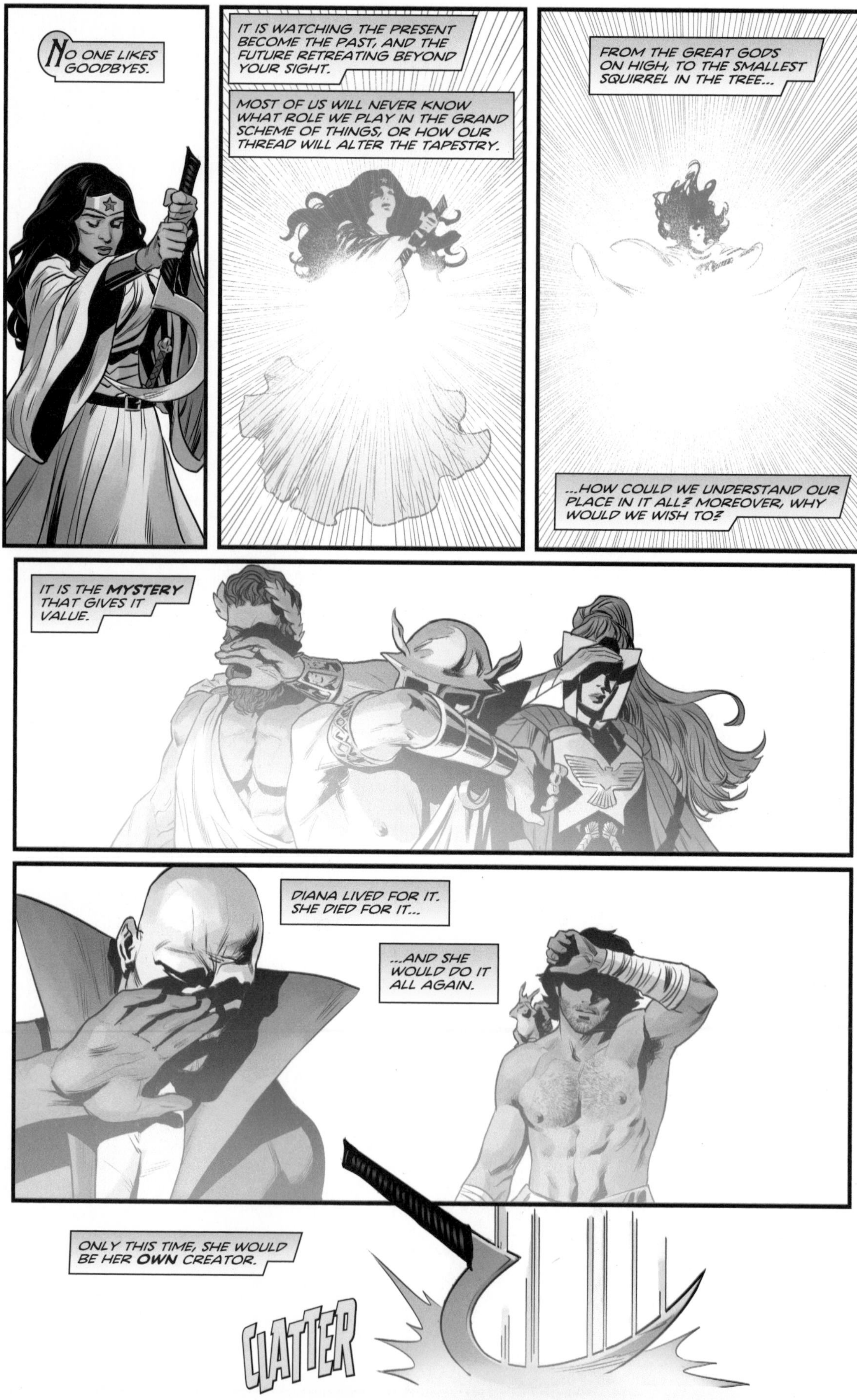
NO ONE LIKES GOODBYES.
IT IS WATCHING THE PRESENT BECOME THE PAST, AND THE FUTURE RETREATING BEYOND YOUR SIGHT.
MOST OF US WILL NEVER KNOW WHAT ROLE WE PLAY IN THE GRAND SCHEME OF THINGS, OR HOW OUR THREAD WILL ALTER THE TAPESTRY.
FROM THE GREAT GODS ON HIGH, TO THE SMALLEST SQUIRREL IN THE TREE...
...HOW COULD WE UNDERSTAND OUR PLACE IN IT ALL? MOREOVER, WHY WOULD WE WISH TO?
IT IS THE MYSTERY THAT GIVES IT VALUE.
DIANA LIVED FOR IT. SHE DIED FOR IT...
...AND SHE WOULD DO IT ALL AGAIN.
ONLY THIS TIME, SHE WOULD BE HER OWN CREATOR.
CLATTER

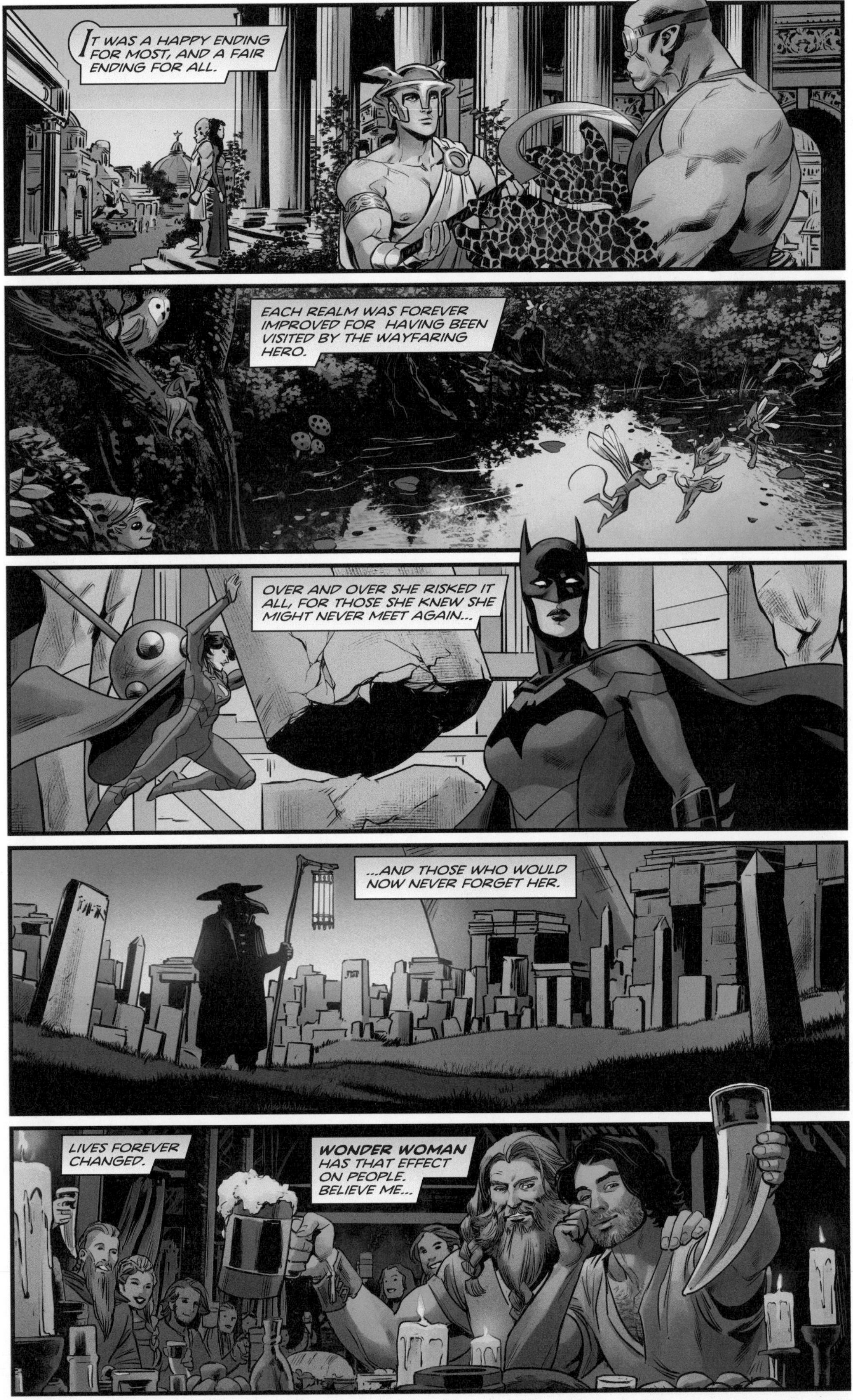
IT WAS A HAPPY ENDING FOR MOST, AND A FAIR ENDING FOR ALL.
EACH REALM WAS FOREVER IMPROVED FOR HAVING BEEN VISITED BY THE WAYFARING HERO.
OVER AND OVER SHE RISKED IT ALL, FOR THOSE SHE KNEW SHE MIGHT NEVER MEET AGAIN...
...AND THOSE WHO WOULD NOW NEVER FORGET HER.
LIVES FOREVER CHANGED.
WONDER WOMAN HAS THAT EFFECT ON PEOPLE. BELIEVE ME...

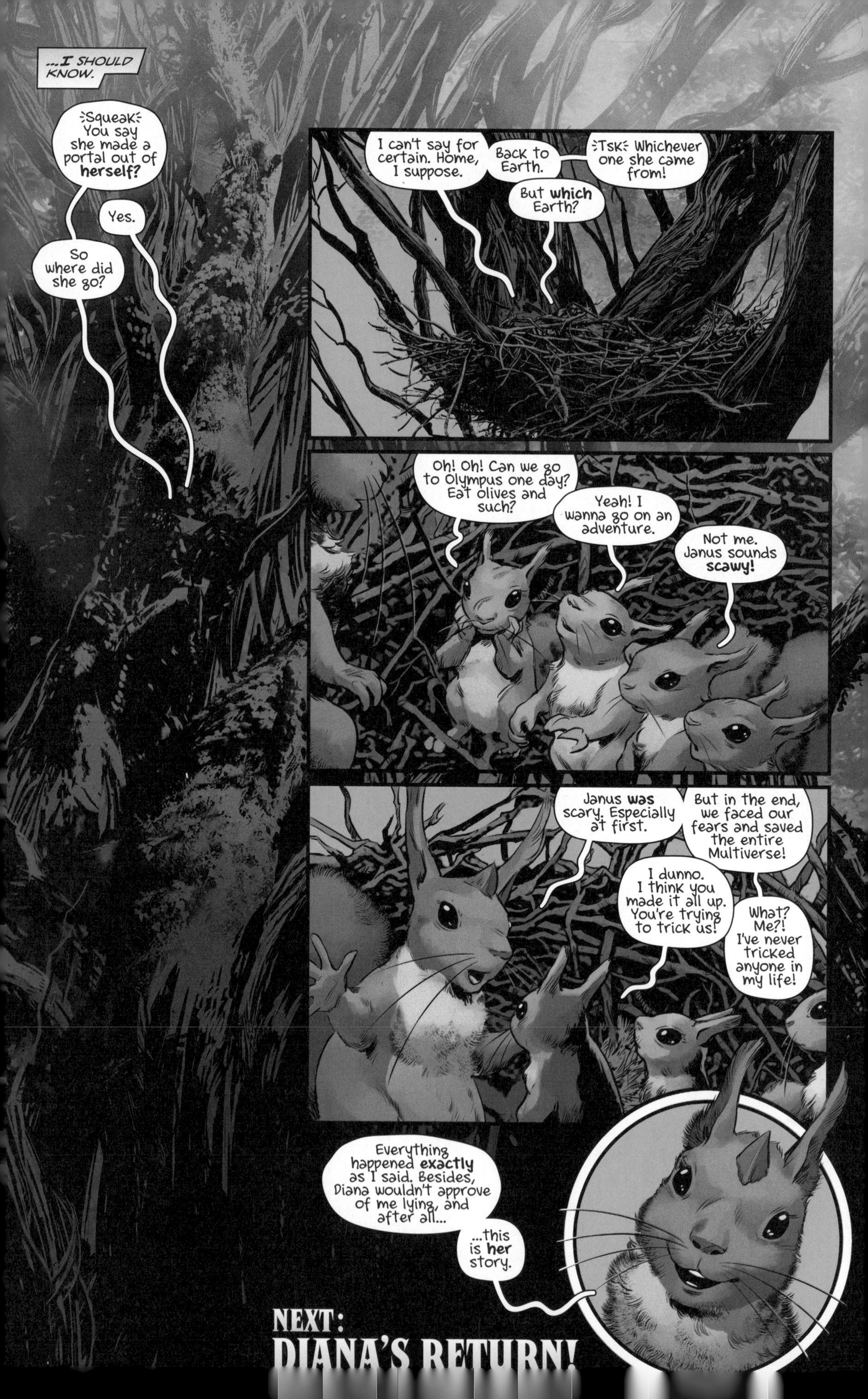
...I SHOULD KNOW.
Squeak! You say she made a portal out of **herself?**
Yes.
So where did she go?
I can't say for certain. Home, I suppose.
Back to Earth.
Tsk! Whichever one she came from!
But **which** Earth?
Oh! Oh! Can we go to Olympus one day? Eat olives and such?
Yeah! I wanna go on an adventure.
Not me. Janus sounds **scawy!**
Janus **was** scary. Especially at first.
But in the end, we faced our fears and saved the entire Multiverse!
I dunno. I think you made it all up. You're trying to trick us!
What? Me?! I've never tricked anyone in my life!
Everything happened **exactly** as I said. Besides, Diana wouldn't approve of me lying, and after all...
...this is **her** story.

NEXT: DIANA'S RETURN!

VARIANT COVER & DESIGN GALLERY

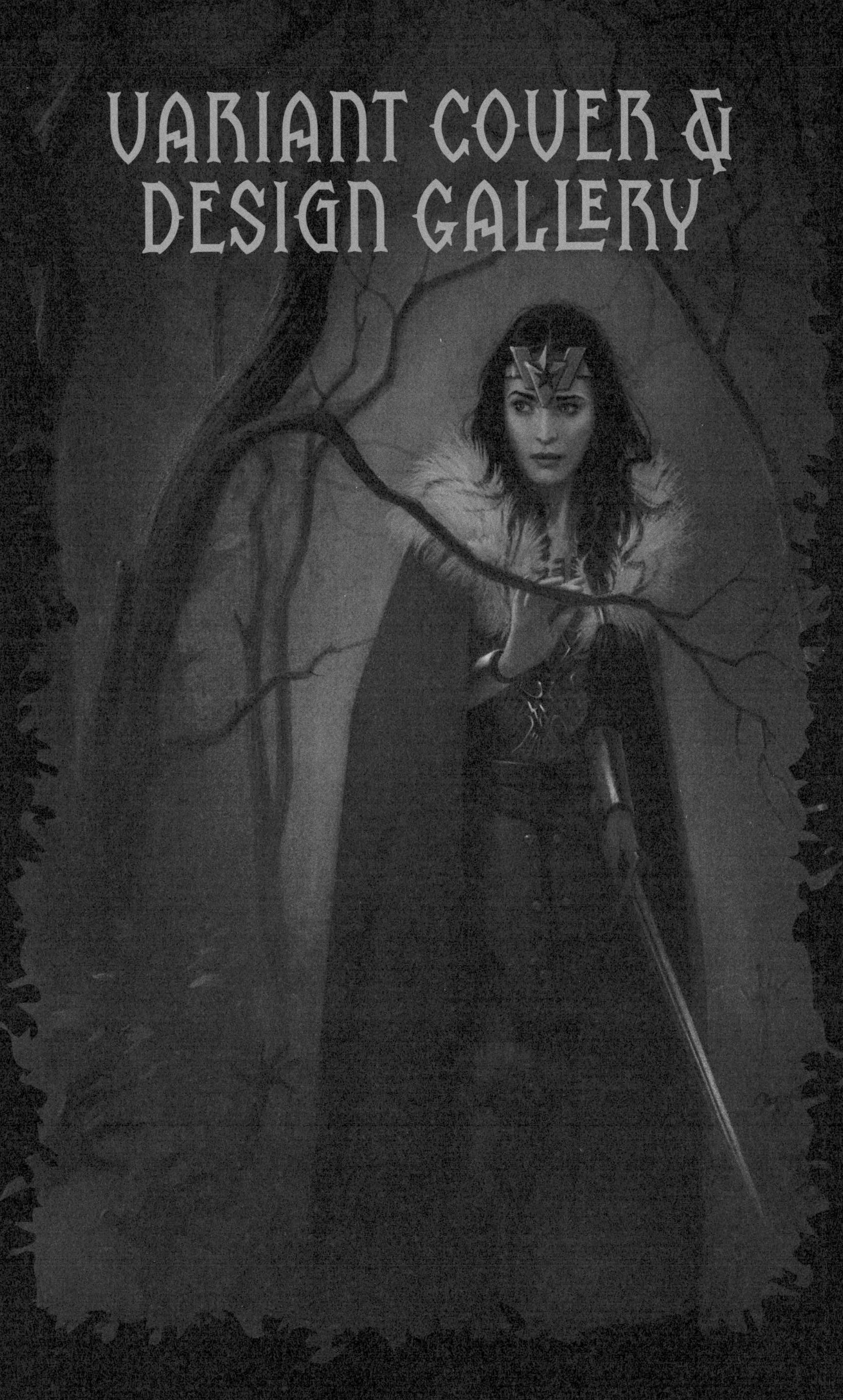

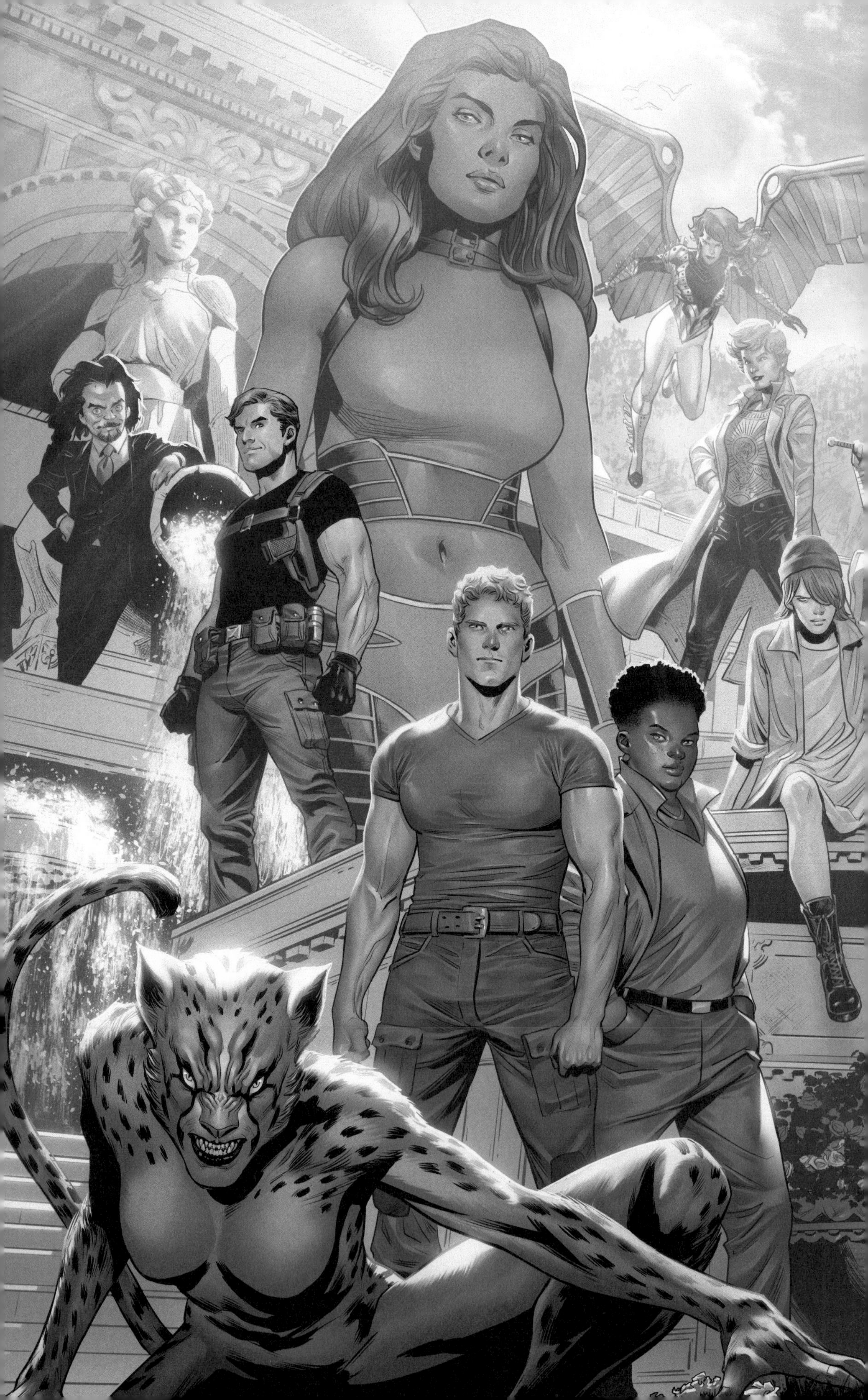

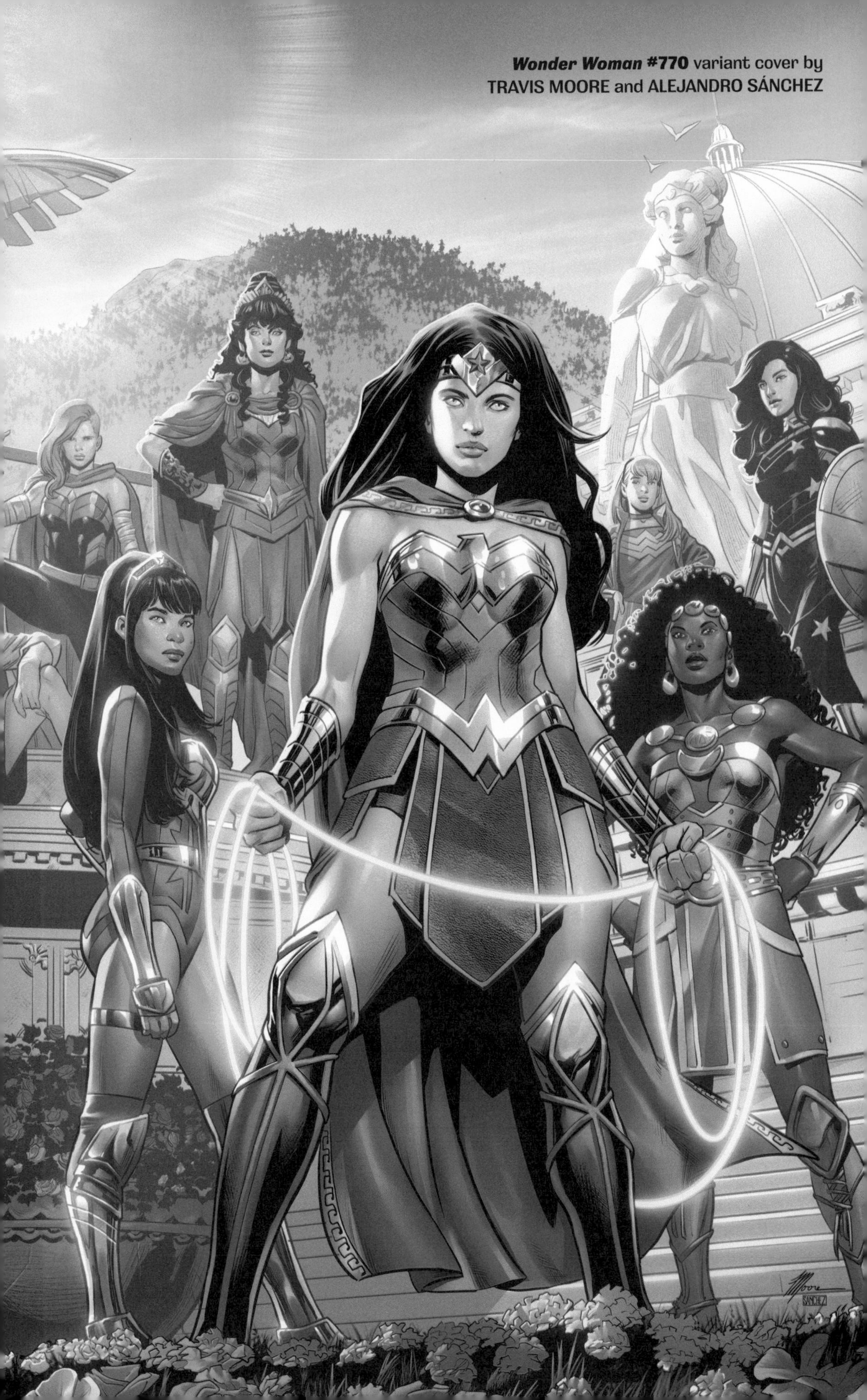

***Wonder Woman* #770** variant cover by
TRAVIS MOORE and ALEJANDRO SÁNCHEZ

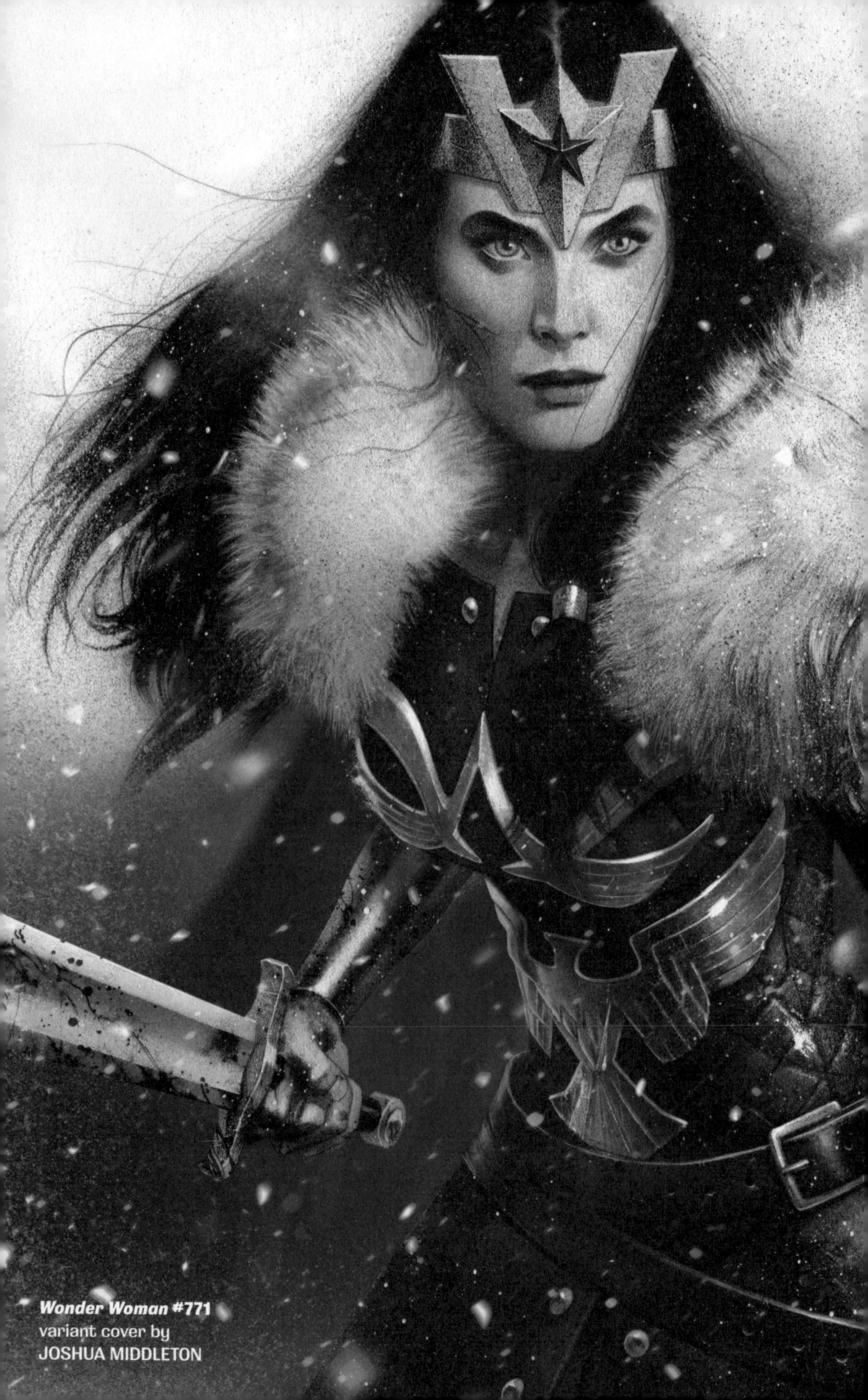

***Wonder Woman* #771**
variant cover by
JOSHUA MIDDLETON

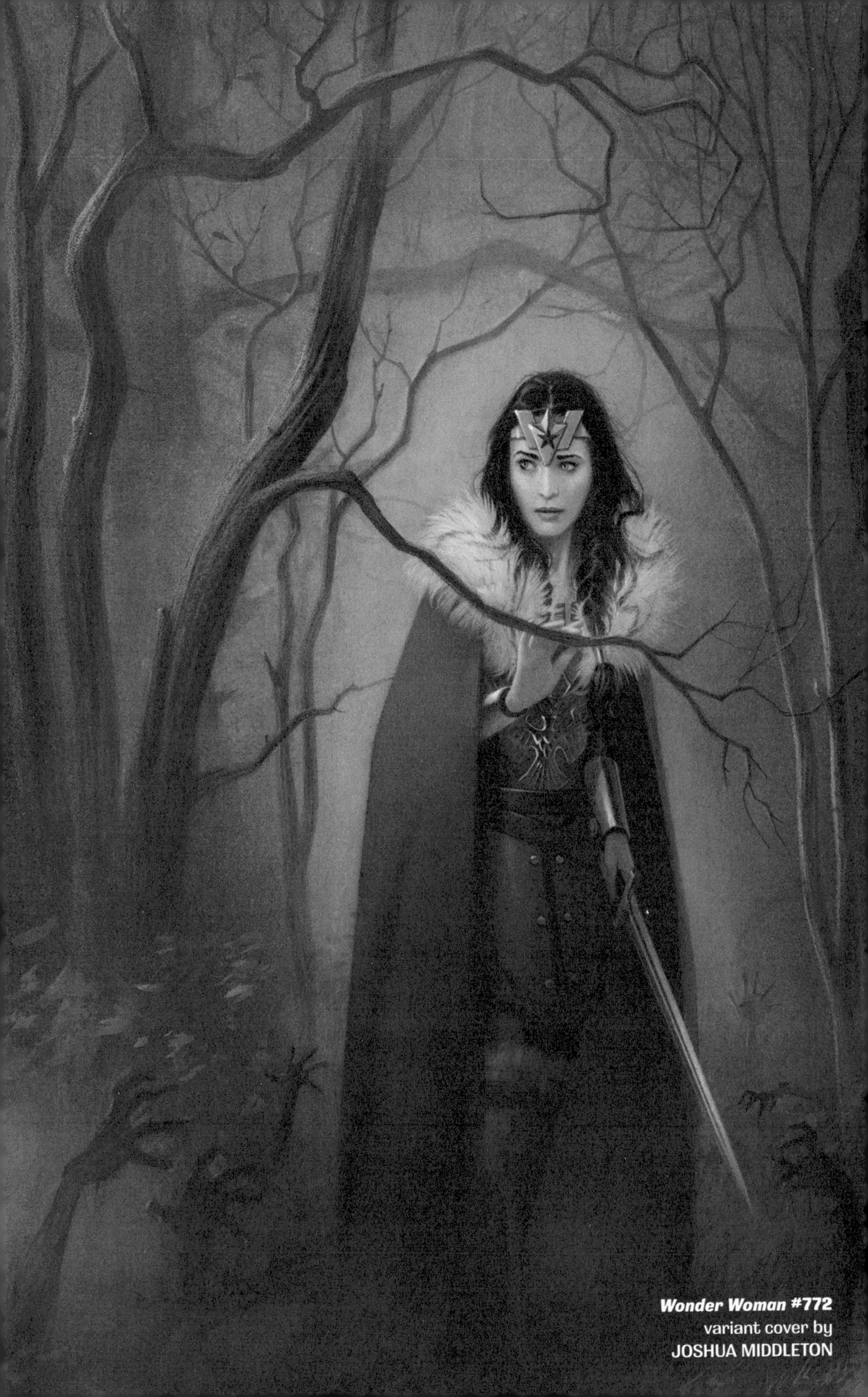

***Wonder Woman* #772**
variant cover by
JOSHUA MIDDLETON

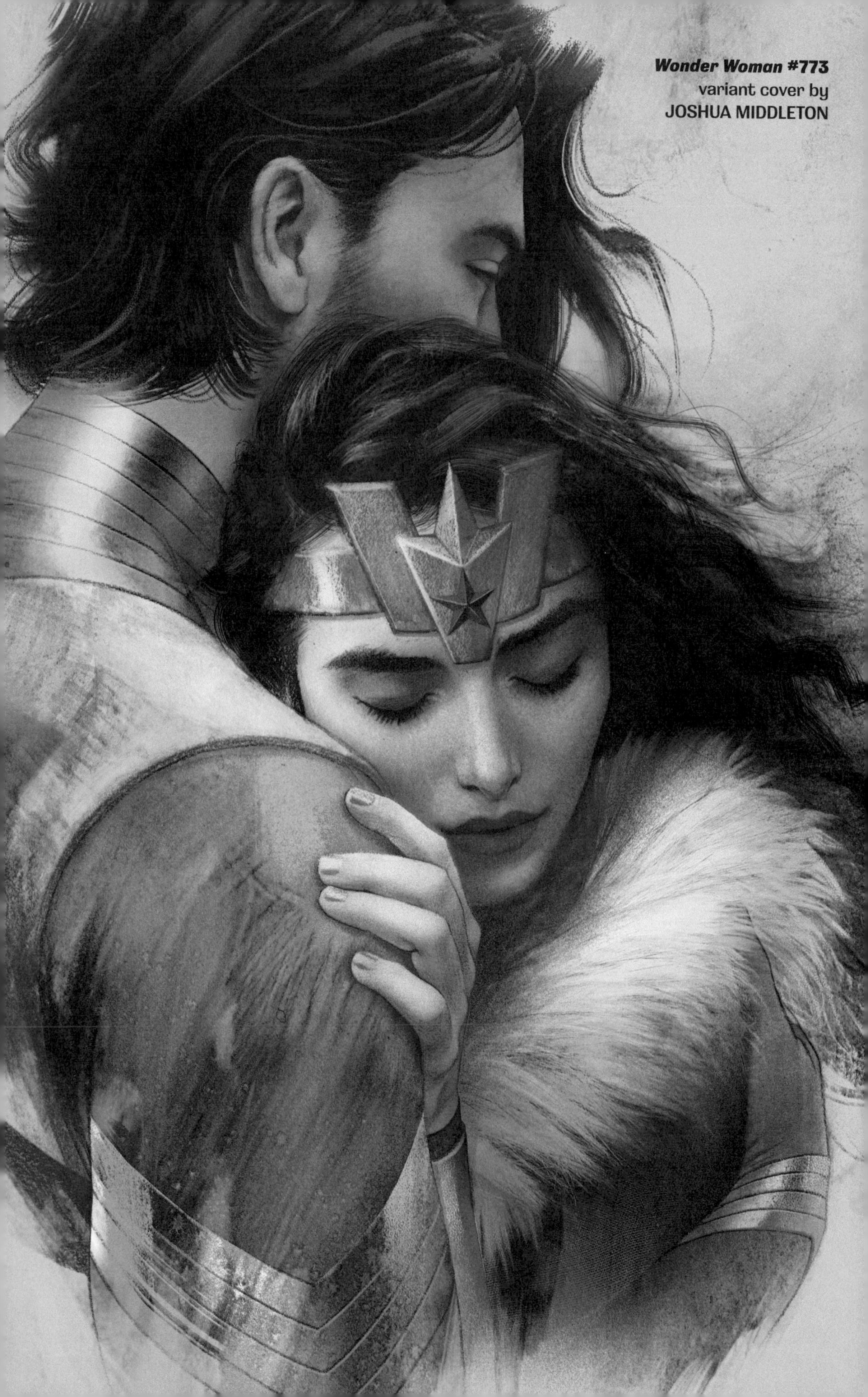

***Wonder Woman* #773**
variant cover by
JOSHUA MIDDLETON

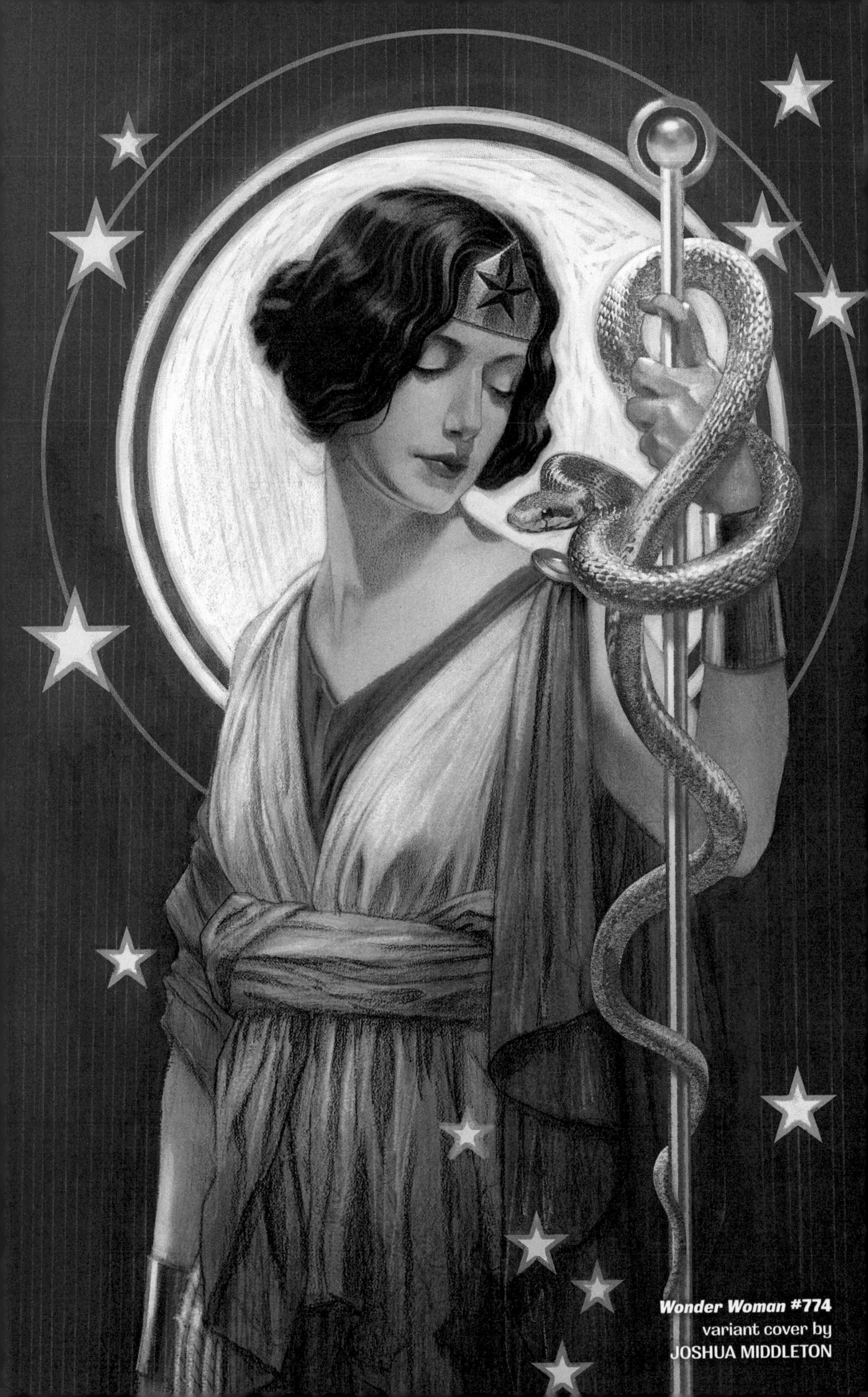

***Wonder Woman* #774**
variant cover by
JOSHUA MIDDLETON

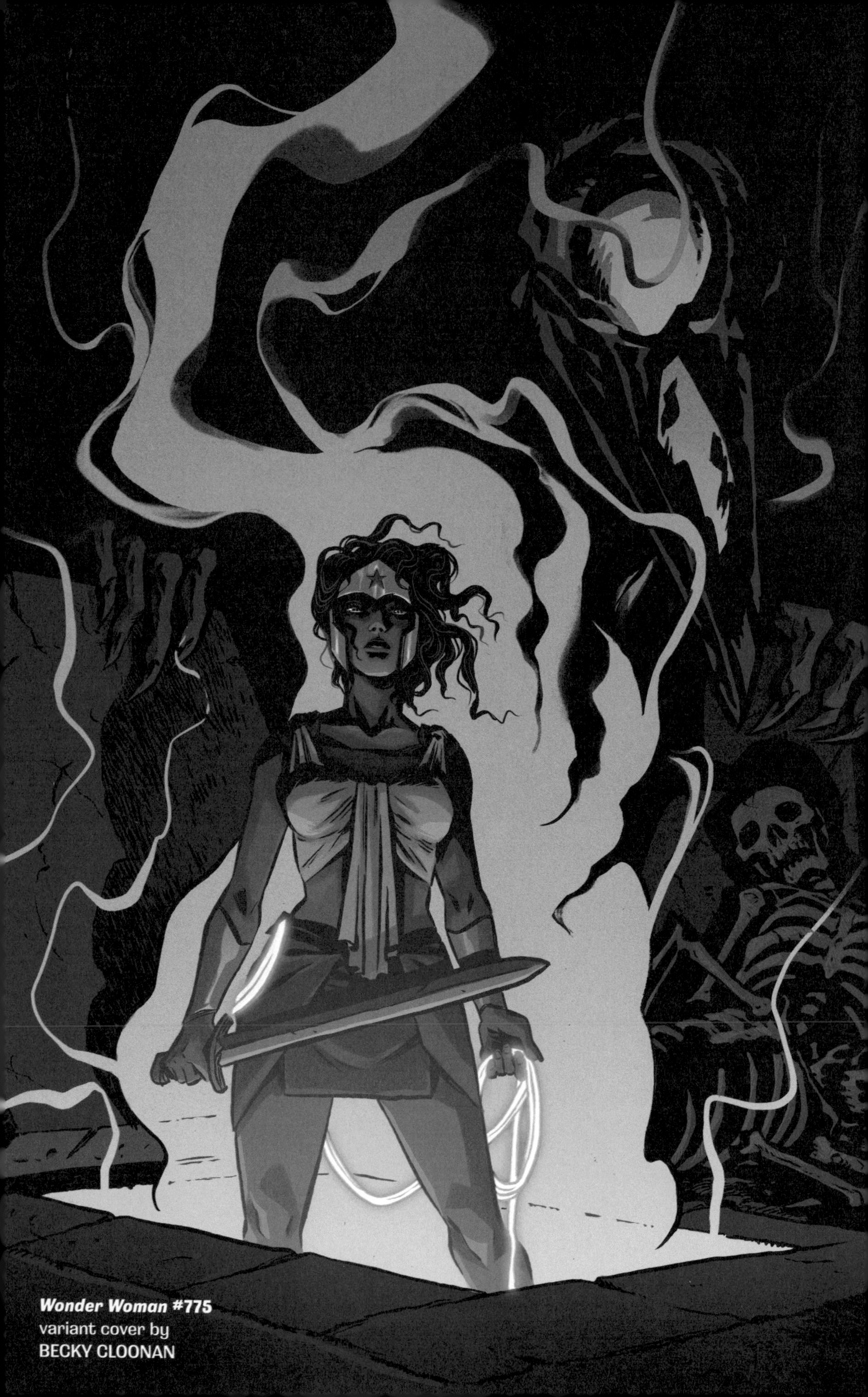

***Wonder Woman* #775**
variant cover by
BECKY CLOONAN

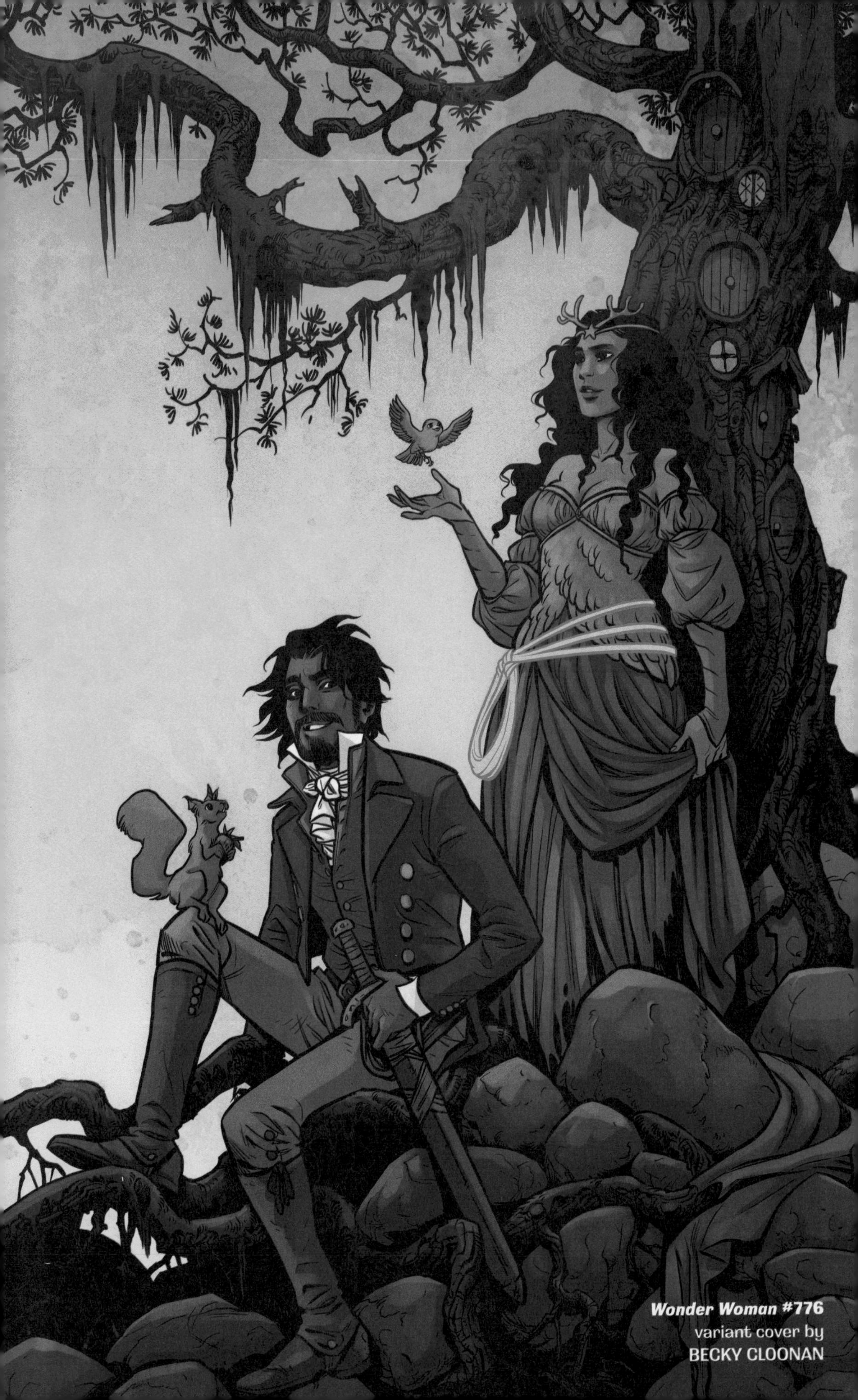

Wonder Woman #776
variant cover by
BECKY CLOONAN

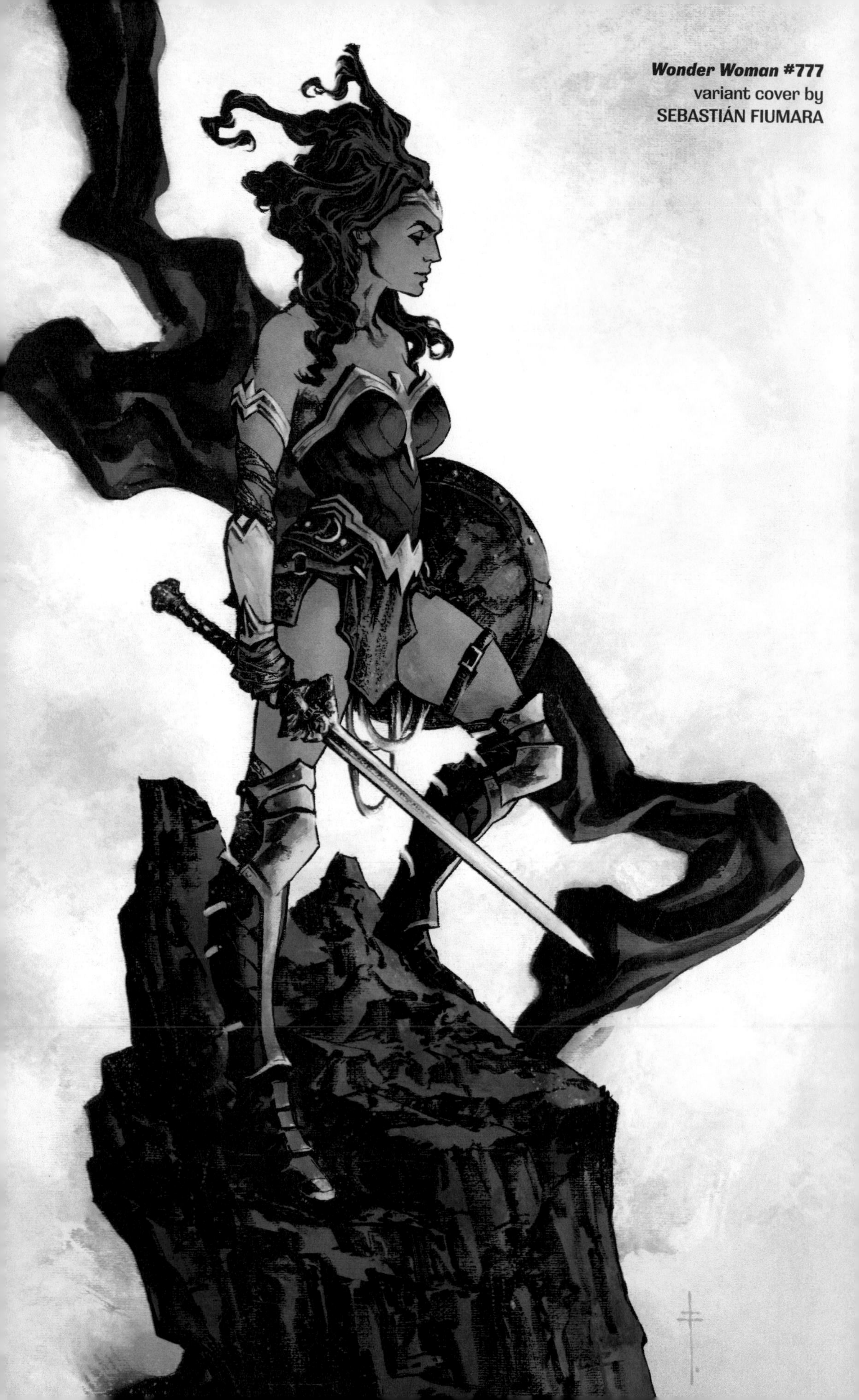

***Wonder Woman* #777**
variant cover by
SEBASTIÁN FIUMARA

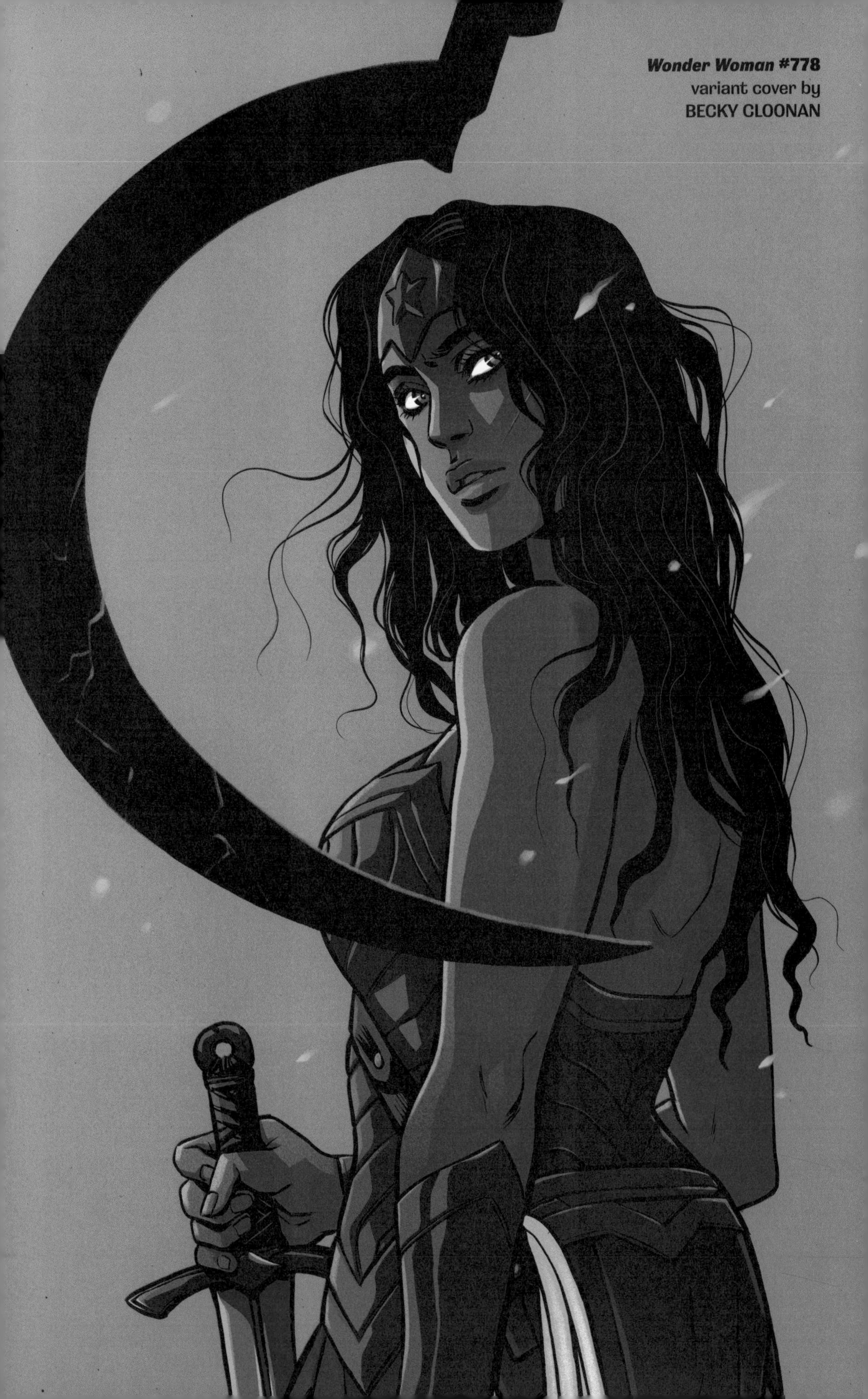

***Wonder Woman* #778**
variant cover by
BECKY CLOONAN

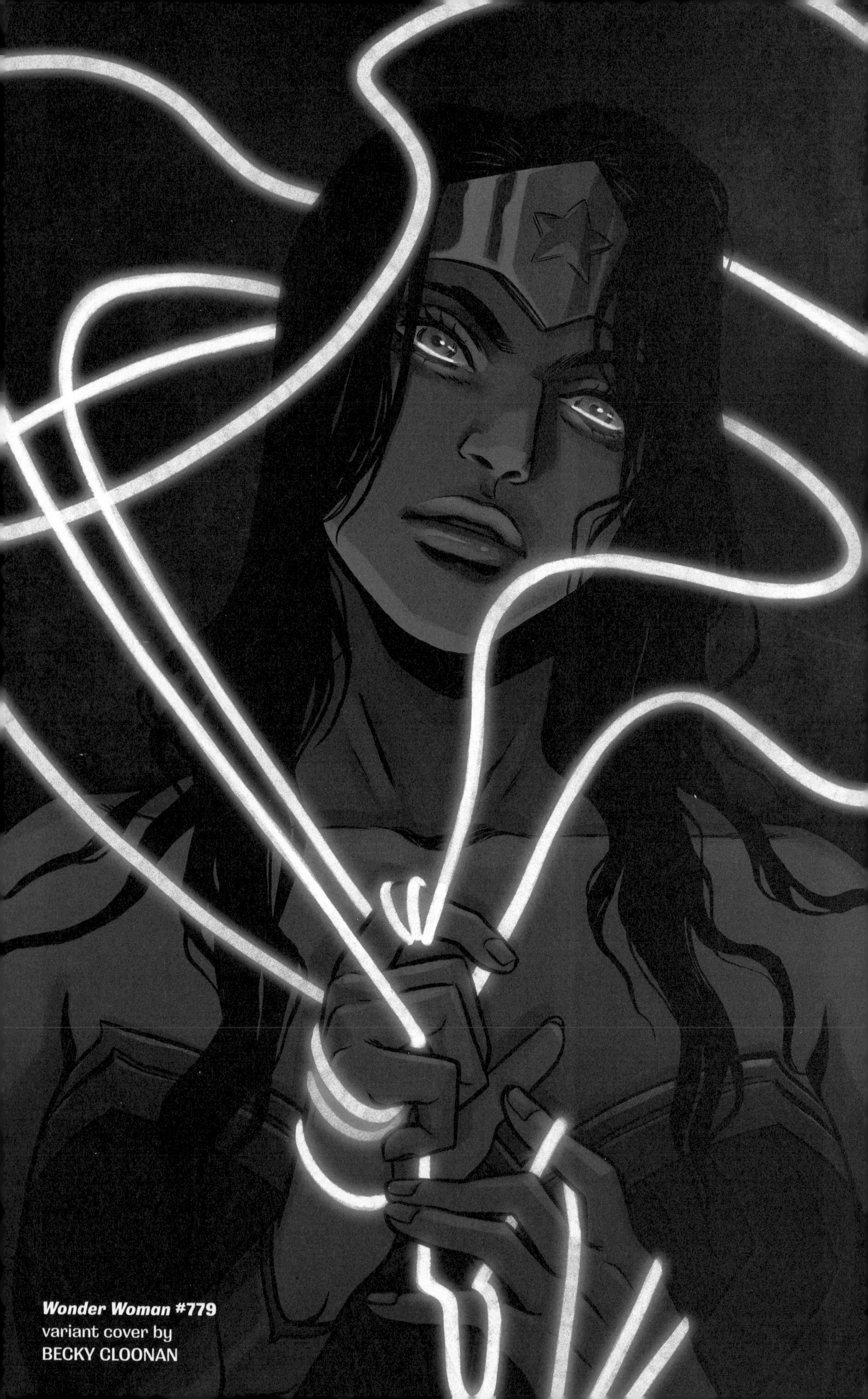

***Wonder Woman* #779**
variant cover by
BECKY CLOONAN

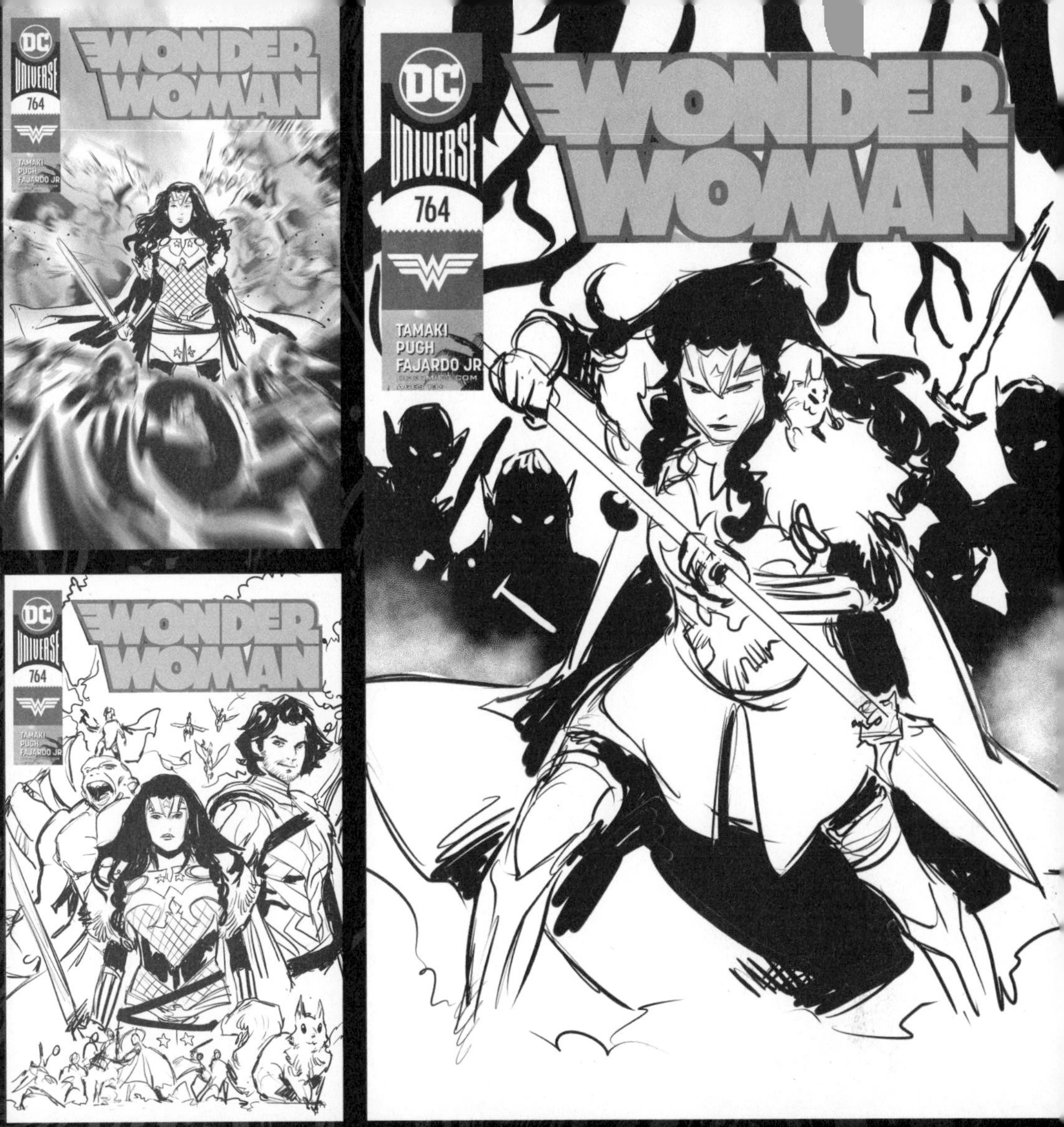
DC
UNIVERSE
764
WONDER WOMAN
TAMAKI
PUGH
FAJARDO JR

Wonder Woman #770-771 cover sketches by TRAVIS MOORE

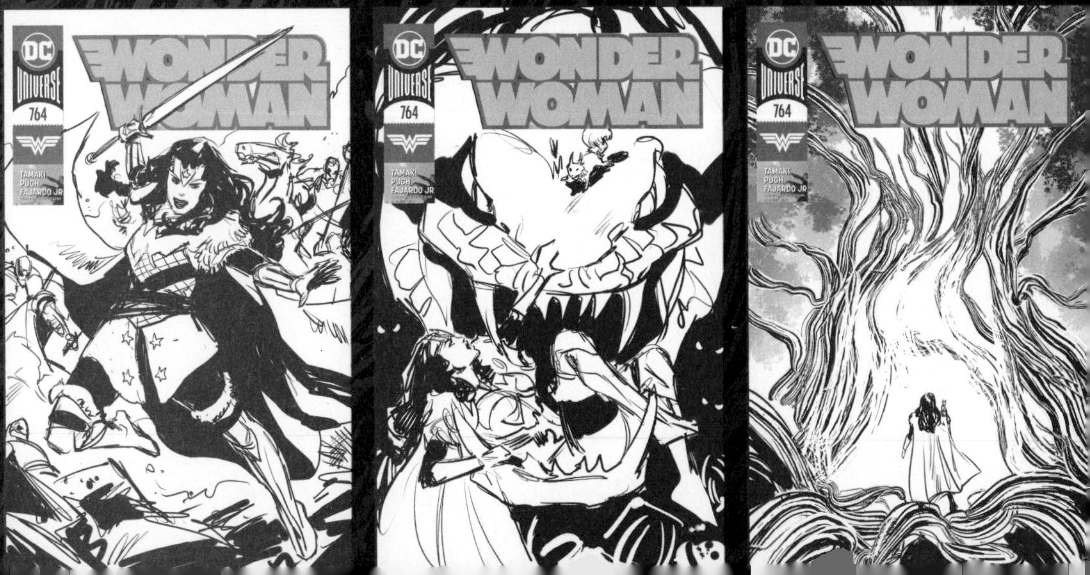
DC
UNIVERSE
764
WONDER WOMAN
TAMAKI
PUGH
FAJARDO JR

Wonder Woman #772-776 cover sketches by TRAVIS MOORE

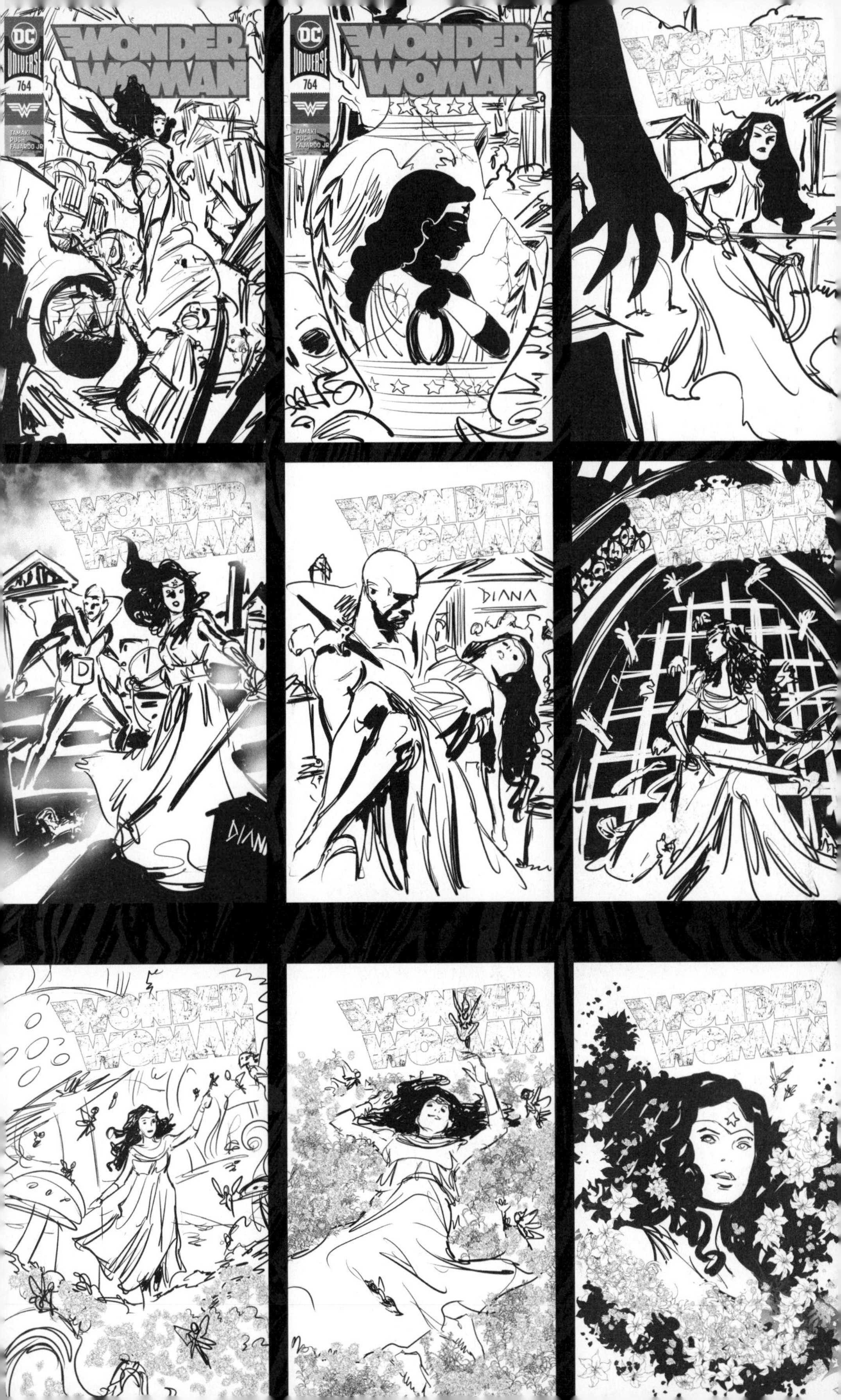
DC UNIVERSE
WONDER WOMAN
764
TAMAKI
PUGH
FAJARDO JR
DC UNIVERSE
WONDER WOMAN
764
TAMAKI
PUGH
FAJARDO JR
WONDER WOMAN
WONDER WOMAN
D
DIANA
WONDER WOMAN
DIANA
WONDER WOMAN
WONDER WOMAN
WONDER WOMAN
WONDER WOMAN

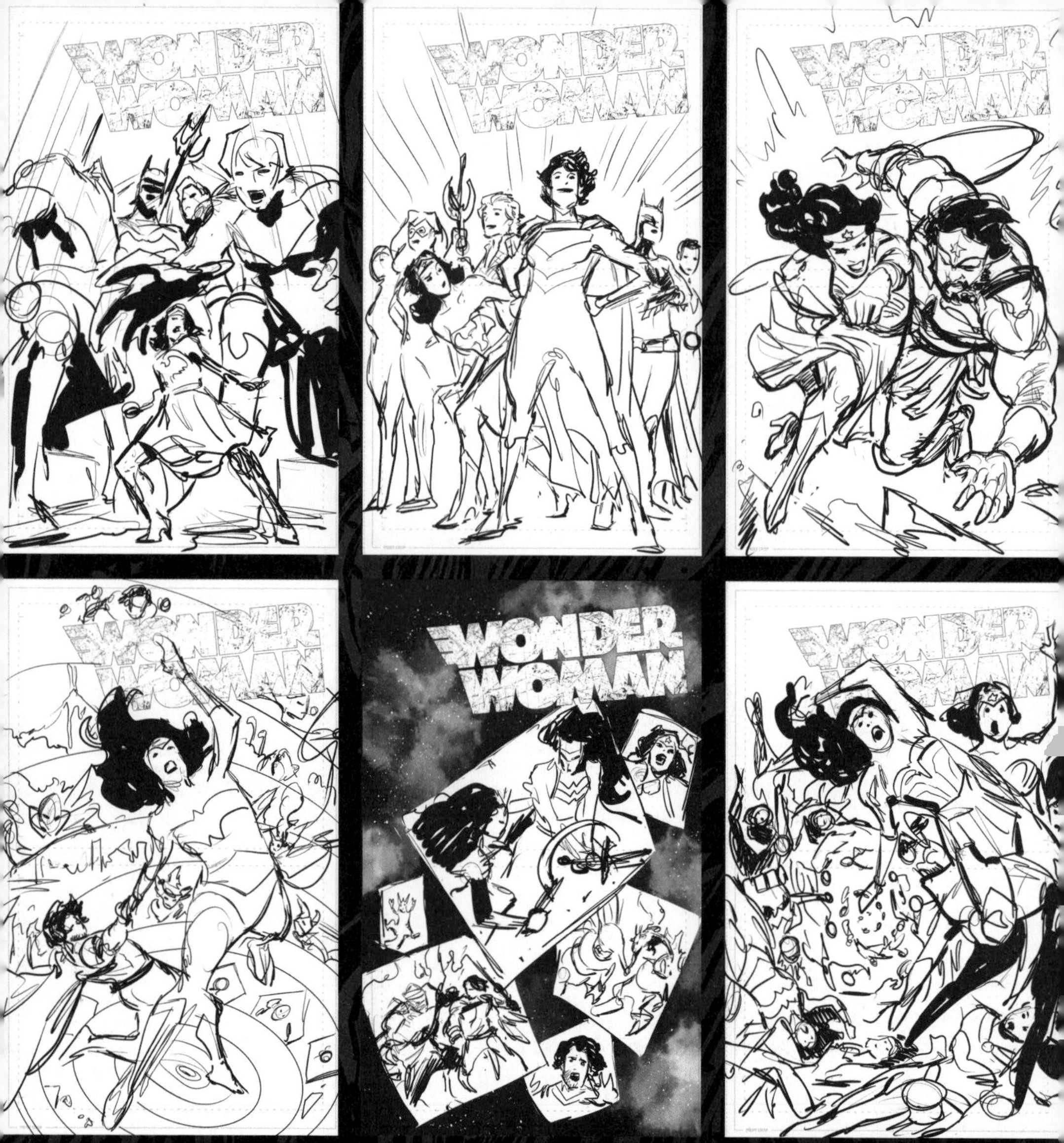
WONDER WOMAN

Wonder Woman **#777-779** cover sketches by TRAVIS MOORE

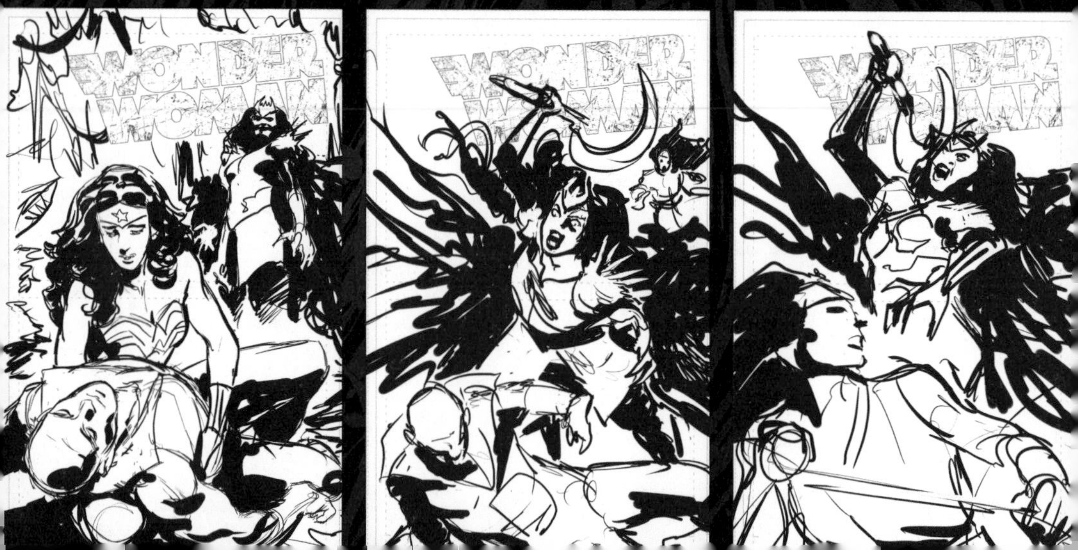
WONDER WOMAN

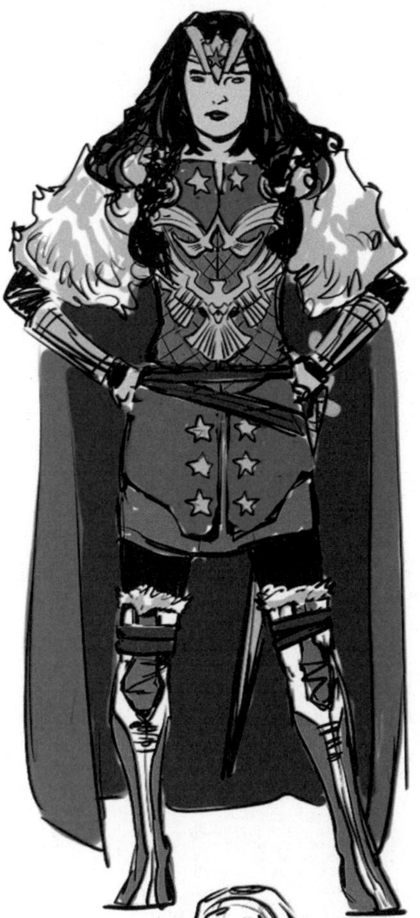

Nordic Wonder Woman sketches
by TRAVIS MOORE

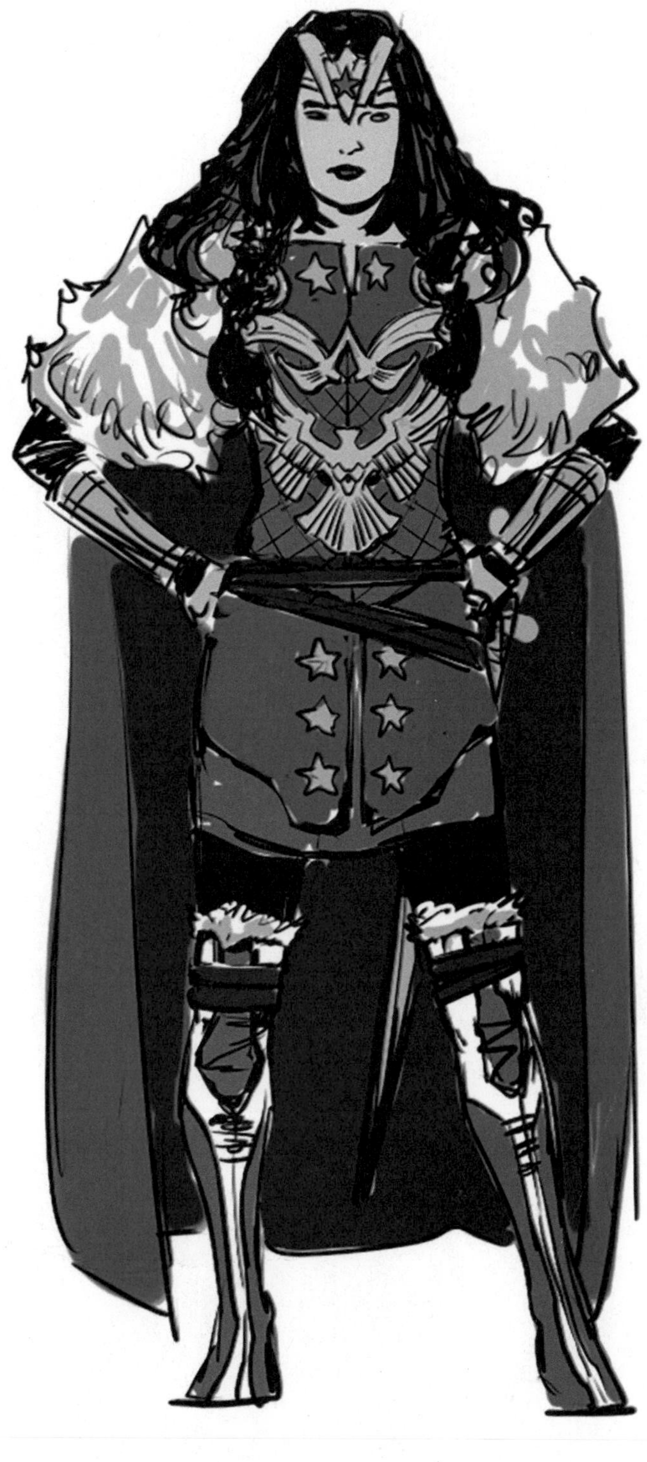

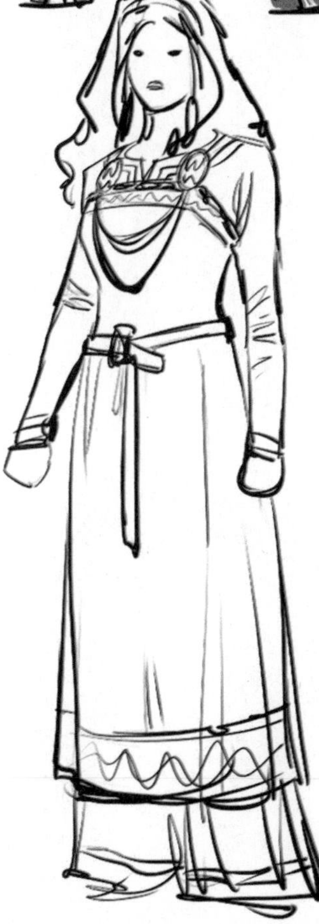

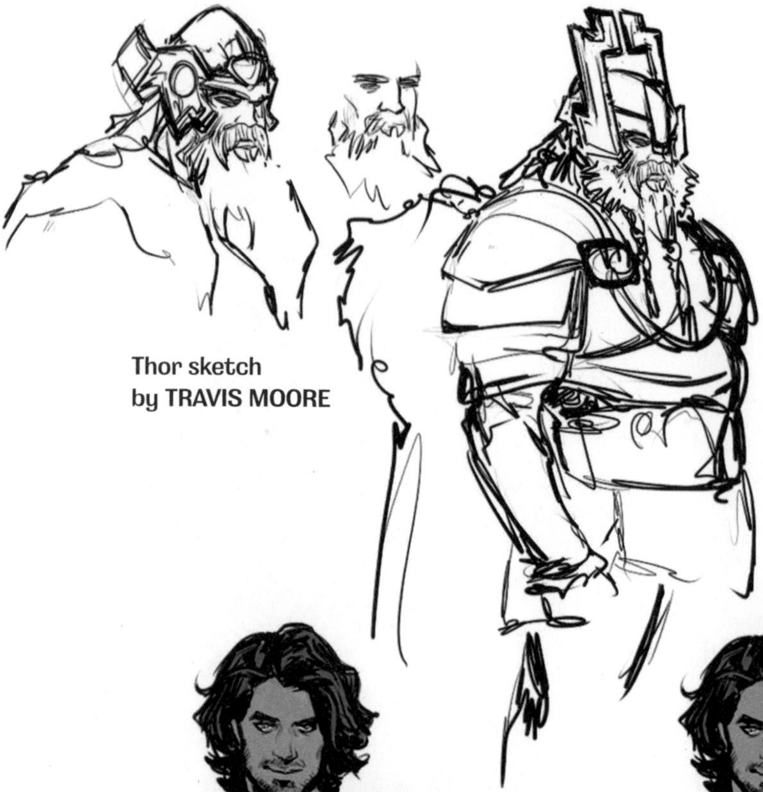

Thor sketch
by TRAVIS MOORE

Siegfried sketches
by TRAVIS MOORE

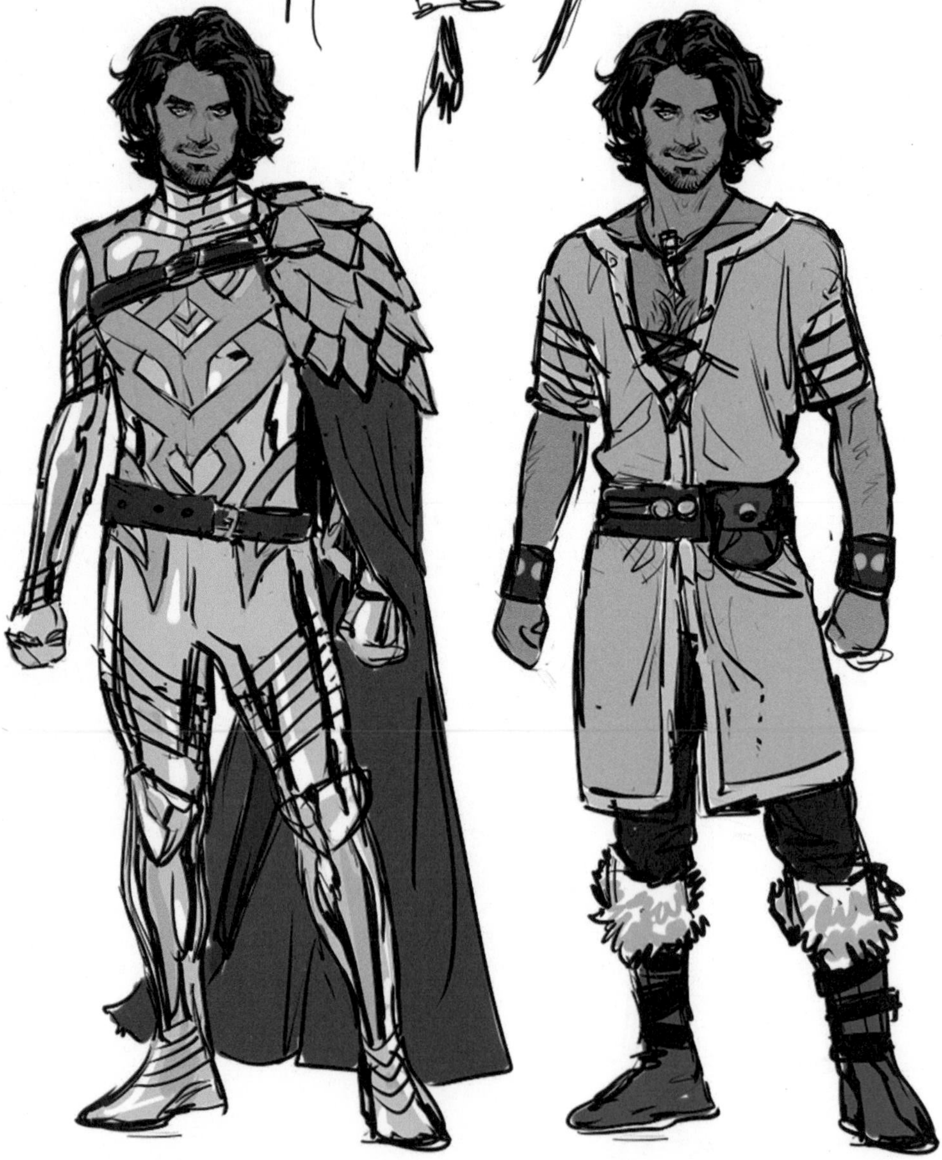

Janus sketch by ANDY MacDONALD

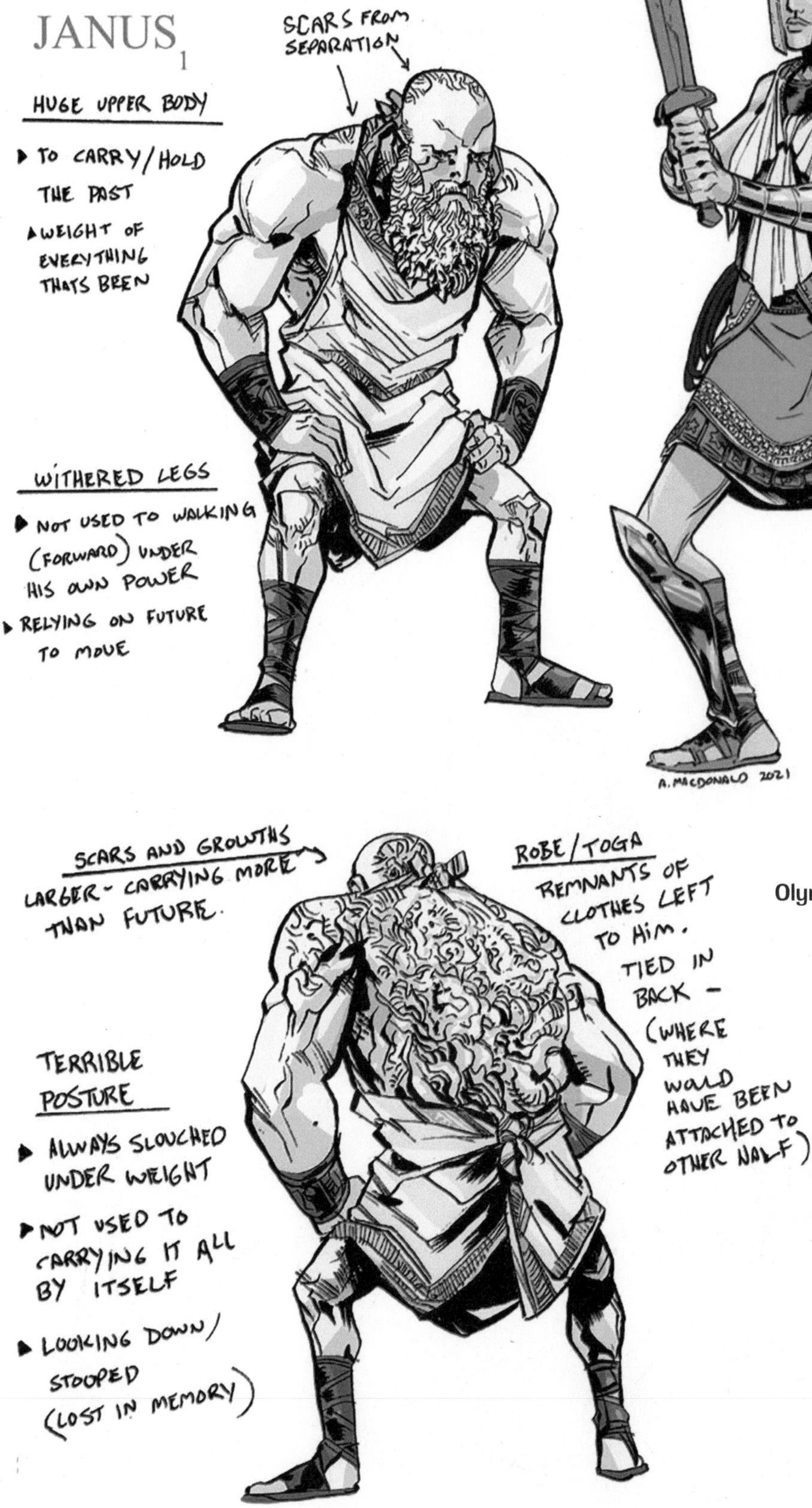
JANUS 1
SCARS FROM SEPARATION
HUGE UPPER BODY
▸ TO CARRY/HOLD THE PAST
▴ WEIGHT OF EVERYTHING THATS BEEN
WITHERED LEGS
▸ NOT USED TO WALKING (FORWARD) UNDER HIS OWN POWER
▸ RELYING ON FUTURE TO MOVE
SCARS AND GROWTHS
LARGER - CARRYING MORE THAN FUTURE.
ROBE/TOGA
REMNANTS OF CLOTHES LEFT TO HIM.
TIED IN BACK - (WHERE THEY WOULD HAVE BEEN ATTACHED TO OTHER HALF)
TERRIBLE POSTURE
▸ ALWAYS SLOUCHED UNDER WEIGHT
▸ NOT USED TO CARRYING IT ALL BY ITSELF
▸ LOOKING DOWN/ STOOPED (LOST IN MEMORY)

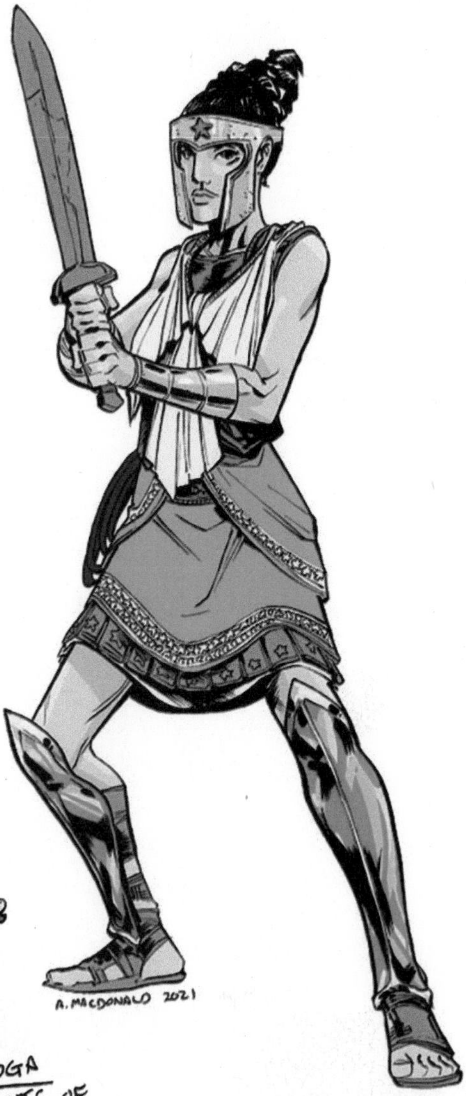
A. MACDONALD 2021

Olympus Wonder Woman sketch by ANDY MacDONALD

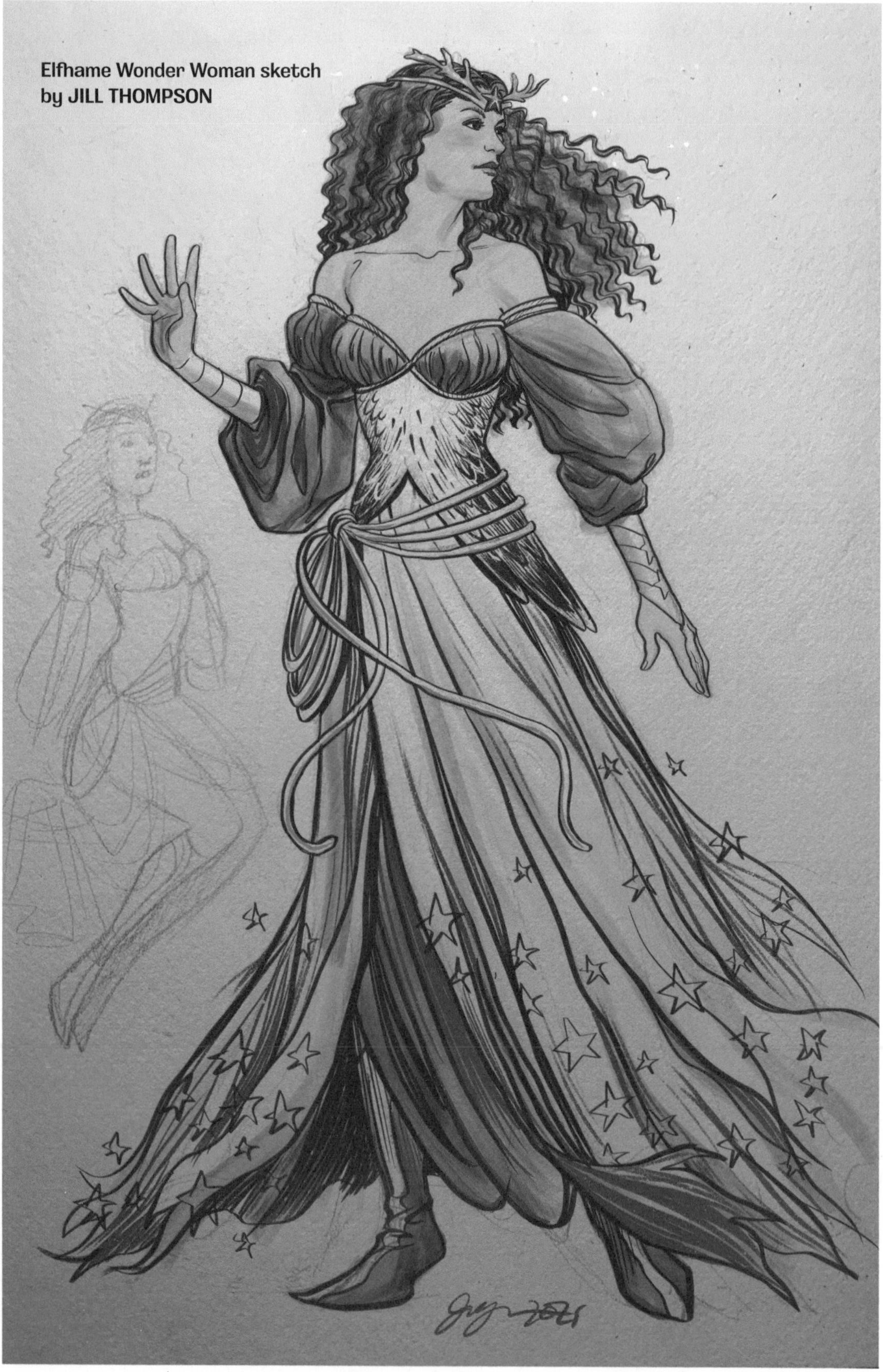

Elfhame Wonder Woman sketch
by JILL THOMPSON